Actors Performers YEARBOOK 2016

Actors & Performers YEARBOOK 2016

Edited by Lloyd Trott

Bloomsbury Methuen Drama
An imprint of Bloomsbury Publishing Plc

B L O O M S B U R Y
LONDON • OXFORD • NEW YORK • NEW DELHI • SYDNEY

Bloomsbury Methuen Drama
An imprint of Bloomsbury Publishing Plc

50 Bedford Square
London
WC1B 3DP
UK

1385 Broadway
New York
NY 10018
USA

www.bloomsbury.com

Bloomsbury is a registered trade mark of Bloomsbury Publishing Plc

Twelfth edition 2016

British Library Cataloguing-in-Publication Data
A catalogue record for this book is available from the British Library.

ISBN: PB: 978-1-4742-3977-6
ePub: 978-1-4742-3976-9
ePDF: 978-1-4742-3975-2

Library of Congress Cataloging-in-Publication Data
A catalog record for this book is available from the Library of Congress.

Printed and bound in Great Britain

About the Editor

Lloyd Trott is the Academy Dramaturg of the Royal Academy of Dramatic Art, London. He has taught actors at RADA for 38 years. He plans and casts the Academy's public repertoire with the Academy's Director. He has two main teaching strands, Dramaturgy and Professional Development. Lloyd is the Academy's primary liaison with actors' agents and casting directors in the UK and shepherds the acting students through their third year and into the profession. Alongside his RADA commitments Lloyd has worked as an Arts researcher and lobbyist and been an elected politician. He represented Dulwich in the last years of the Inner London Education Authority (1986–90) where he set up and chaired a Cultural Review of Inner London, as well as chairing the Arts and Libraries Committee of the Association of Metropolitan Authorities. In the mid-nineties he was Dramaturg at Theatr Clwyd. He taught dramaturgy on the MA Writing for Performance at Goldsmiths College 1998–2005, since when he has worked full-time at RADA. Lloyd is an Associate of the Wrestling School – the theatre company devoted to producing the plays of Howard Barker. Lloyd was the 2011 Winner of the Kenneth Tynan Award for services to dramaturgy in the UK.

Contents

Media

Disabled actors

Resources

Foreword

Equity (see page 380) is a relatively small union covering a wide variety of issues – not just contracts – of importance to those working in the performing arts. Despite our size we are expert in all the issues we cover, thanks to a dedicated staff with a wide variety of specialist knowledge to support our members.

However, you, as lone actor, also have a range of other concerns that are outside Equity's remit. For instance, how do you go about finding a specialist photographer capable of capturing the essential 'you'? What unforeseen pitfalls can you expect to encounter on a small-scale tour? Which agents and casting directors are happy to receive unsolicited showreels?

The joy of this wonderfully comprehensive book is that it gives you not only detailed listings for every aspect of work-related issues, but also great insights into the experiences of seasoned practitioners. The really helpful introductions and articles are written with warmth and humour. It is a valuable companion and an essential tool for all actors at whatever stage in their careers.

Christine Payne
General Secretary of Equity

Introduction

We start with a very sad note as the Yearbook's founding Editor, Simon Dunmore, who was already seriously ill when I took over the editorship last year, has now passed away. I remain deeply grateful to Simon in having inherited such a wealth of information on being an actor and/or performer and managing those careers. After nearly 40 years of teaching at RADA I find the Yearbook's ''Training' section the most comprehensive and honest guidance manual, not only to young aspirant actors, but their parents, teachers and careers' advisors, who otherwise have very little to illuminate the apparently quixotic pathways into our mysterious and reputedly risky profession. It really does bear reading and re-reading throughout the whole process of auditioning for drama schools. For those progressing to recall auditions and beyond, it is very important to read through the rest of the Yearbook's articles and browse the directory sections both of which are aimed at any actor, but give those eager to join our profession a very salutary indication of the myriads of non-acting personnel, who are essential support to an actor sustaining an income over a lifetime.

With actors' incomes very much at the forefront of my mind, I am very pleased we have included as one of this year's new articles 'Actors and Gamesters: Video games are very good news for the actor' by Mark Estdale. As Mark reveals there is a surprising amount of very well-paid employment for actors in this new and creatively provoking sector.

Our printed edition has now grown to such a size that we are having to take some immediate measures in the withdrawal of certain articles before being able to add new ones, and before producing an overall editorial strategy for our expanded remit – to performers. Mark's video games' article would seem to lead naturally to an entries' section for this work, while the vast area of comedy would bridge both actors and performers, and those are just two of the possible new sections. The archived articles will still continue to be available online (at www.actorsandperformers.com). The first two articles to become online only are 'Training in America' by David Taylor-Sharp, and 'Gaining an acting foothold in the USA' by Mark Pitt. This is not to say that we think the notion of acting in American has diminished in interest, far from it. Brendan Thomas's 'Are you ready for Pilot Season?' was commissioned especially to demonstrate and assist British actors' growing fascination, with much practical advice. Equity was a step ahead of us when it launched its Los Angeles network in the Autumn of 2013.

Finally, John O'Donovan, Commissioning Editor at Bloomsbury Methuen Drama, and I are very pleased that Judy Tither has joined us as our new Project Editor.

Lloyd Trott, Consultant Editor

Training
Introduction

This section is largely devoted to those who are 18 and older. This is not to dismiss the fact that there is training (of varying kinds) for those under that age. However, the field is so wide that the confines of this book limit listings only to the major organisations.

In spite of the fact that a minority of well-known actors did not formally train, it is very important for today's aspirant to do so. An ever-increasing number of people want to become actors, so those with 'casting clout' (agents, casting directors and directors) have more and more people to choose from. Doesn't it make sense to select from those who've undergone the rigours of a respected training process? It is an essential fact that the acting industry works on very tight time-scales and budgets – trained actors should be quicker, more reliable and, usually, more inventive than their untrained counterparts. For instance, an untrained voice that cracks up after a few days of live performance is time-consuming and costly for a management – only the larger productions can afford understudies. An untrained actor, who may look good on camera, will take time to learn how to work on a television set, where time spent keeping technicians waiting is very, very expensive. A fight (in a theatre or on camera) has to be staged so that it (a) looks real, (b) is safe for the participants and (c) can be seen properly by camera and/or audience – actors who've been trained in the essentials of combat will make this staging process much quicker. Moving correctly in period costumes, performing all kinds of formal dance and using microphones properly are just a few of the other time-saving skills that the trained actor can bring to a production. It is only an exceptional few who, nowadays, have the opportunity to 'learn on the job'.

For today's aspiring actor, it is important to train on a professionally recognised course. The established drama schools are the focus of such training. There are acting-related university degree courses which have a reasonable proportion of vocational training (as well as academic work) and there are numerous part-time, short-term and 'foundation' courses which will give you basic insights into the many crafts involved in acting. However, because of the intense competition, a full-time drama school course of at least a year is essential for most people.

For those who have already trained, there are opportunities to learn new skills and refine those already acquired, or simply to keep them in trim when the acting work is not coming in. The latter is very important, as you can be asked to demonstrate your skills at very short notice. Being an actor is a bit like being a fireman – without the regular salary. Also, the more you can legitimately add to the 'Skills' section of your CV, the more you can enhance your chances of finding work.

Editor's Note: It is especially important to **check for the latest information on all fees listed** under all headings in this section. *Actors and Performers Yearbook* makes every effort to ensure that such information is correct and up-to-date, but prices are especially liable to ongoing amendment.

Training for the under-18s

It is a fact that many child stars do not succeed as adult actors. There are notable exceptions – Nicholas Lyndhurst, Dennis Waterman and Jenny Agutter, for instance – but they are the exceptions that prove the rule. I also wonder whether a childhood largely devoted to performing is entirely healthy: what about learning about life? And what about learning other essential skills in order to earn one's living when the acting work is not coming in? Generally speaking, the best thing for the stage-struck child is to send him or her to one of the numerous youth theatre groups and drama workshops that exist in almost every town and city. These are often listed in *Yellow Pages*, and many are members of the National Association of Youth Theatres – see below. Public productions are often the last priority of such groups – especially for the younger ages – but a terrific amount can be learnt by the young from what seem like simple, make-believe games. Children in such groups won't learn many of the technical skills necessary to acting, but they will learn a lot of important social skills and the fundamental business of 'interacting' that is so important to an acting ensemble – that it's not just what you can create that matters, but what you can create with other people. Some youth theatres are allied to agencies who will promote their members for professional work, but it is important to note that employment of the under-16s is very strictly regulated.

National Association for Youth Drama (NAYD)

7 North Great George's Street, Dublin 1
tel 353-1 878 1301 *fax* 353-1 874 9816
email info@nayd.ie
website www.youthdrama.ie

NAYD is the development organisation for youth theatre and youth drama in Ireland. It supports youth drama in practice and policy, and supports the sustained development of youth theatres in Ireland.

NAYD advocates the inherent value and the unique relationship between young people and theatre as an artform, and is committed to extending and enhancing young people's understanding of theatre and to raising the artistic standards of youth theatre across the country. The organisation supports youth drama in practice through an annual programme that includes the National Youth Theatre, National and Regional festivals of youth theatres, commissioning new writing, publications, resources, training and other services, as well as research and policy development.

With a membership of 60 youth theatres throughout the country, NAYD supports the sustained development of youth theatres in partnership with local authorities, youth services, theatres and arts centres. Its productions are of a professional standard and are cast from youth theatres around Ireland. Previous productions include: *A Dream Play*, directed by Jimmy Fay; *The Seagull*, directed by Wayne Jordan; *A Midsummer Night's Dream*, directed by Gyorgy Vidovsky; *Young Europeans*, directed by Gerard Stembridge; and *The Crucible*, directed by Ben Barnes. For further details about NAYD's work, please refer to the website.

National Association of Youth Theatres (NAYT)

c/o Friargate Theatre, Lower Friargate, York YO1 9SL
tel (07804) 254651
email info@nayt.org.uk
website www.nayt.org.uk

Founded in 1982, the National Association of Youth Theatres (NAYT) is the development agency for youth theatre practice in England. The organisation supports the development of youth theatre activity through training, advocacy, participation programmes, and information services. Registration is open to any group or individual using theatre techniques in their work with young people, outside formal education. NAYT is an educational charity (No. 1046042) and a company limited by guarantee (No. 2989999).

NAYT responds to enquiries from young people, teachers, parents, carers, youth workers and social services looking for information and advice about youth theatre provision or career or educational opportunities. This free service puts young people in direct contact with youth theatres.

National Youth Arts Wales (NYAW)

245 Western Avenue, Cardiff CF5 2YX
tel 029-2026 5060 *fax* 029-2026 5014

email nyaw@nyaw.co.uk
website www.nyaw.co.uk/e_nytw.html
Creative Activist for 2014/15 Jain Boon

NYAW represents the National Youth Brass Band of Wales, National Youth Wind Orchestra of Wales, National Youth Jazz Wales, National Youth Choir of Wales, National Youth Chamber Ensemble of Wales, National Youth Dance Wales, National Youth Orchestra of Wales, and National Youth Theatre of Wales (NYTW).

The National Youth Theatre of Wales was founded in 1976 and has since provided opportunities for hundreds of young people, many of whom are now actively involved with the theatre as professional actors, directors, writers, designers and stage managers. The NYTW is aimed at young people aged 16-21 who are drawn from all over Wales. With guidance from its Creative Activist, the youth theatre prepares and rehearses during the summer of each year for a series of high-profile public performances.

In addition, the NYTW spearheads a development programme of workshops and education activities, designed to increase interest and participation in youth theatre.

National Youth Music Theatre (NYMT)

Adrian House, 27 Vincent Square,
London SW1P 2NN
email enquiries@nymt.org.uk
website www.nymt.org.uk

The National Youth Music Theatre exists to produce challenging music theatre work (both major productions and workshops) for young people of all backgrounds as participants. It helps them to explore new and existing works, to inspire themselves and each other – giving them the opportunity to achieve their highest aspirations and to realise their talent, imagination and creativity.

National Youth Theatre of Great Britain (NYT)

443-45 Holloway Road, London N7 6LW
tel 020-7281 3863
website www.nyt.org.uk
Artistic Director Paul Roseby *Executive Director* Sid Higgins *General Manager* Alexa Cruickshank

Founded in 1956, the NYT is the UK's premier youth arts organisation, providing young people aged 13-21 with the opportunity for creative participation and learning through theatre arts. Courses are offered in Acting, Stage Management, Lighting & Sound, Scenery & Prop Building and Costume Making at a professional standard, which culminate in a season of productions and community projects around the UK and abroad, in professional theatres and site-specific locations.

Many leading names in the creative industries started out at the NYT, including Sir Ben Kingsley, Sir Derek Jacobi, Dame Helen Mirren, Daniel Craig, Daniel Day Lewis, Chiwetel Ejiofor, Timothy Spall, Liza Tarbuck and Matt Smith.

The NYT auditions approximately 3,000 applicants each year at one of 20 audition centres across the UK. Approximately 650 new members are recruited annually. Successful applicants are offered a place on one of the courses, and, having completed a course, members are eligible to audition for the NYT's production season or to become Peer Mentors within the Creative Learning programme. Major productions are mounted each year.

The NYT also has a robust Creative Learning programme which embeds learning throughout all projects. It runs accredited courses for those not in education or training, as well as many open access projects and community productions.

Scottish Youth Theatre

The Old Sheriff Court, 105 Brunswick Street,
Glasgow G1 1TF
tel 0141-552 3988 *fax* 0141-552 7615
email info@scottishyouththeatre.org
website www.scottishyouththeatre.org
Artistic Director Mary McCluskey

Founded in 1977, Scottish Youth Theatre is Scotland's national theatre for and by young people. Using the youth theatre/drama process to develop not only creativity and performance skills but also transferable skills in participants, Scottish Youth Theatre puts particular emphasis on each individual's personal and social development. It offers weekly drama and dance classes for young people aged 2½ to 25, performances for all the family and the flagship Summer Festival, which includes performance and technical theatre courses, open to young people across Scotland aged 8 to 25.

For participants who have shown promise and are interested in a career in any aspect of theatre, film and television, there is Scottish Youth Theatre's high-quality, high-profile project and performance group, SYT Productions.

Scottish Youth Theatre also works in partnership with schools, youth theatres, youth groups and national agencies to deliver tailor-made Special Projects.

Youth Music Theatre UK

London Office Youth Music Theatre UK,
Lyric Hammersmith, Lyric Square, King Street,
London W6 0QL
tel 020-8563 7725
Edinburgh Office Youth Music Theatre UK, c/o YTAS,
Summerhall, 1 Summerhall, Edinburgh EH9 1PL
tel tel 0131-538 2723
website www.youthmusictheatreuk.org

Youth Music Theatre UK (also known as YMT) is the UK's national company providing musical theatre activities for young people across the UK. It is one of the nine National Youth Music Organisations (NYMOs) supported by Arts Council England and the DfE (Music and Dance Scheme); its core programme links young people from local/regional productions into formal training at drama school – so successful auditionees will be talented, with many going on into the creative industries. YMT has a strong relationship with the UK's largest teaching union, the NASUWT, who are its principal sponsors, and with Trinity College London, who formally assess the activities.

Auditions for young performers take place around the UK in January and February, and successful applicants join the companies of 8 fully staged productions at venues and festivals around the country in the summer holidays.

YMT The Explore Programme is a series of workshops, courses and projects that help young people develop their skills and abilities in the performing arts. This includes the opportunity to work with artistic teams to create new music theatre. YMT also creates similar pathways for young writers, composers and musicians as well as those interested in technical theatre. YMT offer a wide range of outreach opportunities with schools, youth services and cross-cultural groups.

Training opportunities for graduate directors, assistant directors, assistant MDs, designers and choreographers working alongside its professional staff are also available.

Drama schools

Currently there is a core of established drama schools which belong to an organisation called Drama UK (**www.dramauk.co.uk**) – which is a recent amalgamation of the Conference of Drama Schools (CDS) and the National Council for Drama Training (NCDT). See Ian Kellgren's article on page 22 for more about Drama UK. These drama schools run courses that are 'accredited'; that is, quality assured by experienced professionals. However, there are also a few well-respected courses that are currently not 'accredited' and/or not part of Drama UK.

It is important to check the current funding arrangements for each course you intend applying for. Don't simply rely on what arrangements were in place last year, as things have a habit of changing. Many three-year accredited courses have 'degree' status – in spite of the fact that there is little or no written component to the courses, let alone formal, written exams. (Historically, the schools took the 'degree' route to help students get funding on the same basis as those following conventional academic courses.) Degree status actually means very little in the acting profession, and courses with degree status are not necessarily better than those without it. Some schools have been quite vociferous about not wishing to become embroiled in the whole philosophy and bureaucracy that is fundamental to degree education – believing that joining with a university would compromise the purely vocational character of their courses. One such adds: "Universities are academic institutions, and the intelligence required of an academic is different from that required of an actor. While some are blessed with both kinds, many talented and intelligent actors are of indifferent academic ability. We would not wish to exclude them." Degree status will enable you to go on to a higher degree and enhance your employment prospects outside the profession – but not within it.

Funding for some accredited one- and two-year courses is available, but not with the same frequency as for three-year courses. However, there is advice on finding funds from private sources on Drama UK's website, and some schools have scholarships and/or are good at helping students with this task.

It is worth spending time checking through all the courses listed below – also, read through the *Guide to Professional Training in Drama and Technical Theatre*, which is available from Drama UK's website. Look too at **www.theessentialsguide.co.uk** for a very thought-through list of what to look for in a course. (Additionally, if possible seek the opinion of those with recent knowledge of drama schools.) Then get prospectuses for any school that you feel could be viable for you – and read each one thoroughly. Important considerations include whether you could be eligible for funding for your fees (and a maintenance loan), and potential living costs – central London is significantly more expensive to live in than Manchester, for example. (Bear in mind, too, whether a degree qualification at the end of the course is important to you.) Above all, it's important to try to assess which courses you feel would suit you best, and to apply – some require application via UCAS **www.ucas.ac.uk** or **www.cukas.ac.uk** – to as many as you can afford the audition fees and travel costs for. Don't forget to factor in the cost of overnight accommodation, if necessary. The plain truth is that competition for places is so intense (especially for women) that you need to audition for as many places as possible. Every time you do another audition you will learn more about the techniques of auditioning than any book or class can teach you. It is important to take on board the fact that many people take two or three years of auditioning, and sometimes more, before they get places. If you are determined to become a professional actor, you have to take rejection in your stride – learn from it, and keep on trying until you succeed.

Finally, carefully check the application deadlines, funding details and audition specifications of each school to which you intend to apply – there are some considerable variations (see the Checklist following the listings given below). You may find it useful to read *An Applicant's Guide to Auditioning and Interviewing at Dance and Drama Schools*, which is available from Drama UK's website. Andrew Piper's website (**www.andrew-piper.com**) contains useful advice on auditioning and fundraising for drama school, as well as an account of his own first year.

Notes:

• For general information on funding for fees and maintenance loans, see **www.gov.uk/browse/education/student-finance**.

• Places on some accredited courses are currently funded through Dance and Drama Awards (DaDAs). These were introduced in the late 1990s, and provide funding for about two-thirds of successful applicants. For more details, check each relevant school's prospectus and website – also look at **www.gov.uk/dance-drama-awards**.

• For the latest details on course accreditation, please see Drama UK's website **www.dramauk.co.uk**.

* denotes membership of Drama UK

The Academy of Live and Recorded Arts (ALRA)*

Studio 24, The Royal Victoria Patriotic Building, John Archer Way, London SW18 3SX
tel 020-8870 6475
email info@alra.co.uk
North West Campus, ALRA, Turner Street, Wigan WN1 3SU
website www.alra.co.uk
Principal Adrian Hall

Full-time acting courses:

• BA (Hons) Acting. A full-time, 3-year course to prepare students for a varied career as a professional actor. This course is also available at ALRA North.
• MA Acting. A full-time, intensive 15-month course to prepare students for a career in the stage and screen industries. This course is also available at ALRA North.
• Stage Management & Technical Theatre Foundation Degree. A 2-year course to equip students with the necessary skills to gain employment in the theatre industry. This course is also available at ALRA North.
• Foundation Course in Acting. Available part-time and full-time, aimed at those considering full-time actor training and those considering a career change. Part-time also available at ALRA North, full-time only available at ALRA North.

See **www.alra.co.uk** for more details.

American Musical Theatre Academy London (AMTA)

Europa House, 13-17 Ironmonger Row, London EC1V 3QG
tel 020-7253 3118
email info@americanacademy.co.uk
website www.americanacademy.co.uk
Principals/Directors Kenneth Avery-Clark, Christie Miller

Courses offered:

• One Year Full Time Acting Programme for Stage and Screen. No specific academic requirements; entry is by audition only. Trainfor a week in USA.

Welcomes candidates with disabilities and will consider each on a case-by-case basis, according to the strength of their audition. Please note that current premises are not wheelchair accessible.

Arts Educational Schools, London (ArtsEd)*

Cone Ripman House, 14 Bath Road, London W4 1LY
tel 020-8987 6666 *fax* 020-8987 6699
email drama@artsed.co.uk
website www.artsed.co.uk
Principal Jane Harrison *Deputy Principal and Director of the School of Musical Theatre* Chris Hocking *Head of Acting* Gareth Farr *Head of Film Acting* Caroline Jeffries

Part of the Dance and Drama Awards scheme. Applications for courses and awards should be made direct to the school. Only students taking an approved Trinity College London qualification will be eligible to apply for an award. All courses are accredited by Drama UK or the Council for Dance Education and Training, and validated by Trinity College London (Diplomas and Certificates) and City University London (degrees).

Full-time acting courses:

- BA (Hons) Acting/Level 6 Diploma in Professional Acting (3 years). Applicants must be aged 18 or over.
- BA (Hons) Musical Theatre Programme/Level 6 Diploma in Professional Musical Theatre (3 years). Applicants must be aged 18 or over.
- MA Acting/Level 5 Certificate in Professional Acting (1 year postgraduate). Applicants must be aged 21 or over.

Birmingham School of Acting*

Millennium Point, Curzon Street,
Birmingham B4 7XG
tel 0121-331 7200 *fax* 0121-331 7221
email info@bsa.bcu.ac.uk
website www.bcu.ac.uk/bsa
Principal Stephen Simms

Full-time acting courses:

- BA (Hons) Acting (3 years). Applicants must be aged 18 or over by the time the course commences with 2 A levels (grade E or above) or equivalent. Admission is by two-stage audition.
- MA/PgDip Acting (1 year). Applicants must have a first degree and some relevant experience. Admission is by audition.
- BA (Hons) Applied Performance (Community and Education) (3 years). Applicants must be aged 18 by the time the course commences with a minimum of 2 A levels or equivalent (240 points). Candidates will be invited to an interview and workshop assessment.
- BA (Hons) Stage Management (3 years). Applicants must be aged 18 by the time the course commences, with a minimum of 2 A Levels or equivalent (240 points). Candidates will be invited to interview.
- MFA Acting (The British Tradition) (2 years). Applicants must have a first degree and some relevant experience. Admission is by audition in the USA, Birmingham or by DVD.
- MA/PgDip Professional Voice Practice (1 year). Applicants must have a first degree and some relevant experience. Admission is by audition.

The Birmingham Theatre School

The Old Fire Station, 285-287 Moseley Road,
Highgate, Birmingham B12 0DX
tel 0121-440 1665
email info@birminghamtheatreschool.co.uk
website www.birminghamtheatreschool.co.uk
Principal Chris Rozanski *Key contact* Fiona Allison

Full-time acting courses:

- HND Performing Arts/Theatre Acting (2 years). Applicants must be aged 18 or over with 12 points at A level or BTEC.
- BTEC Extended National Diploma in Performing Arts (Acting) (2 years). Applicants must be aged 16 or over.
- Professional Acting Diploma (1 year). Applicants must be aged 18 or over.
- Open Access Foundation in Acting (1 year). Applicants must be aged 16 or over.

The Bridge Theatre Training Company

90 Kingsway, North Finchley, London N12 0EX
tel 020-7424 0860
email admin@thebridge-ttc.org
website www.thebridge-ttc.org
Joint Artistic Directors Mark Akrill, Judith Pollard
Administrator Connie Mensah

The Bridge is a non-profit organisation which provides intensive training for a professional acting career. Courses include comprehensive career guidance, and a graduating season of public productions in London theatres, with a West End showcase at the Criterion Theatre in front of agents, directors and casting directors.

Full-time acting courses:

- Professional Acting Course (2 years). Applicants must be aged 18 or over.
- Professional Acting Course (1 year postgraduate/post-experience). Applicants must be aged 21 or over, with a university degree or significant relevant experience.

Bristol Old Vic Theatre School*

2 Downside Road, Clifton, Bristol BS8 2XF
tel 0117-973 3535 *fax* 0117-923 9371
email enquiries@oldvic.ac.uk
website www.oldvic.ac.uk
Principal Paul Rummer *Artistic Director* Jenny Stephens

An affiliate of the Conservatoire for Dance and Drama. All courses are entirely vocational and are validated by the University of West England.

Full-time acting courses: Applications should be made direct to the school. All applicants auditioned, with further 1-day recalls.

- BA Hons Professional Acting (3 years)
- FdA Professional Acting (2 years)
- MA in Professional Acting (1 year, 40 weeks, for International students)

The City Lit

Keeley Street, Covent Garden, London WC2B 4BA
tel 020-7492 2542
email drama@citylit.ac.uk
website www.citylit.ac.uk/dramaschool
Head of Drama, Dance & Speech Vivienne Rochester
Patron Jonathan Miller

For the Diploma below, you will work with directors, teachers, agents and casting directors, preparing you for the industry. Our expert Drama Tutors are all professional practitioners with extensive experience of working in major drama schools and the profession. The first year of the Diploma course combines robust technical training with in-depth methodological grounding. In the second year, while continuing training, the focus shifts to performance, and the students form a self-contained theatre company working on a range of projects both within and outside City Lit. You will receive individual mentoring and work within a tight collaborative unit.

Financial assistance is available for those in need, including several bursaries of £1,000 or £2,000, as well as short-term loans and Professional and Career Development Loans. Two Jonathan Miller Scholarships (worth 50% of the second-year fees) are available to second-year students.

By graduation, you will have achieved: a showreel; an audio reel; an agents' showcase performance; and a personal business plan. You will also be entitled to a Student Equity Card, and entry to the Spotlight directory and its services. For more details, please see the course brochure or go online.

Full-time acting courses:

• Two Year Professional Acting Diploma. A two-year intensive acting course for those wishing to progress from vocational study to a professional career in the arts. A full-time course over 4 days from Monday to Thursday, leaving 3 days in the week for further study and/or work (32 contact hours). Entry is by audition.

A note on eligibility: "Our programme is designed for those with previous experience or relevant undergraduate qualifications. We welcome the following people to audition: students from our City Lit Drama community; students from other universities and drama schools; working professionals from the Performing Arts industry; artists returning to performance with new life skills. Our mission is to recruit a diverse collective of professionally focused individuals who can feed off each other's passion, uniqueness, culture and life experiences."

Court Theatre Training Company

The Courtyard Theatre, Bowling Green Walk,
40 Pitfield Street, London N1 6EU
tel 020-7739 6868
email info@courttheatretraining.org.uk
website www.courttheatretraining.org.uk
Principal/Director June Abbott *Key contact* Sarah Meadows

As well as the BA (Hons) Acting 2 Years (see below), offers a postgraduate acting course and training for directors and stage managers – please consult the website for further details. The site has wheelchair access and there is a support system for students who are dyslexic.

Full-time acting courses:

• BA (Hons) Acting (2 years) – a distinctive course specially designed for the practical training of the actor; work can take place within the professional environment of an acclaimed working theatre. Applicants must be aged 19+ with 120 UCAS points. Some public funding is available. Applications should be made directly or via UCAS/CUKAS by the end of July.

Cygnet Training Theatre*

Cygnet Theatre, Friars Gate, Exeter EX2 4AZ
tel (01392) 277189
email info@cygnettheatre.co.uk
website www.cygnettheatre.co.uk
Principal Rosalind Williams *Artistic Director* Alistair Ganley

Cygnet offers a 1-year foundation course and a 3-year full-time training based in its own studio theatre. Functions as a small touring company, drawing its members from all over the UK and abroad. The small number of applicants selected each year (6-8) are chosen for their flexibility, maturity, awareness and self-discipline.

Students are expected to work with professional commitment from the first day in this ensemble training. Financial assistance is occasionally available to third-year students. People may enter straight from school, after a university degree or as a career change. All need stamina, commitment and an ability to put the work of the ensemble first.

Applicants must be aged 18 or over. Professional Acting Certificate.

The Dorset School of Acting

Lighthouse, 21 Kingland Road, Poole,
Dorset BH15 1UG
tel (01202) 922675
email admin@dorsetschoolofacting.co.uk
website www.dorsetschoolofacting.co.uk
Co-founders/Principals James Bowden & Laura Roxburgh

The 1 year diploma course in Acting & Musical Theatre has a 100% success rate in placing students at reputable drama schools for further training or into professional work. It is designed to provide a real insight into the rigours of drama school training, giving classes in acting, dance, voice and singing, tutorial sessions, theatre visits and business advice. Holds at least 3 masterclasses a year, taught by major, current industry professionals who are leaders in their field. The school welcomes applications from students with disabilities, and is happy to make adjustments to ensure that its courses are inclusive. It does not expect applicants to be strong in all disciplines when they audition.

Acting courses offered:

• 1 Year Diploma in Acting & Musical Theatre (30 weeks) – the qualification gained is Trinity ATCL Level 4 in Drama & Speech. Applicants should be

aged 16+. Applications should be made directly to the school by the end of July.
• 2 Year Diploma in Acting & Musical Thatre (78 weeks) – the qualification gained is Trinity LTCL Level 6 in Drama & Speech. Applicants should be aged 18+. Applications should be made directly to the school by the end of July.

Drama Centre London*

Granary Building, 1 Granary Square,
London N1C 4AA
tel 020-7514 7023
email drama.centre.admissions@csm.arts.ac.uk
website www.arts.ac.uk/csm/drama-centre-london
Principal Jonathan Martin *Key contact* Annette Welland

Trains students to become professional actors, directors and writers. Established in 1963, it is now part of the University of the Arts London, and is a member of Drama UK. The school awards 3 Foundation Scholarships; 1 Reeves Scholarship; 5 UK/EU Leverhulme Scholarships; and 2 International Leverhulme Scholarships. For detailed information on Scholarships and Bursaries, see the website under 'Apply and Funding'.

Full-time acting course:

• BA (Hons) Acting (3 years). Applicants must have 2 A levels or equivalent. 16 places are available. Public funding/student loans available for all UK/EU students doing their first degree. Applications should be made through UCAS.
• MA Acting (45 weeks). 20 places are available.
• MA Screen: Acting (60 weeks over 16 months). 18 places are available.

Note that applicants for both MA courses must have a related degree, a diploma in dance or drama, an honours degree in another discipline supported by performance-related experience (professional, amateur or student), or significant professional experience. Applications are made direct to the school.
• Diploma in Foundation Studies (Performance) (30 weeks). Applicants must have 1 A level or a BTEC National Diploma in Performing Arts or equivalent. 20 places are available. Applications are made direct to the school.

Drama Studio London (DSL)*

1 Grange Road, London W5 5QN
tel 020-8579 3897 *fax* 020-8566 2035
email admin@dramastudiolondon.co.uk
website www.dramastudiolondon.co.uk
Principal Chris Pickles *Managing Director* Kit Thacker

Drama Studio London (DSL) provides full-time, professional acting training for mature and postgraduate students aged 21 and over. A 1-year course of 44 weeks (beginning in August) and a 2-year course of 36 weeks (beginning in October) are offered each year. Auditions and open days are held from November or June. For a prospectus, information or an application form, contact **admin@dramastudiolondon.co.uk** or visit the website. Some Dance and Drama Awards are available; all candidates are automatically assessed for a DaDA at recall. Successful graduates will receive the Drama Studio London Diploma, and may also take the Trinity College London National Certificate in Professional Acting, if they wish.

East 15 Acting School*

Hatfields, Rectory Lane, Loughton IG10 3RY
tel 020-8508 5983 *fax* 020-8508 7521
email east15@essex.ac.uk
website www.east15.ac.uk
Director Professor Leon Rubin *Key contact* Catherine Williams (Admissions Officer)

Full-time acting courses:

• BA Acting (3 years), BA Acting (International), BA Acting and and Community Theatre, BA Acting and Cointemporary Theatre, BA Acting and Stage Combat, BA Physical Theatre. Deadline for applications is June. All courses require a successful audition, plus A-level; 160 points including CE at A-level. BTEC Extended Diploma: MPP.
• BA World Performance (3 years) requires a successful audition, plus A-levels: 260 points including CE at A-level. BTEC Extended Diploma: MPP.
• MA/PG Acting (1 year). Selection for this course is based upon experience and potential. All applicants must be over the age of 21; there is no upper age limit. Applicants must hold a BA degree (normally at least a 2:1) or have suitable previous life professional or academic experience.

Other full-time acting courses:
• Certificate of Higher Education in Theatre Arts
• MA/MFA in Acting (International)

Please see the website for details of the above courses.

École Internationale de Théâtre Jacques Lecoq

57 Rue du Faubourg Saint-Denis, 75010 Paris
tel 33 (0)1-4770 4478 *fax* 33 (0)1-4523 4014
email contact@ecole-jacqueslecoq.com
website www.ecole-jacqueslecoq.com
Principal Mrs Pascale Lecoq

Founded in Paris in 1956, with the aim of producing a young theatre of new work, generating performance languages which emphasise the physical playing of the actor. Focuses on art theatre, but with the view that theatre education is broader than the theatre itself: "It is a matter not only of training actors, but of educating theatre artists of all kinds." Provides as broad and durable a foundation as possible for every student. Also offers part-time courses. See also the company's entry under *Short-term and part-time courses* on page 31. As a movement school, all classes require a great degree of physical movement, so applicants must be physically fit.

Full-time acting courses:

• Professional Course (Certificate – Master Level; 2 years). No public funding available. Applications should be made direct to the school by September. Applicants must be aged 21+ with initial theatre training and stage experience.

Fourth Monkey

The Monkey House, 97-101 Seven Sisters Road, London N7 7QP
tel 020-7281 0360
email office@fourthmonkey.co.uk
website www.fourthmonkey.co.uk
Artistic Director Mr Steven Green

A training provider with a difference, offering full- or part-time ensemble-based contemporary Rep training and professional performance opportunities. Shortlisted for *The Stage*'s School of the Year award.

Full-time acting courses:

• Two Year Rep (2 year full-time actor training programme, 40 hours per week. Based in London and includes a month-long residential programme in Italy). Applicants must be aged 18 and over. Performance experience and A-Level qualifications or similar desirable, but not compulsory.
• Year of the Monkey (1 year full-time actor training programme, 20-35 hours per week variable, concluding at the Edinburgh Fringe Festival). Applicants must be aged 18 and over. Performance experience and A-Level qualifications or similar are desirable, but not compulsory.

Fourth Monkey accepts applications from all areas of society; the only factor impacting suitability on any training programme is the presence of talent, a desire to learn and develop and an equal desire to work as an ensemble company member.

The Giles Foreman Centre for Acting

Studio Soho,
entrance in Royalty Mews (next to Quo Vadis),22-25 Dean Street, London W1D 3AR
tel 020-7437 3175
email info@gilesforeman.com
website www.gilesforeman.com
Director Giles Foreman *Key contact* Lindsay Richardson

An exciting professional acting studio housing some of the country's top coaches in the disciplines of screen- and theatre-acting, movement, voice, improvisation, on-camera, Meisner technique, movement psychology and character analysis – directing and text analysis.

Comprises 2 easy-access large bright air-conditioned studios plus changing room, chillout area and kitchen, props store. (Wheelchair-accessible, entrance lift and step-free studio facilities.) Plus separate airy daylight-studio and meeting-rooms. Wi-Fi throughout. Offers the opportunity for professional actors to develop their skills through regular acting classes and workshops, and to create projects in both film and theatre. Specialised intensive masterclass short courses offered by internationally renowned practitioners from all over the world. Due to its location at the heart of the the UK film, TV and theatre industry, also offers many opportunities to meet casting directors, directors and producers through industry showcases, casting-network and Q&A evenings.

Professional coaches available to prepare actors for auditions and self-tapes, and develop characters for projects they have secured.

Full-time courses:

• Post-Graduate-Equivalent Intensive Diplomas in Acting and Directing (15 months). One half-scholarship available. Applicants should be aged 20 or over. PCDL registered.
• Foundation ATCL Diploma (11 months, evening and weekend-mode). Validated by Trinity College London. Applicants should be aged 17 or over.

GSA, Guildford School of Acting*

University of Surrey, Stag Hill Campus, Guildford GU2 7XH
tel (01483) 560701 *fax* (01483) 535431
email info@gsauk.org
website www.gsauk.org
Head of GSA Terrie Fender

GSA was founded in 1935, and from 1964 onwards has concentrated on the vocational training of actors and stage managers. Since 1987 the Musical Theatre Course has held a leading position in the world of actor training.

Full-time acting courses: Applications for undergraduate courses should be made via UCAS. Applications for the BA (Hons) Theatre (conversion by distance learning) and for postgraduate courses should be made direct to the University of Surrey.

• BA (Hons) Theatre (1-year conversion by distance learning). Applicants must be aged 18 or over and hold a level 5 or above performing arts diploma.
• BA (Hons) Acting (3 years). Applicants must be aged 18 or over, with 3 A levels.
• BA (Hons) Musical Theatre (3 years). Applicants must be aged 18 or over, with 3 A levels.
• BA (Hons) Actor Musician (3 years) [subject to validation]. Applicants must be aged 18 or over, with 3 A levels.
• BA (Hons) Professional Production Skills. Applicants must be aged 18 or over, with 3 A levels.
• MA in Acting (1 year). Applicants must be aged 21 or over.
• MA in Musical Theatre (1 year). Applicants must be aged 21 or over.
• MA Creative Practices and Leadership (1 year). Applicants must be aged 21 or over.

Guildhall School of Music & Drama*

Silk Street, Barbican, London EC2Y 8DT
tel 020-7628 2571 *fax* 020-7256 9438
email registry@gsmd.ac.uk
website www.gsmd.ac.uk
Director of Acting Wyn Jones

Full-time acting courses:

• BA (Hons) Acting (3 years). Applicants are normally at least 18 years old with a minimum of 2 A-level passes or equivalent. Applications should be made direct to the school as early as possible, and by mid-January at the latest. Student Support from the UK Government is available for most EU students.
• MA in Acting (3 years). Designed for students who have a university degree and wish to have a full professional training in acting. The MA students work in the same classes, rehearsals and performances as the students on the 3-year BA in Acting, with additional tutorials in support of achieving the Masters level outcomes. Entrance is by audition. At the point of audition, no distinction is made between applicants to the BA and the MA. Once a graduate applicant has received an offer, he or she can opt to follow either the MA or the BA programme. MA students have the same practical training as the BA students. They take additional modules developing their critical and reflective skills and are required to achieve more demanding learning outcomes and a higher standard overall.

In the final year of training, clear guidance is given on starting in the acting profession. There are regular talks and visits by regional theatre directors, agents, casting directors, income tax advisers and representatives from Equity.

International School of Screen Acting

The Old Lab, 3 Mills Studios, Three Mills Lane, London E3 3DU
tel 020-8709 8719
email office@screenacting.co.uk
website www.screenacting.co.uk
*Key contact*Alexandra Webb

Founded in 2001, ISSA is a drama school dedicated to preparing actors for today's TV and film industry. Based within 3 Mills Studios, the school is at the heart of a creative and successful media village.

Full-time acting courses:

• One Year Full Time Advanced Screen Acting.
• Two Year Screen Acting.

Italia Conti Academy of Theatre Arts*

'Avondale', 72 Landor Road, London SW9 9PH
tel 020-7733 3210 *fax* 020-7737 2728
email acting@italiaconti.co.uk
website www.italiaconti-acting.co.uk
Programmes Director (Acting) Chris White

A member of Drama UK, the Academy offers a 3-year BA (Hons) Acting Degree, validated by the University of East London, as well as a 1-year Foundation Acting course which is in preparation for full-time actor's training. Italia Conti Academy of Theatre Arts is a world-renowned centre for actor training. Its graduates populate the performance industries and it is this commercial edge that makes the BA (Hons) Acting course unique. It is one of the country's leading vocational acting courses with an emphasis on professional development and employability.

Full-time acting courses:

• BA (Hons) Acting (3 years). Applicants must be aged 18 or over with 5 GCSEs (grade C or above), including English, and 2 A levels (grade E or above) or equivalent.
• Foundation Acting (1 year). Applicants must be aged 17 or over with 5 GCSEs (grade C or above), including English.

Kogan Academy of Dramatic Art

9-15 Elthorne Road, Archway, London N19 4AJ
tel 020-7272 0027 *fax* 020-7272 0026
email info@scienceofacting.com
website www.scienceofacting.com
Principal Neil Sheffield *Office Manager* Dennis McGeown

Formerly known as The Academy of the Science of Acting and Directing.

Full-time acting courses: No public funding is available for the courses listed below, but students may apply for a limited number of scholarships. There are daytime and evening courses.

• Three Year Acting Course. offering a BA (Hons) in Acting accredited by Kingston University. Applicants must be aged 18 or over. Offers 30 places each year.
• Two Year Acting Course. Applicants must be aged 18 or over. Offers 30 places each year.
• One Year Acting Course. Applicants must be aged 18 or over. Offers 30 places each year.
• Evening Courses. "One to One" sessions, workshops and other training also available.

LAMDA (London Academy of Music & Dramatic Art)*

155 Talgarth Road, London W14 9DA
tel 020-8834 0500 *fax* 020-8834 0501
email admissions@lamda.org.uk
website www.lamda.org.uk
Principal Joanna Read

LAMDA (London Academy of Music & Dramatic Art) is an internationally renowned drama school, providing exceptional vocational training for students of promise in the dramatic arts. We prepare actors for sustainable careers in the industry. You can see our alumni at the National Theatre, the RSC, Shakespeare's Globe, on London's West End, in Broadway and on the big and small screen worldwide.

As an affiliate of the Conservatoire for Dance and Drama, LAMDA receives funding from the Higher Education Funding Council for England (HEFCE). This means that eligible UK/EU students are able to access loans to assist with their tuition fees and maintenance costs. LAMDA and the Conservatoire also have a range of scholarships and bursaries available to ensure that the most talented students can access our training, regardless of their financial circumstances.

Committed to recruiting on talent alone, LAMDA auditions and/or interviews everyone who submits their application by the advertised deadline, providing they meet the age requirements for the training. We do not ask applicants for specific academic qualification; we ask only for talent, passion and a commitment to learn.

Full-time acting courses:

• BA (Hons) Professional Acting (3 years). Minimum entry age is 18. Admission is by audition and interview.
• Foundation Degree in Acting (2 years). Minimum entry age is 18, but due to experience necessary for this course, most students are 21 and over. Admission is by audition and interview.
• MA Classical Acting for the Professional Theatre (1 year). This course is for international students with a BA or BFA degree or eqivalent. Students without this qualification must demonstrate a comparable level of knowledge and experience gained in a professional company or vocational drama school. Admission is by audition and interview.
• LAMDA Semester Diploma in Classical Acting (14 weeks). Minimum entry age is 18 and admission is by application only. Applicants may apply to LAMDA directly or through their home university or college.

Please visit **www.lamda.org.uk** for further details, application deadlines and course fees, as well as information on all other LAMDA courses.

The Liverpool Institute for Performing Arts (LIPA)*

Mount Street, Liverpool L1 9HF
tel 0151-330 3232/3116/3084/3022 *fax* 0151-330 3131
email admissions@lipa.ac.uk
website www.lipa.ac.uk

"We aim to produce disciplined, multi-skilled and creative practitioners; thoughtful actors who want to take responsibility for shaping their own careers. Acting talent alone is not enough to sustain a career. So, we encourage you to broaden your skills and entrepreneurial outlook and hence increase your opportunities for work."

Full-time acting courses:

• BA (Hons) Acting (3 years). Applicants must be aged 18 or over; there is no upper age limit. Educational attainment, relevant experience and interdisciplinary interest and ability will be taken into account when applying. Applications should be made through UCAS. If invited to audition, further information will be required.
• Foundation Certificate in Acting and Musical Theatre (1 year). Applicants must be aged 18 or over; there is no upper age limit. Educational attainment, relevant experience and interdisciplinary interest and ability will be taken into account when applying. Applications should be made through UCAS. If invited to audition, further information will be required.

London Academy of Radio, Film & TV

1 Lancing Street, London NW1 1NA
tel 0870-626 5100
website www.media-courses.com
Director of Courses Andy Parkin *Key contact* Estelle Burton

The school has more than 30 teaching staff; around 1,200 students take one or more of its 100+ courses. It is situated opposite Euston Station.

Full-time acting courses:

• Diploma in Screen Acting. Application deadline is June. Age range: 16+. Entry is by audition: 1 modern and 1 classical speech.

London School of Dramatic Art

4 Bute Street, London SW7 3EX
tel 020-7581 6100
email enquiries@lsda-acting.com
website www.lsda-acting.com
Principal Jake Taylor *Administrator* Lydia Palmese

Offers a range of comprehensive courses designed to develop individual creative talents, and to provide a thorough grounding in all aspects of performance as part of a student's preparation for a working life as an actor. There is currently no wheelchair access to the main building or training rooms: if this affects applicants who would like to know when these spaces become accessible, please let the school know. All auditions are free and no international student fees are charged. No formal qualifications are required as the training is vocational: "We look more at potential and at levels of creativity."

Full-time courses:

• Advanced Diploma in Acting (1 year). No public funding available. Applications should be made direct to the school by the end of September. Applicants must be aged 18 or over.
• Foundation Diploma in Acting (1 year). No public funding available. Applications should be made direct to the school by the end of September. Applications must be aged 18 or over.

London School of Musical Theatre

c/o Prince Studios, 110 York Road,
London SW13 3RD
tel 020-7407 4455

email info@lsmt.co.uk
website www.lsmt.co.uk
Principal/Course Producer Adrian Jeckells

Full-time courses:

• Musical Theatre Diploma Course (1 year). Age range for entry is 18-35.

London Studio Centre (LSC)

Artsdepot, 5 Nether Street, Tally Ho Corner, North Finchley, London, N12 0GA
tel 020-7837 7741
email info@londonstudiocentre.org
website www.londonstudiocentre.org
Director Nic Espinosa *Audition Enquiries* Sarah Tudor
Dean of Studies/Programme Leader Robert Penman

London Studio Centre is a professional dance college validated by the Council for Dance Education and Training. Courses include: BA (Hons) Theatre Dance (validated by Middlesex University), a foundation course, the LSC Diploma and Saturday Associate Programmes.

LSC's facilities include state-of-the-art dance and drama studios and access to fully equipped theatres. LSC graduates are regularly seen performing in London's West End and with international dance companies around the world.

Manchester School of Theatre at MMU*

School of Theatre, Mabel Tylecote Building, All Saints, Manchester M15 6BH
tel 0161-247 1933 *fax* 0161-247 6875
email msaprogteam1@mmu.ac.uk
website www.theatre.mmu.ac.uk
Course Director David Shirley Key contact MSA Programme Team 1

Full-time acting courses:

• BA (Hons) Acting (3 years). Applicants must be aged 18 or over with 2 A levels or equivalent. Applications should be made through UCAS by January.

Mountview Academy of Theatre Arts*

Kingfisher Place, Clarendon Road, London N22 6XF
tel 020-8881 2201 *fax* 020-8829 0034
email enquiries@mountview.org.uk
website www.mountview.org.uk
Principal Stephen Jameson

Full-time acting courses: Applications for the courses listed below should be made direct to the school, by February for the BA (Hons) in Acting or Musical Theatre and by June for the Actor Musician BA (Hons) postgraduate courses.

• BA (Hons) Acting (3 years). Applicants must be aged 18 or over, usually with A levels but these are not essential. Dance and Drama Awards are available for a significant number of students.
• BA (Hons) Actor Musician (3 years). Applicants must be aged 18 or over, usually with A levels but these are not essential. Dance and Drama Awards are available for a significant number of students.
• BA (Hons) Musical Theatre (3 years). Applicants must be aged 18 or over, usually with A levels but these are not essential. Dance and Drama Awards are available for a significant number of students.
• PG Dip in Acting/MA in Performance (1 year). Applicants must be aged 21 or over, usually with a university degree.
• PG Dip in Musical Theatre/MA in Performance (1 year). Applicants must be aged 21 or over, usually with a university degree.

MTA (The Musical Theatre Academy)

Bernie Grant Arts Centre, Town Hall Approach Road, Tottenham Green, London N15 4RX
tel 020-8885 6543
email info@theMTA.co.uk
website www.theMTA.co.uk
Principal Annemarie Lewis Thomas

The MTA run the UK's first accelerated learning programme for triple-threat performers, meaning that their students are industry-ready in 2 years as opposed to the more traditional 3. The acting component of the musical theatre course is split 50/50 between stage and screen acting. The school only employs working professionals ensuring that students are taught current and relevant industry thinking. The school has received industry plaudits for its work and is extremely successful at gaining students agent representation on completion of the course, with nearly three-quarters of graduates now working under professional contracts.

Oxford School of Drama*

Sansomes Farm Studios, Woodstock, Oxford OX20 1ER
tel (01993) 812883 *fax* (01993) 811220
email info@oxforddrama.ac.uk
website www.oxforddrama.ac.uk
Principal George Peck *Executive Director* Kate Ashcroft

The smallest of all the drama schools with accredited status. Awarded Beacon Status by the Minister for Education in 2006. Provides a significant number of Dance and Drama Awards for its 1- and 3-year courses. Also offers its own Hardship fund which is distributed each year to students on full-time courses at the school. Students not in receipt of a DaDA are prioritised for funding. The Lionel Bart Foundation and the Sir John Gielgud Charitable Trust currently support the school; in addition, students have also won the Laurence Olivier Bursary, the Henry Cotton Memorial Fund Award, the *Evening Standard*/Patricia Rothermere Award, the Alan Bates Award, and the BBC Carleton Hobbs bursary award.

Full-time acting courses: Applications for the courses listed below should be made direct to the school by May.

• Three Year Acting Course. Applicants must be aged 18 or over.
• One Year Acting Course. Applicants must be aged 21 or over.

Poor School

242 Pentonville Road, London N1 9JY
tel 020-7837 6030 *fax* 020-7837 5330
email acting@thepoorschool.com
website www.thepoorschool.com
Principal Paul Caister

The school was created in 1986 with the aim of providing high-quality acting training that is financially within the reach of all, or almost all. Training lasts 2 years and operates in the evenings and at weekends until the final 2 terms, when daytime work is involved. Since March 1993 the Poor School has owned its own theatre, the Workhouse; this is a flexible studio theatre seating 50-80.

Full-time acting courses:

• Two Year Acting Course (6 terms). Most students are in their early 20s but the school offers many places to older and younger people. Auditions are held throughout the year. In their graduating year, students present 2 showcases for the profession only as well as a season of plays for the public.

Royal Academy of Dramatic Art (RADA)*

62-64 Gower Street, London WC1E 6ED
tel 020-7636 7076 *fax* 020-7323 3865
email enquiries@rada.ac.uk
website www.rada.ac.uk
Key contact Sally Power

The Royal Academy of Dramatic Art (RADA) offers vocational training for actors, stage managers, directors, designers and technical stage craft specialists.

Full-time acting courses:

• BA (Hons) Acting (3 years). Applicants must be over the age of 18
• MA Theatre Lab (1 year)
• Foundation Course in Acting (12 weeks)

RADA also runs courses in technical theatre training and masters courses in Directing and Text and Performance, as well as short courses throughout the year in both technical and acting disciplines. Courses at RADA are intensive and require a high level of commitment; in return students receive an extremely high level of teaching with almost unparalleled links to the industry.

More details on all the courses are available on the RADA website **www.rada.ac.uk.**

The REP College

17 St Mary's Avenue, Purley on Thames, Berks RG8 8BJ
email tudor@repcollege.co.uk
website www.repcollege.co.uk
Key contact David Tudor

Provides acting students with 1 year of practical education, including 14 public performances.

Full-time acting courses:

• Acting Course (1 year plus shorter courses). Applicants must be aged 18 or over.

Rose Bruford College*

Lamorbey Park, Burnt Oak Lane, Sidcup DA15 9DF
tel 020-8308 2600 *fax* 020-8308 0542
email enquiries@bruford.ac.uk
website www.bruford.ac.uk
Principal Professor Michael Earley

Full-time acting courses: Applicants for the BA degree courses listed below must be over the age of 18 with the equivalent of a minimum of 2 A levels at grade C or above. Applications should be made through UCAS.

• BA (Hons) Acting (3 years)
• BA (Hons) Actor Musicianship (3 years)
• BA (Hons) American Theatre Arts (3 years)
• BA (Hons) European Theatre Arts (3 years)

Royal Academy of Music

Musical Theatre Department, Marylebone Road, London NW1 5HT
tel 020-7873 7483 *fax* 020-7873 7484
email mth@ram.ac.uk
website www.ram.ac.uk/mth
Head of Musical Theatre Bjorn Dobbelaere MMus
Programme Leader Louise Shephard *Musical Theatre Company Coordinator* Stephen Minay

Students are enrolled at the Royal Academy of Music, an institution of world renown, training students for more than 190 years. Students study for University of London degrees. Fellow students include instrumentalists, composers, jazz and commercial musicians, pianists and opera singers.

Full-time acting courses:

• One Year Musical Theatre Programme. Aimed at graduates, mature students and experienced performers wishing to undertake a career in musical theatre. The course provides an intensive training in singing, acting, movement and voice to students of postgraduate (or equivalent) level. Includes extensive one-to-one tuition with expert tutors and industry showcase, projects for invited industry guests and public performances.

The Royal Central School of Speech and Drama*

64 Eton Avenue, London NW3 3HY
tel 020-7722 8183 *fax* 020-7722 4132
email enquiries@cssd.ac.uk
website www.cssd.ac.uk
Principal Gavin Henderson

Scholarships/Bursaries Central has a range of scholarships, bursaries and awards available for students on its undergraduate and postgraduate programmes. Visit the website for further details.

Undergraduate courses:

BA (Hons) Acting – Offers three specialist courses Acting, Acting Collaborative and Devised Theatre and Acting Musical Theatre. Entry requirements are 2 A levels at grade C, 3 GCSEs at grade C and selection by audition. Normal offers may be higher and depend upon expected grades and audition performance. Exceptionally, applicants who do not meet this requirement, but demonstrate appropriate potential, may be accepted. Applications should be made through UCAS by January.

BA (Hons) Theatre Practice (Performance Arts) – 3 A Levels at BBC and subject to an interview and participation in a selection day. Normal offers may be higher and depend upon expected grades, their portfolio and performance at interview. Exceptionally, applicants who do not meet this requirement, but demonstrate appropriate potential, may be accepted. Applications should be made through UCAS by January.

Postgraduate Courses

All MA courses listed below are for postgraduates or actors (aged 21 or over) with significant professional experience. Applications for all postgraduate courses should be made direct to the school:

- Acting
- Acting for Screen
- Actor Training and Coaching
- Movement Studies
- Musical Theatre
- Performance Practices and Research

Royal Conservatoire of Scotland*

100 Renfrew Street, Glasgow G2 3DB
tel 0141-332 4101 *fax* 0141-332 8901
email dramaadmissions@rcs.ac.uk
website www.rcs.ac.uk
Principal John Wallace

Full-time acting courses: Applications for the undergraduate courses listed below should be made via Conservatoires UK (**www.cukas.ac.uk**) by 15 January 2016 (UK/EU) or 31 March 2016 (overseas). Applications for postgraduate courses listed below should be made via Conservatoires UK (**www.cukas.ac.uk**) by 30 April 2016. Applications for BA Performance in British Sign Language / English should be made direct to the Royal Conservatoire of Scotland. Please email dramaadmissions@rcs.ac.uk for more information. Applications for this course should be made by 15 January 2016 (UK/EU) or 31 March 2015 (overseas). Applications for the courses listed below should be made direct to the school by March. Public funding is available for some students.

Courses available:

- BA Acting (full-time, 3 years)
- BA Performance in British Sign Language/English
- BA Musical Theatre (full-time, 3 years)
- BA (Hons) Contemporary Performance Practice (full-time, 4 years)
- MA Musical Theatre (full-time, 1 year)
- MA Classical and Contemporary Text (full-time, 1 year)

Royal Welsh College of Music and Drama*

Castle Grounds, Cathays Park, Cardiff CF10 3ER
tel 029-2039 1361
website www.rwcmd.ac.uk
Principal Hilary Boulding *Drama Admissions Officer* Luise Moggridge

Full-time acting courses:

- BA (Hons) Acting (3 years). Applicants should normally be at least 18 years old by the time of enrolment. There is a range of support in place to help cover the cost of tuition, the details of which will depend on where the student normally lives. Applications should be made through CUKAS.
- Postgraduate Diploma in Acting for Stage, Screen and Radio (1 year). Applicants should normally be at least 21 years old by the time of enrolment. Applications should be made directly to the college.
- MA in Acting for Stage, Screen and Radio (4 terms – September until January). Applicants should normally be at least 21 years old by the time of enrolment. Applications should be made directly to the college.
- MA in Musical Theatre (3 terms – January until December). Applicants should normally be at least 21 years old by the time of enrolment. Applications should be made directly to the college.

Checklist of drama school deadlines, audition requirements, audition fees and funding systems

Only Drama UK member schools are included, and postgraduate courses often have different application deadlines and funding systems. Compiled by Lloyd Trott.

School	Definition of 'Classical'	Definition of 'Modern/ Contemporary'	Other Parameters	Audition Fee	Funding System	Application Deadline
ALRA	Shakespeare/Jacobean	After 1980 – with some camerawork	No longer than 2mins each	£45	DaDA	1st April
Arts Ed	Classical (preferably Shakespeare) "8-10 lines of heightened text"	Written after 1980 – no more than 2mins	Short dialogue – provided by school – to camera	£45	DaDA	27th February
Birmingham School of Acting	Elizabethan/Jacobean (they provide you with a list that you MAY choose from)	"Last 20 years"	No longer than 2mins each; a song for the recall, with sheet music – no more than 3mins	£46	Maintained	Mid-May
Bristol	Classical	Modern – "in prose"	Speeches should not exceed 4mins in total; an unaccompanied song; sight-reading from a given text	£50	Maintained	27th February
Central	Two from supplied list	After 1960	None	£55	Maintained	Mid-January – via UCAS
Drama Centre	Shakespeare/His Contemporaries	After 1830	Speeches should not exceed 3mins	£50	Maintained	Mid-January – via UCAS
Drama Studio	Classical	After 1955		£45	DaDA	No set deadline

School	Definition of 'Classical'	Definition of 'Modern/ Contemporary'	Other Parameters	Audition Fee	Funding System	Application Deadline
East 15	Shakespearean/Jacobean – "no more than 1.5mins"	After 1950 – "no more than 2mins"	A 3rd speech that contrasts well with the modern speech – no longer than 2mins	£55	Maintained	Mid-April – via UCAS
Guildford (GSA)	Written before 1800	Written after 1950	A Shakespeare sonnet	£45	DaDA/ Maintained	Mid-January – via UCAS
Guildhall	Shakespeare/Jacobean – verse	Written after 1956	And a contrasting speech from any period; no longer than 2mins each; a short unaccompanied song	£63	Maintained	30th January
Italia Conti	One from supplied list	After 1870	No more than 1.5mins each	£45	Maintained	31st March – via UCAS
LAMDA	Elizabethan/Jacobean	Modern	No longer than 3mins each and clearly contrasting; asked to sing at recall	£49 (UK credit/ debit card)) £63 (UK paper/online) £77 (international card) £87 (international paper/online)	Maintained	2nd March
LIPA	One from supplied list	After 1945	Musical Theatre song and 2min devised piece	£35	Maintained	Mid-January – via UCAS
Manchester School of Theatre	Shakespeare – blank verse	After 1970	And a contrasting speech from any published play; no more than 2mins each	£45	Maintained	Mid-January – via UCAS
Mountview	Shakespeare	After 1979	No longer than 2mins each	£45	DaDA	1st February
Oxford	Elizabethan/Jacobean	After 1950	No more than 2mins each	£45 (EU) £55 (non-EU)	DaDA	31st May

School	Definition of 'Classical'	Definition of 'Modern/ Contemporary'	Other Parameters	Audition Fee	Funding System	Application Deadline
RADA	Elizabethan/Jacobean	After 1960	Second Classical speech may be required; a song in recall	£45 before 11th December, £85 after 11th December	Maintained	27th February
Rose Bruford	16th/17th/18th century or Ancient Greek	After 1960 – "not verse"	No more than 1.5mins each	£45	Maintained	Mid-January – via UCAS
Royal Conservatoire of Scotland	Shakespeare – "preferably in verse"	A contrasting contemporary speech	No less than 1min and no more than 3mins each; song	£45 + admin £20	Maintained	UK/EU 15th January – via CUKAS. International 31st March
Royal Welsh	Elizabethan/Jacobean	20th/21st century	No longer than 2mins each	£45	Maintained	Mid-January – via CUKAS

Notes:

- When only 'Classical' is specified, this can mean anything written before about 1800.
- When only 'Modern' or 'Contemporary' is specified, you should be fine with anything written after 1945 – and speeches written between 1900 and 1945 have often proved acceptable in this category.
- 'Verse' is sometimes specified – this doesn't mean that it necessarily needs to rhyme. In fact, some schools specify 'blank' (i.e. non-rhyming) verse.
- You'll find various definitions in the 'Classical' column – "Shakespearean/ Jacobean", "Elizabethan/Jacobean", "Shakespeare/Contemporaries". Strictly, these all imply slightly different (but overlapping) periods in history. In practice, anything written between about 1560 and 1640 should be fine.
- All schools ask that there is sufficient contrast between 'Classical' and 'Modern/ Contemporary' speeches.
- See individual schools' websites for more detailed audition requirements and advice.
- UCAS & CUKAS (www.cukas.ac.uk) fee (where appropriate) is in addition to each school's audition fee.
- Musical Theatre & other specialist courses usually have additional audition requirements.
- Some schools will allow late applications, but they can't guarantee you an audition and may charge a higher audition fee.
- Some schools offer free auditions to those from low-income households.
- Also see *Effective audition speeches* on page 149.

Warning:

Some of these details may change for entry in future years. Please inform the Editor of any such changes at **lloydtrott@rada.ac.uk**.

What are drama schools looking for?

Geoffrey Colman

A lifelong contract

Many underestimate the fact that becoming an actor is about signing a sort of lifelong and extraordinary contract which contains the most incredible clause – one that requires the artist to metaphorically go to places both dark and light; to represent, live and die for us. Seven times a week or in 14 takes.

To successfully navigate such moments one must posses a licence, for to 'go there' is not something that everybody can or wants to do. Not everybody has the skill. Not everybody is prepared to dedicate the years of preparation required to become an actor. Alas many also underestimate the phenomenal personal responsibility of such an undertaking, and delude themselves that it can be achieved by just wanting it very much – like a child wants ice cream. I have not found this to be the case.

In the last ten years there has been significant expansion in the field of professional actor-training. The sector consists of 21 schools that subscribe to, and are measured by, a set of overarching industry-approved principles held by the accrediting body, Drama UK (**www.dramauk.co.uk**), which was until recently known as CDS/NCDT. Many thousands apply to drama school each year, and yet in spite of the much publicised increase to higher education tuition fees by the Higher Education Funding Council for England (**www.hefce.ac.uk**) – which approved a top-up funding maximum of £9000 per year – the numbers of wannabe Oliviers and Redgraves are most definitely on the up. Add this to the vast catalogue of non-professional diploma and degree awarding courses offering performance-related study, and it becomes very clear that acting is a much sought-after pursuit.

What are you looking for? Do your research

In spite of excellent regulating bodies like Drama UK (and additionally for those schools in Higher Education, the Quality Assurance Agency – **www.qaa.ac.uk**), there is actually no real sector uniformity in terms of funding (including tuition top-up fees), quality of training, award outcomes (certificate, diploma, degree), and most certainly graduate employment prospects, which vary from school to school. So set aside the question about what are drama schools looking for – what are *you* looking for? The first task is not to perfect some extraordinarily well-honed accent or radical audition monologue interpretation, but rather, many months prior to this process, to undertake a sleeves-rolled-up systematic approach to a lot of very necessary research into the sector itself. If you are going to commit three years of your life to something, you really should find out what that something is!

All drama schools publish their entry requirements in either a glossy prospectus or more typically on a website, but as such these only really describe required entry criteria, a brief course outline and in at least three cases a list of permitted classical audition speeches with the names of successful alumni who spoke those same speeches many years before. The real answers required are sometimes just a little bit more abstract. Many drama schools now offer open day events: these afford a terrific and all-important onsite 'experience' of the building, its community of staff and students, and the general but nevertheless important 'feel' of the place. If possible, attend a few plays or musicals performed by final year students from different schools; this can be extremely useful in that it demonstrates a very public slice of the quality of teaching and professional guidance that a particular school might offer.

Once started, this level of nerdy cultural forensic work will certainly enable you to identify at least where you would actually like to study. But why do you want to become an actor? This is the real question that you must ask. Not so that you can decorate your personal statement with incredible but quite useless prose (as audition candidates often do), but rather, in order for you to align all future coordinates to it. You will need to refer to this answer for the rest of your life.

Audition actively, with clarity and commitment

It was the jaded theatre producer Emmanuel Azenberg who pessimistically described how successful entry into the ranks of the professional Broadway musical chorus required an alarming but necessary process of becoming a kind of fabulous invalid – a gradual giving up of self and becoming unable to do or cope with anything other than being in the chorus itself. Never really knowing who deals the cards – and in fact never really knowing what the game is in the first place! Having been involved with drama school auditions for many years, I would suggest that his observation might just as well apply as a cautionary tale to those many thousands of audition candidates that approach the day with all too little consideration for the task and commitment ahead. The necessary forms completed, speeches learnt and black tee-shirt specially ironed for the occasion, they arrive all psyched up and ready to do two incredible speeches to knock 'em dead.

But most candidates have a seriously limited, almost passive expectation about what drama schools actually want at audition, as well as of the actual training itself. The audition day is not merely there to equip the candidate with a jolly site tour, a space within which to recite a contrasting classical and contemporary speech, and even, just possibly, to offer some sort of snatched insight into how the course might be taught. To enter the world of drama school depends upon something far more fundamental than a set of well-worn clichéd, seen-it-in-the-movies assumptions.

The craft of acting is not limited to a single method or approach; it is joyfully promiscuous. But for every actor we witness on our screens or in the theatre itself we also encounter a different sort of promiscuity. Some actors are famously trained and some are just famous, possessing a peculiar but much-desired cultural tag. The 'celebrity' is often 'untrained' but connected to the performance industry by events that afford measurable charisma, enigma or sensation. As such, celebrities may not in the short term need a drama school training but rather, a constant stream of tabloid stories showing hasty late-night retreats from exclusive bars and restaurants. Such activities can (and occasionally do) open doors and give entry into the industry – but the hinges that hold them are tissue thin, and the doors will rarely remain permanently open!

Drama school entry requirements are published, so there is no mystery. Typically schools will be looking for 'evidence of ongoing commitment to acting', 'evidence of a trainable voice and body', 'evidence of intellectual, emotional and physical skills' and so on. These competencies are all there waiting on the audition panellist's check list. There is not a section that refers to 'tingle factor' or 'star quality' because this is only found on the fame TV panellist's laminated sheet. Equally there isn't an additional sub-criteria requirement listing one blonde, one tall, one fat, one thin to balance future casting designs not yet discussed.

The choice of speech preoccupies many candidates, who unearth an astounding range of two-minute extracts – often material inappropriately sourced from the Internet and disallowing any creative placement of their own heart and mind. And oh, how audition candidates obssess about contrasting this, that or the other! Just select an extract from a play that is simple, clear, unfussy and – most important of all – one that allows for you to enter its world without a fight (and most certainly without the need to show that you are entering it). People do bring much worked-upon accents, props, shouts, peculiar moves, glances and screams as though volume alone will do the deal. This should be avoided. Remember too that audition panellists have experienced the gamut of human suffering in two-minute chunks many times before. But emotion in itself is not the gold medal if it is false, inappropriate or showy (especially without real context).

Look diligently before you leap

Drama school training is not casual but actually quite conservative and very ordered indeed. One class follows another and then another. How to fit into this delightful regime? It can be repetitive and exhausting. The audition panel will therefore look for signs of one who can cope with this, or not. A professional training is a physical, emotional, muscular assimilation of many processes. Learning lines is really not the issue – but learning the difficult routine and discipline of acting can be. The audition is as much about assessing this point as to whether a given Juliet or Hamlet is believable.

Like many momentous occasions in life, the drama school audition can be so very memorable. Like the first day of the school summer holidays or the first page of a new novel or even the first kiss! For there to be a first day at drama school is an achievement in itself! And yet to audition is to be part of an occasion mixed with both excitement and fear. Excitement in that all the waiting and preparation is over ... but also fear in that what happens if a place is not offered?

To be an acting student at an accredited drama school is not to be part of something that is either casual or meaningless. But success in the current climate is now also measured by other indictors. Most students juggle outside work commitments with a very heavy work-load of study, and somehow exist on far less money than is possible. Drama school training is impacting – it marks all those who come into contact with it. Yes, every move, every gesture and vocal shift is catalogued for later dissection. But this is why to be trained is not to take an unfathomable leap in the dark. Sacrifices will have to be made, and we must ensure that in the new funding climate, becoming an artist will not render a fearful, voiceless future to all but a privileged few.

What drama schools actually want is to restore the helplessness of our own lives through the long, productive and meaningful careers of future artists like you. Don't take an unfathomable leap – only if you're utterly convinced should you sign the training contract – but prepare for this moment with diligence, care and humility. Good Luck!

Geoffrey Colman is Head of Acting at The Royal Central School of Speech and Drama.

Drama UK and Quality Assured

Championing quality drama training through Advocacy, Assurance and Advice – Ian Kellgren explains

Drama UK was formed in 2012 following the merger of the National Council of Drama Training (NCDT) and the Conference of Drama Schools (CDS). It continues to fulfil the work of these two organisations, and its Board is drawn from influential figures in the industry and the provision and support of training.

Drama UK aims to act as an advocate for the drama training sector. Recently, against the background of an economic downturn, student fees have gone up and funding to Higher Education teaching has gone down. Despite this, the performing arts industry continues to be a massive contributor to the economy and needs a skilled workforce. An organisation to champion the sector at the highest levels of government was needed that could also maximise information to potential students and their families. Drama UK was created to do just this.

Drama UK therefore provides students of all ages with advice and a route map for all drama training, from early years through vocational training to professional development for those working in the industry. This advice is primarily available through the Drama UK website, **www.dramauk.co.uk**.

In addition, Drama UK awards a quality kite mark to the very best drama training available. Just as you might look for a quality kite mark when buying electrical goods, so Drama UK provides just this for the best vocational drama training to reassure you that it is fit for purpose, safe and gives you every chance of making a lasting career in the profession.

Until recently, quality drama training was identified by NCDT accreditation. The National Council for Drama Training was formed in 1976, after a Gulbenkian Foundation report, 'Going on the Stage', recommended its establishment. There were fears then that a severe increase in unemployment in the profession, coupled with a multiplication of training establishments, was leading to a critical situation for vocational drama training. NCDT was created to provide some way to judge which courses were truly vocational, realistically leading to a career.

Back in 1976, there were only seven universities offering drama degrees: there are now over 2,000 courses with drama or performance in the title. The need for potential students and the current funders to have some way of knowing which are vocational is stronger than ever.

In addition, many changes have taken place over the last 36 years. For example, Equity is no longer a closed shop,where you need to be a member to gain employment (although there are around 37,000 members, and extensive use of Equity contracts by employers persists). The profession has undergone massive change. Few, if any, reps exist in the way that they did in the early 70s. Musical theatre is a much more dominant force, demanding a supply of 'triple threat' performers; that is, those who can act, sing and dance, all to a high standard. Technological advances are continuing to revolutionise the ways in which the recorded media operate. The major vocational drama schools are now in Further Education and Higher Education, subject to the relevant Quality Assurance requirements.

Drama UK now accredits conservatoire training drama schools rather than individual courses. Each school has to show that its key courses comply with extensive industry-endorsed criteria, and that all the courses the school puts forward as being 'vocational' satisfy Drama UK's hallmarks of conservatoire training. The Board of Drama UK agrees these requirements and then delegates the operation of the system to a QA Board, which is responsible for ensuring that experienced professionals scrutinise documentation and a panel of experts conduct an onsite visit. The panel talk to the staff and to the students as well as visiting classes and seeing examples of recorded and live work. They are looking all the time at the professional relevance of the training.

Reports with recommendations are viewed by the QA Board, which in turn makes recommendations to the Board of Drama UK, which is obliged to accept them unless they are perverse or illogical, so maintaining a 'Chinese wall' of impartiality.

The QA Board has up to seven members, all of whom are experts in their fields and include major casting directors, artistic directors and Equity members; other experts are co-opted for meetings when required.

Drama UK advocates that conservatoire-level vocational training for performers is still the primary preparation route for a career in acting and musical theatre. However, given the complex needs of the performance industry, there is increasing demand for detailed information on other routes to a wide range of careers in the Creative and Cultural Industries. With that in mind, Drama UK has recently reviewed and expanded its approach to wider quality assurance, reflecting the complex needs of the performance industry. The Drama UK website was developed to provide this information. Drama UK Accreditation will still only be available to fully vocational courses, but courses with some vocational content will be Quality Assured and pre-vocational courses will also be assessed, providing some comfort as to their safety and value.

Finally, Drama UK has begun a study of the employment landscape for actors who trained at drama schools, giving, for the first time, sound data on which to develop a picture of where graduates find work. This is of value to potential students and their families, the training providers and the industry.

The discerning shopper will want the electrical goods they buy to be not only fit for purpose and safe, but also to have benefited from development and innovation. Through quality assurance, Drama UK offers to the discerning, a means of identifying those vocational drama courses that are fit for purpose and safe but, as well, are based on the best practices of over a hundred years of drama training combined with the benefits of development and innovation; and an understanding of the landscape of employment and how to navigate it.

Ian Kellgren is an award-winning theatre director who began as an assistant director at the Royal Court in London, rising to Literary Manager, before becoming Artistic Director of Durham Theatre Company and the longest-serving Artistic Director of the Liverpool Playhouse. Currently, he is Chief Executive of Drama UK.

Starting later in life

Hugh Osborne

The actor's life – and it's almost a cliché to point it out – is one filled with uncertainty, disappointment and, often, severe financial hardship. The prospective actor needs to think very carefully about the importance s/he attaches to securing a long-term partner, setting up a home and raising a family; it's highly likely that pursuit of an acting career will militate against all three. Would you really want to jeopardise all that, and the happiness which accrues from it, purely in order to stand – very occasionally – on a stage, in a silly costume, saying things like 'Good my lord, thrice hath the bell sounded; therefore, hie thee hither' (or, if you'd prefer, to stand – very occasionally – in a field, in a dull costume, saying things like 'Guv, you'd better come and take a look at this')? The answer, based on a balanced, sober and careful consideration, would have to be a resounding 'No.'

But what if you've already attained the home, the partner, the family? What if pursuing your dream of being an actor entails not jeopardising what you've never had, but, far more scarily, endangering what you've already got? Or, to formulate the problem more optimistically, can you enter – or try to enter – the acting profession later in life without doing so? This article addresses some of the practical advantages and disadvantages of being a mature entrant to the profession, as I was. It in no way offers itself as a definitive 'how to' guide, or as a prescriptive set of rules for the would-be actor to follow. Rather, it riffs on my own experiences, observations and, I suppose, prejudices, in order to give an idea of some of the hurdles you may have to overcome, and of how best to overcome them.

Professional training is mandatory ...

My first prejudice is this: anyone considering a career in acting should regard training at a reputable drama school as mandatory. The pros and cons of training (including issues of cost) are a constant source of debate within the business, and rehearsing them here is outside the scope of this article; but there are, I maintain, a number of specific advantages for the mature applicant.

For eliminating bad habits ...

Firstly, the mature applicant (whom I shall now address as 'you') has usually done a lot of amateur dramatics. You were probably bitten by the acting bug while appearing with your local am-dram society. A decade or two of amateur acting may well have given you plenty of experience; but, be assured, you will have picked up a multitude of bad habits, mannerisms and tics that will need to be pointed out to you before you can move into the professional arena. I had a terrible habit of blinking excessively every time it was my turn to speak; I also stooped badly. I left drama school with the blinking corrected, a full inch taller. Am-dram societies also tend to foster antics (temper tantrums, unpunctuality, divaish behaviour, etc.) that simply aren't tolerated in the business itself. Drama school is the perfect place to address these issues.

... And playing catch-up

Secondly, you will have to play catch-up. Someone with ten-odd years of professional experience over you will, of course, have ten-odd years' worth of professional contacts;

attending drama school lets you make a tranche of contacts in one fell swoop, from the staff and visiting tutors to your fellow-students. (One general note about this whole business of making contacts: do not fall into the trap of thinking that it is all about schmoozing and bumping into casting directors at cocktail parties. Rather, you should only consider someone – be it an actor, director, producer or casting director – a 'contact' if you have had a professional relationship with them. The people you encounter at drama school are the first who will meet this criterion.)

The ultimate opportunity for playing catch-up, of course, is the end-of-course showcase mounted for industry professionals. My own showcase was attended by some 300+ industry folk; sure enough, both my first and second jobs (a small part plus cover in a No.1 tour; an understudy job in a West End play) derived from auditions gained by having been seen by casting directors at that same showcase. In fact, the importance to your career of these showcases can't be understated: never again will you get the opportunity to impress (or repel) simultaneously so many influential figures.

View your age as an advantage

This last point highlights the one great advantage you have as a mature entrant: your age. The uncertainties and instabilities of the acting life are immense: for every one person embarking on a performing career, there is another giving up in disgust, disillusionment or because of financial necessity. This is all to your advantage: the overwhelming majority of new actors are going to be much younger than you; those falling by the wayside, however, will be much nearer your own age. And you will only ever be in direct competition with people who are in the same casting bracket as yourself.

Moreover, the sorts of roles you will be offered, in the first instance, are virtually tailored for the mature beginner: one-line TV roles; small parts with covers in plays; understudy jobs. This leads to another factor in your favour: actors who have been in the business for twenty-odd years will not be interested in doing the sort of parts you will be auditioned for. With regard to understudy jobs, for instance, I found that producers and directors can tend to prefer late starters precisely because they don't bring any of the 'that-should-have-been-me-up-there' bitterness which can characterise the older actor. As a late starter, you will possess the twin attributes that are actually a rare combination: maturity of years and fresh-faced enthusiasm.

With regard to the above, however, it should be pointed out that – as ever – women have 3,000 years of patriarchy ranged against them. As a late female starter, you will face a number of obstacles to gaining a professional foothold that simply don't apply to your male counterpart. Firstly, you will be in competition with an awful lot of women who, having trained or performed in their twenties, took time off to raise a family and are now trying their hand in the professional arena again. In other words, they will not only have a CV of professional credits, they will also be comparatively happy to take smaller parts. Secondly (in theatre, at least), just as there are many more leading roles for middle-aged and older males, so there are a concomitant number of smaller ensemble/covering jobs for men of the same age. Add in the fact that there are more parts for men generally (look at the cast list of any Shakespeare play, for instance), and you will see that the late female starter needs extra reserves of resilience and financial capital to embark on an acting career.

Have realistic expectations

In all of this there is an implicit point that should now be rendered explicit: don't expect leading roles. These, assuredly, will go to people who have been in the business a long time.

You may well find you are able to carve out a successful career as an actor (by successful, I mean 'working'; and by working, I mean 'working sporadically'); however, you will also find that you may – against your will and expectations – find yourself being constantly seen for small roles (and some roles can be very small: my first theatre job had nine lines, one of which was 'Yes,' another of which was 'No.'). The fact you played Curly five times for the Bloggs-on-Sea Amateur Operatic Society will cut no ice whatsoever. If you are hoping to be parachuted suddenly to stardom, forget it.

One detrimental consequence of your being determined to play leading roles at all costs is that you may find yourself being drawn to performing in 'fringe' and – the often laughably-misnamed – 'profit-share' productions. My own view is that working for no money is to be not working at all: a dilettante existence, because you have retired on a nice pension, playing King Lear either Upstairs at the Bunch of Grapes or Downstairs at the Bricklayers' Arms, may well satisfy your own ego, but cannot be regarded as an acting career as such. Such actors – and there are more than a few – are detrimental to the profession, precisely because they contribute to a culture wherein actors are expected to work for nothing. (Let this be my second prejudice.)

Always be pragmatic

One final practical consideration you must make, as I stated at the outset, is of the toll an acting career will take on you personally. Maintaining a family life while, say, being off on tour for six months is no mean feat, especially if your partner is used to you having a conventional working pattern. Conversely, if you are single, finding a partner can be tricky because the instability of your lifestyle, and the lack of security it represents, means that you are – to be frank – an unattractive proposition. I suppose I am expressing this in the bleakest possible terms, but I feel the most important attribute you need, as a late entrant to the acting profession, is pragmatism.

My conclusion is a brief one: the work is definitely out there for the late beginner – although it may not necessarily be the work you originally envisaged – provided you approach the task of carving out your new life with humility, practicality and emotional hardiness. Good luck, and welcome to the profession!

Hugh Osborne became an actor at the age of 37. He trained at the Bristol Old Vic Theatre School. Since graduating, he has appeared in numerous plays and musicals all over the country. West End shows include: *And Then There Were None*, *Donkeys' Years*, *Footloose*, and *The Last Cigarette*. He also appeared in *Afterlife* at the Royal National Theatre, and *The King and I* at the Albert Hall. Tours include: *The Lady in the Van*, *Noises Off*, *The Sound of Music* and, most recently, *To Sir With Love*. His own play, *Diary of a Nobody*, premiered at the Royal & Derngate, Northampton; a nationwide tour is currently in preparation.

Short-term and part-time courses

This section lists both 'taster' opportunities for drama school aspirants, and further training for professional actors.

Pre-drama-school courses

Competition for drama school places seems to be growing even more ferocious, and many applicants will enhance their chances if they go on a pre-drama-school course. You may, for example, have done A level Drama, but the actual acting training on such courses is often limited – generally geared more towards the exam-passing university entrant than auditioning for drama school. Whatever your acting background, a 'taster' course (for just a week, for instance) can give you a good idea of what further help/training you need in order to prepare you properly for drama school auditions.

Additional skills

As well as the organisations listed below, there are periodic 'one-off' workshops around the country. These are usually 'trailed', and sometimes advertised, in *The Stage*. Equity occasionally subsidises such enterprises (some, away from the major cities), so it is worth checking with your local Branch/Organiser. Actors Centres are not just places to sharpen up your existing skills and develop new ones, but also great meeting places for actors to exchange ideas and information.

Academy of Creative Training

8/10 Rock Place, Brighton, East Sussex BN2 1PF
tel (01273) 818266
email info@actbrighton.org
website www.actbrighton.org
Principal/Director Janette Edisford

All classes are in the evenings and at weekends to allow students to undertake actor training whilst maintaining their domestic and financial commitments. Monthly payment options are available by arrangement. Entry onto long courses is via audition (*Fee*: £30) or attendance on a 2-week intensive workshop (*Fee*: £100) held monthly throughout the year and designed as an introduction to actor training. Students embarking on the Diploma in Acting are eligible to audition for a bursary. Range of short courses and Summer Schools. The school operates an equal opportunities policy that includes disabled students, but there is limited access to the dance studio and washroom facilities.

Courses offered:

- ATCL Diploma in Acting (2 years). For students aged 18+. *Audition requirements*: as above
- Intensive Foundation Course (1 year, 10 hours per week). For students aged 16+. *Audition requirements*: as above
- Creative Playground (12 weeks of 3 hour Masterclasses, runs each term)
- Introduction to Playwriting (2 terms)
- Musical Theatre (12 weeks of 3 hour classes, runs each term).

Academy of Performance Combat (APC)

mobile (07963) 206803
email info@theapc.org.uk
website www.theapc.org.uk

APC is dedicated to bringing combat in any form in any media into the 21st century. "We are absolutely committed to safer, more exacting techniques than any other organisation." Please see the website for more details of courses and qualifications offered.

Actor Works

First Floor, Raine House, Raine Street, Wapping, London E1W 3RJ
tel 020-7702 0909
email ask@actorworks.org
website www.actorworks.org
Director Daniel Brennan

Full-time evening and weekend course: This course is designed for those who may:

- need to work during the day to pay for their training;
- have family commitments that prevent them from studying in the day;
- be considering changing their career and need to keep 'the day job' until the acting bug finally bites for good.

It is an intensive, 2-year vocational training, which covers all aspects of an actor's work. Subjects covered include: acting for stage, screen acting, actors' movement, speech, voice, reading, audition technique, stage combat, dance, singing and theatre history. During the course students will take part in up to 5 different productions, normally at the end of every term.

The course culminates in an agents' showcase at a major theatre and a season of graduation plays on the London fringe.

Students on this course must be aged 20+. There is no upper age limit.

There are 6 terms in all.

Postgraduate course: This course is designed for those who:
• studied drama at university and would like some more 'hands on' experience;
• have had actor training and would like to hone their skills.

This is a 1-year daytime course, which offers full actor training. Subjects covered include: acting for stage, screen acting, actors' movement, speech, voice, reading, audition technique, stage combat, dance, singing and theatre history. During the course students will take part in up to 4 different productions, normally at the end of every term.

The course culminates in an agents showcase at a major theatre and a season of graduation plays on the London fringe.

Students on this course must be aged 21+. There is no upper age limit.

There are 3 terms in all.

Foundation course: This course is designed for younger students who:
• need guidance and support through the gruelling process of auditioning for major drama schools;
• have not yet decided whether acting is for them;
• want to do something productive with their gap year.

This 1-year daytime course is not full actor training as such, but it prepares students for what they will experience should they choose to take up acting as a career. Emphasis is placed on preparation, application and discipline. We encourage confidence and a feeling of self-worth which helps students through the audition process. Subjects covered include: voice, speech, actors' movement, audition preparation, stage combat, theatre history and reading. Students can expect to take roles in 3 different productions over the year.

Students on this course must be between the ages of 17 and 20.

There are 3 terms in all.

Other courses offered: Also now runs a part-time course designed for those who wish to pursue acting as a leisure interest. "You may wish to 'test the water' before considering full-time training; to improve your self-confidence in group situations; to improve your public-speaking skills; or perhaps simply enjoy a new activity one night a week." These qualifications are currently NVQ Level 3 equivalent and from 2008 count for between 20 and 65 points towards UCAS tariffs. The cost for 10 Tuesday evenings is £350. For LAMDA tuition on Thursdays, an extra £100 (plus the cost of exam – £40-£50).There is no need to audition, though "please phone us in the first instance to reserve a place, before sending payment".

Actors Centre

1A Tower Street, Covent Garden,
London WC2H 9NP
tel 020-7240 3940
email act@actorscentre.co.uk
website www.actorscentre.co.uk
Chief Executive Louise Coles

Full membership is open to Equity members, registered graduates from the Conference of Drama Schools (now Drama UK) in their first year of registration (must hold a student Equity card), and foreign actors holding an Equity letter of exemption. Members are entitled to a wide range of subsidised classes and workshops led by experienced directors and tutors who are active in the industry, plus full use of the centre, café facilities when available and a quarterly schedule.

Regular classes and workshops include Acting, Tool Box, TV and Film, Auditions, Advice, Labwork, Voice, Shakespeare, Stage Combat, Directing, Musical Theatre and Writing. In addition, members can book individual sessions to work on singing, acting, sight-reading, Alexander Technique, dialect, voice and movement.

Please see the website for details of other types of membership and fees.

Actors Temple

Studio Theatre, 13-14 Warren Street,
London W1T 5LG
tel 020-3004 4537
email info@actorstemple.com
website www.actorstemple.com
Directors Mark Wakeling, Ellie Zeegen *Key contact* Tanja McGhie

Training and production company specialising in the Meisner technique. Studio theatre in the West End.

Courses offered:

• 5-week intensive 1st term; 5-week intensive 2nd term (20 weeks each).
• Introduction week (monthly; Mon-Fri 5 x 4-hour classes).

"Unfortunately there are stairs to the basement studio, so not good for wheelchair-users; we do however have a disabled toilet. We have a very open policy towards those with disabilities."

American Musical Theatre Academy London (AMTA)

Europa House, 13-17 Ironmonger Row,
London EC1V 3QG

tel 020-7253 3118
email info@americanacademy.co.uk
website www.americanacademy.co.uk
Principals/Directors Kenneth Avery-Clark, Christie Miller

Courses offered:

• One Year Full Time Musical Theatre Programme.
• Two Year Full Time Musical Theatre Programme.

No specific academic requirements; entry is by audition only. Applicants must be skilled in at least 2 of the 3 disciplines: acting, singing, dance. Train for a week in New York (one year course).

Welcomes candidates with disabilities, and will consider each on a case-by-case basis, according to the strength of their audition. Please note that current premises are not wheelchair accessible.

Arts Educational Schools, London (ArtsEd)*

Cone Ripman House, 14 Bath Road, Chiswick, London W4 1LY
tel 020-8987 6666
website www.artsed.co.uk

Courses offered:

• Post-Diploma BA (Hons) in Performance. Validated by City University. A year-long evening conversion course. Open to students who hold a diploma in acting or musical theatre from an NCDT (now Drama UK) or CDET accredited course.
• Foundation in Performance (1 year part-time). Acting or Musical Theatre option. 3 evenings per week running over 3 terms, starting in September.

Part-time evening and holiday courses for 17+ years:
• Various courses in acting and musical theatre disciplines, including stage, screen, voice, dance and audition technique, are offered for varying skill levels throughout the year.

For full details on all courses offered at ArtsEd, please visit **www.artsed.co.uk**.

Associated Studios

The Hub, St Alban's Fulham,
2 Margravine Road London W6 8HJ
tel 0207-3852 038
email info@associatedstudios.co.uk
website www.associatedstudios.co.uk
CEIO/Founding Principal Leontine Hass

Founded in 2007, Associated Studios offers professional development and training for actors, musical theatre performers and opera singers. There are several professional development workshops, masterclasses and short courses throughout the year, giving professional and/or experienced performers the opportunity to work on their skills. There is also a one year full-time training course (4 days per week) in musical theatre.

Full-time courses:

• Musical Theatre (1 year, full-time) – Lasting for 10 months, this course is open to applicants aged 18+. The total cost is £9,800. There are no specific entry requirements, but all potential applicants must audition for a place on the course.
• Musical Theatre Course (part time) – Lasting 4 months.
• Musical Theatre Course (part time) – Lasting 7 months.
• Opera Course (part time) – Lasting 4 months.
• Opera Course (full time) – Lasting 1 year.

For more information and full details of courses on offer, visit the website.

Birmingham School of Acting*

Millennium Point, Curzon Street,
Birmingham B4 7XG
tel 0121-331 7200 *fax* 0121-331 7221
email info@bsa.bcu.ac.uk
website www.bsa.bcu.ac.uk
Principal Stephen Simms *Admissions Manager* Roger Franke

Courses offered:

• Creative Drama (30 weeks part-time). 3 hours of classes per week
• Acting Summer School. 2 weeks in August
• Shakespeare Summer School. 4 days in August
• Musical Theatre Week. 6 days in August
• Musical Theatre Weekend. 2 days in August

The Birmingham Theatre School

The Old Fire Station, 285-287 Moseley Road, Highgate, Birmingham B12 0DX
tel 0121-440 1665
email info@birminghamtheatreschool.co.uk
website www.birminghamtheatreschool.com
Principal Chris Rozanski *Key contact* Fiona Allison (Arts Admin Manager)

Courses offered:

• Part-time Professional Diploma (Evenings & Weekends). Applicants must be aged 18 years or over.
• Acting for Beginners (11 weeks). Covers the basics of character creation, voice, improvisation and performance discipline for acting beginners. Students participate in all aspects of the creative process, from basic exercises to final presentations. Classes take place in the evening.
• Creating Performance (11 weeks). Each term, students will create and perform using a variety of techniques and using both texts and devised work. All aspects of character creation and working with an audience will be explored. Suitable for people with previous experience in acting. Classes take place in the evening.

The Bloomsbury Alexander Centre

Bristol House, 80A Southampton Row,
London WC1B 4BB

tel 020-7404 5348 or 020-8374 3184
email info@alexcentre.com
website www.alexcentre.com
Directors Stephen Cooper, Natacha Osorio

The centre specialises in teaching the Alexander Technique. Teachers are available for private lessons, with discounts available for students and actors. There are ongoing introductory workshops and courses, as well as drop-in vocal work for actors with experience of the AT. The introductory course runs for 4 weeks (1.5 hours a week) and costs £80. The drop-in AT vocal work classes are £15 per session. *Note for disabled actors*: "Our premises are on the ground floor with one step up onto the main entrance and one other just inside."

Boden Studios

99 East Barnet Road, New Barnet, Herts EN4 8RF
tel 020-8447 0909 *fax* 020-8449 5212
email info@bodenstudios.com
website www.bodenstudios.com
Director Adam Boden

Established in 1973. A part-time performing arts school offering 1 full scholarship each year.

Courses offered:

• Acting Performance – 12 weeks, 1.5 hours per week
• Guildhall Drama Exams – 12 weeks, 1 hour per week

British Academy of Dramatic Combat

website www.badc.co.uk

Offers a Performance Certificate in Stage Combat at Foundation, Basic, Basic Level 2, Recommended and Advanced levels. Training is available in the following methods: Broadsword & Shield, Double Handed Broadsword, Quarterstaff, Rapier & Dagger, Rapier & Cloak, Rapier & Buckler, Smallsword, Unarmed Combat. Programmes of workshops are arranged throughout the country, and anyone with suitable venue spaces or wanting to be added to the workshop mailing list should email **workshops@badc.co.uk.**

The British Academy of Stage & Screen Combat

Kemp House, 152 City Road, London EC1V 2NX
mobile (07837) 966559
email info@bassc.org
website www.bassc.org

The British Academy of Stage & Screen Combat was founded in 1993 with the aim of improving the standards of safety, quality and training of stage combat, and promoting a unified code of practice for the training, teaching and assessing of stage combat within the United Kingdom.

All BASSC teachers have undergone a rigorous training programme and the examining members of the BASSC are highly qualified, experienced professionals with a tradition of working in theatre throughout the UK, including the National Theatre, RSC, Royal Opera House, Liverpool Everyman, Theatre Royal York and Newcastle and Shakespeare's Globe, and television and film productions such as: *Alexander*, *Troy*, *Stardust*, *The Last Legion* and *Sherlock Holmes*.

BASSC teachers train students in stage combat at numerous drama schools, universities and colleges including: RADA, Central School of Speech and Drama, Birmingham School of Acting, Drama Studio London and Bath Spa University. They also teach students outside of drama courses at The City Literary Institute, and at independently run classes and workshops including the annual British National Stage Combat Workshop. Teachers run classes and workshops in the USA, Germany and Spain.

Since its formation the BASSC has established a reputation as the invigorating driving force behind stage combat in the United Kingdom, and is respected, both nationally and internationally, as the leading provider of professional-level stage combat training.

As a result of this, British Equity, in 1997, recognised the BASSC's Advanced Certificate as a valid qualification for entry onto the Equity Fight Directors' Training Scheme, and in 2001 the BASSC was appointed by the Equity Council for the training and assessment of Fight Director candidates applying to join the Equity Fight Directors' Register.

The BASSC now has training schemes in place which allow for development from actor/combatant to Certified Teacher, as well as assessment and training of Fight Directors for the Equity register.

The City Lit

Keeley Street, Covent Garden, London WC2B 4BA
tel 020-7492 2542
email drama@citylit.ac.uk
website www.citylit.ac.uk
website www.cltheatre.co.uk
Head of Drama, Dance & Speech Vivienne Rochester

The college offers an eclectic mix of disciplines such as acting, movement, voice, musical theatre, teaching, media, mime, circus, stage fighting, magic, comedy, dance, self-presentation, debating, accents, sight-reading and pronunciation for speakers of other languages, etc., which develop vocational, social and personal skills.

There are various small grants that might cover travel, books or child-care. Students may ring or come into the office for an interview between 12.30pm and 1.30pm (Monday and Wednesday), or 5.30pm and 6.30pm (Monday, Tuesday and Thursday).

The City Lit Theatre Company was set up to train a company of actors to produce work of the highest professional standard, providing a platform for its members to hone their skills and display their talents.

Directors, teachers and practitioners are invited and engaged to facilitate. Its members are made up of a combination of graduates from the accredited courses, or from the advanced/professional provision in the Drama, Dance & Speech department's programme, and experienced practitioners who wish to further their experience with the college. Auditions are held annually. The college has awarded associate status to a number of actors who have produced an excellent body of work with the company. All company members are eligible for the 3 productions staged each year, and some productions transfer on to other venues. Also, artists are invited, if appropriate, to professional castings that are occasionally held at The City Lit. Professional Masterclasses are held throughout the year.

The accredited courses are as follows (Drama UK recognised):

• Professional Acting Diploma (2 year full-time). Entry is by audition
• Drama Foundation course (1 year part-time). Entry is by audition
• Access to HE Diploma (drama) (1 year part-time). Entry is by audition
• Stage Fighting (1 year part-time, plus a number of shorter courses). Applicants must be aged 19 or over. Entry is by interview

A range of acting, voice, movement, TV and film, radio presenting classes and other related disciplines are also available. Courses run for 10-12 weeks or shorter with entry at various points throughout the year as well as a summer school throughout the months of July and August. Contact The City Lit for a prospectus and visit **www.citylit.ac.uk/dramaschool.**

Drama Studio London (DSL)*

1 Grange Road, London W5 5QN
tel 020-8579 3897 *fax* 020-8566 2035
email admin@dramastudiolondon.co.uk
website www.dramastudiolondon.co.uk
Principal Chris Pickles *Managing Director* Kit Thacker

Courses offered:

• 1 Year Diploma in Professional Acting
• 2 Year Diploma in Professional Acting
• Acting Summer School

East 15 Acting School*

Hatfields, Rectory Lane, Loughton IG10 3RY
tel 020-8508 5983 *fax* 020-8508 7521
email east15@essex.ac.uk
website www.east15.ac.uk
Director Leon Rubin *Key contact* Catherine Williams (Admissions Officer)

Courses offered:

For details of the summer 2016 programme please visit the website **www.east15.ac.uk/summercourses.asp**

All of the above courses carry University of Essex credits. Applicants must be aged 17 years or over.

École Internationale de Théâtre Jacques Lecoq

57 Rue du Faubourg Saint-Denis, 75010 Paris
tel 33 (0)1-4770 4478 *fax* 33 (0)1-4523 4014
email contact@ecole-jacqueslecoq.com
website www.ecole-jacqueslecoq.com
Principal Mrs Pascale Lecoq

Founded in Paris in 1956, with the aim of producing a young theatre of new work, generating performance languages which emphasise the physical playing of the actor. Focuses on art theatre, but with the view that theatre education is broader than the theatre itself: "It is a matter not only of training actors, but of educating theatre artists of all kinds." Provides as broad and durable a foundation as possible for every student. As well as the part-time courses listed below, offers a 2-year full-time Professional Course resulting in a Master Level Certificate. See also the company's entry under *Drama schools* on page 9. As a movement school, all classes require a great degree of physical movement, so applicants must be physically fit.

Courses offered:

• LEM (1 season October-June). 7 hours per week. Entry by file
• Introductory Course (1 season October-June). 5 hours per week. Entry by file

Fourth Monkey

The Monkey House, 97-101 Seven Sisters Road, London N7 7QP
tel 020-7281 0360
email office@fourthmonkey.co.uk
website www.fourthmonkey.co.uk
Artistic Director Mr Steven Green

A training provider with a difference, offering full- or part-time ensemble-based contemporary Rep training and professional performance opportunities.

Courses offered:

• Two Year Rep. 2 year, full-time actor training programme, 40 hours a week. Based in London and includes a month-long residential programme in Italy. Applicants must be aged 18 and over. Performance experience and A0-level qualifications or similar desirable but not compulsory.
• Year of the Monkey One Year Course, full-time actor training programme, 22-40 hours a week variable, concluding at the Edinburgh Fringe Festival. Applicants must be aged 18 and over. Performance experience and A-level qualifications or similar desirable but not compulsory.

Accepts applications from all areas of society; the only factor impacting suitability on any training programme is the presence of talent, a desire to learn and develop and an equal desire to work as an ensemble company member.

The Giles Foreman Centre for Acting

Studio Soho,
entrance in Royalty Mews (next to Quo Vadis),
22-25 Dean Street, London W1D 3AR
tel 020-7437 3175
email info@gilesforeman.com
website www.gilesforeman.com
Director Giles Foreman *Key contact* Lindsay Richardson

An exciting professional acting studio housing some of the country's top coaches in the disciplines of screen- and theatre-acting, movement, voice, improvisation on-camera, Meisner technique movement psychology and character analysis, directing and text analysis.

Comprises 2 easy-access large bright air-conditioned studios plus changing room, chillout area and kitchen, props store. (Wheelchair-accessible, entrance lift and step-free studio facilities.) Plus separate airy daylight-studio and meeting-rooms. Wi-Fi throughout.

Courses offered (many run throughout the year):

All ages from 17+.

• Complete Beginners/Introduction to Acting (10 weeks – 3 hours per week). Open entry
• Intermediate Acting (12 weeks – 4 hours per week). Entry by application
• Advanced Acting (12 weeks – 4 hours per week). Entry by application
• Professional Acting (12 weeks – 4 hours per week). Entry by interview/audition
• Movement (10 weeks – 2 hours per week). Entry by application
• Voice (10 weeks – 2 hours per week). Entry by application
• On-Camera (10 weeks – 3 hours per week). Entry by application
• Meisner Technique (10 weeks – 3 hours per week). Entry by application

Other courses offered:

• Meet the Industry Evenings (2 hours), September-July. Application via Spotlight or relevant CV
• Workshops – specialised subjects (12 hours over 2 days). Application by appropriate previous study and/or performing experience

GSA, Guildford School of Acting*

Stag Hill Campus, Guildford GU2 7XH
tel (01483) 560701
email info@gsauk.org
website www.gsauk.org
Head of GSA Terrie Fender

Courses offered:

• Singing in the Theatre (1 week). A summer course designed for students over the age of 17 who wish to improve their singing. Other disciplines relating to the voice will also be explored. Entry is in July
• Musical Theatre (2 weeks). Culminating in a performance in the Bellairs Playhouse, this course is open to students aged 17 or over and takes place in July/August
• Audition Techniques (1 week). Course takes place in August and is geared towards students aged 17 or over
• Intensive Musical Theatre Dance for Beginners (1 week). An intensive course to discover what your body is capable of doing. Explore the foundations of tap, jazz and ballet and get guidance and expert advice on what you need to work on and hopefully gain the confidence to compete in a dance class situation. The course takes place in August and is open to students 17 years and over
• Acting for Camera (1 week). The course takes place in August and is open to students 17 years and over

Other summer schools: Courses are offered at a reasonable cost and provide either a stimulating refresher course or an introduction to basic theatre training. There is no audition procedure, and everyone is welcome. All courses are staffed by members of the GSA faculty.

July/August:
• Youth Theatre (9 days)
• Musical Theatre (2 weeks)
• Intensive Musical Theatre Dance (5 days)
• Intensive Musical Theatre Acting (5 days)
• Intensive Musical Theatre Singing (5 days)
• Audition Technique (2 x 5-day sessions)
• Directing a Musical (5 days)
• Acting for Camera (5 days)

For further information or to download an application form, please refer to the website, or telephone or email (**summerschool@gsauk.org**) for a brochure.

Guildhall School of Music & Drama*

Silk Street, Barbican, London EC2Y 8DT
tel 020-7628 2571 *fax* 020-7256 9438
email dramasummerschool@gsmd.ac.uk
website www.gsmd.ac.uk
Director of Acting Wyn Jones

Founded in 1880, the Guildhall School is acknowledged internationally as a leading conservatoire for both music and drama.

Courses offered: The 2 summer school courses (Acting in Shakespeare & Contemporary Theatre; and Acting in Musical Theatre) each offer 3 weeks of stimulating and inspiring training in acting. Both will include class work or workshops with many of the school's core staff.

• Acting in Shakespeare & Contemporary Theatre. 3 weeks of intensive tuition, workshops and rehearsals. Students have craft-based classes for half of the day; for the other half they work with a director and explore short scenes from Shakespeare and contemporary plays, investigating the texts through

group exercises and improvisation. The aim is to demystify Shakespeare and provide a challenging insight into modern drama. The course concludes with a presentation of work-in-progress to students and staff (not open to the public) which may take the form of a workshop or open class.
• Acting in Musical Theatre. 3 weeks of intensive tuition, workshops and rehearsals. Students have craft-based classes for half the day; for the other half they work as an ensemble with a director on a musical project, exploring a selection of scenes, songs and dances based around a theme. The focus of the course will be upon the craft of acting within the context of musical theatre. It will conclude with a presentation of work-in-progress to students and staff (not open to the public) which may take the form of a workshop or open class. The course is led by Guildhall School tutor Martin Connor, who directs the school's annual musical.

Craft-based classes for both courses include: Acting, Voice, Movement, Improvisation, Mask, Combat, Historical, Dance and Audition Technique. At least 2 visits to attend performances in London theatres are included in the fees of both courses. Applicants must be at least 18 years old by the start of the course; there is no upper age limit. A good standard of English is essential. Accommodation is available. Please consult the website (**www.gsmd.ac.uk/dramasummerschool**) for up-to-date information on fees, curriculum and application procedure, or telephone 020-7382 7183 for details of the application procedure. Email enquiries to **dramasummerschool@gsmd.ac.uk**

"There is no application deadline but, in view of the limited number of places, applicants are strongly advised to book early. If the summer school is full, you will be placed on a waiting list."

Hope Street Ltd

13A Hope Street, Liverpool L1 9BQ
tel 0151-708 8007
email peter@hope-street.org
website www.hope-street.org
Director Peter Ward

Provides professional development for emerging artists: actors, directors, designers, composers, film makers, and production managers. The 6-month programme is led by professional artists from the UK and Europe. 4 or 5 projects are produced during the programme; these are cross-artform productions in the street, in unusual spaces and in non-traditional venues for audiences of between 150 and 30,000. Applications are welcome from anyone over 18 living anywhere in the world. No fees are payable. No training allowance is provided.

The Impulse Company

Twickenham
mobile (07525) 264173
email info@impulsecompany.co.uk
website www.impulsecompany.co.uk
Principal/Director Scott Williams *Key contact* Lindsay Mohun

Established for over 18 years in the UK, Scott Williams' Impulse Company provides Meisner-rooted core training for the adult actor within a supportive and positive atmosphere. It is currently focusing on its Modular part-time Year and Second Year part-time Rehearsal and Performance courses.

Courses offered:

• Modular Year course. 3 self-contained 8-week terms. Entry is by interview, in October and January each year. 8+ hours per week
• Second Year Rehearsal & Performance course. 3 self-contained 11-week rehearsal and performance periods per year. Entry is by completion of the Year course, or by invitation. 7+ hours per week

International School of Screen Acting

3 Mills Studios,Three Mill Lane, London E3 3DU
tel 020-8709 8719
email office@screenacting.co.uk
website www.screenacting.co.uk
*Key contact*Mark Normandy

Founded in 2001 to specialise in offering full-time training specifically in television and film acting, taking a holistic approach to creativity in relation to students' personal development.

Courses offered:

• 'Crash Course' – week-long course offered at various times throughout the year. No audition required
• Summer Course – week-long course offered in Aug/Sept. No audition required

Kogan Academy of Dramatic Art

9-15 Elthorne Road, Archway, London N19 4AJ
tel 020-7272 0027 *fax* 020-7272 0026
email info@scienceofacting.com
website www.scienceofacting.com
Principal Neil Sheffield

Formerly known as The Academy of the Science of Acting and Directing.

Courses offered:

• Three Year Evening Acting Course. Applicants must be aged 16 or over. Offers 14 places each year. *Audition requirements/fee*: see entry on page 11 for details.
• Two Year Evening Acting Course. Applicants must be aged 16 or over. Offers 14 places each year. *Audition requirements/fee*: see entry on page 11 for details.
• Intensive Acting Course (33 weeks). 6 hours of classes per week. No audition required.
• Spring Workshop (2 weeks). Course takes place in March. No audition required.

Training

• Summer Workshop (2 weeks). Course takes place in July. No audition required.

London Academy of Music and Dramatic Arts (LAMDA)*

155 Talgarth Road, London W14 9DA
tel 020-8834 0500 *fax* 020-8834 0501
email enquiries@lamda.org.uk
website www.lamda.org.uk
Principal Joanna Read *Admissions Assistants* Amy Richardson, Elissa Perrau, Philip McDonnell

Courses offered: Short-term courses are offered on the following:

• Shakespeare and His Contemporaries (8 weeks)
• Shakespeare (4 weeks)
• Physical Theatre (2 weeks)
• Audition Technique (2 weeks)
• English Communication Skills Through Drama Workshop (EFL – 3 weeks)
• Introduction to Drama School (2 weeks)
• EFL in Audition Technique (2 weeks)

With the exception of the Introduction to Drama School and Audition Technique courses, where the minimum age is 16, students on all other Summer Courses must be 18 years or above. For more information on all LAMDA's courses, including fees and deadlines, please visit the website.

London Academy of Radio, Film & TV

1 Lancing Street, London NW1 1NA
tel 0870-626 5100
website www.media-courses.com
Director of Courses Andy Parkin *Key contact* Estelle Burton

The academy has more than 30 teaching staff; around 1,200 students take one or more of its 100+ courses. It is situated opposite Euston Station.

Courses offered:

• Acting Masterclass (1 week – 30 hours). No audition required
• Acting for Film & TV (9-week course – 9 x 3 hours). No audition required (*Note*: 2 versions of this course exist – 1 on a weekday evening; 1 on a Saturday)

London School of Dramatic Art

4 Bute Street, London SW7 3EX
tel 020-7581 6100
email enquiries@lsda-acting.com
website www.lsda-acting.com
Principal Jake Taylor *Administrator* Lydia Palmese

Offers a range of comprehensive courses designed to develop individual creative talents, and to provide a thorough grounding in all aspects of performance as part of a student's preparation for a working life as an actor. There is currently no wheelchair access to the main building or training rooms: if this affects applicants who would like to know when these spaces become accessible, please let the school know. All auditions are free and no international student fees are charged. No formal qualifications are required, as the training is vocational: "We look more at potential and at levels of creativity."

Part-time 18+ acting courses:

• Foundation Diploma in Acting (2 years, 7.5 hours per week). Entry is by audition
• Access to Acting (10 weeks, 2 hours per week)

Short-term 18+ acting courses:

• Introduction to Acting (2 weeks in July)
• Introduction to Acting (2 weeks in August)
• Screen Acting (1 week in September)
• Audition Techniques (1 week in September)

Manchester School of Acting

14-32 Hewitt Street, Manchester M15 4GB
tel 0161-238 8900
email info@manchesterschoolofacting.co.uk
website www.manchesterschoolofacting.co.uk
Key contact Mark Hudson

High-profile acting school offering part-time training for actors.

Method Acting London

16-18 Heneage Street, London E1 5LJ
tel 020-7622 9742
email main@methodacting.co.uk
website www.methodacting.co.uk
Principal/Director Sam Rumbelow

Within the specifically defined and well-established structure of the classes, provides a grounded, conscious understanding of the craft of acting is facilitated, while unlocking powerful creativity of your thoughts, impulses and emotions. Entry is after a detailed talk and discussion of class and the applicant, conducted by phone.

Part-time/short-term 16+ acting courses:

• Main Class (4 weeks, 16 hours per week)
• Mid Class (4 weeks, 3 hours per week)

Michael Chekhov Studio

48 Vectis Road,
London SW17 9RG (Administative Office)
tel 020-8696 7372
email info@michaelchekhovstudio.org.uk
website www.michaelchekhovstudio.org.uk
Director Graham Dixon *Key Contact* Ian Bevins

Founded in 2003, the MCSL provides actors (and directors) an opportunity to explore Michael Chekhov's unique approach to the art of acting. Many drama trainings are based upon 'closed systems' that look inside one's own psychology to create a character but Chekhov created an 'open system' that permits actors to enter an objective creative world immediately using an increased ability to imagine and sense. Yearly programs of workshops, classes and intensives on the basic techniques of

Chekhov leading to more advanced work including ensemble initiatives with evolving developments into the area of quantum physics and the holistic views of Steiner, Jung, Tolle and other philosophy as a best practice methodology.

Morley College

61 Westminster Bridge Road, London SE1 7HT
tel 020-7450 1832
email drama@morleycollege.ac.uk
website www.morleycollege.ac.uk
Key contact Dominic Grant

Offers part-time acting classes from entry-level to advanced. Classes are led by specialist acting tutors with extensive professional experience. An Access Hardship Fund and concessionary fees are available to some students.

Courses offered:

• A range of evening and part-time acting skills courses are available, including: Acting level 1, 2 and 3; Acting: The Company; courses in Physical Theatre, Directing, Playwrighting, Voice, Devising, Mask, Mime, and Clowning. Drama skills including courses for actors with moderate learning disabilities, Confidence through Acting Courses, Public Speaking courses and many others. Some courses require tutor approval.

Mountview Academy of Theatre Arts*

Clarendon Road, London N22 6XF
tel 020-8881 2201
email enquiries@mountview.org.uk
website www.mountview.org.uk
Principal Stephen Jameson

Courses offered:

• Foundation Acting (1 year). 9 hours of classes per week. Entry is by audition.
• Foundation Musical Theatre (30 weeks). Full-time. 30 hours of classes per week. Entry is by audition.
• Actors' Masterclass (3 weeks), Course takes place in July/August. No audition required.
• Musical Theatre Bootcamp (3 weeks). Course takes place in JulyAugust. No audition required.
• Amateur Directors' Weekemd (2 days). Course takes place in July. No audition required.

Oxford School of Drama*

Sansomes Farm Studios, Woodstock,
Oxford OX20 1ER
tel (01993) 812883
email info@oxforddrama.ac.uk
website www.oxforddrama.ac.uk
Principal George Peck *Executive Director* Kate Ashcroft

Course offered:

• Six Month Foundation Course in Acting, runs from September to March. Aimed at students aged 18 and over. The course covers acting methods and technique, movement, voice, singing, film and television and stage fighting. 32 hours of classes per week for 22 weeks. Graduates include Philip McGinley (regular in *Game of Thrones*) and Lydia Rose Bewley (regular in *The Royals* and *Drifters*. Entry is by audition.

Pineapple Dance Studios

7 Langley Street, London WC2H 9JA
tel 020-7836 4004 *fax* 020-7836 0803
email studios@pineapple.uk.com
website www.pineapple.uk.com

Pineapple offers more classes than any other studio throughout Europe, and the widest variety of dance styles. The philosophy behind the creation of the Pineapple Dance Studios was to break down the elitist barriers surrounding dance, making it available to everyone – from the absolute beginner to the advanced and the professional dancer. All classes are open, so you do not need to book; you can just come along at any time and join a class. Everybody is welcome: Pineapple offers classes for all levels and all ages. Approx. 200 classes per week, ranging from classical ballet to street jazz, hip hop to Salsa, Egyptian dance to Bollywood grooves plus many more. Opening hours: Mon to Fri: 9am–9pm; Sat: 9am–6pm.

Poor School

242 Pentonville Road, London N1 9JY
tel 020-7837 6030 *fax* 020-7837 5330
email acting@thepoorschool.com
website www.thepoorschool.com
Principal Paul Caister

The school was created in 1986 with the aim of providing high-quality acting training that is financially within the reach of all, or almost all. Training lasts 2 years and operates in the evenings and at weekends until the final 2 terms, when daytime work is involved. Since March 1993 the Poor School has owned its own theatre, the Workhouse; this is a flexible studio theatre seating 50-80.

Short courses:

The Poor School runs 4-day courses through the year, and many take these as an alternative to audition. There is also a summer programme of short acting courses from June to September, incorporating 3-week, 4-day and shorter courses. Accommodation in London may be booked through the school.

The Questors Theatre Ealing

12 Mattock Lane, London W5 5BQ
tel 020-8567 0011 *fax* 020-8567 2275
email enquiries@questors.org.uk
website www.questors.org.uk
Principal David Emmet *Key contact* Andrea Bath (Executive Director)

Provides part-time training for actors in the context of a working theatre. Financial support is available from a private trust fund for a limited number of students.

Courses offered:

• Acting: Foundation and Performance (2 years). 6 hours of classes per week. Entry is by audition.
• Introduction to Acting (1 year). Age range for entry is 17-20. 3 hours of classes per week. Entry is by audition.

Royal Academy of Dramatic Art (RADA)*

62-64 Gower Street, London WC1E 6ED
tel 020-7636 7076 *fax* 020-7323 3865
email enquiries@rada.ac.uk
website www.rada.org
Key contact Sally Power

Courses offered:

• Acting Shakespeare (8 weeks). Designed for experienced actors, this course offers an opportunity to expand, explore and deepen awareness of Shakespeare's texts. Covers all aspects of vocal technique, with classes to develop the resonance and range of each student's voice. The last 2 weeks of the course are spent in full-time rehearsal for a workshop production culminating in 3 performances in a RADA theatre. Entry is deliberately restricted, and places are awarded by competitive audition. Students below the age of 18 are not normally accepted; most students are in their 20s. Course takes place in June and July. *Audition requirements*: 1 speech from Shakespeare and 1 from a modern play, each lasting no longer than 3 minutes.
• The RADA Summer School (4 weeks). Based on exploring Shakespeare from an actor's point of view, this course mixes rehearsing scenes and speeches with intensive classes in essential acting skills. Students below the age of 18 are not normally accepted; most students are in their 20s. Course takes place in July and August. No audition required.
• Musical Theatre (5 days). This course is designed for intermediate and advanced singer-actors who have already received some formal vocal training and are intending to pursue a career in musical theatre. During the course, guidance on casting and help with audition repertoire is given. Students work with a singing tutor, director, choreographer and musical director, both in groups and individually, to develop the necessary skills required by the successful singer-actor in today's musical theatre. At the end of the course there is an informal presentation of selected pieces for an invited audience, followed by individual feedback.
• The RADA Contemporary Drama Summer School (10 days). This course provides the opportunity to work on modern or contemporary texts. Students work in groups led by a director, with support from a voice and a movement instructor. Other playwrights talk about their work during special evening sessions, describing their experience of working with actors and what they expect from them, following presentations of excerpts from their plays by RADA graduates. Students present rehearsed material and receive feedback from the director and the voice and movement teachers on the last day of the course. Students below the age of 18 are not normally accepted; there is no upper age limit.
• European Greats. This 5-day course examines scenes from Chekhov and Ibsen. Fresh approaches to the work of these authors is encouraged, along with looking at how the themes of these plays are still urgent and relevant to us today. Scenes are explored with a director, and participants are asked to thoroughly review their process of rehearsal in accordance with the material. The course is aimed at those with some experience of acting who want the opportunity to explore these writers from the point of view of the performer.

Richmond Drama School

RACC, Parkshot, Richmond TW9 2RE
tel 020-8891 5907 ext. 4018
email IAG@racc.ac.uk
website www.RACC.ac.uk
Course Director Victoria Hobbs

Courses offered:

Richmond Drama School offers established courses; including Access to Drama (HE), Foundation Year in Acting, Foundation Year in Musical Theatre, Audition Techniques, Stage Combat, Improvisation, a Shakespeare summer school and many others. With an exceptional reputation for outstanding teaching and a strong history of placing students in the country's top CDT drama schools; these include RADA, Central, Guildhall, LIPA and ALRA amongst others. Many previous students, who have not desired an academic pathway, have been able to step straight into the professional industry. Up-to-date details are available from the website.

Rose Bruford College*

Lamorbey Park, Burnt Oak Lane, Sidcup DA15 9DF
tel 020-8308 2600 *fax* 020-8308 0542
email enquiries@bruford.ac.uk
website www.bruford.ac.uk
Principal Professor Michael Earley

Courses offered:

• Acting Summer School (2 weeks). Designed for participants over the age of 18 (16+ for non-residential students), this programme includes classes, rehearsals and workshops on voice, movement, acting and improvisation.
• Acting Advanced Intensive (12 weeks). Designed for professionals wanting additional training.
• MA Ensemble Theatre (full time, 13 months). Designed for professional practitioners to develop their practice as a researcher through experiential learning.
• MA Theatre for Young Audiences (part or full time). Designed to work and study with leading TYA figures.

The Royal Central School of Speech and Drama*

64 Eton Avenue, London NW3 3HY
tel 020-7722 8183 *fax* 020-7722 4132
email short.courses@cssd.ac.uk
website www.cssd.ac.uk
Principal Gavin Henderson

A selection of courses offered:

Evening Courses (3 terms a year)

(18+ years)

- Acting – An Introduction
- Acting – Text 1
- Acting – Text 2
- Acting – Shakespeare
- Audition Technique
- Directing – An Introduction
- Voice for Performance – An Introduction
- Singing
- Saturday Youth Theatre for 6-17 year olds

Diplomas

(18+ years)

- Gap Year Diploma (October start)
- Acting Diploma (January start)
- Musical Theatre Diploma (January start)
- Performance Making Diploma for Learning Disabled Adults (January start)

Summer School (from July to August)

Acting

(17+ Years)

- Combat and Stage Fighting
- Summer Musical Theatre
- How to Become an Actor
- Improvisation
- Acting for Beginners
- Actors' Audition Pieces
- Directed Scenes
- Summer Shakespeare
- Summer Theatre Company
- Acting for Camera for Beginners

Voice

(17+ Years)

- Voice Fundamentals 1: Good Voice Use
- Voice Fundamentals 2: Voice in Performance

Youth Theatre

(Ages 6-17 years)

- Youth theatre for Actors I (Age 11-17) (1 week)
- Youth theatre for Actors II (Age 11-17) (2 weeks)
- Youth theatre for Actors (Age 6-11) (1 week)
- Preparing for Higher Education: Studying Drama (Age 15-17)

Theatre Royal Haymarket Masterclass Trust

Theatre Royal Haymarket, London SW1Y 4HT
tel 020-7389 9660
email info@masterclass.org.uk
website www.masterclass.org.uk
Patrons Dame Judi Dench, Sir Peter Hall, Sir David Hare, Maureen Lipman CBE

Masterclass is a theatre charity based at the Theatre Royal Haymarket that opens doors to young people from all backgrounds, aged 16-30, who are interested in the performance industry. The programme provides workshops and talks with leading actors, directors, designers and writers working in theatre today, alongside unique performance experiences, apprenticeship opportunities and community projects.

Previous Masters have included Danny DeVito, Simon Callow, Mike Leigh, Alan Rickman, Joanna Lumley and Idris Elba. For details of forthcoming events, consult the website.

Theatre Workout Ltd

13A Stratheden Road, Blackheath, London SE3 7TH
tel 020-8144 2290
email enquiries@theatreworkout.com
website www.theatreworkout.com
Director Adam Milford

Bespoke theatre workshops and events in the West End. Services include short courses, training, coaching, dramaturgy and other client services. Workshops, courses and events are often on request by groups, but also has a new programme offering short courses throughout the year. Interested parties should either sign up to the company's newsletter or visit the website for more information.

Bespoke workshops and training in London's West End. Programmes include one-off workshops, short courses, private coaching, hospitality and production services.

Youngblood

Top Floor, 57 Paddington Street, Marylebone, London W1U 4HZ
tel 020-7193 3207
email info@youngblood.co.uk
website www.youngblood.co.uk

A company of fight directors and stage-combat teachers. Runs ongoing classes for professional actors in various locations around London. Also provides fight directors and trainers for film, television and theatre projects, including low-budget productions.

Private tutors and coaches

ABI Acting

email stephanie.schonfield@googlemail.com

Specialises in audition technique, relaxation, unlocking and analysing Shakespeare, text preparation and voice training for professional actors and drama school candidates. Charges a basic rate of £35 per hour, but is happy to discuss with each individual client how a session can be made to meet their specific needs. Is happy to provide material for private students to use, and to answer minor follow-up queries after a lesson.

Teaches at home but is happy to travel to a client's home for a small extra cost. The nearest station is Kensal Green tube or Kensal Rise overground station. – a 7-minute walk. Bus routes are 452, 187, 52 and 6. Has taught many actors and aspiring actors for 7 years in a variety of roles. These range from visiting lecturer and audition panelist at several top London drama schools to tutor and private coach. Is also an actress in TV, film and theatre for over 20 years. "My extensive experience means I understand, and can effectively address, both the actor's needs and the industry's demands."

Audition Doctor

South East London
mobile (07764) 193806
email tilly.blackwood@gmail.com
website www.auditiondoctor.co.uk

A bespoke service that provides invaluable help for auditions, whether you are a professional actor dealing with confidence issues or a Drama School applicant. Charges £40 per hour. Is happy to provide material for private students to use, and to answer minor follow-up queries at no extra charge. Teaches from a home location with weekly surgeries conducted at The Actors Centre (both are wheelchair accessible). The nearest station is Borough on the Northern Line, around a 4-minute walk away. "I have been, and continue to be, a professional working actor for the last 20 years, and have been teaching for the last 3. With my sanity intact and an undwindled passion for the business, I am perfectly placed to give up-to-date assistance, direction and information in an ever-changing profession." Audition Doctor has been listed in the top 10 Acting Coaches on the Acting in London website

Barbara Berkery

London N19
tel 020-7281 3139
email barbaraberkery@hotmail.com

Specialises in accents, voice and text. Details of fees and discounts are available upon enquiry. Happy to provide material for private students to use, and to answer minor follow-up queries at no extra charge. Teaches from home and/or studio, both of which are wheelchair accessible. Main teaching location is 10 minutes' walk from Holloway Road tube (bus routes 17, 43, 271 and 263). Further details are available from IMDb. Has taught hundreds of actors/aspiring actors over a period of 30 years, and possesses extensive experience both as an actress and as a director. Works with her Associates at Vox Barbarae, Elspeth Brodie and Eleanor Boyce, which is often more convenient both financially and logistically.

Nancy Bishop Casting

35a WentworthStreet, London E1 7TD
email workshops@nancybishopcasting.com
website www.nancybishopcasting.com

Specialises in on-camera audition coaching. Nancy Bishop is primarily a casting director, but sometimes also works as a coach for on-camera auditioning. She is the founder of the Acting for Film department at the Prague Film School, and teaches her technique in masterclasses throughout Europe, as well as in New York, Los Angeles and internationally. She has lectured at the Actors Centre in London, the National Theater Institute in the US, and the Royal Scottish Academy of Music and Drama. Subject to availability, she can coach in London or via Skype, provided it is not for a film she is casting. For more information, see her book, *Auditioning for Film and TV* (Bloomsbury Methuen Drama). Check her website for an audition masterclass schedule.

Main areas of work are film, TV and commercials. Prefers to meet actors during the production process. Welcomes introductions with CV and one photo by email. Also selcome invitations to theatre or screening in London by email.

Irene Bradshaw

Flat F, Welbeck Mansions, Inglewood Road, West Hampstead, London NW6 10X
020-7794 5721*mobile* (07949) 552915
email irene@irenebradshaw.fsnet.co.uk
website www.voice-power-works.co.uk

Specialises in audition technique, voice/production, RP and accents. Charges £45 per hour, which is a special rate for actors. Provides material for students to use, and all lessons are recorded to CD or memory stick. Is happy to answer minor follow-up queries. Teaches from home (unless a client is disabled, in which case will travel to theirs); the nearest tube is West Hampstead, a 5-minute walk. Bus routes are C11, 139 and 328.

Has taught "countless" actors and aspiring actors over 36 years. An actress for more than 20 years in film, television and theatre, she trained in the Linklater method of voice production at LAMDA with Kristin Linklater, sponsored by the Arts Council of Great Britain. Has taught at the City Lit, the Actors Centre and most of the leading stage and drama schools, as well as running her own theatre company, where she directed several plays in new writing as well as classics. Has trained numerous students for entry into drama school with considerable success, and has helped many actors find their voice.

Ross Campbell

Canalot Studios, Kensal Road,
London W10 and Farnborough, GU14
mobile (07956) 465165
email rosscampbell@ntlworld.com
website www.rosscampbell.biz
website www.musicaltheatreireland.ie

Specialises in acting techniques, audition preparation, college entrance and related examinations and diplomas. Charges £75 per hour. Is happy to provide material for private students to use, and to answer minor follow-up queries after a lesson.

Teaches in a private studio at home in Surrey and a private London studio, the latter of which is wheelchair-accessible. The nearest stations are Ladbroke Grove and Westborne Park – a 7-minute walk. Alternatively, take a number 23 bus. Has taught many actors and aspiring actors for 30 years. Ross is a professor at the Royal Academy of Music London, Head of Singing and Musical Theatre at Musical Theatre Ireland (MTI), a former head of music and singing at Guildford School of Acting (GSA) and a consultant to Musical Theatre Poland (MTP).

Mel Churcher

mobile (07778) 773019
email melchurcher@hotmail.com
website www.melchurcher.com
website www.actinganddrama.com

Teaches in Central London and by Skype. More details are available from www.imdb.com and from own websites.

Has taught thousands of actors and aspiring actors over 30 years. Has worked as an actor and theatre director; taught at most major UK drama schools and at the Actors Centre; coached on more than 50 films; run national and international workshops; and authored 2 books: *A Screen Acting Workshop plus DVD* (Nick Hern Books, 2011), and *Acting for Film: Truth 24 Times a Second* (Virgin Books, 2003). Holds an MA in Performing Arts (Middlesex) and in Voice Research (CSSD). "I am happy to help with most aspects of auditioning and working in theatre and film. I can can advise on understanding the differences between film and theatre, film technique, and building confidence and overcoming nerves."

MJ Coldiron

54 Millfields Road, London E5 0SB
mobile (07941) 920498
fax 020-8533 1506
email jiggs@blueyonder.co.uk

Offers audition coaching for professional and aspiring actors; advice about theatre and performance training in the US and the UK; and coaching in acting technique, public speaking and presentation skills. Charges £45 per hour (3 sessions for £120). Occasional group workshops. Can provide material for clients and is happy to receive minor follow-up queries. Teaches from home studio, with the nearest rail station being Hackney Central Overground. Has taught hundreds of aspiring actors over 25 years: please make contact for more details. Advises clients: "The theatrical profession is very demanding and is not to be sought for fame or fortune. It is also very competitive and you must work hard, but if you have talent, desire and discipline I can help you to improve your technique and gain in confidence."

The Confident Voice

School of Economic Science Building,
11-13 Mandeville Place, London W1V 3AJ
mobile (07976) 805976
email neville@speakwell.co.uk
website www.speakwell.co.uk

Specialises in audition technique and voice. Dialogue coach, Shakespeare, musical comedy and lyrical interpretation. Services include coaching in elocution, communication techniques and self-awareness; also the establishment of confidence and natural performance. Fee details are available on application. Offers special packages and coaching in stage, TV and radio techniques. Teaches from the Mandeville Place address, which is wheelchair-accessible. The nearest station is Bond Street underground, around 3 minutes' walk away (bus route 10). Has taught hundreds of actors and directors over 20 years. Advises clients: "Have complete faith and confidence in *yourself.* Continual work on voice and movement and penetration of Shakespeare – the greatest master Teacher."

Jerry Cox MA BA PGCE

4 Stevenson Close, Barnet, Herts EN5 1DR
mobile (07957) 654027
email jerrymarwood@hotmail.com

Specialises in audition technique and voice. Charges £25 per hour or £40 for 2 hours. Is happy to provide material for private students to use, and to answer minor follow-up queries. Teaches from home or from the client's home. The nearest railway is Oakleigh Park/Totteridge & Whetstone – a 10-15 minute walk from the main teaching location. Bus route 383. Has taught 300-500 actors and aspiring actors over 8 years, and worked as an actor, deviser and director; lots of film, theatre, TIE and touring experience. Advises clients: "To paraphrase Bella Merlin, get the process right, and the results look after themselves."

Bridget de Courcy

19 Muswell Road, London N10

Taught singing at the Actors Centre, Covent Garden for 19 years.

Jane de Florez, LGSM PGDip

West Kensington/Barons Court, London W14
tel 020-7602 0741
email janedeflorez@gmail.com
website www.singingteacherlondon.com; www.janedeflorez.co.uk

Specialises in singing technique, repertoire, performance, auditions. Charges £45 per hour. Is happy to provide material for private students to use, and to answer minor follow-up queries at no extra charge. Teaches from home studio, which is 5 minutes' walk from West Kensington and Barons Court tube stations. Has taught hundreds of actors and aspiring actors for the past 20 years, and now sees at least 10 pupils each week who are performers or aspiring performers. Teaches a strong, versatile technique that is suitable for all types of music. Most students go into classical, musical theatre and cabaret.

Tess Dignan

4 Oregon Building, Deals Gateway,
London SE13 7RR
mobile (07528) 576915
email tess.dignan@gmail.com

Specialises in audition and performance coaching. Charges £50 per hour and is happy to provide material for private students to use. Also happy to answer minor follow-up queries after a lesson.

Teaches at home, which is wheelchair-accessible. The nearest station is Deptford Bridge – a 2-minute walk away. Has taught thousands of actors and aspiring actors for over 21 years. More information on Tess's career can be obtained through her agent Upson Edwards. Her advice to aspiring actors is to "never stop training."

Antonia Doggett

1 Brading Crescent, Wanstead, E11 3RT
tel (07814) 155090
email antoniadoggettcontact@gmail.com
website www.antoniadoggett.co.uk

Specialises in audition preparation, cold reading, text, Shakespeare, voice, LAMDA/Trinity examinations, one to one, courses and workshops. Charges £30 per hour and prefers payment by PayPal or electronic transfer. Is happy to provide material for private students to use, and to answer minor follow-up queries after a lesson.

Teaches at home, or happy to travel to central, south or south east London or client's home. The location is wheelchair accessible and the nearest station is Holborn – a 3-minute walk away. Has taught around actors and aspiring actors for 7 years and previously trained with Teatr Piesn Kozla, Poland, assistant director for Stathis Livathinos, National Theatre of Greece. Also an examinar for London College of Music and New Era examinations. Currently a voice coach for *Waterloo Road.*

Drama School Auditions

mobile (07862) 255402
email matt@dramaschoolauditions.co.uk
website www.dramaschoolauditions.co.uk

Specialises in audition technique (particularly for drama schools), casting, performance confidence and personal management. Offers a range of course options with different pricings; please consult the website for details. Bursaries may be considered in extreme circumstances. Preferred payment methods are cheque or BACS transfer. Has an extensive database of both classical and modern speeches, which are used in conjunction with the courses. Minor follow-up queries are addressed at no extra charge. Courses take place at various studios, and wheelchair-accessible locations can be organised with advance notice. The company has been running for more than 3 years and has taught many actors and aspiring actors. Details about the tutors are available from the website.

Ben Eedle

273 Camberwell New Road, London SE5 0TF
mobile (07587) 526286
email ben@theenglishbears.com
website www.theenglishbears.com

Specialises in voice into acting. Charges £40 per session (min 1.5hr), and offers a free 30-minute consultation. Happy to provide material for private students to use and will answer minor follow-up queries at no extra cost. Teaches at home (not wheelchair accessible) or at the client's home, provided the latter has access to a piano. The nearest tube is Oval on the Northern line, about a 15-minute walk away. Buses are 436, 185, 36 (all direct from Oval tube). Has taught more than 100 actors or aspiring actors. Trained at Webber Douglas and is still a working actor. Has also directed theatre productions. Advises actors: "Your authentic voice is central to the successful playing of any character."

Julia Gaunt

1 Brandreth Drive, Giltbrook, Nottingham
tel (01159) 385689 *mobile* (07712) 624083
email joolsmusicbiz@aol.com
website www.joolsmusicbiz.com

Specialises in singing, musical theatre, secure vocal technique, voice and performance; subsidiary of Jools Music Biz. Charges a minimum of £30, and a maximum of £45, per hour, with discounted rates for block bookings. Happy to provide material for clients and to receive minor follow-up enquiries. Teaches from home, but will travel (if travel costs paid) for a company or group. The nearest railway station is Langely Mill or Nottingham; easily accessible from the M1.

More information can be found on the website. Has taught hundreds of aspiring singers and actors both privately and in association with colleges and universities. She is a member of the British Voice Association and the Incorporated Society of Muscians and has run many workshops and masterclasses. Advises clients: "Remember the 3 Ds: Determination, Dedication and Discipline."

Prue Gillett Actor Training

Cheshire
email coaching@pruegillett.com
website www.pruegillett.com/coaching

Specialises in Meisner Technique, Received Pronunciation and Accent Reduction. Charges from £20 per 3.5-hour session for group classes, and £30 per hour for private sessions. When possible will provide material for students' use, and will answer minor follow-up queries at no extra cost. Teaches from home and studio bases in Altrincham, South Manchester. The nearest station is Altrincham, around 8 minutes on foot from the main teaching location. Buses, trains and trams run from Manchester to Altrincham. Please see website for further details.

John Grayson

2 Jubilee Road, St Johns, Worcester WR2 4LY
mobile (07702) 188031
email jgtutor-performer@yahoo.co.uk
website www.JohnLGrayson.com

Specialises in audition technique, voice, accents, singing, public speaking and coaching. Charges £25 per hour. Can provide material for students and is happy to receive minor follow-up queries. Can teach from home or from a client's house. The nearest station is Worcester Foregate Street (there is a good service from Birmingham), from which the house is 10-15 minutes' walk. Has taught around 20 aspiring actors in about 6 years. Please see website for more details. Is happy to advise students on how to survive when not working.

Martin Harris

32 Baxter Road, Sale, Manchester M33 3AL
tel 0161-969 1444 *mobile* (07788) 723570
email martin@auditioncoach.co.uk
website www.auditioncoach.co.uk

Specialises in audition technique and selection and direction of audition pieces. Offers group acting classes as well as one-to-one tuition for aspiring and professional actors. Also teaches sight reading and gives advice about CVs, agents and jobs. Charges £25 per hour, with a discount of 20% if the client pays for 10 sessions in advance. Accepts payment with cash or cheque, or via Internet banking.

Is happy to provide material for private students to use, and will answer minor follow-up queries at no extra charge. Teaches at home, or at the client's home (with a small extra charge). The home office is wheelchair-accessible. Sale metrolink is the nearest station, around 5 minutes' walk from the office (bus routes: 16, 18, 18A, 19, 41, 86, 99, 245, 263, 264, 266, 267, 268 and 272). Has taught more than 200 actor clients over 10 years. Trained as an actor at Birmingham School of Acting, and has worked as an actor and director since 1995. Currently also Artistic Director of Rocket Theatre in Manchester.

Daniel Hoffmann-Gill

London
mobile (07946) 433903
email danielhg@gmail.com

Specialises in actor confidence-building, improvisation technique, removing actors' blocks, audition technique, casting technique and various practitioner-centred methods such as Guskin, Meisner, Lecoq and Donnellan. Has been a professional actor for more than 16 years, working in film, TV and theatre, and has taught actors for over 14 years. Focuses on one-to-one work, aimed at enabling the actor to do themselves and their imagination justice – also, on practical assistance in audition technique and how to do the very best you can in any casting situation, "no matter how bizarre". Uses real casting briefs and exercises, for students to try out their ideas.

Currently teaches at the Central School of Speech and Drama as a guest lecturer, at the Actors Centre and for the National Theatre, as well as for numerous London agents. References from previous students are available on request. Charges £50 per hour, with special packages available for long-term work or working towards drama school entry: these are tailored on an individual basis, so please email for details. Works from home or from the client's home, and occasionally uses performance spaces, depending on the project. All locations used are wheelchair-accessible. Has taught around 300 actors. Advises clients that "hard graft and positive attitude go a long way in a tough, tough industry".

Jennifer Jane Hooker

Based in Central London
mobile 07725 977146
email jj@jjhooker.com
website www.jjhooker.com

Specialises in character work, scene breakdown, emotional and sensory work, and audition technique. Charges £40 per hour with a free introductory meeting. Teaches both known, named actors and students at college. Trained with Susan Batson of Susan Batson Studios, NYC, who sends her actors to JJ when they are in Europe. Has additional add on to coaching of Human Software Engineering, a 'debugging' technique to get rid of past conditioning and reach your full potential. Will accept cash, cheque and online payments. Is happy to provide material for use by private students and to answer minor follow-up queries at no extra cost. Nearest tube stations are Marylebone, Baker Street and Edgware Road (5 minutes' walk from main teaching location). Bus routes are 205, 2, 18, 27, 74, 113, 13, 139 and 189.

Mark Hudson

MSA, 14-32 Hewitt Street, Manchester M15 4GB
tel 0161-238 8900
email info@manchesterschoolofacting.co.uk
website www.manchesterschoolofacting.co.uk

Film, television and theatre - acting, dialogue and dialect coach.

Charlie Hughes-D'Aeth

Based in Brighton and London
mobile (07811) 010963
email chdaeth@aol.com

Text and Voice Coach. Currently consultant text and voice coach on RSC's *Matilda the Musical* and resident voice coach on Warner Bros' *Charlie and the Chocolate Factory*.

Offers coaching on practical voice technique for text and singing.

Desmond Jones

20 Thornton Avenue, London W4 1QG
tel/fax 020-8747 3537
email enquiries@desmondjones.com
website www.desmondjones.com

Specialises in physical audition techniques and mime and physical theatre. One of the founders of physical theatre; has run his own School of Mime and Physical Theatre for 25 years, with expertise in all aspects of movement. Charges are negotiable, with various packages and discounts available; please make contact for more information. Will provide clients with occasional worknotes and is happy to answer minor follow-up queries. Teaches out of home (a 3-minute walk from Turnham Green station, bus routes 94, 27, H91, 191, 267), or the home of the client – whichever is more suitable. Has taught more than 2,500 aspiring actors over 40 years. Advises clients: "Do it now!"

Lawrence Lambert

c/o The Actors Centre, 1A Tower Street, London WC2H 9NP
email lawrielambo@yahoo.co.uk

Audition, creating character, improvisation, text and voice. Specialist in Method Acting. Work detail can be for beginners, professionals or individuals returning to the profession. Charges £30 per hour, with a discount for block bookings. Happy to provide material for private students to use, and to answer follow-up queries after a lesson.

Will teach at home, at the client's home, or at the Actors Centre; all are wheelchair-accessible. Nearest tube/railway station is Arsenal (home) or Leicester Square (Actors Centre). Bus route is 19.

Has taught professional actors and aspiring actors over 22 years of teaching. Experienced in stage, television and feature film, and is an East 15 graduate. "I cater for all types of experience – from novice to seasoned professional."

Marj McDaid

Stoke Newington, London N16
tel 020-7923 4929 *mobile* (07815) 993203
email marjmcdaid@hotmail.com
website www.voicings.co.uk

Specialises in voice (Estill method – safe techniques for shouting, screaming, etc.), character work, and accents (especially Irish and American). Charges £40 per hour; discounts can be arranged when a number of sessions paid for in advance. Prefers cash or interbank transfer. Is happy to provide audition speeches (not songs) for private students to use, and will answer minor follow-up queries at no extra charge. Teaches from home, which is 10 mins from Stoke Newington (overground; Highbury & Islington tube). Bus routes include 67, 73, 76, 149, 243, 393 and 476. Has taught hundreds of actors and aspiring actors over 20 years.

Martin McKellan

Covent Garden, London WC2
mobile (07425) 204070
email dialectandvoice@yahoo.co.uk
website www.martinmckellan.com

Specialises in auditions, acting classes and all aspects of voice work (accent and dialogue a particular area of expertise). Rates are negotiable and offers are available; please make contact for full details. Is happy to provide material for private students to use, and to answer minor follow-up queries at no extra charge. Will teach from home, from a client's home or at another location. Covent Garden is the nearest tube station, 3 minutes' walk away. Has taught thousands of actors and aspiring actors over the past 15 years, and has extensive experience as a freelance acting/voice coach working in the West End and in Regional Theatre and for both film and television.

Alison Mead

57 Millstrood Road, Whitstable, Kent CT5 1QF
tel 01227-276 217 *mobile* (07770) 672589
email alison.mead49@gmail.com
website www.alisonmead.com

Specialises in audition technique, accent work, sight reading, acting through song, Shakespeare, character building, Stanislavski, Meisner and Laban techniques. Also happy to teach all areas of acting and text work, specifically designed for schools, colleges and theatre groups. Charges are negotiable, but there is a basic rate of £30 per hour for private tuition (£50 for 2 hours). Sessions can be also be shared by two people for £50 per hour. Alison is happy to provide material for private students to use, and to answer minor follow-up queries after a lesson.

Teaches at home, which is wheelchair-accessible or is happy to travel to student's home for a small extra charge. The nearest station is Whistable – a 10-minute walk. Alison is happy to collect her student from the station before the first lesson. Bus routes are 4A and 6A from Canterbury towards Whistable. She has taught many actors and aspiring actors for over 25 years. Alison has taught Drama and Theatre Arts at degree level, A-Level and GCSE. She has adjudicated at 6 drama festivals for both adults and young people. "Make sure this is the career for you and that it is what you want above all else."

Repliedfor2016

Robin Miller

London
mobile (07957) 627677
email robinjenni@hotmail.com
website www.castingcallpro.com/uk/robin.miller and www.spotlight.com/0632-4531-6660

Specialises in audition speeches, accents and dialects. Charges £20 per hour (special packages negotiable; preferred payment methods are cash or cheque), and is happy to answer minor follow-up queries at no extra charge. Teaches at home – no steps up to the house – or at the client's home. Nearest station is St Margaret's, 12 minutes away, or Twickenham, 10 minutes away. Bus routes are H37 or 267. Has 30 years' experience in the acting profession as an actress, writer, workshop leader, teacher and director; please see Spotlight and Casting Call Pro for further details. Advises actors that "choosing the right speech is incredibly important".

Sally Mortemore

7 Groton Road, Earlsfield, London SW18 4ER
tel 020-8576 2192 *mobile* (07973) 835292
email mortemores@aol.com
website www.sallymortemore.com

Fully qualified voice coach and professional actress; specialises in Shakespeare and is very experienced in voice, audition coaching, text and accent softening. Charges £30 per hour or £40 for 1.5 hours. Offers a free half-hour consultation for new students, and a discounted rate of £20 per hour for drama school leavers in their first year as a professional. Is happy to provide material for students to use, and to answer minor follow-up queries. Teaches from home, which is wheelchair-accessible; the nearest station is Earlsfield, only 2 minutes away. Has taught 200+ actors and aspiring actors over 6 years.

Frances Parkes

11 Jasmine Court, 102 Alexandra Road, Wimbledon, London SW19 7JY
tel 020-8542 2777
email frances@maxyourvoice.com
website www.maxyourvoice.com

Specialises in vocal technique, including accents, dialects and dialogue. Also coaches acting on film and preparing for TV/film roles. Charges £95 per hour and may offer reductions for students and Actors Centre members, rates are negotiated for each production. Is happy to provide material for private students to use, and to answer follow-up queries after a lesson.

Teaches at Diorama and Harley Street studios, though is happy to travel to the client if this is more suitable, dependent on the situation. Diorama studios are wheelchair-accessible at all times and Harley Street until 5.30pm. The nearest stations are Oxford Street and Warren Street – both a 5-minute walk from each location. The studios are also served by multiple bus routes. Has taught for over 10 years and has dealt with many actors and aspiring actors during this time. Trained at the Guildhall and worked in the acting profession for 7 years at the same time as coaching for film, TV and theatre work as well as audios/voice overs. "Use your inspiration to fuel your work and your commitment to learn your craft. Practice, practice, practice."

Richard Ryder

9 Kamen House, 17-21 Magdalen Street, London SE1 2RH
mobile (07967) 352551
email richard@therichervoice.com
website www.therichervoice.com
website www.theaccentkit.com

Specialises in accents, voice and text coaching. Charges £90 per hour with a discount for 6 or more sessions booked in advance. Cash or direct payment to bank. Happy to provide material for private students to use, and to answer minor follow-up queries at no extra cost. Teaches at home (wheelchair accessible) or at the client's home (time charged for travel). The nearest station is London Bridge, 6 minutes' walk from the main teaching location (buses 47, RV1 and many others pass through this area). Has more than 14 years' teaching and coaching experience, at the RSC, National Theatre, West End theatre, TV and film.

You can also download The Accent Kit app for iPhone and Android

Rebecca Semark

Epping, Essex
mobile (07956) 850330
email rebecca@semark.biz
website www.semark.biz

Specialises in audition technique, monologues and voice technique. Stage and drama school entrants includes singing. Charges from £25 for half hour, £40 per hour. Offers discounts to sibling groups and students. Fortnightly teaching is preferred, as this gives more time to practise work and allows for other commitments. Is happy to provide material for students to use, and to answer minor follow-up queries. Teaches from home; the closest station is Epping on the Central Line, which is a 5-10 minute walk. Has taught many performers, actors and aspiring actors over a 20-year period. Since 1973 has worked extensively in theatre and television as a dancer, actress and singer in many genres, including Musical Theatre.

Ros Simmons

120 Hillfield Avenue, Crouch End, London N8 7DN
tel 020-8347 8089
email info@realspeaking.co.uk
website www.realspeaking.co.uk

Coaching Rates:

- 1.5 Hours £90.00: New Accent Study; allowing time to learn and connect with any accent
- 2 Hours: £120.00: New Accent Study with text
- 1 Hour: £65.00: follow up to any accent study
- Student rate: £55 per hour

Specialises in accents and dialects, voice and auditions, as well as Spoken English skills for those with Englsh as a second language. Provides full accent breakdowns and is happy to answer minor follow-up queries. Teaches mainly from home base, with Finsbury Park the nearest tube (overground, Hornsey Station on Tottenham Lane, just around the corner from the premises). Buses from Finsbury Park tube are W3 to Tottenham Lane or W7 to Crouch End Broadway. Has taught around 1,000 actors and aspiring actors, in drama schools and privately, over a period of 10 years. Trained as an actor at the Polytechnic School of Theatre in Manchester, and has worked extensively in theatre, film, TV and radio.

Giles Taylor

mobile (07973) 960681
email gilestaylor@ukgateway.net

Specialises in Shakespeare and audition speeches. Is a verse specialist, but works too on prose texts – classical and modern. Charges £40 per hour. Discounts are available: 3 sessions for £100, and students £30 per hour. Is happy to provide material for private students to use, and to answer minor follow-up queries after a lesson.

Teaches from home, but other locations can be arranged (please note that these may incur travel costs). The nearest tube station is Highgate and bus routes are 43 and 134. Has taught more than 100 actors and aspiring actors over 6 years. "I have been in the business for nearly 20 years, working in theatre, music theatre, television, film and radio. I am a regular teacher at the Actors Centre."

Paul Todd

3 Rosehart Mews, London W11 3JN
tel 020-7229 9776 *mobile* (07813) 985092
email paultodd@talk21.com

Specialises in singing, acting, piano, music theory and voice. Charges £30 per hour; discounts are available on application. Happy to provide material for students to use, and to answer minor follow-up queries at no extra charge. Teaches from home, the nearest tube stations are Notting Hill/Bayswater/ Queensway around 8-9 minutes away. Bus routes are 7, 23, 27, 28, 31 and 328. More details about services offered are available from Forward Talent/Yellow Pages. Has taught very many actor/singers and aspiring actor/singers over 40 years. Has extensive experience as Musical Director at numerous theatres around the UK, including Theatre In The Round, Scarborough and The Royal National Theatre. Advises: "Get on with it. Get the right teacher. Do it."

Vocal Confidence with Alix Longman

Melbourne, Australia
mobile 61 (0) 401 798 258
email alix@vocalconfidence.com
website www.vocalconfidence.com

Skype: Sessions available worldwide.

"Vocal Confidence technique is a unique, fast and effective method that fixes all vocal problems with speech, presentation and singing." Audition technique and dialect work also offered. Charges £50 (AU$100) per hour. 10% discount for students and members of Equity/Spotlight. Initial and follow-up queries provided for no extra fee. Has successfully reconnected thousands of actors to their vocal confidence over 25 years. Further details and testimonials available on website. "Once reconnected to Vocal Confidence, the tone of emotional integrity instantly connectsintension with every person in your audience, both personaly and professionally.

Genevieve Walsh

37 Kelvedon House, Guildford Road, Stockwell, London SW8 2DN
mobile (07801) 948864

Specialises in coaching for auditions and public speaking (presentation technique). Charges £30 per hour (£20 for students). Happy to help in the selection of material for students' use, and to answer minor follow-up queries, time permitting. Teaches from home (nearest station is Stockwell, a 5-minute walk away; bus routes 2 or 88). Has taught dozens of actors and aspiring actors over a 35-year period, and has extensive experience as an actor, teacher and director. "Know your material inside out and all the background to the speech. It is very basic advice, but it is essential."

Mark Westbrook – Acting Coach Scotland

ACS Studio, 2nd Floor, 19 Queen Street, Glasgow G1 3ED
tel 0800-756 9535

email mark@actingcoachscotland.co.uk
website www.actingcoachscotland.co.uk

Areas of specialism are practical aesthetics, audition technique and group acting classes. Charges £30 per hour for private tuition, and £125 for a 10-week evening class. Packages are available (£75 for 3 hours, £130 for 6 hours). Preferred payment methods are PayPal or cash. Provides audition material for students to use, and is happy to give feedback after lessons at no extra charge. Teaches at a city-centre studio, but would travel to the home of wheelchair users. The closest station is St Enochs tube or Queen Street station (5 and 10 minutes away respectively). Has taught hundreds of actors over a period of 10 years. Wide experience as a professional theatre director, former lecturer in acting and head of acting at a conservatory for musical theatre. Advises actors: "You can unlock any scene if you know the right questions to ask."

Anne Wittman

North London
mobile (07956) 602508
email info@spokenstates.com
website www.spokenstates.com

Specialises in coaching British and other non-US actors in a range of American dialects for audition and performance. Also works with accent correction for foreign speakers who would like to attain greater clarity of speech and to correct or soften their existing accent towards General American. Coaches RP for both native and foreign speakers; also coaches acting for audition and performance. Enjoys working with poets and other writers on presentation of their own material at readings.

Charges £40 per hour. Happy to provide material for private students to use, and to answer minor follow-up queries at no extra cost. Teaches from home (wheelchair accessible), but is also connected with various institutions. Nearest tube stations are Finsbury Park or Highgate: the most direct route to the main teaching location is the W3 or W7 bus from Finsbury Park. Has taught at least 400 actors since 1994. Further details are available from the website – also see Anne's article on dialect published in the 2013 edition of *Contacts*, under Drama Training.

Tessa Wood

43 Woodhurst Road, London W3 6SS
tel 020-8896 2659 *mobile* (07957) 207808
email TessaRosWood@aol.com

Specialises in physical voice including centring, alignment, tension release, breath, articulation, range, projection, tone. Also Standard English, RP and period RP, and audition technique. Fee is negotiable and there is a 20% discount for students and sometimes for actors who aren't working. Can provide copies of audition material, but generally does not lend books as they never seem to be returned. Will give minor follow-up advice for no extra charge. Teaches from home or the client's home (for an additional charge). Nearest train link is the Silverlink (North London Line) and the station, Acton Central, is 5 minutes away. Acton Town (Piccadilly/District Lines) is about 15-minutes' walk, and Acton Mainline (1 stop from Paddington) is about 10 minutes away. Many of the buses from Shepherd's Bush going in the direction of Ealing pass within 5-6 minutes of the house (route 207 plus others).

Has taught well over 3,000 actors and aspiring actors over a 20-year period. Pursued a full-time acting career for 15 years, and still does some acting every year. Has coached well-known TV presenters and actors on a one-to-one basis. "Whether or not an actor has full-time training (which I would highly recommend), they should keep up their process with classes, both one-to-one and in the form of group workshops."

A professional mindset: some pointers

Lee Ravitz

For a trainee performer, one of the toughest hurdles to be negotiated in the earliest part of a career is the transition between leaving a drama school or course and entering into the full-time profession of the working actor. In essence, this involves a shift in environment – from a (relatively) closed and nurturing situation into a competitive and emulative atmosphere – and a shift in focus – from learning acting principles as an end in itself to attempting to apply those principles daily in order to win work. Coping with the shifts can require some important changes in mindset, and this article aims to offer some ideas about what those might be.

If you turn to the back of this Yearbook and read Tim Bentinck's *An Actor's Guide to Keeping Sane*, you will encounter an ebullient account of how an actor can maintain their commitment to a tough career, and keep their head above water, year after year. But this piece aims its message at those of you who are just beginning to establish yourselves as career actors, if you, as yet, have little notion of what might be expected of a life within the industry, and what mental strategies may be needed to cope with it. I hope it'll prove a useful primer.

Persistence

The first vital quality you will need is the determination to persevere with your craft, come what may. Acting can bring you many rewards over time, but you must be clear that your intent is, first and foremost, to grow personally through your acting as a human being, to find individual creative fulfilment, to learn how to move audiences and, not least, to learn how to run yourself as a successful business.

Pursuing these values is all the more important in that instant recognition within the profession, however much talent you may possess, is offered only to a select few (and those few tend to have been 'fast tracked' by virtue of attending the most prestigious drama schools and securing high-powered agents with connections at an early point). Most drama training, solid though it may be, will not guarantee you work (though it will have made you a better actor). A course which, by default, focuses on acknowledging your contribution may, no less crucially, fail to prepare you for the fact that, once within the industry, no-one has a need to recognise your presence. It is really up to you to ensure that the industry begins to take notice of what you can offer, and this can, in turn, involve years' worth of resilience and persistence – at sourcing work, winning work, and seeing work through solidly. But it is this persistence and resilience that will pay dividends over time.

To say this is no platitude. In practical terms, winning a good reputation and networking successfully are what make you competitive, over the long run, in an increasingly deregulated actors' market. You wish to be seen as a performer who is reliable and capable, one who possesses the sheer determination to rise to challenges, to nurture contacts, and to build up your skills, your self-awareness and your marketplace visibility year on year. This takes sticking power. It takes commitment. Above all, it takes time. So, learn to persist.

Maturity

The acting industry can be a truly capricious business. This may not be entirely surprising. A degree of immaturity can play an essential part in any creative personality, and a quality of wilfulness may be as significant in conditioning the behaviour of a director as any actor. There are those out there (thankfully in the minority) who will pay more attention to their paperwork in the audition room than your diligently prepared performance, however hard you try. Yet the truth remains that, should you find yourself faced with situations in which the behaviour of other professionals appears fickle and immature, it is attendant upon you, for the sake of your own professionalism, to respond with dignity, restraint and maturity.

It's not a question of toeing lines; it's a question of knowing that anything you perceive as a lack of professionalism in others shouldn't be allowed to encourage a lack of professionalism in your own responses. So, don't assume that it's fair to get to an audition late (or fail to notify someone in advance if you can't make it) just because you were seen an hour and a half later than scheduled at your last audition. Don't start writing scrappy covering letters, just because one agency office didn't have the grace to return you a compliments slip.

Not being in training means that you are no longer being cosseted, and to function in the industry you have to grow a tough hide. But that doesn't mean you forgo behaving like a professional because of it. By the same token, you shouldn't be afraid to question bad decisions if they are made, or of learning to treat those who employ you as your equals. That's a form of maturity, too, and adopting such an approach earns respect ... a signal that you have moved beyond the deference of training, and are ready to be treated as an actor who knows their own mind, and their own business.

Self-awareness

At the outset of your career, it's worth asking yourself the question: how are you going to ensure that you secure consistent work which will suit your particular playing style? There may be no hard or fast solutions to this, but one important consideration is to become aware of what strengths and qualities, what look and feel, you generate as a performer. As all actors have to sell on the market is themselves, it's crucial to gauge a sense of this early, and you can even start to derive a sense of it from your training feedback. Did you find that you were praised more for your comedy work than for your drama? Were tutors of the opinion that you offered more as a face for screen than as a stage performer? And what do you especially engage with working on: do you love to play the villain, rather than the hero? Are you happiest in a supporting part, or a leading one? Have you got special skills that complement your acting, and you want to put to use?

Too often, actors come into the marketplace unfocused. They have no clarity over the problem of what they may or may not be considered suitable to play, and are forever disappointed that they secure no auditions or interest. Much of the difficulty stems from the fact that they aren't demonstrating to potential employers that they know themselves, know what they are skilled at offering, and have a sense of what – essentially – makes them the actor that they are.

This isn't to suggest you should place arbitrary limitations on yourself, or fail to push yourself. But having a sense of self-awareness – what your look, your strengths and skills offer to the industry – is one of the greatest benefits you can hold for securing work in a competitive market. You don't want to be a frustrated actor; you want to become a fulfilled actor. Become self-aware.

Keeping solvent

This is a point that almost goes without saying, and elsewhere this Yearbook gives clearer details on how you may find secondary work to support you when acting work is thin on the ground. However, it is worth restating that some degree of financial flexibility is crucial to supporting your most central need as a jobbing actor: continuing in the industry year upon year. It's all too easy to fall by the wayside for the simple reason that you can't afford to support yourself, if you're not careful.

Day jobs can be tough: not only tough to find, but tough to endure. The principal irony is that many support jobs are extremely routine and dull, and most actors are, by default, driven by a need for self-expression that directly conflicts with the demands of their (necessary) day job. When you train as an actor, your time is taken up with a continuous round of acting exercises, acting workshops, set performances: it can be a shock to the system to realise that acting will constitute only a small element of your day-to-day routine once you leave the training behind (unless you are very lucky).

There are important benefits to be gained by taking on a support job – sometimes lateral benefits, like gaining new stimuli and experiences that may inform your acting, or grounding your perspective on life. And some actors are canny enough, and adaptable enough, to secure the kind of support jobs for themselves that they can also take pride in. But above all, the most important function a support job has is as a means to an end: holding one is your insurance that you will be able to continue to pursue the work that you really love when money from it is scarce. Acting has never paid well, and it has rarely paid regularly: the debate about whether or not jobbing actors should be working in e.g. fringe theatre for little or no pay at all (an increasingly common tendency in the earliest years of a career) will run and run. It's certain, however, that if you as an actor are already supporting yourself by means of a day job, you are at least freeing yourself up to cover your costs on such projects, whilst hopefully using them as a springboard to build up your base of contacts, your review notices, and your market visibility.

It goes without saying that all of this advice is derived from experience. Above anything else, the keynote attitude I'm advocating is that you need to be capable of coping with the day-to-day realities of the business. If you are lucky enough to make it big quickly, then these principles can be safely ignored; but if you are one of the many thousands of actors who will have to make their own luck, then having coping strategies in place will prove invaluable to you. Working as an actor can be the most stimulating, exhilarating, expressive and emotionally fulfilling ride you will ever take in your life – but it's often up to you to make it so.

Lee Ravitz is a character actor, who joined the profession in 2006 after some years spent training as a history lecturer. He has always loved applying his gifts for enquiry to the issues surrounding performers' lives, the development of specific stage and screen modes, and the internal politics of the industry, and has gained something of a reputation on the Casting Call Pro forums as a commentator and pundit on acting matters. Alongside his stage and screen work, he serves on Equity's Independent Theatre committee, and writes radio plays for the Bunbury Banter Theatre Company.

An actor's toolkit

Compiled by Simon Dunmore

You need to organise the following essential items before you even get your first interview, let alone an agent and/or your first job. You should start planning for all these in good time, before the end of your training – ready for your first public production.

1 Join Equity! You can join (very cheaply) as a student member (see **www.equity.org.uk/about-us/join-us**) and, for a small extra fee, reserve your professional name: details of how to go about this are on the website.

2 A good, strong professional name. If you can't (or don't want to) use your real name, it's important to select an alternative that you're completely comfortable with.

3 Well-designed headed paper. Beatrice Warde, the passionate typography expert, said, "Typefaces are the clothes words wear." Find a typeface that 'dresses' your professional name well.

4 Secure and reliable telephone and Internet connections for professional use. *Note*: It is very important that your outgoing message and email address sound professional and not like hangovers from your adolescence.

5 A reliable computer with printer. *Tip*: Laser printers provide a much crisper quality when printing text – and laser toner is much cheaper, per page, than ink.

6 An up-to-date copy of *Actors and Performers Yearbook*. *Tip*: It is worthwhile not only reading the rest of this book to get a feel for how different parts of the profession function, but also reading through websites.

7 A good set of photographs and sufficient copies. See Angus Deuchar's article and the introduction to Photographers and Repro Companies starting on page 391.

8 A well-laid-out and up-to-date CV. *Notes*: It's important to ensure that all spellings of proper names (directors, play titles, etc.) are correct. Also, to understand how to convert your CV into Portable Document Format (PDF) for email transmission.

9 A good standard letter that you can adapt for individual circumstances, and use in emails, etc. See Ian Liston's article *Marketing Yourself – A Producer's Viewpoint* on page 129.

10 Half-a-dozen (or more) varied audition speeches. See my *Effective Audition Speeches* article on page 149.

11 Half-a-dozen (or more) varied audition songs. See Jennifer Reischel's article *Cattle Calls and How to Survive Them* on page 158.

12 A mental list of things (not just acting ones) you could talk about in order to respond to the almost inevitable question(s), "What have you been doing recently?" and/or "Tell me a bit about yourself."

13 An entry in *Spotlight* – details at **www.spotlight.com/join**. *Note*: Entry into *Spotlight* is strictly limited to professionally trained and/or professionally experienced performers, and applications are always vetted.

14 A reasonable selection of clothes for interviews and auditions. Essentially, you need to feel comfortable and appropriately dressed for each individual circumstance … and you will face a wide variety of such circumstances.

15 An up-to-date passport – jobs which require travelling abroad at short notice are becoming more frequent.

16 A budget. The costs of the above can accumulate quite quickly – before you've earned a penny. And there are many other minor things not listed: postage; Equity entry fee and annual subscription; subscriptions to *The Stage* and other professional publications; travel costs to interviews, and so on. All the above items can easily add up to much more money than you might think: you need to calculate your potential professional expenses and budget for them. *Notes*: Although many of the above are allowable against tax (see Philippe Carden's article *Tax & National Insurance for Actors* on page 440), don't forget to include your potential tax bill! Also, at the outset of your career, consider carefully the cost-effectiveness of items like personal websites, showreels, etc. These are only worthwhile if you have sufficient high-quality material that makes you look 'professional'. Also see Nancy Bishop's article, *Marketing and the Internet: maintaining your online presence* on page 388.

17 Sources of non-acting income that are flexible enough for you to drop at 24 hours' notice. At an educated guess, only about 10 per cent of the profession earn a living *solely* from acting. And, even for those, incomes can be incredibly variable – £200 one year to over £20,000 the next, to quote just one example (see Andrew Piper's article *Between Engagements* on page 444).

18 A working knowledge of the nation's transport systems (especially London's): you will often not know where you might be required for audition/interview (even work) until very late in the day. *Tip*: As a general rule it is wise to double your estimated travelling time to allow for the almost inevitable foul-ups.

19 A great deal of patience, persistence, determination, cunning and resourcefulness.

20 A stoical source of solace for the bad times. *Tip*: Find another activity that absorbs you as much as acting does.

21 A copy of my *An Actor's Guide To Getting Work* for reading on the loo (published by Methuen).

General points:

(a) Can you organise yourself? Acting can be an instant business. For days/weeks/months/years nothing happens, and then a few minutes/hours/days/weeks/months/years later it can *all* be happening. You must always be ready, but not constantly on tenterhooks. In spite of the popular image of the chaotic, dizzy actor, you have to be personally organised or you could significantly harm your employment prospects.

(b) As an actor you are your own business. You are not only your own work-force, but also your publicity and public relations office, accountancy division, transport manager, and – above all – your managing director. Of course, you may well have an agent, an accountant, etc., but none of these people can do anything unless you give them clear direction. You are finally responsible for your success or failure in the business.

Simon Dunmore has been directing productions for over 30 years – nearly 20 years as a resident director in regional theatres and, more recently, working freelance. In that time there have been more than 200 productions (of all styles, colours, shapes and sizes), most recently several Drama School Showcases, Maugham's *Home and Beauty* and new plays about sex, WB Yeats' up-and-down relationship with Maud Gonne, one set inside a pyramid, and another about Bismarck. Past favourites include: *The Promise* (Alexei Arbuzov), *Antigone* (Jean Anouilh), a seven-handed version of *Antony & Cleopatra* and too many others to mention. He also teaches acting, and has worked in many drama schools and other training establishments around the country. He has written several books: *An Actor's Guide to Getting Work* (fifth edition, 2012), the *Alternative Shakespeare Auditions* series, and was formerly the Consultant Editor for *Actors' Yearbook*.

Agents and casting directors

Introduction

Actors have probably existed since before the invention of writing; actors' agents have only been around since the invention of the telephone, just over a century ago. Prior to this, work-seeking actors had to make themselves known in person to potential employers – for instance, certain hostelries in the Covent Garden area of central London were well-known 'talent-spotting' haunts. Actors would also 'catch a ride' with one of the touring companies in the hope of proving themselves to the manager – and then being put on the payroll. Others would pay managers to let them play small parts, in the hope of being noticed. All this meant a lot of hard work and/or expense (let alone the time needed to earn his/her living by other means) for the pre-electronic-age actor. The invention of actors' agents seemed to fill a vital gap.

In the 1970s, a number of actors, dissatisfied with the (by then) traditional agent system, formed the first co-operative agencies (see page 88). This apparently simple idea – with all members taking turns to 'man' the office – took a while to become established. Like many 'simple ideas', the pioneers found that there were more complications involved than they'd initially envisaged, and employers were slow to accept the idea. Nearly forty years later, the best 'co-ops' have as much professional credibility as their conventional counterparts.

It used to be the case that only the biggest companies used casting directors. The administrative burden inherent in running such a company (let alone directing productions) meant that assistance in the casting process became essential. The 1990s saw a rise in the use of casting directors and in the number of freelancers working on short-term contracts: most of the latter work in a wide variety of fields.

The simple fact is that a significant proportion of properly paid acting work is 'brokered' by casting directors and agents.

Agents and casting directors have very distinct functions – see the articles. The term 'casting agents' is used to describe walk-on agents who take the responsibility for casting walk-ons/extras in television and film. They have client bases comprising lots of different types, and on request can supply a suitable crowd for any occasion. Thus they fulfil the roles of both agent and casting director for non-speaking parts that don't need to be auditioned.

Agents

A good agent understands contracts, knows the current rates in every field of work and – most importantly – has plenty of professional contacts and access to far more casting information than most individuals can ever possess. Directors and casting directors rely on the agents they know and trust to help with the filtering process of whom to interview. A good agent will work hard at promoting each of his/her clients; in return, it is not unreasonable that they charge commission on every contract they negotiate for you – generally, 10-20 per cent (plus VAT, if appropriate). A good agent will also (a) have only as many clients as they can reasonably handle, and (b) ensure that they have a good range of ages and types of actors in order to cover as many casting opportunities as possible.

When you are seeking representation, it is advisable to contact agents by post in the first instance – unless specifically informed otherwise. It is a good idea to include a separate 10x8in (25x20cm) photograph, and it is important that all your enclosures give your name and the best way to contact you (not a long list of confusing alternatives). Agents receive many requests for representation, and photographs can become separated from their accompanying letters and CVs, so proper labelling is essential.

Use the listings that follow to (a) target your submission as accurately as possible (for example, by writing to a specific, named person – unless advised otherwise), (b) check for any details that could inform the content of your letter, and (c) find out whether each would be interested in any extras, like a showreel. Time spent checking such details can save money and enhance your chances of being noticed more than the next person. Unless you have a good collection of professional credits, it is generally best to write to agents when there's an opportunity for them to see you performing in something.

If you are invited to meet an agent, that is often a good sign. You should approach the occasion in much the same way as you would an interview for a production. The major difference is that you should be prepared to ask (reasonable) questions – rates of commission, for instance.

When seeking representation, it can be a good idea to target only those agencies that you think might suit you. For instance, might you feel lost in a large agency, but feel more comfortable with a smaller one? On the other hand, some larger agencies have huge 'clout' and can be the first 'port of call' for the casting of prestigious productions.

When you've been taken on by an agent, it is important to establish how your working relationship will function. Be clear about any areas of work that you don't want to be suggested for, discuss your availability for auditions and interviews, agree how much promotion you should do for yourself, and so on.

These listings only contain agents who represent adult actors – there are many others who represent children, models, extras and so on.

PMA following an agency's name denotes membership of the Personal Managers' Association, the leading professional body of talent agencies in the UK. It was set up more than 60 years ago with the intention of encouraging good practice among agents through better communication between agents and from agents to the industry.

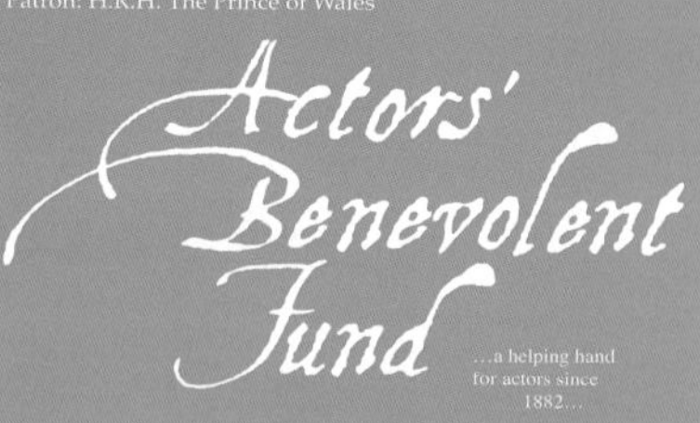
Actors' Benevolent Fund
...a helping hand
for actors since
1882...

drama uk
recognised

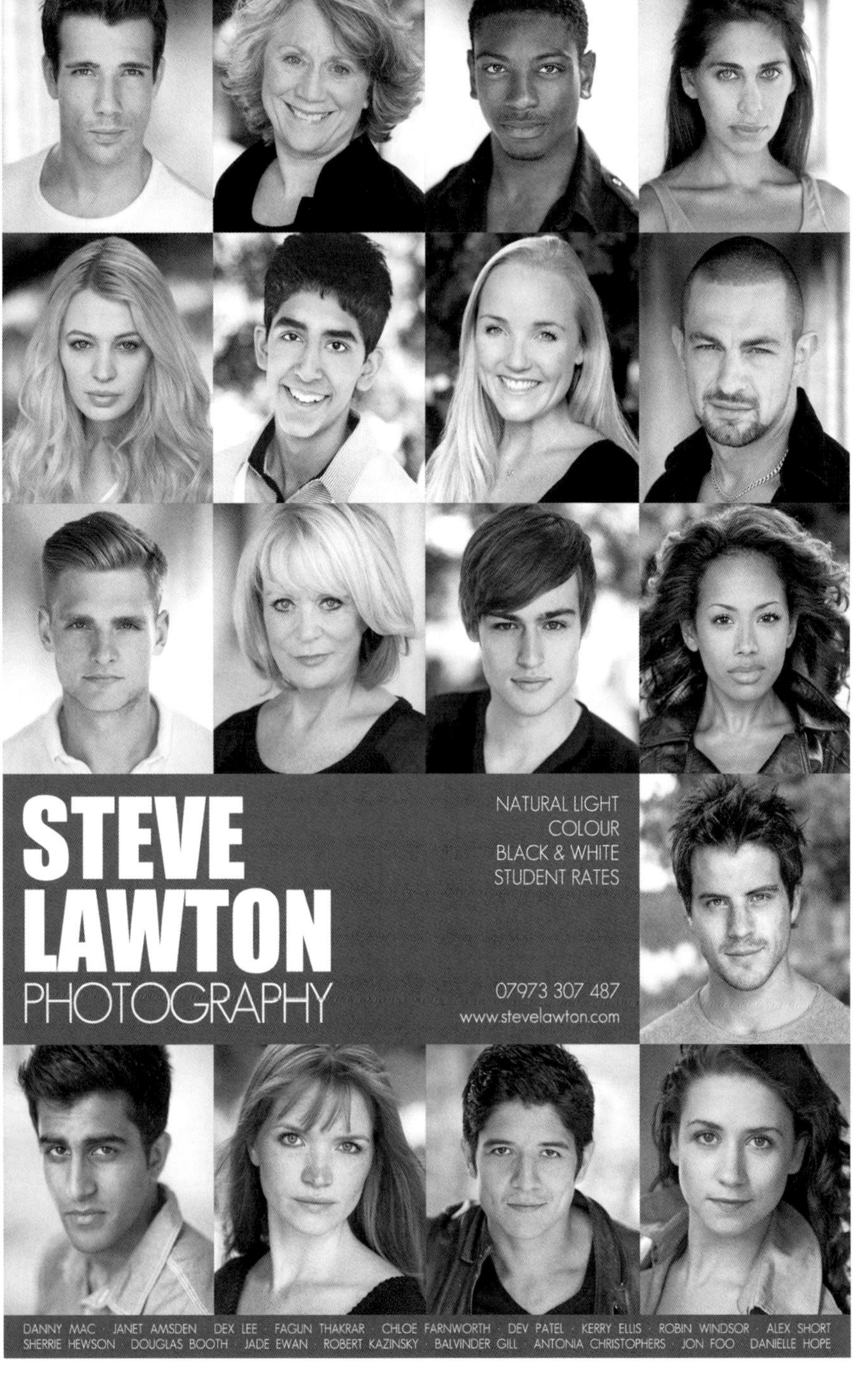
STEVE
LAWTON
PHOTOGRAPHY
NATURAL LIGHT
COLOUR
BLACK & WHITE
STUDENT RATES
07973 307 487
www.stevelawton.com
DANNY MAC · JANET AMSDEN · DEX LEE · FAGUN THAKRAR · CHLOE FARNWORTH · DEV PATEL · KERRY ELLIS · ROBIN WINDSOR · ALEX SHORT
SHERRIE HEWSON · DOUGLAS BOOTH · JADE EWAN · ROBERT KAZINSKY · BALVINDER GILL · ANTONIA CHRISTOPHERS · JON FOO · DANIELLE HOPE

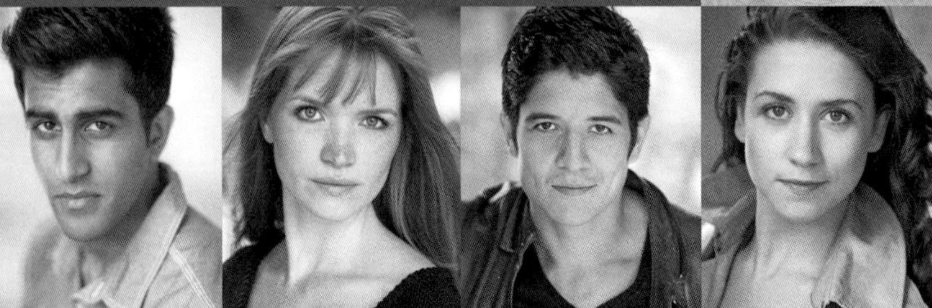

42 M&P PMA

First Floor, 8 Flitcroft Street, London WC2H 8DL
tel 020-7292 0554
email mollycowan@42mp.com
website www.42mp.com
Partner Kate Buckley, assisted by Molly Cowan *Senior Agents* Molly Wansell and Georgina Monkland

Established 2003. Main areas of work are theatre, TV, film, commercials and musicals. Represents 97 actors. Also respresents directors, casting directors, writers and producers. Welcomes performance notices nationwide given a week's notice. Welcomes letters (with CVs and photographs), CVs and photographs sent by email and show reels. Respresents actors with disabilities.

A&J Management

242A The Ridgeway, Botany Bay, Enfield EN2 8AP
tel 020-8342 0542 and 020-8342 0842
email info@ajmanagement.co.uk
website www.ajmanagement.co.uk
Managing Director Joanne McLintock *Key contact* Joanne McLintock

Established in 1984. 2 agents represent actors. Areas of work include theatre, musicals, television, film, commercials, corporate and voice-overs.

Will consider attending performances at venues within Greater London with a minimum of 2 weeks' notice. Accepts submissions (with CVs and photographs) from actors previously unknown to the company if sent by email. Invitations to view individual actors' websites are also accepted.

Chris Abakporo

47 Chatsworth Road, Stratford, London E15 1RB
mobile (07903) 192413
email chrisabak@hotmail.co.uk
Agent Chris Abakporo

Established in 2010. Areas of work include TV, film and commercials. Welcomes CVs and photographs sent by email. Also accepts showreels and invitations to view actors' websites.

Access Artiste Management Ltd

71-75 Shelton Street, Covent Garden,
London WC2H 9JQ
tel 020-7866 5444
email mail@access-uk.com
website www.access-uk.com
Manager Sarah Bryan

Established in 1999. Areas of work include theatre, musicals, television, film, commercials, corporate. Also represents directors, musical directors, choreographers, composers, playwrights and musical works.

Will consider attending performances in Greater London and elsewhere with 1 month's notice. Accepts submissions (with CVs and photographs) from professional actors previously unknown to the company. Showreels, voicereels and details of individual actors' websites should only be sent upon request. Welcomes enquiries from disabled actors.

Actors Direct Associates (ADA)

11 St George's Crescent, Rhyl, Clwyd,
Wales LL18 3NN
mobile (07951) 477015
email ada.actors@gmail.com
email casting@actorsdirectassociates.net
website www.actorsdirectassociates.net
Agent and *Managing Director* Rachael Power

Established in 2010. 1 agent represents 30 actors. Areas of work include theatre, TV, film, commercials, corporate and voice-overs.

Will consider attending performances at venues in London, Manchester, Liverpool or Dublin. Welcomes emails with links to online CVs only. Happy to consider applications for representation from disabled actors. *Commission*: Varies dependent on contract.

Actors International Ltd

Soho, London
020-7025 8777 *fax* 020-7025 8001
email mail@actorsinternational.co.uk
website www.actorsinternational.co.uk
Agents Caroline Taylor, Lee Thomas

Established in 2000. 2 agents represent around 70 actors. Areas of work include theatre, musicals, television, film, commercials and corporate.

Will attend showcases/performances within Central London given as much notice as possible. Accepts email submissions ONLY; no postal submissions will be considered.

Actors World Casting

13 Briarbank Road, London W13 0HH
mobile (07960) 332846
email katherine@actors-world-production.com
Agent Katherine Pageon

Established in 2005. 1 agent represents 40 actors. Areas of work include theatre, musicals, television, film, commercials, corporate, voice-overs.

Will consider attending performances in Greater London with at least 2 weeks' notice. Notices of performances should be sent via email only. Accepts submissions sent via email (with CVs and 1 photograph only) from actors previously unknown to the company. Invitations to view individual actors' websites also accepted, as are enquiries from disabled actors. *Commission*: Theatre 15%; Other 20%.

AFA Associates

Unit 101A, Business Design Centre, 52 Upper Street,
London N1 0QH
tel 020-7682 3677 *mobile* (07904) 962779

email afa-associates@hotmail.com
Agent Rhiannon Mosson

Established in 2009. Works in theatre, film, TV, commercials, corporate, musicals and promos.

Welcomes performance notices within the Greater London area if given at least 7 days' notice. Accepts approaches from actors by post and email, and welcomes showreels and invitations to view individual actors' websites. Represents actors with disabilities.

The Agency

9 Upper Fitzwilliam Street, Dublin 2
tel 353-1661 8535
email admin1@tagency.ie
website www.theagency.ie
Directors Teri Hayden, Karl Hayden

The Agency has been representing Ireland's foremost acting talent for stage and screen since its establishment 30 years ago. In that time its multi-award-winning clients have appeared in numerous productions worldwide, and the company continues to set the standard for excellence in acting.

AHA Talent Ltd PMA

74 Clerkenwell Road, London EC1M 5QA
tel 020-7250 1760
email mail@ahatalent.co.uk
website www.ahatalent.co.uk
Agents Amanda Fitzalan Howard, Mark Price, Darren Rugg, Kirsten Wright, Kevin Brady, Chloe Brayfield, Gemma Allsopp

8 agents represent around 200 actors and creatives working in theatre, musicals, television, radio, film, commercials, corporate role-play and voice-overs. Other clients include writers, broadcasters, designers, directors and composers.

Will consider attending performances within Greater London given 2-3 weeks' notice. Welcomes submissions (with CVs, photographs, showreels, voicereels and sae) from actors previously unknown to the agency if sent by post. Does not accept email applications or invitations to view an actor's website. *Commission*: 10-15% depending on the medium.

All Talent – Sonia Scott Agency

Unit 325, 95 Morrison Street, Glasgow G5 8BE
tel 0141-418 1074 *mobile* (07971) 337074
email enquiries@alltalentuk.co.uk
website www.alltalentuk.co.uk

Established in 2005. 2 agents represent 50-60 actors. Also represents other skills within the profession.

Will consider attending performances in Central London and Glasgow with at least 2-3 weeks' notice. Accepts submissions (with CVs and photographs) from actors previously unknown to the company; postal submissions preferred. Invitations to view showreels or voicereels and individual actors' websites also accepted, and follow-up calls welcomed. Welcomes enquiries from disabled actors. *Commission*: 15%

Anita Alraun Representation

1A Queensway, Blackpool, Lancashire FY4 2DG
tel (01253) 343784
Sole Proprietor/Agent Anita Alraun

1 agent represents 40-45 actors. Areas of work include theatre, musicals, film, television, commercials, radio drama, corporate and some voice-overs.

Attendance at performances is dependent on potential client submissions/interviews. Accepts submissions (with CV, photograph and sae – essential for reply) by post only from trained/experienced actors previously unknown to the company. Emailed submissions will not be considered. Please do not send showreels or voicereels unless requested. *Commission*: Radio 10%; Theatre 12.5%; Film and TV 12.5%; Commercials 15%

Jonathan Altaras Associates Ltd PMA

53 Chandos Place, London WC2N 4HS
tel 0207-812 6461/2/3
email info@jaalondon.com
Agents: Wim Hance, Helen Filmer

Established in 1991, areas of work are theatre, musicals, TV, film, commercials, corporate and voice-over.

Welcomes performance notices in Great Loondon area, given as much notice as possible. Welcomes letters with CVs, photographs, showreels, voice tapes with sae. Invitations, CVs, photographs, showreel link by email. No follow-up phone calls please. Does not currently represent actors with diabilities but is open to the idea of respresenting disabled actors.

ALW Associates

1 Grafton Chambers, Grafton Place,
London NW1 1LN
tel 020-7388 7018 *fax* 020-7813 1398
email alw_carolpaul@talktalk.net

Established in 1977 as Vernon Conway Ltd. Sole representation of 50 actors. Areas of work include theatre, television, film and commercials.

Will consider attending performances at venues within Greater London and occasionally elsewhere with 1 week's notice. Accepts submissions (with CVs and photographs) from actors previously unknown to the company, sent by post or email. Also accepts invitations to view individual actors' websites. Showreels and voicereels should only be sent on request. *Commission*: Theatre and Radio 10-12.5%; Film and TV 12.5%; Commercials 15%

Amber Personal Management Ltd PMA

Room A, Plumtree House, 21-31 Oldham Street,
Manchester M1 1JG

tel 0161-228 0236 *fax* 0161-228 0235
email info@amberltd.co.uk
website www.amberltd.co.uk
Principal Agent Sally Sheridan *Agent* Jasmine Parris
Associate Agent Estelle Jenkins

Works in theatre, musicals, television, film, commercials, corporate and voice-over. 3 agents represent 90-100 actors. Recommends the photographer John Nicholls (**868online@googlemail.com**). Will consider attending performances in Manchester, Leeds and Liverpool if given a minimum of 2 weeks' notice.

Welcomes letters (with CVs and photographs) from individual actors previously unknown to the company if sent by post. Does not welcome email approaches or follow-up telephone calls. Encourages enquiries from actors with disabilities. Will accept showreels, voicereels and invitations to view individual actors' websites. *Commission*: Recorded Media (TV/Film/Commercial) 15%; Theatre, Musicals, Corporate 10%

The American Agency

14 Bonny Street, London NW1 9PG
tel 020-7485 8883
email americanagency@btconnect.com
Agent Ed Cobb

Areas of work include theatre, musicals, television, film, commercials, corporate and voice-overs. 2 agents represent 80 actors.

Will consider attending performances within the Greater London area. Accepts submissions (with CVs and photographs) from actors previously unknown to the agency if sent by post or email. Invitations to view individual actors' websites, showreels and voicereels are also accepted. Welcomes enquiries from disabled actors. *Commission*: Theatre 10%; Other 15%

Angel & Francis Ltd PMA

1st Floor, 12 D'Arblay Street, London W1F 8DU
tel 020-7439 3086 *fax* 020-7437 1712
email agents@angelandfrancis.co.uk
Director Kevin Francis

Established in 1976. 3 agents represent about 75 actors and TV/film casting directors. Areas of work include theatre, television, film and commercials. *Commission*: 10-12.5%

Christopher Antony Associates

Studio F5, Grove Park Studios,
188-192 Sutton Court Road, London W4 3HR
tel 020-8994 9952
email info@christopherantony.co.uk
website www.christopherantony.co.uk
Agents Chris Sheils, Kerry Walker

Christopher Antony Associates has been operational since 2006. Offers a personal management service specialising in Musical Theatre. As theatre agents, represents a small and diverse list of artistes in the West End, UK Tours and Overseas.

APM Associates

Elstree Film Studios, Shenley Road,
Borehamwood WD6 1JG
020-8953 7377*mobile* (07918) 166706 or (07760) 625551
email apm@apmassociates.net
website www.apmassociates.net
Managing Director Linda French

APM Associates represent clients in all fields of the entertainment industry, including television, film, theatre, musical theatre, commercials and dance.

Welcomes applications from both experienced performers and graduates of accredited drama schools via post or email. *Commission*: Brochure and specimen contract available upon offer of interview.

ARG (Artists Rights Group Ltd) PMA

4A Exmoor Street, London W10 6BD
tel 020-7436 6400
email comiskey@argtalent.com
website www.argtalent.com
Agents: Sue Latimer (assisted by Sarah Spahovic), Claire Cominsky (assisted by Katherine Darke), Tiffany Grayson

Established on 2001, main area of work are theatre, musicals, film, TV and corporate. Represent approximately 60 actors, as well as presenters amd production.

Welcomes performance notices UK wide, ideallly with a week or more notice. Welcomes letters (with CV and photographers), CVs, showreels and photographs by email.

Argyle Associates

43 Clappers Lane, Fulking, West Sussex BN5 9ND
mobile (07905) 293319
email argyle.associates@me.com
Director Richard Linford *Key personnel* Geraldine Pryor

Established in 1995. 2 agents represent 30 actors. Areas of work include theatre, musicals, television, film, commercials and corporate.

Will consider attending performances at venues in Sussex and Surrey (e.g. Eastbourne, Brighton, Guildford, Dorking, Windsor) with 2 weeks' notice. Accepts submissions (with CVs and photographs) from actors previously unknown to the company if sent by post. Invitations to view individual actors' websites are also accepted. "Be clear about what you think you have to offer the agency – your type and roles. Your photograph should look like you and be a high-grade holiday snap." *Commission*: Theatre and Radio 10%; TV 12.5%; Commercials, Film, Corporate and CD Rom 15%

The Artists Partnership PMA

101 Finsbury Pavement, London EC2A 1RS
tel 020-7439 1456 *fax* 020-7734 6530

email email@theartistspartnership.co.uk
website www.theartistspartnership.co.uk
Managing Director Roger Charteris; *Agents* Kimberley Donovan, Annalisa Gordon, Emily Hayward-Whitlock, Justine Hodgkinson, Saskia Mulder, Gilly Sanguinetti, Zoe Stoker, Robert Taylor, Jan Thornton

Formerly Ken McReddie Associates. 8 agents represent actors, directors and writers for theatre, television, film, commercials and voice-overs.

Jonathan Arun Ltd PMA

37 Pearman Street, London SE1 7RB
tel 020-7840 0123
email info@jonathanarun.com
website www.jonathanarun.com
Agents Jonathan Arun, assisted by Max Latimer, Amy O'Neill, Maria Girod-Roux (Commercials)

Established in 2007. Main areas of work are theatre, film, television, musical theatre, commercials, and American TV/film. 2 agents represent 80 actors plus a commercials list of 35. Will consider attending performances if given at least 3 weeks' notice.

Please approach the agency by email only, with Spotlight link and showreel. Tries to respond to all, but if interested in taking a contact further will always respond within a week. Will consider representing actors with disabilities.

Asquith & Horner

The Studio, 14 College Road, Bromley BR1 3NS
tel 020-8466 5580 *fax* 020-8313 0443
website www.spotlightagent.info (view PIN 9858-0919-0728)
Senior Partner Anthony Vander Elst *Partner* Helen Melville

Established 1989. 2 agents represent 70 actors. Also represented are directors, choreographers, presenters, singers, dancers and commercial models. Areas of work include theatre, musicals, television, film, commercials, corporate and voice-overs.

Will consider attending performances at venues within Greater London and elsewhere, but requests as much notice as possible. Accepts submissions (CVs and photographs) from actors previously unknown to the company; also accepts showreels and voicereels, and invitations to view actors' websites. "Unsolicited enquiries should always be accompanied by an appropriately stamped and addressed envelope for return of answer, photo, voicereel, etc." Email applications are discouraged.

Associated International Management (AIM)

4th Floor, 7 Hatton Garden, London, EC1N 8AD
tel 020-7831 9709
email info@aimagents.com
website www.aimagents.com
Key personnel Derek Webster, Stephen Gittins, Nicola Mansfield

An international management established in 1984. 3 agents represent around 70 actors. Areas of work include theatre, television, film and commercials.

Will consider attending performances within the Greater London area with at least 3 weeks' notice. Accepts submissions (with CVs and photographs) from actors previously unknown to the agency if sent by post, but not by email. *Commission*: 10-12.5%

BAM Associates (UK) Ltd

Benets, Dolberrow, Churchill, Bristol BS25 5NT
tel (01934) 852942
email bam@louisealexander.plus.com
website www.ebam.tv

2 agents represent 60 actors. Areas of work include theatre, musicals, television, film, commercials, corporate and voice-overs.

Welcomes hardcopy or emailed submissions from actors seeking representation (with CVs and 10x8in b&w photographs). Welcomes enquiries from disabled actors. *Commission*: Theatre 10%; Mechanical Media 15%

Gavin Barker Associates Ltd PMA

2D Wimpole Street, London W1G 0EB
tel 020-7499 4777 *fax* 020-7499 3777
email assistant@gavinbarkerassociates.co.uk
website www.gavinbarkerassociates.co.uk
Managing Director Gavin Barker *Associate Director* Michelle Burke

Established in 1998. 3 agents represent 55 actors and a handful of creatives. Areas of work include theatre, musicals, television, film, commercials, corporate and voice-overs. Also represents directors and choreographers.

Will consider attending performances at venues in Greater London given at least 3 weeks' notice. Accepts submissions (with CVs and photographs) from actors previously unknown to the company if sent by email. Follow-up calls are not welcome. Happy to receive showreels and voicereels. "We do not currently represent any disabled actors, but would consider each applicant on a case by case basis." *Commission*: 10-12.5%

Becca Barr Management

97 Mortimer Street, London W1W 7SU
tel 0203-1372 980
email info@beccabarrmanagement.co.uk
website www.beccabarrmanagement.co.uk

Areas of work include theatre, TV, film, commercials, corporate and voice-overs. Also represents presenters and experts.

Accepts submissions by email (with CVs and photographs). Showreels and voicereels are also welcome.

Eamonn Bedford Agency

2nd Floor, 10 Warwick Street, London W1B 5LZ
tel 020-7734 9632

email info@eamonnbedford.com
(enquiries@eamonnbedford.com for Submissions)
website www.eamonnbedford.com

Established in 2012. 1 agent represents around 60 clients. Areas of work include theatre, film and TV.

Accepts CVs with photographs from those seeking representation, via email. *Commission*: TV and Film 12.5%, Theatre 10%

Olivia Bell Management PMA

193 Wardour Street, London W1F 8ZF
tel 020-7439 3270 *fax* 020-7439 3485
email xania@olivia-bell.co.uk
Managing Director Xania Segal; *Agents* Robin Hudson, Gavin Mills, Antony Read

Established in 2001. 2 agents represent 90 actors. Areas of work include theatre, musicals, television, film and commercials.

Will consider attending performances at venues within Greater London with a minimum of 1 week's notice. Accepts submissions (with CVs and photographs) from actors previously unknown to the company if sent by post. Invitations to view individual actors' websites and showreels or voicereels are also accepted. *Commission*: 12.5-20%

Benjamin Management Ltd (formerly Audrey Benjamin Agency)

Garden Studios, 71-75 Shelton Street,
Covent Garden, London WC2H 9JQ
tel 020-7866 5412 *mobile* (07921) 212360
email agent@benjaminmanagement.co.uk
Key personnel Ziggie Ward, Katie Cameron, Joanne Benjamin, Clive Chenery

Established in 1985. Represents actors across the board.

Will consider attending performances within Greater London, given 2-3 days' notice. Welcomes letters (with CVs and photographs) from individual actors previously unknown to the agency, hard copies preferred over email, unless accompanied by showreel and/or performance footage. Encourages enquiries from actors with disabilities. Does not welcome follow-up calls, showreels, voicereels or invitations to view individual actors' websites. *Commission*: Theatre 10%; Film, TV, Commercials 15%

Jorg Betts Associates PMA

2 John Street, London WC1N 2ES
tel 020-3405 4546 *fax* 020-7903 5301
email agents@jorgbetts.com

Established in 2001. Areas of work include theatre, musicals, television, film, commercials and corporates. Also represents directors, casting director, choreographers and presenters.

Accepts submissions (with CVs and photographs) from actors previously unknown to the company if sent by post.

Billboard Personal Management

45 Lothrop Street, London W10 4JB
tel 020-7735 995 *mobile* 07791 970773
email daniel@billboardpm.com
website www.billboardpm.com
Agent Daniel Tasker

Established in 1985. 1 agent represents 55 actors. Areas of work include theatre, musicals, television, film, commercials, corporate and voice-overs.

Will consider attending performances at venues in Greater London given a minimum of 2 weeks' notice. Accepts submissions by email only, no bigger than 1MB, from actors if they are currently performing. *Commission*: Commercials 16%; Film and TV 13.5%; Other 11%

Rebecca Blond Associates PMA

69A Kings Road, London SW3 4NX
tel 020-7351 4100 *fax* 020-7351 4600
email info@rebeccablond.com
Agent Rebecca Blond

Established in 1991. 2 agents represent around 60 actors in all areas of acting work; also represents directors.

Welcomes performance notices for shows within Greater London with 2 weeks' notice. Welcomes representation enquiries (with CV and photographs) by post or email, as well as showreels and invitations to view individual actors' websites. Does not welcome follow-up calls. *Commission*: Varies

Bloomfields Welch Management PMA

77 Oxford Street, London W1D 2ES
tel 020-7659 2001 *fax* 020-7659 2101
email info@bloomfieldsmanagement.com
website www.bloomfieldsmanagement.com
Director Emma Bloomfield

Established in 2004. Areas of work include theatre, musicals, television, film, commercials and corporate. 3 agents represent 40 actors.

Will consider attending performances anywhere, given at least 2 weeks' notice. Accepts submissions (with CVs and photographs) from actors previously unknown to the company if sent by post, but not by email. Invitations to view individual actors' websites, showreels and voicereels are also accepted. Welcomes enquiries from disabled actors.

Blue Star Associates

7-8 Shaldon Mansions, 132 Charing Cross Road, London WC2H 0LA
tel 020-7836 6220
email bluestar.london.2000@gmail.com
Directors Barrie Stacey, Keith Hopkins

Established in 2007 (formerly Barrie Stacey Promotions, established 1960). Works in theatre, musicals, pantomime, television, film and commercials. Around 70 actors represented. Will consider attending performances in the Greater London area.

Welcomes letters (with CVs and photographs) sent by post or email. Does not represent actors with disabilities. *Commission*: Theatre 10%; TV/Film 15%

Sandra Boyce Management PMA

125 Dynevor Road, London N16 0DA
tel 020-7923 0606 *fax* 020-7241 2313
email info@sandraboyce.com
Agent Sandra Boyce (MD)

2 agents represent 70 actors in all areas of acting work; directors also represented.

Welcomes performance notices if given at least 2 weeks' notice, and is prepared to travel within the Greater London area. Happy to accept letters (by post) with CVs and photographs from individuals previously unknown to the company, but does not welcome follow-up calls. Encourages approaches from disabled actors. Also welcomes showreels and voicereels.

Michelle Braidman Associates Ltd PMA

2 Futura House, 169 Grange Road, London SE1 3BN
tel 020-7237 3523
email info@braidman.com
website www.braidman.com
Agents Michelle Braidman, Nicola Whitworth, Rebecca Kirby

Established in 1983. A leading international theatrical agency representing artists and creative talent.

Submissions should be sent by post. They should include a covering letter with CV, headshot, contact details and sae.

Eva Bridge Management

Ryden Grange, Bisley, Surrey GU21 2TH
tel (01635) 799454 *mobile* (07788) 725164
email info@evabridge.com
website www.evabridge.com
Agent Eva Bridge *Assistants* Jessica Galt, Leanora Adds

Established in 2012. Main areas of work are theatre, musicals, film, television, commercials and voice-over.

Will consider attending performances in London and in the Surrey/Berkshire areas, given 2 weeks' notice. Is happy to receive approaches by actors previously unknown to the agency. Does not currently represent actors with disabilities, but would certainly consider it. *Commission*: Commercials 15%; Film, TV, Voice-overs, Corporate 12%; Theatre 10%

BROOD PMA

49 Greek Street, London W1D 4EG
tel 020-3489 4949
website www.broodmanagement.com
Main Agent Brian Parsonage-Kelly

Represents 60 actors and personalities. Clients work throughout the industry from Hollywood to Fringe, corporates to cruises and soaps to commercials. Prospective clients please visit the website, apply by email only **broodapplication@aol.com**.

Jeremy Brook Ltd

37 Berwick Street, London W1F 8RS
tel 020-7434 0398 *fax* 020-7287 8016
email info@jeremybrookltd.co.uk
website www.jeremybrookltd.co.uk
Managing Director/Senior Agent James Foster

Originally Jean Clarke Management established in 1995. Areas of work include theatre, musicals, television, film, commercials, corporate and radio.

Will consider attending performances in Greater London with at least 3-4 weeks' notice. Accepts submissions from actors previously unknown to the agency by email. Showreels, voicereels and invitations to views an actor's website are also accepted, but follow-up calls and emails are not welcome.

Valerie Brook Agency

10 Sandringham Road, Cheadle Hulme, Cheshire SK8 5NH
tel 0161-486 1631
email colinbrook@freenetname.co.uk

2 agents represent 25 actors. Areas of work include theatre, musicals, television, film, commercials and corporate role-play.

Will consider attending performances at venues outside Greater London with 2 weeks' notice. Accepts postal submissions (with CVs and photographs) from actors previously unknown to the company. Invitations to view individual actors' websites are also accepted. *Commission*: Negotiated with clients individually

Brown, Simcocks & Andrews (UK) LLP

504 The Chandlery, 50 Westminster Bridge Road, London SE1 7QY
020-7953 7484020-7953 7494
email info@bsaagency.co.uk
website www.brownsimcocksandandrews.co.uk
Partners Carrie Simcocks, Kelly Andrews

Established in the 1970s; 2 agents represent 65-70 actors. Areas of work include theatre, musicals, television, film, commercials and corporate.

Will consider attending performances within the Greater London area, given 2-4 weeks' notice. Accepts submissions (with CVs and photographs) from actors previously unknown to the company if sent by post. Unsolicited emails are not welcome. *Commission*: 10-15%

Brunskill Management Ltd

Suite 8A, 169 Queen's Gate, London SW7 5HE
tel 020-7589 8668 *mobile* 020-7589 9460
email mark@brunskill.com
Director Mark Holden-Hindley

For artist representation see the entry for Stanton Davidson Associates under *Agents* on page 83.

Bronia Buchanan Associates Ltd

1st Floor, 23 Tavistock Street, London WC2E 7NX
tel 020-7631 2004 *fax* 020-7631 2034
email info@buchanan-associates.co.uk
website www.buchanan-associates.co.uk
Director Bronia Buchanan *Agents* Gina Rowland, Laura Justice, Alex Gottschall, Chadd Garvie

Sole representation of approximately 25 creatives and 150 actors. Areas of work include theatre, musicals, television, film and commercials.

Will consider attending performances at venues within Greater London and elsewhere, but requests as much notice as possible. Accepts submissions by post or email (with CVs and photographs) from actors previously unknown to the company. Showreels and voicereels are also encouraged. *Commission*: 12% plus VAT

Burnett Crowther Ltd PMA

3 Clifford Street, London W1S 2LF
tel 020-7437 8008 *fax* 020-7287 3239
email associates@bcltd.org
website www.bcltd.org
Agents Barry Burnett, Lizanne Crowther

Established in 1965. 2 agents represent 140 actors.

Will consider attending performances at venues within Greater London, with 3 weeks' notice. Accepts submissions by email (with CVs and photographs) from actors previously unknown to the company. *Commission*: 10-12%

Burningham Associates

4 Victoria Road, Twickenham TW1 3HW
mobile (07807) 176287
email info@burnassoc.org
website www.burnassoc.org
Director Susan Burningham *Associate (Germany)* Margaret Nieman

Established in 2012. Main areas of work are theatre, film, television, radio, commercials, voice-over and corporate (films and training). Also represents playrights.

Accepts letters (with CV and photographs and sae) only. Actors with disabilities are welcome to apply. The agency will only consider actors who have attended a full-time accredited drama school, who are members of Spotlight and intend to become full members of Equity. All actors are expected to have a showreel and voicereel. *Commission*: Theatre, 10%, Film, Television, Radio, Voice Overs Commercials, Corporate 15%

The BWH Agency Ltd PMA

5th Floor, 35 Soho Square, London W1D 3QX
tel 020-7734 0657 *fax* 020-7734 1278
email info@thebwhagency.co.uk
website www.thebwhagency.co.uk
Agents and Company Directors Joe Hutton, Bill Petrie, Lisa Willoughby and Andrew Braidford *Agent* Holly Davidson, all assisted by Eleanor Cairns and Maddie Burdett-Couts (accountant)

Established in 2004, main areas of work are theatre, musicals, TV, film, commercials and radio. Welcomes letters (with CVs and photographs), CVs and photographs sent by email, showreels and voice tapes.

Paul Byram Associates (THE AGENCY) PMA

Suite B0079, The Long Lodge,
265-269 Kingston Road, Wimbledon, SW19 3FW
020 3137 3385 *tel* +1 310 531 8673
email contact@paulbyram.com
website www.paulbyram.com
Senior Agent Paul Byram *Agent* Jason Jenkins

Established in 2010 main areas of work are TV, theatre, film, commercials, corporate and musicals. Represents 50 actors, as well as casting directors and directors. Charges commission on a sliding scale.

Welcomes perfomance notices within central London and Fringe venues with 2 weeks' notice; will occasionally go further afield with greater notice.All contact via the company website contact page or, worst case, vai email only. No post please. Represents actor with disabilities.

Jessica Carney Associates PMA

4th Floor, 23 Golden Square, London W1F 9JP
tel 020-7434 4143
email info@jcarneyassociates.co.uk
website www.jessicacarneyassociates.co.uk

Established in 1950. Areas of work include: theatre, television, films, commercials and musicals. Also represents technicians and craftspeople.

Cannot consider actors for representation unless they can be seen in performance (not showcase) within Greater London (requires 2-3 weeks' notice), or possess good mainstream TV credits. Only accepts submissions if sent by email to **representation@jcarneyassociates.co.uk**. Emails should contain a link to their Spotlight CV and showreel. *Commission*: TV/Film 12.5%; Theatre 10%; Commercials 15%

CBL Management

20 Hollingbury Rise, Brighton BN1 7HJ
mobile (07956) 890307
email enquiries@cblmanagement.co.uk
website www.cblmanagement.co.uk
Agents Claire Carpenter, Beth Eden, Linda Edwards

Established in 2007. 3 agents represent 90 artistes. Works in theatre, musicals, television, film, commercials, corporate and voice-over. Directors, choreographers, musical directors and technicians also represented.

Welcomes CVs and photographs by email only.

CDA PMA

167-169 Kensington High Street, London W8 6SH
tel 020-7937 2749 *fax* 020-7373 1110
email cda@cdalondon.com
Agents: Belina Wright, Theresa Hickey

3 agents represent 60 actors.

Will consider attending performances at venues within Greater London with 3 weeks' notice. Accepts submissions (with CVs and photographs) from actors previously unknown to the company if sent by post. Showreels, voicereels and invitations to view individual actors' websites are also accepted. *Commission*: Variable

Center Stage Agency

7 Rutledge Terrace, South Circular Road, Dublin 8
tel 353 (0)1-4533599
email geraldinecenterstage@eircom.net
website www.centerstageagency.com

Founded 1994, areas of work include theatre, television, film, musicals, voice-over, commercial and web-based work.

Will consider attending performances at venues in Dublin with 1 weeks' notice. Accepts submissions by email (with CVs and photographs). Showreels are also welcome. *Commission*: 10-15%.

Esta Charkham Associates

16 British Grove, Chiswick, London W4 2NL
tel 0208-7412 843
email office@charkham.net
website www.charkham.net

Boutique talent agency established in 2000. Areas of work include theatre, film, TV, radio, voice-over and comedy.

Will consider attending performances at venues in Greater London area with at least 2 weeks' notice. Accepts submissions of CV and photograph along with a covering letter by way of a request for representation. Does not welcome email enquiries.

Peter Charlesworth & Associates

67 Holland Park Mews, London W11 3SS
tel 020-7792 4600 *fax* 020-7792 1893
email info@petercharlesworth.co.uk
Director Peter Charlesworth *Associate* Sharry Clark

Does not welcome unsolicited contact – including performance notices – from actors previously unknown to the company.

Cinetea

9 rue des Trois Bornes, 75011 Paris
tel 33 (0)1 4278 1717
email cinetea@orange.fr
website www.cinetea.fr
Agent Marie Claude Schwartz

Will accept European actors speaking French; CVs and photographs should be sent by email. Showreels and voicereels also accepted.

Claypole Management

PO Box 123, Darlington DL3 7WA
tel 0845-650 1777
email info@claypolemanagement.co.uk
website www.claypolemanagement.co.uk

Established in 2000. Areas of work include: theatre, musicals, television, film, commercials and corporate.

Will consider attending performances at venues within the north or north-east of England. Welcomes both CVs and letters from clients previously unknown to the company and unsolicited CVs and photographs. These should be sent via email or post. Also welcomes invitations to view individual actors' websites, showreels or Spotlight links. Happy to receive applications for representation from disabled actors.

Clic Agency

7 Ffordd Seion, Bangor, Gwynedd LL57 1BS
tel (01248) 354420
email clic@btinternet.com
website www.clicagency.co.uk
Proprietor Helen Pritchard

Established in 2006. 1 agent represents around 50 actors in all areas of work.

Accepts submissions (with CVs and photographs) from actors previously unknown to the company, sent by email. Encourages enquiries from disabled actors and welcomes showreels, voicereels, follow-up calls and invitations to view individual actors' websites. *Commission*: Varies, but not more than 15%

Elspeth Cochrane Personal Management

Now amalgamated with Asquith & Horner. See the company's entry under *Agents* on page 56.

Cole Kitchenn Personal Management Ltd PMA

ROAR House, 46 Charlotte Street, London W1T 2GS
tel 020-7427 5681
email info@colekitchenn.com
website www.colekitchenn.com
Managing Director/Agent Stuart Piper *Senior Agent/Director* Oliver Thomson *Associate Agents* Alex Segal, Ashley Vallance *Assistant* Dominique Baxter

The agency is a team of 5 representing a select list of actors and creatives, from directors and choreographers to designers and musical directors.

Welcomes performance notices within Greater London given 2-3 weeks' notice. Happy to receive letters and emails (with CVs, photographs and showreels) from new actors, but prefers not to receive follow-up telephone calls.

Shane Collins Associates PMA

Suite 112, Davina House, 137-149 Goswell Road, London EC1V 7ET
tel 020-7253 1010 *fax* 0870-460 1983
email info@shanecollins.co.uk
website www.shanecollins.co.uk
Agent Shane Collins

Established in 1986, the agency represents around 85 actors working in all areas of the industry.

Will consider attending performances within Greater London given as much notice as possible. Accepts submissions (with CVs and photographs) from actors previously unknown to the company; however, follow-up telephone calls, emails, showreels, voicereels and invitations to view an actor's website are not welcomed. Photos, CVs and showreels will only be returned if the actor includes a stamped, addressed envelope.

Conway Van Gelder Grant PMA

3rd Floor, 8-12 Broadwick Street, London W1F 8HN
tel 020-7287 0077 *fax* 020-7287 1940
Agents Nicholas Gall; Nicola van Gelder and Kat Oliver, assisted by George Davies and Rachael Swanson; John Grant, assisted by Deborah Charlton and Alice Smith and Liz Nelson, assisted by Vena Dacent.

5 agents represent actors working in all areas of the industry.

Will consider attending performances within Greater London and occasionally elsewhere, given 3-4 weeks' notice. Accepts postal submissions (with CVs, photographs and sae to ensure reply) from actors previously unknown to the agency, along with invitations to view an actor's website. Showreels and voicereels should only be sent if requested after initial contact has been made. Follow-up telephone calls and emails are not welcomed. *Commission*: Varies according to contract

Howard Cooke Associates (HCA)

19 Coulson Street, London SW3 3NA
tel 020-7591 0144
Managing Director/Senior Agent Howard Cooke
Associate Agent Bronwyn Sanders

2 agents represent 40 actors. Areas of work include theatre, musicals, television, film, commercials and corporate.

Will consider attending performances at venues within Greater London and elsewhere (if within easy travelling distance) with 3 weeks' notice. Hard-copy applications (with CVs, photographs and sae) from actors previously unknown to the company are welcome, but email submissions are not accepted. *Commission*: 10-20%

Cooper Searle Personal Management Ltd

St Martin's Theatre, West Street, London WC2H 9NZ
tel 020-7183 4851
email admin@coopersearle.co.uk
website www.coopersearle.co.uk
Agent/Director Emily Rose

Established in 2010. Represents around 45 clients. Main areas of work are theatre, musicals, television, film, commercials, corporate, pantomime and stills.

Emily will try to attend performances if it is possible, but welcomes approaches from actors. Emily will always see clients perform. Applications should be via email containing actor's CV, headshots, and any material or links that can help the agency see their work.The agency considers every application based on performance ability and marketability.
Commission: 12.5-15%

Clive Corner Associates

'The Belenes', 60 Wakeham, Portland DT5 1HN
tel (01305) 860267
email cornerassociates@aol.com
Key personnel Clive Corner, Duncan Stratton

Established in 1988. 2 agents represent 40 actors. Areas of work include theatre, musicals, television, film, commercials and corporate.

Will consider attending performances at venues within Greater London if given 3 weeks' notice. Rarely prepared to travel elsewhere. Accepts submissions by email. *Commission*: 20%

Coulter Management Agency PMA

Siute 418, The Pentagon Centre, Washington Street, Glasgow G3 8AZ
tel 0141 204 4058
email info@coultermanagement.com
Agent Julie Hamilton

Areas of work include theatre, television, film, commercials, corporate and voice-overs.

Will consider attending performances at venues in Scotland with 3 weeks' notice. Accepts submissions (with CVs and photographs) from actors previously unknown to the company if sent by email. Showreels and voicereels are also accepted. *Commission*: 7.5-15% (sliding scale)

Covent Garden Management

Cida, 7-15 Greatorex Street, London E1 5NF
tel 020-7392 7324 *fax* 020-7240 8409
email info@coventgardenmanagement.com

Established in 2002. The agency represents around 30 actors. Areas of work include theatre, musicals, television, film, commercials, corporate and voice-overs. Also represents directors.

Will consider attending performances at venues within Greater London with 2 weeks' notice. Accepts submissions (with CVs and photographs) from actors previously unknown to the company if sent by post. *Commission*: 10-15%

Curtis Brown Ltd PMA

Haymarket House, 28-29 Haymarket,
London SW1Y 4SP
tel 020-7393 4400 *fax* 020-7393 4401
email info@curtisbrown.co.uk
website www.curtisbrown.co.uk
Agents Oriana Elia, Richard Gibb, Jessica Jackson, Alistair Lindsey-Renton, Frances Stevenson, Sam Turnbull, Olivia Woodward, Lara Beach, Grace Clissold, Jacquie Drewe, Mary FitzGerald, Maxine Hoffman, Lucy Johnson, Sarah MacCormick, Grant Parsons, Sarah Spear, Kate Staddon

One of Europe's oldest and largest independent literary and media agencies. Established over 100 years ago, there are now more than 20 agents within the Book, Media, Actors and Presenters Divisions, 5 of whom represent actors. Also represents writers, directors, playwrights and celebrities.

Submissions should be sent by post and addressed to 'Actors Agents'. They should include a covering letter with email address, CV, photograph, showreel (if actor has one) and sae for the return of the showreel. Tries to respond within 4-6 weeks. Does not meet potential clients before viewing their work. Does not accept email or faxed submissions. *Commission*: 12.5-15%

DAA Management PMA

Welbeck House, 66-67 Wells Street,
London W1T 3PY
tel 020-7255 6123
email info@daamanagement.co.uk
website www.daamanagement.co.uk
Key personnel Debi Allen, Charlene McManus, Jess Molloy, Becky Williams, Michael Ford, Lucy Nooshin, Craig Latto, Lucy O'Meara

Established in 2009. Main areas of work are theatre, musicals, television, film, commercials and corporate. Will usually respond within 14 days to performance notices; productions must be within the M25 radius or at a major arts festival.

Welcomes letters (with CVs and photographs) from actors previously unknown to the agency, sent by email to **representation@daamanagement.co.uk**. Also accepts showreels, voice tapes and invitations to view actors' websites. Represents actors with disabilities.

David Daly Associates

586 King's Road, London SW6 2DX
tel 020-7384 1036 *fax* 020-7610 9512
email agent@daviddaly.co.uk
Manchester office: 16 King Street, Knutsford WA16 6DL
tel (01565) 631999 *fax* (01565) 755334
email north@daviddaly.co.uk
website www.daviddaly.co.uk
Agents David Daly, Louisa Miles (London); David Daly, Mary Ramsay (Manchester)

An established actors' agency bring 30 years of experience to the entertainment industry.

Elizabeth Davies Associates

Suite 279, 116 Ballards Lane, Finchley,
London N3 2DN
tel 020-3138 0950 *mobile* (07534) 196166
email edaviesassociates@yahoo.com
Agents Elizabeth Davies, Omar Hunte

Established in 2007. Areas of work include theatre, musicals, TV, film, commercials, corporate, voice-over, touring, booker, PR and marketing. Books are currently closed.

Will consider attending performances at venues within Greater London. Accepts submissions (with CVs and photographs), showreels, voice tapes and invitations to view individual actors' websites. *Commission*: 20-25%

Chris Davis Management PMA

Tenbury House, 36 Teme Street, Tenbury Wells, Worcestershire WR15 8AA
tel (01584) 819005 *fax* (01584) 819076
email cdavis@cdm-ltd.com
website www.cdm-ltd.com
Managing Director Chris Davis

Areas of work are theatre, musicals, television, film, commercials and corporate. 2 agents represent 80 actors; directors, choreographers, designers and musical directors are also represented.

Will consider attending performances within Greater London and elsewhere, given as much notice as possible. Welcomes letters (with CVs and photographs) from actors previously unknown to the agency, sent by post or email. Does not welcome follow-up calls. Accepts showreels, voicereels and invitations to view individual actors' websites. Encourages applications from actors with disabilities.

Davis Bishop Associates

Cotton's Farmhouse, 28 Whiston Road, Cogenhoe, Northamptonshire NN7 1NL
tel (01604) 891487
email admin@cottonsfarmhouse.org
Agents Lena Davis, John Bishop

Established in 1986. Areas of work include theatre, musicals, television, film, commercials, corporate, voice-overs. Also represent other skills within the profession.

Will consider attending performances in Greater London with plenty of notice. Accepts submissions (with CVs and photographs) from actors unknown to the company. Follow-up calls and email submissions are not welcomed. *Commission*: 10-20%

Felix de Wolfe PMA

20 Old Compton Street, London W1D 4TW
tel 020-7242 5066 *fax* 020-7242 8119
email info@felixdewolfe.com

Areas of work include film, television, theatre, musicals, commercials, corporate and radio. Also represents directors, producers and writers.

Accepts submissions by email to **info@felixdewolfe.com** which must be marked Re: representation.*Commission*: Variable

Devine Artist Management

115 Tempus Building, 9 Mirabel Street, Manchester M3 1NP
tel 0161-726 5726
email manchester@devinemanagement.co.uk
website www.devinemanagement.co.uk

Works in all areas. A paperless office which only accepts applications by email. Prefers to view showreels via a link. Does not welcome follow-up calls. Welcomes applications from young performers. Currently represents several disabled actors and presenters, and encourages applications from such individuals.

Diamond Management PMA

31 Percy Street, London W1T 2DD
tel 020-7631 0400
email jd@diman.co.uk
website www.diamondmanagement.co.uk
*Agents:*Lesley Duff, Jean Diamond, Clare Partridge, Charlie Cox

Established in 2003. Main areas of work are TV, theatre, commercials and film; also represents directors, MDs, writers and costume designers.

Welcomes letters (with CVs and photographs), follow-up phone calls, CVs and photographs sent by email, showreels, voice tapes and invitations to view actors' websites. Represents actors with disabilities. *Commission* 12.5%

DQ Management

27 Ravenswood Park, Northwood, Middlesex HA6 3PR
tel 01273-721221 *mobile* (07713) 984633
email dq.management1@gmail.com
website www.dqmanagement.com
Senior Partners Peter Davis, Kate Davis

Established in 2003. Areas of work include theatre, musicals, television, film, commercials and corporate. 2 agents represent 80 actors.

Will consider attending performances within the Greater London area and elsewhere with at least 2 weeks' notice. Accepts submissions (with CVs and photographs) from actors previously unknown to the company if sent by post. Invitations to view individuals' websites, showreels or voicereels are also accepted. Welcomes enquiries from disabled actors. *Commission*: Theatre 10%; West End 12.5%; TV/Film/Commercials 15%

Kenneth Earle Personal Management

214 Brixton Road, London SW9 6AP
tel 020-7274 1219 *fax* 020-7274 9529
email kennethearle@agents-uk.com
website www.kennethearlepersonalmanagement.com

Established in 2000. 3 agents represent around 40 actors. Areas of work include theatre, musicals, television, film, commercials, corporate and voice-over.

Accepts submissions (with CVs and photographs) from actors previously unknown to the company if sent by post or email. No telephone calls. Please include any showreels, voicereels, demos, links, websites and invitations. *Commission*: 15%

Susi Earnshaw Management

The Bull Theatre, 68 High Street, Barnet, Herts. EN5 5SJ
tel 020-8441 5010 *fax* 020-8364 9618
email casting@susiearnshaw.co.uk
website www.susiearnshawmanagement.com
Agents Susi Earnshaw, Melissa Gillespie, Jessie Tsang, Robin Parsons

Established in 1989. 4 agents and bookers represent 30 adult actors, 60 child performers, and various tribute bands. Areas of work include theatre, musicals, television, film, corporate, live entertainment, dance videos, radio and commercials.

Prefers submissions via email (with CVs and photos). *Commission*: Theatre 10%; TV, Film and Commercials 15%

Elite Talent

54 Crosslee Road, Blackley, Manchester M9 6TA
mobile (07787) 342221
email paul@elitetalent.co.uk
website www.elitetalent.co.uk
Senior Agent Paul Newbery

Established in 2007. London and Manchester representation. Main areas of work are theatre, musicals, television, film, commercials and corporate.

Will consider attending performances in Manchester/Northern areas, given 14 days' notice. Welcomes letters (with CVs and photographs) sent by post or email, but prefers email submissions. Also accepts showreels, voicereels (online only), and invitations to view actors' websites. Encourages submissions from actors with disabilities. *Commission*: Theatre 10%, TV, Film, Corporate 15%, Commercials 20%

Emptage Hallett PMA

2nd Floor, 3-5 The Balcony, Castle Arcade, Cardiff, CF10 1BU
tel (02920) 344205
email cardiff@emptagehallett.co.uk
website www.emptagehallett.co.uk
Agents Claire Symons, Gemma McAvoy

Founded in 1999, main area of work is theatre, musicals, TV, film, commercials, voice-over and corporate. Represents 85 actors, and also directors, presenters, writers and casting directors. Charges standard PMA rates. They will make every effort to attend performances in Cardiff. Happy to receive emails with links to view showreels, voicereels and Spotlight CV link. Also welcome applications from actors with disabilities who have a link to their showreel and Spotlight CV.

June Epstein Associates

62 Compayne Gardens, London NW6 3RY
tel 020-7328 0864 or 020-7372 1928
fax 020-7328 0684
email june@june-epstein-associates.co.uk

Established in 1973; represents approximately 40 actors working in theatre, musicals, television, film commercials and corporate role-play. Recommends the photographers Jonathan Dockar-Drysdale (**fact-d@lineone.net**) and Peter Simpkin (**petersimpkin@aol.com**).

Will consider attending performances within Greater London given 2-3 weeks' notice. Accepts postal submissions (with CVs and photographs) from actors previously unknown to the agency. Welcomes voicereels from singers, follow-up telephone calls and showreels, but prefers not to receive emails. *Commission*: 10%; Commercials 15%

The Jane Estall Agency

37 Madeira Drive, Hastings TN34 2NH
mobile (07703) 550006
email thejaneestallagency@gmail.com
website www.thejaneestallagency.webeden.com
Owner/Director Jane Estall

Established in 2010. Represents around 25 actors. Areas of work include theatre, musicals, TV, film, commercials, corporate and voice-over. Also represents stand-up comedians and chaperones.

Will consider attending performances, given 1 week's notice. Welcomes submissions (with CVs and photographs) from actors previously unknown to the agency, sent by post and email; also accepts showreels, voice tapes and invitations to view individual actors' websites. Represents actors with disabilities.

Ethnics Artiste Agency

86 Elphinstone Road, Walthamstow, London E17 5EX
tel 020-8523 4242 *fax* 020-8523 4523
email info@ethnicsaa.co.uk
website www.ethnicsartisteagency.com
Managing Director Pauline Oni

Founded in 1997. 2 agents represent 60 actors in all areas of acting work. The company represents multicultural and international performers and artistes from across the globe, including actors, singers, dancers, musicians and martial artists from Asia, Africa and Europe, and performers of ethnic-minority British origin. Specialises in representation of performers of colour and those with fluent foreign-language skills.

Welcomes performance notices 2-3 weeks in advance; will consider travelling to shows within Greater London. Welcomes letters (with CVs and photographs) from individuals previously unknown to the company if sent by post, but not by email. Welcomes showreels, but not invitations to view individual actors' websites. Welcomes representation enquiries from disabled actors.

– **see entry under WIS Celtic Management** on page 88

Stephanie Evans Associates

Rivington House, 82 Great Eastern Street, London EC2A 3JF
tel/fax 0870-609 2629
email steph@stephanie-evans.com
website www.stephanie-evans.com
Director Stephanie Evans

Established in 2003. 1 agent represents 60 actors. Areas of work include theatre, musicals, television, film, commercials and corporate.

Will consider attending performances in England and Wales with at least 1 month's notice. Accepts submissions (with CVs, photographs and showreels) from actors previously unknown to the company if sent by post. Invitations to view individual actors' websites are also accepted. Welcomes enquiries from disabled actors. *Commission*: 12%

Excess All Areas

3 Gibbs Square, London SE19 1JN
tel 020-8761 2384
email info@excessallareas.co.uk
website www.excessallareas.co.uk
Director Paul L Martin

Agency dedicated to cabaret, burlesque, circus and variety acts. Corporate work, private parties, etc. for already existing self-contained acts.

Paola Farino

109 St George's Road, London SE1 6HY
tel 020-7207 0858
email info@paolafarino.co.uk
website www.paolafarino.co.uk

Established in 2007. Sole agent, works in theatre, TV, film, commercials, corporate and photography. Will consider attending performances within Greater London. Prefers to receive performance notices and all other approaches by email – include Spotlight PIN. "Check website first to see if there is anybody else represented with a similar MO."

Feast Management PMA

1st Floor, 34 Upper Street, London N1 0PN
tel 020-7354 5216 *fax* 020-7354 8995

email office@feastmanagement.co.uk
Agent Sadie Feast

3 agents represent actors. Areas of work include theatre, musicals, television, film, commercials, corporate and voice-overs.

Will consider attending performances in the London area if plenty of notice is given. Accepts submissions (with CVs and photographs) from actors previously unknown to the company.

First Act Personal Management

2 St Michaels, New Arley, Coventry CV7 8PY
tel (01676) 540285 *fax* (01676) 542777
email firstactpm@aol.com
website www.spotlightagent.info/firstact
Agent John Burton

Established in 2003. 1 agent represents 25 actors. Areas of work include theatre, musicals, television, film, commercials, corporate and voice-overs.

Will consider attending performances in England and Wales with at least 2 weeks' notice. Accepts submissions (with CVs and photographs) from actors previously unknown to the company if sent by post. Invitations to view individual actors' websites, showreels or voicereels are also accepted. Welcomes enquiries from disabled actors. *Commission*: 10-15%

Flatlined Talent

Unit 2, Campbell Street, Preston PR1 5LX
tel (07557) 434680
email office@flatlinedtalent.co.uk
website wwwflatlinedtalent.co.uk
Agents Jacklyn Cooksley-Pekepo, Kay Purcell

Established in 2011. Main areas of work are theatre, musicals, television, film, commercials and corporate. 2 agents represent 20 actors.

Will consider attending performances anywhere in Great Britain, and preferably in the North West, given at least 2 weeks' notice. Accepts letters and emails from individuals previously unknown to the agency, if accompanied by CVs and photographs. Currently represents no disabled actors, but offers positive discrimination to all. *Commission*: Rep Theatre/Corporate/low-paid work 5-10%; TV/Film 15%

Kerry Foley Management Ltd

Communications House, 26 York Street, London W1U 6PZ
mobile (07747) 864001
email contact@kfmltd.com
website www.kfmltd.com
Director Kerry Foley

Established in 2011. Main areas of work are theatre, musicals, television, film, commercials and corporate. Also represents creatives, including directors, musical directors and choreographers. Will consider CVs and photographs sent by email. Agency is open to all actors on their merits.

Sharon Foster Management

15A Hollybank Road, Birmingham B13 0RF
mobile (07919) 417812
email mail@sharonfoster.co.uk
website www.sharonfoster.co.uk

1 agent represents around 40 actors working in theatre, musicals, television, radio, film, commercials and corporate role-play.

Will consider attending performances given sufficient notice. Accepts submissions (with CVs and photographs) from actors previously unknown to the agency, sent by post or email. Follow-up telephone calls, showreels, voicereels and invitations to view an actor's website are also accepted. *Commission*: 10-15%

Julie Fox Associates

tel (01628) 777853
email agent@juliefoxassociates.co.uk
website www.juliefoxassociates.co.uk
Agents Julie Fox, Corrine Murray

Agency works in all areas of live and recorded media. 2 agents represent 50 actors; directors and casting directors also represented. Accepts email approaches only (letters, CVs, showreels or links to Spotlight).

Cinel Gabran Management

Ty Cefn, 14-16 Rectory Road, Canton, Cardiff, CF5 1QL and Adventure House, Newholm, Whitby, North Yorkshire YO21 3QY
tel 029-2066 6600 and 019-4760 5376
email mail@cinelgabran.co.uk
website www.cinelgabran.co.uk
Managing Director/Agent David Chance

Established in 1992. 1 agent represents 40 actors. Also represents presenters and directors.

Accepts submissions, (with CVs and photographs), from actors previously unknown to the company if sent by email. *Commission*: Theatre 10%; Film 15%; all other media 12.5%

Hilary Gagan Associates PMA

187 Drury Lane, London WC2B 5QD
tel 020-7404 8794 *fax* 020-7430 1869
email hilary@hgassoc.co.uk
Assistant Shiv Coard

3 agents represent approximately 100 actors. Areas of work include theatre, musicals, television, film, commercials, corporate, voice-overs. Also represents directors and choreographers.

Will consider attending performances in Greater London with at least 2 weeks' notice. Accepts submissions (with CVs and photographs with name on back of photograph) from actors previously unknown to the agency (include sae). Invitations to view individual actors' websites, showreels and voicereels are also accepted. Follow-up calls are welcomed, as are enquiries from disabled actors. *Commission*: 7.5-15%

Galloways

Suite 410, Henry Wood House,
2 Riding House Street, London W1W 7FA
email info@gallowaysagency.com
website www.gallowaysagency.com
Head Agent Jilly Moore; *Agent* Romany Hoyland; *Commercials Agent* Miranda Heffernan

Established in 1985, and represents actors for stage, screen, radio and commercials.

Galloways is a small, close-knit team who focus on the individual needs of our actors. Many of our clients have been with us since the inception of the company but we are also constantly looking for fresh talent to add to our list. We also work with agents in New York and Los Angeles.

Submissions for representation can be made either by post or email. No phone calls please. We will respond to all postal applications which include a self-addressed envelope.

Gardner Herrity PMA

24 Conway Street, London W1T 6BG
tel 020-7388 0088 *fax* 020-7388 0688
email info@gardnerherrity.co.uk
Key contact Andy Herrity

Areas of work include feature films, television, theatre and radio drama.

Will consider attending performances within the Greater London area with at least 3 weeks' notice. Accepts submissions (with CVs and photographs) from actors previously unknown to the company if sent by post, but not by email. Also accepts showreels, voicereels, and invitations to view individual actors' websites. Welcomes enquiries from disabled actors. *Commission*: 10%

Garricks PMA

Angel House, 76 Mallinson Road,
London SW11 1BN
tel 020-7738 1600 *fax* 020-7801 0088
email info@garricks.net
Key personnel Megan Willis

Established in 1981. Areas of work include theatre, television, film, commercials and corporate.

Will consider attending performances at venues within Greater London and elsewhere. Accepts submissions (with CVs and photographs) from actors previously unknown to the company, sent by post or (preferably) email. Invitations to view individual actors' websites are also accepted. *Commission*: TV, Film and Theatre 10%; Commercials 15%

Gilbert & Payne Personal Management

Room 236, 2nd Floor, Linen Hall,
162-168 Regent Street, London W1B 5TB
tel 020-7734 7505 *fax* 020-7494 3787
email ee@gilbertandpayne.com
Director Elena Gilbert *Key personnel* Elaine Payne

Established in 1996. 2 agents represent 50 actors. Areas of work include theatre, musicals, television, film, commercials and corporate, with a particular emphasis on musical theatre. Also represents choreographers.

Will consider attending performances at venues in Greater London with a minimum of 1 week's notice. Accepts submissions (with CVs and photographs) from actors previously unknown to the company if sent by post. Follow-up telephone calls are also accepted. *Commission*: Theatre 10%

Global Artists PMA

23 Haymarket, London SW1Y 4DG
tel 020-7839 4888 *fax* 020-7839 4555
email info@globalartists.co.uk
website www.globalartists.co.uk

A personal management company representing professional actors and actresses. Areas of work include theatre, musical theatre, television, film, commercials and corporate. Also represents a limited number of theatre designers, choreographers, directors and musical directors.

Accepts submissions from actors previously unknown to the company, sent by post or email. Does not welcome telephone enquiries.

Grantham-Hazeldine Ltd PMA

Suite 427, The Linen Hall, 162-168 Regent St,
London W1B 5TE
tel 020-7038 3737/8 *fax* 020-7038 3739
email agents@granthamhazeldine.com
website www.granthamhazeldine.com
Directors John Grantham, Caroline Hazeldine *Agent* Claire O'Sullivan and Nicholas Errington

Established in 1984. 4 agents represent 120 actors and creatives. Areas of work include theatre, musicals, television, film, commercials, corporate and voice-overs. Also represents writers and stunt co-ordinators.

Will consider attending performances at venues in Greater London and elsewhere with 1 month's notice. Accepts submissions (with CVs and photographs) from actors previously unknown to the company if sent by post. Will not accept showreels and voicereels at the initial stage of contact. *Commission*: Theatre and Radio 10% plus VAT; TV and Film 15% plus VAT

Darren Gray (Management)

2 Marston Lane, Portsmouth, Hampshire PO3 5TW
tel 023-9269 9973 *fax* 023-9267 7227
email darren.gray1@virgin.net
website www.darrengraymanagement.com
Managing Director Darren Gray

Established in 1994. 2 agents represent 60 actors in both England and Australia. Agency mainly represents Australian actors, the majority of whom come from Australian soap operas. Areas of work include theatre, musicals, television, film, commercials, corporate and voice-overs. Also represents directors, producers, writers and presenters.

Will consider attending performances at venues within Greater London and elsewhere at whatever notice possible. Accepts submissions (with CVs and photographs) from actors previously unknown to the company, sent by post or email. Showreels, voicereels and invitations to view individual actors' websites are also accepted. Welcomes enquiries from disabled actors. *Commission*: 10%

Sandra Griffin Management Ltd

6 Ryde Place, Richmond Road,
East Twickenham TW1 2EH
tel 020-8891 5676 *fax* 020-8744 1812
email office@sandragriffin.com
website www.sandragriffin.com
Key personnel Sandra Griffin, Howard Roberts

Established in 1989. Represents actors in theatre, musicals, television, film, commercial and corporate work.

Welcomes written enquiries from actors seeking representation (with CV, photograph and sae to ensure reply), but does not accept unsolicited voicereels, DVDs or showreels. Will consider seeing potential clients in current theatre productions, if in easily accessible locations. *Commission*: Varies according to contract

Rob Groves Personal Management PMA

Hudson House, 8 Tavistock Street,
London WC2E 7PP
020-7125 0207
email rob@robgroves.co.uk
website www.robgroves.co.uk
Agent Rob Groves assisted by Annemarie Hardy

Established in 2007. Main areas of work are theatre, musicals, TV, film, commercials, corporate, video games. Currently represents 40 actors. Welcomes Spotlight Link or link to actor's own website sent by email, no attachments. Doesn't currently represent disabled actors but would do so where appropriate.

Commission: Live Performance 10%, Screenwork 15%, Commercials 20%

Louise Gubbay Associates

69 Paynesfield Road, Tatsfield, Kent TN16 2BG
tel 01959-573 080
email alex@louisegubbay.com
website www.louisegubbay.com
Managing Director Louise Gubbay

Founded in 2006. Works in theatre, musicals, television, film, commercials and corporate. LGA represents 40 actors.

Welcomes CVs from professionally trained actors only, by post or email. LGA is a full member of the Agents Association (London region) and now has an LA division. *Commission*: Varies

Hall James Personal Management

12 Melcombe Place, London NW1 6JJ
tel 020-3036 0558
email info@halljames.co.uk
website www.halljames.co.uk
Directors Sam Hall, Stori James

Established in 2006. Areas of work include musicals, television, film, commercials and corporate. 2 agents represent around 50 actors; also represents theatre directors and choreographers.

Welcomes performance notices and letters (with CVs) from individual actors previously unknown to the agency, as well as showreels. *Commission*: 10%

Hamilton Hodell Ltd PMA

Fifth Floor, 66-68 Margaret Street,
London W1W 8SR
tel 020-7636 1221 *fax* 020-7636 1226
email info@hamiltonhodell.co.uk
website www.hamiltonhodell.co.uk

3 agents represent 80 actors, working in leading roles in film, television, theatre and radio productions.

The Harris Agency Ltd

71 The Avenue, Watford, Herts WD17 4NU
tel (01923) 211644
email theharrisagency@btconnect.com
Agent Sharon Harris

In association with The Harris Drama School. Evening acting workshops for all clients and actors seeking representation. Established in 1977. 2 agents represent 40 clients.

Accepts invitations for productions at any time of year. Welcomes letters (with CVs and photographs) from actors previously unknown to the agency, sent by post or email. Also accepts follow-up calls, showreels, voicereels, and invitations to view individual actors' websites. Encourages enquiries from actors with disabilities. *Commission*: Theatre 10%; TV, Film, Commercials 15%

HarveyStein Associates Ltd

020-7175 7937
email info@harveystein.co.uk
website www.harveystein.co.uk
Managing Director Lois Harvey

Established in 2015, with 1 agent and 1 assistant, managing a small client list working throughout the industry. Happy to receive respresentation requests by email, but no large files, just links.

Hatton McEwan Penford PMA

Unit 3, Chocolate Studios, 7 Shepherdess Place,
London N1 7LJ
tel 020-7253 4770 *fax* 020-7251 9081

email mail@hattonmcewanpenford.com
website www.hattonmcewanpenford.com

Established in 1988, the agency represents actors working in theatre, musicals, television, film and commercials.

Will consider attending performances within Greater London (but rarely elsewhere) given 4 weeks' notice. Accepts submissions (with CVs and photographs) from actors previously unknown to the company, sent by post or email. Showreels, voicereels and invitations to view an actor's website are also accepted, but follow-up telephone calls are not welcomed.

Cheryl Hayes Management

85 Rothschild Road, London W4 5NT
tel 020-8994 4447 *mobile* (07767) 685560
email cheryl@cherylhayes.co.uk
website www.cherylhayes.co.uk

Established in 2008. Primarily represents comedy writer/performers; sole agent represents actors and writer/performers.

Will consider attending performances if given 2-3 weeks' notice. Welcomes approaches from actors, comedy writers and performers with CVs and photographs by post or email, and will accept showreels, voicereels and invitations to view individual actors' websites. *Commission*: 15%

Henry's Agency

53 Westbury, Rochford, Essex SS4 1UL
tel (01702) 541413 *fax* (01702) 541413
email info@henrysagency.co.uk
website www.henrysagency.co.uk

Established in 1995; 1 agent represents 35 actors. Areas of work include theatre, musicals, television, film, commercials and corporate.

Will consider attending performances at venues within Greater London with 2 weeks' notice. Accepts submissions (with CVs and photographs) from actors previously unknown to the company if sent by post. Emails are accepted if attachments consist of Word documents or small jpeg files. Follow-up telephone calls, showreels and voicereels are also accepted. Recommends the photographer Ash (**ash@ashphotomedia.com**). *Commission*: Varies

Hobson's Actors

62 Chiswick High Road, Chiswick, London W4 1SY
tel 020-8995 3628 *fax* 020-8996 5350
website www.hobsons-international.com
Drama Agent Christina Beyer *Commercial Agent* Linda Sacks

Areas of work include theatre, musicals, television, film, commercials and corporate.

Will consider attending performances at venues within Greater London given 2 weeks' notice. Accepts submissions (with CVs and photographs) from actors previously unknown to the company if sent by post. Showreels are also accepted.

Jane Hollowood Associates Ltd

17/113 Newton Street, Manchester M1 1AE
tel 0161-237 9141 *tel* 020-8291 5702
mobile (07712) 436566
email info@janehollowood.co.uk
website www.janehollowood.co.uk
Agents Jane Hollowood, Java Bere

Established in 1998; 2 agents represent approx. 85 actors working in many areas of the industry.

Will consider attending performances within Greater London and potentially elsewhere, depending on diary commitments and provided that 2-3 weeks' notice is given. Accepts postal and email submissions (with CVs and photographs) from actors previously unknown to the agency. Showreels and voicereels should only be sent on request, and follow-up telephone calls are unwelcome. *Commission*: Theatre 10%; Radio, Role-play and Voice-overs 12%; Television, Film and Commercials 15%

HR Creative Artists (HRCA)

tel 020-3286 8830
email contact@hrca.eu
website www.hrca.eu

Representing a culturally rich mix of artists from across Europe and worldwide. Applications must be made electronically via email, following the submissions guidelines on the website.

Nancy Hudson Associates PMA

50 South Molton Street, London W1K 5SB
tel 020-7499 5548
email agents@nancyhudsonassociates.com
website www.nancyhudsonassociates.com
Director/Agent Nancy Hudson

Established in 1999. 1 agent represents 75 actors. Areas of work include theatre, television, film, commercials, radio, corporate and voice-overs.

Welcomes submissions by email (with CVs and photographs).

Steve Hughes Management Ltd

tel 0844-556 4670
email management@stevehughesuk.com
website www.stevehughesuk.com
Artist Manager Steve Hughes

Founded in 2012. Management company and theatre producer based in London, with an extensive network of contacts in all areas of the entertainment and music business. Client portfolio includes a range of high-profile celebrities. A strong emphasis on developing new and exciting talent.

Welcomes letters (with CVs and photographs) from individual actors previously unknown to the agency, sent by post but not email. Will consider invitations to view actors' websites and to visit productions.

Hunwick Hughes Ltd

Hudson House, 8 Albany Street, Edinburgh EH1 3QB
tel 0131-271 5900 *fax* 0131-225 4535
email maryam@hunwickhughes.com
website www.hunwickhughes.com
Agent Maryam Hunwick *Assistant* Amanda Stewart

Personal management agency established in 1999. 1 agent represents actors in all media including several BAFTA and BIFA award-winning stage, screen and television artists.

Will consider attending performances at venues within Greater London and in Scotland given 4 weeks' notice. Accepts submissions (with CVs and photographs) from actors previously unknown to the company if sent by post. Will also accept showreels. *Commission*: Theatre 10%; TV and Broadcast Media 12.5%; Commercials 15%

Icon Actors Management

Tanzaro House, Ardwick Green North,
Manchester M12 6FZ
tel 0161-273 3344
email info@iconactors.net
website www.iconactors.net
Agent Nancy Lang

Established in 2000. Areas of work include theatre, musicals, television, film, commercials, corporate and voice-overs.

iD Agency Limited

6 Paramount Court, 41 University Street,
London WC1E 6JP
mobile (07528) 381833
email info@theidagency.co.uk
website www.theidagency.co.uk
Company Directors Hannah Burt, Barbara Adie

Established in 2011. Works in theatre, musicals, TV, film, commercials, corporate and presenting. 2 agents represent 30 clients (actors and presenters).

Will consider attending performances in London. Actors should send CVs and photographs by email to **info@theidagency.co.uk**. *Commission*: 12.5%

IDAMOS Agency

1 Frederick Court, 63 Albert Road, London E18 1LE
tel 020-3318 0244
email idamosagency@gmail.com
website www.idamos.com
Director Liz Isaac *Assistant Head Agent* Phillip Barnes

Established in 2012, IDAMOS represents actors with unique skills in a variety of performance fields, including theatre, musicals, film, TV, commercials, corporate and voice-over. 2 agents represent 55 actors.

Will consider attending performances at venues within Greater London with 2 weeks' notice. Accepts submissions (with CVs and photographs), and also happy to receive showreels, voicereels and invitations to view individual actors' websites, all via email. Does not currently represent disabled actors.

Imperial Personal Management Ltd

102 Kirkstall Road, Leeds LS3 1JA
tel (0113) 244 3222
email katie@ipmcasting.com
website www.ipmcasting.com
Managing Director Katie Ross

Established in 2007. 4 agents represent 30-50 actors working in television and film; also has a subsidiary company, IPM Crew. Recommends Imperial Photography (**info@ipmcasting.com**).

Welcomes performance notices within the Greater London and Northern areas (within 50 miles of the company's postcode), and prefers 1 month's notice if possible. Welcomes letters (with CVs and photographs) from individual actors previously unknown to the agency, sent by post or email. Accepts follow-up telephone calls, showreels and voicereels, and welcomes invitations to view individual actors' websites. Encourages enquiries from actors with disabilities. *Commission*: 10-15%

Independent Talent Group Ltd PMA

40 Whitfield Street, London W1T 2RH
tel 020-7636 6565

Areas of work include theatre, musicals, television, film, commercials, corporate and voice-overs. Also represents directors, writers, technicians and presenters.

Will consider attending performances at venues within Greater London. Accepts submissions (with CVs and photographs) from actors previously unknown to the company if sent by post. SAE must be included. We do not accept email submissions. *Commission*: 12.5%

Inter-City Casting

27 Wigan Lane, Wigan,
Greater Manchester WN1 1XR
tel (01942) 321969
email intercitycasting@btconnect.com
Agent Caroline Joynt

Established in 1983. 2 agents represent approximately 60 actors. Areas of work include theatre, musicals, television, film, commercials and corporate.

Will consider attending performances at venues in Manchester and Liverpool. Accepts submissions (with CVs and photographs) from actors previously unknown to the company if sent by post. Showreels, voicereels and invitations to view individual actors' websites also accepted. Recommends the photographer Michael Pollard (see entry under *Photographers and repro companies* on page 391). *Commission*: 10-12.5% plus VAT

International Actors London (IAL)

Penthouse 11, Bickenhall Mansions,
London W1U 6BR

tel 020-7125 0539
email ialagents@gmail.com
website www.ialagency.com
Key contact John Riordan

Established in 2011. Works in theatre, TV, film and commercials. 2 agents represent ethnically diverse and international actors based in the UK.

Will consider attending performances within the Greater London area, given 2-4 weeks' notice. Actors should apply by emailing their Spotlight link, which should have their showreel attached. Does not currently represent actors with disabilities, but applications are welcome. *Commission*: Theatre 10%; Voice-over, Commercial Theatre 12.5%; TV, Film, Commercials 15%

Irish Actors London Ltd

Penthouse 11, Bickenhall Mansions, London W1U 6BR
tel 020-7125 0539
email irishactorslondon@gmail.com
website www.irishactorslondon.co.uk
Key contact John Riordan

Established in 2010. 2 agents represent Irish actors working in theatre, TV, film and commercials.

Will consider attending performances within the Greater London area, given 2-4 weeks' notice. Actors should apply by emailing their Spotlight link, which should have their showreel attached. Does not currently represent actors with disabilities, but applications are welcome. *Commission*: Theatre 10%; Voice-over/Commercial Theatre 12.5%; TV, Film, Commercials 15%

JB Associates

PO Box 173, Manchester M19 0AR
tel 0161-237 1808 *fax* 0161-249 3666
email info@j-b-a.net
website www.j-b-a.net
Proprietor John Basham

Established in 1996. 2 agents represent 65 actors. Areas of work include theatre, musicals, television, film, commercials, corporate and voice-overs.

Will consider attending performances at venues in the North and occasionally elsewhere, given 3-4 weeks' notice. Accepts submissions (with CVs and photographs) from actors previously unknown to the company preferably by email. Will also accept showreels, voicereels, and invitations to view individual actors' websites. *Commission*: Theatre 10%; TV 15%

Jeffrey & White Management Ltd PMA

No. 2 Ladygrove Court, Hitchwood Lane, Preston, Hitchin, Herts. SG4 7SA
tel (01462) 433752
email info@jeffreyandwhite.co.uk
Partners Judith Jeffrey, Jeremy White *Key personnel* Laura Elgar

Established in 1986. 3 agents represent 85 actors. Areas of work include theatre, musicals, television, film, commercials and corporate.

Will consider attending performances given as much notice as possible. Accepts submissions (with CVs and photographs) from actors previously unknown to the company if sent by post. *Commission*: Theatre, Film and TV 12.5%; Commercials 15%

Mark Jermin Management

Swansea Metropolitan University, Mount Pleasant Campus, Swansea SA1 6ED
mobile (01792) 458855
email info@markjermin.co.uk
website www.markjermin.co.uk
Agents Mark Jermin, Charlotte Robb, Kelly Smith

Established in 2007. Areas of work include theatre, musicals, television, film, commercials, corporate and voice-overs.

Will consider attending performances at venues within London, Manchester and south and west Wales, given 2 weeks' notice. Accepts submissions by email (with CVs and photographs) for actors unknown to the agents. Also accepts unsolicited CVs (with photgraphs), via email. Happy to receive invitations to view actors' websites and to consider applications for representation from disabled actors. *Commission*: Negotiable

Jewell, Wright Ltd

17 Percy Street, London W1T 1DU
tel 020-7462 0790
email agents@jwl-london.com
website www.jwl-london.com
Director/Agent Jimmy Jewell *Agent* Neal Wright
Junior Agent Peter Bliss

Established in 2005. Main areas of work are theatre, musicals, television, film, commercials and radio. 3 agents represent 90 actors; also represented are directors, choreographers, writers and musical directors.

Will attend performances in Greater London only, if given at least 2 weeks' notice. Welcomes letters (with CVs and photographs, plus showreel) from individual actors previously unknown to the company if sent by post only; does not accept unsolicited emails, follow-up calls, or invitations to view individual actors' websites. Actively encourages enquiries from actors with disabilities. *Commission*: Theatre 12.5%; Television/Film 15%; Commercials 17.5%

Johnston & Mathers Associates Ltd

PO Box 3167, Barnet, London EN5 2WA
tel 020-8449 4968 *fax* 020-8449 4968
email Johnstonmathers@aol.com
website www.johnstonandmathers.com
Key personnel Dawn Mathers, Suzanne Johnston

Established in 2001. Areas of work include theatre, musicals, television, film, commercials and corporate. A small agency of around 40 actors.

Will consider attending performances within the Greater London area with at least 1 month's notice. Accepts submissions (with CVs and photographs) from actors previously unknown to the company if sent by email. Invitations to view individual actors' websites are accepted, as are showreels and voicereels. Welcomes enquiries from disabled actors.

JPA Management PMA

30 Daws Hill Lane, High Wycombe,
Buckinghamshire HP11 1PW
tel (01494) 520978
email agent@jpaassociates.co.uk
website www.jpaassociates.co.uk
Agent Ben McDougall

Established in 1995, main areas of work are theatre, musicals, TV, film, commercials, corporate, voice overs and radio. Represents over 40 actors, and musical directors and writers. *Commission*: 10%-15%. Does not welcome performance notices. Welcomes CVs and photographs sent by email. Represents actors with disabilities.

K Talent Artist Management

43 Aldwych, 4th Floor, London WC2B 4DN
tel 020-7379 1616
email mail@ktalent.co.uk
website www.ktalent.co.uk
Agents Mel Wildey, Sheri Copeland, Hailey Budd, Stephanie Fisher, David Stoller and Ros Bolton

Established in 2003. 5 agents represent 30 actors each. Areas of work include theatre, musicals, television, film, commercials, corporate and voice-overs.

Welcomes both CVs and letters from actors previously unknown to the Company and unsolicited CVs and photographs. These should be sent via email. Also welcomes showreels and voice tapes. Happy to consider applications for representation from disabled actors.

KAL Management

95 Gloucester Road, Hampton,
Middlesex TW12 2UW
tel 020-8783 0039 *fax* 020-8979 6487
email kaplan222@aol.com
website www.kaplan-kaye.co.uk
Key personnel Kaplan Kaye

Established in 1982. Sole representation of approximately 25 actors. Areas of work include theatre, musicals, television, film, commercials, corporate and voice-overs.

Will consider attending performances at venues within Greater London given as much notice as possible. Accepts submissions (with CVs and photographs) from actors previously unknown to the company if sent by post. Showreels and voicereels should only be sent on request. *Commission*: Theatre 10%; TV 15%

Roberta Kanal Agency

82 Constance Road, Twickenham,
Middlesex TW2 7JA
tel 020-8894 2277 *fax* 020-8894 7952
email roberta.kanal@dsl.pipex.com
Director Roberta Kanal

Established in 1972; 1 agent represents approximately 30 actors working in all areas of the industry.

"Take a simple approach: phone first; send a CV if requested, with a clear letter and one photograph, along with an sae for their return. As with casting directors, only use email if requested. Unsolicited items will be ignored due to the growing number of applications becoming impossible to handle."

Keddie Scott Associates PMA

31 Hatton Garden, London EC1N 8DH
tel 020-3490 1050 *fax* 020-7147 1326
mobile (07786) 070543
email info@keddiescott.com
website www.keddiescott.com
Managing Director Fiona Keddie-Ord; *Agent* Alex France, assisted by Danielle Crockford. *Scottish Book* Paul Michael (*email* scotland@keddiescott.com) *Northern Book* Anthony Williams(*email* north@keddiescott.com)

Keddie Scott Associates Ltd has been established since 2003.. Works in all areas of the performing arts industry, including TV, film, commercials, theatre, musical theatre (small- mid- large-scale) and corporate assignments of every nature. Please note that KSA operates on a Personal Exclusive Management basis.

Robert Kelly Associates PMA

10 Greek Street, London, W1D 4DH
email rep@robertkellyassociates.com
website www.robertkellyassociates.com

Established in 2006. Robert Kelly represent clients in television, film, theatre, musical theatre, radio and commercials. Recommends the photographer Brandon Bishop (**www.brandonbishopphotography.com**). Will consider attending performances within Greater London, at repertory theatres nationally and at Number 1 touring venues in the South East if given 4-6 weeks' notice.

Welcomes letters (with CVs) from individual actors previously unknown to the agency. Submissions should be sent by post or email. Showreels, voicereels and invitations to view individual actors' websites are also accepted. *Commission*: Theatre 10%; Corporate & Radio 12.5%; TV & Film 15%

Steve Kenis & Co PMA

95 Barkston Gardens, London SW5 0EU
tel 020-7434 9055 *fax* 020-7373 9404
email sk@sknco.com
Agents Steve Kenis, Karen Holmes

Founded in 2000. 2 agents represent 14 actors, as well as writers, directors and technicians. *Commission*: 10%

Kew Personal Management

PO Box 679, RH1 6EN
mobile (07876) 457402
email info@kewpersonalmanagement.com
website www.kewpersonalmanagement.com
Company Manager Kate Winn

Works in theatre, musicals, TV, film, commercials, corporate, voice-over and presenting.

Will consider attending performances in the Greater London area. Accepts letters (with CVs and photographs) from actors previously unknown to the company, but email is preferred. Accepts showreels, voicereels and links to Spotlight pages. Happy to accept submissions from disabled actors.

Keylock Management

58 Plymouth Road, Tavistock, Devon PL19 8BU
mobile (07943) 593404
email agent@keylockmanagement.com
website www.keylockmanagement.com

2 agents represent 35 actors working in TV, film, commercial, theatre and corporate.

Will consider attending performances, given sufficient notice. Accepts email submissions and CVs (with Spotlight link) from actors with professional training and previously unknown to the agency.

LA Management

10 Fair Oak Close, Kenley, Surrey CR8 5LJ
tel 020-7183 6211 *mobile* (07507) 276211
email lee-ann@lamanagement.biz
website www.lamanagement.biz
Actors' Agent/Talent Director Lee-Ann Robathan

Established in 2006. Main areas of work are television, film, commercials, corporate, theatre and radio. Also represents presenters, singers and voice-over artists. Will see actors perform, but requires 1 week's notice.

Welcomes letters with follow-up calls, emails, showreels and voicereels. LA Management is open to representing all actors, with or without disabilities. *Commission*: 10% Theatre; 20% TV/Film

Laine Management

131 Victoria Road, Salford M6 8LF
tel 0161-789 7775 *fax* 0161-787 7572
email info@lainemanagement.co.uk
website www.lainemanagement.co.uk
Company Director Samantha Greeley

Areas of work include theatre, television, film, commercials and corporate.

Will consider attending performances at venues in Manchester and the surrounding area with 2-4 weeks' notice. Accepts CVs and photographs from individuals previously unknown to the agency, but emails, showreels and invitations to view individual actors' websites are not welcomed. *Commission*: 15%

Langford Associates Ltd

17 Westfields Avenue, Barnes, London SW13 0AT
tel 020-8878 7148
website www.langfordassociates.com
Key personnel Barry Langford, Simon Hayes

Established in 1987. 1 agent represents 40-45 actors. Areas of work include theatre, television, film, commercials, corporate and voice-overs.

Will consider attending performances at mainstream venues within Greater London, given 2 weeks' notice. Accepts submissions (with CVs and photographs) by post or email. Email submissions should include no more than 1 small image (emails with multiple attachments will be deleted unread). 'Name' actors seeking representation may ring and speak to Barry Langford in complete confidence.

"I am always happy to receive details by post and I regularly meet with new actors. When writing, please include an sae if you would like your details to be returned. Please do not send unsolicited showreels. I prefer to receive 10x8in photographs, and would suggest that you use a good photographer and update your photo at least every 18 months. Make sure you are listed in Spotlight, as this is a prerequisite for all professional actors."

Nina Lee Management

Suite 36, 88-90 Hatton Garden, London EC1N 8PN
mobile (07989) 135216
email nina@ninaleemanagement.com
website www.ninaleemanagement.com
Agent Nina Lee

Areas of work include theatre, TV, film, commercials, corporate and radio.

Welcomes performance notices, each one will be considered on its individual merits. Accepts submissions by email (with CVs and photographs).

Jane Lehrer Associates PMA

PO Box 66334, London NW6 9QT
tel 020-7435 9118 *fax* 020-7482 4899
email jane@janelehrer.co.uk
Sole Proprietor Jane Lehrer

Established in 1986. 2 agents represent 80 actors. Areas of work include theatre, musicals, television, film, commercials, corporate and voice-overs. Also represents presenters.

Will consider attending performances at venues in Greater London with 2-3 weeks' notice. Accepts submissions (with CVs and photographs) from actors previously unknown to the company if sent by email. An sae must always be included. Showreels and voicereels should only be sent on request.

Mike Leigh Associates

11-12 Great Sutton Street, London EC1V 0BX
tel 020-7017 8757 *fax* 020-7486 5886
email mail@mikeleighassoc.com
website www.mikeleighassoc.com
Agents Mike Leigh, Janie Jenkins

Established in 2007. Works in all areas except voice-over. 2 agents represent 60 actors; also represented are presenters, comedians, DJs and writers. Recommends the photographer Steve Ullathorne (**steve@steveullathorne.com**).

Will consider attending performances within Greater London given 1 month's notice. Welcomes letters (with CVs and photographs) from actors previously unknown to the agency if sent by post, but not by email. Will accept showreels, voicereels, and invitations to view individual actors' websites. *Commission*: 15%

Leno Martin Associates Ltd

Personal Management/Theatre Production/Casting, 3B Nettlefold Place, London SE27 0JW
tel 020-8655 7656
email info@lenomartinassociates.com
website www.lenomartinassociates.com
Senior Agent Antony Stuart-Hicks (Theatre/Screen)
Senior Agent Paul Leno (MT/Commercials/ International/Cruise)*Senior Agent* Leon Kay (Musical Theatre)

Established in 2014. Main areas of talent management are theatre, musical theatre, television, film, commercials, cruise ships, UK/International tours and pantomime. Will consider attending performances within the London/Greater London area, given 2-4 weeks' notice.

Welcomes letters and emails (with CVs and headshots); also accepts showreels and invitations to view individual actors' websites. Emails accepted. "We would prefer, where possible, to attend a performance." Currently looking to expand representation of versatile performers. An Equal Opportunities company. *Commission*: Stage 12.5%; Screen 15%; Self-sourced 10%. Contract: 12 month minimum term.

Lime Actors Agency & Management Ltd

Nemesis House, 1 Oxford Court, Bishopsgate, Manchester M2 3WQ
tel 0161-236 0827 *fax* 0161-228 6727
email georgina@limemanagement.co.uk
Director Georgina Andrew

Established in 1999. 1 agent represents 70 actors. Areas of work include theatre, musicals, television, film, commercials, corporate and voice-overs. Also represents musical directors.

Will consider attending performances at venues within Greater London and elsewhere given 4 weeks' notice. Accepts submissions (with CVs and photographs) from actors previously unknown to the company if sent by post. Follow-up telephone calls, showreels, voicereels and invitations to view individual actors' websites are also accepted.

Linkside Agency

57 High Street, Ashford, Kent TN24 8SG
tel 020-7384 1477 *fax* (01372) 801972
email info@linksideagency.com

Established in 1986. 2 agents represent 40 actors. Areas of work include theatre, musicals, television, film, commercials, corporate and voice-overs.

Will consider attending performances at venues within Greater London given a minimum of 2 weeks' notice. Accepts submissions (with CVs and photographs) from actors previously unknown to the company if sent by email. Showreels and voicereels are also accepted.

Eva Long Agents

107 Station Road, Earls Barton, Northants NN6 0NX
mobile (07736) 700849
fax (01604) 811921
email EvaLongAgents@yahoo.co.uk
Key personnel Eva Long

Established in 2003. 1 agent represents 40 actors. Areas of work include theatre, musicals, television, film, commercials, corporate and voice-overs.

Will consider attending performances within the Greater London, Midlands and East Anglia areas, with at least 1 month's notice. Prefers to receive submissions (with CVs and headshots) by email, rather than by post. Showreels, voicereels and invitations to view individual actors' websites are also accepted. Welcomes enquiries from disabled actors. *Commission*: 15%

Gina Long (Longrun Artistes)

32 Ashburnham Road, Belvedere, Kent DA17 6DA
tel (01322) 400387
email longrunartistes@icloud.com
Founder/Director Gina Long

Established in 2005. Works in theatre, musicals, TV, film, commercials, corporate, voice-over and dance. 2 agents represent 120 clients. Will accept unsolicited applications from actors previously unknown to the agency, as hard copy (with photographs). Is happy to represent actors with disabilities. *Commission*: 10-20%

Lovett Logan Associates

40 Margaret Street, London W1G 0JH
tel 020-7495 6400 *fax* 020-7495 6411
email london@lovettlogan.com (London)
email edinburgh@lovettlogan.com (Edinburgh)
Scottish office: 2 York Place, Edinburgh EH1 3EP
tel 0131-478 7878 *fax* 0131-557 8787
website www.lovettlogan.com

Established in 1981. Areas of work include theatre, musicals, television, film, commercials, corporate and voice-overs.

Will consider attending performances at venues in Greater London and Scotland (handled by Scottish office) with 2-3 weeks' notice. Accepts submissions (with CVs and photographs) from actors previously unknown to the company if emailed to

representation@lovettlogan.com. Invitations to view individual actors' websites are also accepted.

LSW Promotions

PO Box 31855, London SE17 3XP
tel 020-7793 9755 *fax* 020-7793 9755
email londonswo@hotmail.com
website www.londonshakespeare.org.uk
Executive Director Bruce Wall *Development Associate* James Croft

Established in 1998. 2 agents represent 20 actors. Areas of work include theatre, musicals, television and film.

Will consider attending performances at venues within Greater London and elsewhere, given 2 weeks' notice. Accepts submissions (with CVs and photographs) from actors previously unknown to the company, sent by post or email. Invitations to view individual actors' websites are also accepted. *Commission*: 10% donation to charity (LSW Prison Project)

Dennis Lyne Agency PMA

503 Holloway Road, London N19 DD
tel 020-7272 5020
email info@dennislyne.com
website www.dennislyne.com
Agent Dennis Lyne *Associate* Sharon Levinson

Established in 1995. 2 agents represents 50 actors. Areas of work include film, television and theatre.

Will selectively consider attending performances within Central London, given at least 2 weeks' notice. *Commission*: 10%; Commercials 15%

MacFarlane Chard Associates PMA

33 Percy Street, London W1T 2DF
tel 020-7636 7750 *fax* 020-7636 7751
email enquiries@macfarlane-chard.co.uk
website www.macfarlane-chard.co.uk
Agents Thyrza Ging, Derick Mulvey

Founded in 1994. Works in all areas. 3 agents represent 120 actors, as well as directors, writers, producers, technicians and authors.

Will consider attending performances in Greater London, given as much notice as possible. Welcomes letters (with CVs and photographs) from actors previously unknown to the agency if sent by post, and encourages enquiries from actors with disabilities. Does not welcome follow-up calls, invitations to view individual actors' websites, or unsolicited approaches by email. Will accept showreels and voicereels. *Commission*: Varies

MacFarlane Doyle Associates

90 Long Acre, Covent Garden, London WC2E 9RZ
tel 020-3600 3470
email enquiries@macfarlanedoyle.com
website www.macfarlanedoyle.com
Agents Ross MacFarlane, Don Rogers, Perry Doyle, Mel Devine

Established in 2009. Main areas of work are theatre, musicals, television, film, corporate, commercials and voice-overs. Each agent represents around 20 actors; directors and choreographers are also represented.

Welcomes performance notices and will travel to any area, given 3 weeks' notice. Prefers submissions as hard copy by post (letters, CVs and photographs) or by email. Represents actors with disabilities. *Commission*: Theatre, TV & Film 12.5%; Commercials 15%

Mahoney Bannon Associates (MBA) ADD

Concorde House, 18 Margaret Street, Brighton BN2 1TS
tel (01273) 685970 *fax*
email info@mbagency.co.uk
website www.mbagency.co.uk
Key personnel Derek 'Bo' Keller, Stephen Holroyd, Alan Kite

Established in 1960. Represents 60-70 actors. Areas of work include theatre, musicals, television, film, commercials and corporate.

Please check submission details on website prior to seeking represention. Will consider attending performances at venues within Greater London and on the South Coast with 1 month's notice. Accepts submissions (with clearly written CVs and photographs) from actors previously unknown to the company if sent by post. Photographs should be of a good quality. Enclose an sae for return of personal details. Showreels, voicereels and invitations to view individual actors' websites are also accepted. *Commission*: 10-17% depending on the type of work

Management 2000

11 Well Street, Treuddyn, Flintshire CH7 4NH
tel (01352) 771231 *fax* (01352) 771231
email jackey@management-2000.co.uk
website www.management-2000.co.uk

Established in 2000. 1 agent represents 30 actors. Areas of work include theatre, musicals, television, film, commercials, corporate and voice-overs.

Accepts submissions (with CVs and photographs) from actors previously unknown to the company if sent by post. Follow-up telephone calls, showreels and voicereels are also accepted. *Commission*: 10-15%

Marcus & McCrimmon Management

Winston House, 3 Bedford Square, London WC1B 3RA
tel 020-7323 0546
email info@marcusandmccrimmon.com
website www.marcusandmccrimmon.com

Founded in 1999. Main areas of works are musicals, television film and commercials. 2 agents represent around 100 actors.

Will consider attending performances within Greater London given 4 weeks' notice if the actor is playing a substantial role. Welcomes letters (with CVs and photographs) from actors previously unknown to the agency if sent by post (with sae if contents need to be returned). Also accepts submissions by by email, but with no large files. Follow up calls are not welcome.

Markham, Froggatt & Irwin PMA

4 Windmill Street, London W1T 2HZ
tel 020-7636 4412 *fax* 020-7637 5233
email admin@markhamfroggattirwin.com
website www.markhamfroggattirwin.com
Key personnel Alex Irwin, Stephanie Randall, Jonty Brook, Anna Dudley, Tamsyn Manson, Ellie Martin-Sperry, Emily MacDonald, Pippa Markham (Consultant)

Works in theatre, musicals, television, film, commercials, corporate and voice-overs.

Ronnie Marshall Agency

66 Ollerton Road, London N11 2LA
tel 020-8368 4958

Established in 1970. 2 agents represent 20 actors in theatre, musicals, television, film, commercials, radio, corporate work and voice-overs.

Will consider attending performances at venues within the Greater London area subject to 2 weeks' prior notice. Accepts businesslike submissions (with CVs and photographs) from actors previously unknown to the agency if sent by post. Photographs should be a good likeness and accompanied by an sae for their return. Follow-up telephone calls and invitations to view individual actors' websites are also accepted. *Commission*: 5% if instigated by the client; 20% otherwise

Scott Marshall Partners PMA

2nd Floor, 15 Little Portland Street, London W1W 8BW
tel 020-7637 4623 *fax* 020-7636 9728
email smpm@scottmarshall.co.uk
Agents/Company Directors Amanda Evans, Suzy Kenway, Manon Palmer

Areas of work include theatre, musicals, television, film, commercials, corporate and voice-overs. Also represents directors (theatre and TV) and sound designers.

Will consider attending performances at venues within Greater London if given as much notice as possible. Accepts submissions (with CVs and photographs) from actors previously unknown to the company if sent by email only to **submissions@scottmarshall.co.uk**. No postal submissions accepted.

McLean-Williams Management

Gainsborough House, 81 Oxford Street, London W1D 2EU
tel 020-7223 8683 *fax* 020-7631 3739
email info@mclean-williams.com

Established in 2002; 1 agent represents approximately 40 clients working in theatre, musicals, television, film, commercials and corporate role-play.

Will consider attending performances within Greater London given 2 weeks' notice. Welcomes submissions (with CVs, photographs, showreels and voicereels) from actors previously unknown to the agency. Will also accept follow-up telephone calls, emails and invitations to view an actor's website.

Bill McLean Personal Management

23B Deodar Road, London SW15 2NP
tel 020-8789 8191 *fax* 020-8789 8192

Established in 1972. Will consider attending performances in Greater London with sufficient notice. Accepts submissions (with CVs and photographs) from actors previously unknown to the company if sent by post. Follow-up telephone calls are also accepted. *Commission*: Theatre 10%; TV 12.5%; Commercials 15%

McMahon Management

28 Cecil Road, London W3 0DB
tel 020-8752 0172
email mcmahonmanagement@hotmail.co.uk (Industry Use)
email info@mcmahonmanagement.co.uk (Submissions)
website www.mcmahonmanagement.co.uk
Agent Thomas McMahon *Assistant Agent* Brian Morse

Established in 2009. Works in theatre, TV, commercials, corporate and film. Will consider attending performances within London and Greater London given 2 weeks' notice. Welcomes letters (with CVs and headshots) from individuals previously unknown to the agency; these can only be returned with an appropriate sae. Happy to receive email requests with Spotlight link included. Does not welcome follow-up phone calls. *Commission*: Theatre 12.5%; TV, Commercial and Corporate 15%

MCS Agency

47 Dean Street, London W1D 5BE
tel 020-7734 9995 *fax* 020-7734 9996
email info@mcsagency.co.uk
Key contact Fay Carnell

Established in 1994. 2 agents represent actors. Areas of work include theatre, musicals, television, film, commercials and voice-overs. Also represents presenters.

Will consider attending performances at venues within Greater London with 2 weeks' notice. Accepts submissions (with CVs and photographs) from actors previously unknown to the company if sent by post. Showreels, voicereels and invitations to view individual actors' websites are also accepted. *Commission*: 15-20%

Middleweek Newton Talent Management PMA

95A Rivington Street, London EC2A 3AY
tel 020-3394 0079 (Office)
email agents@mntalent.co.uk
website www.mntalent.co.uk
Agent Lucy Middleweek

Established in 2013. Areas of work include theatre, television, film and commercials.

Accepts submissions by email (with CVs and photographs). Also welcomes showreels and invitations to view individual actors' websites.

Mime The Gap

17 Cromer Road, Southend, Essex SS1 2DU
mobile (07970) 685982
email mimethegap@mac.com
email richard@mimethegap.com
website www.mimethegap.com
Agent Richard Knight

Established in 1992. Areas of work include theatre, film, corporate and festivals.

Will consider attending performances, though this is dependent on client. Accepts submissions by email (with CVs and photographs) and links to showreels. Happy to consider applications for representation from disabled actors. *Commission:* Varies

Mitchell Maas McLennan Ltd

29 Thomas Street, Woolwich, London SE18 6HU
tel 020-8301 8745
email agency@mmm2000.co.uk
website www.mmm2000.co.uk

Established in 2005. 2 agents represent approximately 60 actors. Areas of work include theatre, musicals, television, film, commercials, corporate. Also represents choreographers. Recommends the photographer John Clark (see entry on page 397).

Will consider attending performances in Greater London and elsewhere with at least 2-4 weeks' notice. Accepts submissions (with CVs and photographs) from actors previously unknown to the agency. Showreels, voicereels and invitations to view individual actors' websites also accepted. Follow-up calls are welcomed. *Commission*: 10%

Morello Cherry Actors Agency

c/o Morello Cherry Ltd DNA Performance Resource, 1st Floor Manchester House, 84 Princess Street, Manchester M1 6NG
tel 0207-993 5538 *mobile* (07886) 846938 and (07842) 707100
email info@mcaa.co.uk
website www.mcaa.co.uk

Established in 2007. 3 agents represent 40 actors. Areas of work include theatre, television, film, commercials, corporate and voice-overs.

Accepts submissions via email with links to online CV, footage and images. Does not welcome postal applications and requests no large file downloads. *Commission*: Standard Equity rates

Lee Morgan Management

4 Bloomsbury Square, London WC1A 2RP
tel 020-7430 1006 *mobile* (07949) 729639
email lee@leemorgan.biz
website www.leemorgan.biz

Established in 2005. Represents clients working in musicals, television, film and commercials.

Welcomes performance notices in the London areas, given 2 weeks' notice. Is happy to receive letters (with CVs and photographs) from individual actors previously unknown to the agency, sent by post or email. Accepts showreels and voicereels, and encourages enquiries from actors with disabilities.

MR Management PMA

67 Great Titchfield Street, London W1W 7PT
tel 020-7636 8737
email info@mrmanagement.net
website www.mrmanagement
Mark Pollard Ross Dawes

Established in 2001. Main areas of work are theatre, musicals, TV, film, commercials and corporate. Represents approximately 100 actors. Also represents directors, presenters and writers. Welcomes letters (with CVs and photographs), follow-up phone calls, CVs and photographs sent by email, showreels and voice tapes. Open to clients with disabilities but not currently representing any disabled actors. *Commission* 10-12% theatre, 15% film and TV

Mrs Jordan Associates PMA

Communications House, 26 York Street, London W1U 6PZ
tel 020-3151 0710
email apps@mrsjordan.co.uk
website www.mrsjordan.co.uk
Associates Sean D Lynch, Guy Kean, Felicity Coleman

Established in 2008. Areas of work include stage, television, film, commercials, corporate and voice-overs. Represents some regionally based actors. Does not represent walk-ons, extras, models or under-16s. 2 principal agents plus associates represent around 75 actors.

Will consider attending performances but would need to meet in advance first. Unsolicited applications accepted by email only. Spotlight link imperative. Happy to consider applications from actors with disabilities, on the understanding that, unfortunately, casting opportunities are very limited. Advises actors: "We have a very small client list and a strict 'no clash' policy. Check our website to see if we have a vacancy for your type before you email us. We cannot consider applicants unless we have seen a showreel or performance." *Commission*: 10-15%

MSFT Management

email agent@msftmanagement.com
website www.msftmanagement.com

Established in 2009. Main areas of work are theatre, film and commercials. Will only travel in London Zones 1-4, with 1 month's notice. Actors please post Spotlight link only on **www.facebook.com/msftlondon**. Open to receiving applications from actors with disability. *Commission*: 20%

Elaine Murphy Associates

Suite 1, 50 High Street, London E11 2RJ
tel 020-8989 4122 *fax* 020-8989 1400
email elaine@elainemurphy.co.uk
Director Elaine Murphy

Established in 1990. 2 agents represent 50 actors. Areas of work include theatre, musicals, television, commercials, corporate and voice-overs.

Will consider attending performances within Greater London with plenty of notice. Accepts submissions (with CVs and photographs) from actors previously unknown to the agency; showreels, voicereels and invitations to view individual actors' websites are also accepted.

The Narrow Road Company PMA

1st Floor, 37 Great Queen Street, London WC2B 5AA
tel 020-7831 4450
email amy@narrowroad.co.uk
Agents Amy Ireson, James Ireson, Chloe Oxbury, Richard Ireson

Established in 1986, the agency has 3 offices with each agent representing approximately 40 actors. Areas of work include theatre, musicals, television, film, commercials, corporate and voice-overs. In addition, the Surrey office represents writers, directors, lighting designers, fight directors and choreographers.

Will consider attending performances within the Greater London area, given 1-2 weeks' notice. Accepts submissions (with CVs and photographs) from actors previously unknown to the company if sent by post, but does not welcome email submissions. Showreels and voicereels should be sent only if requested. "We always try to be helpful and informative, but callers should be aware of how busy we often are." *Commission*: 10-15%

Manchester office

Grampian House, 4th Floor, 144 Deansgate, Manchester M3 3EE
tel 0161-833 1605 *fax* 0161-833 1605
email manchester@narrowroad.co.uk
Agent Elizabeth Stocking

Steve Nealon Associates PMA

3rd Floor, International House, 1-6 Yarmouth Place, London W1J 7BU
tel 020- 7125 0468 *mobile* (07904) 671877
fax 020-7629 1317
email admin@stevenealonassociates.co.uk
website www.stevenealonassociates.co.uk
Agents Steve Nealon and Alexis Conway Keane

Works in theatre, film, television, commercials, musicals and corporate.

Depending on the production and the actor, will attend performances anywhere in the UK, given a week's notice. Welcomes letters, with CVs and photographs, sent by post and email, and accepts showreels. Plans to represent actors with disabilities. *Commission*: 10-15%

Nelson Browne Management Ltd PMA

40 Bowling Green Lane, London EC1R 0NE
tel 020-7970 6010 *fax* 020-7837 7612
email enquiries@nelsonbrowne.com
website www.nelsonbrowne.com
Company Director Mary Elliott Nelson

Established in 2007. 2 agents represent 80-90 actors working in musicals, television, film, commercials, corporate and voice-over; also represents directors and actor/musicians.

Welcomes performance notices within the Greater London area, given 2 weeks' notice. Welcomes letters (with CVs and photographs) from individual actors previously unknown to the agency, sent by post or email. Accepts follow-up telephone calls and invitations to view individual actors' websites. No showreels or voicereels. Encourages enquiries from actors with disabilities. *Commission*: Theatre 10%; TV and Film 15%

North West Actors – Nigel Adams

64 Nuttall Street, Bury, Manchester BL9 7EW
tel 0161-761 6437
email nigel.adams@northwestactors.co.uk
website www.northwestactors.co.uk
Proprietor Nigel Adams

Established in 2007. Main areas of work are theatre, musicals, television, film, commercials, corporate, radio and voice-overs. 1 agent represents 42 actors. Recommends the photographer Michael Pollard (**info@michaelpollard.co.uk**).

Will consider attending performances within the Greater Manchester area, given 2 weeks' notice, or London, given 4 weeks' notice. Welcomes letters (with CVs and photographs) from individual actors previously unknown to the agency, sent by post or email. Also accepts showreels, voicereels and invitations to view individual actors' websites.

Northern Lights Management

Dean Clough Mills, Halifax, Yorkshire HX3 5AX
tel (01422) 330101
Agents Maureen Magee, Angie Cowton

Established in 1998. 2 agents represent 45 Northern and Northern-based actors. Areas of work include theatre, musicals, television, film, commercials, corporate and voice-overs.

Will consider attending performances at venues within Greater London and elsewhere, given 2 weeks' notice. Accepts submissions (with CVs and photographs) from actors previously unknown to the company if sent by post. Showreels and voicereels are also accepted. Enclose an sae for the return of items sent. Telephone calls and emails with attachments are not accepted. Advises actors that the agency is small and rarely takes on new clients.

NS Artistes' Management

10 Claverdon House, Hollybank Road, Billesley, Birmingham B13 0QY
tel 0121-684 5607 *mobile* (07870) 969577
email administrator@nsartistes.co.uk
website www.nsartistes.co.uk
Managing Director Neale Stephen McGrath *Director* Arali Niamh McGrath

Founded in 2004, and representing 75 actors in all areas of acting work including role-play, presenting and training, the company also represents individuals for writing, consultancy, design, stage management, presenting, drama tutoring and fight arranging. "If you have a talent in the business, even if I have not mentioned it, then I am interested – no matter what age, creed or colour you are, or whether you are disabled or able-bodied."

Welcomes performance notices a fortnight in advance; will consider attending performances around the UK. Welcomes letters (with CVs and photographs) from actors previously unknown to the company if sent by post, but not by email. Does not welcome unsolicited showreels or invitations to view individual actors' websites. *Commission*: Theatre 12.5%; Stage Management 10%; Other 15%

Nyland Management

93 Kinder Road, Hayfield, High Peak SK22 2LE
tel (01633) 745629 *mobile* (07902) 246157
email casting@nylandmanagement.com
website www.nylandmanagement.com

2 agents represent 60 actors. Areas of work include theatre, musicals, television, film, commercials, corporate and voice-overs.

Accepts submissions from Spotlight members. Email only.

Otto Personal Management Ltd

Hagglers Corner, 586 Queens Road, Sheffield S2 4DU
tel (01142) 372432 *mobile* 07587 133212
email admin@ottopm.co.uk
website www.ottopm.co.uk

Established in 1985. 41 actors. Areas of work include theatre, musicals, television, film, commercials, corporate and voice-overs.

Will consider attending performances at venues in the UK with approximately 1 month's notice. Accepts submissions (with CVs and photographs) from actors previously unknown to the company, sent by post or preferably by email. Will also accept showreels, voicereels and invitations to view individual actors' websites.*Commission*: 10-13%

Pan Artists Agency

Cornerways, 34 Woodhouse Lane, Sale M33 4JX
tel 0161-969 7419
email panartists@btconnect.com
website www.panartists.co.uk

Established in 1973. Accepts submissions (with CVs and photographs, "which must be up to date") from actors previously unknown to the company, sent by post or email. Postal submissions must be accompanied by an sae.

Paul Pearson – London Theatrical

18 Leamore Street, London W6 0JZ
tel 020-8748 1478
email agent@londontheatrical.com
website www.londontheatrical.com
CEO Paul Pearson *Head of Media* Chris Read

Established in 2009. 2 agents represent 35 clients. Main areas of work are film, television, theatre and commercials.

Only accepts CVs and photographs sent by email. Has an equal opportunities policy. *Commission*: 15%

Pelham Associates PMA

Albert House, 82 Queen's Road, Brighton BN1 3XE
tel (01273) 323010
email petercleall@pelhamassociates.co.uk
website www.pelhamassociates.co.uk
Agents Peter Cleall, Dione Inman

Established in 1993. Areas of work include theatre, musicals, television, film, commercials, corporate and voice-overs.

Will consider attending performances at venues within Greater London and elsewhere, given at least 2 weeks' notice. Accepts submissions (with CVs and photographs) from actors previously unknown to the company if sent by post. *Commission*: 8-12.5%

Pemberton Associates Ltd

51 Upper Berkeley Street, London W1H 7QW
tel 020-7734 4144 *fax* 0161-235 8442
www.pembertonassociates.com

Established in 1989. 5 agents represent 150 clients. Areas of work include theatre, musicals, television, film, commercials, corporate and voice-overs.

Will consider attending performances at venues in the North West, with 2-3 weeks' notice, if looking for new clients. Accepts submissions (with CVs and photographs) from actors previously unknown to the company if sent by post.

Frances Phillips PMA

89 Robeson Way, Borehamwood, Herts. WD6 5RY
tel 020-8953 0303 *mobile* (07957) 334348

email frances@francesphillips.co.uk

Established in 1983 and representing 50 actors aged 16 upwards. Areas of work include theatre, musicals, television, film, commercials, corporate and voice-overs. Submissions by email only considered if Spotlight View PIN number and date of birth details are included. CVs and photos will be requested at a later date if required.

Piccadilly Management

23 New Mount Street, Manchester M4 4DE
tel 0161-212 8522 *mobile* (07930) 834891
tel 020-3322 7457 London office
email info@piccadillymanagement.com
website www.piccadillymanagement.com
Agent Peter Foster

Established in 1985. Main areas of work include television, theatre, stage, commercials, corporate and voice-overs. Represents around 50 actors.

Welcomes approaches from actors previously unknown to the company, sent by post or email. Accepts invitations to view individual actors' websites and welcomes enquiries from actors with disabilities.

Janet Plater Management Ltd

Floor D, Milburn House, Dean Street,
Newcastle upon Tyne NE1 1LF
tel 0191-221 2490
email info@jpmactors.com
website www.jpmactors.com

Established in 1997. 1 agent represents approximately 65 actors. Areas of work include theatre, musicals, television, film, commercials, corporate and voice-overs Extras department has over 800 extras in the North East region.

Will consider attending performances at venues in North East England with a few weeks' notice. Accepts submissions (with CVs and or photographs or Spotlight link) from actors previously unknown to the company if sent via email. Links to showreels welcome; if applying by email no large attachments. *Commission*: Maximum of 15%

Premier Acting

tel 0141-255 0255
email info@premieracting.com
website www.premieracting.com
Agent Allan Jones

Established in 2013. Based in Glasgow, Premier Acting is an amalgamation of Glasgow Acting and the Cairns Agency.

Will consider attending performances at venues in Scotland with 3-4 weeks' notice. Accepts submissions (with CVs and photographs) from actors previously unknown to the agency. A Spotlight Link should be included if possible. Also welcomes showreels.

Morwenna Preston Management

49 Leithcote Gardens, London SW16 2UX
tel 020-8835 8147
email info@morwennapreston.com
website www.morwennapreston.com

2 agents represent 60 actors for theatre, musicals, television, film, commercials and corporate. Also represents some presenters.

Welcomes performance notices 4 weeks in advance, and is prepared to travel within the Greater London area. Welcomes letters (by email) from individuals previously unknown to the company. Does not welcome follow-up calls. Welcomes showreels and invitations to view individual actors' websites. *Commission*: 12.5%

Price Gardner Management PMA

BM 3162 London WC1N 3XX
tel 020-7610 2111
email info@pricegardner.co.uk
website www.pricegardner.co.uk
Contact Sarah Barnfield

Television, film, theatre, musical theatre, commercials, radio, voice-over and corporate. Submissions can be made via the website contact form or via email.

Principal Artistes

Suite 1, 57 Buckingham Gate, London SW1E 6AJ
tel 020-7637 2120 *mobile* (07881) 623708
email info@principalartistes.co.uk

Established in 1993. 2 agents represent 60 actors. Areas of work include theatre, musicals, television, film, commercials and corporate.

Will consider attending performances at venues in Greater London with at least 1 week's notice. Accepts submissions (with CVs and photographs) from actors previously unknown to the company if emailed to enquiries@principalartistes.com or uploaded to the website www.principalartist.com. If sent by post please ensure it bears the correct posage. *Commission*: Theatre 10%; Other 15%

Pure Actors Agency & Management Ltd

4th Floor, 20-22 High Street, Manchester M4 1QB
tel 0161-832 5727
email enquiries@pure-management.co.uk
website www.pure-management.co.uk
Director Debbie Pine

Established in 2005. 1 agent represents 40 actors. Areas of work include television, film, theatre, commercials, radio and corporate.

Will consider attending performances within the Manchester area, given at least 6 weeks' notice. Recommends the photographer Michael Pollard (see entry on page 403). Accepts submissions (with CVs and photographs) from actors previously unknown to the agency – but be sure to include an sae. Showreels, voicereels and invitations to view individual actors' websites are also accepted. Welcomes enquiries from disabled actors. *Commission*: 15%

Qtalent PMA

2nd Floor, 161 Drury Lane, Covent Garden, London WC2B 5PN

Qtalent is the new name for the combined agencies International Artistes and JLM Personal Management. These 2 agencies between them have 100 years of expertise and know-how in the British entertainment industry. This combined management resource now forms a unique and powerful force in the fields of film, television, and theatre in the UK and beyond. Qtalent are part of Qdos Entertainment, which is one of the largest entertainment groups in the UK. Together they represent a diverse client base, including numerous high-profile performers and actors.

Accept submissions via email with CVs and headshots. For further information on how to apply, please visit: **www.qtalent.co.uk**.

RBM Actors

3rd Floor, 1 Lower Grosvenor Street, London SW1W OEJ
tel 020-7976 6021
email info@rbmactors.com
website www.rbmactors.com
Agent Sarah London

Works mainly in theatre, television, film and commercials. 2 agents represent around 30 actors, and comedians/writers.

Will consider attending performances within Greater London, given 2-3 weeks' notice. Welcomes letters (with CVs and photographs) from individual actors previously unknown to the company, sent by post only, but not follow-up calls. Accepts showreels and voicereels, as well as invitations to view individual actors' websites. Encourages enquiries from actors with disabilities. "We advise you to contact us when you are appearing in something. We don't represent actors we don't know or haven't seen."

Redeeming Features

190 Westcombe Hill, Blackheath, London SE3 7DH
tel 020-7138 1822
email artists@redeemingfeatures.co.uk
website www.redeemingfeatures.co.uk
Head of Talent/Casting Andrew Fawn *Assistant Agent* Georgia Lester *Agent* Zack Miller *MD and Founder* Nate Wiseman

Production company founded in 2006; agency established in 2010. Main areas of work are commercials, television, film, emerging platforms and stage. "We are growing at present, but it is important to us that each client is given full support and direction – so our aim is not to represent more than 10 actors per agent or assistant agent. Because we are an offshoot of a production company, we feel our understanding of the realities of production from the point of view of scheduling, budgeting, casting and shooting puts us in a unique position to supply the right talent for the right production."

Will consider attending performances within Greater London, given as much notice as possible. Can only represent actors who have a head shot and showreel, and are on Spotlight. *Commission*: around 20% across the board

Redroofs Associates

26 Bath Road, Maidenhead, Berkshire SL6 4JT
tel (01628) 674092 *fax* (01753) 785443
email agency@redroofs.co.uk
website www.redroofs.co.uk

Established in 1947, the agency only represents Redroofs graduates and current students. It does not, therefore, welcome performance notices or representation enquiries from actors unknown to the school. Areas of work include theatre, musicals, television, film, commercials, corporate and voice-overs. *Commission*: 15%

Redrush Talent

22 Burnsall Street, London SW3 3ST
tel 02891 878 146 *mobile* (07803) 594961
email janice@redrushtalent.com
website www.redrushtalent.com
Founder and Agent Janice Rush *Assistant* Louise Statham

Founded in 2009, 1 agent represents 10 actors and also represents presenters and writers. Main areas of work include film, theatre, musicals, TV, commercials, corporate and voice-over.

Will consider attending performances at venues within Greater and Central London, given at least 1 weeks' notice. Accepts submissions (with CVs and photographs) from actors previously unknown to the company if sent by email. Showreels, voicereels and invitations to view individual actors' websites are also accepted. Redrush are happy to consider applications for representation from disabled actors. *Commission:* 15%

Lisa Richards Agency

108 Upper Leeson Street, Dublin 4
tel 353 1 637 5000 *fax* 353 1 667 1256
email info@lisarichards.ie
website www.lisarichards.ie
Managing Director Lisa Cook *Agents (Actors)* Lisa Cook, Richard Cook, Jonathan Shankey, *(Voice-over)* Lorraine Cummins *(Literary)* Faith O'Grady *(Comedy)* Ami Burke, Christina Dwyer *(Corporate)* Eavan Kenny

The Lisa Richards Agency was founded in 1989 by Lisa and Richard Cook. Originally established as a theatrical agency, Lisa Richards now provides representation for actors, comedians, voice-over artists, authors, playwrights, directors and designers. The company employs a staff of 13 people across the different departments. 3 agents and 1 assistant represent 90-100 actors, and there is 1 voice-over agent, 2 comedy agents, and 1 literary agent as well as 1 receptionist.

Welcomes performance notices if sent 3 weeks in advance, and is prepared to travel around Ireland. Welcomes letters (with CVs and photographs) from actors previously unknown to the company if sent by post, but not by email; does not welcome follow-up calls. Happy to receive showreels and invitations to view individual actors' websites. Welcomes enquiries from disabled actors. Submission guidelines on site for authors. Also operates a London office (details on website).

Room 3 Agency Ltd

Head Office: The Old Chapel, 14 Fairview Drive, Redland, Bristol BS6 6PH
tel 0845-5678 333 / 020-7183 1872 / 0117-944 1477
email kate@room3agency.com
website www.room3agency.com
Director Kate Marshall

Established in 2009. Main areas of work are television, film, commercials, corporate, voice-overs. 1 agent represents 20 actors; presenters also represented.

Will consider attending performances in London and the South West, with 1 month's notice. Accepts letters, CVs and photographs sent by post or email, showreels and invitations to view actors' websites. Does not represent actors with disabilities. *Commission*: 20%

Frances Ross Management

Higher Leyonne, Golant, Fowey, Cornwall PL23 1LA
tel (01726) 832395 *mobile* (07593) 994050
email francesross@btconnect.com
Director Frances Ross

Established in 2006. Main areas of work are theatre, film, television and commercials. 1 agent represents 20 actors.

Will consider attending performances in the South West region. Welcomes CVs, photographs and showreel links by email only – no CDs or DVDs. Happy to represent actors with disabilities. *Commission*: 15-20%

Rossmore Management PMA

Broadley House,
48 Broadley Terrace. London NW1 6LG
tel 020-7258 1953
email agents@rossmoremanagement.com
website www.rossmoremanagement.com

Established in 1993. 3 agents represent 80 actors. Areas of work include theatre, musicals, television, film, commercials, corporate and voice-overs.

Will consider attending performances at venues within Greater London. Accepts submissions (with CVs and photographs) from actors previously unknown to the company if sent by post. Please include sae. *Commission*: Theatre and Radio 10%; Film, TV and Commercials 15% plus VAT

Royce Management

121 Merlin Grove, Beckenham BR3 3HS
tel 020-8650 1096
email office@roycemanagement.co.uk
website www.roycemanagement.co.uk

Established in 1980. 2 agents represent 50-60 actors. Areas of work include theatre, musicals, television, film, commercials, corporate and voice-overs.

Will consider attending performances at venues within Greater London with a minimum of 1 week's notice. Accepts submissions with a link to actors' Spotlight page by email. No attachments. *Commission*: Commercials 15%; All other work 10%

St James's Management

7 Smyatts Close, Southminster, Essex CM0 7JT
tel (01621) 772183
Managing Director Jacqueline Leggo

Established in 1965. 1 agent represents approximately 40 actors. Areas of work include theatre, musicals, television, film, commercials, corporate and voice-overs. Actors should approach the company by letter and enclose an sae.

Saraband Associates

39-41 North Road, London N7 9DP

Areas of work include theatre, musicals, television, film and commercials.

Will occasionally consider attending performances at venues in Greater London, given 1 month's notice. Accepts submissions (with CVs and photographs) from actors previously unknown to the company if sent by post. An sae should be included with CVs and photographs. *Commission*: Varies

SCA Management

Abbey Business Centre, Wellington Way, Brooklands Business Park, Weybridge, Surrey KT13 0TT
tel (01932) 268375 *fax* (01932) 268500
email agency@sca-management.co.uk
email scamanagement@aol.com

Established in 1980. 2 agents represent 50 actors. Areas of work include theatre, musicals, television, film, commercials and corporate.

Will consider attending performances within Greater London given sufficient notice. Accepts submissions (with CVs and photographs) from actors previously unknown to the company if sent by post. Showreels and voicereels are also accepted. All submissions must be sent with an appropriately sized sae for reply. *Commission*: 15%

Tim Scott

PO Box 63856, London N6 9BQ
tel 020-8347 8705

email timscott@btinternet.com

Established in 1988. Areas of work include theatre, television, film, and commercials.

Accepts postal submissions (with CVs and photographs) from actors previously unknown to the company.

SDM (formerly Simon Drake Management)

14 Ivor Court, Gloucester Place, London NW1 6BJ
tel 020-7183 8995 020-7183 9013
email admin@simondrakemanagement.co.uk
website www.simondrakemanagement.co.uk
Agent Simon Drake

Established in 2007. Works in theatre, musicals, TV and film. Unsolicited approaches should be made via email only, giving Spotlight PIN.

Dawn Sedgwick Management

3 Goodwins Court, London WC2N 4LL
tel 020-7240 0404 *fax* 020-7240 0415
email dawn@dawnsedgwickmanagement.com
website www.dawnsedgwickmanagement.com
Key personnel Dawn Sedgwick, Nicola Mason-Shakespeare

Established in 1992. 3 agents represent 20 actors. Areas of work include theatre, television, film, commercials, corporate and voice-overs. Also represents presenters, comedians and writers.

Accepts submissions (with CVs and photographs) from actors previously unknown to the agency if sent by post, but not by email. Showreels, voicereels and invitations to view individual actors' websites are also accepted. Welcomes enquiries from disabled actors. *Commission*: 15%

Select Management

PO BOX 748, London, NW4 1TT
mobile (07956) 131494 and (07855)794747
email mail@selectmanagement.info
website www.selectmanagement.info
Agent Venetia Suchdev

Established in 2008. Areas of work include theatre, TV, film, commercial, voice over, print, modeling, corporate, dance, presenting.

Will consider attending performances at venues within Greater London with at least 1 week's notice. Accepts CVs and photographs if sent by email. Also welcomes voice tapes and showreels or invitations to view individual actors' websites as well as applications for representation from disabled actors. *Commission*: 20%. No commission on any work obtained by actors themselves.

Sharkey & Co. Ltd PMA

44 Lexington Street, London W1F 0LP
tel 020-7287 1923
email info@sharkeyandtrigg.com
website www.sharkeyandco.com
Agent Simon Sharkey

Established in 2012, main areas of work are theatre, musicals, cabaret, TV, film, radio, commercials, voice-over, talking books and corporates. Represents 60 actors and also directors and choreographers. Does not represent children. *Commission* 12.5% for everything except feature films and commercials which are 15%.

Welcomes CVs and photographs sent by email with links to showreels and websites. Welcomes perfomance notices with a minimum of two weeks' notice, Greater London preferred. Doesn't currently represent actors with disabilities but very happy to consider applications.

Shepherd Management Ltd PMA

4th Floor, 45 Maddox Street, London W1S 2PE
tel 020-7629 5268 *fax* 020-7499 7535
email info@shepherdmanagement.co.uk
Agent Christina Shepherd

2 agents and 1 junior agent represent 120 actors, 1 director and 1 designer. Areas of work include theatre, musicals (occasionally), television, film, corporate and voice-overs.

Will consider attending performances within Greater London given as much notice as possible. Accepts postal submissions (with CVs, photographs and sae) from actors previously unknown to the agency. Showreels and voicereels will also be accepted. Emails and follow-up telephone calls are not welcomed.

Shepperd-Fox PMA

2nd Floor, 47 Bedford Street, London WC2E 9NH
tel 020- 7240 2048
email info@shepperd-fox.co.uk
website www.shepperd-fox.co.uk
Agents Jane Shepperd, James Davies

A boutique theatrical agency based in Covent Garden, representing a select list of clients in theatre, TV, film, musical theatre, commercials and radio.

Sandra Singer Associates

21 Cotswold Road, Westcliff-on-Sea, Essex SS0 8AA
tel (01702) 331616
email sandrasingeruk@aol.com
website www.sandrasinger.com
Key personnel Sandra Singer

Main areas of work are with leads and featured artists for feature films, film, television, commercials and musical theatre. Specialises in artistes under 25 years of age, but is also a boutique agency of established artistes.

Accepts applications by email. No zip files, jpgs, or emails with large files unless requested. Showreels should only be sent on request.

Camilla Storey Management

30 Percy Street, London W1T 2DB
tel 020-3051 8360
email camilla@csmagt.com
Agent Camilla Story

Areas of work include TV, film, theatre, commercials, corporate, musicals and pantomimes.

Accepts submissions by email (with CVs and photographs), and also welcomes showreels.

Smart Management

PO Box 64377, London EC1V 1ND
tel 020-7837 8822
email smart.management@virgin.net
Agent Mario Renzullo

Established in 2000. Areas of work include theatre, musicals, television, film, commercials, corporate and radio.ntact by post/email.

Will consider attending performances given 1 month's notice.

Paul Spyker Management

PO Box 48848, London WC1B 3WZ
tel 020-7462 0046
email belinda@psmlondon.com

Works in all areas of the entertainment industry; also represents directors and choreographers. Recommends the photographer Jorge de Reval.

Will consider seeing performances given a month's notice. Welcomes letters (with CVs) from individual actors previously unknown to the agency, if sent by post or email; also accepts invitations to view individual actors' websites. Encourages enquiries from actors with disabilities.

Stanton Davidson Associates PMA

RADA Studios, 16 Chenies Street,
London WC1E 7EX
tel 020-7581 3388
email contact@stantondavidson.co.uk
website www.stantondavidson.co.uk
Agents Geoff Stanton, Roger Davidson

Formerly Brunskill Management Ltd. See also the company's entry under *Agents* on page 58. Agency represents approximately 80 clients, actors, producers, directors, designers, composers and musical directors. Areas of work include theatre, musicals, opera, film, television, commercials, corporate and voice-overs.

Will consider attending performances both in and outside of Greater London, but request as much notice as possible. Accepts submissions from actors previously unknown to the company, preferably by email with a limited number of small attachments. If you can't resist the temptation to send a CV and photograph by post, please include an appropriately sized envelope for their return.

Stevenson Withers & Associates Ltd PMA

Studio 7C, Clapham North Arts Centre,
Voltaire Road, London SW4 6DH
tel 020-7720 3355 *fax* 020-7720 5565
email talent@stevensonwithers.com
website www.stevensonwithers.com
Agents Natasha Stevenson, Jennifer Withers, Lindsay Kutner *Assistant* Perry Antoniou

3 agents represent 100 actors. Areas of work include theatre, musicals, television, film, commercials, corporate and voice-overs. Actors should approach the company by email.

Stirling Management

490 Halliwell Road, Bolton, Lancashire BL1 8AN
tel (01204) 848333
email admin@stirlingmanagement.co.uk
website www.stirlingmanagement.co.uk
Agents Glen Mortimer, Judith Bailey

Established in 2008. 2 agents represent 80-100 actors and performers. Areas of work include theatre, TV, film, commercials, corporate, voice-overs and photo shoots. Also represents cruise-ship singers and entertainers.

Will consider attending performances at venues in the north west given at least 1 weeks' notice, though preferably more. Accepts submissions by email (with CVs and photographs). Asks that Spotlight links and showreels be included if available. *Commission:* Theatre 15%, Voice-over and Photoshoots 20%

Stiven Christie Management

1 Glen Street, Tollcross, Edinburgh EH3 9JD
tel 0131-228 4040
email info@stivenchristie.co.uk
website www.stivenchristie.co.uk
Proprietor Douglas Stiven

Founded in 1983 (and incorporating The Actors Agency of Edinburgh). Agency represents actors for theatre, musicals, television, film, commercials, corporate and voice-overs.

Katherine Stonehouse Management

PO Box 64412, London W5 9GU
tel 020-8560 7709
email katherine@katherinestonehouse.co.uk
website www.katherinestonehouse.co.uk
Senior Agent Katherine Stonehouse

Established in 2008. Works mainly in theatre, musicals, TV, film, commercials, corporate, voice-over and presenting.

Will consider attending performances in Greater London and North-East England, given 4 weeks' notice. Welcomes letters (with CVs and photographs) sent by post or email. Also accepts showreels and invitations to view individual actors' websites.

The Talent Agency Ltd

Freshwater House, Outdowns, Effingham KT24 5QR
tel (01483) 281500 *fax* (01483) 281501
email info@thetalentagencyltd.co.uk
Managing Director Mike Smith *Producer* Daryl Smith
Consultant Sally James

A management company established in 1974 and covering all aspects of clients' career and long-term development; represents around 10 actors. Areas of work include television, film, commercials, corporate and voice-overs. Also represents radio and TV presenters and sports stars.

Will consider attending performances at venues in Greater London and elsewhere, given 2-3 weeks' notice. Accepts submissions (with CVs and photographs) from actors previously unknown to the company, sent by post or email. Also accepts showreels and voicereels. Invitations to view individual actors' websites are only accepted if sent via email. Submitted CVs should be as complete as possible, and separate clearly professional experience from student productions. Applicants should always state if they have yet to acquire a professional role. *Commission*: 15-20% according to press, accountancy, and PR agreements

Talent Artists Ltd

59 Sydner Road, London N16 7UF
tel 020-7923 1119 *fax* 020-7923 2009
Director Jane Wynn Owen

Talent Artists Ltd represents actors working in all fields of the industry, with a particular emphasis on musical theatre.

The Talent Scout

email connect@thetalentscout.org
website www.thetalentscout.org

Established in 2009. Main areas of work are film, theatre and television – primarily in Los Angeles, New York and London. Represents actors, models, recording artists and bands.

Welcomes contact by actors previously unknown to the agency, if made by email with cover note, links to online CVs, photos, websites and reels. No attachments. Please visit our website and read our contact policy before approaching. "Invitations to shows are always welcome."

Tavistock Wood PMA

Tavistock Wood, 45 Conduit Street,
London W1S 2YN
tel 020-7494 4767 *fax* 020-7434 2017
email info@tavistockwood.com
website www.tavistockwood.com
Agents Angharad Wood, Charles Collier, Molly Wansell

Specialist boutique agency and management company representing around 100 clients across the fields of acting, writing and direction. The agency is now well know for an approach which places a strong focus on pan-European talent. Accepts submissions, (with CVs and photographs), from actors previously unknown to the company by post only – these should be accompanied by a covering letter and a sae.

TCG Artist Management Ltd

14A Goodwin's Court, London WC2N 4LL
tel 020-7240 3600 *fax* 020-7240 3606
email info@tcgam.co.uk
website www.tcgam.co.uk

Established in 1998. 1 agent represents 70 actors, with 2 assistants. Areas of work include theatre, musicals, television, film and commercials. Accepts submissions via email with Spotlight link.

Lisa Thomas Management

Unit 10, 7 Wenlock Road, London N1 7SL
tel 0845-900 5511
email lisa@lisathomasmanagement.com
website www.lisathomasmanagement.com

Areas of work include stand up comedy, television, film, commercials and corporates.

Katie Threlfall Associates PMA

13 Tolverne Road, London SW20 8RA
tel 020-8879 0493
email katie@ktthrelfall.co.uk
Agent Katie Threlfall

Founded in 1996 as Hillman Threlfall; changed its name in 2006 to Katie Threlfall Associates. 1 agent represents 90 actors in theatre, musicals, television, film, commercials and corporate.

Will attend performances at venues within Greater London if given 1 month's notice. Accepts submissions (with CVs and photographs) from actors previously unknown to the company. Welcomes showreels and invitations to view individual actors' websites. "Address letters correctly to the agent. Only write in if you have a showreel, or with an invitation to a show: we do not take on or meet people whose work we do not know." *Commission*: Commercials 15%, Television 12.5%, Theatre 10%

Janice Tildsley Associates

71A Grove Road, London E17 9BU
tel 020-8521 1888
email kathryn@janicetildsleyassociates.co.uk
website www.janicetildsleyassociates.co.uk
Agents Kathryn Kirton

Established in 2003. 1 agent represents 40 actors. Areas of work include television, film, commercials and theatre, with a particular focus on musical theatre.

Will consider attending performances within the Greater London area. Accepts submissions (with CVs and photographs) from actors previously unknown to the agency if sent by post, but not by email. Welcomes enquiries from disabled actors. *Commission*: 10-15%

TMG Associates

4 Cavendish Square, London W1G 0PG
tel 020-7437 1383 *mobile* 07866 589905
email tanya.greep@googlemail.com
Proprietor Tanya Greep *Key personnel* Natalie Elliott

Established in 1981. 2 agents and 1 assistant represent 70-80 actors. Areas of work include theatre, musicals, television, film, commercials, corporate and voice-overs.

Will consider attending performances at venues within Greater London with 2 weeks' notice if an actor is playing a substantial role. Accepts submissions by email. Showreels and voicereels should only be sent on request. *Commission*: 12.5%

Top Talent Agency (TTA Adults)

PO BOX 860, St Albans, Hertfordshire AL1 9BR
01727-855903
email admin@toptalentagency.co.uk
website www.toptalentagency.co.uk
Director & Head Agent Warren Bacci *Child Division* Toni Browne *Adult Actors Division & Director of TTA Adults* Leoni Kibbey & Andy Musgrove *Junior Agent* Laura Jayne

Established in 2008. 3 agents represent 300 actors (children and adults). Areas of work include theatre, musicals, television, film, commercials, corporate and voice-overs.

Will consider attending performances with 1 week's notice. To be considered for representation, please apply through the Top Talent website, www.toptalentagency.co.uk, and go to the 'join us' page. *Commission*: 15% for adults and 20% for child actors. Does not currently represent disabled actors.

Total Vanity Ltd

15 Walton Way, Aylesbury, Bucks HP21 7JJ
mobile (07739) 381788
email richardwilliams@totalvanity.com
website www.totalvanity.com
Agent Richard Williams

Established in 2000. 1 agent represents 50 actors. Areas of work include theatre, musicals, television, film, commercials, corporate and voice-overs. Also represents presenters.

Will consider attending performances within the Greater London area with at least 1 week's notice. Accepts submissions (with CVs and photographs) from actors previously unknown to the company if sent by post. Showreels, voicereels and invitations to view individual actors' websites are also accepted. Welcomes enquiries from disabled actors. *Commission*: 20%

Troika PMA

10A Christina Street, London EC2A 4PA
tel 020-7336 7868
email casting@troikatalent.com
website www.troikatalent.com
Agents Michael Duff and Sarah Stephenson, assisted by Aine O'Sullivan and Harrison Davies; Kat Gosling, assisted by Tom Holcroft; Gary O'Sullivan, assisted by Jill Regan; Conor McCaughan and Sam Fox, assisted by Kirsty Beaton, Kate Morrison and Alex Pudney; Melanie Rockcliffe, Dylan Hearn and Sophie Chapman, assistaed by Becca Kinder and Hannah Fletcher

Established in 2005, main areas of work are film, theatre, TV and musicals. Represents approximately 250 clients, includng actors, directors, presenters, writers, comedians, casting directors and producers. Welcomes performance notices for productions in London. Accepts email submissions only with a showreel link if possible. Represents actors with disabilities. *Commission*: 12.5%

United Agents PMA

12-26 Lexington Street, London W1F 0LE
tel 020-3214 0800 *fax* 020-3214 0802
email info@unitedagents.co.uk
website www.unitedagents.co.uk
Agents Jess Alford, Hannah Begbie, Julia Charteris, Kate Davie, Charlotte Davies, Sean Gascoine, Duncan Hayes, Olivia Homan, Chris Keen, Lindy King, Kitty Laing, Thea Martin, Lucia Pallaris, Helen Robinson, Joanna Scarratt, Dallas Smith, Lisa Toogood, Maureen Vincent, Kirk Whelan-Foran, Ruth Young

Established in 2007. Represents about 500 actors. The agency also represents writers, directors, producers, designers and other creatives.

"We now only accept submissions by email. Please email your CV and headshot to **submissions@unitedagents.co.uk** and expect a reply within 4-6 weeks. Any physical submissions will not receive a response."

Universal Artists

480 Upper Newtownards Road, Belfast BT4 3GZ
tel 028-9065 2200 *mobile* (07838) 235792
email mark@universalartists.co.uk
website www.universalartists.co.uk
Agent Mark McCrory

Established in 2005. Main areas of work are film, TV, theatre, commercials, voice-over and radio. 1 agent represents 65 artists. Also represents Gillian Reynolds (Casting Director).

Will consider attending performances within Northern Ireland and Greater London. Welcomes applications as emailed CVs, showreels and voice tapes. Is open to representing actors with disabilities. *Commission*: 10%

Urban Talent

Nemesis House, 1 Oxford Court, Bishopsgate, Manchester M2 3WQ
tel 0161-228 6866 *fax* 0161-228 6727
email liz@nmsmanagement.co.uk
Key personnel Liz Beeley

Urban Talent represents 30-50 actors. Areas of work include theatre, television, film, commercials, corporate and voice-overs. Also represents presenters.

Will consider attending performances at venues in the North West with 2 weeks' notice. Accepts submissions (with CVs and photographs) from actors previously unknown to the company, sent by post or email. Also accepts invitations to view individual actors' websites. *Commission*: 15%

UVA Management

Pinewood Studios, Pinewood Road, Iver Heath, Buchinghamshire SL0 0NHL
tel 0845-370 0883
email info@uvamanagement.com
website www.uvamanagement.com
Head agent Wayne Berko

Established in 2004. Main areas of work are theatre, musicals, television, commercials and corporate. 2 agents represent around 8 actors; also represents presenters.

Welcomes letters (with CVs and photographs) from actors previously unknown to the company if sent by post or email, but prefers not to receive invitations to view individual actors' websites. Does not accept showreels or voicereels. Welcomes enquiries from actors with disabilities. *Commission*: Theatre 10%; TV and Film 13%

VSA Ltd PMA

186 Shaftesbury Avenue, London WC2H 8JB
tel 020-7240 2927 *fax* 020-7240 2930
email info@vsaltd.com
website www.vsaltd.com

VSA has a long and very fine heritage as an agency, having been created by the theatrical agent and impresario Vincent Shaw back in the 1950s. Since then the agency has maintained its position as a top theatrical management looking after many successful artists, including the legendary Jessie Matthews, as well as giving many industry leaders such as Bill Kenwright an opportunity to get started in the industry.

Andy Charles took over the agency in 2002, after working alongside Vincent Shaw as his head agent, and today runs VSA with fellow agent and business partner Tod Weller. Their combined experience of the industry from both sides of the fence (Andy's from his career as an actor, and Tod's from his career in TV, advertising and commercials production) ensures an in-depth understanding of the demands of an ever-changing business, as well as an empathy and insight into the daily challenges of an artist's life. "Our continued success depends on our relationships with our clients and with casting professionals – relationships we nurture and never take for granted; friendly, professional and very personal management is paramount to all that we do."

Roxanne Vacca Management PMA

73 Beak Street, London W1F 9SR

2 agents represent 45 actors. Does not welcome performance notices, but will accept letters (with CVs and photographs) from individual actors previously unknown to the agency if sent by post. Also accepts showreels, voicereels, and invitations to view individual actors' websites. *Commission*: Film & TV 12.5%; Theatre 10%; Commercials 15%

Louise Dyson at VisABLE People

PO Box 80, Droitwich WR9 0ZE
tel (01386) 555 170 *mobile* (01905) 776631
email louise@visablepeople.com
website www.visablepeople.com
Agent Louise Dyson

Production details: Founded in 1994, VisABLE is the UK's first agency representing only disabled people for professional engagements. It represents artistes with a wide range of impairments and in every age group, including children. 2 agents represent around 150 artistes in all areas of acting, including presenting.

Casting procedures: Does not welcome performance notices: "Sorry, usually no time to get out and see them; existing clients only." Happy to receive other enquiries (with CVs and photographs) from disabled actors via website only. Showreels should always be accompanied by an sae for return. Also happy to receive invitations to view individual actors' websites. Recommends the photographer Simon Donnelly. *Commission*: 10%-17.5% (commercials: 20%).

VM Talent Ltd PMA (Vic Murray Talent)

Unit 40, Battersea Business Centre, 99-101 Lavender Hill, London SW11 5QL
tel 0207-112 8938
email info@vmtalent.com
website www.vmtalent.com
Agent: Vic Murray; *Junior Agent:* Ellie Blackford

Established in 2009, and currently representing 35 clients. Areas of work include theatre, TV, film and radio; also represents presenters and writers. Welcomes CVs, photographs and showreels sent by email. Committed to a policy of equal opportunity.

Suzann Wade

9 Wimpole Mews, London W1G 8PB
tel 020-7486 0746 *fax* 020-7486 5664

email admin@suzannwade.com
website www.suzannwade.com
Director Suzann Wade & Assistants

Areas of work include theatre, musicals, film, TV, commercials, corporate and voice-over. Talent agency with a personalised service.

Welcomes performance notices for London venues only (West End and Central), if received as hard copy by post and at least 2 weeks' notice is given. Welcomes letters (with CVs and photographs) from individual actors previously unknown to the company if sent by post with sae. No emails, follow-up calls or voicereels, but will accept showreels if they are sent with an sae for return. It is best to provide links to voice/showreel or CV on hard copy submissions. Encourages enquiries from disabled actors, linguists and high-physicality actors sent by post, and currently represents, or plans to represent, actors with disabilities.

Waring & McKenna Ltd PMA

44 Maiden Lane, Covent Garden,
London WC2E 7LN
tel 020-7836 9222 *fax* 020-7836 9186
email dj@waringandmckenna.com
Agents Daphne Waring, John Summerfield

Established in 1993. 2 agents represent approximately 80 actors. Areas of work include theatre, musicals, television, film, commercials, corporate and voice-overs.

Will consider attending performances at venues within Greater London and occasionally elsewhere, given at least 1 month's notice. Accepts postal submissions (with CVs and photographs) from actors previously unknown to the company. Follow-up telephone calls are also accepted. Showreels and voicereels should only be sent on request. *Commission*: Theatre 10%; TV and Low-Budget Films 12.5%; Commercials and Feature Films over £4 million 15%

Janet Welch Personal Management

Old Orchard, The Street, Ubley, Bristol BS40 6PJ
tel (01761) 463238
email info@janetwelchpm.co.uk

Established in 1990. Areas of work include theatre, musicals, television, film, commercials, corporate and voice-overs.

Will consider attending performances at venues within Greater London and sometimes elsewhere, given sufficient notice. Accepts submissions (with CVs and photographs) from actors previously unknown to the company if sent by post.

Penny Wesson Management

26 King Henry's Road, London NW3 3RP
tel/fax 0207-722 6607 and 020-7483 2890
email penny@pennywesson.com
Agent Penny Wesson

Founded 2002, Penny Wesson represents 12 theatre professionals and directors. *Comisson*: 10%

Meredith Westwood Management Ltd

Suite A, 236 Cambridge Heath Road, Bethnal Green, London E2 9DA
mobile (07411) 503007
email meredithwestwoodmanagement@gmail.com
website www.meredithwestwoodmanagement.co.uk
Senior Casting Agent and Primary Enquiries Contact Tara.

Established in 2011. Works in film, TV, commercials, theatre, musicals, events, corporate, presenting and voice-over (does not represent sole voice-over or presenting clients). 2 agents represent 30 clients.

Will consider attending performances in London, for which short notice is encouraged. Welcomes emails from actors with links to showreels and websites or dates of performances. No follow-up phone calls, although follow-up emails are accepted. Happy to hear from actors with disabilities; all are judged equally regardless of disabilities or race. *Commission*: 20% across filmed and digital media, 15% across theatre and events

Wilde Management

11 Wilton Road, Manchester M21 9GS
mobile (07759) 567639
email info@wildemanagement.com
website www.wildemanagement.co.uk
Agent Rebecca Jenner *Assistant Agent* Phil Minns

Established in 2010. Main areas of work are theatre, TV and film. 1 agent represents approximately 10 actors. Welcomes CVs and photographs sent by email only. *Commission*: 10-15%

Williamson & Holmes

51 St Martin's Lane, London WC2N 4EA
tel 020-7240 0407
email info@williamsonandholmes.co.uk
website www.williamsonandholmes.co.uk
Agents Jackie Williamson, Michelle Holmes, Danica Pickett

Established in 2005, the agency represents 80 actors. Areas of work include theatre, musicals, television, film, commercials and corporate.

Will consider attending performances at venues within Greater London with 2 weeks' notice. Accepts submissions (with CVs and photographs) from actors previously unknown to the company if a link to Spotlight page is emailed (no large attachments). *Commission*: Theatre 10%; TV/Film/Commercials/ Radio 15%

Willow Personal Management

151 Main Street, Yaxley, Peterborough PE7 3LD
tel (01733) 240392

email office@willowmanagement.co.uk
website www.willowmanagement.co.uk
Director Peter Burroughs

Established in 1995. 1 agent represents more than 150 actors. Specialises in the representation of short actors (under 5ft) and tall actors (over 7ft). Areas of work include theatre, musicals, television, film, commercials, corporate and voice-overs.

Accepts submissions (with CVs and colour photographs) from actors previously unknown to the company if sent by email. *Commission*: 15%

Wintersons PMA

59 St Martin's Lane, London WC2N 4JS
tel 020-7836 7849
email info@nikiwinterson.com
website www.nikiwinterson
Agents Niki Winterson and Lawrence James *Trainee Agent* Faye Timby

Established in 2011. Main areas of work are theatre, musicals, TV, film, commercials and corporate. Represents 100 actors. Also represents directors, presenters, prodcuers, writers and composers. Welcomes performance notices and will attend whenever possible within London. Welcomes letters, CVs via email with Spotlight links only. Please do not atach images or large files to emails.

WIS Celtic Management

86 Elphinstone Road, London E17 5EX
tel 020-8523 4234 *fax* 020-8523 4523
email wis.celtic@ethnicsaa.co.uk
Managing Director Pauline Oni

Established in 2004, specialising in Welsh, Irish and Scottish actors. Areas of work include theatre, musicals, television, film, commercials, corporate and voice-overs. One agent represents 12 actors.

Will consider attending performances within Greater London with at least 3 weeks' notice. Accepts submissions (with CVs and photographs) from actors previously unknown to the agency if sent by post, but not by email. Welcomes showreels and voicereels, and enquiries from disabled actors. *Commission*: Varies

Edward Wyman Agency

23 White Acre Close, Thornhill, Cardiff CF14 9DG
tel 029-2075 2351
email wymancasting@yahoo.co.uk
website www.wymancasting.co.uk
Managing Director Judith Gay

Areas of work include television, film, commercials, corporate, photo shoots and voice-overs.

Accepts submissions from actors previously unknown to the company. Actors should download an application form from the website. All submissions should include CVs and photographs. Books are open in January each year. Welsh actors are particularly welcome. *Commission* 15%

CO-OPERATIVE AGENCIES

Before making an approach, it is important to understand what being a member of one of these entails, and to be clear about your reason(s) for wanting to join. Many Co-ops have clear details for applicants on their websites.

21st Century Actors Management

206 Panther House, 38 Mount Pleasant, London WC1X 0AP
tel 020-7278 3438 *fax* 020-7833 1158
email 21centuryactors@gmail.com
website www.21cam.co.uk

Co-operative management established in 1992. Represents 21 actors. Areas of work include theatre, musicals, television, film, commercials and corporate. Members are expected to work 3 days in the office per month.

Will consider attending performances at venues in and around London. Accepts submissions (with CVs and photographs) from actors previously unknown to the company if sent by email. Actors requesting representation should write stating why they wish to join a co-operative, and outlining their casting type and skills. *Commission*: Theatre, TV, Commercials & Film 10%

1984 Personal Management Ltd

Suite 508, Davina House, 137 Goswell Road, London EC1V 7ET
tel 020-7251 8046 *fax* 020-7250 3031
email info@1984pm.com
website www.1984pm.com

Co-operative management (CPMA member) representing 25 actors. Areas of work include theatre, musicals, television, film, commercials, and corporate. Members are expected to work 4 days in the office per month unless paying commission.

Will consider attending performances at venues in Greater London with 1 month's notice. Accepts letters (with CVs and photographs) from actors previously unknown to the company, following an initial telephone call. Please visit website first. Actors should always enquire whether the agency is recruiting before sending CVs. Will also accept showreels and follow-up telephone calls. *Commission*: 5%

Actors Alliance

Disney Place House, 14 Marshalsea Road, London SE1 1HL
tel 020-7407 6028 *fax* 020-7407 6028
email actors@actorsalliance.co.uk
website www.actorsalliance.co.uk

A co-operative group of actors established in 1976 to advance one another's careers. Currently there are 19 members, who are all in Spotlight and belong to Equity. Areas of work include theatre, musicals, television, film, commercials, corporates and voice-overs. Members are expected to work in the office at least 1 day a week.

When interested, and given a minimum of 2 weeks' notice, will attend an applicant's performance in Greater London. Apply (with CV and photograph) by post only, enclosing an sae for reply. Do not send a showreel unless requested to do so. Actors Alliance is not funded from commission.

Actors' Creative Team

Panther House, 38 Mount Pleasant,
London WC1X 0AN
tel 020-7278 3388
email office@actorscreativeteam.co.uk
website www.actorscreativeteam.co.uk

Founded in 2001, this co-op agency has members working in theatre, musicals, television, film, commercials and corporate projects. Members are expected to work 3 days in the office each month. Welcomes performance notices for events, given at least 2 weeks' notice. Will also accept emails (with CVs, cover letter & headshots), see website for more details. Prospective clients need to include their reasons for choosing a co-operative agency in a covering email. Commission: Theatre 10%; Recorded Media up to 12.5% (7.5% for low-paid jobs)

Actors Direct Ltd

Number 5, 651 Rochdale Road, Manchester M9 5SH
tel 0161-237 1904 *fax* 0161-237 1904
email info@actorsdirect.org.uk
website www.actorsdirect.org.uk
Administrators Eilis Hetherington, Jonathan Byrne

Established in 1994. Co-operative management. Sole representative of approximately 25 actors. Areas of work include theatre, musicals, television, film, commercials, corporate and voice-overs. Members are expected to work 2-3 days in the office each month.

Will consider attending performances at venues in the North (Manchester, Leeds, and Liverpool areas) if given 2 weeks' notice. Accepts submissions (with CVs and photographs) from actors previously unknown to the company if sent by post. Also accepts showreels and voicereels. Will consider applications from trained professional actors with excellent IT and communications skills and the ability to perform office duties to a high standard. "Actors Direct is constantly striving to maintain a high professional image and to provide a first-class service to casting directors." *Commission*: 10% for members

The Actors File

The White House, Oval House,
52-54 Kennington Oval, London SE11 5SW
tel 020-7582 7923
email theactorsfile@btconnect.com
website www.theactorsfile.co.uk

Established in 1983. Co-operative management representing 20-25 actors. Areas of work include theatre, musicals, television, film, commercials, corporate and voice-overs. Members are expected to work 4 days in the office per month and to attend business meetings.

Will attend performances at venues in Greater London and occasionally elsewhere. Accepts submissions by post or email which include CV, photograph and covering letter detailing interest iin a co-op. Will also accept showreels.

The Actors' Group

Swan Buildings, 20 Swan Street, Manchester M4 5JW
tel/fax 0161-834 4466
email enquiries@theactorsgroup.co.uk
website www.theactorsgroup.co.uk

Established in 1980. Co-operative management representing actors. Areas of work include theatre, musicals, television, film, commercials, corporate and voice-overs. Members are expected to carry out various office duties.

Will consider attending performances at venues in the North West with 2-4 weeks' notice. Accepts submissions (with CVs and photographs) from actors previously unknown to the company if sent by post. Will also accept follow-up telephone calls, showreels, voicereels and invitations to view individual actors' websites.

Actors Network Agency

55 Lambeth Walk, London SE11 6DX
tel 020-7735 0999 *fax* 020-7735 8177
email info@ana-actors.co.uk
website www.ana-actors.co.uk
Coordinator and Administrator Sandie Bakker

Established in 1985. Co-operative management representing 20-30 actors. Areas of work include theatre, musicals, television, film, commercials and corporate. Also represents role-play. Members are expected to work 4 days in the office per month.

Will consider attending performances at venues in Greater London and occasionally elsewhere, given as much notice as possible. Accepts submissions (with CVs and photographs) from actors previously unknown to the company if sent by post. Will also accept showreels. "An interest in, and commitment to, this type of agency is essential." *Commission* 10%; Commercials 12.5%

Actorum Ltd

c/o Theatre Delicatessen, The Annexe,
25 Eccleston Place, London SW1W 9NF
tel 020-7636 6978
email info@actorum.com
website www.actorum.com

Co-operative management representing 35 actors.We operate on the principle of collective self-determination in the entertainment business with each actor working 4 days a month in the office when not working professionally.

Will consider attending performances at venues in Greater London and elsewhere, given 4 weeks' notice. All applications sent to **newaps.actorum@gmail.com**. Showreels, voicereels and invitations to view individual actors' websites accepted. *Commission*: Theatre 10%; TV, Commercials and Film 15%

Alpha Actors

Studio B4, 3 Bradbury Street, London N16 8JN
tel 020-7241 0077 *fax* 020-7241 2410
email alpha@alphaactors.com
website www.alphaactors.com

A co-operative agency established in 1983, Alpha Actors currently represents 25 actors working in theatre, musicals, television, film, commercials and corporate work. Members are expected to work 4 days in the office each month.

Welcomes submissions by email or by post with letter, CV and photograph, and will consider attending performances within Greater London, given as much as notice as possible.

Arena Personal Management Ltd

E11 Panther House, 38 Mount Pleasant, London WC1X 0AN
tel 020-7278 1661
email arenapmltd@aol.com
website www.arenapmltd.co.uk

Co-operative management representing 20 actors. Areas of work include theatre, musicals, television, film, commercials, corporate and voice-overs. Members are expected to work 1 day in the office per week.

Will consider attending performances at venues in Greater London given 3-4 weeks' notice. Accepts submissions (with CVs and photographs) from actors previously unknown to the company if sent by post or email. Will also accept follow-up telephone calls, showreels, voicereels and invitations to view individual actors' websites. *Commission*: Theatre 10%; Commercials 12.5%

AXM (Actors Exchange Management Ltd)

Unit J302, J Block, Biscuit Factory, 100 Clement's Road, London SE16 4DG
tel 020-7837 3304
email info@axmgt.com
website www.axmgt.com

Established in 1983. Co-operative management representing 20 actors. Areas of work include theatre, musicals, television, film, commercials, corporate and voice-overs. Members are expected to work 4 days in the office per month.

Will consider attending performances at venues in Greater London, given sufficient notice. Accepts submissions (with CVs and photographs) from actors previously unknown to the company if sent by post or email. Showreels and voicereels should only be sent on request following an interview. *Commission*: Variable depending on work type.

Bridges: The Actors' Agency Ltd

Studio S12, Out of the Blue Drill Hall, 36 Dalmeny Street, Edinburgh EH6 8RG
tel (0131) 5543073 *fax* (07718) 122477
email admin@bridgesactorsagency.com
website www.bridgesactorsagency.com

Established in 2008. At present the only co-operative agency active in Scotland. Areas of work include theatre, television, film, commercials, radio and corporate. Members are expected to contribute to the running of the office, and to attend meetings; therefore all prospective members must be based a commutable distance from Edinburgh.

Accepts submissions via letters and emails: include a CV and headshot. Will also accept showreels, voicereels and invitations to view individual actors' websites. Welcomes invitations to attend performances and showcases.

Entry to the agency is via audition. If successful, a stakeholder donation of £100 is required to join the agency. Prospective members must also be registered with Spotlight. *Commission*: Non-Electronic 10%; Electronic 12%

Castaway Actors Agency

30-31 Wicklow Street, Dublin 2
tel 353-1671 9264/9059 *fax* 353-1761 9133
email office@castawayactors.com
website www.castawayactors.com

Established in 1989. A co-operative agency representing 34 actors. Members are expected to fulfil office duties throughout the year. Areas of work include theatre, musicals, television, film, commercials, corporate and voice-overs. Accepts submissions with CVs, photographs and a cover letter from Dublin-based actors.

CCM

Unit 6, Second Floor, Aztec Row, 1 Berners Road, London N1 0PW
tel 020-7183 3425
email casting@ccmactors.com
website www.ccmactors.com

Secretary David Shackleton *Administrator* Neil Patrick

Established in 1993. Co-operative management representing up to 30 actors. Areas of work include theatre, film, television, musicals and commercials. Members are expected to work up to 3 days in the office per month, and need office skills.

Members will consider attending performances, with notice. The agency accepts letters and emails (with photographs and CVs – hard-copy submissions preferred) from actors previously unknown to the membership, and will also accept invitations to view actors' personal websites. Entry to the agency is via audition, which prospective members will be invited to attend. Actors must be aware of how co-operatives work, and their role within them. Information is available from Equity and Spotlight. A Training Fee of £250 (in 2 instalments) is required to join the agency. Prospective clients must also be registered in *Spotlight.*

Central Line

11 East Circus Street, Nottingham NG1 5AF
tel 0115-941 2937
email centralline@btconnect.com
website http://thecentralline.co.uk

Established in 1984. Co-operative management representing 15-25 actors. Areas of work include theatre, musicals, television, film, commercials, corporate and voice-overs. Also represents directors. Members are expected to work in the office as and when appropriate.

Will consider attending performances at venues in Greater London and elsewhere. Accepts submissions (with CVs and photographs) from actors previously unknown to the company, sent by post or email. Will also accept follow-up telephone calls, showreels, voicereels and invitations to view individual actors' websites. *Commission*: 10%

Circuit Personal Management Ltd

Suite 31 Progress Centre, Charlton Place, Ardwick Green, Manchester M12 6HS
tel 0161 425 0763*fax* (01782) 206821
email mail@circuitpm.co.uk
website www.circuitpm.co.uk

Established in 1988. Co-operative management representing actors in the West Midlands, North West and West Yorkshire area. Areas of work include theatre, musicals, television, film, commercials, corporate and voice-overs. Members are expected to work approximately 15 days annually and to attend monthly meetings.

Will consider attending performances at venues within the operating area, preferably with 3-4 weeks' notice. Accepts submissions from actors (with CVs and photographs) sent by post or email. Will also accept follow-up telephone calls.

City Actors' Management

Oval House, 52-54 Kennington Oval, London SE11 5SW
tel 020-7793 9888
email info@cityactors.co.uk
website www.cityactors.co.uk

Co-operative management representing 29 actors with 1 permanent, office-based rep. Areas of work include theatre, musicals, television, film, commercials and corporate. Members are expected to work 4 days in the office per month.

Will consider attending performances at venues in Greater London with a minimum of 2 weeks' notice. Submissions (with CVs and photographs) should be sent by post and email. Advises actors to contact the agency when appearing in a show, or with a showreel, as new members will not be admitted without their work being seen. Will also accept follow-up telephone calls. *Commission*: Theatre 10%/12.5% depending on income; Media 15%

Crescent Management

Southbank House, Black Prince Road, London SE1 7SJ
tel 020-8987 0191
email mail@crescentmanagement.co.uk
website www.crescentmanagement.co.uk

Established in 1991, the agency has 20-25 members working in theatre, musicals, television, film, commercials and corporate drama. Members are expected to work 3 days in the office each month.

Will consider attending performances within Greater London given 2 weeks' notice. Accepts submissions (with CVs and photographs) from actors previously unknown to the agency: please read the advice on how to apply given on the website. Will also accept follow-up telephone calls, showreels, voicereels and invitations to view an actor's website. *Commission*: Theatre 10%; Television 12.5%; Film 15%

Denmark Street Management

Unit 77b, Eurolink Office Building, 49 Effra Road, Lambeth, London SW2 1BZ
tel 020-7700 5200 *fax* 020-7084 4053
email mail@denmarkstreet.net
website www.denmarkstreet.net

Established in 1985. Co-operative management representing up to 30 actors working in theatre, musicals, television, film, commercials, corporate and voice-overs. Members are expected to work 1 office day per week.

Will consider attending performances if given notice. Accepts submissions via the 'apply' link on the website only (applicants must be members of Spotlight) from actors previously unknown to the company. Showreels and voicereels should only be sent on request. Applicants should state why they would like to join a co-operative. Ethnic-minority and older actors are particularly welcome. *Commission*: 10% for all work.

Direct Personal Management

Duke Studios, 3 Sheaf Street, Leeds LS10 1HD
tel/fax (0113) 266 4036
email office@directpm.co.uk
St John's House, 16 St John's Vale, London SE8 4EN
tel/fax 020-8694 1788

website www.directpm.co.uk

Established in 1984 (formerly Direct Line Personal Management). Co-operative management representing 25 actors. Areas of work include theatre, musicals, television, film, commercials, corporate, role-play and voice-overs. Members are expected to work 2 days in the office each month.

Will consider attending performances at venues within Greater London and elsewhere, with 1 month's notice. Accepts submissions (with CVs and photographs) from actors previously unknown to the company, sent by post or email. Follow-up telephone calls, showreels, voicereels and invitations to view individual actors' websites are also accepted. "Please consult our website before applying. Every applicant's enquiry is discussed at a monthly meeting. We do reply, but would appreciate it if actors enclosed an sae to help reduce our costs." *Commission*: 5-15%

Frontline Actors' Agency

30-31 Wicklow Street, Dublin 2
tel (353) 1 6359882
email frontlineactors@eircom.net
website www.frontlineactors.com
Chair Bríd Ní Chumhaill

Established in 2000. Main areas of work are theatre, television, film, commercials, corporate and voice-overs. Co-operative agency with 24 actor members who are expected to work approximately 1 week per quarter in the office. Will attend performances in Ireland only, given 2 weeks' notice.

Welcomes letters (with CVs and photographs), showreels, and invitations to view actors' websites. Encourages submissions from actors with disabilities.

IML

The White House, 52-54 Kennington Oval, London SE11 5SW
tel 020-7587 1080 *fax* 020-7587 1080
email info@iml.org.uk
website www.iml.org.uk

Co-operative management established in 1980. Represents 22 actors. 2 members work in the office each day on a rotational basis. Areas of work include theatre, musicals, television, film and commercials. Members are expected to work 4 days in the office per month.

Will consider attending performances at venues in Greater London given 3 weeks' notice. Accepts submissions (with CVs and photographs) from actors previously unknown to the company if sent by post. Will also accept follow-up telephone calls. Showreels and voicereels should only be sent on request. *Commission*: 5-15% depending on the job

Inspiration Management

Unit 6, Panther House, 38 Mount Pleasant, London WC1X 0AN
tel 020-7833 2912
email mail@inspirationmanagement.org.uk
website www.inspirationmanagement.org.uk

Established in 1986, Inspiration is a co-operative actors' agency. Areas of work include theatre, television, film, commercials, corporate, audio and role-play. Members work 30 days in the office per year, when not engaged in professional acting work, and attend regular meetings.

Actors can apply to join by email or post, with details of their shows where applicable, and are encouraged to consult the website prior to applying. Successful applicants will be invited to interview and audition. *Commission* 10%

MV Management

Ralph Richardson Memorial Studios, Kingfisher Place, Clarendon Road, London N22 6XF
tel 020-8889 8231 *fax* 020-8829 1050
email theagency@mountview.org.uk
website www.mvmanagement.org.uk

Represents actors in all areas of the industry: television, film, theatre, musicals, commercials, radio and voiceover. "MV Management is a co-operative agency exclusively for actors who attended and have graduated from Mountview Academy of Theatre Arts. Please do not contact the agency regarding representation unless you are a Mountview graduate."

North of Watford Actors Agency

The Creative Quarter, The Town Hall, St George's Street, Hebden Bridge, West Yorks HX7 7BY
tel (01422) 845361 or 020-3601 3372
fax (01422) 846503
email info@northofwatford.com
website www.northofwatford.com
New Applications Coordinator Chris Orton

Established in 1992. Co-operative management representing 25-30 actors. Areas of work include theatre, musicals, television, film, commercials, corporate and voice-overs. Members are expected to work 3-4 days in the office per month.

Will consider attending performances at venues in Northern locations (Leeds, Manchester, etc.) but requests as much notice as possible. Accepts submissions (with CVs and photographs) from actors previously unknown to the company if sent by post. Will also accept follow-up telephone calls, showreels, voicereels and invitations to view individual actors' websites. *Commission*: Varies depending on the work

NorthOne Management

The Biscuit Factory, Unit B202.6, Tower Bridge Business Complex, 100 Clements Road, London SE16 4DG
tel 020-7359 9666
email actors@northone.co.uk
website www.northone.co.uk

Established in 1987. Co-operative management representing 30 actors. Areas of work include theatre, television, film, commercials and corporate. Members are expected to work 2 days in the office per month.

Will consider attending performances at venues within Greater London given at least 1 week's notice. Accepts submissions (with CVs and b&w 10x8in photographs) from actors previously unknown to the company if sent by post, with an explanation of why they wish to be representd by a co-operative agency. Will also accept follow-up telephone calls, showreels and voicereels. Prefers to hear from actors when currently performing. Administration and technical skills are advantageous. Applicants must be on Spotlight. *Commission*: 10%

Oren Actors Management

Chapter Arts Centre, Market Road, Cardiff CF5 1QE
(02920) 233321
email info@orenactorsmanagement.co.uk
website www.orenactorsmanagement.co.uk

Established in 1981. Co-operative management representing 20-25 actors. Areas of work include theatre, musicals, television, film, commercials, corporate and voice-overs. Members are expected to work 4 hours in the office per week.

Will consider attending performances at venues in Greater London, Cardiff, South West England and Wales given 2 weeks' notice. Accepts submissions (with CVs and photographs) from actors previously unknown to the company. Will also accept follow-up telephone calls, showreels, voicereels and invitations to view individual actors' websites. Applicants are asked to state clearly why they have approached a co-operative. *Commission*: Theatre 8%; Mechanical Media 10%

Performance Actors Agency

137 Goswell Road, London EC1V 7ET
tel 020-7251 5716 *fax* 020-7251 3974
email info@performanceactors.co.uk
website www.performanceactors.co.uk
Key personnel Lionel Guyett

Established in 1984. Co-operative management representing 30+ actors. Areas of work include theatre, musicals, television, film, commercials, corporate and voice-overs. Members are expected to work 3-4 days a month in the office.

Will consider attending performances at venues within Greater London and occasionally elsewhere. Accepts submissions (with CVs and photographs and an SAE – NOT by email) from actors previously unknown to the company. Will also accept showreels and voicereels. "We only recruit new members when specific categories are required. Call first." *Commission*: 10%

RbA Management Ltd

37-45 Windsor Street, Liverpool L8 1XE
tel 0151 708 7273
email info@rbamanagement.co.uk
website www.rbamanagement.co.uk

Established in 1995, RbA is a co-operative management representing up to 20 actors. Areas of work include theatre, musicals, television, film, radio, commercials, corporate and voice-overs. Many of the actors have other, additional skills. Members are expected to contribute 5 working days in the office every 2-3 months.

Will consider attending performances at venues in the North West (Manchester, Liverpool, North Wales) and nationally with 3-4 weeks' notice. Accepts brief, straightforward submissions (with CVs and photographs along with a covering letter) from actors previously unknown to the company if sent by post or email. Showreels, voicereels and invitations to view individual actors' websites are also accepted. *Commission*: 15%

Rogues & Vagabonds Management

The Print House, 18 Ashwin Street, London E8 3DL
tel 020-7254 8130
email rogues@vagabondsmanagement.com
website www.vagabondsmanagement.com

Co-operative management representing 28-30 actors. Areas of work include theatre, television, film, commercials and corporate. Members are expected to work in the office 3 days per month.

Will consider attending performances anywhere, if given at least 3-4 weeks' notice. Accepts submissions (with CVs and photographs) from actors previously unknown to the company if sent by post or email. Showreels, voicereels and invitations to view individual actors' websites are also accepted. Welcomes enquiries from disabled actors. *Commission*: TV/Film 10% on first £200, 15% thereafter; Theatre 10%

Rosebery Management Ltd

87 Leonard St, London EC2A 4QS
tel 020-7684 0187 *fax* 020-7684 0197
email admin@roseberymanagement.com

Established in 1984. Represents 40 actors in theatre, musicals, television, film, commercials, corporate work and voice-overs. Rosebery has a full-time Lead Agent. Members are expected to work 18 days in the office per year.

Will consider attending performances at all venues within Central London. Submissions by email to **rosebery.applications@gmail.com.** *Commission*: 10% on all acting work

Stage Centre Management Ltd

41 North Road, London N7 9DP
tel 020-7607 0872
email info@stagecentre.org.uk
website www.stagecentre.org.uk

Established in 1982. Co-operative management agency. Areas of work include theatre, musicals, television, film, commercials and corporate. Members are expected to work 1 day in the office per week when not acting.

Will consider attending performances at venues within Greater London and elsewhere, given at least 2 weeks' notice. Accepts submissions (with CVs and photographs) from actors previously unknown to the company, sent by post or email. Will also accept follow-up telephone calls, showreels, voicereels and invitations to view individual actors' websites. Applicants should not apply if they are unable to provide visible evidence of their work (e.g. performance notice, showcase or showreel). *Commission*: 10-15% depending on job

West Central Management

E4 Panther House, 38 Mount Pleasant, London WC1X 0AN
tel 020-7833 8134 *fax* 020-7833 8134
email mail@westcentralmanagement.co.uk
website www.westcentralmanagement.co.uk

Established in 1984. Co-operative management representing 15-20 actors. Areas of work include theatre, musicals, television, film, commercials and corporate. Members are expected to work 4 days in the office per month.

Will consider attending performances at venues within Greater London with 2 weeks' notice. Accepts submissions (with CVs and photographs) from actors previously unknown to the company, sent by post or email. Will also accept invitations to view individual actors' websites. "We would need to see an applicant's live performance or showreel, but only after an initial meeting/audition." *Commission*: 10%

Being an agent

Howard Roberts

There are a number of unfortunate stereotypes of agents, and – particularly among younger actors – misconceptions about an agent's role. Whilst popular belief would have us all enjoying long lunches between bouts of shark-like behaviour, the truth is somewhat more akin to that of any other hard-working facilitator.

What does an agent do?

There is no definitive job description for an agent; you will find that different agents have different styles, and work in different ways. Broadly speaking, however, we can divide the agent's role into four broad aims, as follows:

• to maintain contacts across the industry, in order to secure work for their clients – most commonly in terms of obtaining casting information;
• to negotiate fees on behalf of those clients, in order to maximise rewards for the artist, and to ensure that those fees are paid;
• to manage the artist's diary in order not to miss the next job opportunity; and
• to advise the artist on their career choices and options.

Bear in mind that your agent is working for you all the time, even when you might not be earning. It is for this reason that you pay them commission for all performing work in which you are engaged whilst they represent you.

When you see agents at showcases and first nights, or when you hear that an agent is coming to your production, remember that this is usually after they have already worked a full day in the office. Attending these events is a key part of their business: it is their opportunity to network, to keep abreast of new developments and new performers, and to maintain good relationships – for example, with a casting director. The job of an agent can be immensely rewarding, but those rewards come as a result of long hours and hard work.

How do I get an agent?

Sadly, anyone can call themselves an agent, because there are no entry restrictions to the profession. In this book, you will find more than 50 pages listing agents: some of them belong to the Personal Managers' Association (PMA), a body that requires members to have at least three years' trading in the industry prior to joining. However, many other established and reputable agents choose not to belong to the PMA. So take advice. Talk to other performers, to casting directors and to established industry advisers like John Colclough, and endeavour to establish a shortlist of suitable contacts.

A phone call or an email may establish whether an agency is currently considering new clients. Don't be too disheartened if they say that their list is full – persevere with other approaches. And do be careful with emailed requests: many agents now find themselves inundated with email traffic from actors seeking representation, and could choose not to respond.

If an agency asks you to send in your details, check what they require: this will usually be a current CV, a clear 10x8in head shot and a covering letter. See if they want a DVD showreel, or a CD voicereel, but be careful of sending these unsolicited. I would suggest that you always send a correctly stamped and addressed envelope with your submission, as this will make it easier for the agent to respond.

The CV should contain your relevant professional experience, details of where you trained, and any other marketable skill(s) you may possess (for example, a clean driving licence, sports at which you are proficient, languages you might speak, musical instruments you can play, whether you can safely ride a horse, and anything else that might add to your performance).

Photographs should be clear and as up to date as possible. Remember, on the Spotlight site your photo will appear slightly smaller than a passport photo, so you want the best possible definition, at the smallest size. You are in an image-led profession, and your picture is likely to be the first point of contact. Always go to a professional photographer, but be careful of spending too much money on photos until you have an agent; chances are, they might want something different. And always put your contact details on the back of your photo; in a busy office it can get separated from your letter and CV.

Keep your letter businesslike: check to whom you are writing, date the letter and spell their name correctly. Finally, ensure that you use the correct postage: it will not improve your chances if the agent has to pay a surcharge on your letter. Of course, the agent might be happy to receive an emailed submission, using your Spotlight PIN number to access your details. Always ensure that your Spotlight entry is up to date with your correct playing age, latest credits and full list of marketable skills.

Interviews

Turn up on time – never late, but not too early either. Check where you are going in advance so that you don't arrive flustered. You are going to see a busy person, who may be in a position to help your career, so treat the meeting seriously. If you fail to attend at the agreed time, they may think that you will treat castings in a similar manner.

Before 'the day', have your questions ready and prepared in your mind. How long have you been established? How many agents work here? How many clients do you represent? What are your commission rates? (It is unusual for these to be higher than 15% – and be very wary of any agency who would charge you for enrolment.) Are you VAT registered? (If so, remember that this means you will be paying VAT on top of your commission.) Where would you fit in with this agency, and would you clash with any of their existing clients?

This is all information that you need to glean – but at interview, do be careful *how* you ask your questions. Some agents might be more reticent than others; you will need to carefully judge the mood and tone of the meeting. The agent might want to make it clear that they are interviewing you, and not the other way round. Remember, agents will vary in their style and way of working: you must be sensitive and able to adapt.

Offers of representation

Agencies come in all shapes and sizes. Larger, well-established West End concerns certainly have the attraction of the star names they represent, and if they offer you a place it could work for you. They will have the first look at film scripts, and the international cachet. However, what are sometimes referred to as the 'boutique agencies' might also be advantageous: with them, you are likely to have direct access to the principal partners, and you are more likely to be important to them. Smaller agencies have the motivation to secure as much work as possible for their clients, for as much time as possible. They will not want 'passengers'.

If you do get an offer, or offers, of representation, take time to think about it, and *always* seek advice. This is an important decision. Remember that you are entering into a business relationship, not looking for a new best friend. Of course, the best sort of actor to be is a working actor, and so the agency that works best for you is the one that helps you to keep working, irrespective of its size and location or how long it has been established.

Contracts

A contract should place your business relationship on a professional basis, clearly stating not just commission rates, but also such important issues as the required notice period for terminating your agreement. Don't be afraid of being contractually committed, but neither should you ever sign a contract on the spot. Take it away and get a second opinion, be it from another performer, from Equity, or from someone with specialist knowledge.

Problems?

How often do agents hear actors complain that their agent never puts them up for anything – or that they are not seen, even though they are ideal for a part? The harsh reality is that it is a buyer's market. You face vast amounts of competition for every job, and despite your agent's best efforts, the casting director still might not want to see you.

If you really do feel that the actor-agent relationship is not working, the first person you should talk to is your agent! Try to work out if there has been any misunderstanding about your skills, or playing age, or photo; often such issues can easily be resolved by honest discussion.

If there are irreconcilable differences, then try hard to part amicably. It's a small profession, and agents do talk to one another. Attempt to secure new representation before you move, but first check any obligations you have to your existing agent in terms of period of notice, or ongoing work, or work for which you have been submitted.

And finally ...

Always try and work with your agent. Establish how proactive they want you to be. If there are areas of work you do not wish to pursue, make sure that you let your agent know. Always ensure that you keep your agent fully aware of your availability – weekends and holidays included.

Remember: actors face huge amounts of competition, and it is the agent's job to improve the odds in a client's favour. It is a very tough profession, and experience often indicates that you have to work very hard just to be lucky.

Howard Roberts MSc is a partner in Sandra Griffin Management Ltd. He has been an actors' agent for more than 20 years, initially as an assistant and then as a co-director. Prior to this he was a lecturer in Economics and Politics in Further Education. He lives in West London.

CPMA: the Co-operative Personal Management Association

Almost all actors' co-operative agencies belong to the Co-operative Personal Management Association (CPMA), which was created in 2002 to promote co-op agencies in the profession, encourage the highest professional standards, and represent the interests of co-op agencies to outside bodies, such as Equity and Government departments.

Actors represented by co-operative agencies run the agency themselves, through a democratic structure, and work as unpaid agents for each other. Some co-ops employ a co-ordinator or administrator (who is not an actor). Co-op agencies are non-profit-making, and any surplus funds are put back into the business. Co-op agencies began in the UK in 1970, since when many more have been established and thrive. Co-ops access the same casting information as conventional agents and suggest actors for jobs, negotiate contracts and fees, take commission on jobs, and recommend and promote their clients to casting directors (CDs) and others. There is often a fee to join a co-op, which is refunded when you leave. Other, non-refundable, fees may be charged, and there could also be a voluntary monthly levy to cover office costs, co-ordinator's fees, etc. Co-op members work in the office (typically two to four times a month), attend business meetings (usually monthly) to discuss aspects of running the agency, oversee the work of other co-op members (often with CDs), and consider the work of applicants.

Belonging to a co-op has many advantages: ·

- You quickly learn how the industry works, which can be very useful for newcomers and those returning to the profession.
- You are in contact with many industry professionals, which could help you get work.
- You are supported by other actors in the agency, some of who will have a lot of experience.
- You know which jobs you have been suggested for, and can monitor them.
- You have more influence over how you are represented, and can be more pro-active in your career.
- You can say which type of work you will or won't do, without fear of being asked to leave the agency.
- Usually, more than one person decides whom to suggest for a job. Many CDs acknowledge that co-ops often know their clients much better, and can sell them with honesty and confidence.
- Co-ops have smaller lists of clients, tend to avoid clashes, and commission rates are lower.

However, you should be aware that there can be drawbacks to being part of a co-op. As with conventional agents, standards vary; a co-op is only as good and professional as its members. Can you be sure that other members are working as hard for you, as you are for them? Continuity can also be a problem, with so many people involved. Although co-ops with a co-ordinator may have an advantage in this respect, measures such as detailed note-taking and not changing negotiators on a contract still need to be taken. And CDs tend to send breakdowns for major TV and film roles to the top agencies in the industry – although other parts will be sent to good co-ops.

To join a co-op you need to be a good agent (not just a good actor), committed, reliable and keen to support fellow actors. You must be able to use a computer and learn the software the agency uses. You must be prepared to get on the phone, talk to CDs, and sell your clients with knowledge and conviction, making intelligent and credible suggestions for roles. Consider, too, your personal commitments, such as doing non-acting jobs to earn money, and expenses, such as travel to and from the office, and joining/training fees.

If you are thinking of applying to a co-op, first ask if applications are being considered – and if so, how they should be submitted. Many co-ops, like conventional agents, do not accept email applications. Check CVs and photos on the agency's website to identify potential gaps. Send your photograph and CV, saying why a co-op agency interests you, and stressing skills and any contacts you have which could be useful. Co-ops usually want to see an applicant's work, so send a showreel or details of the show you're in (they tend not to go to drama school shows or showcases, unless someone has expressed interest).

To find out more about the agency, talk to current and former members. You might want to know when the agency was established; if any ex-members have returned; the extent of their contacts with CDs and with theatres; the range of casting information they receive; and whether they belong to the CPMA, which has a code of conduct (Equity particularly welcomed the creation of the CPMA for this reason). If the co-op is interested in your application, you will be interviewed by all available members. If offered a place, you will usually have a three- to six-month trial period. After discussion to see how both sides feel, you may then be offered full membership.

Please visit **www.cpma.coop** for further information.

Voice-over agents

This section lists agencies that specialise in voice-overs. Check the details of how each wishes to be approached, and refer to the 'Showreel, Voicereel and Website Services' section for more about getting a voicereel (or 'voice demo') made. Some of the larger conventional agencies have their own voice-over departments – generally for their existing clients only.

Accent Bank

420 Falcon Wharf, 34 Lombard Road,
London SW11 3RF
tel 020-7223 5160
email enquiries@accentbank.co.uk
website www.accentbank.co.uk
Director Lisa Paterson

Areas of work include television, film, commercials, audio books, radio, corporate and training material. 3 agents represent more than 200 clients. Has in-house facilities to produce voicereels for clients and other actors. See the website for current rates.

Accepts submissions from actors previously unknown to the agency. Will also accept submissions sent via email. Voicereels and invitations to view individual actors' websites are also accepted. Follow-up calls are welcome. Will consider representing disabled actors. *Commission*: 15%

Ad Voice

Oxford House, 76 Oxford Street, London W1D 1BS
tel 020-7323 2345 *fax* 020-7323 0101
email info@advoice.co.uk
website www.advoice.co.uk
Key personnel Susan Barritt

1 agent represents clients working in television and radio commercials, documentaries, corporate, animations and audiobook recordings. Submission via **info@advoice.co.uk**

Calypso Voices

27 Poland Street, London W1F 8QN
tel 020-7734 6415 *fax* 020-7437 0410
email calypso@calypsovoices.com
website www.calypsovoices.com
Manager Jane Savage

2 agents represent 80 clients for voice-over work. Areas of work include television and radio commercials, documentaries, animation, corporate, audio books and on-air promotions.

Conway Van Gelder Grant

Third Floor, 8-12 Broadwick Street,
London W1F 8HW
tel 020-7287 1070 *fax* 020-7287 1940
email voices@conwayvg.co.uk
website www.conwayvangeldergrant.com
Agents Kate Pulmpton, Hayley Ori, Neil McNulty

Areas of work include animated film, commercials, documentary, audio books, gaming and camapigns. *Commission*: 15%

Earache Voices

177 Wardour Street, London W1F 8WX
tel 020-7287 2291 *fax* 020-7287 2288
email enquiries@earachevoices.com
website www.earachevoices.com
Agent Alex Lynch-White

Provides voice-overs for commercials, documentaries, audio books and animation.

Accepts voicereels via email only. *Commission*: 15%

Foreign Versions

tel 0333 123 2001
email info@foreignversions.co.uk
website www.foreignversions.com
Directors Margaret Davies, Anne Geary *Project Manager* Bérangère Capelle

Foreign Versions works with advertising agencies for foreign markets, corporate clients, companies producing audio guides, and film and television companies.

As the agency specialises in foreign languages, all voices must be mother-tongue speakers. Voice samples should be sent on MP3 (or similar) via email, together with a CV.

Hamilton Hodell Ltd

20 Golden Square, London W1F 9JL
tel 020-7636 1221 *fax* 020-7636 1226
email info@hamiltonhodell.co.uk
website www.hamiltonhodell.co.uk
Head of Voice and Commercials Louise Donald

Main areas of work are television, film, commercials and audio books. 1 agent in the Voice department and 4 in the Acting department represent around 124 clients in total.

Welcomes letters (with CVs) from individual actors previously unknown to the agency, sent by post only. Will accept follow-up telephone calls, unsolicited voicereels, and invitations to view individual actors' websites. Currently represents, or plans to represent, actors with disabilities. *Commission*: 15%

Hobson's Voices

2 Duke's Gate, Chiswick, London W4 5DX
tel 020-8995 3628 *fax* 020-8996 5350

email voices@hobsons-international.com
website www.hobsons-international.com
Managing Director Donna Lampton *Company Co-ordinator* Sue Horrix

6 agents represent 160 artists. Welcomes submissions for representation *by email only*. MP3 files to **submissions@hobsons-international.com**.

iCan Talk Ltd

tel (01858) 466749
email hello@icantalk.co.uk
website www.icantalk.co.uk
Key contact Katie Matthews

Established in 2009. Voice-over agency.

Inter Voice Over

72 Charlotte Street, London W1T 4QQ
tel 020-7262 6937
email info@intervoiceover.com
website www.intervoiceover.com
Casting Director Liliane Goudriaan

Established in 1998. Main areas of work are voice-over, voice acting, television, film, commercials and corporate videos. Welcomes voice demos by email to **casting@intervoiceover.com**. Does not currently represent actors with disabilities.

Lip Service

60-66 Wardour Street, London W1F 0TA
tel 020-7734 3393 *fax* 020-7734 3373
email bookings@lipservice.co.uk
Managing Director Alex Mactavish

4 agents solely represent over 100 clients and a number of foreign clients. Areas of work include television, film, commercials and audio books.

Accepts submissions (with CVs and voicereels) from individual actors previously unknown to the company, sent by email or post. Please enclose an sae for their return.

Kate Moon Management

PO Box 648, Harrington, Northampton NN6 9XT
Voice-Overs & Corporate Television Agent Kate Moon (*Director*)

Areas of work include television, commercials and audio books.

Accepts submissions (with CVs and voicereels) from individual actors (experienced only) previously unknown to the company, if sent by email.

Rabbit Vocal Management Ltd

94 Strand on the Green, London W4 3NN
tel 020-7287 6466 *fax* 020-7287 6566
email info@rabbitvocalmanagement.co.uk
website www.rabbitvocalmanagement.co.uk
Managing Director Rebecca Fuller *Senior Agent* Tania Bruce *Junior Agent* Amy Howell; *Agent's Assistant* Sophie Marsh.

Representing 200 artists. Covers all areas of voice work including TV and radio, commercial, documentaries, audio books, promos and continuity, and animation.

Accepts submissions (with CVs) from actors previously unknown to the agency if sent by email but not by post. Invitations to view individual actors' websites are also accepted. Represents disabled actors.

Red 24 Voices

The Hospital Club, 3rd Floor, 24 Endell Street, London WC2H 9HQ
tel 020-7559 3611
email info@red24management.com
website www.red24management.com
Managing Director Paul Weedon

Main areas of work are television, commercials and radio. 2 agents represent around 50 clients. Recommends the company The Showreel for the production of voicereels.

Welcomes letters (with CVs) from individual actors previously unknown to the agency, sent by post or email. Will accept unsolicited voicereels and invitations to view individual actors' websites. Currently represents, or plans to represent, actors with disabilities. *Commission*: 20%

Rhubarb Voices

1st Floor, 1A Devonshire Road, Chiswick, London W4 2EU
tel 020-8742 8683 *fax* 020-8742 8693
email enquiries@rhubarbvoices.co.uk
website www.RhubarbVoices.co.uk
Key personnel Johnny Garcia

Leading UK voice talent agency with experience casting voices into all platforms of the spoken word, including commercials, continuity & promos, corporate pieces, animation, games, ADR/lip-synch and more. Represents around 90 exclusive UK and North American artists, and more than 100 foreign-language artists.

Actors seeking representation should email their CV (including any voice-over work to date), a photo and an MP3 showreel. Please note that the agency prefers not to receive follow-up calls.

Shining Management Ltd

81 Oxford Street, London W1D 2EU
tel 020-7734 1981 *fax* 020-7734 2528
Director Clair Daintree *Key personnel* Jennifer Taylor

2 agents represent 55 clients. Areas of work include voice-overs for television, film, commercials and audio books.

Accepts submissions (with CVs and voicereels) from individual actors previously unknown to the company if sent by post. Include an sae for the return of submissions. "Please do not ring with submission enquiries." *Commission*: 15%

Talking Heads
Argyll House, All Saints Passage, London SW18 1EP
tel 020-7292 7575
email voices@talkingheadsvoices.com
website www.talkingheadsvoices.com

Areas of work include commercials, television, film, animation, corporate videos, audio books and foreign voices.

Accepts submissions (with CVs and voicereels) by email or post. Invitations to view websites are also accepted. *Commission*: 15%

Sue Terry Voices Ltd
4th Floor, 35 Great Marlborough Street,
London W1F 7JF
tel 020-7434 2040 *fax* 020-7434 2042
email sue@sueterryvoices.co.uk
website www.sueterryvoices.co.uk
Managing Director Sue Terry

3 agents represent around 200 actors working in voice-overs only. Does not welcome unsolicited approaches by actors unknown to the company. *Commission*: 15%

Tongue & Groove
PO Box 173, Manchester M19 0AR
tel 0161-228 2469 *fax* 0161-249 3666
email info@tongueandgroove.co.uk
website www.tongueandgroove.co.uk
Producers Bev Ashworth, John Basham

2 agents represent 50 clients. Areas of work include voice-overs for television, commercials and audio books.

Accepts submissions (with CVs and voicereels) from individual actors previously unknown to the company if sent by post. Also accepts voicereels and invitations to view individual actors' websites.

Vocal Point
131 Great Titchfield Street, London W1W 5BB
tel 020-7419 0700 *fax* 020-7419 0699
email enquiries@vocalpoint.net
website www.vocalpoint.net
Agent Ben Romer Lee

Areas of work include television, commercials and audio books. 2 agents represent approximately 85 clients.

Accepts submissions from actors previously unknown to the company. Invitations to view individual actors' websites are also accepted. Follow-up calls are not welcomed. *Commission*: 15%

Voice Shop
First Floor, 1A Devonshire Road, London W4 2EU
tel 020-8742 7077 *fax* 020-8742 7011
email info@voice-shop.co.uk
website www.voice-shop.co.uk
Key contact Maxine Wiltshire

3 agents represent 42 clients working in television, film, commercials and audio-book recording.

Welcomes emails with MP3 audio samples from new actors, but prefers not to receive follow-up telephone calls or voicereels. All audio samples should contain appropriate material, and be professionally produced. *Commission*: 15%

Voice Squad
76 Park Avenue North, London NW10 1JY
tel 020-8450 4451
email voices@voicesquad.com
website www.voicesquad.com
Director Neil Conrich

2 agents represent more than 70 clients. Areas of work include television, film, commercials and audio books.

Accepts submissions (with CVs and voicereels) from individual actors previously unknown to the company if sent by post. *Commission*: 15%

VoiceBank Ltd
PO Box 825, Altrincham, Cheshire WA15 5HH
tel 0161-973 8879
email elinors@voicebankltd.co.uk
website www.voicebankltd.co.uk
Director Elinor Stanton

Works in all areas: musicals, television, film, commercials, audio books and radio. Represents 42 clients.

Welcomes unsolicited voicereels and invitations to view individual actors' websites. Does not currently represent any actors with disabilities, but "this would not be a barrier to joining the company".

Voicebank, The Irish Voice-Over Agency
35 Thomastown Rd, Dun Laoghaire, Co. Dublin
tel +353 1 235 0838
email info@voicebank.ie
website www.voicebank.ie
Company Manager/Owner Deborah Pearce

Voicebank are a voice-over agency only and represent actors, comedians and presenters for all aspects of voice work. Main areas of work include musicals, television, film, commercials, audio books and radio. 3 agents represent more than 120 clients.

Welcomes letters (with CVs and photographs) from individual actors previously unknown to the agency, sent by post only. Accepts unsolicited voicereels and invitations to view individual actors' websites. Voice-over demos of no longer than 2 minutes should be submitted on MP3 to info@voicebank.ie. Currently represents, or plans to represent, actors with disabilites. *Commission*: Varies

The Voiceover Gallery
First Floor, 1 Ridgefield, 16-18 King Street,
Manchester M2 6EG

tel 0161-881 8844 *fax* 0161-881 8951
email manchester@thevoicegallery.co.uk
12 Cock Lane, London EC1A 9BU
tel 020-7987 0951
email london@thevoiceovergallery.co.uk
website www.thevoicegallery.co.uk
London: *Managing Director* Marylou Thistleton-Smith *Voice Agent* Martyna Szmytkowsk; Manchester: *Head of Production* Kathryn Fox *Voice Agent* Hannah Ralph

Areas of work include corporate, documentary, new media, television and radio advertising. 3 agents represent 60 English voices and multiple foreign voices.

For all representation enquiries and instructions for submissions to the agency, visit the 'Our Services' section of the website, and click on 'Artist Services'. *Commission*: 15%

VSI (Voice & Script International)

Aradco House, 132 Cleveland Street, London W1T 6AB
tel 020-7692 7700 *fax* 020-7692 7711
email info@vsi.tv
website www.vsi.tv
Head of Voice-Over Department Jose Alonso/Isobel George *Voice-Over Project Managers* Laura Caines, Lyndsey Warren, Martyna Komorowska, Ellen De Venter, Aleksandra Kulicka, Giulia Parker, Rebecca Ormshaw, Maria Perdiki *Key contact* Jose Alonso

6 voice-over agents represent approx. 1500 foreign-language voice-over clients. Areas of work include voice-overs for television, film, corporate and commercials.

Accepts submissions (with CVs) from individual actors and presenters previously unknown to the company, sent by post or email (**voices@vsi.tv**). Also accepts voicereels and invitations to view individual actors' websites. "We only use mother-tongue foreign-language speakers."

Suzy Wootton Voices

72 Towcester Road, Far Cotton, Northampton NN4 8LQ
tel (01604) 765872 *mobile* (07970) 263991
email suzy@suzywoottonvoices.com
website www.suzywoottonvoices.com

1 agent represents 46 clients. Areas of work include television, film, commercials and audio books.

Accepts submissions via email only, and invitations to view individual actors' websites. *Commission*: 15%

Yakety Yak All Mouth Ltd

56 Broadwick Street, London W1 7AJ
tel 020-7430 2600 *fax* 020-7404 6109
email info@yaketyyak.co.uk
website www.yaketyyak.co.uk
Proprietor Jolie Williams

3 agents represent 177 clients. Areas of work include voice-overs for television, film, commercials, animation and audio books.

Books are currently closed, but submissions can be sent to **submissions@yaketyyak.co.uk** in MP3 format. *Commission*: 15%

Presenters' agents

James Grant Media

94 Strand on the Green, London W4 3NN
tel 020-8742 4950 *fax* 020-8742 4951
website www.jamesgrant.co.uk

5 agents represent 21 presenter clients; also represents television presenters and stage actors.

Welcomes letters (with CVs and showreels) from individuals previously unknown to the agency, sent by post or email.

Jeremy Hicks Associates Ltd

3 Stedham Place, London WC1A 1HU
email info@jeremyhicks.com
website www.jeremyhicks.com
Agents Jeremy Hicks, Sarah Dalkin *Agents' Assistant* Charlotte Leaper *Assistant* Julie Dalkin

2 agents represent presenters, writers and chefs.

Welcomes letters (with CVs and showreels) from individuals, and emails. *Commission*: 15% (10% for scriptwriters)

Red 24 Management

First Floor, Kingsway House, 103 Kingsway, London WC2B 6QX
tel 020-7559 3611
email info@red24management.com
website www.red24management.com
Managing Director Paul Weedon

Welcomes letters (with CVs and showreels) from individual presenters previously unknown to the company, sent by post or email, and accepts invitations to view individuals' websites.

Sandra Singer Associates

21 Cotswold Road, Westcliff on Sea, Essex SS0 8AA
tel (01702) 331616
email sandrasingeruk@aol.com
website www.sandrasinger.com

2 agents represent approximately 40 main clients. "We are a specialist boutique agency representing some of the best talent in the UK for Acting and Musical Theatre." Also a leading Young Performers agency. Email requests in the first instance regarding representation. *Commission*: 10% Stage; 20% Screen

Triple A Media

30 Great Portland Street, London W1W 8QU
tel 020-7637 5839
email info@tripleamedia.com
website www.tripleamedia.com
Owner/Agent Andy Hipkiss *Agent* James Hancock

Established in 2007. Areas of work include television, radio and corporate. Also represents a number of other media professionals, including DJs, presenters and experts. Member of the Personal Managers Association (PMA).

Accepts submissions by email (with CVs and photographs), and welcomes showreels. Happy to represent actors with disabilities.

Jo Wander Management

110 Gloucester Avenue, London NW1 8HX
tel 020-7209 3777 *fax* 020-7209 3770
email jo@jowandermanagement.com
website www.jowandermanagement.com
Managing Director Jo Wander

1 agent represents 15-20 presenter clients.

Welcomes letters (with CVs and showreels) from individual presenters previously unknown to the agency, sent by post or email; will accept invitations to view individuals' websites.

Casting directors

Essentially, casting directors take on the 'nitty-gritty' work involved in the casting process – it is usually the director, and sometimes the producer, who actually 'directs' the casting decisions. The crucial thing to remember is that each one is employed – by someone else. Some casting directors are employed on a full-time basis; a significant number work freelance and can be as concerned about where their next job is coming from as you are. Therefore, if one gets you to meet their director-employer, it is important that you live up to that casting director's expectations: carefully absorb any brief that s/he gives you. If you suddenly decide to take a radically different approach, s/he will be put into a difficult position with that director-employer.

Fundamental to the job of being a casting director is a wide knowledge of all kinds of actors. Therefore a good one will have seen as many productions as possible. Like squirrels storing nuts for the winter, they keep extensive notes and are continually adding to their collections of actor-profiles. An empathetic, intuitive and imaginative casting director has immeasurable value to both actors and director.

You should approach casting directors in much the same way as you would agents: however, it's even more important that there's something they can see you in. It's also important to remember that they are more project-oriented than talent-oriented. In other words, whilst an agent is looking for talent to add to their client list, a casting director is usually concentrating on specific talent for a specific project. Research what the casting director is currently casting, and target them accordingly. You can keep reasonably up to date with the activities of some casting directors by looking at the website of the Casting Directors Guild (CDG) – **www.thecdg.co.uk**.

Jo Adamson-Parker

mobile (07787) 870211
email jo@northerndrama.co.uk

Main areas of work are theatre, television and film. Casting credits include: *The Bill*, *Chucklevision*, *Red Riding*, and theatre for Hull Truck, Pilot Theatre Company.

Will consider attending performances at venues in Greater London and elsewhere given 1-2 weeks' notice. Accepts submissions (with CVs and photographs) from actors previously unknown to the casting director sent by email. Will also accept showreels – preferably an emailable link. "I am eager to arrange general meetings with actors."

Pippa Ailion CDG

Unit 67B, Eurolink Business Centre, 49 Effra Road, London SW2 1BZ
tel 020-7738 7556
Pippa Ailion, Jim Arnold, Natalie Gallacher

Main areas of work are theatre and musicals. Current West End/tours: *Bend it Like Beckham*, *Gypsy*, *Sunny Afternoon*, *Memphis*, *Charlie and the Chocolate Factory*, *The Book of Mormon*,*Wicked*, *Billy Elliot*,*The Lion King*, *Top Hat*, *The Rise and Fall of Little Voice*. Recent other work includes: *Here Lies Love* (Dorfman); *The Pajama Game* (Shaftesbury); *We Will Rock You* (Dominion); *From Here to Eternity* (Stratford East and UK tour); *Legally Blonde* (Savoy); *Fela* (NT, Broadway and US tour); *The Fairy Queen* (Glyndebourne, Paris, New York); *Million Dollar Quartet*, *Waiting for Godot*, *Decade*, *Spring Awakening*, *Marguerite*, *The Drowsy Chaperone*, *Porgy and Bess*, and *Blue Man Group*. For Chichester: *Gypsy*, *Guys and Dolls*, *Kiss Me Kate* (and Old Vic); *Sweeney Todd* (and Adelphi); *The Pajama Game* (and Shaftesbury); *Love Story* (and Duchess); *The Magistrate* (and Savoy); *Misalliance*, *Suzanna Andler*, *Song of Singapore* (and Mayfair Theatre). For Regent's Park: *Porgy and Bess*, *The Sound of Music*, *Ragtime*, *A Midsummer Night's Dream*, *Into the Woods*, *Lord of the Flies* (and UK tour), *The Importance of Being Earnest*. Future theatre: *Guys and Dolls*, *Dreamgirls*, *Motown*, *The Wind in the Willows* (West End).

Will consider attending performances at venues in Greater London and occasionally elsewhere (such as Chichester or Stratford) given 2-3 weeks' notice. Accepts submissions (with CVs and photographs) from actors previously unknown to the casting director if sent by post. Does not welcome email enquiries.

Dorothy Andrew Casting

Kings Cottage, 409 Kings Road, Ashton-Under-Lyne, Lancashire OL6 9EX
tel 0161-344 2709
email dorothyandrewcasting@gmail.com

Casts mainly for television, film and commercials. Recent credits include: *Hollyoaks*, *Grange Hill* and *Court Room*.

Will accept postal submissions (with CVs and photographs) from actors previously unknown to the company, but unsolicited emails and showreels are not welcomed. "When writing, make your letter short and to the point. Always include a photograph (10x8in b&w) and a CV. Only send in a showreel if requested."

Ashton Hinkinson Casting

Unit 15, Panther House, 38 Mount Pleasant, London WC1X 0AN
tel 020-7580 6101
email casting@ahcasting.com
website www.ashtonhinkinson.com
Casting Directors Emma Ashton, Debs Hinkinson

Areas of work include television, film and commercials. Recent credits include: *Brother* (commercial for Bacon, Copenhagen); *Galaxy* (commercial for RSA, London); *Hostel 1 & 2* (for International Production Co.).

Will consider attending performances in Greater London with at least 1 week's notice. Invitations to showcases are also welcomed. Accepts submissions (with CVs and photographs) from actors previously unknown to the company; invitations to view individual actors' websites are also accepted.

Amy Ball

See the entry for the Royal Court Theatre under *Producing theatres* on page 143.

Derek Barnes CDG

BBC Drama Series Casting, BBC Elstree, Room N221, Neptune House, Clarendon Road, Borehamwood WD6 1JF
tel 020-8228 7096 *fax* 020-8228 8311
email derek.barnes@bbc.co.uk

Main areas of work are film and television. Casting credits include: *Casualty*, *Holby City*, *Doctors* (BBC Drama Series) and *Down To Earth* (Series 5, BBC).

See also the entry for BBC (Drama Production) under *BBC network television* on page 305.

Lesley Beastall Casting

41E Elgin Crescent, London W11 2JD
tel 020-7727 6496
email lesley@lbcasting.co.uk
Casting Director Lesley Beastall

Works in commercials. Recent credits include: *Sunshine* (ITV1); *Built with You in Mind* (Thompson's Holidays); and voice-overs for The Natural Confectionary Company.

Does not welcome performance notices or unsolicited submissions by actors previously unknown to the company, but will accept invitations to view individual actors' websites. Any such approach should be made by email only.

Lauren Beauchamp Casting

34A Brightside, Billericay, Essex CM12 0LJ
mobile (07961) 982198
email laurenbeauchamp@talktalk.net
Head Casting Director Lauren Beauchamp *Assistant Casting Director* Dee Atkins

Main areas of work are theatre, television, film and commercials. Recent casting credits include: *Itch* (short film; Director, Antony Gallagher for Itchka Productions); and *Bacon Sandwich* (theatre; Director, Emily North for Interact Productions).

Will consider attending performances within the Greater London and Essex areas, given at least 2 weeks' notice. Welcomes unsolicited CVs and photographs, sent by email only. Accepts showreels and invitations to view individual actors' websites.

Rowland Beckley

See the entry for BBC (Drama Production) under *BBC network television* on page 305.

Charlotte Bevan

See the entry for the National Theatre under *Producing theatres* on page 139.

Lucy Bevan CDG

Ealing Studios, Ealing Green, London W5 5EP
tel 020-8567 6655
email lucy@lucybevan.com

Main areas of work are film and television. Credits include: *An Education* (BBC films), *Pirates of the Caribbean: On Stranger Tides* (Walt Disney Pictures), *300: Rise of an Empire* (Warner Bros.) and *Quartet* (Headline Pictures).

BBC Drama Series Casting

See the entry for BBC (Drama Production) under *BBC network television* on page 305.

Sarah Bird CDG

PO Box 32658, London W14 0XA
tel 020-7371 3248 *fax* 020-7602 8601
email sarah@sarahbird.com

Casts for film, television, theatre and commercials. Casting credits include: *You Don't Have To Say You Love Me*, directed by Simon Shore (Samuelson Productions); *Ladies in Lavender*, directed by Charles Dance (Scala Productions); *Fortysomething* (Carlton

TV); and *Calico*, directed by Edward Hall (Sonia Friedman Productions).

Siobhan Bracke CDG

Basement Flat, 22A The Barons, St Margaret's, Middlesex TW1 2AP

Main area of work is theatre. Theatre credits include: Head of Casting for the RSC (1986-91); Shakespeare's Globe for Mark Rylance; Lyric Hammersmith for Neil Bartlett; Hampstead Theatre for Tony Clark/ Lucy Bailey; Cheek By Jowl for Declan Donnellan; Chichester – *Nicholas Nickelby* for Philip Franks; *I Am Shakespeare* for Mark Rylance; *When We Are Married* for Ian Brown, West Yorkshire Playhouse. Television credits include: *A Doll's House* and *Measure for Measure* for David Thacker; *Buddha of Suburbia* and *Persuasion* for Roger Michell.

Will consider attending performances at venues in Greater London and occasionally elsewhere, given as much notice as possible (preferably 4-5 weeks). Accepts submissions (with CVs and photographs) from actors previously unknown to the casting director if sent by post. Does not welcome email enquiries.

Candid Casting

2G Woodstock Studios, 36 Woodstock Grove, London W12 8LE
tel 020-7490 8882
email mail@candidcasting.co.uk
Casting Director Amanda Tabak CDG *Assistant* Jennifer Smith

Main areas of work are television, film and commercials. Casting credits include: *Kidulthood*, *Britain's Got the Pop Factor*, and *MI High*.

Will consider attending performances at venues in central London given at least 2 weeks' notice. Accepts submissions (with CVs, photographs and showreel) from actors previously unknown to the casting director if sent by email to **mail@candidcasting.co.uk**. Does not welcome post enquiries without an sae, or invitations to view individual actors' websites.

John Cannon CDG

BBC Elstree, (Rm N208) Neptune House, Clarendon Road, Borehamwood WD6 1JF
tel 020-8228 7122
email john.cannon@bbc.co.uk

Currently Casting Director for *Holby City*.

Other recent television credits include: *Mr Stink*, *Gangsta Granny*, *The Boy in the Dress*, *Big School*, *WPC 56*, *32 Brinkburn Street*, *The Coroner* and *Father Brown* – all BBC. Was Resident Casting Director for the Royal Shakespeare Company. Recent theatre credits include: *See How They Run* (tour, W/E); *Hedda Gabler* (WYP/Liverpool Playhouse); and *Yellowman* (tour for Liverpool Everyman).

Welcomes performance notices with at least 2 weeks' notice. Also happy to receive letters and emails (with CVs and photographs) from actors, as well as invitations to view individual actors' websites or online showreels.

See also the entry for BBC (Drama Production) under *BBC network television* on page 305.

Cannon Dudley & Associates

43A Belsize Square, London NW3 4HN
tel 020-7433 3393 *fax* 020-7813 2048
email cdacasting@blueyonder.co.uk
Casting Director Carol Dudley CDG, CSA *Casting Associate* Helena Palmer

Main areas of work are film, theatre and television. Recent credits include: *The Third Mother – Mother of Tears* (Director: Dario Argento); *Master Harold and the Boys* (Director: Lonny Price); and theatre productions for Hampstead, Edinburgh and the West End.

Will consider attending performances at venues in Greater London given as much notice as possible. Accepts submissions (with CVs and photographs) from actors previously unknown to the casting director if sent by post. Does not welcome email enquiries. CVs which are not submitted for specific projects or with reference to current shows or television performances cannot be kept for future reference. Telephone enquiries about current casting projects or progress of mailed submissions are not welcomed.

Anji Carroll CDG

email anji@anjicarroll.tv

Main areas of work are theatre, television, film and radio. Casting Associate for the New Vic Theatre, casting all in-house shows. Recent theatre castings include: *The Borrowers*, *Around The World In 80 Days*, *Inherit The Wind*, *The 101 Dalmatians*, *A Christmas Carol*, *The Widowing of Mrs. Holroyd*, *A Fine Bright Day Today*, *Far From The Madding Crowd*, *Where Have I Been All My Life*, *The Glass Menagerie*, *Proof* and *The Admirable Crichton*. Other theatre credits include 2 seasons for the Bristol Old Vic, various productions at the Northcott, *The Thrill Of Love* (St James Theatre); *Judgement Day* (The Print Room) and *Precious Little Talent* (Trafalgar Studios).

Recent feature film castings include: *Papadopoulos & Sons*, *West is West*, *Mrs Ratcliffe's Revolution*, *Out of Depth*, and *The Jolly Boys' Last Stand*.

Recent television castings include: *Titanic: Flesh & Steel vs Nature*, comedy drama series *The Cup* (for BBC 2); *The Bill* (over 50 episodes); *The Sarah Jane Adventures: Invasion of the Bane*, 32 episodes of *London's Burning*, four 90-minute episodes of *The Knock* and *Coming Up*.

Radio castings include: BBC 4's political drama series *Number Ten*.

The Casting Angels (London and Paris)

Suite 4, 14 College Road, Bromley BR1 3NS
fax 020-8313 0443
Director Michael Ange
Key personnel Michael *(Big Decisions)*, Gabriel *(Announcements)*, Raphael, Uriel *(The Daily Grind)*, Lucifer *(Special Consultant)*

Main areas of work are television, musicals, film and commercials with "casting across the board". Casts for the UK and other countries within Europe.

Will consider attending performances at venues in Greater London and elsewhere, given as much notice as possible. Accepts showreels.

Casting Couch Productions Ltd

213 Trowbridge Road, Bradford-on-Avon, Wiltshire BA15 1EU
mobile (07932) 785807
email moira@everymansland.com
Casting Director/Producer Moira Townsend

Moira Townsend is currently producing children's shows but is still available for casting. Main areas of work are television, film and commercials. Casting credits include: *Who Killed Tutankhamen?* (documentary) and advertisements including British Airways, Curry's Electrical Stores, Heal's, Sugar Puffs, DVLA and Lunn Poly. Producers, please call for Bristol/Bath-based castings.

Will consider attending performances at venues in Greater London and elsewhere (especially Bath/ Bristol area), given 2-3 weeks' notice. Accepts submissions from actors previously unknown to the casting director if sent by email. Actors will only receive a response if the casting director is able to attend a performance.

Suzy Catliff CDG

tel 020-8442 0749
email soosecat@mac.com

Casts mainly for television, film and theatre. Co-author of *The Casting Handbook* published by Routledge. Most recent credits include: for television, all UK casting on *The Murdoch Mysteries* (Series 1-9); UK casting on *Primeval New World* and final two series of *Primeval UK* (ITV); *Silent Witness* (Series IX & X); *Blitz* (Channel 4); *D-Day* (BBC 1); *Sir Gadabout* (ITV); *Casualty* (3 series); *Ny-Lon* (associate). For film: *A Bunch of Amateurs, Stormbreaker, The Swimming Pool, Sense and Sensibility*, and *The English Patient* (associate).

Urvashi Chand CDG

Cinecraft, 69 Teignmouth Road, London NW2 4EA
tel 020-8208 3861
email urvashi@chandcasting.com
website www.chandcasting.com

Main area of work is film. Recent credits include: *Daylight Robbery* (directed by Barry Leonti), and *Red Mercury* (directed by Roy Battersby).

Will consider attending performances within the Greater London area and elsewhere with at least 2 weeks' notice. Accepts submissions (with CVs and photographs) from actors previously unknown to the agency, by email. Showreels, voicereels and invitations to view individual actors' websites are also accepted.

Charkham Casting

Suite 361, 14 Tottenham Court Road, London W1T 1JY
tel 020-7927 8335 *fax* 020-7927 8336
email charkhamcasting@btconnect.com
Casting Directors Beth Charkham, Gary Ford

Areas of work include theatre, musicals, television, film and commercials. Recent credits include: *Charlie and the Chocolate Factory, Silent Witness* and *The Bill.*

Andrea Clark Casting

tel 020-7381 9933
email andrea@aclarkcasting.com
website www.aclarkcasting.com
Casting Director Andrea Clark

Works mainly in film, television and commercials.

Accepts showreels, links and invitations to view individual actors' websites or links to view Spotlight, Casting Call Pro or IMDb pages. Emails with multiple or very large attachments cannot be viewed. "When an actor has an agent, I prefer contact to be made via the agent."

Sam Claypole

PO Box 123, Darlington DL3 7WA
email contact@samclaypolecasting.com
website www.samclaypolecasting.com
Casting Director Sam Claypole

Established in 2005. Works in film, TV and commercials. Recent credits include: *Scintilla, Harrigan, Almost Married*, and *In Our Name* (all Feature Films).

Welcomes letters (with CVs and photographs), showreels, invitations to view actors' websites, and performance notices.

Ben Cogan

See the entry for BBC (Drama Production) under *BBC network television* on page 305.

Jayne Collins

The Price Building, 110 York Road, London SW11 3RD
tel 020-7223 0471 *fax* 020-7240 5323
email info@jaynecollinscasting.com
website www.jaynecollinscasting.com

Areas of work include theatre, musicals, television, film and commercials.

Will consider attending performances within the Greater London area and elsewhere, given at least 1 week's notice. Accepts submissions (with CVs and photographs) from actors previously unknown to the company if sent by post, but not by email. Welcomes showreels.

Alistair Coomer

See the entry for the Donmar Warehouse under *Producing theatres* on page 135.

Lin Cordoray

66 Cardross Street, London W6 0DR

Main areas of work are television and commercials.

Will consider attending performances at venues in Greater London. Accepts submissions (with CVs and photographs) from actors previously unknown to the casting director if sent by post. Does not welcome email enquiries.

Irene Cotton Casting

25 Druce Road, Dulwich Village, London SE21 7DW
tel 020-8299 1595 *fax* 020-8299 2787
email irenecotton@btinternet.com
Director Irene Cotton CDG

Recent credits include: *Americus* (RAI Feature); *The Little Mermaid* (Feature); *Done 4 Jobs Dinner* (Malcrazo Films); *The Little Black Book* (Park Theatre); Dirty Dancing (Aldwych Theatre and tour), *Long Lonely Walk* (film), *Why We Went To War* (Channel 4), *The Bill* (ITV); *The Countess* (Criterion Theatre, London); *Panorama* (BBC); and *Caffe Latte* commercial (Home Productions). Welcomes performance notices as far in advance as possible, and is prepared to travel to performances within Greater London. Does not welcome any other unsolicited form of approach, including CVs, photographs, showreels or invitations to view individual actors' websites. Advises actors to make contact only to inform the casting director "when their work can be seen – TV, film or stage".

Margaret Crawford

92 Castelnau, London SW13 9EU

Casts mainly for television. Casting credits include: *Bad Girls* (Series 2-8); *Footballers' Wives* (Series 1-5); *Footballers' Wives Extra Time* (Series 1 & 2); *Waterloo Road* (Series 1) and *Bombshell* (Series 1).

Will consider attending performances at venues in Greater London and occasionally elsewhere, given as much notice as possible. Accepts submissions (with CVs and photographs) from actors previously unknown to the casting director if sent by post. Does not welcome email enquiries. Also accepts showreels, voicereels and invitations to view individual actors' websites.

Kahleen Crawford Casting CDG

Film City Glasgow, Govan Town Hall,
401 Govan Road, Glasgow G51 2QJ
tel 0141-4251 725
email casting@kahleencrawford.com
website www.kahleencrawford.com
Casting Directors Kahleen Crawford, Danny Jackson and Caroline Stewart

Main areas of work include film, TV and commercials. Recent productions include: *Jimmy's Hall* (dir. Ken Loach); *Under the Skin* (dir. Jonathan Glazer) and *45 Years* (dir. Andrew Haigh).

Welcomes CVs and photographs from actors previously unknown to the casting director (of a reasonable file size), if sent by email. Happy to receive invitations to view productions in London, Glasgow and the surrounding areas, provided 1 week's notice is given. Also accepts links to online showreels, but please bear in mind that receipt may not be acknowledged. Only grants a general interview in special circumstances.

Crocodile Casting

9 Ashley Close, Hendon, London NW4 1PH
tel 020-8203 7009 *fax* 020-8203 7711
email croccast@aol.com
website www.crocodilecasting.com
Casting Directors Tracie Saban, Claire Toeman

Established in 1996 with the aim of constantly accessing new faces and fresh talent. The company casts mainly for commercials, pop videos and corporate work; sometimes holds general auditions to meet new actors and models.

Gary Davy CDG

Top Floor, 15 Crinan Street, York Way,
London N1 9SQ
tel 020-7713 0888
email casting@garydavy.com

Casts for film and television. Casting credits include: Steve McQueen's Cannes/BAFTA-winning *Hunger*; Nick Love's *The Business* and *The Sweeney*; *Revengers Tragedy* (dir. Alex Cox); Nick Cave's *The Proposition* (dir. John Hillcoat); *44 Inch Chest*; and the upcoming Helen Mirren film *Woman in Gold*, directed by Simon Curtis. Television credits include: *Strike Back* (HBO Cinemax/SKY); *Death Comes to Pemberley* (BBC); *Fleming: The Man Who Would be Bond* (SKY Atlantic/BBC America); Jed Mecurio's *Critical* (early 2015) and UK Casting on *Band of Brothers*.

Stephanie Dawes

13 Nevern Square, London SW5 9NW
tel (07802) 566642
email stephaniedawes5@gmail.com

Works in television and voice-over. Recent credits include: *Blue Murder*, *Stockwell*, and *Britannia High* (all ITV1).

Gabrielle Dawes CDG

PO Box 52493, London NW3 9DZ
tel 020-7435 3645

email gdawescasting@tiscali.co.uk

Gabrielle Dawes is Associate for Casting at Chichester Festival Theatre, and a freelance Casting Director. See also the entry for Chichester Festival Theatre under *Producing theatres* on page 134.

Theatre includes: *The Norman Conquests, All About My Mother, New Voices 24-Hour Plays* (Old Vic); *Cat on a Hot Tin Roof, Three Days of Rain, Treasure Island* (West End); Rupert Goold's *Macbeth* (Chichester/West End/Broadway); *Wallenstein, The Grapes of Wrath, Separate Tables, Hay Fever, Aristo, Funny Girl, The Circle, Taking Sides/Collaboration* (and West End); *Hobson's Choice, The Waltz of the Toreadors, Twelfth Night* (all Chichester); *The English Game* (Headlong Theatre); *The Elephant Man* (Sheffield); *As You Like It* (Watford).

As Deputy Head of Casting at the National Theatre 2000-2006, award-winning productions included *Caroline, or Change*; *His Dark Materials*; *Elmina's Kitchen*; *The Pillowman* and *Coram Boy*.

Television credits include: Harold Pinter's *Celebration* and *Elmina's Kitchen* by Kwame Kwei-Armah. Films include *Perdie* (BAFTA award for Best Short Film) and *The Suicide Club*.

Kate Day CDG

Pound Cottage, 27 The Green South, Warborough, Oxfordshire OX10 7DR

Main areas of work are television, film and commercials.

Will consider attending performances at venues in Greater London and occasionally elsewhere, given as much notice as possible. Accepts submissions (with CVs and photographs) from actors previously unknown to the casting director if sent by post. Does not welcome email enquiries.

Paul De Freitas

16 Wimpole Mews, London W1G 8PE
tel 020-7486 5407 *fax* 020-7486 1817
email info@pauldefreitas.com
website www.pauldefreitas.com

Main areas of work are film, television and commercials. Casting credits include: *Dog Boy* (BBC2); *Lazarus & Dingwall* (BBC2); *Bernard & The Genie* (Talkback/Attaboy); *The Princess Academy* (Weintraub Productions); and *What Larry Says* (Platypus Productions).

The Denman Casting Agency

Burgess House, Main Street, Farnsfield, Notts NG22 8EF
Key personnel Jack Denman FEAA

Main areas of work are theatre, musicals, television, film and commercials. Casting credits include: *Peak Practice, Doctors*, and *Crimewatch* (television); and videos for PC World and Boots. Awarded Preferred Agents status by the BBC for supporting artists and walk-ons.

Accepts submissions (with CVs and photographs) from actors previously unknown to the casting director if sent by post. Does not welcome email enquiries. No short film enquiries.

Malcom Drury CDG

34 Tabor Road, London W6 0BW
tel 020-8748 9232

Casts mainly for television. Casting credits include: *The Bill, Heartbeat, The Beiderbecke Affair* and Laurence Olivier's *King Lear*.

Carol Dudley CDG, CSA

See entry for Cannon Dudley & Associates.

Julia Duff CDG

First Floor, 11 Goodwins Court, London WC2N 4LL
tel 020-7863 5557
email julia@juliaduff.co.uk

Casts mainly for television. Casting credits include: *New Tricks, Hotel Babylon, Secret Diary of a Call Girl, Persuasion, Monarch of the Glen*, and *The Amazing Mrs Pritchard*.

Maureen Duff CDG

PO Box 47340, London NW3 4TY
tel 020-7586 0532 *fax* 020-7681 7172
email info@maureenduffcasting.com

Main areas of work are film, television and theatre. Credits include: *Closing The Ring* (Richard Attenborough); *The History of Mr Polly* (Granada Media); *Poirot* (several episodes for Granada Media); and *Dancing At Lughnasa* (and several other productions for the Northcott Theatre, Exeter).

Jennifer Duffy CDG

11 Portsea Mews, London W2 2BN
tel 020-7262 3326
email casting@jennyduffy.co.uk

Main areas of work are film and television. Credits include: *Life 'n' Lyrics* (Fiesta Productions, BBC Films, Universal); *Wallace & Gromit: The Curse of the Wererabbit* (Aardman/Dreamworks); *Macbeth* (BBC) and *Dunkirk* (BBC2, Huw Wheldon BAFTA Award 2005).

Irene East Casting CDG

40 Brookwood Avenue, Barnes, London SW13 0LR
tel 020-8876 5686 *fax* 020-8876 5686
email IrnEast@aol.com

Main areas of work are theatre and film. Casting Director for Love and Madness Productions. Theatre credits include: Rising Tides/High Tides Festival, *Bunny's Vendetta* (Derry); *Aristocrats* (Letterkenny); *Richard III* (Riverside and Tower of London); *Fool for Love, Macbeth, Ajax* (dir. Jack Shepherd); *A Skull in Connemara, The Tempest, The Playboy of the Western World*. Features include: *Begin* (Jack Shepherd); *A*

Distant Mirage (Harbajan Verdi); *A Small Dot on the Landscape* (Alice D. Cooper).

Will attend performances at venues in Greater London and occasionally elsewhere, given a couple of days' notice. Please, no showreels unless requested.

EJ Casting

PO Box 63617, London W9 1AN
tel 020-7564 2688 *mobile* (07891) 632946
email info@ejcasting.com
Director Edward James

Casts for theatre, musicals, film, commercials and corporate work. Casting credits include: *Into the Woods* and *Sweet Charity* (theatre); commercials for AOL, Lloyds Bank, Sony BMG, Universal Music, and Cadbury's Fingers; and *Air on a G String* (film).

Will consider attending performances at venues in Greater London and occasionally elsewhere. Accepts showreels containing work that has been broadcast. Due to the overwhelming number of CVs sent, is unable to accept general enquiries. "Please only send an application if it is a performance notice or in response to a specific breakdown."

ET Casting Ltd.

2 Sterne Street, London W12 8AD
tel 020-3010 3030
email emily@etcasting.com
website www.etcasting.com
Casting Director Emily Tilelli *Casting Assistant* Ana Friere De Andrade

Established in 2011. Main areas of work are commercials, television series, feature films and corporate videos. Recent credits include: *Nina Forever* (feature film); *Dead Folk* (feature film), *Open Wounds* (TV film); and *Metamorphosis Titian 2012* (Short Film). Will consider attending performances in the Greater London area, with a minimum of 3 weeks' notice.

Welcomes CVs and photographs sent by email, showreels and voice tapes, and invitations to view individual actors' websites.

Richard Evans CDG

10 Shirley Road, London W4 1DD
tel 020-8994 6304
email richard@evanscasting.co.uk
website www.evanscasting.co.uk and www.auditionsthecompleteguide.com

Main areas of work are theatre, musicals, television, film and commercials. Casting credits include: *The Rat Pack – Live From Las Vegas* (theatre).

Will consider attending performances at venues in Greater London and occasionally elsewhere, given sufficient notice. Requests 1-2 weeks before the opening night for theatre productions, and 2-3 days prior to transmission for television shows. Accepts follow-up telephone calls after a production has opened. Welcomes submissions (with CVs and photographs) from actors previously unknown to the casting director if sent by post, and email enquiries with links to Spotlight page, online showreel, etc. (but no large attachments).

Advises actors to: "Be specific, find out what people cast and their current projects, suggesting yourself for particular roles whenever possible. When inviting casting personnel to see your work, always ensure that the part you are playing is worth them coming to see, and offer complimentary tickets. Unless a part is very specific or hard to cast, we usually only invite artists in to audition whose work we have seen or have met, as this enables us to speak honestly and accurately about them to the creative teams with whom we are working. It is worth keeping in touch when you have something to say as your career progresses especially if you have met or know someone."

Fawn Casting Ltd

86-90 Paul Street, London EC2A 4NE
mobile (07766) 501553
email andrew@fawncasting.com
website www.fawncasting.com
Owner/Casting Director Andrew Fawn

Established in 2012. Main areas of work are television, film, commercials, corporate, voice-over and shorts. Recent credits include: *The Craftsman*, *The Watcher Self*, and *Drive-Thru*. Will consider attending performances in Greater London/Brighton given a minimum of 1-2 days' notice – 2 weeks preferred.

Bunny Fildes Casting CDG

56-60 Wigmore Street, London W1U 2RZ
tel 020-7935 1254 *fax* 020-7298 1871

Casts mainly for theatre, television, film and commercials.

Will consider attending performances within Greater London given 2 weeks' notice. Accepts postal submissions (with CVs and photographs) from actors previously unknown to the company. Unsolicited emails and showreels, however, are not welcomed.

Sally Fincher CDG

tel 020-8347 5945
email sallyfincher@btinternet.com

Main area of work is television. Credits include: *Murder In Suburbia*, *Sweet Medicine*, *Barbara*, *Kiss Me Kate*, *Outside Edge* and *The Upper Hand*.

Fruitcake London

Studio 125, 77 Beak Street, London W1F 9DB
tel 020-7993 5165
email casting@fruitcakelondon.com
Casting Directors Thomas Adams, Andrew Mann

Casts mainly for TV commercials and digital media. Casting credits in 2012 include: commercials for San

Miguel, Vauxhall, Sky TV, M&S and Nike; and pop promos for Chase & Status, Paulina Rubio and Ayumi Hamasaki.

Will consider attending performances at venues in Greater London given 2 weeks' notice. Accepts submissions (with CVs and photographs) from actors previously unknown to the casting directors if sent by post. Does not welcome email enquiries.

Caroline Funnell

25 Rattray Road, London SW2 1AZ
tel 020-7326 4417

Areas of work include theatre and musicals. Will consider attending performances within the Greater London area with at least 2 weeks' notice.

Artistic Director of Sixteenfeet Productions (25 Rattray Road, London SW2 1AZ, info@sixteenfeet.co.uk).

Martin Gibbons Casting

Manchester
mobile (07976) 912776
email info@martingibbons.com
website www.martingibbons.com
Casting Director Martin Gibbons

Established in 2011. Main areas of work are film, television, commercials, theatre, music videos, corporate and voice-over. Recent credits include: Beady Eye (Music Video), Co-operative Food Campaign, and National Lottery. Will consider attending performances in any area.

Welcomes CVs and photographs sent by email, as well as showreels and voice tapes.

Tracey Gillham CDG

tel 01932-562 112
email tracey@traceygillhamcasting.co.uk
email michelle@traceygillhamcasting.co.uk
Associate Casting Director Michelle Cavanagh

Main areas of work are film and television. For recent credits, please see Spotlight or the CDG website.

Nina Gold CDG

117 Chevening Road, London NW6 6DU
tel 020-8960 6099 *fax* 020-8968 6777
email info@ninagold.co.uk

Main areas of work are film, television and commercials. Casting credits include: *Vera Drake*, directed by Mike Leigh (Thin Man Films); *The Life and Death of Peter Sellers*, directed by Stephen Hopkins; *The Jacket*, directed by John Maybury (Warner Bros); *Daniel Deronda*, directed by Tom Hooper (BBC TV); *Amazing Grace* and *Rome* both directed by Michael Apted; *Starter for Ten* directed by Tom Vaughan; *The Illusionist* directed by Neil Burger; and *Brothers of the Head* directed by Keith Fulton and Louis Pepe.

Miranda Gooch

102 Leighton Gardens, London NW10 3RP

Casts mainly for feature films. Recent credits have included: *True Story* and *Tooth*.

Will consider attending performances within Greater London given as much notice as possible. Accepts submissions (with CVs and photographs) from actors previously unknown to the company, sent by post or email. Showreels are also accepted.

Jill Green CDG

Jill Green Casting, Wellington House, 1st Floor, 125 Strand, London WC2R 0AP
tel 020-7632 4747

Casts for theatre and musicals. Casting credits include: *Kinky Boots* (Adelphi Theatre); *Beautiful - The Carole King Musical* (Aldwych Theatre); *War Horse* (New London Theatre); *The Curious Incident of the Dog in the Night-time* (Gielgud Theatre); *Jersey Boys* (Piccadilly Theatre and UK tour); *The Lion King* International Tour 2014-15; *The Scottsboro Boys* (Garrick and Young Vic Theatres); *I Can't Sing!* (London Palladium); *Rock of Ages* (Garrick and Shaftesbury Theatres and UK tour); *Finding Neverland* (Leicester Curve); *The Producers* (Drury Lane Theatre); *Contact* (Queens Theatre); and *Beyond the Sea* (co-casting credit, film directed by Kevin Spacey).

Will consider attending performances within Greater London and occasionally elsewhere, given a minimum of 4 weeks' notice. Accepts email submissions (with Spotlight links, CVs and photographs attached) from actors who are currently appearing in a production, but does not welcome blanket mailings, unsolicited emails or showreels (unless an sae is enclosed for their return).

David Grindrod CDG

4th Floor, Palace Theatre, Shaftesbury Avenue, London W1D 5AY
tel 020-7437 2506 *fax* 020-7437 2507
email dga@grindrodcasting.co.uk

Casts for musicals and films. Film credits: Dance casting *Nine*, Ensemble casting *Mamma Mia!* and *The Phantom of the Opera*. West End casting: *Chicago*, *Mamma Mia!*, *Ghost*, *Hairspray*, *Love Never Dies*, *Sister Act*.

Will consider attending performances within Greater London and possibly elsewhere, given as much notice as possible. Does not welcome unsolicited submissions from actors. Casting breakdowns are released via Spotlight, therefore actors should only write in with reference to specific productions. See also David's article *Casting for musical theatre* on page 123.

Angela Grosvenor CDG

66 Woodland Road, London SE19 1PA
tel 020-8244 5665
email angela.grosvenor@virgin.net

Established in 1990. Main areas of work include TV and film. Recent credits include: The *Tractate Middoth*, *Topsy and Tim* and *The Cafe*.

Welcomes invitations to productions to view actors for consideration, and casting interviews can be arranged dependent on the situation.

Janet Hall

3 Shaw Road, Littleborough, Oldham OL15 9LG

Main areas of work include television, film and commercials. Casting credits include: AXA commercial, and *The Sound of Music* (theatre).

Will consider attending performances at venues in Greater London and in Manchester, Liverpool and Leeds, given 1 week's notice. Accepts submissions (with CVs and photographs) from actors previously unknown to the casting director, sent by post or email. Also accepts showreels, voicereels and invitations to view individual actors' websites.

Louis Hammond CDG

tel 020-7610 1579
email louis@louishammond.co.uk

Main areas of work are theatre, television and film. Casting credits include: Theatre – *Creditors* (Young Vic); *Romeo and Juliet* (Sheffield Crucible); *The Funfair* (HOME Manchester); *Violence and Son, Who Cares, Fireworks* (Casting Associate at the Roysl Court); *Romeo and Juliet* (HOME, Manchester); *Amadeus* (Chichester Festival Theatre); *The History Boys* (Sheffield Crucible); *The Winter's Tale* (Open Air Theatre, Regents Park); *Driving Miss Daisy* (UK); *Rough Cuts/International Residencies* (Royal Court); *The Resistible Rise of Arturo Ui* (Liverpool/Nottingham); *Batman Live* (World Arena Tour); *All My Sons* (Leicester Curve); *The Member of the Wedding, Dirty Butterfly, The Indian Wants the Bronx* (Young Vic); *The Importance of Being Earnest* (West End); *Testing the Echo, Loot* (Tricycle); *Rock 'n' Roll* (Royal Court/West End). Film – *Mirrormask* and *Arsene Lupin*. TV – *The Bill* (Head of Casting).

Hammond Cox Casting

Units 115 & 116 Panther House, 38 Mount Pleasant, London WC1X 0AN
tel 020-7278 4713
email office@hammondcoxcasting.com
website www.hammondcoxcasting.com
Casting Directors Michael Cox, Thom Hammond

Established in 2012. Works in film, commercials, music video and theatre. Recent credits include: Beady Eye (Music Video); Robinsons (Commercial) and *Flight of the Pompodour* (Short Film).

Gemma Hancock CDG

North Lodge, Weald Chase, Staplefield Road, Cuckfield, West Sussex RH17 5HY
email gemma@hancockstevenson.com
website www.hancockstevenson.com

Main areas of work are theatre, television and film.

Judi Hayfield CDG / Judi Hayfield Ltd

6 Richmond Hill Road, Gatley, Cheshire SK8 1QG
mobile (07919) 221873
email judi.hayfield@hotmail.com

Former Head of Casting for Granada.

HB Casting

tel 020-7871 2969 *mobile* (07957) 114175
email hannah@hbcasting.com
Casting Director Hannah Birkett

Winners of 'Best Casting' at the Film Craft Cristal 2014 Awards and twice at the British Arrow Awards. Areas of work include television, film, commercials, idents, pop promos, voice-overs. Recent credits include work for Nespresso, Nike and Tango.

Will consider attending performances with 1 week's notice via email. Accepts CVs and photographs via email.

Polly Hootkins Casting CDG

tel 020-7692 1184 *mobile* (07545) 784294
email phootkins@clara.net
website www.thecdg.co.uk
Key personnel Polly Hootkins

Prefers all submissions (CVs, photographs, showreels, etc.) via email.

Juliet Horsley

See the entry for the National Theatre under *Producing theatres* on page 139.

Hubbard Casting

14 Rathbone Place, London W1T 1HT
tel 020-7631 4944 *fax* 020-7636 7117
email email@hubbardcasting.com
Casting Directors John Hubbard, Ros Hubbard, Dan Hubbard, Amy Hubbard *Casting Associates* Gemma Sykes, Martin Ware

Casts mainly for film and television. Casting credits include: *Dracula Year Zero, The Hobbit: The Desolation of Smaug*, and *Downton Abbey 4*.

Accepts letters (with CVs and photographs) from actors previously unknown to the agency, sent by post.

Sue Jackson

53 Moseley Wood Walk, Leeds LS16 7HQ

Freelance casting director.

Trevor Jackson CDG

1 Bedford Square, London WC1B 3RA
tel 020-7637 8866 *fax* 020-7436 2683

Casts mainly for musicals produced by Cameron Mackintosh Ltd. Casting credits include: *My Fair Lady, Les Miserables, Miss Saigon, Phantom of the Opera, Mary Poppins, Avenue Q* and *Oliver!*

Will consider attending performances at venues in Greater London given as much notice as possible. Accepts submissions (with CVs and photographs) from actors previously unknown to the casting director if sent by post, but does not welcome email enquiries. Showreels, voicereels and invitations to view individual actors' websites are also accepted.

Janis Jaffa Casting

London W12
email janis@janisjaffacasting.co.uk

Works mainly in television, film and commercials.

Will consider attending performances within Greater London. Welcomes emails (with CVs and photographs attached) from individual actors previously unknown to the agency. Will accept showreels and invitations to view individual actors' websites by email.

Jennifer Jaffrey

136 Hicks Avenue, Greenford, Middlesex UB6 8HB
mobile (07973) 617168
email jennifer.jaffrey@gmail.com
Key personnel Jennifer Jaffrey *(Proprietor)*

Main areas of work are theatre, musicals, television, film and commercials. Casting credits include: *Cross My Heart*, *Ten Minutes Older* and *Such a Long Journey*.

Will consider attending performances at venues in Greater London given as much notice as possible. Accepts submissions (with CVs and photographs) from actors previously unknown to the casting director if sent by post, but does not welcome email enquiries. Photographs should have the actor's name written on the back, and an sae must be included for the return of material. Showreels should only be sent on request.

Matilda James

See the entry for Shakespeare's Globe under *Producing theatres* on page 144.

Lucy Jenkins (Jenkins McShane Casting)

74 High Street, Hampton Wick,
Kingston on Thames KT1 4DQ
tel 020-8943 5328 *fax* 020-8977 0466
email lucy@jenkinsmcshanecasting.com

Casts mainly for film, television, theatre and commercials. Casting credits include: *Babyfather* (BBC); *The Bill* (television); *Top Dog* (short film) and *Emma* (theatre).

Rebecca Jenner

All enquiries via email
email casting@rebeccajenner.com
website www.rebeccajenner.com
Casting Director Rebecca Jenner

Established in 2011. Main areas of work are theatre, TV and film. Recent credits include: (as Casting Director) *JB Shorts* (Manchester); *The Seagull* (Library Theatre); *Wanted! Robin Hood* (Library Theatre).

Will consider attending performances within Greater London and in Manchester/the North West, given at least 1 week's notice. Accepts CVs and photographs sent by email only.

Marilyn Johnson CDG

11 Goodwin's Court, London WC2N 4LL
tel 020-7497 5552 *fax* 020-7497 5530
email casting@marilynjohnsoncasting.com

Main area of work is television. Credits include: *Our Mutual Friend*, *Holding On*, *Murphy's Law*, *Nature Boy* and *Inspector Morse*.

Sam Jones CDG

Flat 3, 56 Trinity Church Square, London SE1 4HT
tel 020-7378 0222 *mobile* (07941) 960998
email samjonescasting@btconnect.com

Previously Head of Casting for the RSC, Sam has just cast the first two award-winning years for the newly formed National Theatre Wales. Her extensive theatre credits include work for Peter Hall, Stephen Berkoff, Kneehigh, Shared Experience, Told By An Idiot, The Opera Group, Lyric Hammersmith, Hampstead Theatre, the Almeida, The Royal Court, Young Vic, Sheffield Crucible and the West Yorkshire Playhouse among others. Her West End work includes: *Another Country*, *Journey's End*, *Dinner*, *A Day in the Death of Joe Egg*, *Up for Grabs!*, *After Mrs Rochester*, *The Children's Hour*, *Betrayal* and *Old Times*. Her recent television work includes: *Love and Marriage*, several series of *Trial and Retribution*, *The Commander* and *Above Suspicion* all for ITV, and the BAFTA award-winning *Occupation*, *Lennon Naked* and *Prisoners' Wives* for the BBC. Recent film work includes: *Resistance*, *Jadoo*, *The Father* and *Panda Eyes*.

Sue Jones CDG

24 Nicoll Road, London NW10 9AB
tel 020-8838 5153 *fax* 020-8838 1130
email sue@suejones.net

Main areas of work are film, television, theatre and commercials. Casting credits include: *The Virgin of Liverpool*, starring Ricky Tomlinson and Imelda Staunton (MOB Films); *The Sound of Thunder*, with Ed Burns, Ben Kingsley and Catherine McCormack; *The Origins of Evil* (CBS/Alliance Atlantis); *Messiah* and *Coriolanus* (both plays directed by Stephen Berkoff); *The Vicar* (BBC television); and *The Politician's Wife* (Channel 4).

Kate and Lou Casting

The Basement, Museum House, 25 Museum Street, London WC1A 1JT
mobile (07976) 252531
website www.kateandloucasting.com

Casts for commercials. Recent credits include: Tilda Rice, McDonalds, Lotto, and Doritos.

Does not welcome performance notices. Will accept letters (with CVs and photographs) from individual actors previously unknown to the company, and unsolicited CVs and photographs, sent via email. Does not welcome showreels or invitations to view individual actors' websites.

Anna Kennedy Casting

8 Rydal Road, London SW16 1QN
email anna@kennedycasting.com
website www.annakennedycasting.com

Welcomes performance notices, for productions within the Greater London area, with 2 weeks' notice. Will accept letters, but not emails, with CVs and photographs from individuals previously unknown to the casting director; also welcomes showreels and invitations to view actors' websites.

Beverley Keogh

29 Ardwick Green North, Ardwick,
Manchester M12 6DL
tel 0161-273 4400 *fax* 0161-273 4401
email beverley@beverleykeogh.tv

Main areas of work are television, film and commercials. Casting credits include: *The Village, In The Flesh, Last Tango in Halifax, Scott & Bailey* and *The Mill.*

Accepts submissions (with CVs and photographs) from actors previously unknown to the casting director, sent by post or email.

Belinda King Creative Productions

Casting Department, BK Studios,
157 Clarence Avenue, Northamptonshire NN2 6NY
01604 720041
email casting@belindaking.com
website www.belindaking.com
*Casting Director*Camilla King

Producers of shows at sea for luxury cruise brands including Seabourn and Holland America Line. International casting with auditions worldwide including London, New York, Sydney, Moscow, Kiev.

Primary casting requirements: West-End calibre singers and classically-trained dancers.

Jerry Knight-Smith CDG

Royal Exchange Theatre, Manchester M2 7DH
tel 0161-615 6761
website www.royalexchangecasting.co.uk

Resident Casting Director for the Royal Exchange Theatre, Manchester. See entry under *Producing theatres* on page 143 for further details.

Suzy Korel CDG

mobile 07973 506793
email suzy@korel.org

Will consider attending performances at venues in Greater London given as much notice as possible. Accepts submissions (with CVs and photographs) from actors previously unknown to the casting director, and invitations to view individual actors' sebsites are also accepted via email.

Karen Lindsay-Stewart CDG

PO Box 2301, London W1A 1PT
email asst@klscasting.co.uk

Main areas of work are television and film. Casting credits include: *Sylvia, Harry Potter and the Chamber of Secrets,* and *Cambridge Spies.*

Will consider attending performances at venues in Greater London with sufficient notice. Accepts submissions (with CVs and photographs) from actors previously unknown to the casting director if sent by post, but does not welcome email enquiries. Do not send sae(s) for replies.

Kay Magson Casting

PO Box 175, Pudsey, Leeds LS28 7LN
tel (0113) 236 0251
email kay.magson@btinternet.com
Casting Director Kay Magson

Recent credits include *Bollywood Jane, Twelfth Night, Alice in Wonderland, Duchess of Malfi* (West Yorkshire Playhouse); national tours of *Singin' In the Rain, Aspects of Love, Round the Horne...Revisited* and *Dracula, Noises Off, Billy Liar, The Flint Street Nativity, The Electric Hills* (Liverpool); *A Model Girl* (Greenwich); *One Last Card Trick, Aladdin* (Watford); *Merrily We Roll Along, Importance of Being Earnest, As You Like It* (Derby); *The Way of the World, Follies* (Northampton); *East Is East* (York/ Bolton); *Rosencrantz & Guildenstern Are Dead, Much Ado About Nothing* (Manchester Library).

Will consider attending performances within the Greater London area and elsewhere, with at least 4 weeks' notice. Accepts submissions (with CVs and photographs) from actors previously unknown to the casting director, via email only.

Lisa Makin

Creative Producer, Chichester Festival Theatre.

See the entry for Chichester Festival Theatre under *Producing theatres* on page 134.

John Manning

4 Holmbury Gardens, Hayes, Middlesex UB3 2LU
tel 020-8573 5463

Works in theatre and musicals. Recent credits include: *The 39 Steps* (Criterion Theatre); *Turandot* (Hampstead) and *An Inspector Calls* (national tour).

Will consider attending performances within the Greater London area, and regularly attends regional theatre – but does request 4 weeks' notice. Welcomes letters (with CVs and photographs) from individual actors previously unknown to the company, sent by post only; will also accept invitations to view individual actors' websites.

Carolyn McLeod

1st Floor, 193 Wardour Street, London W1F 8ZF
mobile (07946) 476425

email info@cmcasting.co.uk
website www.cmcasting.co.uk

Main areas of work are film and television. Recent feature projects include: *High Strung, The Dying of the Light* with Nicolas Cage, *Walking with the Enemy* with Ben Kingsley, *The Liability* with Tim Roth and Jack O'Connell, *The Magnificent Eleven, Payback Season, The Woman in Black* and psychological thriller *Truth Or Die,* along with numerous projects for the SyFy Channel, Hallmark and BBC projects currently in development including: *Inferno, Burning Road, Mr Smith* and *War Wolf.*

Given sufficient notice will consider attending performances at venues in and around Greater London. Will accept emailed broadcast or show notifications, also emailed submissions from actors previously unknown to the casting director. Showreels, voicereels and invitations to view individual actors' websites are also accepted.

Chrissie McMurrich

16 Spring Vale Avenue, Brentford, Middlesex TW8 9QH

Main areas of work are theatre and television. Recent casting includes: the tour of *Scooby Doo and the Pirate Ghost Live on Stage*; the Ludlow Festival/Exeter Northcott Theatre production of *Romeo and Juliet*; *Original Sin, The Blue Room, A Christmas Carol* and *Cyrano de Bergerac* for the Haymarket Basingstoke; and the tour of *Thomas the Tank Engine and Friends.*

Will consider attending performances at venues in Greater London given 2 weeks' notice. Accepts submissions with performance notices (containing photos and CVs) from actors previously unknown to the casting director if sent by post. No unsolicited emails are accepted. "Please be aware of the new postage rates for A4 envelopes. Not everyone will pay the Royal Mail handling charge to get unsolicited photos and CVs."

Anne McNulty CDG

email mcnultyassistant@gmail.com

Former Resident Casting Director for Donmar Warehouse. Now working as a freelance casting director, mainly in theatre. See Anne's article on page 121 for advice on casting for the stage.

Sooki McShane (Jenkins McShane Casting)

8A Piermont Road, East Dulwich, London SE22 0LN
tel 020-8693 7411 *fax* 020-8693 7411
email sooki@jenkinsmcshanecasting.com

Works mainly in theatre, film and television. Casting credits include: *Rainbow Room* (Granada television); *My Brother Rob* (feature film); and casting for the Warehouse Theatre Croydon.

Currently Resident Casting Director for the Nottingham Playhouse. See entry under *Producing theatres* on page 132 for further details.

Thea Meulenberg Casting

Keizersgracht 116, 1015 CV, Amsterdam
tel (31) 2 0626 5846
email info@theameulenberg.com
website www.theameulenberg.com
website www.kftv.com/thea-meulenberg-casting

Established in 1980. Works in TV, film, commercials, corporate, print and photography. Recent credits include: Grolsch for Worldwide; Job.TV (Swiss); Chocolate, Lease Plan Toyota. Around 3000 actors represented.

Accepts CVs and photographs sent by email (also links to TV commercials – send by email).
Commission: 20%

Hannah Miller

See the entry for the Royal Shakespeare Company under *Producing theatres* on page 143.

Helena Palmer

See the entry for the Royal Shakespeare Company under *Producing theatres* on page 143.

Simone Pereira Hind Casting CDG

Argyll House, 37 Castle Terrace, Edinburgh EH3 2EL
email simonepereirahind@gmail.com
website www.simonepereirahind.com

Established in 1990. Main areas of work are in film and television, with recent credits including *Outlander, Tea Cup Travels* and *Moondogs.*

Will consider attending performances primarily in Edinburgh or Glasgow and sometimes London. Accepts CVs with photographs and showreels via email only. Happy to receive enquiries from actors previously unknown to the casting director, particularly those based in Scotland. The casting director is not always able to respond though may keep details on file for future reference.

Kate Plantin CDG

4 Riverside, Lower Hampton Road,
Sunbury On Thames TW16 5PW
mobile (01932) 782350
email kate@kateplantin.com
website www.kateplantin.com
Key Contact Kate Plantin

Established in 2000. Main areas of work include: theatre, film, television, corporate and commercials. Recent castings include: Theatre: *McQueen* (dir. John Caird); *Sweeney Todd* (dir. Bill Buckhurst) and *Stop* (dir. John Schwab). Film: *We Still Steal the Old Way* (dir. Sacha Bennett); *Index Zero* (dir. Lorenzo Sportiello) and *We Are Tourists* (dir. Oar Pali).

Will consider attending performances at venues outside of London given 3 weeks' notice and 1 weeks' notice if within Greater London. Accepts submissions by email (with CVs and photographs). Also welcomes showreels and invitations to view actors' websites.

Carl Proctor CDG

15B Bury Place, London WC1A 2JB
tel 020-7681 0034 *mobile* (07956) 283340
email carlproctorcasting@gmail.com
website www.carlproctor.com

Casts mainly for film and television. Casting credits include: *Son of God* (Christopher Spencer); *Blood Creek* (Joel Schumacher); *Shadow of the Vampire* (E. Elias Merhige); *The Wedding Date* (Clare Kilner); *Mrs Palfrey at the Claremount* (Dan Ireland) and *Twelfth Night* (Trevor Nunn).

Asks that actors only contact by email. CVs and photographs are no longer kept on file as these details are available on Spotlight Interactive.

Andy Pryor CDG

31-35 Kirby Street, London EC1N 8TE
tel 020-7851 8535 *fax* 020-7836 8299

Casts mainly for film and television. Casting credits include: *Glorious 39* (dir. Stephen Poliakoff); and *Doctor Who* and *Life on Mars* (for BBC Television).

Gennie Radcliffe

tel 0161 952 1000
email gennie.radcliffe@itv.com

Casting Director for *Coronation Street*. See entry for Granada under *Independent television* on page 306 for further details.

Leigh-Ann Regan Casting (LARCA) Ltd

The Old Rectory Coach House, Leckwith Road, Llandough, Penarth, CF64 2LY
mobile (07779) 321954
email leigh-annregan@btconnect.co.uk

Areas of work include television, film, commercials and theatre. Resident casting director at Clwyd Theatr Cymru (see entry under *Producing theatres* on page 134). Recent credits include: 21-part drama series for S4C/Fiction Factory (Ypris); 4 years casting *Caerdydd* for S4C/Fiction Factory.

Will consider attending performances in Greater London and elsewhere with at least 1 week's notice. Accepts submissions (with CVs and photographs) from actors previously unknown to the casting director.

Nadine Rennie

See the entry for the Soho Theatre under *Producing theatres* on page 144.

Simone Reynolds CDG

60 Hebdon Road, London SW17 7NN
email simonemreynolds@gmail.com

Main areas of work are film, television, theatre and commercials. Casting credits include: *The 39 Steps* (Olivier Award for Best Comedy); *The Vicar of Dibley* (TV); *The Politian's Wife*, BAFTA and Emmy Awards (TV); *Love of my Life* (film); *Happily Ever After* (film); *Jack and Sarah* (film); *Shining Through* (film).

Will consider attending performances at venues in Greater London and elsewhere, given as much notice as possible. Accepts postal submissions (with CVs and photographs) from actors previously unknown to the casting director, but does not welcome email enquiries. Advises actors to: "Keep CVs clear (separate out the part from the director and venue) and keep covering submissions brief."

Danielle Roffe Casting

71 Mornington Street, London NW1 7QE
email danielle@danielleroffe.com
website www.danielleroffe.com

Works in film and television. Recent credits include: *The Upside of Anger*, *She's Gone*, and *Holy Cross*.

Welcomes performance notices and is prepared to travel within Greater London. Does not welcome unsolicited CVs, photographs or showreels, but is happy to receive invitations to view individual actors' websites.

Annie Rowe Casting

98 St Alban's Avenue, London W4 5JR
tel 020-8354 2699 *mobile* 07734 809597
email annie@annierowe-casting.co
website www.annierowecasting.com

Established in 2009. Main area of work includes theatre, commercials, corporate, short and feature films, music videos. Most recent work: commercial for Ariel; music video for Clean Cut Kid; *The Father* at Trafalgar Studio 2. Best known for casting *Yellow Face* at the NT Shed; *Father's Day* TV movie starring Ray Winstone and site-specific show *The Hotel* plays.

Happy to receive performance notcies, given 2 weeks' notification. CVs, photographs, showreels, voice tapes and invitations to view actors' websites welcome, preferably by email. Please submit via Spotlight link for a specific job, rather than unsolicited.

Neil Rutherford Casting

mobile (07960) 891911
email neil@neilrutherford.com
website www.neilrutherford.com

A casting director since 2000, working mainly in theatre in the West End and internationally, having been Head of Casting at ATG until 2012 and now freelance.

Welcomes CVs and letters (with photographs), via email. Also happy to receive casting interview enquiries via the same method.

Jane Salberg

86 Stade Street, Hythe, Kent CT21 6DY
tel (01303) 239277
email janesalberg@aol.com

Works in theatre and musicals. Recent credits include: UK Casting Director for Jean Ann Ryan (Cruise Musicals); *Horrid Henry Live and Horrid* (UK tour); and *The Wizard of Oz* (Royal Festival Hall).

Prefers not to receive performance notices or unsolicited submissions, but will consider invitations to view individual actors' websites.

Ginny Schiller CDG

9 Clapton Terrace, London E5 9BW
tel 020-8806 5363
email ginny.schiller@virgin.net

Main area of work is theatre, but has also casted for television, film, radio and commercials. Recent work includes: *Relative Values* (Bath Theatre Royal and Pinter Theatre); *1984* (Headlong, Almeida and Playhouse Theatres); *Twelfth Night* (Liverpool Everyman); *Ghosts* (Rose Theatre, Kingston/ETT tour); 2014 summer season at Bath Theatre Royal and Ustinov Studio seasons 2011-2014.

Accepts links to view actors' CVs and online profile or showreel via email. Welcomes performance notices via email, if given 2 weeks' notice.

Laura Scott CDG

56 Rowena Crescent, London SW11 2PT
tel 020-7978 6336 *fax* 020-7924 1907
email laurascottcasting@mac.com

Main areas of work are film, television, theatre and commercials. Casting credits include: *Bonekickers* (BBC TV); *William and Mary* (Series 1-3, TV); *Trial and Retribution XIV* (TV) and *The Time of Your Life* (TV).

The Searchers

70 Sylvia Court, Cavendish Street, London N1 7PG
email casting@thesearchers.net
website www.thesearchers.net
Directors Wayne Waterson, Ian Sheppard

Casts mainly for television, film and commercials. Recent credits include: commercials for Pepsi, Nike, Kellogg's and Royal Mail. Has worked for directors including Terry Gillingham, Tarsem and Earl Morris.

Will consider attending performances within Greater London given 1 week's notice. Accepts submissions (with CVs, showreels and photographs) from actors previously unknown to the company, but does not welcome unsolicited emails or invitations to view an actor's website.

Select Casting Ltd

PO Box 748, London NW4 1TT
mobile (07956) 131494
email info@selectcasting.co.uk
website www.selectcasting.co.uk
website http://pro.imdb.com/name/nm3052115/
Casting Venetia Suchdev

In 2004 Select Casting Ltd started up as an in-house extras agency for an already established production house. It gained independent status as a casting agency as well as an extras agency in 2007. Select Management was established in 2008 to look after a handful of professional actors, dancers, presenters and models who are registered on Spotlight.

Initially specialising in the Bollywood market it quickly progressed to more regional film productions by film-makers from other regions in the Indian subcontinent. Also offered serives to film-makers from the Middle East and Russia a wider global market, allowing production companies to make one call and fulfil all their requirements for an international cast and grew globally.

Provides line production services and full accounting packages (including tax credits and day-to-day cash flow services etc).

Recent filmography: Bollywood films include: *Bhagam Bhag, Namastey London, Salaam-E-Ishq* and *Patiala House*; Russian films include: *Platon*; Middle Eastern productions include: *El Malik Farourk (King Farouk)*; Hungarian-US productions include: *Magic Boys*; Chinese productions include: *Dual Crisis, Triumph in the Skies II*; British feature films include: *Keith Lemon - The Film* and *Kick*. Has also worked on several music videos, commercials, idents and promos etc. Works in all forms of media - film, TV, online, modelling in print or on stage.

Phil Shaw

Suite 476, 2 Old Brompton Road, South Kensington, London SW7 3DQ
tel 020-8715 8943
email shawcastlond@aol.com

Main areas of work are theatre, television, film and commercials. Casting credits include: *Deckies* (Channel 4 series pilot); *Days in the Trees* (BBC Radio); *Body Story* (BBC doc/drama series); *Romans 12:20* (BAFTA-nominated short); *Winter Fiction* (NFTS); *The Turn of the Screw*; *Billy Liar*; *The Chalk Garden*; *Cock & Bull Story*; *People Are Living There* (theatre - No. 1 Tour, King's Head, Watford Palace); *The Last Post* (film, BAFTA nominated); *Italian Movies* (feature); and currently, *1066-Conqueror* (TV mini-series).

Will consider attending performances at venues in Central London given a minimum of 2 weeks' notice. Accepts postal submissions (with CVs and photographs) from actors previously unknown to the casting director, but does not welcome unsolicited showreels or email enquiries.

Michelle Smith CDG

220 Church Lane, Woodford, Stockport SK7 1PQ
tel 0161-439 6825 *fax* 0161-439 0622
email michelle.smith18@btinternet.com

Main areas of work are film, television and commercials. Casting credits include: *Steel River Blues* (ITV); *Max and Paddy* (Channel 4); *Phoenix Nights* (Channel 4) and *Cold Feet* series 1-5 (Granada).

Suzanne Smith CDG

3rd Floor, 15 Crinan Street, York Way, London N1 9SQ
tel 020-8993 8118 *fax* 020-7436 9690
email zan@dircon.co.uk

Main areas of work are film and television. Credits include: *Dracula* (NBC/Sky); *Black Sails* for Starz; *Band of Brothers* and *The Pacific*. Films include: *Three Musketeers* and *Mariah Mundi*.

Wendy Spon CDG

c/o National Theatre, South Bank, London SE1 9PX
email wspon@nationaltheatre.org.uk

Main areas of work are film, television, theatre and musicals. Until recently, Head of Casting at Talkback Thames (*The Bill*), and now Head of Casting at the National Theatre (see entry under *Producing theatres* on page 139). Casting credits include: *The Graduate* (theatre, directed by Terry Johnson); *Oklahoma* and *Oh What a Lovely War* (both for the National Theatre); and *Shadow Man* (short film).

Emma Stafford

Royal Exchange, St Ann's Square,
Manchester M2 7BR
tel 0161-833 4263 *fax* 0161-833 4264
email info@emmastafford.tv
website www.emmastafford.tv

Areas of work include television, film and commercials. Recent credits include: *200 Magazine*, Co-op Bank, Robinsons, *If I Were a Butterfly*.

Will consider attending performances within the North West area with at least 2 weeks' notice. Accepts letters (with CVs and photographs) from actors previously unknown to the agency; will also accept CVs and photographs sent by email, and view showreels.

Helen Stafford

14 Park Avenue, Enfield, London EN1 2HP
tel 020-8360 6329
email helenstaffordcasting@gmail.com

Casts in film and theatre, in both the UK and the USA. Recent credits include: films: *A Punter's Prayer*, *Deano and Louise*, *When the Money Runs Out*, *Burning*, *Death Scene* and *The Big Steal*; theatre: New York Broadway production transfers to London West End.

Will consider seeing actors perform in Central and Greater London, with 1 week's notice. Accepts letters (with CVs and photographs) from individuals unknown to the agency, sent by post. Showreels on request only.

Robert Sterne

See the entry for Nina Gold CDG under *Casting directors* on page 112.

Gail Stevens Casting CDG

84-85 London Lane, London EC1A 9ET
email office@gailstevenscasting.com

Main areas of work are television, film and commercials. Casting credits include: *Zero Dark Thirty*, *Slumdog Millionaire* , *Trainspotting* and *Babylon*.

Sam Stevenson CDG

email sam@hancockstevenson.com
website www.hancockstevenson.com

Main areas of work are television, theatre and film. More details are available on the website.

Liz Stoll

BBC Elstree, Room N223 Neptune House,
Clarendon Road, Borehamwood WD6 1JF
tel 020-8228 8285 *fax* 020-8228 8311
email liz.stoll@bbc.co.uk

Has worked in all areas of actor casting and has been casting BBC1 drama for the past 13 years. Work for the BBC includes the series *One Night*, the film *The Night Watch*, 5 series of *Judge John Deed*, 5 series of *Down To Earth* and currently casting on *Holby City*. Happy to receive performance notices at least 2 weeks in advance, and is prepared to travel within Greater London (sometimes further, work permitting) to see shows.

Welcomes emails with CVs and photographs from actors previously unknown to the casting director; prefers Spotlight showreels, and is happy to receive invitations to view individuals' websites.

See also the entry for BBC (Drama Production) under *BBC network television* on page 305.

Charlotte Sutton

See the entry for the National Theatre under *Producing theatres* on page 139.

Syson Grainger Casting

Rooms 7&8, 2nd Floor, 83-84 Berwick Street,
London W1F 8TS
tel 020-7287 5327 *fax* 020-7287 3629

Recent feature films include: *Children of Men*, directed by Alfonso Cuaron; *Syriana*, directed by Stephen Gagan; *Batman Begins*, directed by Chris Nolan; *Troy*, directed by Wolfgang Petersen; *Snatch*, directed by Guy Ritchie; *Spygame*, directed by Tony Scott; and *Fifth Element*, directed by Luc Besson.

Amanda Tabak CDG

See the entry for Candid Casting under *Casting directors* on page 107.

Topps Casting

The Media Centre, 7 Northumberland Street,
West Yorkshire HD1 1RL
tel (01484) 511988 *fax* (01484) 483100
email nicci@toppscasting.co.uk
website www.toppscasting.co.uk
Casting Director Nicci Topping

Works in television, film and commercials. Recent work includes: feature films *Speak No Evil* and *Tribe*; feature trailer *Storage*.

Welcomes performance notices within Greater London and elsewhere (Manchester, Leeds, Sheffield) if given 2 weeks' notice. Accepts letters (with CVs & photographs) from individual actors previously unknown to the agency, sent by post or email.

Moira Townsend

See the entry for Casting Couch Productions Ltd under *Casting directors* on page 108.

Jill Trevellick CDG

92 Priory Road, London N8 7EY
tel 020-8340 2734
email jill@jilltrevellick.com

Main areas of work are film and television. Casting credits include: TV – *Downton Abbey* (series 1-3); *The Hour, White Heat, Merlin, Vanity Fair, North and South, The Canterbury Tales, Merlin* (series 1-5). Film – *What We Did On Our Holiday* (Andy Hamilton & Guy Jenkin, 2013); *Fish Tank* (Andrea Arnold, 2009); *I Know You Know* (Justin Kerrigan, 2009).

Sarah Trevis CDG

PO Box 47170, London W6 6BA
tel 020-7602 5552 *fax* 020-7602 8110

Main areas of work are television and film. Recent casting credits include: work for Granada television, the BBC and Twentieth Century Fox.

Will consider attending performances given 2 weeks' notice. Accepts submissions (with CVs and photographs) from actors previously unknown to the casting director if sent by post. Does not welcome email enquiries.

Sally Vaughan CDG

2 Kennington Park Place, London SE11 4AS
tel 020-7735 6539

Main area of work is theatre. Credits include: *Porridge* (No. 1 UK tour); *'Allo, 'Allo* (No. 1 UK tour); *Dad's Army – The Lost Episodes* (No. 1 UK tour); *Sweet Charity* (Victoria Palace Theatre), *Of Thee I Sing* and *Sweeney Todd* (Bridewell Theatre); and *Anna Weiss* (Whitehall Theatre).

Anne Vosser

156 Lower Farnham Road, Aldershot, Hampshire GU12 4EL
tel (01252) 404716 *mobile* (07968) 868712
email anne@vosser-casting.co.uk
website www.vosser-casting.co.uk

Main areas of work are theatre and musicals. Casting credits include: *What The Butler Saw, Zorro, Taboo, Fame, Saturday Night Fever, Footloose, Never Forget* (all in the West End).

June West

email junewest@junewestcasting.com
website www.junewestcasting.com

Having enjoyed a career as Casting Director at ITV Granada, June has worked on numerous award-winning dramas, comedy series, drama-documentaries and, of course, the longest-running soap in history – *Coronation Street*.

June is now a freelance Casting Director, and with the benefit of more than 30 years' experience working with some of the most celebrated talent in our industry.

Matt Western

150 Blythe Road, London W14 0HD
tel 020-7602 6646
email matt@mattwestern.co.uk

Main areas of work are film, television and commercials. Casting credits include: *Affinity* (ITV1), *Coup!* (BBC2); *Roman Mysteries* (2 series for BBC1); *55 Degrees North* (2 series for BBC1) and *Class of '76* (ITV1).

Toby Whale CDG

80 Shakespeare Road, London W3 6SN
tel 020-8993 2821 *fax* 020-8993 8096
email toby@whalecasting.com
website www.whalecasting.com

Head of Casting at the National Theatre 2003-06. Main areas of work are film, television and theatre. Casting credits include: *The History Boys*; *East is East* (Assassin Films/FilmFour); *The French Film* (Slingshot); *True Dare Kiss* (BBC); *Spoonface Steinberg* (BBC Films); *Wire in the Blood* (Series 1 & 2 – Coastal/ITV); and more than 40 theatre productions for the Royal Court Theatre, Out of Joint, the Almeida Theatre, English Touring Theatre and Sheffield Crucible, among others.

Tara Woodward

Top Flat, 93 Gloucester Avenue, Primrose Hill, London NW1 8LB
tel 020-7586 3487 *fax* 020-7681 8574

Main areas of work are film, television, theatre and commercials. Casting credits include: *The Early Days, Post* and *Hello Friend* (all for Shine/Film Four Lab); *Chasing Heaven* (for Venice Film Festival); *The Browning Version* and *Romeo and Juliet* (theatre); and commercials for Parmalat Aqua and Royal Danish Post. Has worked as Casting Assistant to Nina Gold on films including *All Or Nothing* (directed by Mike Leigh) and *Love's Labour's Lost* (directed by Kenneth Branagh).

Jeremy Zimmermann Casting

36 Marshall Street, London W1F 7EY
tel 020-7478 5161 *fax* 020-7437 4747

Main areas of work are film and television. Recent casting work includes: *Keeping Mum, The Contract, Van Wilder 2, Dog Soldiers* and *Blood And Chocolate.*

Will consider attending performances at venues in Greater London and elsewhere. Accepts postal submissions (with CVs and photographs) from actors previously unknown to the casting director, but does not welcome email enquiries. Invitations to view individual actors' websites are also accepted.

Casting for the stage

Anne McNulty

If the essence of acting on stage is the gathering of a group of people to share a story, then the work of a casting director is to guide and support the director in meeting and choosing the actors to make up that group. The director will have ideas and expectations and it's my job to share the widest possible range of acting talent to achieve the cast. The choice is wide open until we have seen all our actors.

The play, the director, the venue, the timescale, the salary – these are the first things to take into consideration when I am approached to work with a director on a play. We will both read the script in depth. We produce a breakdown describing each of the roles and I may send this out to agents via a Spotlight link; it will depend on size of cast and if the director has strong initial ideas. I will check CVs and perhaps go straight to an offer for the key roles in a production.

I will also compile a list of actors for each of the roles based on my knowledge of their work, details from their agents and their CVs. We will also receive individual submissions and will read these too. The decisions about who and how many actors to meet will depend on the director's schedule and who we feel is suitable. We will also be speculative if there is a credit that interests us on an actor's CV, or if we have seen a review that describes a particular actor who we like the sound of. It is not necessary to have an agent to be considered for casting but sometimes if may be a stipulation that the actor has some professional experience. It all depends on the role and the director.

I may work with an assistant and between us we will book rooms, liaise with the director about the text you should prepare, fix the meetings and read in, if required.

You will be invited to audition because you have been singled out as a potential for the role and one of a small group being met. A fixed time has been allocated for your meeting and you need to use it to show your skills. Please don't make excuses. You should have been given enough time to prepare, but if you are called in at short notice then do all you can and share that in the meeting.

Know the story of the play. The internet can offer a precis for existing texts, and if it is a new play you may be sent the script – if not, interpret what you can from the sides you are sent. It is vital to prepare well and bring your sense of the character into the meeting. You are coming into the room to get the job, so a sense of who you are as a person and as a company member is important. Expect to be asked a question about any shows you have seen lately, or if you have a favourite writer or actor, who they are and why you chose them.

If the role requires an accent then prepare in that accent and also be ready to use your own accent. The director could ask you to give an extreme interpretation of the character to see how far you can stretch in trying something. Do think about how you dress, as being too relaxed and informal can suggest you're not taking the meeting seriously. Shorts and flip-flops simply do not work.

One other crucial piece of advice is to listen carefully and be succinct. The urgency and nerves of wanting to do a good audition can mean you don't hear properly or reply quickly, meaning you may not hear everything that the director has said. Often, this clarity is vital and you can always ask for them to say it again. If you are asked if you have any questions, it usually means 'do you understand?' and it is not an opportunity to stall or to ask the director how they see the part.

You may meet directors who are less forthcoming and simply want you to work on the text. They may give you a note but will not really engage in chat. Don't be alarmed, they will be considering your work just the same and that is their style.

If the meeting does not lead to you getting the role, your work and the inspiration you offered will be recorded by the team and hopefully they will think of you for future projects. You may feel you are totally right for a role but there are many considerations in balancing a company, casting a family, the siblings – even twins! Also, the relationship of the parents, best friend, rival or lover, will decide how the choice is made. I always feed back to agents and actors after their auditions. This can take time but gives you an indication of how it went so you can use that in the future.

When I am in the midst of a casting, the priority will always be the meetings. I will give you as much information as possible, to ensure that your meeting can be open, investigative and a time to really work the text. Make the most of it.

My other source of insight is to see as many shows as I can – every evening and sometimes on the weekend. I will go to regional productions and shows on tour, to watch as many actors, interpretations and styles of direction and production, as they give me lots of information. I cover many of the drama school shows and share the progress of new graduates as they find their first jobs in theatre. I will also see all the current television and films – so there's plenty of input going into each new casting.

I think William Shakespeare sums it up perfectly: 'the readiness is all'. Keep it simple, prepare well and good luck.

Anne McNulty, CDG, is originally from Manchester and moved to London in 1986 to work for a charity, then joined the Young Vic in 1990 as PA to the Artistic and Administrative Directors. This was where she met Sam Mendes and joined the Donmar Warehouse as Casting Director, plus administrative support, in May 1992. After working with both Michael Grandage and Josie Rourke, she left in 2012 to pursue a freelance career and to work in drama schools, with a particular interest in audition workshops.

Casting for musical theatre

David Grindrod

The process of producing/casting a musical can be a very long and costly affair. Everyone is looking for the next *Phantom of the Opera* or *Mamma Mia!*; years of work can go into the production you see on stage today. Workshops have now become a necessity in order to see if a show 'has legs', without spending too much money. In consultation with the producer and creative team, I will assemble a group of actors who may not be totally right for the roles but who work well in a workshop situation. If the green light is given after the workshop presentation, the casting process – in conjunction with everything else – begins.

A casting breakdown is drawn up: this consists of all the details required by agents and artists about the characters, vocal ranges, etc. plus the proposed dates of the production. Open calls are sometimes organised for specific roles, but normally the breakdown gets sent to agents via the Spotlight link, which reaches 500 agents/representatives at the touch of a button.

There is always a 'wish list' of actors whom producers would like in their production, but the bulk of submissions will come through agents, in the form of photos and CVs. Unsolicited mail is also received; sometimes it is difficult to keep all this on file due to sheer number of submissions. Either I or my associates will also attend college shows and presentations to look for specific talent.

When preparing your photos and CVs, always remember that these are the calling cards with which you promote yourself! A good photograph is not 'artistic' (i.e. showing a face half in shadow); rather, it should always present a good full face that really does look like you. Your CV should ideally be just one page stapled to the back of your photograph. It should include all relevant details (*not* forgetting contact details) to show your skills. Make this information clear and precise. If you feel that you are suitable for musical casting, be very accurate and truthful about your vocal range: don't make it complicated – basically, tenor or soprano, with the top of your range noted. We can normally tell your style by the shows you have appeared in.

The audition process normally begins with artists performing two contrasting songs that show range and personality. Make an effort to pick a song that is suitable for the show – not pop, for example, when you are up for Rogers & Hammerstein. Nerves will take over; therefore, don't sing the song you learnt yesterday, but perform something tried and tested (something you would be happy singing naked in Trafalgar Square!). When we ask, "Have you got something else?" we don't want the answer, "My agent said you only wanted two songs,"; have your book of audition pieces with you and give us the chance to choose an alternative. Actors often ask whether I have favourite songs that I like to hear – or songs that I don't: I only really mind when they come in with completely the wrong song for the production.

If an actor is successful, they will receive a call-back for a dance/movement call. This normally causes concerns, but actually it is not usually that specific; we only want to see whether a person is happy with his/her body. If the audition is for a major dance show, hopefully you will know your limitations, and either not audition at all, or be ready to throw yourself into the routine. Again, be honest: then you won't upset the creative team.

Further recalls take place with music and script from the show: the musical supervisor or associate director normally takes these calls. If you come in for the musical supervisor, come back with music prepared and your own song. *Always* bring your own song – it's a good reminder for the team. In addition to any script you are asked to read, you may get asked for a speech: have a couple of acting pieces prepared, and again, nerves will take over, so make sure you know them properly. Remember that these speeches are also to allow the director to assess how well you can respond to direction, and how readily you can take a note.

The culmination of the casting process – 'the finals' – is the most nerve-wracking experience, even for a highly experienced artist. Bring everything with you that you have been given. You may not get *asked* for everything, but have it just in case. You may have been asked to dress in a certain way; always put some thought into that, as directors can be blinkered at times ... I have known artists to arrive with a couple of outfits and ask me to pick one! The panel will consist of the whole creative team and the producers. At this stage I can't do any more for you – though hopefully I can keep the atmosphere in the room happy and 'up'. Stay calm, don't change anything that you have been told, and audition to the best of your abilities.

Now the wait to see if you have the role. Always remember that you have got this far in the process because you can sing and act far better than anyone else. In the end, the decision could come down to height, look, hair colour; funnily enough it may not have anything to do with your singing/acting skills at this point. And you may not get an instant answer; you may have to wait until other meetings have taken place. You may get put on 'hold': normally that means you are not first on the list, but if somebody above you declines the offer you may move up. If you are lucky, the phone call will come with a straight offer. How exciting is that ... Contractual details are then advised and, if all that is agreed, your date for first rehearsal is given. Always remember that you are a small part of the bigger picture – a small part of the jigsaw puzzle that goes together to form: The Musical.

David Grindrod founded David Grindrod Associates (DGA) with Stephen Crockett in January 1998, after 20 years' experience in the theatre in various roles ranging from assistant stage manager to general manager. Current West End casting includes *Chicago*, *Evita*, *The Lord of the Rings*, *Mamma Mia!* (worldwide), *Spamalot*, *The Sound of Music*. Films include *The Phantom of The Opera*. DGA are also casting consultants for *On The Town* and *Kismet* at the English National Opera, and belong to the Casting Directors Guild of Great Britain.

Theatre
Introduction

Theatres and theatre companies/managements abound in all kinds of different forms, and paid opportunities for live performance are not restricted to putting on productions. The days of the permanent repertory company are almost gone, but there is a much wider diversity of work available. The larger companies/managements often use casting directors (see page 105), who should usually be your first port of call with your letter, CV and photograph. However, it can be worth exploiting any personal contacts that you may have.

For all approaches, it is important to send your submissions to the person named – unless you have a personal contact.

Some organisations have regular casting patterns – see The Casting Calendar on page 284 for details.

Producing theatre in the regions

Gemma Bodinetz

There is no such thing as 'regional theatre'.

Every so often I will read an article about the flourishing, or indeed the demise, of 'regional theatre'. Quite often I am asked to contribute to the debate. Do I think too much funding is focused on London and not on regional theatre? Is the quality of the work in the regions as high as that in London? Do we need building-based regional theatre? The questions seem always to be predicated on an assumption that, from Plymouth to Newcastle, Liverpool to Chichester, there is this generic sort of theatre defined simply by the fact that it is NOT IN LONDON.

But, as anyone vaguely familiar with 'London theatre' will tell you, the fact that The Young Vic and The Old Vic both share the same postcode does not mean their ethos, their audience or their vision have much in common. 'London theatre', if it were ever really used, would be a redundant term, useful only to separate it from the rest of the world geographically.

And so it is in the regions. In fact one could go further and contend that any regional theatre doing its job well should be like no other regional theatre. If we have anything in common it is our remit to respond to our audiences, our time and place. And each of those factors are as different as the towns and cities we find ourselves in and the geopolitical forces that act upon them year to year.

I don't think I would have written that paragraph when I first took up my position as artistic director of the Liverpool Everyman and Playhouse theatres in 2003. I think back then I would have spoken very passionately about the universality of 'great theatre' and of my desire to produce work at these theatres as good as any seen in London, nay, *the world*! I would have eschewed localism and talked fervently about 'quality' and 'excellence'. These were my gods. They still are.

BUT . . .

I have discovered that the gods of Quality and Excellence need to be contextualised in terms of my city region of Merseyside.

There is undoubtedly such a thing as 'great universal theatre'. Think of a high-quality chain of shops or restaurants. The sort of chain you hope might move into your local high street. It began in Soho or maybe New York, Berlin . . . but its brand of quality assurance and 'uniqueness' has seen it blossom all over the country. Having one of these in your town centre feels like you're on the way up, your area is aspirational. And the food/clothes/coffee/rose-patterned handbags are always high quality. What it can't do is represent your locale or make your high street feel any different from hundreds of others up and down the country. You'll never say to a friend: 'Oh you must come and stay with us we've got a great ******* in our city centre'.

Liverpool is a potent city. A city defined by its extraordinary history, its idiom, its writers, poets, musicians, actors, footballers, politicians, architecture . . . It was once the second city of the Empire. It has in more recent history registered some of the highest indices of long-term unemployment, teenage pregnancy, dependence on antidepressants, low levels of third-level educated residents. It delivered what was widely acknowledged to be a hugely successful European Capital of Culture in 2008. How could any 'regional' theatre worth its salt ignore the particularity of such a city?

After just a few months in my position, I realised that not only would I never be able to produce work that I did not consider to be 'excellent' without betraying my core sensibilities as an artist, but that truly excellent work in a city with such a strong identity and culture needed to respond to both. Moreover, in a city that had suffered enormous economic hardship over recent decades, as the largest subsidised theatre in the region, we had a duty to nurture the next generation of artists and theatregoers and create theatre that mattered on our stages, in our communities and schools and with our youth theatres.

Of course the tightrope we walked, as we sought to create work that responded to Liverpool, crossed a crocodile-infested river called 'PAROCIALISM'. Heaven help us if we fell in there, for we could potentially plunge these theatres into the nether regions of no national reviews, dwindling numbers of nationally recognised directors, writers and actors wanting to work with us and the lost opportunity of making the national success of these theatres a source of civic pride. No, we quickly realised that if these theatres were to be all we believed they should be for the city, they had to be particular but not inwardly facing. If we were commissioning a new play by a Liverpool writer, (which we have done many, many times), then whilst the play could be set in this city, (it didn't have to be), and should reflect the concerns of this city, it should also be asking a question relevant to any visiting audience member from another place. We wanted big national plays with a 'Liverpool heartbeat'.

Soon our script and programming meetings became very focused on this intangible 'Liverpool heartbeat'. As well as the plays we were commissioning, we passed the classic texts through the same sieve. *Coriolanus* and *Much Ado* felt Liverpool; *Love's Labour's Lost* less so. *The Birthday Party*? *Saved*?

Of course, I realise this all sounds very spurious. Liverpool is many things and the clichés about the people of Liverpool tend to be just that. Never mind that there are as many ways to produce *Coriolanus* as there are directors and actors. But the fact remained that talking about work in terms of our city began to draw into clearer vision all the reasons that we received public money to put on theatre.

If the impulse behind a script or a production didn't seem to embrace the passions of Liverpool, have the potential to bring joy to its audiences, make sense to its communities and schools, develop its artists and bring civic pride by the quality of its execution to its people, then frankly we weren't interested, even if it would potentially have commercial appeal or be generally perceived to be 'where it's at'.

I drew up a manifesto to help clarify, both internally and externally, where our vision was focused. This document is intended as a touchstone as we walk across the tightrope of universal excellence married with local resonance whilst hopefully avoiding parochialism and ubiquitous 'high-quality' theatre. Its somewhat revealing headline is: Joy Beyond Expectation and its major subtitles are: humanity, dare, time and place, brilliance and forward thinking. The whole document can be found on our website. It's by no means an intellectual piece but it is in some ways a love letter from a publicly funded theatre to its city. A promise if you like, to be both aspirational *and* reactive, to be artistically ambitious from the consequences of a profound conversation with a city and its artists.

We work with actors, directors, writers and designers from all around the world. Many of our productions transfer to London and the West End. Our production of *The Caretaker* transferred to New York. We regularly co-produce with other theatres in the regions and with West End and national producers. We are not just putting on plays by, about and starring Liverpool actors. But whether it's the full-blown visceral horror of *Ghost Stories* or the exquisite joy and irreverence of Roger McGough's Molière trilogy the impulse to produce or co-produce the work has been its rightness to the flavour and the particular heartbeat of this unique city.

Every regional theatre in the country is looking at ways to create dazzling theatre; the best of them, and there are many, are able to marry this with the distinction of their region. It's not about doing everything in your local accent but it is, in my opinion, doing all you can to make your work relevant to your audience and your audience relevant to the nation.

Gemma Bodinetz took up her post as Artistic Director for the Liverpool Everyman and Playhouse theatres in September 2003. She has since directed *The Kindness of Strangers*, *The Mayor of Zalamea*, *Intemperance* and *Macbeth* at the Everyman; *Ma Rainey's Black Bottom*, *Who's Afraid of Virginia Woolf?*, *The Lady of Leisure*, *All My Sons*, *Tartuffe*, *The Hypochondriac*, *A Streetcar Named Desire* and *The Misanthrope* at the Playhouse, and *Yellowman* on tour. Gemma was previously an Associate Director at Hampstead Theatre, where she directed *Paper Husband*, *Chimps*, *English Journeys*, *Snake*, *Death of Cool*, *Hand in Hand* and *After the Gods*. Gemma has directed numerous productions nationally – her credits include: *Caravan* and *A Buyers Market* (The Bush Theatre, London); *Yard Gal* and *Breath Boom* (The Royal Court, London); *Meat* (Plymouth Theatre Royal); *Hamlet* (Bristol Old Vic); *Luminosity* (RSC); *Rosencrantz and Guildenstern are Dead* and *Four Nights in Knaresborough* (West Yorkshire Playhouse).

Marketing yourself: a producer's viewpoint

Ian Liston

Anything and everything an actor does in his or her working life is about presentation. A sloppy, badly rehearsed performance is not going to win prizes, let alone get you more work. You may have spent a couple of years or more – and invested many thousands of pounds – developing your talent with a lifelong career in mind, so why risk the good work you've done already by not marketing yourself properly? Hopefully you regard yourself as an actor of some quality, so why jeopardise your potential by failing to promote yourself in a 'quality' way?

Whether you've had formal training or never had a day's tuition in your life, it is still going to take a lot of effort and hard work on your part to find work and ensure that the time and heartache already invested has been worth it. It's inadvisable to rely solely on an agent, no matter how good they may be, to find you work. If you don't have an agent, in order to get one you will have to impress them as much as any other director or company you want to contact – and the ability to market yourself properly and create a good impression is even more essential.

Your most important asset will be your CV. Using even the simplest word processing programme makes it easy to keep this up to date. Not only will your CV contain, ideally, a couple of contrasting recent photographs, but you should also have the ability to 'drop in' a particular photograph that may be more suited to the part you are applying for.

It's worth spending as much as you can afford to obtain decent photographs. Even though you may a have a friend who knows how to use a digital camera, they're unlikely to have the skill and experience of a professional photographer, who will have the expertise to produce pictures that will get you noticed.

Published yearly by Spotlight, *Contacts* provides many and varied examples of the work of specialist photographers; you can also find out more details about individual photographers starting on page 391 of this book. Most have websites, which can help you choose someone who appeals to you.

As with photographs, don't skimp on materials: invest in some decent paper – 100gsm at the very least. CVs usually get passed around various interested parties and, while they may arrive in good condition, for a few pence extra you can enclose them in a plastic folder to prevent them from becoming dog-eared when passed around a busy casting or production office. Most people prefer to print on white paper, but a tint or subtle colour can make your CV stand out even more, and make it easier to locate at a hectic casting session.

In terms of layout, a neat listing of your credits in chronological order is essential. As a producer, I much prefer to see credits categorised into separate sections of Stage, TV, Film, plus other relevant categories (e.g. Radio, Opera, etc.). Most actors are in *Spotlight*, which has a neat and efficient layout in its online publication that is worth adopting.

You should list the year of performance followed by the medium (i.e. Stage, TV, etc.) and then the character name, the title of the piece, the production company and the director. If the productions were at drama school or were unpaid or amateur, make that clear.

Every director/producer will look for their own 'tell-tale' clues in a CV: I put great emphasis on directors and companies with whom an actor has worked. Make sure you spell the names correctly. There's nothing more indicative of a sloppy actor than inaccurate spelling, be it a play title, director or character's name, and poor grammar. Don't be tempted to pad out your CV or fabricate plays, parts and directors, as you can be sure your sins will find you out!

You may have a wealth of leading roles under your belt before you became a professional actor: much better to list them as 'non-professional', 'training' or 'unpaid' work. Sadly there still seems to be a stigma surrounding the word 'amateur' when, in truth, much good work, comparable with the best of fringe or profit-share, is performed by amateur companies.

Let's assume that you've done all your groundwork. You will have familiarised yourself with the various casting services that are available (several offer free trials) and you are developing a network of your own to find out about the possibilities of work. You are reading the trade press (e.g. *The Stage*, which can now be accessed online on a daily basis) and you have invested in a copy of *Contacts* (and this *Yearbook*, of course) so that you have all the names and contact addresses to hand of just about anyone who is anybody.

Now starts the slog – and it's not going to be a one-off afterthought on a Friday afternoon, after the phone hasn't rung about work for yet another week. Treat it as a business: your business. Research the market. Identify the companies whose work most interests you – or who might be most interested in you. A simple telephone call is usually sufficient to find the name of the person to contact. It could be a producer, director or casting director, but getting an individual's name will better your chances. It's useless writing to ask for a general audition or interview if the company never holds any.

To maximise your chance of success, write your short, to-the-point letter and send it with your CV to the identified contact. A brief comment to acknowledge the company's work doesn't go amiss, and gives you a better chance of engaging someone's interest ... but don't be smarmy, smart-assed or clever. There is nothing more annoying to a producer than someone who 'desperately wants to work for your company' when plainly they have no real idea of what the company does.

Avoid gimmicks. I've never forgiven the sender of the childishly folded letter which, when opened, spilled a heap of stars and glitter that took months to get out of clothes and carpet. I may not have forgotten the gimmick about wanting to be a star, but I've certainly forgotten the name!

If you're sending a photo with your CV, then you must remember to *put your name and contact details on the back of the photo*! It never ceases to amaze me how many people omit to do such a simple thing. For at least 50% of the hundreds of applications we receive each year, we have no means whatsoever of identifying the photo – so if it gets separated from a CV, as can often happen, it will have been a total waste of time and money.

First impressions count. You wouldn't (would you?) attend an audition or interview looking scruffy and unkempt. Some people do, but that's another story. Take care with your spelling and grammar and avoid using exclamation marks at the end of every sentence. A neatly addressed, handwritten letter using quality paper certainly grabs my attention:

they're such a rarity these days. Keep it brief and to the point, without being verbose. If you have 'doctors' handwriting', use simple typed labels and a neatly typed letter but, at the very least, handwrite the salutation and the signature. Mass-produced mail-shot letters are easy to spot and they usually end up straight in the bin. Unless a stamped addressed envelope is enclosed (and I only speak for myself) I would not usually offer the courtesy of a reply and the return of a photograph.

There is an increasing tendency these days to include a DVD or similar visual medium as part of the submission. This should be of the highest possible quality and capable of being played on any equipment; and it should comprise a personal introduction from your good self together with a selection of photographs/video clips from recent work. It should *not* be a replacement for the letter and CV. As with every element of your submission, make sure your contact details are clearly marked.

A major factor to get right is the postage. Since the new method of sizing, weighing and pricing for postage came into force in 2007, it's amazing how few people still bother to check they have the right amount of stamps. Too few, and your recipient will have to fork out a few pounds to get something he or she hasn't expected and will likely bin; too many and you're wasting your own hard-earned cash. Useful advice on this matter is included in Simon Dunmore's introduction to this *Yearbook*.

Email is being used increasingly as a method of contact and every recipient has their own way of dealing with it. It can be particularly useful if a potential work opportunity comes to your attention at short notice. It's faster than the post and nothing is more effective than striking whilst the iron is hot – but make sure any files you send are as small as possible. Include your Spotlight link and, if you have a website, the link to that as well.

In similar fashion, always make sure you have ready a good supply of your photographs and CVs, although it's pointless printing too many at one time, as the real worth of a good CV is the fact that it's absolutely up to date. If you're suggesting that your correspondent can look up your entry in *Spotlight*, make sure that too is up to date. In 2007 an agent suggested I look up his client in *Spotlight*; a pointless exercise since the actor's most recent credits were for 1998!

Success is so often a matter of luck. A CV/letter arriving in the right hands, just when a producer/director is looking for someone like you, can open untold doors, but it's astonishing how few actors bother to spend that little bit of extra time and effort getting it right.

Always remember the wise words of Ivor Novello, one of the most successful actor/managers of the 20th century: "If you want to be a success, look it!" – and that goes for your correspondence as well as your appearance.

Good luck! I look forward to hearing from you.

Ian Liston is an actor and producer whose career covers over 40 years' experience as an actor in feature films, on TV and on the stage. His company, Hiss & Boo Ltd, is one of the UK's leading producers of pantomime and revue, and its productions are frequently seen on the UK touring circuit and overseas.

Producing theatres

Included in this section are the national and regional building-based companies that mount their own productions – sometimes in co-operation with others, and sometimes sending out tours. (Almost all also receive touring productions.) The majority are subsidised by the national and regional Arts Councils (and use Equity's regional theatre contract), but a few are not (and use Equity's commercial theatre contract), and a few have their own contractual arrangements. Almost all have websites which can be very useful for keeping track of their activities. A little extra insight into a theatre – beyond that listed on the following pages – might just tip the balance in your favour.

In real terms, rates of pay are better than they were a decade and more ago, but they are still only 'adequate' – especially if you are incurring the extra costs of living away from home. However, rehearsing and performing a production in such a theatre can be an exhilarating experience. A well-run theatre has a wonderful 'family' atmosphere, and in the close-knit working environment you can often make friendships which sustain for many years afterwards – as well as contacts who might be useful in years to come. It is well worth checking each theatre's 'casting procedures' very carefully as there are significant variations between them. It is also worth familiarising yourself with their programmes of productions via *The Stage* and/or their websites.

Abbey Theatre Amharclann na Mainistreach

26 Lower Abbey Street, Dublin 1, Republic of Ireland
tel +353 (0)1 8872200 *fax* +353 (0)1 8729177
email info@abbeytheatre.ie
website www.abbeytheatre.ie
Director Fiach Mac Conghail

Ireland's national theatre. Produces new Irish writing and contemporary productions of classic plays.

Abbey Theatre Amharclann na Mainistreach

26/27 Lower Abbey Street, Dublin 1, Ireland
00 353 1 88772200*fax* 00 353 1 8729177
email info@abbeytheatre.ie
Artistic Director Fiach MacCoghail *Casting Director* Kelly Phelan *Casting Assistant* Jan Schneider

Production details: The Abbey Theatre produces an ambitious annual prgramme of Irish and international theatre across its two stages and on tour in Ireland and internationally. The Abbey Theatre is committed to building the Irish theatre repertoire, through commissioning and producing new Irish writing, and re-imagining national and international classics in collaboration with leading contemporary talent.

Casting procedures: The Abbey Theatre is the only theatre in Ireland with a full time in-house casting department dedicated to seeking out new and emerging talent, as well as keeping abreast of the continued work and development of previously established actors from all over the country and abroad. The Abbey Theatre holds general auditions bi-annually. The casting department attends performances throughout the year, nationally and internationally, as well as drama school showcases in Dublin and London.

Almeida Theatre

Almeida Street, London N1 1TA
tel 020-7359 4404
email info@almeida.co.uk
website www.almeida.co.uk
Artistic Director Rupert Goold

Production details: The Almeida is a 325-seat theatre in the heart of Islington, North London. Produces a diverse range of British and International drama with some of the world's best artists, and has developed a reputation as a local theatre with a world profile. Almeida Projects links the theatre's work with the local community. Stages approximately 6 productions each year. Recent productions include: *Mr Burns*, *King Charles III*, *American Psycho*, *Ghosts* and *Chimerica*.

Casting procedures: Productions are cast by external freelance casting directors on a project-by-project basis. Uses the TMA/Equity Subsidised Rep contract and subscribes to the Equity Pension Scheme. Actively promotes the use of inclusive casting.

Arcola Theatre

24 Ashwin Street, London E8 3DL
tel 020-7503 1645

email production@arcolatheatre.com
website www.arcolatheatre.com
Artistic Director Mehmet Ergen

Production details: Founded in 2000 by Artistic Director Mehmet Ergen and Executive Producer Leyla Nazli, Arcola Theatre is now one of the most respected arts venues in the UK, "blazing a trail in artistic excellence and innovative management from the outset". Housed in a converted factory in Hackney, Arcola is a favourite of established theatre literati as well as young, upwardly mobile innovators. London's largest theatre studio, it has become well known for the variety of its programming, from new writing to classic drama, music and comedy.

Arcola has staged work by some of the best living actors, writers and directors, including productions by William Gaskill, Timberlake Wertenbaker, Ariel Dorfman, Sean Holmes, Dominic Domgoole, Max Stafford-Clark and Frank McGuinness, among others. 2 studio theatres and 4 other spaces suitable for rehearsals and other events.

Yvonne Arnaud Theatre

Millbrook, Guildford, Surrey GU1 3UX
tel (01483) 440077 *fax* (01483) 564071
website www.yvonne-arnaud.co.uk
Director and Chief Executive James Barber

Production details: The Yvonne Arnaud Theatre is a busy producing and presenting house, creating shows in Guildford and touring nationally, with many productions transferring to the West End. On both the main stage and in the Mill Studio an eclectic mix of classical and contemporary work by new, lesser-known and established writers is staged.

The Youth and Education facility offers an exciting mix of activities for young people and adults all year round. The Yvonne Arnaud opened the 80-seat Mill Studio in 1993, to provide a venue for work that would not otherwise be seen in Guildford. It also forms the base for the Youth Theatre's activities.

Belgrade Theatre

Belgrade Square, Coventry CV1 1GS
tel 024-7625 6431
email admin@belgrade.co.uk
website www.belgrade.co.uk
Theatre Director & Chief Executive Hamish Glen
Associate Director – Community & Education Justine Themen

Production details: Recent productions include: *One Night in November* (about the Coventry Blitz); *Scenes from a Marriage* (directed by Trevor Nunn); and 'legendary' annual pantomimes.

Birmingham Repertory Theatre

Centenary Square, Broad Street,
Birmingham B1 3AH
tel 0121-245 2000
email info@birmingham-rep.co.uk
website www.birmingham-rep.co.uk
Artistic Director Roxana Silbert *Associate Director Learning & Participation* Steve Ball *Casting Co-ordinator* Alison Solomon

Production details: Stages 15 productions in the main house each year, and 6 in the studio. Also runs Outreach, Community and Education programmes.

Casting procedures: "The play's director, a casting director and sometimes a producer handle casting for all Main House and Studio productions. We currently make use of freelance casting directors, specific to each production, administered by our in-house Casting Co-ordinator."

Birmingham Stage Company (BSC)

Suite 228, 162 Regent Street, London W1B 5TB
tel 020-7437 3391 *fax* 020-7437 3395
email info@birminghamstage.net
website www.birminghamstage.net
Actor/Manager Neal Foster

Production details: Founded in 1992, the BSC stages 5 shows each year, 4 of which tour nationally. Produces a range of plays with particular emphasis on new writing, and is recognised for its children's shows, which visit 60 venues around the UK. Recent productions include: *Proof* (West End); *Horrible Histories* (UK tour); *The Jungle Book* (UK tour); *Treasure Island* (UK tour); *Danny the Champion of the World*. Offers TMA/Equity approved contracts and subscribes to the Equity Pension Scheme.

Casting procedures: Uses freelance casting directors and sometimes holds general auditions. Casting breakdowns are published on the website, and in *Spotlight*. Submissions by hard copy only – no phone calls. "Do as much research as you can before submitting." Actively encourages applications from disabled actors.

Bristol Old Vic

King Street, Bristol BS1 4ED
tel 0117-949 3993 *fax* 0117-949 3993
email admin@bristololdvic.org.uk
website www.bristololdvic.org.uk
Artistic Director Tom Morris

Production details: Bristol Old Vic is a theatre company founded in 1946 and based in a complex which includes the unique Theatre Royal, opened in 1766 – the oldest theatre auditorium in the UK, which many think the most beautiful. Bristol Old Vic is also unique in its close working relationship with the Bristol Old Vic Theatre School.

The Bush Theatre

7 Uxbridge Road, London W12 8LJ
tel 020-8743 3584
email info@bushtheatre.co.uk
website www.bushtheatre.co.uk
Artistic Director Madani Younis *Associate Director* Omar Elerian

Production details: Founded in 1972, the Bush specialises in developing and producing new writing to the highest professional standard. Stages 5-8 productions a year, totalling around 280 performances. Also tours productions, although the bulk of performances are at the Bush itself. Up to 6 actors are employed on each production, and the company offers TMA/Equity approved contracts. Recent productions include: *Money, the Game Show, Three Birds*, and *Disgraced.*

Casting procedures: Casts in-house, and does not hold general meetings or issue public casting breakdowns. Welcomes letters and emails from actors previously unknown to the company. Does not welcome showreels or invitations to view actors' websites. Actively encourages applications from disabled actors and promotes the use of inclusive casting.

Chichester Festival Theatre

Oaklands Park, Chichester PO19 6AP
website www.cft.org.uk
Artistic Director Jonathan Church *Creative Producer* Lisa Makin *Associate Casting Director* Gabrielle Dawes

Production details: Chichester Festival Theatre (CFT) is one of the UK's flagship theatres with an international reputation for producing work of the highest quality. In 2014 it reopened its completely refurbished 1,310-seat Festival Theatre; the Minerva Theatre has 310 seats. The Festival season normally runs from April-October followed by a programme of high quality touring shows in the winter months. Also has a thriving Learning, Education and Participation Department with a year-round events and community programme, and award-winning Youth Theatre that presents highly successful summer and Christmas productions using the main stage. Recent productions include: *Gypsy, Guys and Dolls, Amadeus* and *Taken at Midnight.*

Casting procedures: No open auditions, casting is done on a production-by-production basis.

Citizens Theatre

Gorbals, Glasgow G5 9DS
tel 0141-429 5561 *fax* 0141-429 7374
email info@citz.co.uk
website www.citz.co.uk
Artistic Director Dominic Hill *Production Administrator (Casting & Contracts)* Jacqueline Muir

Production details: Internationally renowned producing theatre, producing work in Glasgow and on tour as well as a pioneering year-round Citizens Learning and TAG programme for participants of all ages. Stages 7 productions a year, and undertakes 2 tours per annum. Offers TMA/Equity approved contracts.

Casting procedures: Does not use freelance casting directors. Holds limited general auditions once a year in June, and specific casting for individual shows as and when required. Welcomes emails from actors (with CVs and photographs), which should be submitted to **jackie@citz.co.uk**.

Clwyd Theatr Cymru

Mold, Flintshire CH7 1YA
tel (01352) 756331 *fax* (01352) 701558
email mail@clwyd-theatr-cymru.co.uk
website www.clwyd-theatr-cymru.co.uk
Artistic Director Terry Hands *Associate Director* Tim Baker *Casting Director* Leigh-Ann Regan

Production details: The major drama-producing company in Wales. Although most work is presented in English, some pieces are performed in Welsh. Stages 5-6 shows in the main house, and 5-6 in the studio each year, with some mid- large-scale productions touring Wales and England. Also runs TIE programmes.

Recent productions include: *Aristocrats, Season's Greetings, Copenhagen, Under Milk Wood* and *Arms and the Man.* Offers TMA/Equity approved contracts and subscribes to the Equity Pension Scheme.

Casting procedures: Welcomes enquiries from actors: these should be sent to Leigh-Ann Regan at the above address. (More information about Leigh-Ann Regan can be found under Casting directors on page 117.) Will consider applications from disabled actors to play characters with disabilities.

Coliseum Theatre

Fairbottom Street, Oldham OL1 3SW
tel 0161-624 1731
email mail@coliseum.org.uk
website www.coliseum.org.uk
Artistic Director Kevin Shaw

Production details: A traditional repertory theatre producing 8 shows each year, with additional incoming tours and one-off special events. Also runs Outreach and Community programmes (contact Carly Henderson). Recent productions include: *Chicago, Boeing Boeing, Our Day Out* and *Hobson's Choice.*

Casting procedures: Does not use freelance casting directors. Casting breakdowns are available from the website. Welcomes letters and email submissions for specific roles (with CVs and photographs). Also accepts invitations to view individual actors' websites. Offers TMA/Equity approved contracts and subscribes to the Equity Pension Scheme. Will consider applications from disabled actors to play characters with disabilities.

Contact Theatre

Oxford Road, Manchester M15 6JA
tel 0161-274 3434 *fax* 0161-274 0640
website www.contactmcr.com
Artistic Director Matt Fenton

Production details: Since re-opening in 1999, Contact has emphasised its work with young adults (aged 13-30), putting participation at the heart of its ethos and activities. Contact is also one of the most culturally diverse theatres in the country; it was awarded the inaugural ECLIPSE award for cultural diversity, as well as the Arts Council's ART04 Award Northwest for 'outstanding achievement in the arts'.

Contact has striven to rewrite the rulebook on what 'theatre' can be. A wide range of touring theatre, music, dance and mixed-media work complements the theatre's in-house productions. The huge variety of participatory work with young people is integrated as closely as possible with the company's 'professional' programme. High quality and innovation are key to Contact's participatory work; leading companies working with young people at Contact have included: Frantic Assembly, RJC Dance, Quarantine, and Nitro – as well as a huge range of artists from hip hop to forum theatre and from verse drama to contemporary dance. Recent productions include: *Perfect* (Kaite O'Reilly and Paul Clay); *Slamdunk* (Felix Cross, Benji Reid with Nitro); *Dancing within Walls* (by Rani Moorthy with Rasa); *Dreaming of Bones* (with Red Ladder).

Casting procedures: Uses freelance casting directors and does not advertise casting breakdowns publicly. Welcomes letters (with CVs and photographs) from actors, but warns that it is unable to reply to unsolicited submissions. The theatre prefers not to receive showreels, emails and invitations to view actors' websites. Offers TMA/Equity approved contracts. Actively encourages applications from disabled actors and promotes the use of inclusive casting.

Curve

60 Rutland Street, Leicester LE1 1SB
tel 0116-2423560
email contactus@curvetheatre.co.uk
website www.curveonline.co.uk
Artistic Director Paul Kerryson *Associate Director (Community Engagement)* Suba Das *Associate Director (Participation & Learning)* Tim Ford

Production details: A new state-of-the-art theatre designed by world-renowned architect Rafael Vinoly. Has 2 auditoria, one with 750 seats and the other providing a 350-seat flexible smaller space. "A stunning glass façade encloses a magnificent foyer and mezzanine walkway, with views onto the café, bars, dressing rooms and workshop areas. The stage is placed at street level between the 2 auditoria."

Casting procedures: Uses both in-house and freelance casting directors. Holds general auditions; actors may write in for casting breakdowns as soon as productions are announced. Does not welcome unsolicited approaches by post or by email, showreels, or invitations to view individual actors' websites. Offers Equity-approved contracts as negotiated through TMA. Actively encourages applications from disabled actors and promotes the use of inclusive casting.

Derby Theatre

15 Theatre Walk, St Peter's Quarter, Derby DE1 2NF
tel (01332) 593939
website www.derbytheatre.co.uk
Artistic Director Sarah Brigham

Production details: Derby Theatre has a long and rich history of delivering high-quality drama to audiences. Previously Derby Playhouse, Derby Theatre, which sits at the heart of the city, is now owned and run by the University of Derby. The theatre is rooted in the local community but international in its outlook, producing and presenting performances working with the best local, regional and national talent.

In 2012 Derby Theatre was awarded strategic funding by Arts Council England to develop a new model for regional theatre in the 21st century. From 2013, under the new artistic directorship of Sarah Brigham, who works alongside General Manager Gary Johnson, the theatre is transforming from a traditional producing house to an organisation of training, mentorship and artistic excellence. Its aim is to be an examplar – a new way of looking at the role and responsibility of theatre to its community. Derby's focus will ensure that each part of the theatre's process will be open to public learning opportunities, building the organisation's ability to take artistic risks by bringing creatives and audiences along on a creative path via the co-production of narratives.

Stages 6 productions annually in the Main House, and also works in youth theatre and TIE. Offers Equity-approved contracts as negotiated through UK Theatre, and subscribes to the Equity Pension Scheme. Recent productions include (from 2013): *Cooking with Elvis*, *The Seagull*, *Kes* and *The Odyssey*.

Casting procedures: Uses freelance casting directors. Actors are invited to email enquiries to **casting@derbytheatre.co.uk**. Welcomes letters (with CVs and photographs) from individual actors previously unknown to the company, sent by post or email, and accepts showreels as well as invitations to view actors' websites and visit productions. Applications from disabled actors are actively encouraged.

Donmar Warehouse

41 Earlham Street, London WC2H 9LX
tel 020-7240 4882
website www.donmarwarehouse.com
Artistic Director Josie Rourke *Casting Director* Alastair Coomer

Production details: Independent producing house located in Covent Garden. The building originally served as a vat room and hop warehouse for the local brewery. In 1961 it was purchased by Donald Albery and converted into a rehearsal studio for the London Festival Ballet, which he formed with ballerina Margot Fonteyn. The theatre takes its name from them.

In the 1990s the Donmar was redesigned. The current theatre space retains the characteristics of the former warehouse while incorporating a new thrust stage. Recent productions include: *Red*, *Luise Miller*, *The Recruiting Officer*, *Julius Caesar*, *Roots*, *Coriolanus* and *My Night with Reg*.

Casting procedures: Casting breakdowns are not publicly available. Offers TMA/SOLT/Equity approved contracts. Rarely has the opportunity to cast disabled actors.

The Dukes

Moor Lane, Lancaster LA1 1QE
tel (01524) 598500
website www.dukes-lancaster.org
Director Joe Sumison *Theatre Secretary* Jacqui Wilson

Production details: A producing theatre with an independent cinema. Stages several home-produced shows each year in the main house (313 seats) and 1 in the studio (178 seats), with a focus on contemporary drama and outdoor, site-specific productions. Also runs a Youth Arts programme. Recent productions include: *The Life And Times Of Mitchell & Kenyon*, *No Fat Juliets*, *Sabbat* and *Robin Hood* (outdoor walkabout production).

Casting procedures: Does not use freelance casting directors. Casting breakdowns are obtainable through the website, postal application (with sae) and Spotlight. Welcomes letters (with CVs and photographs) but not email submissions. Showreels and invitations to view individual actors' websites are also accepted. Offers TMA/Equity approved contracts. Actively encourages applications from disabled actors and promotes the use of inclusive casting.

Dundee Repertory Theatre

Tay Square, Dundee DD1 1PB
tel (01382) 227684 *fax* (01382) 228609
website www.dundeerep.co.uk
Chief Executive Nick Parr *Artistic Director* Jemima Levick

Production details: Producing theatre housing Dundee Repertory Ensemble – Scotland's only permanent acting company. Stages 6 shows each year in the main house. Home also to Rep Creative Learning, Scotland's largest permanent Creative Learning Department (contact Gemma Nicol). Recent productions include: *Great Expectations* and *The Glass Menagerie*.

Casting procedures: Does not use freelance casting directors. Welcomes letters (with CVs and photographs) but not email submissions.

Gate Theatre

Above Prince Albert Pub, 11 Pembridge Road, London W11 3HQ
tel 020-7229 0906 *fax* 020-7221 6055
email gate@gatetheatre.co.uk
website www.gatetheatre.co.uk
Artistic Director Christopher Haydon

Production details: Presents new writing and undiscovered classics from around the world in original and visually imaginative productions. Stages 5-6 shows each year. Also runs a Community/Education programme. Recent productions include: *The Kreutzer Sonata*, *Grounded*, and *The Body of An American*.

Casting procedures: Does not accept unsolicited CVs/submissions. "Individual directors tend to cast from their own lists – contact with the director is the best way to ensure that your application is considered. The Gate Theatre Company is committed to promoting theatre as an activity for all."

Greenwich Theatre

Crooms Hill, Greenwich, London SE10 8ES
tel 020-8858 4447 *fax* 020-8858 8042
email info@greenwichtheatre.org.uk
website www.greenwichtheatre.org.uk
Artistic & Executive Director James Haddrell

Production details: Currently mainly receiving touring productions, but occasionally produces shows in-house. Specialises in musical theatre, children's theatre and the work of emerging companies, and produces showcases and semi-staged readings at different points of the year; these often involve professional performers. Recent productions include: *Keeping up with the Joans*; *The Secret Market* (site specific) and *Sam Rose in The Shadows* (puppetry). Offers TMA/Equity approved contracts and subscribes to the Equity Pension Scheme.

Casting procedures: Generally uses freelance casting directors. "Please don't send unsolicited applications; do look at the casting section on the website, as we aim to provide advance information on our future productions, and answer standard questions. Most casting is concerned with the pantomime, so the best time to enquire is between May and July. We are keen to hear from locally based musical performers and especially anyone who has experience of working with young people." Does not have a specific policy on casting disabled actors, as the stage is not wheelchair accessible: "It depends on the actor's particular needs."

Hampstead Theatre

Eton Avenue, London NW3 3EU
tel 020-7449 4200 *fax* 020-7449 4201
email info@hampsteadtheatre.com
website www.hampsteadtheatre.com
Artistic Director Edward Hall

Production details: Hampstead Theatre identifies and produces important new plays by new, mid-career and established writers. Plays are bold, relevant and entertaining. Presents 7 productions in the main house each year, and 7 in the studio. Recent productions include: *Chariots of Fire*, adapted by Mike Bartlett (transferred to the West End); *The Judas Kiss* by David Hare (transferred to the West

End); *55 Days* by Howard Brenton; *Di and Viv and Rose* by Amelia Bullmore; *Longing* by William Boyd; *#aiww* by Howard Brenton and *Race* by David Mamet. Studio shows include: *And No More Shall We Part* by Tom Holloway (transferred to the Traverse Theatre); *Donny's Brain* by Rona Munro; *Ignorance* by Steve Waters; *I Know How I Feel About Eve* by Collette Kane; *Hello/Goodbye* by Peter Souter; *Say It With Flowers* by Gertrude Stein and *A Human Being Died That Night* by Nicholas Wright.

Casting procedures: Uses freelance casting directors.

Harrogate Theatre

Oxford Street, Harrogate, North Yorks HG1 1QF
tel (01423) 502710 *fax* (01423) 563205
email info@harrogatetheatre.co.uk
website www.harrogatetheatre.co.uk
Chief Executive David Bown

Production details: Stages 3 productions annually in the main house; also works in Outreach and Community (key contact, Hannah Draper). Recent productions include: *Private Lives*, *Absent Friends*, and *Dick Whittington*.

Casting procedures: Uses freelance casting directors and sometimes holds general auditions. Offers Equity approved contracts as negotiated through TMA, and participates in the Equity Pension Scheme. Will consider applications from disabled actors to play characters with disabilities. Harrogate Theatre has no resident Artistic Director, and so unsolicited approaches are not welcome. Please check the website for any casting opportunities.

HOME

2 Tony Wilson Place,
Manchester M15 4FN (*temporary*)
tel 0161-228 7621
email info@homemcr.org
website www.homemcr.org
Artistic Director, Theatre Walter Meierjohann

Production details: HOME was formed by the merger in 2012 of the Library Theatre Company and Cornerhouse, HOME produces the best in contemporary theatre, visual art and film, learning and participation, creative industries and digital innovation. The company's new venue, opened in spring 2015, comprises a 500-seat theatre, a 150-seat flexible studio space, a 500m^2, four metre-high gallery space, five cinema screens, education spaces, digital production and broadcast facilities, a café bar, restaurant and offices. HOME provides new opportunities for artists and audiences to create work in different ways together and serves as a social and cultural hub – in one building visitors will be able to see original new work across the visual arts, theatre and film. The Library Theatre moved out of its home, the Central Library in Manchester city centre, in July 2010. The company produced 3 shows a year at the Lowry in Salford, plus some site-specific work, including a number of Manchester Theatre Award-winning productions. Offers TMA/Equity-approved contracts.

Casting procedures: Uses freelance casting directors; casting breakdowns are available from the website and Spotlight. Also holds a limited number of general auditions/interviews in the summer. Actors requesting inclusion in these are advised to write in March or April. HOME encourages applications from actors with disability, and promotes inclusive casting.

Hull Truck Theatre

50 Ferensway, Hull HU2 8LB
tel (01482) 224800 *fax* (01482) 581182
email admin@hulltruck.co.uk
website www.hulltruck.co.uk
Artistic Director Mark Babych *Casting* Enquiries to Administration Department

Production details: Founded by Mike Bradwell in 1971, Hull Truck has a national and international reputation for creating new work by living writers. The company moved into a brand new purpose-built theatre in 2009, which houses 2 auditoria. Its core mission is to produce contemporary plays, or adaptations of key classics which influence today's writers. A substantial playwright-support programme works alongside co-producing partners from around the country to nurture and showcase fresh talent nationally. Open submission policy and reader service, open to all writers and in all styles. Hull Truck's education and community projects reach thousands of young people, adults and people with disabilities every year. Hull Truck is one of the most famous names in regional touring, annually reaching more than 80 locations across 40 weeks, on small, mid and large scale.

Key Theatre

Embankment Road, Peterborough,
Cambridgeshire PE1 1EF
tel (01733) 207237
website www.peterboroughkeytheatre.co.uk
Artistic Director Michael Cross *Youth Theatre/TIE Officer* Paul Collings

Production details: Mainly a receiving house with occasional in-house productions including an annual pantomime and TIE tours. Stages up to 4 shows each year with co-production opportunities.

Casting procedures: Does not use freelance casting directors. Occasional general auditions. Unsolicited communications are not advised. Casting requirements are sometimes available through the website, but usually through professional casting services, Spotlight link and *The Stage*. "Actors working in the area (and especially touring to the Key) are always encouraged to make contact with the Artistic Director and introduce themselves. Invitations to see artists working in productions are always welcome, and, wherever possible, accepted!"

Offers TMA/Equity contracts and does not subscribe to the Equity Pension Scheme. Rarely (or never) has the opportunity to employ disabled actors.

Live Theatre

Broad Chare, Quayside,
Newcastle upon Tyne NE1 3DQ
tel 0191-261 2694 *fax* 0191-232 2224
email info@live.org.uk
website www.live.org.uk
Artistic Director Max Roberts *Associate Director* Paul James

Production details: New writing theatre established in 1973. Produces 8-10 shows each year in the main house. Also runs TIE, Outreach and Community programmes (contact Paul James).

Casting procedures: Does not use freelance casting directors. Welcomes submissions (with CVs and photographs), sent by post or email. Actors may write at any time. Showreels and invitations to view individual actors' websites are also accepted. Offers ITC/Equity approved contracts. Actively encourages applications from disabled actors and promotes the use of inclusive casting.

Liverpool Everyman and Playhouse Theatre

5-11 Hope Street, Liverpool L1 9BH
tel 0151-708 3700 *fax* 0151-708 3701
email info@everymanplayhouse.com
website www.everymanplayhouse.com
Artistic Director Gemma Bodinetz

Production details: The Liverpool Playhouse focuses primarily on imaginative interpretations of classic drama, from ancient to modern, new writing forms the core of the programme at the recently re-opened Everyman, while the Playhouse Studio is a crucible to develop new talent. The theatres also host touring companies from around the country, run a busy Literary Department – working to nurture the next generation of Liverpool playwrights – and have an active Community Department, which takes work to all corners of the city and surrounding areas. The theatres' Young Everyman Playhouse scheme provides young people with practical training across all aspects of theatre. Recent productions include: *The Match Box, The Hudsucker Proxy, The Hook, Twelfth Night* and *Hope Place.*

Lyric Hammersmith

Lyric Square, King Street, London W6 0QL
tel 020-8741 6850 *fax* 020-8741 5965
email enquiries@lyric.co.uk
website www.lyric.co.uk
Artistic Director Sean Holmes

Production details: The Lyric Hammersmith aims to produce and co-produce work that is provoking, entertaining, popular, eclectic, messy, contradictory and diverse. The Lyric has recently finished work on a major capital project. As well as providing a large extension to the west of the theatre, the building has also be given its first major facelift in 30 years. The new facilities will enable the Lyric to expand its ground-breaking work with artists and young people working in collaboration with a group of partner organisations. It is the most significant cultural development to take place in West London for decades, and will change the cultural landscape of Hammersmith and the lives of thousands of young people. Recent productions include: the first revival in London in over 10 years of Alan Parker's *Bugsy Malone,* the first revival in over 25 years of Edward Bond's *Saved,* Sarah Kane's *Blasted* (Olivier Award winner – Outstanding Achievement in Affiliate Theatre) and *Ghost Stories,* which transferred to the West End and continues to tour internationally.

Casting procedures: Different directors cast their own productions, using freelance casting directors.

Lyric Theatre

55 Ridgeway Street, Belfast BT9 5FB
email arts@lyrictheatre.co.uk
website www.lyrictheatre.co.uk
Executive Producer Jimmy Fay

Production details: Northern Ireland's leading full-time producing house for professional theatre. Presents a distinctive, challenging and entertaining programme of new writing as well as contemporary and classic plays by Irish, European and American writers. Recent productions include: *Punk Rock, Pentecost, Mistletoe & Crime, The Shadow of a Gunman, Dancing at Lughnasa* and *The Night Alive.*

Casting procedures: Does not use freelance casting directors. Welcomes submissions (with CVs and photographs), sent by post or email. Actors may write in at any time. Advises actors to check the website for its future programme. Offers TMA/Equity approved contracts. Will consider applications from disabled actors to play characters with disabilities.

Manor Pavilion Theatre

Manor Road, Sidmouth, Devon EX10 8RP
tel 020-7636 4343 *fax* 020-7636 2323

Since the death of Charles Vance, the management of the summer season has been taken over by Paul Taylor Mills Ltd.

Menier Chocolate Factory

51/53 Southwark Street, London SE1 1RU
tel 020-7907 7060
email info@menierchocolatefactory.com
website www.menierchocolatefactory.com
Artistic Director David Babani

Production details: The Menier Chocolate Factory, which opened in 2004, is an award-winning 180-seat off-West End theatre which stages plays and musicals, live music and stand-up comedy. "There's nowhere quite like the Chocolate Factory anywhere ... the bubbliest kid on the block and one of London's great theatre hopes." (*Daily Telegraph*)

Mercury Theatre

Balkerne Gate, Colchester, Essex CO1 1PT
tel (01206) 577006 *fax* (01206) 769607
email info@mercurytheatre.co.uk
website www.mercurytheatre.co.uk
Artistic Director Daniel Buckroyd *Associate Director* Tony Casement

Production details: The Mercury is a regional theatre based in Colchester which creates, hosts, and tours performances nationally. Staging classic and contemporary drama, musical theatre, new writing, panto, dance, and comedy, the Mercury also supports new talent and runs a Community programme (contact Thomas Freeth). Recent productions include: *The Butterfly Lion, Dial M For Murder* and *Betty Blue Eyes.*

Casting procedures: For all casting enquiries, email **casting@mercurytheatre.co.uk**

The Mill at Sonning Theatre

Sonning Eye, Reading RG4 6TY
tel 0118-969 6039
email admin@millatsonning.com
website www.millatsonning.com
Artistic Director Sally Hughes

Production details: Popular 'dinner theatre' venue, producing a range of plays for audiences to watch while eating a meal. Recent productions include: *French Without Tears, Time to Kill*, and *It Runs in the Family.*

Casting procedures: Forthcoming productions are listed on the website. Actors should send their details, along with specific casting suggestions, to the Artistic Director 2 months before each show.

National Theatre

South Bank, London SE1 9PX
tel 020-7452 3335 *fax* 020-7452 3340
email info@nationaltheatre.org.uk
website www.nationaltheatre.org.uk
Artistic Director Nicholas Hytner (until March 2015), Rufus Norris (from March 2015) *Head of Casting* Wendy Spon CDG *Casting Associates* Charlotte Bevan, Juliet Horsley *Casting Assistant* Charlotte Sutton

Production details: A National Theatre was first proposed in 1848. In 1951 a foundation stone was laid near the Royal Festival Hall, and in 1962 Sir Laurence Olivier was appointed the National's first director, based at London's Old Vic Theatre. Finally, in 1976, the new NT officially opened with a production of *Hamlet.* Today, the National stages a range of classics, musicals, new plays and entertainment "for all the family". The building is currently undergoing a major redevelopment – whilst continuing with productions. It is hoped this will be completed by the end of 2014 and will include the Cottesloe Theatre re-opening as the Dorfman Theatre. "It is all about opening it up – both metaphorically and physically – to more people."

Casting details: The National Theatre's casting team works with approximately 10 directors a year casting NT shows. Actors known to the theatre may be approached directly, but casting is predominantly carried out through agents. The NT will first approach agents to check actors' availability, then audition a shortlist. New talent is actively sought out, and the casting team sees several performances a week within London and (less frequently) outside. It also attends drama schools' showcases and will sometimes approach other casting directors known to the NT.

National Theatre of Scotland (NTS)

Civic House, 26 Civic Street, Glasgow G4 9RH
tel 0141-221 0970 *fax* 0141-248 7241
email info@nationaltheatrescotland.com
website www.nationaltheatrescotland.com
Artistic Director Laurie Sansom *Associate Director* Graham McLaren *Artistic Development Producer* Caroline Newall

Production details: The National Theatre of Scotland launched to the public in February 2006. It has no building, and instead takes theatre all over Scotland and beyond, working with new and existing venues and companies to create and tour theatre of the highest quality. This theatre takes place in the great buildings of Scotland, but also in site-specific locations, community halls and drill halls, car parks and forests. To date, over 130,000 people have seen or participated in its work. NTS has produced 28 pieces of work in 62 locations, from the Shetlands to Dumfries, and from Belfast to London. In 2007/8 NTS toured to the USA and Australasia.

Scottish theatre has always been for the people, led by great performances, great stories and great playwrights. The National Theatre of Scotland exists to build a new generation of theatregoers, as well as reinvigorating the existing ones; to create theatre on a national and international scale that is contemporary, confident and forward-looking; to bring together brilliant artists, designers, composers, choreographers and playwrights; and to exceed expectations of what and where theatre can be.

Offers actors in-house ITC/Equity approved contracts and does not subscribe to the Equity Pension Scheme.

Casting procedures: Each casting process is led by the director of each production, with advisory support from the NTS Artistic Team and Casting Director. When casting for specific shows, the Casting Director puts out a call to agents through *Spotlight.*

The NTS Artistic team makes every effort to see every theatrical event produced in Scotland, maximising the number of actors that NTS sees. The team also responds to individual requests to see actors' work. All actors' CVs and headshots that NTS receives are acknowledged and kept on file in the NTS office. The NTS Casting Director reviews these files at regular intervals, and Directors are encouraged to go through these files before casting their productions. In addition, NTS holds an annual 2-day casting workshop to connect with actors who have sent in CVs but whose work it has been unable to see during the year. Actively encourages applications from disabled actors and promotes the use of inclusive casting.

National Theatre Wales

30 Castle Arcade, Cardiff CF10 1BW
tel 029-2035 3070
email admin@nationaltheatrewales.org
website www.nationaltheatrewales.org
Artistic Director John E. McGrath *Casting Director* Sam Jones CDG

Production details: National Theatre Wales has been making English-language productions in locations all over Wales, the UK, internationally and online since 2010. It operates from a small base in Cardiff's city centre, but works all over the country and beyond, using Wales' rich and diverse landscape, it's towns, cities and villages, its incredible stories and rich talent as its inspiration.

Casting procedures: See **http://community.nationaltheatrewales.org/group/actors**

New Vic Theatre

Etruria Road, Newcastle-under-Lyme ST5 0JG
tel (01782) 717954 *fax* (01782) 712885
email admin@newvictheatre.org.uk
website www.newvictheatre.org.uk
Artistic Director Theresa Heskins

Production details: Purpose-built theatre-in-the-round with a full programme of in-house drama, concerts and occasional touring productions. Stages 10 shows each year in the main house. Also very active with Outreach and Education programmes (contact Sue Moffat and Jill Rezzano respectively). Recent productions include: *Around the World in 80 Days*, *The Thrill of Love*, *Talking Heads* and *A Christmas Carol*.

Casting procedures: Theatre uses an associate casting director through Spotlight link. Casting breakdowns are posted in the casting section of the website. Submissions should be specific and referenced to a particular role.

Northern Stage (formerly Newcastle Playhouse)

Barras Bridge, Newcastle NE1 7RH
tel 0191-242 7200 *fax* 0191-242 7257
email directors@northernstage.co.uk
website www.northernstage.co.uk
Artistic Director Lorne Campbell

Production details: Northern Stage is the largest producing theatre company in the North East of England. The building, formerly known as Newcastle Playhouse & Gulbenkian Studio, re-opened in summer 2006 as Northern Stage following a £9m redevelopment programme. The new building has 3 stages and presents and produces a wide repertoire of UK and international theatre. Staging 6 shows a year, the company also works on participatory projects, with Kylie Lloyd as the lead contact. Touring productions in 2009/2010 included: *Oh What A Lovely War* and *Apples*; 2012 touring *Close the Coalhouse Door*. Offers TMA/Equity-approved contracts and subscribes to the Equity Pension Scheme.

Casting procedures: Casting breakdowns, when available, are published on the website. Actively encourages applications from disabled actors and promotes the use of inclusive casting.

Nottingham Playhouse

Wellington Circus, Nottingham NG1 5AF
tel (0115) 947 4361
email enquiry@nottinghamplayhouse.co.uk
website www.nottinghamplayhouse.co.uk
Artistic Director Giles Croft *Associate Director* Fiona Buffini *Casting Director* Sooki McShane *Director of Roundabout & Education* Andrew Breakwell

Production details: Nottingham Theatre Trust was founded in 1948 and moved to its current location in 1963. Stages 10 shows each year in the main house and 3 Roundabout productions. Also runs TIE, Outreach and Community programmes. Recent productions include: *Burial at Thebes*, *On the Waterfront*, *Vertigo*, *Whale's Tooth*, *Can You Whistle Johanna?*

Casting procedures: Does not use freelance casting directors. Casting breakdowns are available from the casting director, Sooki McShane. Welcomes letters (with CVs and photographs) but not email submissions. Showreels and invitations to view individual actors' websites are also accepted.

Nuffield Theatre

University Road, Southampton SO17 1TR
tel 023-8031 5500 *fax* 023-8031 5511
email info@nuffieldtheatre.co.uk
website www.nuffieldtheatre.co.uk
Director and Chief Executive Sam Hodges

Production details: A regional theatre performing a range of classic plays and new writing. Stages shows in the main house, and in the studio. Recent productions include: *Tonight at 8.30* by Noël Coward and *The Hudsucker Proxy* written by Ethan Coen, Joel Coen and Sam Raimi. Offers TMA/Equity-approved contracts and subscribes to the Equity Pension Scheme.

Casting procedures: Uses freelance casting directors. Casting breakdowns are sometimes available through the Equity Job Information Service. "We consider applications from disabled actors in exactly the same way as applications from able-bodied actors."

Octagon Theatre

Howell Croft South, Bolton BL1 1SB
tel (01204) 529407 *fax* (01204) 556502
email info@octagonbolton.co.uk
website www.octagonbolton.co.uk
Artistic Director David Thacker

Production details: Stages 8-9 shows each year in the main house and 18 in the studio. Also runs TIE, Outreach and Community programmes (contact Activ8 Department). Recent productions include: *Brassed Off*, *Hobson's Choice*, *Twelfth Night* and *An Inspector Calls*.

Casting procedures: Does not use freelance casting directors. Actors should refer to the casting page of the company's website.

The Old Vic

The Cut, London SE1 8NB
tel 020-7928 2651 *fax* 020-7261 9161
email enquiries@oldvictheatre.com
website www.oldvictheatre.com
Artistic Director Kevin Spacey (until 2015), Matthew Warchus (from Autumn 2015)

Production details: Under Artistic Director Kevin Spacey, and Producer John Richardson, The Old Vic Theatre Company is now in its 11th season. Since the theatre company was launched by The Old Vic's Chief Executive (Sally Greene) in 2004, the theatre has once again become a destination as a producing house. Through Old Vic New Voices, the theatre also supports young and emerging talent; runs extensive education projects to complement the work in the season; and reaches out to the community with the aim of opening up the building to new and diverse audiences.

Casting procedures: The Old Vic is not able to accept CVs or speculative applications for employment, as it does not have an in-house casting department.

Open Air Theatre

Inner Circle, Regent's Park, London NW1 4NR
website www.openairtheatre.org
Artistic Director Timothy Shaeder

Production details: Stages 4 shows each year in the main house, including 1 family show. Recent productions include: *Much Ado About Nothing*; *The Tempest* re-imagined for everyone aged 6 or over; *The Importance of Being Earnest*; and *Hello, Dolly!*

Casting procedures: Uses freelance casting directors, who send full casting breakdowns to agents as required for each production. "Unfortunately we are unable to consider unsolicited CVs."

Orange Tree Theatre

1 Clarence Street, Richmond TW9 2SA
tel 020-8940 0141 *fax* 020-8332 0369
email admin@orangetreetheatre.co.uk
website www.orangetreetheatre.co.uk
Artistic Director Paul Miller

Production details: "The Orange Tree Theatre is wholly concerned with the performance of quality live theatre, and with reaching as wide an audience as possible with its work. Over the 40 years of its existence it has established a reputation for being the leader in its field, and is the only permanent theatre-in-the-round in London." Presents a mixture of new writing, classic plays, re-discoveries, comedies and musicals. Education and Community work forms a major area of activity. Stages 8/9 shows each year.

Casting procedures: Please email **admin@orangetreetheatre.co.uk** for casting enquiries. Actively encourages applications from disabled actors and promotes the use of inclusive casting.

Park Theatre

Clifton Terrace, Finsbury Park, London N4 3JP
tel 020-7870 6876
email info@parktheatre.co.uk
email hire@parktheatre.co.uk
website www.parktheatre.co.uk
Artistic Director Jez Bond *Executive Director* John-Jackson Almond

Production details: Park Theatre programmes a balance of new writing and classics, plays and musicals. Looks for work that has a strong narrative and emotional drive and plays that can flourish within the intimacy of smaller theatres. Maintains a good gender balance of male and female roles on stage within a season and generally prefer productions with smaller casts but uniformally high production values. Recent productions include: *These Shining Lives* (by Melanie Marnich), *Daytona* (by Oliver Cotton) and *Adult Supervision* (by Sarah Rutherford; the theatre's writer in residence), *An Audience with Jimmy Savile* (by Jonathan Maitland) and *Toast* (by Richard Bean).

Across two of its associated theatres (Park90 and Park200), the Company have hosted a number of events including 8 in-house productions, a cabaret, music evening, improvisational festival and other creative learning activities. Additionally, a pantomime is hosted each year from November through to January. *Daytona* has also been toured nationally. Offers Equity-approved contracts and subscribes to Equity pension scheme, with UK Theatre agreement where applicable.

Casting procedures: Uses freelance casting directors, but does not hold general auditions. Casting breakdowns are periodically available via Spotlight. Happy to receive unsolicited CVs, but emphasises that due to time constraints not all requests can be answered. These should be sent via email. Also welcomes invitations to view individual actors' websites, but asks that as much time be given as possible for invitations to attend performances.

Perth Theatre, Horsecross Arts

Horsecross Arts Ltd, Perth Theatre & Concert Hall, 185 High Street, Perth PH1 5UW
tel (01738) 477736
email info@horsecross.co.uk
website www.horsecross.co.uk
Interim CEO Colin McMahon

Production details: Perth Theatre, Horsecross Arts produces 4 shows a year and programmes work from independent touring companies and producing houses under the Associate Artistic Directorship of Kenny Miller. Co-produces work with both Scottish and UK venues and produces a family pantomime. Runs Perth Youth Theatre, a vibrant Creative Learning programme, and is committed to providing innovative and relevant work for Scottish audiences.

Casting procedures: Audition is by invitation only; works with a casting director on a show-by-show basis (email **casting@horsecross.co.uk**)

Pitlochry Festival Theatre

Port-Na-Craig, Pitlochry PH16 5DR
tel (01796) 484600 *fax* (01796) 484616
email admin@pitlochryfestivaltheatre.com
website www.pitlochryfestivaltheatre.com
Chief Executive and Artistic Director John Durnin
Community and Education Director Drew Scott

Production details: Founded in 1951, Pitlochry Festival Theatre is a producing and presenting theatre located in the Perthshire Highlands. Comprises the main house (capacity 538), an extensive production facility, and *Explorers*: The Scottish Plant Hunters Garden, containing a number of open-air performance spaces. Between May and October each year a 14-18 strong acting ensemble presents a season of 6 major productions performed in day-change repertoire. Visiting theatre, music, dance, opera and other activities are presented during the winter months. Also runs TIE and Community programmes. Recent productions include: *Whisky Kisses, Perfect Days, The Admirable Critchton, The Yellow on the Broom, Passing Places, Mr Bolfry, The Ladykillers* and *Miracle on 34th Street.* TMA/Equity contracts are offered.

Casting procedures: Does not use freelance casting directors. Recruits new members of the acting ensemble each autumn and winter, with a detailed casting breakdown published each July and October direct to agents and via Spotlight. The closing date for applications is usually in mid-November; auditions are then held in London and Edinburgh in November, December and January. Submissions at any other time – or not in response to the casting breakdown – will not be considered. The theatre actively encourages applications from disabled actors and promotes the use of inclusive casting.

Queen's Theatre

Billet Lane, Hornchurch, Essex RM11 1QT
website www.queens-theatre.co.uk
Artistic Director Bob Carlton

Production details: Has been a producing theatre since it was first established in 1953. Currently works with actor-musicians in a permanent repertory company model. Stages 8 shows each year in the main house. Also runs TIE, Outreach and Community programmes. Recent productions include: *Return to the Forbidden Planet, The Great Gatsby* and *Godspell.*

Casting procedures: Does not use freelance casting directors. Holds general auditions; actors should write in April or May requesting inclusion. Welcomes letters (with CVs and photographs) from actor-musicians only.

Rose Theatre Kingston

24-26 High Street, Kingston-upon-Thames, Surrey KT1 1HL
tel 020-8546 6983
email admin@rosetheatrekingston.org
website www.rosetheatrekingston.org
Director Emeritus Sir Peter Hall *Chief Executive* Robert O'Dowd *Executive Producer* Jerry Gunn

The Rose Theatre Kingston opened its doors to the public in January 2008 with English Touring Productions' production of *Uncle Vanya*, directed by Sir Peter Hall. The design of the theatre was inspired by the Elizabethan Rose on London's Bankside; Kingston's Rose has the same horse-shoe shaped auditorium and an open lozenge stage, creating a sense of intimacy between actors and audiences. The Rose auditorium has a capacity of more than 850 across 3 tiers of seating, including a pit area where audiences can sit on cushions for just £7. In addition to the main space there is a studio, capacity 120, and a gallery, capacity 60. These spaces host a variety of talks and workshops led by theatre writers and practitioners. The theatre also has a strong connection with Kingston University, where it facilitates the University's MA in Classical Drama.

The Rose presents a combination of home-produced drama and received work. Since opening, it has produced 16 home-grown productions, including *Love's Labour's Lost* and *A Midsummer Night's Dream*, directed by Sir Peter Hall; *The Winslow Boy* and *The Lady from the Sea*, directed by Stephen Unwin; and two rep seasons.

Royal & Derngate Theatres

Guildhall Road, Northampton NN1 1DP
tel (01604) 626222 (Admin), (01604) 627566 (TIE)
website www.royalandderngate.com
Artistic Director James Dacre *Associate Director* Dani Parr

Recently the subject of a £15 million redevelopment project, the theatre offers 2 auditoria and 'Underground', a creativity centre that is home to the Youth Theatre and a wide range of workshops and projects for the local community. The theatre's annual pantomime is produced by Qdos (see entry under *Pantomime producers* on page 226).

Royal Court Theatre

Sloane Square, London SW1W 8AS
tel 020-7565 5050 *fax* 020-7565 5001
email info@royalcourttheatre.com
website www.royalcourttheatre.com
Artistic Director Vicky Featherstone *Casting Director* Amy Ball *Associate Directors* Lucy Morrison, Hamish Pirie, John Tiffany *Artistic Associate* Ola Animashawun *Associate Artists* Katie Mitchell, Simon Stephens, Chloe Lamford

Production details: Since 1956 the English Stage Company at the Royal Court has focused on developing, funding and producing new writing. Productions frequently transfer to the West End and Broadway. Stages about 14 productions a year. Also presents an extensive play development programme incorporating workshops and rehearsed readings. Recent productions include: *Liberian Girl* by Diana Nneka Atuona, *Fireworks* by Dalia Taha, *The Twits* by Enda Walsh, *Who Cares* by Michael Wynne, *hang* by debbie tucker green, *The Low Road* by Bruce Norris, *The Ritual Slaughter of Gorge Mastromas* by Dennis Kelly, *Routes* by Rachel De-lahay and *Birdland* by Simon Stephens. Offers SOLT/TMA/UK Theatre/ Equity-approved contracts and does not subscribe to the Equity Pension Scheme.

Casting procedures: Welcomes submissions (with CVs and photographs) by post or email all year round.

Royal Exchange Theatre

St Ann's Square, Manchester M2 7DH
tel 0161-833 9833
website www.royalexchange.co.uk
Artistic Directors Greg Hersov, Sarah Frankcom *Casting Director* Jerry Knight-Smith *Casting Associate* Polly Jerrold *Education Director* Amanda Dalton

Production details: Manchester's leading producing theatre company, comprising a main theatre and studio space. Presents 8-9 productions, on average, in the main theatre and 4-5 in the studio each year. Also runs Education and Community programmes involving schools, young people, community groups and theatre enthusiasts of all ages. Work is based around the theatre's repertoire and its unique building. Where possible, the department leads sessions in the theatre, and frequently works with other departments around the building to give participants an insight into how theatre, and particularly the Royal Exchange, work. Recent productions include: *The Glass Menagerie*, *Three Sisters*, *Antigone*, and *A Taste of Honey*.

Casting procedures: Has a casting department of 2, who coordinate casting for each show. Actors are contracted for individual plays rather than for a season of work. Releases advance production information to around 200 agents on the website. Detailed casting breakdowns are only available for some shows. Will consider attending performances at venues in the North West and London with sufficient notice. Accepts submissions (with CVs and photographs), but actors should bear in mind that the department expects to receive more than 2000 CVs and photos each season – and more in the summer months following graduation at the drama schools. All submissions are considered but they are not kept on file indefinitely.

Royal Lyceum Edinburgh

Grindlay Street, Edinburgh EH3 9AX
tel 0131-248 4800 *fax* 0131-228 3955
email info@lyceum.org.uk
website www.lyceum.org.uk
Artistic Director Mark Thomson

Production details: The Royal Lyceum is one of Scotland's largest producing theatre companies with a season of in-house drama productions running from September to May. In addition, the theatre stages a children's show every Christmas. Occasionally tours in Scotland and abroad, limited hosting of touring companies, and runs an ambitious and acclaimed Education Department. Recent productions include: *Mary Rose, The Lion, the Witch and the Wardrobe, The Man Who Had All the Luck, Curse of the Starving Class*, and *Copenhagen*.

Casting procedures: Does not offer general auditions. "Casting depends on individual directors' choices."

Royal Shakespeare Company

Royal Shakespeare Theatre, Waterside, Stratford-upon-Avon, Warwickshire, CV37 6BB
tel 020-7845 0500
London Office: 1 Earlham Street, London WC2H 9LL
website www.rsc.org.uk
Artistic Director Gregory Doran *Deputy Artistic Director* Erica Whyman *Casting Director* Helena Palmer *Head of Casting* Hannah Miller

Production details: One of the best-known theatre companies in the world, the RSC has been operating under its present name since 1961, a year after Peter Hall was appointed Artistic Director. The repertoire was widened at this time to include modern writing and classics other than Shakespeare. Over the next 50 years the company continued to expand under the artistic directorships of Peter Hall, Trevor Nunn, Terry Hands, Adrian Noble and Michael Boyd. The RSC is at heart an ensemble company, with actors most often being contracted to perform in several productions in a season of work.

Casting procedures: Welcomes performance notices sent 2-6 weeks in advance, and is prepared to travel around the UK, dependent on workload. Welcomes submissions with CV and photograph via email to **submissions@rsc.org.uk**, and preferably in relation to specific productions.

Salisbury Playhouse

Malthouse Lane, Salisbury SP2 7RA
tel (01722) 320117

email info@salisburyplayhouse.com
website www.salisburyplayhouse.com
Artistic Director Gareth Machin

Production details: Produces up to 7 productions each year in the main house, and up to 3 in the studio – alongside an extensive Take Part programme and Theatre For Young People.

Casting procedures: Offers TMA/Equity-approved contracts. Most productions are cast in-house although occasionally the Playhouse use freelance casting directors. Submissions for specific productions by email are welcome. Promotes inclusive casting, and actively encourages applications from disabled actors.

Shakespeare's Globe

21 New Globe Walk, Bankside, London SE1 9DT
tel 020-7902 1400 *fax* 020-7902 1401
email info@shakespearesglobe.com
website www.shakespearesglobe.com
Artistic Director Dominic Dromgoole (until April 2016) *Casting Director* Matilda James

Production details: A reconstruction of Shakespeare's Globe, the theatre has a repertoire which includes the work of Shakespeare, his contemporaries and new writing. The season runs from April to October with up to 10 productions staged each year. Opened second theatre in 2014, The Sam Wanamaker Playhouse, a reconstruction of an indoor Jacobean theatre. Recent productions include: *A Midsummer Night's Dream, Antony and Cleopatra, Julius Caesar* and *As You Like It.*

Casting procedures: Welcomes letters (with CVs and photographs) but not email submissions: prefers invitations to see actors in performance. Actors should write to the Casting Department. Offers actors Equity-approved contracts through an in-house agreement. Actively encourages applications from disabled actors and promotes the use of inclusive casting. The website has more information about casting procedures.

Sheffield Theatres

55 Norfolk Street, Sheffield S1 1DA
tel 0114-249 5999 *fax* 0114-249 6003
email info@sheffieldtheatres.co.uk
website www.sheffieldtheatres.co.uk
Artistic Director Daniel Evans

Production details: Comprises 3 theatres: the Crucible Theatre (thrust stage, 960 capacity), the Studio Theatre (200-400 capacity) and the Lyceum Theatre (pros. arch, 1,168 capacity). Stages 5-6 shows each year in theCrucible and 3-4 in the Studioand 1-2 in the Lyceum. Also runs learning programmes. Recent productions include: *Anything Goes*The Absence of War, *Playing for Time, The Sarah Kane Season* and *The Effect.*

Casting procedures: Uses freelance casting directors. Welcomes letters (with CVs and photographs). Offers TMA/Equity approved contracts.

Sheringham Little Theatre

2 Station Road, Sheringham, Norfolk NR26 8RE
tel (01263) 822117
email enquiries@sheringhamlittletheatre.com
website www.sheringhamlittletheatre.com
Artistic Director Debbie Thompson

Production details: A professional seaside repertory summer season which runs for 10 weeks from July to September, comprising 5 plays which are traditional comedies, farces, thrillers and classics.

Casting procedures: Holds general auditions. Actors should write between January and March, sending a CV and *recent* photograph. Email submissions not welcome. "As a small venue we are non-Equity, but we do work with Equity to pay a realistic wage; we also pay for accommodation and towards travel costs." Actively encourages applications from disabled actors and promotes the use of inclusive casting.

Sherman Cymru

Senghennydd Road, Cardiff CF24 4YE
tel 029-2064 6901 *fax* 029-2064 6902
website www.shermantheatre.co.uk
Artistic Director Rachel O'Riordan

Production details: Stages 4 shows each year and specialises in work for young audiences. Often uses actor-musicians.

Casting procedures: Does not use freelance casting directors. Sometimes holds general auditions. Welcomes letters (with CVs and photographs) but not email submissions. Also accepts invitations to view individual actors' websites.

Soho Theatre

21 Dean Street, London W1D 3NE
tel 020-7287 5060 *fax* 020-7287 5961
email hires@sohotheatre.com (for hirings)
website www.sohotheatre.com
Artistic Director Steve Marmion *Casting* Nadine Rennie

Production details: Soho Theatre + Writers' Centre aims to discover and develop new playwrights, produce a year-round programme of new plays, and attract new audiences. Founded in 1972, the company premiered the early work of such playwrights as Caryl Churchill, David Edgar, Hanif Kureishi, Tanika Gupta, and Timberlake Wertenbaker; more recently it has presented new plays by Laura Wade, Will Eno, Adriano Shaplin, Debbie Tucker Green, Matt Charman, Rebecca Lenkiewicz and Toby Whithouse.

Soho Theatre + Writers' Centre includes a flexible 144-seat theatre, a large self-contained studio space with 85-seat capacity, theatre bar, restaurant, offices, rehearsal, writing and meeting rooms. All spaces are accessible and available for hire. For bookings and general information, please visit **www.sohotheatre.com.**

Casting procedures: Casting is carried out in-house by Nadine Rennie.

Southwark Playhouse

77-85 Newington Causeway, London SE1 6BD
tel 020-7407 0234 *fax* 020-7407 8350
email admin@southwarkplayhouse.co.uk
website www.southwarkplayhouse.co.uk

Production details: Southwark Playhouse's central vision is that of a vibrant theatre in the heart of the London Borough of Southwark, serving the widest possible constituency within the Borough and beyond, providing a platform for emerging theatre practitioners and a programme of performance, education work and community drama.

Southwark Playhouse will be moving to a location in the London Bridge Station development, which completes in 2018. Please see the website for the latest details.

Stephen Joseph Theatre

Westborough, Scarborough YO11 1JW
tel (01723) 370540 *fax* (01723) 360506
email enquiries@sjt.uk.com
website www.sjt.uk.com
Artistic Director Chris Monks

Production details: Stages 6-7 productions each year with lunchtime shows, late nights, rural and national touring. Most work is new writing. Recent productions include: *Improbable Fiction*, *Playing God*, and *Villette*.

Casting procedures: Sometimes holds general auditions; actors may write at any time requesting inclusion. Welcomes submissions (with CVs and photographs) by post or email. Also accepts showreels and invitations to view individual actors' websites. Offers TMA/Equity approved contracts. Will consider applications from disabled actors to play characters with disabilities.

"Casting Director Sarah Hughes is not resident at the SJT. Casting normally only takes place 2-3 times a year. Please note that unsolicited CVs/photos/ showreels will only be returned if with an sae to the same value as the original."

Suffolk Summer Theatres (Southwold & Aldeburgh)

St Edmund's Hall, Cumberland Road,
Southwold IP18 6JP
(07930) 530948
email peter@southwoldtheatre.org
website www.southwoldtheatre.org
Producers: Peter Adshead and Mark Sterling

Production details: Summer theatre with an extensive programme. Stages 5 productions each year playing in 2 venues and occasional tours. Recent productions include: *Arsenic and Old Lace*, *Dick Barton – Special Agent*, *Move Over Mrs Markham*, *Five Finger Exercise*, *Taking Steps*, *Sleuth* and *The Late Edwina Black*.

Casting procedures: Does not use freelance casting directors. Holds general auditions; actors should write in November requesting inclusion. Does not issue casting breakdowns. Welcomes letters (with CVs and photographs) or email submissions, and advises that it is not possible to see everyone who writes in. Offers non-Equity contracts. Rarely (or never) has the opportunity to cast disabled actors.

The Library Theatre

See the entry for HOME under *Producing theatres* on page 137.

Theatre By The Lake

Lakeside, Keswick, Cumbria CA12 5DJ
website www.theatrebythelake.com
Artistic Director Ian Forrest *Associate Director* Mary Papadima *Casting Coordinator* Sophie Curtis

Production details: Each year, Theatre by the Lake produces a Summer Season of 6 plays in repertoire, an Easter production/Spring Season, and a Christmas production. Also promotes a touring programme of visiting professional work across all artforms, and runs Education and Outreach programmes. Recent productions include: *A Chorus of Disapproval*, *Blackbird*, *The Memory of Water*, and *A Midsummer Night's Dream*. Offers TMA/Equity-approved contracts and subscribes to the Equity Pension Scheme.

Casting procedures: Auditions are held 3 times a year. All casting is in-house; does not use freelance casting directors. Casting breakdowns can be obtained by postal application with sae. Does not accept general submissions from actors. Further information about the casting process can be found on the website.

Theatre Royal Plymouth

Royal Parade, Plymouth PL1 2TR
tel (01752) 668282 *fax* (01752) 230499
website www.theatreroyal.com
Artistic Director Simon Stokes

Production details: Theatre Royal Plymouth is the largest and best-attended regional producing theatre in the UK and the leading promoter of theatre in the South West. It produces and presents a broad range of theatre in three distinctive performance spaces – The Lyric, The Drum and The Lab – including classic and contemporary drama, musicals, opera, ballet and dance.

Specialises in the production of new plays and has built a national reputation for the quality and innovation of its programme. Its extensive creative learning work is pioneering and engages young people and communities in Plymouth and beyond. The award winning waterfront production and learning centre, TR2, is a unique building with unrivalled set, costume, prop-making and rehearsal fcilities.

Theatre Royal, Bath

Sawclose, Bath BA1 1ET
tel (01225) 448815
website www.theatreroyal.org.uk
Director Danny Moar

Production details: One of the oldest theatres in Britain. Comprising three auditoria – the Main House, the Ustinov Theatre and the Egg theatre for children and young people – the Theatre Royal offers a varied programme of entertainment all year round.

Theatre Royal, Bury St Edmunds

Westgate Street, Bury St Edmunds, Suffolk IP33 1QR
email sharron.stowe@theatreroyal.org
website www.theatreroyal.org
Creative Producer Emily Slack

Production details: Seating capacity 358. Built in 1819, the theatre is the only surviving Regency theatre in the country. Produces an annual pantomime at Christmas and 2 other shows a year – a rural tour in the spring and an in-house production in the autumn, often from or about the Regency period. Offers non-Equity contracts.

Casting procedures: Casting breakdowns are published via Spotlight only. Actors wishing to be considered for the pantomime should write to the theatre in August. (The spring and autumn shows are cast in January/February and June/July respectively.) Only welcomes letters and emails (with CVs and photographs) from actors previously unknown to the company during these casting periods. Does not welcome showreels, but is happy to receive performance notices. Rarely or never has the opportunity to cast disabled actors.

Theatre Royal Stratford East

Gerry Raffles Square, London E15 1BN
tel 020-8534 7374 *fax* 020-8534 8381
email theatreroyal@stratfordeast.com
website www.stratfordeast.com
Artistic Director Kerry Michael

Production details: Committed to work which portrays the experiences of different social and ethnic communities, the theatre is constantly striving to present shows which resonate with its diverse local audiences. Stages 8 shows each year. Also runs TIE, Outreach and Community programmes. Recent productions include: *Kingston 14*, *Infidel* and *Antigone*.

Casting procedures: Casting opportunities are advertised on the website. Welcomes submissions (with CVs and photographs) sent by post. Advises actors to research the theatre's work before writing, and to think carefully about their own suitability. Invitations to view individual actors' websites also accepted. Actively encourages applications from disabled actors and promotes the use of inclusive casting.

Theatre Royal Windsor

Thames Street, Windsor SL4 1PS
tel (01753) 863444 *fax* (01753) 831673
email info@theatreroyalwindsor.co.uk
website www.theatreroyalwindsor.co.uk
Chief Executive Bill Kenwright *Executive Director* Robert Miles *Theatre Director* Sian Wiggins

Production details: A long-standing, non-subsidised producing theatre. Shows run for 2-3 weeks. Stages 15 productions each year with some going on to tour. Recent productions include: *Black Coffee*, *Last Of The Duty Free* and *Rock'n'Roll*.

Casting procedures: Does not use freelance casting directors. Welcomes letters (with CVs and photographs) but not email submissions. Offers TMA/Equity-approved contracts. Will consider applications from disabled actors to play characters with disabilities.

Tobacco Factory Theatres

First Floor, Tobacco Factory, Raleigh Road, Southville, Bristol BS3 1TF
tel 0117-902 0345 *fax* 0117-902 0162
email theatre@tobaccofactorytheatres.com
website www.tobaccofactorytheatres.com
Artistic Director Ali Robertson

Production details: Stages 3-6 productions a year in the 2 theatre spaces, and also works with the local community. Does not always offer Equity-approved contracts. Offers contracts where possible.

Casting procedures: Casts in-house and does not hold general auditions. Casting breakdowns are available from the website, and via postal application (with sae). Welcomes letters (by post and email) from actors previously unknown to the company, but does not welcome showreels or invitations to view individual actors' websites. Actively encourages applications from disabled actors and promotes the use of inclusive casting.

Torch Theatre

St Peter's Road, Milford Haven SA73 2BU
tel (01646) 694192 *fax* (01646) 698919
email info@torchtheatre.co.uk
website www.torchtheatre.co.uk
Artistic Director Peter Doran *PA to Artistic Director* Lynn Muir *Casting Director* Christine O'Reilly

Production details: Stages 4-5 productions each year. Recent productions include: *Macbeth*, *One Flew Over the Cuckoo's Nest* and *Blue Remembered Hills*.

Casting procedures: Sometimes holds general auditions; actors should write in June requesting inclusion. Casting breakdowns are available by postal application (with sae) and Equity Job Information Service. Welcomes submissions (with CVs and photographs), sent by post or email. Showreels and invitations to view individual actors' websites are also accepted. Advises actors to join the mailing list so they know what is being planned 6 months in advance. Offers TMA/Equity approved contracts. Actively encourages applications from disabled actors and promotes the use of inclusive casting.

Traverse Theatre

Cambridge Street, Edinburgh EH1 2ED
tel 0131-228 3223 *fax* 0131-229 8443
email casting@traverse.co.uk
website www.traverse.co.uk
Artistic Director Orla O'Loughlin

Production details: Scotland's only theatre committed to new writing. Presents a mixed programme of in-house productions and visiting companies and festivals, across its two theatre spaces. Also runs Engagement Projects and Script Development programmes; see website for more details.

Casting procedures: Does not use freelance casting directors. Welcomes letters (with CVs and photographs) and email submissions. Particularly interested to hear from Scotland-based actors.

Tricycle Theatre

269 Kilburn High Road, London NW6 7JR
tel 020-7372 6611 *fax* 020-7328 0795
email admin@tricycle.co.uk
website www.tricycle.co.uk
Artistic Director Indhu Rubasingham

Production details: Since opening in 1980, the Tricycle has striven to produce a challenging and innovative programme of theatre, cinema and visual arts reflecting the cultural diversity of its neighbourhood – and in particular, plays by Irish, African-Caribbean, Jewish and Asian writers – as well as responding to contemporary issues and events with its ground-breaking 'tribunal' plays. The new Tricycle now comprises a 230-seat theatre, a 300-seat cinema, a large rehearsal studio, a visual arts studio for educational use, a smaller theatre/workshop space, an Art Gallery, and a new room called the Creative Space for educational/social exclusion workshops.

The Tricycle maintains a comprehensive Youth and Education programme in Brent schools, and a thriving youth theatre reaching more than 20,000 children and young people each year through access schemes and community work. The theatre stages 5 plays each year. Recent productions have included: the premières of Harold Pinter's *The Dwarfs* and Athol Fugard's *Sorrow and Rejoicings*; 2 plays about the political situation of Northern Ireland – *As the Beast Sleeps* by Gary Mitchell, and *10 Rounds* by Carlo Gebler; and a collaboration with the Royal National Theatre on Zinnie Harris's *Further than the Furthest Thing*.

Casting procedures: Uses freelance casting directors but also occasionally posts casting breakdowns on the noticeboard section of the website. Does not welcome casting enquiries and submissions from actors unknown to the company. The Tricycle does however keep files on Black/Asian actors for its own information and as a resource for others; in such cases a photograph and CV are welcome.

Tron Theatre

63 Trongate, Glasgow G1 5HB
tel 0141-552 3748 *fax* 0141-552 6657
email casting@tron.co.uk
website www.tron.co.uk
Artistic Director Andy Arnold *Outreach* Lisa Keenan

Production details: The Tron Theatre Company is currently under the leadership of Andy Arnold. The Tron presents the people of Glasgow and Scotland with outstanding professional productions of the finest new writing and contemporary adaptations of classic texts, with an emphasis on world, UK and Scottish premieres. The Tron also provides a supportive environment for emerging and established theatre talent, nurturing the future voices of Scottish Theatre. (Seating capacity: main house 230, studio 50.) 6 Tron productions are staged annually in the main house (including co-productions) and 1 production is staged annually in the studio. Other areas of work include our Education & Outreach programme. Recent productions include: World premiere stage adaptation of *Ulysses* by James Joyce; John Byrne's new adaptation of *Three Sisters*; *Dreams and Other Nightmares of Edwin Morgan* by Liz Lochhead; and in autumn 2015, contemporary adaptation of Ibsen's *Ghosts* by Megan Barker

Casting procedures: Casting is done by liaising with show director and casting directors, and using details of actors on file. Actors can write at any time to request inclusion, as their submissions will be kept on file. Accepts submissions (with CVs and photographs) from actors unknown to the company. Actors are employed under Equity-approved contracts, and the theatre participates in the Equity Pension Scheme. Encourages applications from disabled actors and promotes the use of inclusive casting.

Watermill Theatre

Bagnor, Newbury RG20 8AE
tel (01635) 45834 *fax* (01635) 523726
website www.watermill.org.uk
Artistic and Executive Director Hedda Beeby *Outreach Director* Beth Flintoff

Production details: A producing theatre where actors live onsite. Stages 6 shows each year with runs of 6-8 weeks, and 1 Outreach tour. Recent productions have included: Shakespeare, Music Theatre, New Writing and Classics.

Casting procedures: Does not use freelance casting directors. Welcomes emails (with CVs and photographs) with reference to specific castings only. Offers TMA/Equity-approved contracts and subscribes to the Equity Pension Scheme. The Watermill Theatre is committed to equality of opportunity for all.

Watford Palace Theatre

20 Clarendon Road, Watford WD17 1JZ
tel (01923) 235455 *fax* (01923) 819664
email enquiries@watfordpalacetheatre.co.uk
website www.watfordpalacetheatre.co.uk
Artistic Director and Chief Executive Brigid Larmour

Production details: Producing theatre built in 1908 and recently refurbished, it currently stages 8 shows each year. The theatre presents a varied programme but with an emphasis on new plays and adaptations. Also involved in Education and Community theatre, for which Kirsten Hutton (Head of Learning & Participation) is the lead contact. Offers TMA/Equity-approved contracts and does not subscribe to the Equity Pension Scheme.

Casting procedures: Uses freelance casting directors and is unable to respond to individual CVs. Will consider applications from disabled actors to play disabled characters.

West Yorkshire Playhouse

Playhouse Square, Quarry Hill, Leeds LS2 7UP
tel (0113) 213 7800 *fax* (0113) 213 7250
website www.wyp.org.uk
Artistic Director James Brining

Production details: Founded in 1990, the West Yorkshire Playhouse has 2 auditoria – the Quarry (750 seats), and the Courtyard (350 seats). Works include new writing, classics, Shakespeare and musicals, as well as guest productions from incoming touring companies. Also runs TIE, Outreach and Community programmes (contact Gail McIntyre): the schools company tours 3 times a year. Stages 15-17 productions each year across both theatre spaces. Recent productions include: *The Lion, the Witch and the Wardrobe, Othello, Animal Farm, The Hounding of David Oluwale, When We Are Married* and *Peter Pan.* Offers TMA/Equity contracts and does not subscribe to the Equity Pension Scheme.

Casting procedures: Currently the West Yorkshire Playhouse casts through agents' submissions, and works with casting directors on productions on a show-by-show basis. Replies to individual actors can only be sent on receipt of sae. Casting breakdowns are only available to agents. The West Yorkshire Playhouse is an equal opportunities employer in relation to casting.

The New Wolsey Theatre

Civic Drive, Ipswich IP1 2AS
tel (01473) 295900
email info@wolseytheatre.co.uk
website www.wolseytheatre.co.uk
Artistic Director Peter Rowe *Associate Director* Rob Salmon *Chief Executive* Sarah Holmes

Production details: Mixed producing/receiving house, staging 3-4 productions a year in the main house and specialising in musical theatre using actor-musicians. Alongside these productions, the theatre also produces 4 plays per year in our studio space with its Young Company and Youth Theatres. It also works in creative learning and community outreach; the contact for this is Rob Salmon, Associate Director.

Casting procedures: Uses freelance casting directors and does not hold general auditions. Does not welcome unsolicited approaches from actors, unless in response to a casting breakdown. Offers TMA/Equity-approved contracts. Actively encourages applications from disabled actors and promotes the use of inclusive casting.

York Theatre Royal

St Leonard's Place, York YO1 7HD
tel (01904) 623568 (Box Office)
website www.yorktheatreroyal.co.uk
Artistic Director Damian Cruden

Production details: One of the oldest theatres in the country; seats 863 in the main theatre and 102 in the studio. Productions include classics, new writing and the famous York pantomime every Christmas. Also hosts touring companies, premières and has partnerships with tutti frutti, Belt Up Theatre, Touring Theatre Consortium and Pilot Theatre Company, who are resident at the theatre. Runs Outreach, Community programmes and Youth Theatre. Recent productions include: *The York Mystery Plays 2012, The Crucible, Peter Pan, The Wind in the Willows*, Oliver-Award Winning *The Railway Children, Up the Duff, Twelfth Night, The Homecoming* and *The White Crow.*

Casting procedures: Occasionally uses freelance casting directors; submissions from actors may be sent directly to Katy Nelson.

Young Vic

66 The Cut, London SE1 8LZ
email info@youngvic.org
website www.youngvic.org
Artistic Director David Lan

Production details: The Young Vic present a widest variety of classics, new plays, forgotten works and music theatre. The theatre is especially concerned with the art of directing. Their Directors Programme is the most comprehensive in the UK. This fusion makes the Young Vic one of the most exciting theatres in the world. "Our audience is famously the youngest and most diverse in London. We encourage those who don't think theatre is 'for them'". Recent productions include: *A View From the Bridge* (dir. Ivo van Hove); *Happy Days* (dir. Natalie Abrahami); *The Scottsboro Boys* (dir. Susan Stroman); *A Season in the Congo* (dir. Joe Wright); *Feast* (dir. Rufus Norris) and *Sizwe Banzi is Dead* (dir. Matthew Xia).

Casting procedures: Uses freelance casting directors. Does not welcome direct submissions from actors. Offers TMA/Equity approved contracts. Actively encourages applications from disabled actors and promotes the use of inclusive casting.

Effective audition speeches

Simon Dunmore

Audition speeches may be a fundamental part of the actor's 'toolkit', but a surprising number of otherwise good actors are not very good at doing them – and many make poor choices of material to use. It's true that most castings involve a reading, but sometimes audition speeches are asked for in advance, and occasionally you'll get, "We'd just like to see something else; what can you show us?" It would be very silly to be caught out because you haven't done an audition speech since drama school.

Essentially, audition speeches should be self-contained, well chosen, well researched, well staged and well gauged for the space you are in and for whoever is watching you – just like a good production of a play. In fact an audition speech should be a 'mini-production' (of a 'mini-play') in its own right.

Essential parameters

Length

An audition piece should be no more than two or two-and-a-half minutes long (that's roughly 300 words, depending on pace). Two minutes (or less) can be very effective provided that it contains all the parameters listed elsewhere in this article.

How many?

The important thing is to have a good range of audition material so that you've got a library to choose from to suit each given circumstance. I suggest at least half a dozen.

What types?

Your collection should consist of a good variety of characters you could credibly play. They should be within your 'playing range' and appropriate to your appearance: an audition speech is not an acting exercise; it's part of your marketing portfolio.

You should also aim to find material that rarely (if ever) appears elsewhere on the audition circuit. Judging acting is a highly subjective business, so it is generally better to find 'original' material to heighten your chances of not being compared to others. I suggest that you only use material that is popular if you feel sure you can perform it (them) extremely well – on a bad day ...

Accents

If you choose to do a speech written in a regional accent, make sure you can do that accent well enough to convince a native. (It is important to have at least one in your repertoire that features your own accent if it is a strong and 'characterful' one.) Some people choose to 'translate' a speech into an accent with which they are more comfortable, and this can work. However, watch that in doing this you are not sacrificing too much of the quality of the original language.

Sources of speeches

Don't just rely on plays that you know; you should be steadily expanding your knowledge of dramatic literature. Seeing, reading, sitting in libraries and bookshops (especially secondhand ones); even picking up an audition book to find inspiration for a playwright (previously unknown to you) whom you could explore further.

Look in novels, less well-known films, and good journalism (for instance) for material that could be made into good 'drama'. For example, Shakespeare copied (almost word-for-word) Queen Katherine's wonderful speech beginning "Sir, I desire you do me right and justice ..." (*Henry VIII,* Act II, Scene 4) from the court record.

It's generally inadvisable to write your own speech(es). This rarely works, because very few actors are good playwrights. If you do decide to use a self-written piece, it can be a good idea to use a *nom de plume;* you're selling yourself as an actor, not as a playwright. You should also be prepared to talk about the whole play, even if you haven't written it yet.

Content

Too many people fail because they choose to do an indifferent speech. Even if they do it well, it somehow doesn't have much impact because of indifferent writing, lack of depth, and so on. Essentially you should go for pieces that have good 'journeys' – just like a good play.

It can be useful to find speeches that enable you to show your special skills (singing or juggling, for instance), but don't try to cram so much in that the sense is lost in a firework display of technical virtuosity. At the other extreme, avoid something that requires performance at one pace or on one note.

And, never set out to shock deliberately through content and/or crude language. That is not to say don't do 'shockers'; rather, don't set out with the specific idea of shocking your interviewer(s) as many people seem to intend. We've heard most of it before. I cannot describe how mind-numbingly tedious audition-days can become when peppered with such speeches.

Warning: There is now a lot of free audition material available on the Internet. Much of it is indifferently written; however, I have come across the occasional 'gem'.

Shape

Make sure that each of your pieces has a decent shape. In a sense it should be like a good play, with a beginning, middle and ending. Even if the character ends up back where he/she started, so long as he/she has travelled a 'journey' then that's fine.

Shakespeare and the classics

Traditionally you need to have at least one of these in your armoury. The fact is that most people perform them indifferently. Too many renditions seem as dead as their writers. The problem is that they are remote – in language and in content – from our direct experience, and therefore usually require much more research, thought and preparation than a modern speech.

NB It's very tedious to see comedy Shakespeare speech done in a 'cod' West Country accent. If you can genuinely do one of the many variants of this accent, then that's fine, but his language works in every other regional accent in which I've heard it done.

'Trying on'

Try reading any speech that looks good to you (on the page) out loud, in front of someone else, before you start rehearsing it. If you do this, you'll get an even better idea of whether each speech really suits (and 'grabs') you. It's a bit like buying clothes: you see a pair of trousers (say) that look good on the hanger; sometimes you will feel completely different about them when you try them on. The opposite can also occur: you feel indifferent about a speech on the page; you read it out loud and it feels much, much better.

Rehearsing your speeches

'What are you bringing on stage?'

You must bring your character's life history (gleaned from the play and supplemented by your imagination) into your performance. [As the character (i.e. in the first person), write notes of all the bits of information (big and small) that you find, in order to build his/her life.] Most of what you 'bring' won't be obvious to your auditioner(s). However, it will be immediately obvious if that 'life history' is not present. Just as 90% of an iceberg is underwater, a similar proportion of a good performance is also hidden ... but must be there, underneath, to support that performance.

It is particularly important to be clear about what actually provokes the character to start speaking – the 'ignition' that kicks your 'engine' into life. Try running a brief 'film' in your imagination, culminating in the event (for instance, a statement or a gesture from someone else) that is your cue.

Your invisible partner(s)

If you choose a speech addressing another character, then it is vital that that other person (and how they are reacting through the speech) is clear to you. It is generally better to imagine an adaptation of someone you know rather than to 'borrow' someone you've only seen on a flat screen. There can be a huge difference in how we perceive others between two and three dimensions.

It's not just them (and how they are reacting); it's also important to be clear about your relationship. As well as imagining what your character's lover looks like (for instance), you must also know the feel of their touch, their smell, and so forth – and many more personal aspects.

It is also important that any other people, places and events mentioned in the speech are similarly 'clear' in your imagination.

Your invisible circumstances

You should also bring the setting, clothes and practical items with you – in your imagination. (NB I could have written 'set, costumes and props', but I believe that it's important to think of everything being 'real' and not items constructed for a production.) I believe that actors neglecting these is the cause of a high proportion of failed and indifferent speeches. It's not just the visual images, it is also what the other senses give you: the 'brush' of a summer breeze across your face, for instance. Plays are not performed in 'real' rooms (there will be at least one wall missing) and every play has at least one non-appearing character mentioned. These absences are filled by the actors' imaginations. Do the same with these 'absences' in the audition circumstances.

It isn't just the major features that you should think about, but also the apparently minor details – for instance, the mark on a wall that suddenly catches your character's eye. It can be a good idea to draw a map (or groundplan) so that the whole 'geography' of your 'circumstances' is clear for you. Then fill out your imaginary location with as much detail as possible.

Interpretation

As you are creating a 'mini-production' of a 'mini-play' (the 'child' of its 'parent-play'), I believe that it's legitimate to make changes to the given circumstances of the speech when it occurs in the play, especially if such changes enhance your audition performance. (After all, a 'child' can never lose the genetic code of its 'parents', but he/she will evolve their own personality, which will be different.) However, be prepared to justify it – and don't get defensive. There's usually no harm in honest disagreement.

That voyage of discovery

Be aware of the 'voyage of discovery' that shapes your speech. Don't anticipate the end at the beginning. This is a common fault in rehearsal, which is easily corrected – but a remarkable number of people fall into this trap when performing their audition speeches.

It can be very useful to write out a speech with each sentence (or even each phrase) on a separate line. It then appears less of a 'block' of words on the page and more a series of separate, but connected, thoughts and ideas. It is also a good idea to leave sufficient space between each line to write notes on what is the impulse to go on to say the next thing, and the next, and ...

Beginnings

If you start your speech nebulously, your interviewer probably won't take in what you are doing for the first few seconds and may miss vital information that could make the rest of it a complete puzzle to them. You need to find a way of starting your speech that will grab their attention from the very beginning. This doesn't mean that the beginning has to be loud, simply that it should be positive and effective – almost as if the house lights were faded down and the curtain rising on ... You!

NB It can also be very useful to incorporate a simple movement to start a speech; a turn of the head, for instance.

Endings

It's also important to be clear as to why a character stops speaking after talking for two minutes. You need to be clear what your character's final thought is – crucially stopping his/her flow.

Finally

Ask yourself: "Are my speech and my presentation of it a good piece of 'Theatre'?"

Some practical considerations

Staging

Once you've done all the work set out in the previous paragraphs, you need to think carefully about how you stage each piece. Too many people seem inclined to put in extraneous moves either to compensate for the lack of the other character(s), or because they think the speech is boring if it doesn't contain enough movement. If you are properly 'connecting' to character and 'circumstances', the moves will follow naturally from each 'impulse'. However, much of the effect of your performance will be dissipated if your auditioners don't see enough of your face, and especially your eyes. In general (unless it is an address to the audience), they should be able to see three-quarters of your face for at least half the duration of the speech. To achieve this, orientate the other character(s) and 'circumstances' to suit the audition situation. For instance, place the imaginary person to whom you're talking at around 45 degrees to left or right in front of you. If your map (or groundplan) is clear in your mind, then it should be simple to angle it appropriately.

There is no point in placing a chair specifically to mark another character – or even the hat-stand which I once saw used as the object of some singular passions. If you do use such objects you'll usually find yourself concentrating on that object rather than your 'partner(s)'. They should be clearly lodged in your imagination so that the interviewer can 'see' them through you. Also, don't think that you have to stare at one place continually just to make it clear that he or she is there.

Chairs

A warning about chairs. There is a common variety of chair, as familiar as the bollard is to the motorway, that inhabits many popular audition venues. It can serve all kinds of functions as well as the simple one of being sat upon. However, don't rely on the well-known weight and balance of these plastic and steel functionaries for crucial elements of your well-prepared speech. You may suddenly find only chairs with arms or a room filled with wobbly ones. Be prepared to adapt to whatever form of seating is available.

Tip 1 Do a brief check on the mechanics of your audition-chair before you start your speech. For instance, you don't want to be thrown by the fact that the back is lower than that of the chair you rehearsed with ...

Tip 2 If your audition-chair represents a different type of seat (a low, backless bench, for instance), sit on the chair as though you're sitting on that 'bench'.

Props

Avoid using props. As you haven't got a proper set, costume or lighting, too much of the visual emphasis goes on to the prop and consequently away from you. It is amazing how riveting even a small piece of paper produced for one of the numerous 'letter' speeches can become.

Props can be mimed: that mime doesn't need to be brilliant. And think how much easier it is to put down an imaginary glass on an imaginary table, without making a sound at the wrong moment. In using any imaginary prop, remember not just the shape as you 'hold' it in your hand but also its weight and its impact on your sense of touch.

The only exception to this can be a prop introduced briefly and then quickly discarded. Even then, make sure its impact doesn't take the focus from the rest of the speech.

Performing your speeches

Each presentation of a speech has to have the raw energy of a first performance. Unlike a first night, where the only new factor (in theory, at least) is the audience, you have to face numerous new and possibly unexpected factors when doing your audition speech. You need to be not only well rehearsed but also well prepared for how to cope with all the peripherals that are other people's responsibilities when you are actually doing a production. You are your own stage-management, wardrobe department, front-of-house manager, and so forth.

'Act in here?'

I don't think any audition-room is entirely satisfactory. They can be dirty and unkempt, too hot or too cold, too big or too small, have inconvenient echoes, have barely adequate waiting facilities and/or be hard to find down a maze of corridors. You'll be very fortunate if the whole session has only road traffic as a background noise. You have to be prepared to adjust the presentation of your speech(es) to each context – by fractionally slowing down and enhancing your diction slightly if there's an unavoidable echo, or scaling down your movement in a small room, for instance.

It's your space

You should regard the space in which you are doing your speech as your stage with which to do whatsoever you wish – as long as you have due reverence for the fabric of the building, for your interviewers and their goods and chattels. Move the chairs if you need to, take your shoes off if that's necessary, and so on ... but don't ask if it's 'all right' to do so. It can get very tedious for an interviewer if you keep on asking permission every time you want to change something. Providing it doesn't affect your audience directly, just get on with what is necessary for your performance.

Don't ask where to stand; your actor's instinct should tell you the optimum place for what you are about to do. Especially, don't ask permission to start, even if it's only with one of those pathetic little enquiring looks – another way of undermining yourself in your interviewer's eyes. Once you've been given your cue, it's all yours and in your own time.

Natural hazards

Be aware of natural hazards in the room: for example, a low afternoon sun pouring through the windows that blinds you as soon as you happen to turn into it. Don't, on the other hand, stand in the deepest shadow; nobody wants an actor who cannot find his or her light.

Your interviewer will probably be sympathetic if the unexpected suddenly interrupts you, but it really is your responsibility to spot this kind of thing beforehand and adjust accordingly. If it is something impossible to anticipate, then aim to recover as quickly as possible and get back into your speech. After all, if something goes wrong during a performance, you don't just stop until it's put right; you continue as best you can, and 99.9% of the time nobody in the audience will notice that anything went wrong.

Explanations

Minimise explanations about your speech. Ask yourself if you need them at all. In fact the best speeches are self-contained and don't need explanation beyond the character's name and possibly the title and the writer of the play. Whatever their individual faults, most directors do know a lot of plays, the characters within them and who wrote them. Be careful not to insult directors by telling them what they already probably know. (For example, 'Hamlet from *Hamlet* by William Shakespeare.') On the other hand, make sure you know the title and writer of more obscure plays and be prepared to discuss them.

Sometimes, in the process of getting inside the character, actors forget to give these basic details. I don't think this matters (I enjoy trying to work them out for myself), but some directors have a nasty habit of interrupting actors' preparations with demands like "What are you doing, then?" If you do forget and are so interrupted, don't be so thrown that you rush into your speech.

Your interviewer as the other character

Some people try to use their interviewer as the other character for the purposes of their speech. This is not necessarily a good idea. It can work but is fraught with pitfalls.

First of all, do you need to ask permission beforehand? Politeness dictates that you should. After all, you are asking the auditioner to do the job of being in your play. He or she may say, 'Yes, of course', but has probably been asked the same question in every other session of the day; it can get very tedious. Even if it is all right, the auditioner is probably not an actor, will become self-conscious in the process, not react in the way you anticipated, may well want to drop out of character to write notes and consequently won't be a consistent partner.

Preparation

Do give yourself a moment to position and check your chair and to check the 'geography' of your performance in this particular space.

A pause for thought

Then, also do give yourself that moment of thought before starting a speech – a moment to immerse yourself within your character and circumstances. Almost everybody understands that it can be hard to change gear from chatting to acting. Don't think that you are wasting time; it'll only be a few seconds, and your interviewer will almost certainly have something else to write down before concentrating on you again. (For most actors a 'few seconds' feels much, much longer in these stressed circumstances.)

However, don't take too long to wind up into your speech with lots of heavy breathing or pacing about or even just standing quietly in a corner. That may be what you have to do before you go on stage, but most directors, however understanding, will begin to wonder what kind of lunatic you are and are you going to take up precious rehearsal-time with these warm-ups? Your 'pause for thought' should be as brief as you can make it without showing your inner turmoil. Properly done, this can be riveting to watch.

Starting

One of the hardest aspects of doing a speech is starting it from cold. If you are onstage at the beginning of a stage-production (especially on a first night), you'll experience an immense, and for some, terrifying, feeling of excitement and power as the audience goes quiet. You should aim to recreate this feeling just before you start your speech. It'll give you tingles up your spine and put a real 'kick' into your speech. This will 'communicate' to your auditioners and make them really look at you – even if they've had their heads down scribbling in the preceding seconds.

Tip To help stimulate this process, get the smell of dust into your imagination – it's the pervading smell of any theatre.

Communication

You may well 'feel' your speech, but are you communicating it? Just because you are in a small room with only one person watching, don't mutter your speech at below conversation-level. How do I know you can fill a stage, however small, if you are not filling the room we're in? You have to make that room your stage, the interviewer(s) your audience. Think of them as being in the best seats in the stalls (the ones reserved for the critics on a first night) and aim just beyond the limits of the space. Only a lazy actor will give a smaller performance on stage just because there is a small audience.

Don't blast your interviewer out of his seat, either. Measure the acoustics: a lot of audition-rooms are part of church-hall complexes and tend to have high ceilings with the inevitable echo.

The 'need'

There is a 'need' that drives any speech; two minutes is a long time for someone to keep on talking. A long speech is a series of connected thoughts and ideas; underneath there has to be the 'need' to talk at such length. We all know people who 'go on' too much in everyday life – the odd person is able to sustain attention because of the energy and 'need' to communicate. The same is true on stage and in the audition.

Also, remember that your character hasn't usually planned to say so much. Essentially, the circumstances provoke the 'need' for them to add more, and more, and ...

Stopping

If you do need to stop during a piece – you've dried or it's started badly – do it positively and calmly, and do it without a grovelling apology. You may feel terrible but you have to get yourself out of the mess without becoming embarrassing. You can even capitalise on having handled it well. A brief (and positive) "I'll start again" or whatever won't be held against you. If you dry or make a mistake significantly into a speech, just pause briefly and find your way back, just as you would in a public performance.

Bear in mind that most interviewers do not know how acting works. So if, say, your breathing starts going haywire, that's not a reason to stop unless it really is affecting the speech badly. You have left your teachers behind at drama school.

Finishing

When you finish you should keep the final thought in your mind and gently freeze for a moment, just as you would if you're left onstage at the end of a scene in a play. Then fade the imaginary stage-lighting (and close the curtains) at a suitable rate. (That 'moment' should last about a second. If you're unsure, say a multi-syllable word like 'Mississippi' in your head.) Then – without looking your interviewer(s) in the eye – relax back to your normal self, ready to move on to whatever your interviewer wants to do next. Many find the not 'looking your interviewer(s) in the eye' difficult, and a few even think that it might seem rude. However, if you do make eye contact at that crucial moment, you'll probably start to feel very vulnerable – and give out the 'vibe' that you're unconfident about your performance. Whatever you may really feel about that performance, there's nothing else that you can now do, except wait.

There may be a silence; your interviewer(s) may well want to write notes on what you've done. Just settle down and let them get on with it. Don't be thrown by that aching pause; you should quietly wait. The 'ball' is now very definitely in the interviewer's 'court' to restart the conversation.

'Thank you' (a)

There may be a vague 'Thank you' or 'Right', even 'Mmmm' from the interviewer at the end of your speech. Don't read anything in to these vague expostulations. If you do you'll start to undermine yourself. We directors are usually thinking about what we're going to write down about your efforts. That thinking process is dominant and what comes out of our mouths is merely our acknowledgement that you've finished – an attempt at politeness that doesn't come out quite right. (I hear myself doing this constantly, but have never found a way round it.)

'Thank you' (b)

Some actors opt for a 'Thank you', or 'That's it', at the end. Sometimes this sounds pathetic; on others it comes across as sheer arrogance (watch the way some actors do curtain calls). If you've got a good enough 'ending', you've given the cue. The director may not respond to it immediately, but you should have clearly established that the 'ball' is now firmly in his or her 'court'. It's much better to say nothing.

Switching off

It is respected that it can take a few seconds to come back to reality, particularly if it's a very emotional speech. But it's fundamental to acting that just as you can 'switch on', you can 'switch off' with apparent ease. I will never forget a woman who did a wonderfully passionate speech from Arnold Wesker's *Four Seasons* and ended up in buckets of tears. She had done it extremely well but when it was over she simply could not stop crying and had to be taken from the room and given time to recover. What would have happened if she'd had to get similarly emotional on stage and then immediately go on to do a comic scene, as can occur? This is an extreme example which exemplifies the need to look very carefully at how you change back to reality.

'Why don't you try that again? This time standing on your head'

Don't get so stuck into a way of doing a speech that you cannot do it in any other way put to you. Some directors like to work on speeches. You should understand the insides of each speech so well that you could do it 'standing on your head'.

Advice

Some directors give constructive advice. In general, take that as a compliment, even if they are critical. Nobody will waste time and energy giving notes if they didn't at least like some aspect of you and your work. However, one director's constructive notes can become another's criticisms. In rehearsal an actor will take a note and try it out. Sometimes it doesn't work, and the moment has to be looked at again. Maybe it was only half-right. In an audition there is usually no time to rehearse that note to see if it works for you. So, when you do try it, and it perhaps doesn't quite work, you have no recourse to its originator for further amplification. Take such notes as suggestions to be utilised or discarded as suits you and your speech. That's how rehearsals should be anyway.

Final note

Working on audition speeches can be a wonderful way of keeping your 'acting juices' flowing through periods of unemployment.

Simon Dunmore has been directing productions for over 30 years – nearly 20 years as a resident director in regional theatres and, more recently, working freelance. In that time there have been over 200 productions (of all styles, colours, shapes and sizes) – recently: several Drama School Showcases, Maugham's *Home and Beauty* and new plays about sex, WB Yeats' up-and-down relationship with Maud Gonne, one set inside a pyramid and another about Bismarck. Past favourites include: *The Promise* (Alexei Arbuzov), *Antigone* (Jean Anouilh), a seven-handed version of *Antony & Cleopatra* and too many others to mention. He also teaches acting and has worked in many drama schools and other training establishments around the country. He has written several books: *An Actor's Guide to Getting Work* (fifth edition, 2012), the *Alternative Shakespeare Auditions* series, and was formerly the Consultant Editor for *Actors' Yearbook*.

Cattle calls and how to survive them

Jennifer Reischel

Standing in the same spot for hours in the cold at 7am. Listening to endless renditions of the same songs. Finally, being herded into a small studio with 50 others to try and dance a routine from *Cats* in the back row without kicking the person next to you. Sound familiar? These are all experiences you may encounter when attending the infamous 'cattle calls', also known as open auditions ...

Why are open auditions held?

These 'mass viewings' are often the only possibility for newcomers to the industry, and performers without the required contacts, to get a foot in the audition system door, as literally anyone can attend. Casting directors and production teams use opens to spot those who do not have agent representation, are not fully professional (therefore not found in *Spotlight*, etc.), and those professionals they may have missed in their jam-packed audition schedule. Usually held for large-scale musicals, such as *Les Miserables*, *Phantom* or the recent production of *My Fair Lady*, most open auditions tend to take place for West End shows, although there are also examples of opens for touring productions. As an educated guess, I would say that musicals hold at most around half-a-dozen adult calls (for properly paid work) each year. Other types of open auditions include searches for children and teenagers for musicals, film and television shows, such as *Harry Potter* and *Billy Elliott* (film and musical version), as well as very occasional open auditions for adult parts in screen and stage ventures. Cruise ship auditions also tend to be open calls, as do searches for pop/rock band members and solo music artists for recording deals and similar projects.

How do I find out about when/where they take place?

Opens are usually advertised in the weekly newspaper *The Stage*, and sometimes in other casting services such as Castweb and CastNet. Auditions for children and large nationwide searches are also often found in daily newspapers such as *The Guardian* or in local papers sold in the town hosting the audition. Common audition venues tend to be large theatres, dance studios (such as Pineapple and Danceworks in London), grand buildings such as The Welsh Trust Centre in London, and similar locations that are capable of hosting sizeable numbers of waiting and queuing hopefuls.

Cattle calls ads: what are they actually looking for?

Ads for opens in newspapers tend to be quite general and vague. "Looking for excellent singers and dancers" is a favourite, as are "come prepared to dance and sing", "young, sexy and funny", or "hip, trendy and cool". How do you judge if your particular skills are up to scratch or your look is right? First of all, be honest. Can you really hit that top C like your favourite musical theatre performer? Can you really pass for 25 if you are actually 40? If in doubt, ask an industry professional. The truth about opens is that most of the time, the panel will make up their minds within 10 seconds of seeing you walk in – based on first impressions of your appearance, general persona and whether you fit the general look of the part/show. You have very little control over this process, but you can make sure that you start your audition with the right attitude. Be open, friendly, and full of positive 'ready to perform' energy (a smile always helps). Make sure that your 'hello' or similar greeting is clearly audible. Just be yourself, and be proud of who you are and what you have to offer. After all, if you are not confident in your own abilities, how can you expect anyone else to believe in you?

Being recalled – the next step in the process– often depends purely on whether you have the right look or not, although singing range (which should be indicated on your CV), sometimes where you trained, and whether your dance technique is up to scratch during the few minutes they see you leaping around the room, can also affect your chances. A lot of it is gut feeling, and whoever the panel feels drawn to or stands out for them at that particular moment. They usually have a pretty definite view of what they are looking for, and make decisions very quickly as lack of time forces them to do so.

NB Some open calls may involve members of the casting team going through the queue of waiting hopefuls, telling people then and there to go home/stay to be seen. This often happens if the auditions are running late or they know that they will not be able to see everyone queuing that day.

Physical and age restrictions

Some ads mention size and height restrictions. Most of the time, the panel will stick to these and you may be sent home while queuing if they see that you are not in the required bracket. There are always exceptions, of course, and sometimes an inch or two may not be noticed. Music groups tend to be stricter, especially if they are replacing band members. Children/teenage auditions seem to take height restrictions very seriously. As regards age, if you are underage and the ad specifically states that you should be 18 or over, or 16 or over, there is little point in attending this open call as the age limit has been given for legal reasons.

The procedure on the day – and how to prepare

Preparing for an open calls starts with one important point – having an *early* night the day before. You will be up at the crack of dawn heading to the particular audition venue so you can be there at least two hours before the official start time given in the ad. If you do not turn up early, a) you may have to wait for up to eight hours or b) you may not get seen at all. For example, if the queue officially opens at 9am, get there at 7am. Some auditions will involve you literally queuing until you get seen by the panel, while other opens will give you a number and ask you to return at a specific time to audition with another 50 or so people in the queue. It is impossible to tell beforehand. While you are waiting, your CV and photo will be collected by an assistant and they may also sometimes take a Polaroid of you and ask you to fill out a form. Most open calls will tell you straight after your audition whether you were successful or not, and say that they will be in contact for any recall.

Musicals

Depending on the ad, you will have been asked to prepare to sing, dance or both. Even if the ad only asks for one of these, be prepared for both. You may turn up at *My Fair Lady* thinking you will be giving your best 16-bar rendition of 'I could've danced all night', but once you are in the building you discover that you will actually be dancing to 'Get me to the church on time'. It is best to be prepared for everything. Remember that if your open call is the 'queuing until you get seen' kind, you will not have time to find somewhere to warm up. You will have to warm up beforehand and/or in the queue, dancing and singing. Dance auditions often take place in small, crowded dance studios with anything between 20 and 50 people at a time. You are normally given about 10 minutes to learn a routine (sometimes two routines) taught by the dance captain, and then have to perform this to the panel (who will be in the same room watching as you rehearse) with the entire audition group (and then in smaller groups, usually of four or six). In terms of singing, you will very probably not get past 16 bars (I have been to opens where they cut people off after eight bars). In most cases you will be able to choose your own song and will be required to bring your own sheet music. Do *not* sing anything from the show you are auditioning for unless requested to do so in the ad. The ad will usually ask for material "in the style of the show" or to "show off your vocal range/style" – this is particularly popular if the open is for a new musical. Some opens hold both dance and singing auditions on the same day. Remember this if you are taking time off work, as if you are successful in the first part they may well require you to stay on for a second round. The panel will not excuse you or make arrangements for you to come back on another day. They are usually unsympathetic when it comes to work commitments.

Children

Auditions for child roles often require accompaniment by an adult, height measurements, and proof of age. Sometimes they may involve group auditions/workshops to put children at ease and encourage them to perform to the best of their best abilities.

Cruise ship opens

These are quite similar to open calls for musicals, although it is common to be asked to sing two contrasting songs here. It pays off to bring a selection and let the panel choose, especially for Disney cruises. For cruise ship auditions it is also sometimes acceptable to bring backing tracks instead of sheet music – to be on the safe side, bring both unless the ad definitely states which kind of accompaniment to use. Again, be prepared to sing and dance on the same day, which is common for cruise ship calls.

NB Your audition may be videotaped for later use.

Music groups/solo artists

With no existing production to refer to, these cattle calls can often be the hardest. Ads sometimes state the genre that they are looking for, e.g. "in the style of Beyonce/Michael Jackson/Sugarbabes", etc. – but most of the time you will literally have to turn up and just present what shows you and your talents/skills off best. Again, prepare sheet music and backing tracks if you can. Note that for music auditions your style of dress is very important, as image and look can be a large part of your appeal. Don't be afraid to be yourself. Don't copy anyone or try to sound exactly like anyone referred to in the ad. Use you own style and bring your own interpretation to a piece of music. Feel free to bring along a guitar, etc. if you feel that this represents you and/or the kind of band you are going for.

Plays, soaps, films, other

In this kind of open audition you may be asked to sight-read, meaning you will be given a piece of text in the queue or in a waiting room to study (not learn by heart) and then read in front of a camera and/or the panel once it is your turn to be seen. Auditions for screen productions may also involve a screen test, which simply consists of you saying your name (and sometimes an interesting random fact about yourself) in front of a camera and turning your head from right to left so they can take shots of your profile.

The open call survival guide

• Take along a large bottle of water. You may not be able to get out of the queue for an entire day and the last thing you need is to have a dry throat and 'stick-together' lips when you finally get your 30-second chance to sing!
• Bring easily digestible food. Comfort food such as your favourite takeaway chicken tikka masala may clog up your throat and make you feel too heavy to stand, let alone dance.
• Bring a friend. They really can be lifesavers at opens. It is best if they are also auditioning, as you can share experiences of open calls or warm up together ... and most importantly, they can hold your place in the queue while you go to the toilet at a nearby M&S.
• Buy a reliable alarm clock! There is nothing worse than waking up hours too late because yours failed to wake you.
• Take something to distract you. iPods are good to drown out chatter, tears, screaming fits, family feuds and unbearable warm-up exercises by fellow queue members. If you are able to read surrounded by lots of noise, a book can come in handy.
• Remember to take a copy of your CV and photo! Keep the CV to one page, type it out and follow a professional format. Your photo should be a 10x8 inch black and white professional headshot if you are a professional. For children's auditions, other photos may suffice.
• Have details of your agent and personal details like your measurements, etc. listed somewhere, as you may need them in order to fill out forms handed to you.
• Take a pillow. This is very useful for sitting on the kerb when standing becomes too tiring. Or to hit annoying queue members with if their singing becomes too aggravating.
• Take your demo CD and/or a showreel. Vital for any aspiring recording artists – but also handy for musical theatre and cruise ship auditions, especially if they run out of time and simply collect CVs and photos and say they will be in touch with anyone who looks interesting.
• Choose your dance wear/movement wear carefully. *Always* bring these along to a musical theatre/cruise ship cattle call, even if dance is not mentioned in the initial ad. Remember to bring various types of dance footwear (ballet, jazz, capezios, tap, character shoes or 'heels').
• Dress comfortably. Wear a warm coat, scarf, boots, anything to keep you warm and your voice protected if it is cold. You can always take these off once you get inside the actual building. Standing outside for long periods of time can make weather seem much colder than it actually is. Don't invest in expensive make-up, clothes or hair styling; it is not needed.
• Use sunscreen on a hot summer's day. You don't want to suffer burns from queuing in the blazing sun and look like a tomato when you finally get seen!
• Whatever you do, do *not* forget your sheet music/backing tracks! Have your sheet music photocopied, neat and taped together , and with any key changes, etc. highlighted. Do not bring books (especially if they are new) as these will just fall off the piano once opened and cause delays and embarrassment.
• A mobile phone with free minutes/free text messages is a must-have at an open call queue.

Do's and don'ts for cattle calls

Do ...

• Chat to other people in the queue. Everyone is in the same boat and you may meet some like-minded people and make new friends.
• Warm up physically and vocally beforehand.
• Turn up *early*.
• Remain friendly and polite at all times. You never know who may be watching.
• Make sure your hair is out of your face so the panel/camera can actually see you.

Don't ...

• Take a family member with you (unless you are underage). Most of the time they will not understand the process and will get impatient, cold/hot, worried or embarrass you with overprotective care. This is your audition and you need to deal with it by yourself. It's part of the process of being a professional. (Not to mention the fact that an entourage of family members simply clogs up the queue even further.)
• Wait until you get into the queue to learn/choose your song. Choose and rehearse a couple of songs that are appropriate *beforehand*; take all required sheet music/backing tracks along with you and make your final choice when you get into the audition situation (think about it while waiting). There is nothing worse than an audition hopeful panicking because they have not learnt a song/learnt the words, and rehearsing it at the top of their voice for hours in the queue.
• Dress the part. You turning up in Maria von Trapps' nun's habit, Eponine's rags or the Phantom's mask will do you no favours whatsoever and only cause a lot of giggling and pitiful looks. Equally, don't dress as Britney, Snoop Dogg or a member of ABBA. This is not a fancy dress party. Very occasionally, dressing as the part is specified in the advertisement – this is the only time dressing in costume is appropriate.
• Be put off by someone singing 'your song'. The panel will probably hear the song that you selected a hundred times that day, and for opens your choice of song is not that vital as long as it suits your voice, range and the production they are casting for.
• Practise your song full blast in the queue. It's just annoying for everyone else around you and will not help you. Hum to yourself quietly after a thorough warm-up at home.

Jennifer Reischel is the Business Development Manager (Castings) for The Stage Media Company. Her industry guide, *So you want to tread the boards*, was published in 2007, nominated in the "How-to" category at the 2010 London Book Festival, is recommended by Elaine Paige, and includes a Foreword by Leslie Bricusse. Jennifer completed the three-year musical theatre degree at Mountview Academy in 2002, and first pursued a career as an actor. Migrating into writing, she became a regular feature article contributor and theatre critic (including drama school showcases) for *The Stage*, wrote for the Dear John column, and originated *The Stage* Graduates Club e-newsletter. Additionally, Jennifer has cast plays for The Soho Theatre and hosted nationwide graduate workshops as part of *The Stage* Events. **www.performingarts-auditionguide.com**

Understudying

Andrew Piper

Some Frequently Asked Questions

Why would I want to do it?

What's not to like? Reasonable money, loads of free time, very few responsibilities, and the possibility of playing a meaty role alongside some of your theatrical heroes or belting out the solo of a show-stopper in a West End or major provincial theatre.

What are the 'down sides'?

If you're looking for a fast-track to stardom or are in this job for the glamour and glory, then this is not the job for you. There is no getting away from the fact that the understudies are the B-team. Understudying can be a thankless task – no one pays you much attention unless the actor you're covering is off (which may be never), there's very little to do, and most of the time you're essentially getting paid *not* to act – rather like a tuneless busker being given a tenner to go and play *somewhere else*!

Perhaps more so than almost any other acting job, this is very much 'a job'. If you can squeeze some art or advancement out of it too then that's great (in some cases miraculous), but this is definitely not a contract to go into with starry-eyed optimism.

How should I prepare?

Learn the lines! The amount of actual rehearsal time (as opposed to just watching the principal cast) may be fairly minimal. When you do get to rehearse there will be a lot to learn in a very short space of time, so the more solid you are on lines the more productive your rehearsal time will be, and the sooner you'll feel confident about being ready to go on. Do as much of the usual homework – character, historical research, cultural background, etc. – that you would do for any other part. You'll get less opportunity to discuss this in rehearsal (more on that later), but again it means you'll enjoy yourself more in the rehearsal room.

How much rehearsal will I get?

In short, not a lot – certainly not as much as the principal actors will have – but (depending how soon you're called to go on) enough to get you through. You probably won't start rehearsals at all until the main cast have been rehearsing for a while – at the very least the blocking needs to have been decided before you arrive – so the chances are you'll just get a few days (at best) before production week.

During production week itself, expect to be pretty much ignored completely by everyone: their focus is now purely on the principal cast and the technical running of the show. The job of the understudy during this period is to make notes on changes to his or her blocking, become familiar with lighting, sound and other stage effects, keep working on lines, stay available … but generally just stay out of the way. Keep working on your part(s); you may only have had a few days' rehearsal by this point, but there have been enough instances of principal actors injuring themselves during a tech for you not to be complacent at this point!

Rehearsals are likely to be taken by the assistant director, or possibly even the company manager. If you're lucky, you'll have a little time for discussion about character and intentions (the more homework you've done before rehearsals, the more time you'll have), but an awful lot will be down to you to work out for yourself, simply by working on the script and watching the main cast at work.

Do I have to copy the principal actor's performance?

Understudy rehearsals differ from normal rehearsals in one important respect: all your moves (and many of your character choices) have already been decided and cannot be changed by you. In some ways this can be quite liberating – someone else has done all the hard work for you – but it can be challenging to take on these choices and make them your own. What you certainly don't want to do is produce a 'photocopy' of the principal actor's performance, which risks feeling like a hollow caricature; the challenge is to develop a performance which can slot in seamlessly to the main production, but which nevertheless feels like it's your creation. It can be disheartening to be so restricted in your choices, but trust that the principal actor's (and director's) instincts are good, and find a way to make it work for you.

Once the show is open, what are my responsibilities?

Most of your time will be spent either doing ensemble stuff on stage, or simply waiting in the dressing room. Apart from understudy rehearsals (one a week, perhaps, or possibly once a fortnight; if you're working for the RSC you may not have any understudy rehearsals at all once the show is up) your time is your own. If you're not needed for the curtain call, you may not be required to stay until the very end of the show. The rule of thumb is that you're free to go once the character you're covering has made his or her final entrance, but this can vary from production to production.

How often will I go on?

If you're working on a musical, the vocal demands of the piece will probably mean that principal performers will need to take occasional shows, or even just musical numbers, off to rest their voices, and so an understudy on a musical is pretty much guaranteed to be going on fairly frequently. In a straight play there is the distinct possibility that you will never go on at all, unless it's a long and demanding run. Even in the middle of a flu epidemic, the actor(s) you are covering may have a 'show must go on' mentality. They may be secretly hoping that the company manager will send them home, but will not voluntarily go off unless they are on the verge of being hospitalised.

It won't hurt to develop a good relationship with the actor you're covering, so that (a) they know that you actually want to go on (assuming you do; many understudies are quite happy not to) and (b) they may be more inclined to give you your moment in the sun when illness strikes and they're deciding whether or not they're fit enough to go on.

Incidentally, no company manager will allow a healthy principal to take a show off to give their understudy the chance to go on – that would be breach of contract – but I've heard stories of a few who may be wilfully credulous if the principal calls in sick for a matinee in the understudy's home town.

What's it like to go on?

When you get the call to go on, then just about everyone in the company – including the principal actors – will be focusing their energies on making sure that you have everything you need to give a good performance. Depending on how much notice you are given, you may have an opportunity to run through bits of business on stage with the principals, and they may well offer you notes on how to play it. Some of these notes may be helpful, others won't be; take what you need and discard the rest. For the next few hours you are 'one of them', playing for the A-team, and you have to trust that your skill as an actor and all the preparation you've done will get you through. This isn't the time to try anything new; just do what you've rehearsed and everything will be fine.

Don't get star-struck about the people you're on stage with. These are your colleagues, your fellow artists, and whatever your relationship off stage might be, right now they are your equals, so don't be afraid to give a full-blooded performance. Some nerves are completely understandable, so if you know you tend to rush or be a bit quiet, say, when you're nervous, be aware of this and make a conscious effort to slow down or speak up, as appropriate.

Once the nerves have started to subside, allow yourself to enjoy it. Stay focused and in the moment, remembering all the things you've rehearsed, but now that you're playing with the A-team, take on the energy of the other actors and allow it to lift your own performance. Producers are generally happy if you can just get the lines out in the right order and hit your mark – as far as they're concerned you're just there to stop too many people asking for their money back – and if you can do that, then you've done your job, but if you've done your homework, then there's no reason why you can't take it further than that and give a bloody good performance.

Will I get an understudy matinee?

Depending on the agreement you have with the producers, there may be an opportunity for an understudy performance, especially if not all the understudies have had the chance to go on during the run of the show. It's not guaranteed, but if it is going to happen, it will usually be one afternoon when there's no public performance in the theatre (or a theatre on the tour that's reasonably close to London).

All the understudies will play their covered role (or sometimes roles), and may ask supporting members of the principal cast to come in and play the others. They are not obliged to say yes, since it's not in their contract to give up their afternoon off, and they're not getting paid for it; but if asked nicely, most actors are generally happy to help out if they can. If one of them isn't available for some reason, there may need to be some nifty doubling, or the company manager may go on with a book.

Who should I invite to see me?

The understudy matinee is your chance to invite all your friends, family, former colleagues, potential employers, casts from nearby theatres – just about anyone! – to come and see your performance. Tickets will usually be free, but there may be a limit on the number of tickets available to keep front-of-house staff costs down.

I mention inviting potential employers: this can be tricky, even if the show is in the West End. Excuses for casting directors' non-attendance may be along the lines of "Oh, it's so hard to get away from the office [50 yards from the theatre!] during the day," but in reality, producers' frequent indifference to the actual acting talent of the understudy – or, for that matter, the malaise that can set in in the understudy after years sitting in a dressing room doing crosswords – can result in some really quite uninspiring performances during these matinees, and the casting directors know it. (I'm talking about straight plays here; it's a rather different story in musical theatre, where understudies are usually working members of the ensemble and more regularly pressed into service in principal roles.) It's worth asking, nevertheless, although only if you're confident in giving them a show they'll be impressed with. Don't however think that this is your moment to get seen by every casting director in town – it won't be.

Should I do it again?

A good, reliable understudy is highly prized by producers, and may even be offered work on a new production before the principal actors are cast. But once known as an understudy (with the exception, perhaps, of the RSC), it can be hard to get them to see you as someone they might want to cast in a principal role. That may not be a problem for you – in the West End, at least, it gives you terrific freedom to do other things, especially if you have family commitments or are developing another career as a writer or voice-over, say – but a life of waiting in the wings is not for everyone. If you're coming to the end of one understudy job, you must think carefully (and discuss with your agent) about how much and what kind of understudy work you'd like to be put up for in the future. Regular understudying is not the occupation of the ambitious actor, so think carefully about what the benefits and pitfalls of taking a particular understudy job might be.

Andrew Piper trained at Bristol Old Vic Theatre School and edited *Actors' Yearbook* for the 2007 and 2008 editions. He understudied the role of Bernard Woolley in the original West End transfer of Chichester Festival Theatre's production of *Yes, Prime Minister*. Thanks are due to the more experienced understudies who offered their comments on early drafts of this article. More information about Andrew can be found at **www.andrew-piper.com**.

Independent managements/theatre producers

This section mostly lists commercial organisations that mount West End and touring productions to larger-scale venues – some of which originate in the subsidised sector. Most such productions will be led by well-known actors, but they will usually need supporting actors who can also understudy those leads. (In long-running West End productions, the understudies get a chance to do their own performance – a useful opportunity to 'showcase' for agents and casting directors.) Sometimes, such a production will tour in order to try it out before (hopefully) coming into the West End; at others, a management will tour to 'milk' further profits from a West End success.

On tour, apart from 'Acting ASMs' (assistant stage managers who also understudy), you shouldn't be asked to do any of the graft of get-ins and get-outs – unlike on smaller-scale touring. However, if you are also understudying, you will be expected to do an understudy rehearsal every week until the last stages of the tour. This rehearsal will probably be taken by the company manager (rarely, the director) and the whole ambience will feel very unsympathetic to good acting. Despite this, it is very important to be as fully prepared as possible for the chance that the 'name' you are understudying will be unavoidably delayed one night. Touring is fraught with potential delays, and a reputation for being able to 'deliver the goods' at very short notice will enhance future employment prospects. The downside of playing small parts and understudying is that you can become stuck doing this – a good agent will be able to advise in this area.

Touring is not for everyone: long periods away from home, wide variations in the quality of digs (often costing more in holiday resorts during the 'season'), and the fact that you could miss opportunities to be seen for other work are some of the potential disadvantages. On the plus side, contracts for large-scale tours are usually at least three months with a minimum of a week in each venue, and you should have time to see some of the most beautiful sights in the UK (if not Europe and further afield).

Although not as expensive as major films, such productions do cost a lot of money to mount, and productions have been known to collapse suddenly without any warning. When accepting work in this area it is important to have a proper Equity contract.

Ambassador Theatre Group (ATG)

Duke of York's Theatre, 104 St Martin's Lane,
London WC2N 4BG
Head of Production Meryl Faiers

Production details: ATG is the largest owner and operator of theatres in the UK, with 39 venues. It produces across the UK, Japan, Europe and New York. Anywhere between 3 and 30 actors work on each production. Recent productions include: *Guys and Dolls*, *Sweeney Todd*, Matthew Bourne's *Nutcracker* and *Highland Fling*, *The New Statesman* and *The Rocky Horror Show*. Offers Equity approved contracts and is "happy to make contributions [to the Equity Pension Scheme] on behalf of any members of the scheme that we employ".

Casting procedures: Uses freelance casting directors. Welcomes letters (with CVs and photographs), but not email submissions. Actors may write at any time, but prefers contact to be made via an agent and preferably during pre-production. Advises actors against sending expensive photos 'on spec', especially if unaccompanied by a letter. Actively encourages applications from disabled actors and promotes the use of inclusive casting.

Andy Barnes Productions

5A Irving Street, London WC2H 7AT
tel 020-7839 9003
email andy@andybarnesproductions.com
website www.andybarnesproductions.com
Director Andy Barnes *Associate Producer* Wendy Barnes

Production details: Founded in 2005. Primarily a producer of new musicals with Fringe and West End experience; also produces small plays. Founder and producer of Perfect Pitch Musicals Ltd – a development network for new musical theatre. Stages 2-3 productions each year at various venues, which include arts centres and theatres. Number of actors going on tour varies, and regions covered include London, the South East and New York. Recent productions include: *When Harry Met Sally* (UK Tour); *Days of Hope* (King's Head); *Departure Lounge* (Arts Theatre & Edinburgh Festival); and *Someone Who'll Watch Over Me* (Gene Frankel, NY).

Casting procedures: Uses freelance and in-house casting directors. Holds general auditions; actors should write in March and September to request inclusion. Casting breakdowns are available via Spotlight. Welcomes letters (with CVs and photographs) from individual actors previously unknown to the company. Also welcomes email submissions and showreels, but will not accept invitations to view individual actors' websites.

Blue Star Productions

7-8 Shaldon Mansions, 132 Charing Cross Road, London WC2H 0LA
tel 020-7386 6220/4128 *fax* 020-7836 2949
email hopkinstacey@aol.com
Directors Barrie Stacey, Keith Hopkins *Stage Director* Tony Joseph

Production details: Founded in 1966. Specialises in children's musicals and songbook concerts. Stages 24 productions annually with 100 performances during the course of the year. Tours to 8 different theatres in Southern England, including the London area. In general 8 actors are involved in each production. Recent productions include: *West End to Broadway* and *Movie Memories.* Offers non-Equity contracts and does not subscribe to the Equity Pension Scheme.

Casting procedures: All casting is done in-house. Holds general auditions. Casting breakdowns are available on request. Welcomes letters (with CVs and photographs) but not email submissions. Advises actors: "Don't be grand when just starting." Actively encourages applications from disabled actors and promotes the use of inclusive casting.

Cole Kitchenn Ltd

ROAR House, 46 Charlotte Street, London W1T 2GS
tel 020-7427 5680 (Switchboard)
020-7427 5681 (Personal Management) 020-7427 5682 (Production Department) *fax* 020-7353 9639
email guy@colekitchenn.com
website www.colekitchenn.com
Key personnel Stuart Piper, David Cole, Guy Kitchenn

Production details: Production company established in 1970; personal management established in 2005. Has produced more than 60 productions in the West End over the past 35 years. Offers Equity-approved contracts. Recent London productions include: *The Female of the Species* (Vaudeville Theatre) with Eileen Atkins; *Lifecoach* (Trafalgar Studios) with Phill Jupitus; *Daddy Cool* (Shaftesbury Theatre) with Javine & Michelle Collins. Current personal management clients include: Helen Lederer (*Ab Fab*), Paul McEwan (*Emmerdale*), Stephen Uppal (*Hollyoaks*), Jess Robinson (*Headcases/Dead Ringers*), Sarah Lark (*I'd Do Anything*) and award-winning West End stars Paul Baker, Graham Bickley, Kim Criswell, Frances Ruffelle, Robyn North, Jimmy Johnston and Caroline O'Connor.

Casting procedures: Casting breakdowns available from Spotlight and Castweb. Welcomes letters (with CVs and photographs) from actors previously unknown to the company sent by post or email. Invitations to view individual actors' websites and showreels are accepted. Rarely has the opportunity to cast disabled actors.

Contemporary Stage Co

9 Finchley Way, London N3 1AG
email contemp.stage@hotmail.co.uk
Artistic Director David Graham-Young

Production details: Founded in 1993, The Contemporary Stage Company focus on presenting plays and adaptations of novels, with an emphasis on work from cultures outside the English-speaking world. Recent productions include: *The Master and Margarita* (Almeida Theatre), *Flight* (Lyric Theatre), *Potestad* (Gate, Glasgow Mayfest, BBC Radio 3), *Regressions* (Donmar Warehouse, RSC) and *The Tunnel* (Croydon Warehouse).

Casting procedures: Occasionally uses freelance casting directors and holds general auditions. Casting breakdowns are available via PCR. Welcomes CVs and letters from actors previously unknown to the company. Also welcomes invitations to view individual actors' websites and performance notices. Rarely has the opportunity to cast disabled actors.

Paul Elliott Ltd

1 Wardour Street, London W1D 6PA
tel 020-7379 4870
email paul@paulelliott.ltd.uk
Director Paul Elliott

Production details: Large-scale theatre producers, touring no. 1 venues across the UK with plays and musicals. Stages 2-4 productions a year, touring from between 6 weeks to 2 years or more. May use from 3 to 30 actors in each production. Offers TMA SOLT/ Equity-approved contracts and subscribes to the

Equity Pension Scheme. Recent credits include: *Stones in his Pockets.*

Casting procedures: Casts in-house and also uses freelance casting directors. Actors may write at any time requesting inclusion in auditions. Casting breakdowns are published in *The Stage* and included in Spotlight link. Happy to receive CVs and photographs, by post or email, from actors previously unknown to the company. Also happy to receive showreels and invitations to view individual actors' websites. Will consider applications from disabled actors to play characters with disabilities.

Excess In All Areas

3 Gibbs Square London SE19 1JN
tel 020-8761 2384 *mobile* (07905) 259060
email info@excessallareas.co.uk
website www.excessallareas.co.uk
Director Paul L Martin

11-year-old production house for cabaret and variety shows. Runs a useful database for performers to join free of charge. Previous regular shows produced for Old Vic Pit Bar, Soho Revue Bar, CellarDoor, The Arts Theatre, The Leicester Square Theatre, Theatre Museum and many others.

Vanessa Ford Productions Ltd

Upper House Farm, Upper House Lane,
Shamley Green GU5 0SX
tel (01483) 278203 *fax* (01483) 271509
email vanessa@vanessafordproductions.co.uk
Managing Director Vanessa Ford

Production details: Founded in 1979. Tours to approximately 30 theatres throughout the UK each year. On average, 14 actors work on each production. Recent productions include: *The Hobbit, A Christmas Carol* and *Shirley Valentine.* Offers ITC/Equity-approved contracts and does not subscribe to the Equity Pension Scheme.

Casting procedures: Occasionally uses freelance casting directors, and sometimes holds general auditions. Casting breakdowns are available on the website and through Spotlight. Welcomes submissions (with CVs and photographs) by post and email. Invitations to view individual actors' websites are also accepted. Will consider applications from disabled actors to play disabled characters.

Robert Fox Ltd

6 Beauchamp Place, London SW3 1NG
tel 020-7584 6855 *fax* 020-7225 1638
email info@robertfoxltd.com
website www.robertfoxltd.com
Director Robert Fox

Production details: Founded in 1980. Theatre and film production company specialising in large-scale theatre productions and musicals as well as feature films. Performances are staged in the West End and on Broadway. Recent theatre productions include: *South Downs* and *The Browning Version* (West End) and *Hugh Jackman Back On Broadway* (Broadway). Also co-produced the films *Atonement* and, more recently, *Wilde Salome.*

Casting procedures: Employs casting directors for specific projects and does not welcome unsolicited submissions from actors.

Sonia Friedman Productions

Duke of York's Theatre, 104 St Martin's Lane,
London WC2N 4BG
tel 020-7854 8750 *fax* 020-7854 7059
email queries@soniafriedman.com
website www.soniafriedman.com
Producer Sonia Friedman *Associate Producer* Lucie Lovatt

Production details: Sonia Friedman Productions is one of the West End's most prolific and significant theatre producers, responsible for some of the most successful theatre productions in London and on Broadway over the past few years. Since 1990 SFP has produced more than 135 new shows.

Recent West End productions include: *Hamlet* (Benedict Cumberbatch); *Farinelli and The King* (Mark Rylance); *Electra* (Kirstin Scott Thomas); *The River* (Hugh Jackman); *The Sunshine Boys* (Danny DeVito); *Hay Fever* (Lindsay Duncan); *Absent Friends* (Reece Shearsmith); *Master Class* (Tyne Daly); *Legally Blonde: The Musical* (Sheridan Smith).

David Graham Entertainment Ltd

3rd Floor, 14 Hanover Street, London W1S 1YH
tel 020-7175 7170
email info@davidgraham.co.uk
website www.davidgrahamentertainment.com
Director David Graham

Production details: Theatre producer and concert promoter. Stages around 4 productions in 80 theatres and concert halls on an annual basis, with more than 300 performances per year. Countries covered include Britain, Holland, Germany, Canada, Spain, Norway and Ireland. In general, 12 performers work on each production. Recent productions include: *Rising Damp, Birds Of A Feather, The Wonderful West End* and *Hold Tight, It's 60s Night.*

Casting procedures: Does not use freelance casting directors or hold general auditions. Casting breakdowns available via Script Breakdown, CastCall and other casting publications.

The Derek Grant Organisation

13 Beechwood Road, West Moors, Dorset BH22 0BN
tel (01202) 855777
email admin@derekgrant.co.uk
website www.derekgrant.co.uk
Directors/Producers Derek Grant, Michael Jones

Production details: Producer of nationwide theatre tours, celebrity 'evening withs', children's shows, comedy, concerts and plays. On average stages 3-4 projects annually, with around 80 performances in arts centres, theatres and community venues across the UK. In general 6 actors are involved in each production. Recent productions include: Hans Andersen's *The Snow Queen* (13 performances at Lichfield Garrick Theatre); *Pinocchio* (at Bolton Albert Halls); Vince Hill in Concert (at North Pier Blackpool); and *Goldilocks and the Three Bears* (nationwide tour).

Casting procedures: Does not use freelance casting directors. Sometimes holds general auditions and actors are advised to write in September and January requesting inclusion. Welcomes letters (with CVs and photographs) from individual actors previously unknown to the company, sent by post or email. Accepts showreels and will consider invitations to view individual actors' websites. Considers applications from disabled characters to play characters with disabilities. "We treat all our artistes with respect and have a high reputation in the business."

Hartshorn Hook

65 Chapel Street, Greater Manchester M3 5BZ
tel 0161-375 4400
email louis@hartshornhook.com
website www.hartshornhook.com
Directors Louis Hartshorn, Brian Hook

Production details: Founded 2007, Hartshorn Hook Productions are a commercial theatre company based in Manchester. They provide consultancy services to theatre companies across the UK, whether professional productions or community projects. Recent productions include: *Away From Home* (UK tour), *The Blues Brothers – A Tribute* (Lowry Theatre, Manchester and West End) and *Beulah* (UK tour). Hartshorn Hook also lead workshops and contribute to events such as the 2014 UK Theatre Touring Symposium.

Casting procedures: Welcomes invitations to attend productions in Greater London or Greater Manchester.

Hiss & Boo Theatre Company Ltd

Nyes Hill, Wineham Lane, Bolney,
West Sussex RH17 5SD
tel (01444) 881707
email email@hissboo.co.uk
website www.hissboo.co.uk
Artistic Director Ian Liston

Production details: Established in 1977. Pantomime producers also specialising in touring plays and revues in the UK and overseas.

Casting procedures: Works with a known pool of performers. Casting and auditions are only available via Spotlight Interactive Casting. Does not welcome unsolicited CVs by post or email. Offers actors UK Theatre/Equity contracts.

Paul Holman Associates

Morritt House, 58 Station Approach, South Ruislip, Middlesex HA4 6SA
tel 020-8845 9408 *fax* 020-8582 2557
email enquiries@paulholmanassociates.co.uk
website www.paulholmanassociates.co.uk
Directors Paul Holman, John Ogle, Lee Waddingham

Production details: Established in 1990. Produces pantomimes, summer shows and one-night attractions. See entry under *Pantomime producers* on page 225 for more details.

Thelma Holt Ltd

Noel Coward Theatre, 85 St Martin's Lane,
London WC2N 4AU
tel 020-7812 7455 *fax* 020-7812 7550
email Thelma@dircon.co.uk
website www.thelmaholt.co.uk
Managing Director Thelma Holt

Production details: Founded in 1990. Theatre producer of classic plays in the West End, on tour and internationally (particularly Japan). Stages 4-5 productions annually with a total of 250 performances. Tours 6 theatres across the UK each year. On average, 18 actors work on each production. Recent productions include: *Measure for Measure, Twelfth Night, Ghosts, Hamlet, The Taming of the Shrew, All's Well that Ends Well, Othello, Pericles, Titus Andronicus* and *Kean*. Offers Equity/TMA/ SOLT approved contracts and subscribes to the Equity Pension Scheme.

Casting procedures: Uses freelance casting directors. Does not hold general auditions. Advises that the company does not encourage unsolicited approaches with letters or photographs, as they will be ignored if not in production. When casting, requirements are made well known via casting directors. "I have employed disabled actors and will continue to do so – not necessarily to play characters with disabilities. When an actor's good, it's horses for courses."

Image Musical Theatre

23 Sedgeford Road, Shepherd's Bush,
London W12 0NA
tel 020-8743 9380 *fax* 020-8749 9294
email brian@imagemusicaltheatre.co.uk
website www.imagemusicaltheatre.co.uk
Producer/Director Brian Thresh *Composer/Lyricist* Robert Hyman

Production details: Founded in 1988. Stages 4 productions annually, with around 900 performances in 70 venues including arts centres, theatres, schools and other educational venues throughout the UK. In general 3-4 actors are involved in each production. *Recent productions* include: *The Jungle Book, The Secret Garden, Tom's Midnight Garden, The Snow Queen, The Wind in the Willows*, and *Alice in Wonderland.*

Casting procedures: Sometimes holds general auditions. Actors should write in June, October and late January to request inclusion. Casting breakdowns are publicly available via the website, from Equity Job Information Service, and from CastNet and Castweb. Welcomes letters (with CVs and photographs) from individual actors previously unknown to the company only if sent by post. No emails and no showreels, but will accept invitations to view individual actors' websites. Rarely (or never) has the opportunity to cast disabled actors.

Colin Ingram Ltd

Suite 526, Linen Hall, 162-168 Regent Street, London W1B 5TE
tel 020-7038 3905 *fax* 020-7038 3907
email info@coliningramltd.com
website www.coliningramltd.com
Director Colin Ingram *Production Associate* Simon Ash

Production details: Theatrical producers and general managers. The company offers Equity-approved contracts and participates in the Equity Pension Scheme. "Please see the website for details of recent productions and venues."

Casting procedures: Uses freelance casting directors. Does not welcome unsolicited approaches from individual actors previously unknown to the company.

Jendagi (UK) Ltd

PO Box 5597, Glasgow, G77 9DH
tel 0141-533 5856
email robert@robertckelly.co.uk
website www.robertckelly.co.uk
Managing Director Robert Kelly

Production details: The company has thirty years of experience of hosting productions across UK, Ireland, Australia and New Zealand, with over 200 performances each year. Recent productions include: *Mum's the Word, 50 Shades of Maggie* and *Fame the Musical.* Each production consists of 5-10 actors and the company also presents 1 pantomime production per year, touring at the University Concert Hall in Limerick. Offers Equity-approved contracts and subscribes to the Equity Pension Scheme.

Casting procedures: Uses freelance casting directors. Actively encourages applications from disabled actors and promotes the use of inclusive casting.

Gareth Johnson Ltd

1st Floor, 19 Garrick Street, London WC2E 9AX *and* Plas Hafren, Eglwyswrw, Crymych, Pembrokeshire SA41 3UL
tel (07770) 225227 and (01239) 891368 *fax* (01239) 800089
email gjltd@mac.com
website www.garethjohnsonltd.com

Production details: Founded in 2000, this general management company produces (for a client) up to 6 shows a year, West End, UK and overseas. Recent productions include *Beyond Bollywood* (London Palladium); *The King's Speech* (tour); *Oh What a Lovely War* (tour); Mossovet State Theatre Chekhov Season (Wyndham's Theatre); *From Here To Eternity* (Shaftesbury Theatre); *Wonderful Town* (Royal Exchange, Hallé and Lowry – tour); *Journey's End* (tour and West End); *Cowardy Custard* (tour); *Touched* (Trafalgar); *Imagine This* (Theatre Royal Plymouth and New London Theatre); *Crown Matrimonial* (UK tour); *Miss Bollywood – The Musical* (UK and European tour); *The Far Pavilions* (Shaftesbury Theatre). Offers Equity contracts.

Casting procedures: Uses freelance casting directors and does not welcome unsolicited contact of any kind from actors. Policy on disabled actors as instructed by client.

Andy Jordan Productions Ltd

130 Newland Street West, Lincoln LN1 1PH
mobile (07775) 615205
email andy@andyjordanproductions.co.uk
Director Andy Jordan

Production details: Founded in 2000. Commercial production company, largely producing new plays of all genres. Stages 2-4 productions annually with 50-100 performances per year. Performs annually in 4-10 theatres across the UK, including Northern Ireland and the Republic of Ireland. Also tours overseas. On average, 3-7 actors work on each production. Recent productions include: *Lies Have Been Told: An Evening with Robert Maxwell* (2 seasons in West End, 2006), *2Graves* (West End 2006), *Worlds End* (Edinburgh Festival), and *Escaping Hamlet* (Edinburgh Festival). Usually offers Equity-approved contracts (either TMA or ITC).

Casting procedures: Uses freelance casting directors. Actors may write at any time requesting inclusion. Casting breakdowns are published on Spotlight Link. Welcomes submissions (with CVs and photographs) sent by post and email. Rarely has the opportunity to cast disabled actors but will consider submissions to play disabled characters.

Richard Jordan Productions Ltd

Mews Studios, 16 Vernon Yard, London W11 2DX
tel 020-7243 9001 *fax* 020-7313 9667
email info@richardjordanproductions.com
Director Richard Jordan

Production details: Founded in 1998. Produces theatre in the West End, throughout the UK and internationally. Main area of work is new writing and revivals of plays; occasionally produces musicals.

Company works as general managers and consultants for a wide range of producers and theatres in the UK and abroad. Stages around 10-20 productions annually with 300 performances during the course of the year. Recent productions include: Tony Award-winning *Vanya and Sonia and Masha and Spike*; *Lady in the Van*, *Big Mouth*, *Glasgow Girls* (a new musical, the work of Belgian Performance group Ontroerend Goed), the Olivier Award-winning *Roadkill*, the Tony-nominated *Behanding in Spokane*.

Casting procedures: Uses freelance casting directors. Sometimes holds general auditions. Welcomes letters (with CVs and photographs) but not email submissions. Applications are particularly welcome if actors are currently in a production that the company can go and see. Advises that applicants should have an awareness of the type of work produced by the company before sending CVs.

Bill Kenwright Ltd

BKL House, 1 Venice Walk, London W2 1RR
tel 020-7446 6200 *fax* 020-7446 6222
email info@kenwright.com
website www.kenwright.com

Production details: Commercial producing management presenting revivals and new works for the West End and for touring theatres. Recent productions include: *Blood Brothers*, *Dreamboats and Miniskirts*, *Joseph and the Amazing Technicolor Dreamcoat* and *The Sound of Music*. Currently not receiving or responding to unsolicited scripts.

Casting procedures: In-house and freelance casting directors. Enquiries (with CVs and photographs) to **info@kenwright.com**.

Limelight Productions

Unit 13, The io Centre, The Royal Arsenal, Seymour Street, London SE18 6SX
tel 020-8853 9570 *fax* 020-8853 9579
email enquiries@thelimelightgroup.co.uk
website www.thelimelightgroup.co.uk
Artistic Director Richard Lewis *Executive Producer* Martin Ronan

Production details: Established in 1996. Stages 2-3 productions annually, touring to 100 theatres and arenas.

Recent productions include: *LazyTown Live*, *Octonauts Live*, *Peppa Pig Live* and *Ben and Holly's Little Kingdom Live*. Offers Equity-approved contracts.

Cameron Mackintosh Ltd

1 Bedford Square, London WC1B 3RB
tel 020-7637 8866 *fax* 020-7436 2683
Chairman Cameron Mackintosh *Managing Director* Nicholas Allott *Executive Producer and Head of Casting* Trevor Jackson *Casting Director* James Orange *Casting Assistant* Paul Wooller

Production details: Stages musical theatre productions worldwide. Recent productions include: *Les Miserables*, *Miss Saigon*, *The Phantom of the Opera*, *Oliver!*, *Betty Blue Eyes*, *Avenue Q*.

Casting procedures: In-house casting. Does not hold general auditions. Welcomes letters (with CVs and photographs) but not email submissions. Also accepts showreels and invitations to view individual actors' websites.

Johnny Mans Productions Ltd

PO Box 196, Hoddesdon, Herts. EN10 7WG
tel (01992) 470907 *mobile* (07974) 755997
email johnnymansagent@aol.com
website www.johnnymansproductions.co.uk
Key contact Johnny Mans

Production details: Founded as a limited company in 1989. Activities include producing and promoting one-night stands, celebrity concerts, musicals and touring productions; casting for television, pantomime and cruise ships; and artiste and personal management for Sir Norman Wisdom's estate, Max Bygraves' estate, Nicholas Parsons, Buddy Greco, Lezlie Anders, Dave Prowse, Kenny Baker, Trevor Marriott, Georgia Brown-Tuohey, Jeremy Spake, Jess Conrad, Leah Bell, Gerry George and many others. Stages about 30 different productions annually, totalling around 250 performances during the course of the year. Tours concert productions to more than 300 different theatres and arts centres across the UK and Ireland each year. Recent productions include: *Calamity Jane*, *Beatlemania*, *The Spirit of Pavarotti*, *Rock'n'Roll Paradise*, *A Slice of Nostalgia Pie*, *Jukebox & Bobbysox*, *Be Bop A Lula*, *Silver Belles* and *Truly Bassey*. Johnny Mans Productions also publishes and edits *Encore Magazine*, the popular light-entertainment magazine for the showbusiness professional, which is a bi-monthly, full-colour periodical. For details contact **encoremags@aol.com** or telephone 0845-4670792.

Casting procedures: In the first instance, contact **johnnymansagent@aol.com** by email, or write in with photograph and CV/biography to the address given above. Prospective future clients will then be contacted accordingly. Johnny Mans Productions offers Equity-approved contracts.

Meadow Rosenthal Limited

26 Goodge Street, London W1T 2QG
tel 020-7436 2244 *fax* 0870 762 7882
email info@meadowrosenthal.com
website www.meadowrosenthal.com
Producers Jeremy Meadow, Suzanna Rosenthal

Production details: The company produces West End, Off-West End and touring theatre shows both nationally and internationally. Also runs Something for the Weekend which promotes, tours and manages comedy and festival shows.

Casting procedures: Uses freelance casting directors and Spotlight. Actors should only apply in response to advertisements.

Middle Ground Theatre Co.

3 Gordon Terrace, Malvern Wells,
Malvern WR14 4ER
tel (01684) 577231 *fax* (01684) 574472
email middleground@middlegroundtheatre.co.uk
website www.middlegroundtheatre.co.uk
Artistic Director Michael Lunney

Production details: Theatre company producing drama to tour No. 1 UK theatre venues and arts centres. Stages 1 or 2 productions a year with 180 performances across around 25 venues. Covers the whole of Britain and Northern Ireland. Size of cast varies from show to show. Offers actors non-Equity contracts and does not participate in the Equity Pension Scheme. Recent productions include: *Meeting Joe Strummer, The Importance of Being Earnest, Billy Liar, Dial M for Murder*, and *Tunes of Glory*.

Casting procedures: Casts in-house. Casting breakdowns are not publicly available (Spotlight only). Welcomes submissions from actors (with CV and photograph) if sent by post or email. Also welcomes showreels and invitations to view individual actors' websites. Will consider applications from disabled actors to play disabled characters.

Norwell Lapley Productions Ltd

Tenbury House, 36 Teme Street, Tenbury Wells,
Worcestershire WR15 8AA
tel (01584) 819005 *fax* (01584) 819076
email info@cdm-ltd.com
website www.norwelllapley.com
Director Chris Davis *Artist Manager* Triona Adams

Production details: Produces theatre in the West End and touring productions. Stages 4-5 productions annually and gives 40-50 performances during the course of the year at theatres nationwide. Recent productions include *Zipp*. Offers TMA/SOLT/Equity-approved contracts and subscribes to the Equity Pension Scheme.

Casting procedures: Uses freelance casting directors and does not deal directly with actors. Rarely has the opportunity to cast disabled actors.

Popular Productions Ltd

448 Muswell Hill Broadway, London N10 1BS
tel 020-8292 5305
email lm@popularproductions.com
website www.popularproductions.com
Producers John Payton, Lucy Magee

Production details: International theatre producer. Stages 4-6 productions annually, with around 80 performances in 4 theatres in the UK and Dubai. Anything from 2 to 100 actors may be involved in each production. Recent productions include: *The Sound of Music* (International; Middle East Premiere); *When Harry Met Sally* (Dubai); *The Woman in Black* (Dubai).

Casting procedures: Uses freelance casting directors. Sometimes holds general auditions. Casting breakdowns are available from Spotlight and Casting Call Pro. Does not welcome unsolicited approaches by actors unknown to the company, but will consider invitations to view individual actors' websites. Rarely, or never, has the opportunity to cast disabled actors.

David Pugh & Dafydd Rogers

Wyndham's Theatre, Charing Cross Road,
London WC2 0DA
tel 020-7292 0390 *fax* 020-7292 0399
Directors David Pugh, Dafydd Rogers

Production details: Theatre production company staging 2-3 productions annually in the West End and Broadway, and touring to theatres throughout the UK. Recent productions include: *Art, The Play What I Wrote* and *Blues Brothers*.

Casting procedures: Sometimes holds general auditions. Actors should address requests for inclusion to Sarah Bird CDG (see entry under *Casting directors* on page 105), who is responsible for all casting.

PW Productions Ltd

2nd Floor, 80-81 St Martin's Lane,
London WC2N 4AA
tel 020-7395 7580 *fax* 020-7240 2947
email info@pwprods.co.uk
website www.pwprods.co.uk
Chief Executive Peter Wilson

Production details: The company, which Peter Wilson founded in 1983, specialises in the production, general management and bookkeeping/accountancy for theatre presentations. Recent productions include: *The Woman in Black*, Stephen Daldry's production of *An Inspector Calls*, and *Honour* at the Wyndham's Theatre London, starring Dame Diana Rigg, Martin Jarvis OBE and Natasha McElhone.

James Quaife Productions

London
website www.jamesquaife.com
Producer James Quaife

Production details: Established in 2008, James Quaife is an independent theatre producer and general manager working in the West End. Works mainly in theatre with new writing, and employs actors in drama, comedy and musicals. Committed to producing high-quality theatre in the UK; dedicated to the production and staging of ambitious theatre and, by doing so, contributing to the vibrancy and development of the theatre industry. Recent productions include: *Good People* starring Imelda Staunton (Noël Coward Theatre); *Barking In Essex* starring Lee Evans, Sheila Hancock and Keeley Hawes (Wyndham's Theatre); *Happy Never After* (Edinburgh Fringe Festival 2013, Pleasance

Courtyard); the world premiere of *People Like Us* and *Happy Never After* (Pleasance Theatre, London); *Step 9 (of 12)* starring Blake Harrison (Trafalgar Studios); the London premiere of *Precious Little Talent* by Ella Hickson (Trafalgar Studios, 2011 London Theatre Award for Best New Play); *Molière*, *Little Fish* and *Death Of Long Pig* (Finborough Theatre).

Casting procedures: Uses freelance casting directors. Casting breakdowns are sent to agents and available from Spotlight.

The Really Useful Group Ltd

17 Slingsby Place, London WC2E 9AB
tel 020-7240 0880 *fax* 020-7240 1204
website www.reallyuseful.com

Production details: The Really Useful Group (RUG) was founded in 1977 by Andrew Lloyd Webber. It is an international entertainment company actively involved in theatre ownership and management, theatrical production, film, television, video and concert productions, merchandising, records and music publishing.

Rho Delta Ltd

26 Goodge Street, London W1T 2QG
tel 020-7436 1392 *fax* 020-7436 1395
email info@ripleyduggan.com
Director Greg Ripley-Duggan

Production details: Founded in 1991. Produces West End and touring commercial theatre. Stages 1 production annually which tours to 6 theatres. Recent productions include: *The Old Masters, Life x 3* and *The Memory of Water*. Offers actors TMA/SOLT/Equity-approved contracts and subscribes to the Equity Pension Scheme.

Casting procedures: Uses freelance casting directors and does not deal directly with actors. Will consider applications from disabled actors.

Showcase Entertainments Productions Ltd

2 Lumley Close, Newton Aycliffe,
Co. Durham DL5 5PA
Managing Director/Executive Producer Geoffrey JL Hindmarch *Director/Choreographer* Paul W Morgan

Production details: A professional theatrical touring company. Stages 5 productions annually, with around 100 performances in 60 theatres across England, Scotland and Wales. In general 10 actors are involved in each production. Recent productions include: *Musical Magic* starring Paul Daniels and full showcase company (Harlow Playhouse, Litchfield Garrick, Palace Theatre Mansfield).

Casting procedures: Sometimes holds general auditions; actors may write at any time to request inclusion. Welcomes letters (with CVs and photographs) from individual actors previously unknown to the company, sent by post or email. Also welcomes showreels. Rarely, or never, has the opportunity to cast disabled actors.

Marc Sinden Productions Group of Companies

1 Hogarth Hill, London NW11 6AY
tel 020-8455 3278
website www.sindenproductions.com, www.onenightbooking.com, www.uktheatreavailability.co.uk, www.montecarlotheatre.co.uk
Director Marc Sinden

Production details: A West End and touring theatre producer, reaching theatres and arts centres across the UK and Europe. For details of recent productions, please consult the website. Also runs the UK Theatre Availability System (**www.uktheatreavailability.co.uk**) which allows touring companies to check the availability and suitability of theatre spaces.

Casting procedures: Uses freelance casting directors and does not welcome casting enquiries and submissions from actors.

Squaredeal Productions Ltd

24 De Beauvoir Square, London N1 4LE
tel 020-7249 5966
email jenny@jennytopper.com
website www.jennytopper.com
Director Jenny Topper

Production details: Established in 2003. An independent theatre producer staging on average 2-3 productions annually and performing in the West End and 20 theatre venues across the UK. Recent productions include: *The Clean House* (10-week tour); *Martha, Josie and Chinese Elvis* (12-week tour); *Duet for One* (West End); *End of the Rainbow* (West End, tour and Broadway); *Daytona, The Three Lions*.

Casting procedures: Does not hold general auditions. Will accept letters (with CVs and photographs) from actors previously unknown to the company, sent by post or by email. Offers Equity-approved contracts as negotiated through TMA. Rarely has the opportunity to cast disabled actors.

Stanhope Productions Ltd

4th Floor, 80/81 St Martins Lane,
London WC2N 4AA
tel 020-7240 3098 *fax* 020-7504 8656
email admin@stanhopeprod.com
Producer Kim Poster

Production details: Founded in 2001. Theatrical producing company. Stages 4-5 productions annually and gives 576 performances during the course of the year. Tours to 2-4 different theatres, primarily in the West End and London area. In general 18 actors are involved in each production. Recent productions include: *All My Sons, A View from the Bridge, Prick*

Up Your Ears, Carousel, Fiddler on the Roof, Summer and Smoke, Epitaph for George Dillon, A Woman of No Importance, and *Brand*. Offers SOLT/Equity-approved contracts.

Casting procedures: Uses freelance casting directors. Holds general auditions. Casting breakdowns are available via Equity Job Information Service. Will consider applications from disabled actors to play disabled characters.

UK Productions

Churchmill House, Ockford Road, Godalming, Surrey GU7 0NB
tel (01483) 423600 *fax* (01483) 418486
email mail@ukproductions.co.uk
website www.ukproductions.co.uk
Director Martin Dodd

Production details: Established 1995. Produces pantomime, musicals and drama for No. 1 touring, nationally and internationally. (See entry under *Pantomime producers* on page 227.) Offers non-Equity contracts ("roughly in line with Equity") and does not subscribe to the Equity Pension Scheme. Recent productions include: *Seven Brides for Seven Brothers, 42nd Street, Disney's Beauty & The Beast, South Pacific.*

Casting procedures: Casting is done in-house. Does not hold general auditions. Casting breakdowns are distributed via Spotlight or direct to agents. Welcomes performance notices but not any other unsolicited form of correspondence. "Unsolicited CVs are generally a waste of time." Will consider applications from disabled actors to play characters with disabilities.

Ulster Theatre Company

17 Duncrun Road, Limavady,
Co. Londonderry BT49 0JD
mobile (02877) 750240
email michaelpoynor@hotmail.com
website www.ulstertheatrecompany.com
Artistic Director Michael Poynor

Production details: Originally set up as a training company touring mid-scale musical productions in the UK and Ireland. The Company also produces an annual original pantomime, and tours other productions from time to time. Recent productions include: *Comedy of Errors: The Musical, Jonathan Harker and DRACULA* and *Scrooge's Christmas.*

Each production consists of around 8 actors and, on average, the company present 2-3 productions per year. This equates to between 60 and 100 performances annually at venues across the UK and Ireland, mainly small theatres and arts centres. The Company offers Equity/ITC-approved contracts.

Casting procedures: Uses in-house casting directors and holds auditions as required. Casting breakdowns are available via email. Welcomes both CVs and letters from actors previously unknown to the Company, and unsolicited CVs and photographs. These should be sent via email. Also asks that applicants are aware that actors based locally are preferred due to inability to pay travel costs. Welcomes invitations to view individual actors' websites, but only attends invitations to productions within Ireland. Does not welcome showreels. Rarely has the opportunity to cast disabled actors due to the physical nature of most productions.

Anthony Vander Elst Productions

The Studio, 14 College Road, Bromley BR1 3NS
tel 020-8466 5580
Director Anthony Vander Elst

Productions details: Established in 1977. Produces 1-2 productions per year touring the UK.

Recent productions include: *Appearances* (Mayfair Theatre, London); *The Teddy Bears Picnic* (Chester Gateway Theatre); and *Last of the Red Hot Lovers* (London). Unsolicited approaches from actors are discouraged. Offers TMA/Equity-approved contracts.

West End International

The Old Brewhouse, Chesham Road, Wigginton, Hertfordshire HP23 6EH
tel (01442) 824557
email info@westendinternational.com
website www.westendinternational.com
Directors Martin Yates, Alison Price

Production details: Concert and theatre producers. Will accept casting enquiries and letters (with CVs and photographs) from actors previously unknown to the company, sent by post or email. Does not welcome unsolicited showreels.

Middle and smaller-scale companies

This section covers a huge range of companies, from the very prestigious, often subsidised (like Out of Joint), which usually only perform in theatres with around 500 seats (or more), to the very small, which frequently have little or no public subsidy and perform wherever they can find a paying audience. The bigger companies operate much like the commercial 'big boys' in the previous section – except they tend to have longer rehearsal periods. The smaller companies rarely use casting directors, tend to do only one or two performances in each venue, and often pay below Equity rates – and it's probable that you'll have to help with get-ins and get-outs. It's very hard work and you have to rise to the peak of performance every time, in spite of travelling in cramped vans, sharing unsatisfactory digs and rarely, if ever, being seen by anyone who could advance your career. However, some very prestigious companies have grown from such very small beginnings, and a number of now highly respected directors, playwrights and actors have started this way. It is important to assess the potential quality of the product (as well as the pay, and terms and conditions) before accepting such a job.

As such companies tend to come and go with great rapidity, the listings only contain companies that have been in existence for three years or more.

Note Some of the companies listed are members of the Independent Theatre Council (ITC) – **www.itc-arts.org**.

20 Stories High

Toxteth TV, 37-45 Windsor Street, Liverpool L8 1XE
tel 0151-708 9728
email info@20storieshigh.org.uk
website www.20storieshigh.org.uk
Co-Artistic Directors Julia Samuels, Keith Saha
Participation Manager Leanne Jones

Production details: Established in 2006. Creates dynamic, challenging theatre which attracts new audiences, artists and participants. Arts Council NPO from April 2012. Generally stages 1 project annually, with around 40 performances in 20 theatres, schools and youth clubs in the North West and nationally. In general 2-5 actors are involved in each production. Offers Equity-approved contracts as negotiated through ITC. Recent productions include: *Black* by Keith Saha (directed by Julia Samuels – national tour); *Tales from the MP3* verbatim production edited by Julia Samuels (directed by Julia Samuels – national tour); *Melody Loses Her Mojo* by Keith Saha (directed by Keith Saha – co-production with Liverpool Everyman Playhouse and Curve Theatre – national tour); *Whole* by Philip Osment (directed by Juia Samuels – national tour); *Blackberry Trout Face* by Lawrence Wilson (directed by Julia Samuels – national tour); and *Ghost Boy*by Keith Saha (co-production with Contact Theatre and Birmingham Rep– national tour).

Casting procedures: Holds general auditions. Casting breakdowns are available from the website and Equity Job Information Service. Welcomes letters (with CVs and photographs) from individual actors previously unknown to the company, sent by post or email, and is happy to consider invitations to view individual actors' websites. Actively encourages applications from BME and disabled actors and promotes the use of integrated casting.

1623 Theatre Company

QUAD Market Place, Cathedral Quarter,
Derby DE1 3AS
mobile (01332) 285434
email messages@1623theatre.co.uk
website www.1623theatre.co.uk
Artistic Director Ben Spiller *Creative Producer* Christopher Lydon

Production details: 1623 is a theatre company dedicated to seeing Shakespeare differently through theatre/digital performance, learning workshops, participatory activities and training courses. Recent productions include: *Lear/Dementia* (Derby Theatre Studio), *unclepandarus.com* (for the World Shakespeare Festival) and *Emergency Shakespeare* (for *Watch This Space* at the National Theatre).

Casting procedures: Welcomes both CVs and letters from actors previously unknown to the Company and unsolicited CVs and photographs. These should be sent via email. Also welcomes invitations to view individual actors' websites or productions. Happy to accept showreels. Actively encourages applications from disabled actors and promotes inclusive and diverse casting.

Accidental Theatre

Unit E, Lyndon Court, Queen Street, Belfast BT1 6EF
email info@accidentaltheatre.co.uk
website www.accidentaltheatre.co.uk
Artistic Director Richard Lavery

Production Details: Founded in 2012, the company works with playwrights, actors, filmmakers, DJs, choreographers, musicians, poets, painters, technicians and curators to craft plays for Ireland and the world stage. Every production is a fresh invention, each play's architecture defined by the artists with whom we build it. Accidental's theatre represents a collusion of perspectives, art forms and unusual collaborations – curious stories told through vibrant, ambitious performances, opening theatre up to new audiences. Recent productions include: *The Kitchen, the Bedroom and the Grave* (by Donal O'Hagan), *DEATH (on a shoestring)* (by Dave Kinghan) and *The Writers' Room* (by Michael Shannon).

"Collective risk-taking is the inspiration that jolts our work into new theatrical territories and opens it up to new audiences. Accidental walks the tightrope between the unexpected and the impossible, exploring the intersection between British narrative and European aesthetic styles of theatre."

Casting Procedures: Uses in-house casting directors and hold general auditions. Welcomes enquiries, CVs and letters from actors previously unknown to the theatre. Also happy to receive unsolicited CVs, letters, showreels and invitations to view individual actors websites. Casting breakdowns are available from the theatre's website, Spotlight and *The Stage*. Promotes inclusive casting, actively encourages applications from actors with disabilities to play characters with disabilities.

Actors of Dionysus (AOD)

25 St Luke's Road, Brighton BN2 9ZD
tel 01273-810268 *fax* 01273-810268
email info@actorsofdionysus.com
website www.actorsofdionysus.com
Artistic Director Tamsin Shasha; *General Manager* Angela Simou; *Education Officer* Mark Katz

Production details: National and international touring company founded in 1993. Not regularly funded. **aod**Productions specialises in performing new adaptations of Ancient Greek drama and new writing inspired by myth (often with an aerial dimension), through a fusion of poetry, music and movement. "Our mission statement is to make magic from myth, creating beautiful work that transforms, resonates and inspires a wide range of audiences."

Via its outreach arm, **aod**Education, we offer an established educational programme of workshops, pre-show talks, publications, audio-CDs and DVDs. Can tour througout the year; venues include national and international touring venues. In general 1-5 actors work on each production. Recent productions include: *Paris Alexandros* (2015); *Helen* (2014); *Medea* (2013); *Lysistrata* (2010-2011), *Bacchic* (2006-2008). Recent DVDs include *Helen* (2014) and *Medea* (2013). Recent Audio CDs include *Sappho: The Sweetness of Honey* (2014). Also holds one-off high-profile events as part of **aod**Events.

Casting procedures: Does not use freelance casting directors. Holds general workshop auditions; actors should write to request inclusion in early spring and summer. Casting breakdowns are available via the website and Spotlight. Does not welcome general submissions from actors but will accept invitations to view individual actors' Spotlight links and websites.

Actors Touring Company (ATC)

Institute of Contemporary Arts,
12 Carlton House Terrace, London SW1Y 5AH
tel 020-7930 6014
email atc@atctheatre.com
website www.atctheatre.com
Artistic Director Ramin Gray

Production details: Established in 1979. 2 productions are staged annually, touring to theatres in the UK and internationally, employing roughly 4-6 actors. Offers ITC/Equity-approved contracts. Recent productions include: *The Golden Dragon* (UK, India, Iraq, Ireland), *Crave* (UK), *Illusions* (UK), and *The Events* (UK/International).

Casting procedures: Unsolicited approaches from actors are discouraged. Works with specified casting directors on casting productions.

Admiration Theatre

mobile (07010) 041579
email email@admirationtheatre.com
website www.admirationtheatre.com (blog: admiration theatre.wordpress.com)
Director John Seaforth

Admiration Theatre is an experimental theatre company

In 2010 Admiration created *Visions*, adapted from Brecht's *The Visions of Simone Marchard*, and *Tower Hamlet* in 5 Theatre Forms: Traditional British Shakespeare, Stanislavski, Lecoq, Mime, Grotowski. John's books *Theatre Visions* (2012) and *Creative Life In Theatre and Performance* (2013) are available for download on Amazon Kindle. See also *Formed and Unformed Again and Again* (2012), available on YouTube.

ARC Theatre Ensemble

PO Box 1146, Barking, Essex IG11 9WB
tel 020-8594 1095

email carole@arctheatre.com
website www.arctheatre.com
Chief Executive Officer/Artistic Director Carole Pluckrose *Creative Director* Clifford Oliver (Olly)

Production details: Founded in 1984, Arc has built a strong core Management and Associate team bringing together an exceptional range of creative skills, educational experience and business and social expertise. The company is governed by an equally diverse and committed Board of Management. "We also benefit from a first-class pool of highly skilled, trained actors, storytellers, facilitators, workshop leaders, production managers and designers who are individually hand-picked to suit each programme or bespoke project." See the website for more details of its work.

Casting procedures: "To register your interest in working with Arc, please submit your details via the website. We will keep your details on record and contact you when a suitable opportunity arises. Alternatively you can email your details to our General Manager, Nita Bocking: **nita@arctheatre.com**."

Attic Theatre Company

Mitcham Library, 157 London Road,
Mitcham CR24 2YR
tel/fax 020-8640 6800
email info@attictheatrecompany.com
website www.attictheatrecompany.com
Artistic Director Louise Hill

Production details: Attic was founded over 25 years ago when two actors and a musician created a theatre in the ballroom next door to Wimbledon Theatre. In 1994 the ballroom theatre became Wimbledon Studio and Attic Thatre Company was officialy formed. From its new base above Mitcham Library, Attic now makes theatre for both traditional and non-traditional theatre spaces and combines the development of new work with revivals of neglected classics. Many of Attic's productions are staged within Merton in theatres, parks and historic buildings. Attic also runs an extensive community programme. It has produced over 50 productions including world premieres, revivals and new work. For recent and forthcoming poductions see (**www.attictheatrecompany.com**).

Casting procedures: Uses freelance casting directors. Does not hold general auditions and does not accept casting enquiries or submissions from actors.

Badapple Theatre Company

PO Box 57, Green Hammerton, York YO26 8WQ
tel (01423) 339168
email office@badappletheatre.com
website www.badappletheatre.com
Director Kate Bramley

Production details: Founded in 1998. Specialises in new comedy. Stages between 2 and 5 productions per year at a local rural touring level and/or national arts centre/small- to mid-scale theatre level. Uses 6-8 actors per year.

Casting procedures: Uses direct mail castings to agencies. Actors with an interest in the company are free to contact the office at any time. Directors prefer to see actors in performance prior to castings, so welcomes updates of performances in the Yorkshire region that company directors would be able to attend.

Big Telly Theatre Company

c/o Flowerfield Arts Centre, 185 Coleraine Road, Portstewart, Co. L'Derry BT55 7HU
tel 028-7083 2588 *fax* 028-7083 2588
email info@big-telly.com
website www.big-telly.com
Director Zoë Seaton

Production details: Big Telly Theatre Company is Northern Ireland's longest established professional, not-for-profit theatre company, formed in 1987 and based in Portstewart on the North Coast. The company produces theatre, interactive workshop programmes and community creativity projects, which tour throughout Great Britain, Ireland and internationally. It concentrates on the visual potential of theatre through fusion with other art forms such as dance, music, circus, magic and film to create a unique sense of spectacle. "Big Telly's work is driven by a determination to offer audiences entertainment that surprises, stimulates and ignites the imagination."

Casting procedures: Does not use freelance casting directors. Casting breakdowns are available through Spotlight, Equity and other job-information services, and are also released to agents. Welcomes submissions (with CVs and photographs) from actors previously unknown to the company sent by post or email. Invitations to view individual actors' websites are also accepted. Offers ITC/Equity contracts, and endeavours to employ disabled actors when casting for disabled characters.

The Bike Shed Theatre

162/3 Fore Street, Exeter EX4 3AT
mobile (01392) 434169
email info@bikeshedtheatre.co.uk
website www.bikeshedtheatre.co.uk
Director David Lockwood

Production details: Established in 2010. The theatre holds 60 people and produces at least 6 shows a year in-house, specialising in new writing. Will always first consider actors from or based in the South West. Offers Equity contracts when a project is ACE funded. The normal duration of run for a show is 3 weeks (in-house), and up to a week for visiting companies. There are no hire rates; everything is box-office split.

Casting procedures: Uses in-house casting directors. Casting breakdowns are available from Spotlight.

Welcomes approaches (with CVs and photographs) from actors by post and by email, and accepts showreels and invitations to view individual actors' websites. Actively encourages applications from disabled actors.

Border Crossings

13 Bankside, Enfield EN2 8BN
tel 020-8829 8928 *fax* 020-8366 5239
email info@bordercrossings.org.uk
website www.bordercrossings.org.uk
Director Michael Walling

Production details: Established in 1995. International company, working in theatre and combined arts, that creates dynamic performances by fusing many forms of world theatre, dance and music. Stages 1 or 2 productions per year touring to up to 15 venues including arts centres and theatres. Roughly 3-9 actors are used in each production. Recent credits include: *Consumed* (UK tour 2013); *Re-Orientations* (Soho Theatre 2010); *The Dilemma of a Ghost* (2007); *Bullie's House* (Riverside Studios); *Orientations* (Oval House); *Dis-Orientations* (Riverside Studios); and *Double Tongue* (UK tour). "We don't offer Equity contracts, although our own contracts are modelled on the ITC/Equity contract, and we usually pay above the minimum." Does not subscribe to the Equity Pension Scheme.

Casting procedures: Welcomes letters (with CVs and photographs) from actors previously unknown to the company if sent by post, but not by email. Invitations to view individual actors' websites and showreels are accepted. Actively encourages applications from disabled actors and promotes the use of inclusive casting.

Borderline Theatre Co.

Ayr Gaiety, Carrick Street, Ayr KA7 1NU
email enquiries@borderlinetheatre.co.uk
website www.borderlinetheatre.co.uk
Producer Dave Shea

Production details: Founded in 1974, the company stages 2-3 productions each year with an average annual total of 60-90 performances. Each tour normally runs for 31 performances across 13 different venues. Venues include arts centres and theatres across Scotland. In general 4 actors work on each production. Recent productions include: *Tally's Blood, Women on the Verge of HRT* and *Angel's Share.*

Casting procedures: Does not use freelance casting directors. Currently releases casting breakdowns to agents, but may publish these on the website in future. Welcomes submissions (with CVs and photographs) from actors previously unknown to the company sent by post or email. Also accepts showreels.

Bottlefed

email info@bottlefed.org
website www.bottlefed.org
Artistic Directors Kathrin Yvonne Bigler, Rebeca Fernandez Lopez

Production details: Bottlefed, led by artistic partners Kathrin Yvonne Bigler (director) and Rebeca Fernandez Lopez (choreographer), is an award-winning, London- and Bern-based performance company that works and tours nationally and internationally. "Our work is multi-disciplinary and at home in the areas of contemporary performance, installation, dance theatre and free improvisation. The company works as a platform for artistic development, research, collaboration and performance in both professional and community settings. Through the company's participation strand, we run extensive learning and engagement projects and workshops in diverse community and professional settings. Since our professional inception in 2006, we have won the Jury Prize at 100° Berlin festival at Sophiensaele (2010); were shortlisted for a Total Theatre Award for Best Performance as an Ensemble (Edinburgh Fringe 2007); and a Lost Theatre Award for Best Direction (2006)."

Casting procedures: Is not auditioning at the moment.

Bruiser Theatre Company

BEAT Carnival Centre 11-47 Boyd Street, Belfast BT13 2GU
tel 028-9024 3731 *mobile* (07553) 463613
email info@bruisertheatrecompany.com
website www.bruisertheatrecompany.com
Artistic Director Lisa May *Company Manager* Carly McConnell

Production details: Founded in 1997, Bruiser focus on producing exciting and innovative theatre, presenting existing texts using physical theatre techniques. Recent productions include: Cabaret (in association with The MAC, Belfast), *The Secret Diary of Adrian Mole, Candide, Oh, What a Lovely War!* and *The Government Inspector*. Each production consists of 2-14 actors and musicians and, on average, the company present 2 productions per year. This equates to a tour of around 45 performances at 16 venues across Ireland and Scotland. Recently toured productions include: *The 25th Annual Putnam County Spelling Bee* (with music and lyrics by William Finn, based on the book by Rachel Sheinkin.)

Casting procedures: Uses in-house casting directors; casting breakdowns are available on the website. Welcomes both CVs and letters from actors previously unknown to the Company and unsolicited CVs and photographs throughout the year. These should be sent via email. Also welcomes performance notices, invitations to view individual actors' websites and showreels. Rarely has the opportunity to cast disabled actors.

Cahoots Theatre Company

PO Box 118, 43 Bedford Street, London WC2E 9HA
tel 020-8743 7777 *mobile* (07711) 245848

email ds@denisesilvey.com
website www.cahootstheatrecompany.com
Artistic Director Denise Silvey

Production details: Founded in 1999. Produces theatre, cabaret and CD recordings, as well as acting as a general management and press agent (see also !!Link!! entry under Agents). Stages 3-4 productions a year, with 100 performances over 15 venues (arts centres, theatres and cabaret venues) in London, Edinburgh and New York. Productions may involve from 1 to 17 performers. Offers Equity approved and non-Equity contracts. Recent credits include: *Dead Sheep* and *An Audience with Jimmy Savile* at Park Theatre, and *The Man Called Monkhouse* on tour.

Casting procedures: Casting in in-house. Also publishes casting breakdowns on the Equity JIS. Welcomes emails (but not letters) with CVs and photographs from individuals previously unknown to the company. Does not welcome showreels, but is happy to receive invitations to view actors' websites. Will consider applications from disabled actors to play characters with disabilities.

Cambridge Shakespeare Festival

11 Crossways House, Anstey Way, Trumpington, Cambridge CB2 9JZ
mobile (07955) 218824
email mail@cambridgeshakespeare.com
website www.cambridgeshakespeare.com
Artistic Director Dr David Crilly *Associate Directors* Simon Bell, David Rowan

Production details: The Festival Company was established in Oxford in 1988 by Artistic Director Dr David Crilly. The main focus for the Company is the annual Cambridge Shakespeare Festival, which runs throughout July and August. Situated in the gardens of the Colleges of Cambridge University, its pastoral setting is one of the loveliest in the world.

Cardboard Citizens

77a Greenfield Road, London E1 1EJ
tel 020-7377 8948 *fax*
email mail@cardboardcitizens.org.uk
website www.cardboardcitizens.org.uk
Artistic Director Adrian Jackson

Production details: The UK's only homeless people's professional theatre company. Specialises in making forum theatre, but has broadened its scope to the provision of a range of performance-based cultural actions with, for and by homeless and previously homeless people. Productions include: *Glasshouse, A Few Man Fridays, Mincemeat, Woyzeck* – national tour; *Timon of Athens* – national tour with RSC; *Visible* – national tour, 'down and out' community production.

Casting procedures: Uses in-house casting directors. Holds general auditions; actors may write at any time requesting inclusion. Casting breakdowns are publicly available. Welcomes letters, CVs and photographs from individual actors previously unknown to the company, sent via post or email. Also welcomes showreels and invitations to view individual actors' websites. Offers Equity-approved contracts. Actively encourages applications from disabled people and promotes the use of inclusive casting.

The Castle Players

PO Box 17, Barnard Castle, Co. Durham DL12 9YS
(07748) 708619
email enquiries@castleplayers.co.uk
website www.castleplayers.org.uk
Artistic Director Simon Pell

Production details: An amateur community theatre company limited by guarantee. Established in 1987. Undertakes major open-air summer productions in specially constructed tiered-seat theatre. Stages minimum of 1 touring production annually. Recent productions include: *The Merry Wives of Windsor, Romeo and Juliet* and *The 39 Steps.*

Casting procedures: Uses in-house casting directors and holds general auditions; actors should write in January to request inclusion. Will accept unsolicited CVs and photographs sent by email only. Rarely or never has the opportunity to cast disabled actors.

Chain Reaction Theatre Company

Millers House, Three Mill Lane, London E3 3DU
tel 020-8981 9527
email mail@chainreactiontheatre.co.uk
website www.chainreactiontheatre.co.uk
Artistic Director Sarah Smit

Production details: Established in 1994. An award-winning theatre company producing informative, entertaining and thought-provoking theatre, workshops and video productions for people of all ages. Aims to create quality accessible theatre experiences, and engage audiences with writing and performances that explore contemporary issues and perceptions of everyday life. Currently has 12 educational shows in its repertoire, each designed for a specific age range from 5 to 16 years. Performances tackle sensitive and controversial topics including drug-awareness, sexual health, bullying, healthy eating and exercise, and emotional wellbeing. Also designs bespoke pieces of theatre and video productions for a range of professionals, which may be used at corporate workshops, training events and conferences, and also works in TIE and Outreach.

Since 2003 has produced original musical theatre for adult audiences. Its first production, *Everyone Loves Me*, won an award for best musical, and its most recent production, *Pretty Please*, premiered in London in 2007.

Tours up to 4 shows each year. Recent productions include: *Food 4 Thought*; *It's Your Body*; *Movin' On Up*; and *Totally Together*. For more information, contact Sarah Smit.

Casting procedures: Uses freelance casting directors and sometimes holds general auditions. Check website for details of when applications will be accepted.

Cheek by Jowl

Stage Door, Barbican Theatre, Silk Street, London EC2Y 8DS
email info@cheekbyjowl.com
website www.cheekbyjowl.com
Artistic Directors Declan Donnellan, Nick Ormerod

Production details: The company was founded in 1981 by Declan Donnellan and Nick Ormerod. The name conveys an intimacy between the actors, the audience and the text; the phrase 'cheek by jowl' is quoted from *A Midsummer Night's Dream* ("Follow! Nay, I'll go with thee cheek by jowl" (Act III Sc II)) Recent productions include: *Measure for Measure* (in Russian), *Ubu Roi* (in French) and *Tis Pity She's a Whore* (in English).

Casting procedures: "Like the vast majority of other British theatre companies, our actors are on fixed-term contracts. However, many actors come back regularly to work with us. For each new Cheek by Jowl production, a Casting Director is appointed. Please do not send unsolicited CVs as we are unable to accept them."

Chicken Shed Theatre

290 Chase Side, Southgate, London N14 4PE
tel 020-8351 6161 *fax* 020-8292 0202
email info@chickenshed.org.uk
website www.chickenshed.org.uk
Artistic Director Mary Ward

Production details: An inspirational theatre company that produces "beautiful and memorable" performances by working on the basis that everyone should be included, regardless of background, age, race or ability. Runs a Children's and Youth Theatre for 800 young people, operates 3 nationally accredited education courses, engages in community outreach projects, and has established a growing network of satellite 'Sheds' across the country (plus 2 in Russia).

Produces on average 3 productions in the main house (seats 300) and 4 in the studio theatre (seats 100). Recent productions include: *Globaleyes, The Night Before Christmas, An Awfully Big Performance, Paula's Story, The Government Inspector* and *Tales from the Shed.*

Casting procedures: Uses in-house casting directors. Does not hold general auditions; actors may write at any time to request inclusion. Welcomes letters (with CVs and photographs) from actors previously unknown to the company if sent by post or email, but no showreels please. Accepts invitations to view individual actors' websites. Offers Equity approved contracts. Actively encourages applications from disabled actors, and promotes the use of inclusive casting.

Clean Break

2 Patshull Road, London NW5 2LB
tel 020-7482 8600 *fax* 020-7482 8611
email general@cleanbreak.org.uk
website www.cleanbreak.org.uk
Executive Director Lucy Perman

Production details: Clean Break was founded in 1979 by 2 women prisoners at HMP Askham Grange. The company's artistic mission is to create bold new plays by the best women playwrights, telling the stories about women and crime that are not being told elsewhere, and taking this work into prisons and onto stages across London, the UK and the world. The company generally stages 1 production, presenting 35 performances each year. Tours to around 5 theatres and prisons across England and Scotland annually. The average cast size is 3-4. Recent productions include: *Dream Pill* (Edinburgh Festival Fringe), *Recharged* (Soho Theatre, Latitude festival), *Charged* (Soho Theatre), *it felt empty when the heart went at first but it is alright now* (Arcola Theatre), and *This Wide Night* (Soho Theatre). Offers ITC/Equity-approved contracts and does not subscribe to the Equity Pension Scheme.

Casting procedures: Uses freelance casting directors. Does not issue breakdowns. Auditions are organised via actors' agents and personal management. Unable to accept unsolicited CVs or showreels from actors. "Clean Break only employs women (section 7(2)(a) of the Sex Discrimination Act applies). We also actively seek to work with artists with an offending background." Actively encourages applications from disabled actors and promotes the use of inclusive casting.

Clod Ensemble

Unit 1-2 Crown Works, Temple Street, London E2 6QQ
tel 020-7749 0555 *fax* 020-7749 0597
email admin@clodensemble.com
website www.clodensemble.com
Artistic Directors Suzy Willson, Paul Clark

Production details: A small- to mid-scale company established in 1996. Creates theatre, music and performance events, workshops and courses in London, the UK and internationally. Stages on average 1 production each year in the main house; also works in Outreach and Community. Recent productions include: *Red Ladies* and *Greed.*

Casting procedures: Producer does the casting. Sometimes holds general auditions and actors should write in winter and spring to request inclusion. Welcomes unsolicited CVs and photographs if sent by email. Also accepts invitations to view individual actors' websites. Offers Equity-approved contracts as negotiated through ITC. Actively encourages applications from disabled actors and promotes the use of inclusive casting.

Close for Comfort Theatre Company

34 Boleyn Walk, Leatherhead, Surrey KT22 7HU
tel (01372) 378613
email close4comf@aol.com
website www.closeforcomforttheatre.co.uk
Director Janet Gill *Co-director* Glenn Johnson

Production details: Founded in 2001. "Takes theatre to living rooms across the south of England."

Casting procedures: Does not use freelance casting directors or hold general auditions.

Cloud Nine Theatre Productions

5 Marden Terrace, Cullercoats,
North Shields NE30 4PD
tel 0191-253 1901
email cloudninetheatre@blueyonder.co.uk
website www.cloudninetheatre.co.uk
Artistic Director Peter Mortimer *Associate Director* Colette Stroud

Production details: Established in 1997. Dedicated to commissioning and producing new work from Northern playwrights. Has produced plays by more than 24 Northern dramatists, in leading North-East venues. On average stages 2-3 productions each year. Recent productions include: *Death at Dawn - A Soldier's Tale from the Great War* (2014) and *A Parcel for Mr Smith* (2015).

Casting procedures: Uses in-house casting directors. Depends on production; our small-scale productions tend to use members of our ensemble, but we audition for larger scale productions. Enquire first. As a North East-based company, we tend to cast with actors from this region, and generally would not encourage other actors to apply unless specifically requested.

The Common Players

72 West End Road, Exeter
email anthony@common-players.org.uk
website www.common-players.org.uk
Artistic Director Anthony Richards

Production details: Founded in 1989, The Common Players focus on presenting both original productions and the classic texts for, and in partnership with, the communities of the West Country. Recent productions include: *Jerusalem* (by Jez Butterworth), *Educating Rita* (Willy Russell) and *Smuggler's Gold* (an educational programme). Each production consists of 2-16 actors and, on average, the company present 2-3 productions per year. This equates to 30-40 performances at 30 venues across the south west, ranging from small theatres, to arts centres, community spaces, schools and outdoor venues.

Casting procedures: Uses in-house casting directors, but does not hold general auditions. A casting breakdown is available on the website. Rarely has the opportunity to cast disabled actors.

Communicado Productions

The Old Schoolhouse Newlandrig,
Midlothian EH23 4NS
mobile (07525) 181183
email gerrymulgrew@yahoo.co.uk
website www.communicadotheatre.co.uk
Artistic Director Gerry Mulgrew

Production details: Founded in 1983, Communicado is a theatre company that has presented the classics and new stories, live music and visual and physical theatre for over 20 years. It also holds teaching workshops and does exploratory theatre work. Its productions include: *Tam O Shanter* (with Assembly Productions), *The Government Inspector* (with Aberystwyth Arts Centre) and *Calum's Road* (with National Theatre of Scotland).

Each production consists of around 10 actors and, on average, the Company present 2 productions per year. This equates to around 60 performances across Scotland, mainly arts centres, theatres and community spaces. Communicado also take their work to the Edinburgh Fringe Festival. Offers Equity/ITC approved contracts.

Casting procedures: Welcomes invitations to view individual actors' websites and to attend performances. Actively encourages applications from disabled actors and promotes the use of inclusive casting.

Company of Angels

Unit J307, The Biscuit Factory, 100 Clements Road, London SE16 4DG
tel 020-7928 2811
email admin@companyofangels.co.uk
website www.companyofangels.co.uk
Directors Teresa Ariosto, Virginia Leaver

Production details: Established in 1999. New and experimental work for young audiences, with a particular focus on new European writing. Stages 1-4 productions annually, performing in arts centres, theatres, educational and community venues throughout the UK. In general 4-6 actors are involved in each production. Offers Equity approved contracts as negotiated through ITC. Recent productions include: *World Factory* (Young Vic and New Wolsey Theatre) and Theatre Cafe Festival (venues including The Tramshed and York Theatre Royal).

Casting procedures: Sometimes holds general auditions, and actors may write at any time to request inclusion. Casting breakdowns are available from the website, *The Stage*, the Arts Council mailing list, and ITC. Welcomes letters (with CVs and photographs) from individual actors previously unknown to the company, sent by post only. Also welcomes showreels and invitations to view individual actors' websites. Actively encourages applications from disabled actors and promotes the use of inclusive casting.

Complicite

14 Anglers Lane, Kentish Town, London NW5 3DG
tel 020-7485 7700 *fax* 020-7485 7701
email email@complicite.org
website www.complicite.org
Artistic Director Simon McBurney

Production details: Award-winning theatre company founded in 1983. Constantly evolving its ensemble of performers and collaborators. Work ranges from entirely devised pieces to theatrical adaptations and revivals of classic texts. The average cast size is 7 but can be up to 18. Recent productions include: *The Master and Margarita, A Dog's Heart, Shun-kin, A Disappearing Number, Endgame, The Elephant Vanishes* and *Measure for Measure.* Contracts vary: some are TMA/Equity-approved; some (as for *The Elephant Vanishes*) are non-Equity.

Casting procedures: Occasionally uses freelance casting directors. Welcomes invitations to see work (accompanied by a CV and photograph), but unable to respond to everyone. "We are always more inclined to meet actors previously unknown to us if they are familiar with our work (i.e. if they have seen a Complicite show or participated in an Open Workshop). Complicite's Education Department programmes up to 2 Open Workshop seasons for actors each year." Join the Open Workshop mailing list at **www.complicite.org**. Actively encourages applications from disabled actors and promotes the use of inclusive casting.

Concordance

Finborough Theatre, 118 Finborough Road, London SW10 9ED
tel 020-7244 7439
email admin@concordance.org.uk
website www.concordance.org.uk

Production details: Concordance is a theatrical production company, founded by Neil McPherson in 1981, and is resident at the Finborough Theatre, London – see entry under *Fringe theatres* on page 248. The company presents new writing, revivals of neglected work and music theatre.

CragRats Theatre

Vine Court, Chalkpit Lane, Dorking, Surrey RH4 1AJ
tel (08444) 774100 *fax* (01306) 881591
email enquiries@cragrats.com
website www.cragrats.com
Managing Director Will Akerman *Business Support Manager* Nicky Miles

Company's work: A theatrical communications company founded in 1989, specialises in corporate training, TIE and issue-based theatre nationwide. Events draw on a unique mix of live theatre, dynamic workshops, e-learning, video and inspirational ambassadors with every element supported by in-depth research.

Employs 500 actors a year. Project managers and facilitators are trained in-house. Clients include: ASDA, NHS, British Airways, Learning & Skills Councils and the Royal Bank of Scotland.

Recruitment procedures: Extends its actor-base each month. Recruits actors through the website and through agents, Equity Job Information Service and advertisements in The Stage. Welcomes submissions (with CVs and photographs) by post or email from actors with at least 3 years of training at an approved drama school. Accepts invitations to view individual actors' websites and showreels. Actively encourages applications from disabled actors.

Creation Theatre Company

3rd Floor, Cherwell House, 1-5 London Place, Oxford OX4 1BD
tel (01865) 761393 *fax* (01865) 245745
email enquiry@creationtheatre.co.uk
website www.creationtheatre.co.uk
Director David Parrish *Associate Director* Charlotte Conquest

Production details: Produces site-specific Shakespeare. Stages 2-5 productions annually in unusual, non-traditional theatre venues (e.g. open air shows in parks, factory spaces, and a spiegeltent) with approximately 150 performances per year, mostly in Oxford. 8 actors work on each production. Recent productions include *The Snow Queen* and *King Lear.*

Casting procedures: Does not use freelance casting directors or hold general auditions. Casting breakdowns are available by postal application (with sae) and via Castcall. Welcomes letters and emails (with CVs and photographs) from actors previously unknown to the company at any time of year.

Dark Horse

Lawrence Batley Theatre, Queen's Street, Huddersfield HD1 2SP
tel (01484) 484441 *fax* (01484) 484443
email info@darkhorsetheatre.co.uk
website www.darkhorsetheatre.co.uk
Artistic Director Vanessa Brooks

Production details: Established in 2000. Production company exploring a range of projects that include actors with learning disabilities and promote inclusive working practices. Approximately 1 production per year touring to 10-15 venues, including arts centres and theatres in Yorkshire, the North West and internationally. Roughly 5-8 actors are used in each production.

Casting procedures: Occasionally uses freelance casting directors. Does not welcome unsolicited CVs. Actively encourages applications from disabled actors and promotes the use of inclusive casting. Offers Equity-approved contracts.

Dead Earnest Theatre

Applied Theatre Specialists, Sheffield Design Studios, 40 Ball Street, Sheffield S3 8DB
tel 0114-321 0450
email info@deadearnest.co.uk
website www.deadearnest.co.uk
Artistic Director Ashley Barnes *Drama Project Leaders* Vic Roberts, Stacey Sampson, Charlie Barnes

Production details: Dead Earnest is an applied theatre company, using theatre techniques to pursue social goals and in particular to impact on how people act and interact. The main focus of activity is in 3 key areas: Creative Learning (working with schools and universities and developing new techniques); Health and Well-being (CPD with health professionals and service user delivery focused on mental well-being); and Changing Communities (community consultation and looking at issues such as equality and diversity). The company works through forming strong partnerships with clients in the Public, Voluntary and Community sectors in order to bring creative thinking and theatre techniques to their specific needs. Clients are spread the length and breadth of the country. There is also a strong link to Sheffield Hallam University, where Artistic Director, Ashley Barnes, teaches in Applied Theatre.

Stages around 30 productions each year (mainly forum theatre), which all rehearse in Sheffield but are shown throughout the country, and supplies role-play simulators to local hospitals. Does not offer Equity-approved contracts and does not subscribe to the Equity pension scheme.

Casting procedures: Uses freelance casting directors. Sometimes holds general auditions. Welcomes postal or email submissions (with CVs and photographs) from actors previously unknown to the company. Applicants should live locally or have a local base, since company resources do not often extend to assistance with accommodation. The company aims to employ 1 new actor per project. Actively encourages applications from disabled actors.

Dirty Market Theatre Company

6 Grace's Mews, Camberwell, London SE5 8JF
tel 020-7701 8429
email info@dirtymarket.co.uk
website www.dirtymarket.co.uk
Co-directors Georgina Sowerby, Jon Lee

Production details: A collective of theatre makers with classical training; aims to integrate classical backgrounds with contemporary practice to create imaginative and exciting live performance. Applies for funding on a project-to-project basis, and is a member of ITC.

Casting procedures: Uses freelance casting directors. Casts from open workshops, and actors are advised to participate in these to get to know the company's work. Advertises via the website, Casting Call Pro, agents, SPF, etc. Welcomes approaches by actors by post and by email, but prefers to receive showreels by website link. Actively encourages applications from disabled actors.

DV8 Physical Theatre

Toynbee Studios, 28 Commercial Street,
London E1 6AB
tel 020-7655 0977 *fax* 020-7247 5103
email dv8@artsadmin.co.uk
website www.dv8.co.uk
Artistic Director Lloyd Newson

Production details: Creates and tours a new production every 3 years. Currently touring new verbatim theatre production *JOHN* throughout Europe and the UK untill December 2015. Recent productions include: *Can We Talk About This?* (verbatim theatre production); *To Be Straight With You* (verbatim theatre production); *Just for Show* (stage production); *The Cost of Living* (film); *Living Costs* (stage production); *Enter Achilles* (film/stage); *Strange Fish* (film/stage).

Casting procedures: Uses in-house casting directors. Performers should write in when advertised. Does not welcome unsolicited approaches but will accept showreels and invitations to view individual actors' websites. Actively encourages applications from disabled actors and promotes the use of inclusive casting.

Eastern Angles Theatre Company

Sir John Mills Theatre, Gatacre Road,
Ipswich IP1 2LQ
tel (01473) 218202 *fax* (01473) 384999
email info@easternangles.co.uk
website www.easternangles.co.uk
Director Ivan Cutting *Executive Director* Kate Sarley

Production details: Founded in 1982, the company tours theatre productions around East Anglia. New writing and a flavour of the region colour all of its original work. Stages 4-5 pieces each year, with an average annual total of 220 performances at 80 different venues. These include arts centres and theatres, educational and community venues, and site-specific locations. Tours mainly to East England but also nationally on occasion. In general, 6 actors work on each production. Offers ITC/Equity contracts; does not subscribe to the Equity Pension Scheme.

Casting procedures: Does not use freelance casting directors or hold general auditions. Casting breakdowns are not publicly available but may occasionally be posted on the website. Welcomes letters (with CVs and photographs, but not saes); email attachments will not be opened. Advises applicants to consult the website to get an idea of the sort of work the company produces. Applicants should only write once and should specify in their letter if they are local or native to the region. Will consider applications from disabled actors to play characters with disabilities.

Waters Edge

Manchester Road, Chorlton, Manchester M21 9JG
tel 0161-2829 776
email info@edgetheatre.co.uk
website www.edgetheatre.co.uk
Artistic Director Janine Waters

Production details: The Edge is a receiving and a producing theatre. They are a member of the Big Imaginations Theatre Consortium and Paines Plough Small Scale Touring Network and have a particular interest in musical theatre, new writing and theatre for children. Recent productions include: *Love Shift* (Royal Exchange Theatre 2010), *Spinach* (Royal Exchange Theatre, 2011 and Kings Head, 2012) and *Dreaming Under a Different Moon* (Edge Theatre, 2012). Edge stage 1 in-house production every 2 years. Edge offer Equity/ITC-approved contracts.

Casting procedures: Uses in-house casting directors, but does not hold general auditions. Welcomes unsolicited CVs and photographs and showreels from actors who are strong singers only. Also happy to receive invitations to view productions in the north-west. Actively encourages applications from disabled actors and promotes the use of inclusive casting.

English Touring Theatre

25 Short Street, London SE1 8LJ
tel 020-7450 1990
email admin@ett.org.uk
website www.ett.org.uk
Director Rachel Tackley

Production details: As the national touring theatre company of Great Britain, English Touring Theatre creates emotionally and intellectually engaging theatre of outstanding quality, imagination and ambition. The company works with the country's leading directors and designers to produce and remount artistically ambitious theatre that is vigorous, challenging and entertaining, and tours to mid- to large-scale venues nationwide. 4-20 actors are involved in each production. Offers UK Theatre/ Equity contracts and subscribes to the Equity Pension Scheme.

Casting procedures: Uses freelance casting directors and does not atccept unsolicited submissions from actors.

European Theatre Company

39 Oxford Avenue, London SW20 8LS
tel 020-8544 1994 *fax* 020-8544 1999
email admin@europeantheatre.co.uk
website www.europeantheatre.co.uk
Directors Adam Roberts, Jennie Graham

Production details: Founded in 1992, the company produces French-language theatre which tours the UK. Stages 3 or more productions a year, with around 250 performances in arts centres, theatres, schools and community venues. Normally employs 5 actors for each production.

Casting procedures: Casts in-house. Welcomes letters (not emails) with CVs and photographs from French-speaking actors previously unknown to the company.

The Faction

17 Vanbrugh Park, London SE3 7AF
email info@thefaction.org.uk
website www.thefaction.org.uk
Artistic Director Mark Leipacher *Co-Artistic Director*Rachel Valentine Smith

Production details: Founded in 2008, an independent theatre company dedicated to innovative revivals of classical texts. Aims to generate and sustain an ensemble of actors who share and develop skills, and who can explore a 21st-century solution to the extinct repertory system. "We question what constitutes a 'classical text', and work to determine which authors' works complement and enhance our understanding and enjoyment of Shakespeare and his contemporaries and thus should be a permanent part of the repertoire."

Stages 3+ productions annually, with around 120 performances at 4 venues (arts centres/theatres/ outdoor/educational). In general 8-20 actors are involved in each production. Recent productions include: Highsmith's *The Talented Mr Ripley* (Greenwich Theatre); Shakespeare's *Romeo and Juliet* (Greenwich Theatre); Schiller's *Joan of Arc* (New Diorama Theatre); Lorca's *Blood Wedding* (New Diorama Theatre); Schiller's *Mary Stuart* (New Diorama Theatre/UK tour/Qatar).

Casting procedures: Casts in-house. Casting breakdowns are available from the website, mailing list, email and Casting Call Pro. Welcomes letters (with CVs and photographs) from individual actors previously unknown to the company, sent by email. Also accepts showreels and invitations to view actors' websites and visit other productions. Encourages applications from disabled actors and promotes the use of inclusive casting.

Feather Productions Ltd

Unit 3, Blade House, 77 Petersham Road, Richmond, Surrey TW10 6UT
tel 020-8940 2335
email anna@featherproductions.com
website www.featherproductions.com
Artistic Directors Tim Whitnall, Anna Murphy

Production details: Has produced 2 new plays at the Old Red Lion, Islington. Welcomes scripts from new writers.

Casting procedures: Uses in-house casting directors. Sometimes holds general auditions; actors should write in Jan-Feb to request inclusion. Welcomes letters (with CVs and photographs) from individual actors previously unknown to the company sent by post or email. Also accepts showreels and invitations to view individual actors' websites. Offers Equity-approved contracts. Will consider applications from disabled actors to play characters with disabilities.

Fluellen Theatre Company

14 Devon Place, Swansea SA3 4DR
tel (01792) 368269
email fluellentheatre@aol.com
website www.fluellentheatre.co.uk
Artistic Director Peter Richards *Associate Director* Claire Novelli

Production details: Fluellen is a small-scale classical theatre company producing work from Greek drama to Harold Pinter via Shakespeare. Recently included new drama into programming. All productions premiere at the Grand Theatre Swansea. Recent productions include: *The Merry Wives of Windsor* (Shakespeare), *Antigone* (Sophocles) and *The Late Marilyn Monroe* (a new play by Francis Hardy). Each production consists of a variable number of cast members and, on average, the company present 4 main productions per year, alongside 9 shorter 'Lunchtime Theatre' productions. This equates to around 60 performances at 10 venues in Wales, including arts centres, theatres and outdoor community spaces.

Casting procedures: Uses in-house casting director. General auditions are held several times throughout the year. Welcomes both CVs and letters from actors previously unknown to the Company and unsolicited CVs and photographs. These should be sent via email. Also welcomes invitations to view individual actors' websites and showreels. Happy to consider applications from disabled actors and will consider inclusive casting.

Forbidden Theatre Company

56 Handsworth Road, London N17 6DE
email info@forbidden.org.uk
website www.forbidden.org.uk
Artistic Director Steve Brownlie

Production details: Physical and visual theatre company. Produces small-scale productions of adaptations of classics and devised work. Stages 1 production annually and gives approximately 40 performances per year. Tours 2 venues on average and performs in arts centres and theatre venues in London and Scotland. In general, 4-6 actors work on each production. Recent productions include: *Goddess*, *Stung*, and *Mrs Wobble the Waitress and Friends.*

Casting procedures: Does not use freelance casting directors. Sometimes holds general auditions. Actors can write at any time requesting inclusion. Welcomes letters (with CVs and photographs) but not email submissions. Advises that the company will only reply to actors if inviting them to audition. CVs are kept on file.

Forced Entertainment

The Workstation, 15 Paternoster Row, Sheffield S1 2BX
tel 0114-279 8977 *fax* 0114-221 2170
website www.forcedentertainment.com
Key personnel Tim Etchells (*Artistic Director*), Robin Arthur, Richard Lowden, Claire Marshall, Cathy Naden, Terry O'Connor

Production details: Since forming the company in 1984, the 6 core members of the group have sustained a unique artistic partnership, confirming their position as "trailblazers in contemporary theatre". The company's substantial canon of work reflects an interest in the mechanics of performance, the role of the audience, and the machinations of contemporary urban life. Its work, framed and focused by Artistic Director Tim Etchells, is distinctive and provocative, delighting in disrupting the conventions of theatre and the expectations of audiences. Forced Entertainment's trademark collaborative process – devising work as a group through improvisation, experimentation and debate – has made them pioneers of British avant-garde theatre, and touring all over the world has earned them an unparalleled international reputation. Visit the website for a full archive of work.

Forest Forge Theatre Co.

The Theatre Centre, Endeavour Park, Crow Arch Lane, Ringwood, Hants BH24 1SF
tel (01425) 470188 *fax* (01425) 471158
email info@forestforge.co.uk
website www.forestforge.co.uk
CEO/Artistic Director Kirstie Davis *Associate Director* David Haworth

Production details: Tours 3 productions a year into studios, village halls and arts centres, and has a large Creative Learning programme. The company is particularly interested in commissioning new work with rural or regional themes, and second productions. Recent commissions include: *Free Folk* by Gary Owen, and *For the Record* by Joyce Branagh.

Found Theatre

The Byways, Church Street, Monyash, Derbyshire DE45 1JH
tel (01629) 813083
email found_theatre@yahoo.co.uk
website www.foundtheatre.org.uk
Artistic and Casting Director Simon Corble

Production details: Small-scale touring and site-specific theatre.

Casting procedures: Does not hold general auditions; actors should write for specific projects only, when advertised. Welcomes unsolicited CVs and photographs sent via email and invitations to view individual actors' websites.

Frantic Assembly

31 Eyre Street Hill, London EC1R 5EW
tel 020-7841 3115
email admin@franticassembly.co.uk
website www.franticassembly.co.uk
Artistic Director Scott Graham

Production details: Established in 1994. Produces thrilling, energetic and unforgettable theatre. The company attracts new and young audiences with work that reflects contemporary culture. Vivid and dynamic, Frantic Assembly's unique physical style combines movement, design, music and text. Has toured widely throughout the UK and internationally, building a reputation as one of the country's most exciting companies.

In addition to its productions, Frantic Assembly operates an extensive Learn & Train programme introducing 9,000 participants a year to the company's process of creating theatre, in a wide variety of settings. Frantic Assembly also delivers Ignition, an innovative vocational training project for young men, particularly targeting those with little previous experience of the arts.

Casting procedures: Does not hold open auditions. Does not accept unsolicited CVs. External casting directors are used to cast for productions.

Frantic Theatre Company

32 Wood Lane, Falmouth TR11 4RF
0870 7350
email bookings@frantictheatre.com
website www.frantictheatre.com

Production details: Founded in 1990. Stages 2 productions annually with around 900 performances in venues throughout the UK and Ireland every year. Venues include arts centres, village halls, theatres, outdoor venues, educational and community venues, private homes and hospitals. On average 2 actors work on each production. Recent productions include: *You Hum It, I'll Play It.*

Casting procedures: Holds general auditions. Actors should write in May and November to request inclusion. Casting breakdowns are available at Call Pro. Actors are advised not to telephone and to send their details only when they have researched the company's very specific work and explain their suitability

Freedom Studios

Bradford Design Exchange, 34 Peckover Street, Little Germany, Bradford BD1 5BD
tel (01274) 730077
email hello@freedomstudios.co.uk
website www.freedomstudios.co.uk
Creative Producer Deborah Dickinson

Production details: Established in 2007. A national touring, devising theatre company. Stages theatrical events and experiences at arts centres, theatres and outdoor venues across the UK. In general 2-4 actors are involved in each production. Offers Equity-approved contracts as negotiated through ITC. Recent productions include *Street Voices 2*. Also holds the Asian Theatre School for a 15-week period each year, for aspiring Yorkshire British Asian, Black and ethnic minority artists; and Unit 4, "a twice-yearly platform event for some of the most exciting voices in the UK contemporary arts scene".

Casting procedures: Sometimes holds general auditions. Welcomes letters (with CVs and photographs) from individual actors previously unknown to the company, sent by post or email; also accepts showreels and invitations to view individual actors' websites. Will consider applications from disabled characters to play characters with disabilities.

Galleon Theatre Company Ltd

50 Openshaw Road, London SE2 0TE
tel 020-8310 7276
email boxoffice@galleontheatre.co.uk
website www.galleontheatre.co.uk
Artistic Director Alice de Sousa *Theatre Director* Bruce Jamieson

Production details: For recent productions, please see the website. Also has a film company, Galleon Films Ltd, which is developing a slate of 4 feature films.

Casting procedures: Uses an in-house casting director. Holds general auditions; actors should write to request inclusion when the company is casting for a specific project. Casting breakdowns are available through CastNet and advertisements in *The Stage*. Welcomes letters (with CVs and photographs) but not email submissions. Showreels and invitations to view individual actors' websites are also accepted.

Goat and Monkey

email info@goatandmonkey.co.uk
website www.goatandmonkey.co.uk
Director Joel Scott *Producer* Sally Scott

Productions details: Founded in 2004, Goat and Monkey create immersive and site-specific theatre that is highly visual, detailed and ambitious. Their work is influenced by traditional myths and folk tales, and looks to provide a unique experience for audiences in a variety of different environments. Recent productions include: *The Perils of Poisonous Plants* (Kew Gardens); *The Seed* (live performances, online story and real-world treasure hunt); *A Little Neck* (Hampton Court Palace) and *The Knucker* (Amberley Chalk Pits Museum). Each production can include 1-45 actors and, on average, the company present 1 production and several smaller university-based projects per year. Performances take place at theatres, community and outdoor venues across London and the south-east. Offers ITC-based contracts.

Casting procedures: Uses freelance casting directors and only holds production specific auditions. Welcomes both CVs and letters from actors previously unknown to the company if sent by email. Also welcomes invitations to view individual actors' websites, but does not welcome showreels. Casting breakdowns are available through the website and Spotlight. Would welcome the chance to cast disabled actors.

Gomito Productions

52 Malletts Road, Cherry Hinton, Cambridge CB1 9HA
email sam@gomito.co.uk
website wwww.gomito.co.uk
Producer Sam Worboys

Production details: Founded in 2001, Gomito is a collaboration of artists making new visual theatre. The company is an ever-changing family of performers, designers, directors, musicians and writers who want to share stories in a certain way;

with creativity, entertainment, humour, emotion and homespun roughness; with theatricality at its simplest. Recent productions include: *The Achemystorium, Woodland* and *Roost*. Each production consists of 3-6 actors and, on average, the company present 1-3 productions per year. This equates to over 50 performances at over 25 venues, including art centres, theatres and educational establishments. Productions also tour nationally.

Casting procedures: Gomito primarily uses its open workshops for casting at various times throughout the year. Email or join the mailing list on the website for details. Welcomes both CVs and letters from actors previously unknown to the company and unsolicited CVs and photographs. Also welcomes invitations to view individual actors' websites and showreels.

Graeae Theatre Company

Bradbury Studios, 138 Kingsland Road, London E2 8DY
tel 020-7613 6900 *fax* 020-7613 6919
email info@graeae.org
website www.graeae.org
Artistic Director Jenny Sealey

Production details: Founded in 1980. Produces theatre made by disabled people (actors, directors and other theatre practitioners) with physical and sensory impairments. Stages 3 productions annually and gives 70 performances at 50 venues each year. Venues include arts centres and theatres in England, Scotland, Wales and Ireland. 3-6 actors are involved in each production. Recent productions include: national tour of *Blasted* by Sarah Kane and *Whiter Than Snow* by Mike Kenny, which was a co-production with Birmingham Rep. Graeae and New Wolsey Theatre co-produced *Flower Girls* by Richard Cameron in autumn 2007, and Graeae co-produced a new play in spring 2008 with with Suspect Culture.

Casting procedures: Sometimes holds general auditions. Welcomes postal or email submissions (with CVs and photographs) from actors with physical and sensory impairments. Also accepts showreels and invitations to view individual actors' websites. Offers ITC/Equity-approved contracts.

Into The Scene is a new Arts Council England initiative led by Graeae. Works with leading drama schools on inclusive practice to encourage drama schools to recruit more disabled actors onto their training courses.

Scene Change is a Graeae initiative working with venues, drama schools and colleges, offering taster workshops to encourage more young people to apply to drama schools.

The company offers Continued Professional Development workshops for actors. Past workshops have included Comedy Acting with director Gordon Anderson (ATC/Catherine Tate), and Singing with Barb Jungr.

Grassmarket Project

email info@grassmarketproject.org
website www.grassmarketproject.org
Director Jeremy Weller

Production details: Founded in 1989. Independent theatre company producing new work in theatres across Europe, USA and the UK. Stages 2 productions annually and gives 30-40 performances every year. On average, 5-6 actors work on each production. Recent productions include: *De Andre (The Others)*; *Fathers & Sons* (Betty Nansen Theatre, Copenhagen); *Bus Stops* (Glasgow); and *The Foolish Young Man* (Roundhouse Theatre, London). Has also worked in film, notably on Lars von Trier's *Limboland*.

Casting procedures: Productions are cast by freelance casting directors or the company's artistic director. Sometimes holds general auditions. Employs a mixture of trained and untrained actors. Welcomes letters (with CVs and photographs) by post or email. Showreels and invitations to view individual actors' websites are also accepted. Offers non-Equity contracts. Will consider applications from disabled actors to play characters with disabilities.

Green Ginger

Unit 18, Albion Dockside Estate, Hanover Place, Bristol BS1 6UT
mobile (07977) 465850
email mail@greenginger.net
website www.greenginger.net
Artistic Directors Chris Pirie, Terry Lee *Associate Directors* Dan Danson, Laurence De Jonge *Patron* Terry Gilliam

Production details: Founded in 1978, Green Ginger is a theatre company based in Bristol, UK and Wiseppe, France that creates theatre and films with complementary educational activities for most ages and all abilities. Green Ginger enjoys collaboration with major arts organisations, including Welsh National Opera and Aardman Animations. Its members teach at University of Bristol, École Supérieure Nationale de la Marionette (France) and the Royal Welsh College of Music and Drama. Recent productions include: *Les Drames Des Autres* (2011), *Lionel the Vinyl* (2013) and *Outpost* (2014).

Each production consists of 3-4 actors and, on average, the company presents 3 productions per year. This equates to around 120 annually. The company tours extensively, having staged its productions across the world, from the UK to Europe and the Far East. These tours will be hosted at a variety of venues including schools, theatres, community spaces and outdoor and non-traditional theatre spaces. Offers Equity/ITC approved contracts.

Casting procedures: Uses freelance casting directors and only occasionally holds general auditions. Casting breakdowns are available online and on social media. Welcomes both CVs and letters from actors previously unknown to the company and unsolicited CVs and photographs. Also welcomes invitations to view individual actors' websites and showreels. Rarely has the opportunity to cast disabled actors.

Grid Iron Theatre Company

Suite 4/1, 2 Commercial Street, Edinburgh EH6 6JA
tel 0131-555 5455
email admin@gridiron.org.uk
website www.gridiron.org.uk
Director Ben Harrison

Production details: Founded in 1995. Produces new writing and site-specific theatre. Stages 1-3 productions annually and gives 20-50 performances every year. Performs in theatres, outdoor and site-specific venues in Scotland, England and Northern and the Republic of Ireland. Recent productions include: *Huxley's Lab, Barflies, Once Upon a Dragon* and *Roam.*

Casting procedures: Sometimes holds general auditions. Actors may write requesting inclusion at any time throughout the year. Welcomes submissions (with CVs and photographs) sent by post and email. Showreels and invitations to view individual actors' websites are also accepted.

Happystorm Theatre

11 Old Mill Close, Pendlebury, Salford M27 4DW
mobile (07547) 711839
email info@happystormtheatre.co.uk
website www.happystormtheatre.co.uk
Joint Artistic Directors Susi Wrenshaw, Matthew Ganley

Production details: Established in 2010. Award-winning production company specialising in immersive, site-specific theatre. 360-degree adventures that cut to the core of contemporary Salford. Recent productions include *Borderline Vultures* and *The Crypt Project.*

Casting procedures: Uses in-house casting directors and does not hold general auditions. Casting breakdowns are available as Spotlight submissions or by email and via the Equity Job Information Service. Actors should approach the company only for specific casting requirements. Will consider individual performance notices. Actively encourages applications from disabled actors and promotes the use of inclusive casting.

Headlong Theatre

3rd Floor, 34-35 Berwick Street, London W1F 8RP
tel 020-7478 0270 *fax* 020-7434 1749
email info@headlongtheatre.co.uk
website www.headlongtheatre.co.uk
Artistic Director Jeremy Herrin *Key contact* Henny Finch

Production details: National touring theatre company dedicated to new ways of making theatre by exploring revolutionary writers and practitioners of the past, present and future. Stages 4-6 projects annually, performing 24-32 weeks of the year. Tours nationally and internationally. Recent productions include: *Romeo and Juliet* (UK Tour); *Decade* (St Katharine Docks); *Earthquakes in London* (National Theatre/UK Tour); and *ENRON* (Chichester Minerva/Royal Court/West End/Broadway/UK Tour).

Casting procedures: Offers TMA/Equity approved contracts. Casting not dealt with in-house. Independent casting directors used on a show-by-show basis. Show invitations can be sent via email.

Hidden Talent Productions Ltd

50D Wickham Road, Brockley, London SE4 1NZ
mobile (07905) 175934
email info@hiddentalent.org.uk
website www.hiddentalent.org.uk
Artistic Director Adam Linsson *Casting Director* Andrew Miller

Production details: Established in 2006 as a not-for-profit, small-scale theatre producing company. Stages primarily new musicals and cabarets. Aims to raise the profile of musical theatre in the community by producing new works. Tours to small venues across the UK. Offers closed workshop performances and readings through to fully staged musical productions in larger theatres. Stages on average 1 production in the main house and 2 in the studio each year. Recent productions include: *Heaven Sent, A New Musical Comedy* (World Premiere – New Wimbledon Studio); *Manhattan Melodies in the West End* (Dominion Theatre Studio) and numerous cabarets.

Casting procedures: Uses in-house casting directors. Sometimes holds general auditions; actors may write in at any time, but preferably when the company is casting specific projects. Casting breakdowns are available via the website or on postal application with an sae. Welcomes letters (with CVs and photographs) from individual actors previously unknown to the company sent by post or email. Accepts showreels and invitations to view individual actors' websites. Will consider applications from disabled actors to play characters with disabilities.

Highly Sprung Performance Company

Studio 3, 54 Grafton Street, Coventry CV1 2HW
tel (07810) 267660
email mail@sprunghq.fsnet.co.uk
website www.highlysprungperformance.co.uk
Co-Artistic Directors Sarah Worth, Mark Worth

Production details: Founded in 1999. Aims to create original and innovative performances exploring the relationship between dance, text and physical theatre. Also runs community and educational activities alongside productions. Stages 1 production annually with 25 performances every year. Tours 10-15 venues annually: these include arts centres, theatres, outdoor and educational venues in the West Midlands, London, Manchester and Edinburgh. On average 2-8 actors work on each production. Recent productions include: *Pretend I'm Not Here* and *More Than Kisses.*

Casting procedures: Holds general auditions. Actors should send CVs and photographs by post or email. These will be kept on file for future auditions. Casting breakdowns are available on the website, by postal application and via Equity Job information Service and advertisements in *The Stage*. Showreels and invitations to view individual actors' websites are also accepted.

Hijinx Theatre

Wales Millennium Centre, Bute Place,
Cardiff CF10 5AL
tel 029-2030 0331
email info@hijinx.org.uk
website www.hijinx.org.uk
Artistic Director Ben Pettitt-Wade

Production details: Founded in 1981, the company stages professional theatre performed by actors with and without learning disabilities; tours to theatres, festivals and communities in the UK and Europe.

Offers ITC/Equity-approved contracts and does not subscribe to the Equity Pension Scheme.

Casting procedures: Shows are cast by the Artistic Director. Welcomes letters, CVs and photographs from actors previously unknown to the company. Welcomes applications from disabled and non-disabled actors.

Historia Theatre Co

8 Cloudesley Square, London N1 0HT
tel 020-7837 8008 *fax* 020-7278 4733
email historiatheatre@yahoo.co.uk
website www.historiatheatre.com
Artistic Director Catherine Price

Production details: Established in 1997. "Historia presents plays that have their source or inspiration in history." 1 production annually with 20-30 performances. Touring productions visit theatres, arts venues, National Trust houses, museums, churches, schools and village halls both nationally and in London. Roughly 6-8 actors are used in each production. Recent productions include: schools tour of *The Sound of Breaking Glass* by Sally Sheringham (about the Suffragettes) 2012-2013; *Judenfrei: Love and Death in Hitler's Germany* (2011 – New End Theatre, Hampstead; 2010 – Henley Fringe Festival and tour); *An African's Blood* (2007, and a limited season in 2008; tour); *Five Eleven or the Powder Treason* (2005; tour), and *Evelina* (2004; Pentameters Theatre). Offers ITC/Equity rates where possible.

Casting procedures: Does not use freelance casting directors or hold general auditions. Breakdowns are published via Equity's Job Information Service and Spotlight link. Unsolicited approaches from actors are discouraged. Will consider applications from disabled actors when casting for characters with disabilities.

Hoipolloi Theatre

Office F, Dale's Brewery, Gwydir Street,
Cambridge CB1 2LJ
tel/fax (01223) 322748
email info@hoipolloi.org.uk
website www.hoipolloi.org.uk
Director Shôn Dale-Jones *Associate Director* Stephanie Müller

Production details: Founded in 1994, the company creates visually and physically dynamic, imaginative and comic work which tours to small-and middle-scale theatres and arts centres throughout the UK. It is also involved in educational work. Stages 1-2 productions annually, presenting 100 performances every year at 60-70 venues. On average 4-5 actors work on each production. Recent productions include *My Uncle Arly*.

Casting procedures: Sometimes holds general auditions. Actors may write at any time requesting inclusion. Welcomes letters (with CVs and photographs) but not email submissions. Invitations to view individual actors' websites are also accepted. Advises actors approaching the company to have some knowledge of its work.

Hollow Crown Productions

Rose Cottage, Stone Street, Spexhall, Halesworth, Suffolk IP19 0RN
mobile (07930) 530948
email peter@hollowcrown.co.uk
website www.hollowcrown.co.uk
Artistic Director Peter Adshead

Production details: A theatrical production company with a difference. Provides an extension to the young graduate actor's training through the professional production experience. Offers ongoing vocational support to develop and enhance the foundation skills conferred through recognised drama school training, so that each company member may achieve their full potential.

Casting procedures: Uses in-house casting directors. Sometimes holds general auditions via workshops; actors may write in at any time. Casting breakdowns are available from CastNet. Welcomes letters (with CVs and photographs) from actors not previously known to the company if sent by post; no email submissions. Does not accept showreels. Offers own contract based on Equity Fringe/TMA. Will consider applications from disabled actors to play characters with disabilities. "The company is especially keen to hear from actors whose philosophy/approach to text resonates with its artistic policy, and who would be keen to explore often neglected classical texts – including Shakespearean texts in their quarto/folio forms."

Horse and Bamboo Theatre

The Horse and Bamboo Centre, 679 Bacup Road, Waterfoot, Rossendale, Lancashire BB4 7HQ
tel (01706) 220241 *fax* (01706) 831166
email info@horseandbamboo.org
website www.horseandbamboo.org
Key personnel Bob Frith, Alison Duddle, Esther Ferry-Kennington, Phil Milston

Production details: Established in 1978. A visual touring theatre using masks, puppetry, video and movement in theatre. Produces approximately 3 productions per year, touring to 60 venues including arts centres and outdoor venues in the UK, Europe and the USA. Performers must have mask/puppetry or dance experience to a professional level. Offers Equity contracts but does not subscribe to the Equity Pension Scheme. Members of ITC.

Casting procedures: Welcomes letters (with CVs and photographs) from actors previously unknown to the company if sent by post, but not by email. Invitations to view individual actors' websites are also accepted. Will consider applications from disabled actors to play characters with disabilities.

Icarus Theatre Collective

4 Ivor Court, 209 Gloucester Road, London NW1 6BJ
tel 020-7998 1562 *fax* 0871-528 9755
website www.icarustheatre.co.uk
Artistic Director Max Lewendel

Production details: "Explores the the harsh, brutal side of contemporary and classical drama." Aims to produce mid-scale productions of theatre using new writing and under-appreciated classics in diverse performance formats. Teams artists from the international community with British artists, and experienced artists with promising young professionals. Also works in Education, Outreach & Community, for which the key contact is **edu@icarustheatre.co.uk**. Recent productions include: *Macbeth*, *Othello* and *Hamlet* by William Shakespeare; *The Trials of Galileo* by Nic Young; H.P. Lovecraft's *At the Mountains of Madness* adapted by Max Lewendel; *Hedda Gabler* by Henrik Ibsen; *The Lesson* by Eugène Ionesco; *Journey's End* by R.C. Sherriff and *Vincent in Brixton* by Nicholas Wright.

Casting procedures: Uses in-house casting directors. Holds general auditions; actors should write in when advised to do so by the company's newsletter. Casting breakdowns are available from the website and are advertised in Spotlight. Welcomes letters (with CVs and photographs) sent by post, but not email, and does not accept showreels or invitations to view individual actors' websites.

Ichiza Theatre Company

2 Bradford Court, Bloxham, Oxon OX15 4RA
tel (01295) 720500 *fax* (01295) 722118
email office@ichiza.co.uk
website www.ichiza.co.uk
Artistic Director Togo Igawa *Associate Director* Masumi Kako

Production details: Established in 2007. Produces Japanese plays, from traditional theatre to contemporary works, in collaboration with artists from different backgrounds. Recently completed its first production, *The Face of Jizo* by Hisashi Inoue, at Arcola Theatre, to acclaim from wide audiences. Plans to start work in TIE/Outreach in the near future.

Casting procedures: Uses in-house casting directors and holds general auditions; actors are advised to write in only when auditions are announced. Casting breakdowns are available from Equity Job Information Service and *The Stage*. Does not welcome unsolicited approaches by email, but will accept letters (with CVs and photographs) and showreels sent in response to specific, announced auditions. Actively encourages applications from disabled actors and promotes the use of inclusive casting.

Incisor

41 Edith Avenue, Peacehaven, East Sussex BN10 8JB
mobile (07979) 498450
email sarahmann7@hotmail.co.uk
website www.theatre-company-incisor.com
Artistic/Casting Director Sarah Mann *Associate Director* James Madden

Production details: Recent productions include: *Pinter's People*, *The Odd Couple* and *Abigail's Party*.

Casting procedures: Uses in-house casting directors and does not hold general auditions. Casting breakdowns are available from Casting Call Pro/ Castweb/CastNet. Welcomes letters (with CVs and photographs) from actors previously unknown to the company, sent by post or by email. Does not accept showreels but will respond to invitations to view individual actors' websites. Actively encourages applications from disabled actors and promotes the use of inclusive casting. "Incisor's style is big and bold, especially as a lot of our work is outdoors. Large characters and voices needed."

Indigo Entertainments

Tynymynydd, Bryneglwys, Corwen, Denbighshire LL21 9NP
tel (01978) 790211
email info@indigoentertainments.com
website www.indigoentertainments.com
Director Emma Hands

Production details: Founded in 2000. Takes existing small-scale theatre productions, usually with a literary theme, and tours them around the UK and internationally. Stages 5-10 productions annually with 50 performances in 50 venues every year. These include arts centres, theatres, outdoor and educational venues, community venues and hotels all over the UK and in the Middle East and Far East. On average 1-3 actors work on each production. Recent productions include: *The Tale of Beatrix Potter*, *Testament of Youth*, *Hic! The Entire History of Wine (Abridged)*, *Red Wings*, *Richard Bucket Overflows*, *Emily Dickinson & I*, *My Darling Clementine* and *How Pleasant to Know Mr Lear*. Offers non-Equity contracts and does not subscribe to the Equity Pension Scheme.

Casting procedures: Does not welcome unsolicited CVs. Will accept showreels if they demonstrate productions of interest and are not just an actor's general showreel. Advises that the shows presented are usually intelligent, light, witty commercial pieces rather than experimental work.

Jam Theatre Company

45a West Street, Marlow, Buckinghamshire SL7 2LS
tel 01628-483 808
email office@jamtheatre.co.uk
website www.jamtheatre.co.uk
Artistic Director Jo Noel-Hartley *Producer, Production Design and Management* Mark Hartley

Production details: Founded in 2006, Jam Theatre Company is a professional theatre company writing and producing original productions for their own studio theatre and for transfer to commercial theatres. Shows are available for co-productions and licensing in the UK and America with Samuel French, London or via the Jam Theatre website. Jam also offer full-time and e-learning programmes in theatre and performing arts. Jam pays above Equity minimums, but doesn't offer approved contracts. Recent productions include: *Cinderella and the 7 Dwarfs*, *Santa's Secret Escape* and *Spots and Stripes.*

Casting procedures: Casting breakdowns are available through the website, Spotlight and Castweb. Welcomes CVs and letters from actors previously unknown to the company via email and online links to showreels. Also happy to receive production notices and invitations to view individual actors' websites. Will consider applications from disabled actors to play characters with disabilities.

Jasperian Theatre Company

Milsrof, Eglos Road, Ludgvan Churchtown, Penzance TR208HG
tel (01736) 740907 *mobile* (07941) 616177
email tony.jasper@btinternet.com
website www.jasperian.org
Artistic Director Tony Jasper *Production Directors* Kenneth Pickering, Peter Moreton, Harry Gostelow, Clare Davidson

Production details: Founded in 1992, JTC specialises in plays and revues that have a religious underpinning and/or deal with the human condition. The company is a member of ITC and casts all shows on artistic ability – not on any religious affiliation. Normally stages 2-3 productions each year with possibly a total of around 100 performances. Tours to a variety of different venues including theatres, churches and private houses across the UK. In general 3-7 actors work on each production. Recent productions include: *Charles Wesley 1707* (100 venues), *Stories of Grace, It Happened One Friday* and *God's Trombones.*

Casting procedures: Uses freelance casting directors. Actors may write requesting inclusion in the next round of auditions at any time, but the beginning of February, June and September are normally good times. Casting breakdowns are available through casting agencies. Prefers actors to send in their details by post but will accept the occasional email. Showreels are also accepted. Advises actors to read audition notices carefully and only come if suitable and available over the time period specified. A member of ITC, offers non-Equity contracts; however, "Apart from usually £250-£350 I also offer all accommodation and meals paid, and in some instances this is better than a basic Equity contract. I attempt to cast only Equity members. In 18 years, no-one has been owed money [by me]." Actively encourages applications from disabled actors and promotes the use of inclusive casting.

Kabosh

The Old Museum Arts Centre,
7 College Square North, Belfast BT1 6AR
tel 028-9024 3343 *fax* 028-9023 1130
email artisticdirector@kabosh.net
website www.kabosh.net
Artistic Director Paula McFetridge

Production details: Founded in 1994. Produces innovative physical and visual theatre for local, national and international touring and site-specific work. Stages 2-4 productions annually with 56 performances during the course of the year. Tours to around 30 venues annually, including arts centres and theatres, and site-specific locations. In general 2-6 actors are involved in each production. Countries covered include Northern Ireland, Republic of Ireland, England (including London), Scotland, Wales, parts of Europe and North America. Recent productions include: *Rhinoceros* and *Todd.*

Casting procedures: Auditions are by invitation only. Actors should write requesting inclusion in July (for autumn productions) and November (for spring productions). Welcomes applications (with CVs and photographs) sent by post and email. Also accepts invitations to view individual actors' websites. Any actor known to the company is welcome to send a CV and headshot (which will be kept on file) and to notify the director of performances where their work may be seen. The director will endeavour to see new actors. Any unseen actor who has sent a CV will be notified of open auditions, should they arise.

Kali Theatre Company

The Albany, Douglas Way, Deptford,
London SE8 4AG
tel 020-8694 6033
email info@kalitheatre.co.uk
website www.kalitheatre.co.uk
Artistic Director Janet Steel

Production details: Founded in 1991 to encourage, support and promote new writing by Asian women. "We focus on content and ideas as much as style, aiming to present memorable theatre events based on challenging and innovative ideas." Stages on average 1 main house production and 1 studio productioon each year, playing to audiences that are increasingly diverse. Nurtures novice playwrights through its multistrand Writer Development Programme, and has worked with writers such as Tanika Gupta, Rukhsana Ahmad, Gurpreet Bhatti and Shelley Silas among others. Recent productions include: *Zameen, Bhena, Tagore's Women* and *Mustafa*. The company also has a regional Outreach Programme for Asian Women. See website for further details.

Casting procedures: Welcomes letters (with CVs and photographs) from actors previously unknown to the company if sent by post, but not by email. Does not accept showreels or invitations to view individual actors' websites. Rarely (or never) has the opportunity to cast disabled actors. "Phone to find out what we are casting before sending CVs and photos".

King's Fool Productions

mobile (07745) 763543
email james@kingsfool.net
website www.kingsfool.net
Artistic Director James McAnespy

Production details: Established in 2011, King's Fool Productions produces work by the playwright and actor, James McAnespy and selected other works. In 2012 the company produced the premiere tour of *Sitting Up for Michael* across Northern Ireland and revived it in 2014 in the White Bear Theatre. The company has since relocated to London and is currently developing the new work, *Goolie's Human Taxidermy*. Stages 1 major production annually, but aims to increase the number of smaller productions from 2013 onwards. Gives 5-10 performances each year in 5 arts centres and theatres in Northern Ireland and London. In general 3-7 actors are involved in each production.

Casting procedures: Casts in-house. Auditions are held ahead of each project, with appropriate notices posted on Spolight and Casting Call Pro – please note that casting notices posted on other sites have not been placed there by the company, and your application may be overlooked if you do not use the Spotlight casting procedure. Actors are invited to email a CV to the Artistic Director, together with a link to their Spotlight entry and showreel, especially if they are willing to volunteer their time during the development stages for table reads, etc. Actors are given the full script beforehand and groups are invited to audition the scenes together. Postal applications are not welcomed, but emailed CVs with covering letters are accepted throughout the year, although it may not be possible to respond to these individually. Welcomes invitations to productions, and encourages disabled actors to apply for all roles if their disability has no bearing on the part they will be applying for. Parts are written for characters of varying disabilities, and for authenticity it is preferred to cast actors with these disabilities for such parts.

Kneehigh Theatre

14 Walsingham Place, Truro, Cornwall TR1 2RP
website www.kneehigh.co.uk
Artistic Director Emma Rice

Production details: Stages 3 productions annually with 130 performances during the course of the year. On average tours to 15 venues annually. Performs in arts centres, theatres, outdoor and "out of the ordinary" indoor venues across the UK and internationally. Recent productions include: *A Matter of Life and Death, Cymbeline, Rapunzel* and *Brief Encounter*. Offers ITC/Equity-approved contracts but does not subscribe to the Equity Pension Scheme.

Casting procedures: Does not hold general auditions. Advises that the company works with a pool of performers, but is interested in meeting new actors – either by personal recommendation or by seeing their work. Actively encourages applications from disabled actors and promotes the use of inclusive casting.

Language Laid Bare Productions

Top Floor, 298 Brockley Road, London SE4 2RA
mobile (07545) 704016
email languagelaidbare@yahoo.co.uk
Producer Darren Batten

Production details: Aims to produce high-quality performances of new writing and rarely played drama from the UK and overseas. To discover and develop new work and playwrights, and to provide a platform for new and emerging actors and creatives. Stages around 2 productions each year, with 30 performances in 6 arts centres/theatres nationwide. In general 5 actors are involved in each production. Recent productions include: *Deirdre & Me, You Don't Kiss,* and *Nina and Shaz.*

Casting procedures: Uses in-house casting directors. Casting breakdowns are available from Castweb, Castnet and Casting Call Pro. Does not welcome unsolicited approaches by actors, but will accept invitations to view individual actors' websites. Actively encourages applications from disabled actors and promotes the use of inclusive casting.

LipService

Z-Arts, 335 Stretford Road, Manchester M15 5ZA
tel 0161-232 6093/4 *fax* 0161-881 0061
email info@lip-service.net
website www.lipservicetheatre.co.uk
Joint Artistic Directors Sue Ryding, Maggie Fox

Production details: Over the past 20 years, LipService has established itself as one of the leading comedy touring companies, producing shows for the theatre which have a strong base in popular culture. These include: *The Picture of Doreen Gray; Inspector Norse* (a self-assembly Swedish crime thriller); *Desperate to be Doris; Jane Bond* (blonde and dangerous; a spoof of all things Bond); *Very Little Women* (a comic version of Louisa May Alcott's *Little Women*); *Hector's House* (an epic tale of togas and taramasalata); *The Importance of Being Earnest* (a trivial comedy for serious people); *Women on the Verger* (a hilarious look at romantic women's fiction); *Move Over Moriarty* (an impenetrable case for

Sherlock Holmes and Doctor Watson); and *Withering Looks* (a slice of life with the Brontë Sisters).

LipService attracts audiences from a wide social mix and age range. Based in Manchester, the company has built up a solid touring circuit in the North of England and throughout the rest of Britain. Challenges its audience by setting up a recognisable form and subverting it. This is partly achieved by two women playing all the characters, but also by ingenious theatrical surprises. "Along with the National Theatre of Brent, LipService is one of our great 2-person ensembles." (*Guardian*)

Casting procedures: Uses casting directors of co-producing venue. Does not hold general auditions. Actors should write requesting inclusion when extra performers are needed for a new production. Casting breakdowns are available direct from the co-producing theatre; details of co-producers are available via the website. Welcomes invitations from actors to view their work and from actors familiar with the company's work. Offers TMA/Equity-approved contracts.

London Actors Theatre Co.

Unit 5A, Spaces Business Centre, Ingate Place, London SW8 3NS
tel 020-7978 2620 *fax* 020-7978 2631
email latchmere@fishers.org.uk

Production details: Founded in 1987 and normally stages 1-2 productions annually, employing 6-8 actors on non-Equity contracts.

Casting procedures: Casting breakdowns are published in *The Stage*. Any approaches not relating to a specific breakdown are discouraged.

London Bubble Theatre Co.

5 Elephant Lane, London SE16 4JD
tel 020-7237 4434
email admin@londonbubble.org.uk
website www.londonbubble.org.uk
Creative Director Jonathan Petherbridge *Associate Director, Creative Learning* Adam Annand

Production details: The company's mission is "to attract and involve a wide range of audiences and participants, particularly those experiencing theatre for the first time, to inventive and unpredictable events that reflect the diversity of our city and its people".

To this end, the company has the following aims:

• To work particularly with and for people who do not normally have access to theatre for geographical, financial or cultural reasons
• To encourage and enable people to develop their own theatre and related skills
• To work to create a popular theatre form which is open, exciting and accessible
• To produce events which demonstrate and celebrate the creative abilities of all those taking part
• To examine issues of common concern to all those involved through the choice of material for workshops, projects and professional performances
• To challenge prejudice and bigotry through the company's organisation, working processes and final product
• To achieve a diversity of influence that is discernible throughout the company's work and consciousness

Recent productions include: *Hopelessly De-Voted, From Docks to Desktops, Blackbirds, The Sirens of Titan.*

Louche Theatre

Oakleigh, Waun Fawr, Aberystwyth SY23 3QD
tel 01970- 625170 (Admin) and 01970-612617 (Box Office)
email louche.theatre@hotmail.co.uk
website www.louchetheatre.com
Artistic Director Harry Durnall *Production Manager* Lisa Lewis

Production details: Founded in 1981, Louche Theatre presents 3-4 productions per year which are performed in Aberystwyth then tour Wales. Most years, one of theses are taken to the Edinburgh Festival Fringe. Recent productions include: *Portrait of Dylan, The Snow Queen* and *Lilies on the Land.* Each production consists of 10 actors and this equates to around 30 performances; including a tour of 5 venues, specifically small theatres and community centres.

Casting procedures: Uses in-house casting directors and holds general auditions in January. A casting breakdown can be requested by email. Welcomes both CVs and letters from actors previously unknown to the company and unsolicited CVs and photographs. These should be sent via email. Also welcomes invitations to view individual actors' websites and showreels. Encourages applications from disabled actors.

Lurking Truth

Gwynfryn, Newtown Road, Machynlleth, Powys SY20 8EY
tel 01654-702 200
email ddr@aber.ac.uk
website www.theatre-wales.co.uk/companies/company_details.asp?ID=21
Artistic Director and Secretary David Ian Rabey

Production details: Founded in 1986, Lurking Truth present contemporary work and premieres by dramatists such as Howard Barker, David Ian Rabey, David Rudkin and Arnold Wesker. This is sometimes done in association with Aberystwyth University Department of Theatre, Film and Television Studies, and several alumni of the department have gone on to work with the company.

Casting procedures: Uses in-house casting directors, but does not hold general auditions. Welcomes unsolicited CVs (with photographs) sent by email. Also welcomes invitations to view individual actors' websites, but does not welcome showreels. Rarely has the opportunity to cast disabled actors.

Mad Dogs and Englishmen

The Old Post Office, Green Lane, Quidenham, Norfolk NR16 2AP
tel (01953) 888499 *fax* (01953) 888499
email info@mad-dogs.org.uk
website www.mad-dogs.org.uk
Director Ann Courtney

Production details: Founded in 1995. Theatre company based in Norfolk whose policy is to provide well-balanced, entertaining and educational drama. Main areas of work are new writing, adaptations and classical work. Stages 2 productions annually with 70 performances during the course of the year, plus 30 workshops for schools. Tours to rural venues (churches, public houses) as well as arts centres, theatres, outdoor venues, educational venues, and community venues. On average 4-9 actors are involved in each production. Recent productions include: *The Magician's Box*, commissioned by Wilkin and Sons of Tiptree and *David Copperfield*, celebrating the Charles Dickens bicentennial.

Casting procedures: Sometimes holds general auditions.

Magnetic North Theatre Productions

Arto Domo, Argyle House, 3 Lady Lawson Street, Edinburgh EH3 9SH
email mail@magneticnorth.org.uk
website www.magneticnorth.org.uk
Director Nicholas Bone; *Producer* Verity Leigh

Production details: Founded in 1999. Commissions and produces new plays: 5 full productions and 1 film have been produced. Also produces 'Rough Mix', a creative development programme for writers and other practitioners. Stages 1-2 productions annually and gives 20-40 performances during the course of a year. Tours on average to 12 venues annually. About 5 actors are involved in each production. Recent productions include: *Sex and God*, *Pass the Spoon* and *Walden*.

Casting procedures: Sometimes holds general auditions. Actors should write to request inclusion when productions are announced on the website. Casting breakdowns are publicly available through the website. Welcomes submissions (with CVs and photographs) sent by post or email. Also accepts invitations to view individual actors' websites. Advises that the company has a low turnover of productions and a small staff, and finds it difficult to respond to general enquiries about available work.

MANACTCO (formerly Manchester Actors Company)

31 Leslie Street, Manchester M14 7NE
tel 0161-445 8477 *fax* 0161-332 7867
email admin@manactco.org.uk
website www.manactco.org.uk
Artistic Director Stephen Boyes

Production details: Established in 1980 and now the North West's leading provider of theatre in schools. "We are emphatically *not* a TIE company." Reaches well over 80,000 young people each year with around 6 touring productions. Recent productions include: *The Tempest*, *Of Mice and Men*, *The Pirate Queen*, *Much Ado About Nothing*, and *Poetry in Motion*.

Casting procedures: Uses in-house casting directors and sometimes holds general auditions. Actors may write in June/July requesting inclusion. Casting breakdowns are available via Equity Job Information Service and specific casting websites, for example Casting Call Pro. Welcomes letters (with CVs and photographs) from individual actors previously unknown to the company, sent by post or email; also welcomes showreels and invitations to view individual actors' websites. Actively encourages applications from disabled actors and promotes the use of inclusive casting. "We give priority to formally trained actors who have completed recognised courses at drama school. We like actors who can face the rigours of touring with good humour!"

Guy Masterson Productions

email guy@guymasterson.com
Artistic Director Guy Masterson

Production details: Olivier Award-winning producer of small- to mid-scale touring theatre work. Stages 4-6 productions annually with up to 400 touring performances a year. Touring access to 500 different national and international venues, including arts centres, theatres, arts festivals and outdoor, educational and community venues. Recent productions include: *Morecambe* (Olivier Award for Best Entertainment), *Shylock*, *The Odd Couple*, *Twelve Angry Men*, *Animal Farm* and *Under Milk Wood*.

Casting procedures: Rarely holds auditions. Mainly works with actors seen previously or by invitation.

Meeting Ground Theatre Co.

4 Shirley Road, Nottingham NG3 5DA
tel 0115-962 3009
website www.meetinggroundtheatrecompany.co.uk
Artistic directors Tanya Myers and Stephen Lowe

Production details: Work is based on the belief that, by taking artistic work across barriers and frontiers – whether they be national, psychological, intellectual, cultural, spiritual or disciplinary – new sources of energy and creativity can be engendered.

Since 1985 Meeting Ground has been celebrating the meeting of artists from different disciplines and cultures. Administered from its Nottingham base, the company draws together writers, actors, musicians, directors, puppeteers, designers and digital artists, and encourgaes community participation. At the heart of the company's artistic policy and vision is the theatrical exploration of what we call the "politics of the imagination; issues and questions that control the imagination and shape all our destinies. We actively seek to listen and give voice to the unheard."

Casting procedures: Offers ITC/Equity contracts and does not subscribe to the Equity Pension Scheme. Actively encourages applications from disabled actors and promotes the use of inclusive casting.

Midland Actors Theatre (MAT)

25 Merrishaw Road, Northfield,
Birmingham B31 3SL
tel 0121-608 7144 *fax* 0121-608 7144
email news@midlandactorstheatre.co.uk
website www.midlandactorstheatre.co.uk
Director David Allen *Associate Director* Gillian Adamson

Production details: Founded in 1999. Produces classics and new work. Specialises in theatre tours, community productions and schools-based projects. Stages 1-2 productions annually with 30-40 performances during the course of the year. Tours on average to 40 different theatres, schools, and other venues in the West Midlands, East Midlands, and nationally each year. Around 2-5 actors are involved in each production. Recent productions include: *Macbeth*, *Prospero's Island*, *The Children*, *The Mothers*, *The Good Person of Sezuan* and *The White Shining Land*. Offers ITC/Equity-approved contracts and does not subscribe to the Equity Pension Scheme.

Casting procedures: Sometimes holds general auditions. Actors should write requesting inclusion when auditions are advertised; general casting enquiries are most welcome in January and June. Casting breakdowns are publicly available via Equity Job Information Service. Advises that the company is primarily interested in actors who are Midlands based. Actively encourages applications from disabled actors and promotes the use of inclusive casting.

Mikron Theatre Company

Marsden Mechanics, Peel Street, Marsden,
Huddersfield HD7 6BW
tel (01484) 843701
email admin@mikron.org.uk
website www.mikron.org.uk
Artistic Director Marianne McNamara

Production details: Theatre anywhere for everyone, by canal, river and road. Has been touring for 43 years: "Mighty little Mikron" (*Guardian*). Tours on Tyseley, the company's historic narrowboat, on the inland waterways of Britain in the summer, and by road in the autumn months. Recent productions include: *Till The Cows Come Home* by Deborah McAndrew, and *Troupers* by Maeve Larkin.

Casting procedures: Does not hold general auditions. Actors may write in Dec/Jan to request inclusion, and are strongly advised to keep an eye on the website. Casting breakdowns are publicly available from the website, via Equity Job Information Service, Castweb, and on Facebook. Welcomes letters and emails (with CVs and photographs) from actor musicians only. Does not accept showreels, but accepts invitations to view individual actors' websites. Rarely (or never) has the opportunity to cast disabled actors "because of the nature of our tour – however, our Honorary Artistic Director is disabled". Asks actors to "please bear in mind that this is a hard tour: boating all day and shows and get-ins every night. Do consult the website before applying".

Mimbre

Unit 1, Energy Centre, Bowling Green Walk,
London N1 6AQ
tel 020-7096 1129
email info@mimbre.co.uk
website www.mimbre.co.uk
Artistic Directors Lina Johnansson, Silvia Fratelli, *Associate Artistic Director* Emma Norin

Production details: A local and international circus and street theatre company, using circus skills and dance to produce innovative work and promote a strong, positive image of women. Works in unconventional settings, creating moments of the unexpected and reclaiming some beauty in the urban environment. Mimbre's performances and participation programme are designed to reach beyond social, financial and cultural boundaries and find fresh ways to engage, encourage and inspire audiences, both nationally and internationally. Stages 1-2 main shows and 1-2 cabaret acts annually, with 50-60 performances in 15-20 arts centres, outdoor and festival venues, and theatres across the UK and Europe. In general 3-5 actors are involved in each production. Latest production (premiered April 2014): *A Room of Her Own* (premiered March 2015), *Bench* is still on tour.

Casting procedures: Uses in-house casting directors; holds general auditions only when producing a new show. Welcomes letters (with CVs and photographs) from individual actors previously unknown to the company, sent by post or email. Accepts showreels, performance notices and invitations to view actors' websites. Actively encourages applications from disabled actors and promotes the use of inclusive casting.

New Perspectives Theatre Co.

8 Park Lane Business Centre, Park Lane,
Nottingham NG6 0DW
tel 0115-927 2334 *fax* 0115-927 1612
email info@newperspectives.co.uk
website www.newperspectives.co.uk
Artistic Director Jack McNamara

Production details: Founded in 1973. A leading East Midlands touring theatre company; also tours nationally. On average stages 3-5 productions each year, touring all over the county including theatres, arts centres and rural venues. Equity-approved contracts as negotiated through ITC. Recent productions include: *The Lovesong of Alfred J Hitchcock* (Leicester Curve, regional tour); *The Boss*

Of It All (Assembly, Edinburgh); *Farm Boy* (Edinburgh Festival, national tour); *Dolly* (Curve, regional tour); *Those Magnificent Men* (regional tour) and *Lark Rise to Candleford* (national tour).

Casting procedures: Does not welcome unsolicited approaches. Promotes the use of inclusive casting. Casting breakdowns are available through Spotlight Link and from the website.

New Shoes Theatre

01892 710122*mobile* (07972) 395634
email admin@newshoestheatre.org.uk
website www.newshoestheatre.org.uk
Artistic Director Nicolette Kay

Production details: Currently producing *Hurried Steps* by award-winning writer, Dacia Mariani. The company stages 1 or 2 productions annually in arts centres, theatres, educational and community venues. In general up to 5 actors are involved in each production.

Casting procedures: Uses in-house casting directors. Casting breakdowns can be found on the website, *The Stage*, Spotlight, Casting Call Pro and Arts Jobs.

NITRO

Unit 36, 88-90 Hatton Gardens, London EC1N 8PG
tel 020-7609 1331
email info@nitro.co.uk
Artistic Director Felix Cross

Production details: Founded in 1978; formerly known as Black Theatre Co-operative Ltd. National touring theatre company that generates and produces contemporary black musical theatre. First established to provide training for black writers, directors and artists. Aims to explore ways of using black music as a means of attracting new audiences to theatre. Stages 1-2 productions annually with 1-2 performances during the course of the year. Recent productions include: *Nitrobeat* and *A Nitro at the Opera.*

Casting procedures: Sometimes uses agents when casting. Also holds general auditions; actors should write at the start of the year to request inclusion. Welcomes submissions (with CVs and photographs) sent by post or email. Accepts invitations to view individual actors' websites. Advises that the company keeps an up-to-date catalogue of black actors and would particularly welcome CVs from actors of different ethnic backgrounds. Offers TMA/Equity-approved contracts and does not subscribe to the Equity Pension Scheme. Actively encourages applications from disabled actors and promotes the use of inclusive casting.

No Limits Theatre

Studio 2, Arts Centre Washington, Fatfield, Tyne & Wear NE38 8AB
tel 0191-4154966 *fax*
email info@nolimitstheatre.org.uk
website www.nolimitstheatre.org.uk
Artistic Director/Chief Executive Janet Nettleton
Associate Director Alan Parker

Production details: Founded in 1995, No Limits is a touring theatre company that works with adults with and without learning disabilities. Aims to produce high-quality, devised work that challenges traditional perceptions of theatre and disability, staging 1 production in 20 different venues across the UK each year. It also has a strong commitment to outreach and development work. In general 5-8 actors work on each production. Recent productions include: *Attic, The Winged State* and *Cuckoo Jack.*

Casting procedures: Welcomes letters, CVs and photographs from actors previously unknown to the company, but does not accept emails or unsolicited showreels. Advises that the company already has a core acting team but often takes on new actors in workshop training sessions.

Northern Broadsides

Dean Clough, Halifax HX3 5AX
tel (01422) 369704
website www.northern-broadsides.co.uk
Artistic Director Barrie Rutter *Associate Director* Conrad Nelson

Production details: Formed in 1992 by Artistic Director Barrie Rutter, Northern Broadsides is a multi-award winning touring company based in the historic Dean Clough Mill in Halifax, West Yorkshire. The company has built up a formidable reputation performing Shakespeare and classical texts with an innovative, popular and regional style, often in unconventional locations (The Tower of London, cattle markets, churches, indoor riding stables, Victorian mills). As well as touring extensively in the UK, the company has delighted audiences across the world, touring to India, Brazil, the USA, Greece, Cyprus, the Czech Republic, Poland, Germany, Austria and Denmark.

The company repertoire consists mainly of Shakespeare and classical texts. These plays possess a timeless resonance and their universal exploration of the human condition has currency in any day and age, appealing directly to the soul, the emotions and the imagination. Northern Broadsides are dedicated to interpreting the classics in a manner which makes what is often regarded as 'difficult' work extremely accessible. Their lively 'no frills' approach, with simple storytelling and minimal sets, has not only won the company many plaudits and awards, but enabled both established and new audiences to enjoy Shakespeare regardless of language or theatrical convention.

Northern Broadsides' work is characterised by its vitality and humour; the passion of the performers, whose acting style is far less 'mannered' than conventional theatrical productions; an ensemble style which adds coherence to the performances (the result of working with a group of actors over a period of time, in some cases many years) and precise direction which results in work of remarkable clarity.

NTC Touring Theatre Company

The Playhouse, Bondgate Without, Alnwick, Northumberland NE66 1PQ
tel (01665) 602586 *fax* (01665) 605837
email admin@ntc-touringtheatre.co.uk
website www.ntc-touringtheatre.co.uk
Director Gillian Hambleton

Production details: Founded in 1978 as Northumberland Theatre Company. Small-scale touring theatre company performing at village halls, small theatres and community venues in predominantly rural areas. Main areas of work are new writing and physical theatre pieces. Stages 3 productions annually with more than 100 performances during the course of the year. 5 actors are usually involved in each production.

Casting procedures: Sometimes holds general auditions for locally based actors (best time to write is early June or September), but most casting is done through agents. Casting breakdowns are available on the website, via Equity JIS and Arts Jobs. Welcomes submissions (with CVs and photographs) sent by post. Also accepts invitations to view individual actors' performances and will always reply to individual actors. Particularly interested in locally based actors or actors with local origins, and will keep details on file for future reference unless requested to do otherwise. Actively encourages applications from disabled actors and promotes the use of inclusive casting.

The Okai Collier Company Ltd

39 Morris House, Roman Road, Bethnal Green, London E2 0HP
tel 020-8980 5716
email info@okaicollier.com
website www.okaicollier.com
Artistic Directors Omar F. Okai, Simon James Collier

Production details: The Okai Collier Company was formed in 1994 by artistic directors Omar F. Okai and Simon James Collier to explore and push the boundaries of everyday ideas, opinions and opportunities in the creative arts: music, theatre, dance, painting and the written word. Using a variety of media including IT, the company aims to break down contemporary social barriers and encourage new talent by developing a range of projects in this field. These projects include award-winning theatrical productions, opera, creative writing with young people, exhibitions for new artists and community arts projects, as well as its innovative publishing division. Okai Collier is committed to maintaining a balanced portfolio of work, divided between the commercial and charitable spheres and drawing on a diverse range of people and disciplines.

Open Clasp Theatre Company

The Stephenson Building, 173 Elswick Road, Newcastle-upon-Tyne NE4 6SQ
tel 0191-272 4063 *fax* 0191-272 4137
email info@openclasp.plus.com
website www.openclasp.org.uk
Artistic Director Catrina McHugh

Production details: Open Clasp is a women's theatre company specialising in creating high-quality theatre from a female gaze for mixed audiences. Open Clasp's work is created in collaboration with women from the North East. "The company exists to make truthful, risk-taking theatre which is informed by the lived experiences of the women and young women we work with. We want our work to make space for social debate and to encourage our audiences to walk in the shoes of women, including those who are the most disempowered in our society. Our work is performed in a range of settings including regional producing theatres, village halls, conferences and community centres. We have a developing audience and a loyal following which includes women who share the life stories of the characters we depict. We know of no other organisation that works the way that we do." On average stages 1 touring production per year, usually in Feb-March, with approximately 35 performances in 20+ arts centres, theatres, and educational and community venues in North East UK, Scotland, North West UK and Yorkshire. Recent productions include: *The Space Between Us*, *Swags & Tails*, *BlueGiro*, and *Rattle & Roll*.

Casting procedures: Sometimes holds general auditions; actors requesting inclusion should write in September. Casting breakdowns are available from the website, by postal application with sae, and from online casting services. Welcomes letters (with CVs and photographs) from individual actors previously unknown to the company, sent by post or email, but does not accept showreels. Will consider invitations to view individual actors' websites if accompanied by a full CV. Will also consider applications from disabled actors to play characters with disabilities. "It is paramount that our actors share the ethos of the company. Open Clasp ensures that casting is representative of the diverse groups we work with, the issues explored, and the characters they have created."

The Original Theatre Company

Dovedon Hall Office, Chedburgh Road, Whepstead, Bury St Edmunds, Suffolk IP29 4UB
tel 0870-803 0158
email info@originaltheatre.com
website www.originaltheatre.com
Director Alastair Whatley

Production details: Established in 2004. Stages 3-4 productions annually, with 200 performances in 40-50 mid to large-scale theatres across the UK in 2013. In general 8-13 actors are involved in each production. Offers Equity-approved contracts. Recent productions include: Sebatian Faulk's *Birdsong* (2013 and 2014), *Private Ear & The Public Eye* (Yvonne Arnaud Theatre and tour), *Three Men in a Boat*

(Yvonne Arnaud Theatre and tour), *Our Country's Good* (Kingston Rose, Theatre Clywd and tour); *Dancing at Lughnasa* (Glasgow Citizens and tour); *See How They Run* and *Twelfth Night* (produced in rep and touring); *Vincent in Brixton* (Yvonne Arnaud, Theatre Royal Windsor, Northcott Exeter); *Othello* (Harrogate Theatre, Buxton Opera House).

Casting procedures: Sometimes holds general auditions; actors may write in March and July to request inclusion. Casting breakdowns are available from the website, by postal application with sae, and from Spotlight. Welcomes letters (with CVs and photographs) from individual actors previously unknown to the company, sent by post only. Also welcomes showreels and invitations to view individual actors' websites. Actively encourages applications from disabled actors and promotes the use of inclusive casting.

Out of Joint

7 Thane Works, Thane Villas, London N7 7PH
tel 020-7609 0207 *fax* 020-7609 0203
email ojo@outofjoint.co.uk
website www.outofjoint.co.uk
Director Max Stafford-Clark *Administrator and Education Manager* Natasha Ockrent

Production details: Stages 2 productions annually with approximately 230 performances during the course of the year. Tours both nationally and internationally playing to around 12-15 arts centres and theatres each year. Recent productions include: *Duck*, *The Permanent Way*, *Macbeth* and *Talking to Terrorists*.

Casting procedures: Welcomes letters (with CVs and photographs) but not email submissions. Also accepts performance notices from individual actors. Offers Equity-approved contracts. Will consider applications from disabled actors to play characters with disabilities.

Ovation Productions

Upstairs at The Gatehouse, Highgate,
London N6 4BD
tel 020-8340 4256
website www.ovationtheatres.com
Directors John Plews, Katie Plews *Theatre Manager* Claire Thorn

Production details: Founded in 1985. Owns and operates Upstairs at the Gatehouse, a fringe theatre in North London (see entry under *Fringe theatres* on page 246). Recent productions include: *Kiss Me, Kate* and *Singin' in the Rain*.

Casting details: Casting breakdowns are always posted on **www.upstairsatthegatehouse.com** and on Spotlight. Welcomes email submissions. Offers non-Equity contracts. Will consider applications from disabled actors to play characters with disabilities.

The Oxford Shakespeare Company

98 Galloway Road, London W12 0PJ
07581-751198
email info@osctheatre.org.uk
website www.osctheatre.org.uk
Directors Nicholas Green, Emma Randle, Charlotte Windmill

Production details: Founded in 2001. Stage Shakespeare and other classic plays. The OSC are celebrated for their open air, site-specific performances both at their summer residency at Wadham College and across the Historic Royal Palaes sites of Hampton Court, Kensington Palace, Tow of London and the Banqueting House, Whitehall. Stages 3 productions with up to 100 performances during the course of the year. Acting company of up to 12 including actor/musicians. Recent productions include: *As You Like It* (Michael Oakley and Nick Lloyd Webber); *A Midsummer Night's Dream* (Gemma Fairlie and *The Tempest* (Mick Gordon and Nick Lloyd Webber).

Casting procedures: Casting breakdowns are released to agents and are available via Spotlight.

Oxfordshire Theatre Company

c/o Mercer Lewin, 41 Cornmarket Street,
Oxford OX1 3HA
tel (07802) 287703
email info@oxfordshiretheatrecompany.co.uk
website www.oxfordshiretheatrecompany.co.uk
Artistic Director Karen Simpson

Production details: Tours high-quality, challenging, entertaining and accessible theatre to audiences in Oxfordshire and beyond. The company has a unique reputation for taking theatre to non-theatre venues, especially in rural areas. Creates a minimum of 3 productions each year, each of which has a resonance with both adults and younger audiences. The autumn production appeals to families with young children; the spring show embraces narratives that challenge, engage and excite adult audiences. From 2009 the company has produced a summer production that actively encourages both young people and older people to become a more promiment part of its audience.

Casting procedures: The company casts by audition. Breakdowns are published on the website as well as in Castcall and Casting Call Pro, among others. Is unable to consider unsolicited submssions at other times. Actively encourages applications from disabled actors and promotes the use of inclusive casting.

Paines Plough

4th Floor, 43 Aldwych, London WC2B 4DN
tel 020-7240 4533 *fax* 020-7240 4534
email office@painesplough.com
website www.painesplough.com
Artistic Directors James Grieve, George Perrin

Production details: Founded in 1974, the company is dedicated to producing and touring new writing. Recent work includes: Kate Tempest's *Hopelessly Devoted*, Sam Burns' *Not The Worst Place*, Mike

Bartlett's *An Intervention*, The 'Roundabout' season and *Come To Where I'm From*.

Casting procedures: Casts all productions in-house. Does not accept unsolicited CVs or photographs, but holds open auditions throughout the year to meet new actors.

Pendle Productions

Bridge Farm, 249 Hawes Side Lane, Blackpool, Lancashire FY4 4AA
tel (01253) 839375 *fax* (01253) 792930
email admin@pendleproductions.co.uk
website www.pendleproductions.co.uk
Director TS Lince

Production details: Touring professional theatre company. Stages between 10 and 15 productions each year, with 600 performances nationally in 300 venues of all types. Recent productions include: *Cinderella*, *Sinbad* and *Treasure Island*.

Casting procedures: Sometimes holds general auditions; actors should write in April-June requesting inclusion. Casting breakdowns are publicly available via the usual channels. Welcomes letters (with CVs and photographs) from individual actors previously unknown to the company sent by post or email. Accepts showreels but prefers not to receive invitations to view individual actors' websites. Actively encourages applications from disabled actors, and promotes the use of inclusive casting.

Pentabus Theatre Company

Bromfield, Ludlow, Shropshire SY8 2JU
tel (01584) 856564 *fax* (01584) 856254
email info@pentabus.co.uk
website www.pentabus.co.uk
Artistic Director Elizabeth Freestone

Production details: Pentabus Theatre Company develops and produces new plays about the contemporary rural world. The company tours around the country with bold new theatre that has local impact and national resonance. 2014 was the company's 40th anniversary.

Always at the forefront of groudbreaking new theatre, highlights over the years have included: *Milked* (by Simon Longman, a black comedy about rural unemployment); *Each Slow Dusk* (by Rory Mullarkey); *Every Brilliant Thing* (by Duncan Macmillan & Jonny Donahoe, a co-production with Pains Plough); *In This Place* (by Lydia Adetunji and Frances Brett, an audio theatre walking adventure); *White Open Spaces* (a series of monologues about racism); *Strawberry Fields* by Alecky Blythe (a verbatim piece about migrant workers); *Silent Engine* (by Julian Gardner about climate change) and *For Once* (by Tim Price, about teenage car crashes on rural roads).

The company produces around 4 shows a year that tour a range of venues including studio theatres, village halls and arts centres. The company also makes site-responsive shows in particular locations.

Casting procedures: Occasionally uses freelance casting directors. Casting breakdowns are available via Equity Job Information Service and the website. No CVs or email enquiries; instead invite to see in a show.

The People's Theatre Co

69 Manor Way, Guildford, Surrey GU2 7RR
email ptc@ptc.org.uk
website www.ptc.org.uk
Director Steven Lee

Production details: Established in 2003. The company has built an international reputation for its unique brand of sophisticated original pop musicals. Stages 120+ performances per year, touring across the country to Receiving Houses and number 1/number 2 venues. 2-7 actors are generally involved in each production. Recent productions include: *How The Koala Learnt To Hug, There Was An Old Lady Who Swallowed A Fly, The Witch's Bogey* and the award-winning Bink trilogy of full-scale family musicals.

Casting procedures: Casting is done in-house. Holds general auditions. Actors should only write requesting inclusion in response to casting calls. Actors can also register on The PTC's website for first alerts to castings. Casting breakdowns are obtainable via Castweb, Casting Call Pro, CastNet and through the PTC mailing list. Accepts submissions (with CVs and photographs) from individual actors previously unknown to the the company; submissions sent by email are also accepted. Applications from disabled actors are considered to play disabled characters. "We want a well-presented CV with personal information, training, experience and detailed skills – particularly singing, as most of our work is musicals. New actors and recent graduates welcome."

People Show

Brady Arts Centre, 192-196 Hanbury Street, London E1 5HU
tel 020-7729 1841 *fax* 020-7739 0203
email people@peopleshow.co.uk
website www.peopleshow.co.uk
Company: Fiona Creese, Gareth Brierley, George Khan, Jessica Worrall, Mark Long, Sadie Cook

Production details: The longest-running experimental theatre company in the UK, touring nationally and internationally since 1966, creating work for arts centres, theatres, and outdoor and site-specific venues. Anything from 3 to 65 actors are involved in each production. Offers Equity-approved contracts as negotiated through ITC. Recent works includes: *People Show 127: The Crypt Project: People Show 127: Hands Off.* People Show have an exciting line up of shows planned for 2016 to celebrate their 50th anniversary year.

Casting procedures: People Show is an ensemble company with a core group of 7 artists, and an extended network of 45 plus associate artists. Does not use freelance casting directors or hold general auditions. Welcomes approaches from performers previously unknown to the company.

Pilot Theatre

York Theatre Royal, St Leonards Place,
York YO1 7HD
tel (01904) 635755
email info@pilot-theatre.com
website www.pilot-theatre.com
Artistic Director Marcus Romer

Production details: Pilot Theatre is an international touring theatre company based in York, UK. They devise and develop projects with particular focus on working for and with young audiences. They also work across platforms to produce and distribute work digitally, run training conferences, livestream events and performances, provide a wide range of online educational resources.

A wide range of work over the last few years includes the six-camera livestream of the York Myserty Plays for The Space and a range of specially commissioned plays including: *Loneliness of the Long Distance Runner*, *Running on the Cracks*, *Blood + Chocolate* and more recently the new adaptation of *Antigone* by Ry Williams.

"We work with established artists, leading practitioners and diverse teams alongside nurturing young and emergent talent to develop our practice across all platforms of delivery. The audiences and communities we aim to reach are reflected by the diverse teams who make and deliver our work."

Casting procedures: The company regularly posts casting information online. "Please try and avoid sending surface mail for casting, as we are trying to minimise wastage and energy usage." Please email your details to: **casting@pilot-theatre.com**.

Point Blank

The Riverside, 1 Mowbray Street, Sheffield S3 8EN
tel 0114-249 3650/51 *fax* 0114-249 3655
email info@pointblank.org.uk
website www.pointblank.org.uk
Creative Director Steve Jackson

Production details: Established in 1999. Small-scale national touring theatre producing new work, devised, physical theatre and new writing. Stages 1 production annually. 30-60 performances per year touring 18 venues which include art centres, theatres, outdoor venues, educational and community venues. Regions covered include North, North West, Yorkshire, West Midlands, South East, London, Scotland, Ireland and Wales. 2-4 actors are involved in each production. Actors are employed under Equity approved contracts negotiated through ITC. Recent productions include: *Operation Wonderland* (15 venues including The Crucible, Latchmere and The Traverse); *Roses and Morphine* (18 venues including The Crucible, Royal Exchange and Aberystwyth Arts Centre); and *Last Orders* (Sheffield, site-specific).

Casting procedures: Casting is carried out by in-house casting director. Hold general auditions. Actors can write at anytime to request inclusion; details will be kept on file. Casting breakdowns are obtainable via casting websites. Accepts submissions (with CVs and photographs) from individual actors previously unknown to the company. Applications from disabled actors are considered to play disabled characters wherever possible.

"Research the company first to check it's appropriate. We will get back with details of shows as appropriate. Yorkshire-based actors are particularly welcome to apply".

Powerhouse Theatre Company

58 Oak Hill, Wood Street Village,
Guildford GU3 3ER
mobile (01483) 232690
email powerhousetheattre@hotmail.co.uk
website www.powerhousetheatre.co.uk
Artistic Director Geoff Lawson

Production details: Founded in 2007, Powerhouse focuses on presenting high quality, accessible and entertaining productions that deal with important social issues, as well as as well as educational history shows for young people and site-specific work. Recent productions include: *Our Tudors*, *Suffragette* and *Pretty Ugly*. Each production consists of 3-4 actors and, on average, the company tours 3-4 productions per year. This equates to around 50 performances at 4-5 venues, mainly theatres, arts centres, schools and community spaces.

Casting procedures: Uses in-house casting directors, but does not hold general auditions. Casting breakdowns through Casting Call Pro and individual agents. Welcomes both CVs and letters from actors previously unknown to the company and unsolicited CVs and photographs. Also welcomes invitations to view individual actors' websites and showreels. Happy to consider applications from disabled actors and promotes inclusive casting.

Primecut Productions

285A Ormerth Road, Belfast BT7 3GG
tel 028-90645101 *fax* 028-90645101
email info@primecutproductions.co.uk
website www.primecutproductions.co.uk

Production details: An independent touring company based in Belfast and bringing the best of contemporary international playwrights to Irish audiences. Recent productions include: a double bill of *The Mercy Seat* and *Ashes to Ashes* at the Belfast Lyric and touring productions of Caryl Churchill's *A Number* and Owen McCaffery's *Cold Comfort*. The company stages 2-3 productions per year and tours to 10-15 venues across Northern and the Republic of Ireland.

Casting procedures: Does not publish casting breakdowns, but welcomes CVs and photographs from individual actors whose work is previously unknown to the the company; also welcomes invitations to view actors' websites. Will consider applications from disabled actors when casting for characters with disabilities. Offers ITC/Equity-approved contracts.

Proteus Theatre Company

Proteus Creation Space, Council Road, Basingstoke, Hants RG21 3HF
tel (01256) 354541 *fax* (01256) 350186
email info@proteustheatre.com
website www.proteustheatre.com
Artistic Director Mary Swan

Production details: Established in 1981. Touring theatre company operating nationally. Stages 2-3 productions annually touring to 80 venues including arts centres, theatres, outdoor venues, educational and community venues and churches. Recent credits include: *The Secret Garden* and *Missing in Action.*

Casting procedures: Casting breakdowns available via the website and Equity Job Information Service. Does not welcome unsolicited CVs. Actively encourages applications from disabled actors and promotes the use of inclusive casting. Offers ITC/Equity-approved contracts.

Purple Fish Productions

22 Newton Avenue, London W3 8AL
mobile (07976) 809693
email info@purplefishproductions.co.uk
website www.purplefishproductions.co.uk
Artistic Director Michelle Seton

Production details: Founded in 2001. Aims to produce both established work and exciting devised pieces for adults and children. Michelle Seton trained in London and at Le Coq in Paris. Stages 3 productions with 75 performances during the course of the year. Tours to 20 different arts centres, theatres, educational and community venues annually. Tours have covered Greater London, Ireland and Canada. In general 2 actors are involved in each production. Recent productions include: *Told by a Dodo* and *The Two of Us.*

Casting procedures: Casting breakdowns are available via the website. Welcomes letters (with CVs and photographs) but not email submissions. Actors should write only when the company advertises. Invitations to view individual actors' websites are also accepted.

Pursued by a Bear Productions

The Maltings, Bridge Square, Farnham, Surrey GU9 7QR
email pursuedbyabear@yahoo.co.uk
website www.pursuedbyabear.co.uk
Artistic Director Helena Bell

Production details: Theatre and digital film company specialising in new writing commissions. PBAB produces and tours 1 new (Arts Council funded) theatre production annually and creates large-scale community and educational film (most recently funded by Heritage Lottery). Recent theatre tours include: *Kalashnikov: In the Woods by the Lake* by Fraser Grace (Theatre 503 & South East Tour); *Footprints in the Sand* by Oladipo Agboluaje and Rukhsana Ahmad (Oval House & South East tour). Forthcoming theatre production: *Kabaddi-Kabaddi-Kabaddi* by Satinder Chohan (National UK Touring 2012/13). Forthcoming Film: *On Hungry Hill* (Screening November 2012).

Casting procedures: Welcomes submissions (with CVs and photographs) sent by post or email.

Raised Eyebrow Theatre Company

Low Hall Cottage, Carr Lane, Brompton, Scarborough YO13 9DH
tel/fax (01723) 850538
email lizipatch@aol.com
website www.raisedeyebrow.co.uk
Artistic Director Lizi Patch *Associate Director* Jon Stokes

Production details: A community and TIE company staging 2-3 productions each year and presenting approximately 220 performances in schools and community venues across England. The company also runs youth theatres and workshops. In general 5 actors work on each production. Recent productions include: *Farmer Charles*, Raised Eyebrow Youth Theatre; *Destination 2014*, for Capacity Builders conference in Birmingham; *The Street Never Ends* and *The Wave*, Filey Festival; *The Past on Your Doorstep*, Chaddeston Park and Osmaston Park, Derby; *A Midsummer Murder*, The Old Mill, Langtoft Abbey House (in partnership with Derbyshire-based Orange Box Design); *Space Pirates – Adventures on Planet Maths*, tour; *Spike* (in partnership with Scarborough Safer Communities); and *A Midsummer Night's Dream* (Raised Eyebrow Youth Theatre).

Casting procedures: Casting is done in house and with the help of freelance casting directors. Casting breakdowns are available by postal application (with sae), and in *The Stage*. Welcomes letters and emails (with professional CVs and 10x8 photographs) from actors previously unknown to the company. Will also accept showreels and emails. Advises that professional applications will be given priority over photocopies, passport photos and holiday snaps.

Real Circumstance Theatre Company

22 Erle Havard Road, West Bergholt, Colchester CO6 3LH
email info@realcircumstance.com
website www.realcircumstance.com
Artistic Director Dan Sherer *Creative Producer* Anna Bewick

Production details: Real Circumstance is an East of England theatre company dedicated to exploring new ways of playmaking; to working with new writers and emergent artists; and to raising the profile of the East as a source of creative work. Tours 1 studio production each year, to the community. Recent productions include: *Our Share of Tomorrow* by Dan Sherer, *LOUGH/RAIN* by Declan Feenan and Clara Brennan, and *LIMBO* by Declan Feenan (all co-produced with York Theatre Royal and ran at the Edinburgh Fringe).

Casting procedures: Uses in-house casting directors. Sometimes holds general auditions; actors may write at any time to request inclusion. Welcomes letters (with CVs and photographs) from actors previously unknown to the company, and accepts submissions by email. Welcomes showreels and invitations to view individual actors' websites. Offers Equity-approved contracts negotiated through ITC.

Red Ladder Theatre Co.

3 St Peter's Buildings, York Street, Leeds LS9 8AJ
tel 0113-245 5311 *fax* 0113-245 5351
email rod@redladder.co.uk
website www.redladder.co.uk
Artistic Director Rod Dixon

Production details: Red Ladder's mission is to create theatre based around, and influenced by, human struggle. They aim to create galvanising and life-affirming productions that redefine and reclaim notions of the popular, the political and the radical in a theatre context. The company, founded in 1968 in London, has a colourful history. It spans 40 years, from the radical socialist theatre movement in Britain known as agitprop, to its current position.

The company moved to Leeds in the 70s and is still based in the city. During the 80s it redefined itself, changing its cooperative structure to a hierarchy and specialising in targeted work for youth audiences. Acknowledged today as one of Britain's leading national touring companies producing high-quality new plays for youth audiences.

Recent productions include: *Big Society!* (by Boff Whalley, starring stand-up comedian Phill Jupitus); *Promised Land* (by Anthony Clavane); *Wrong 'Un* (a one-woman show about a suffragette); *We're Not Going Back* (Boff Whalley); *Hurling Rubble at the Sun* (Avaes Mohammad, co-production with Park Theatre).

The Red Room

Garden Studios, 71-75 Shelton Street, Covent Garden, London WC2H 9JQ
tel 020-7470 8790 *fax* 020-7379 0801
email info@theredroom.org.uk
website www.theredroom.org.uk
Artistic Director Topher Campbell

Production details: Founded in 1995. Produces new theatre and film work which frees the imagination to challenge the status quo. Creates groundbreaking collaborations between writers, artists and communities to provoke and influence wider social debate. Engages in cultural activism, including bi-monthly RRPlatform events. Stages 1-2 productions annually with 25-50 performances during the course of the year. Tours to international and national locations. In general, fewer than 5 actors (often with ability to work in a devised way) are involved in each production. Recent productions include: *Unstated, Journeys to Work, Hoxton Story, Animal, The Bogus Woman* and *Stitching*.

Casting procedures: Accepts emailed CVs and photographs – no letters or telephone enquiries, please. Offers ITC/Equity-approved contracts where possible. Does not subscribe to the Equity pension scheme. Actively encourages applications from disabled actors and promotes the use of inclusive casting.

Red Rose Chain

Gippeswyk Hall, Gippeswyk Avenue, Ipswich, Suffolk IP2 9AF
tel (01473) 603388 *fax* (01473) 601122
email info@redrosechain.com
website www.redrosechain.com
Directors Joanna Carrick, David Newborn, Jimmy Grimes

Production details: A film and theatre company which spends every summer outdoors with its theatre-in-the-forest event. Runs workshops and develops new writing. "Our diverse work all serves to underpin Red Rose Chain's aim: to use theatre and film to challenge thinking and make connections with those who are normally ignored or avoided by mainstream arts." Stages 4 productions annually, with 50 performances in 20 venues including arts centres, theatres, and outdoor, educational and community venues in East Anglia. In general 3-12 actors are involved in each production. Recent productions include: *A Winter's Tale* (Rendlesham Forest); *Slide Down the Rainbow* (Nowton Park); and *I love Kitkats* (Red Rose Chain).

Casting procedures: Sometimes holds general auditions; casting breakdowns are available via the website. Welcomes letters (with CVs and photographs) from individual actors previously unknown to the company, sent by post or email. Also welcomes showreels and invitations to view individual actors' websites. Actively encourages applications from disabled actors and promotes the use of inclusive casting.

Reveal Theatre Company

The Creative Village,
Staffordshire University Business Village,
72 Leek Road, Stoke on Trent ST4 2AR
tel (01782) 294871

email enquiries@revealtheatre.co.uk
website www.revealtheatre.co.uk
Creative Director Robert Marsden *Director of Productions* Julia Barton

Production details: Established in 1999. A professional small- to middle-scale producing company for touring and residency. Also has a strong outreach department. Stages on average 3 productions each year. Recent productions include: *Beauty and the Beast* (directed by Alex Shepley) and Stephen Sondheim's *Into The Woods* (directed by Robert Marsden).

Casting procedures: Uses in-house casting directors; casting breakdowns are available via the website. Actors may write at any time requesting inclusion. Welcomes submissions (with CVs and photographs) sent by post, but not by email. Also welcomes showreels, and invitations to view individual actors' websites. Offers Equity-approved contracts as negotiated through ITC. Will consider applications from disabled actors to play characters with disabilities.

Richmond Productions

47 Moor Mead Road, St Margaret's,
Twickenham TW1 1JS
website www.richmondproductions.co.uk
Director Alister Cameron

Production details: Founded in 1993. International touring company producing small-cast comedies. Stages 2 productions annually. Tours to hotels in the Middle East and Eastern Europe. Offers non-Equity contracts. Rarely (or never) has the opportunity to cast disabled actors.

Casting procedures: Advises that the company only uses actors already known to it.

Riding Lights Theatre Company

Friargate Theatre, Lower Friargate, York YO1 9SL
tel (01904) 655317
website www.ridinglights.org
Artistic Director Paul Burbridge *Artistic Associates* Sean Cavanagh, Bridget Foreman

Production details: Initially a community theatre project founded in York in 1977, today Riding Lights is touring up to 3 diverse companies simultaneously throughout the UK and abroad. The company is recognised both as a pioneer in reinstating the value of theatre in Christian communication and for significant original and artistic achievement. Recent productions include: *Flight Cases* and *African Show* (co-production with York Theatre Royal).

Rifco Arts

Watford Palace Theatre, 20 Clarendon Road,
Watford WD17 1JZ
tel (01923) 810305
website www.rifcoarts.com
Artistic Director Pravesh Kumar

Production details: An award-winning Theatre Company that develops and creates vibrant, accessible and high-quality theatre which reflects and celebrates the contemporary British Asian experience. Stages 1 mid-scale touring production annually, in theatres across the UK and internationally with around 70 performances in 6 arts centres and theatres in the UK and Pakistan. In general 2-17 actors go on tour. Offers Equity-approved contracts as negotiated through ITC. Recent productions include: *Britain's Got Bhangra, Break The Floorboards* and *MummyJi Presents.*

Casting procedures: Via website and Spotlight. Welcomes letters, (with CVs, photographs and relevant links), from individual actors previously unknown to the company, via email.

Rocket Theatre

32 Baxter Road, Sale, Manchester M33 3AL
tel 0161-969 1444 *mobile* (07788) 723570
email martin@rockettheatre.co.uk
website www.rockettheatre.co.uk
Director Martin Harris

Production details: Rocket Theatre was set up in 1995. It has produced work from its base in Manchester and toured throughout the UK with completely new work and regional premieres of work originally staged by some of London's new-writing venues (particularly the Royal Court, the Bush and the National). The company has won several awards. Previous productions include: *I Licked a Slag's Deodorant* by Jim Cartwright; *Howie the Rookie* by Mark O'Rowe; *A Skull in Connemara* by Martin McDonagh and *Dealer's Choice* by Patrick Marber, as well as several new plays by Jim Burke. The company is currently taking bookings for its brand new 2-man adaptation of Oscar Wilde's *Lord Arthur Savile's Crime* and is also developing several new projects – see the website for details. Rocket Theatre is keen to hear about any interesting collaboration opportunities with other companies or individuals.

Casting procedures: Casting breakdowns are available on the Rocket website and through various industry casting resources. Does not welcome applications from actors unless casting is called for specific parts. No emailed applications.

Scamp Theatre Ltd

44 Church Lane, Arlesey, Bedfordshire SG15 6UX
tel (01462) 734843 *fax* (01462) 730878
email admin@scamptheatre.com
website www.scamptheatre.com
Directors Jennifer Sutherland, Louise Callow

Production details: Established in 2003. An independent production company staging 4 shows annually, with more than 100 performances in the same number of theatres across the UK. In general 3 actors are involved in each production. Offers Equity-approved contracts as negotiated through ITC. Recent productions include: *Private Peaceful* by

Michael Morpurgo (West End, UK Tour); *Pirate Gran* (UK Tour); *Tiddler and Other Terrific Tales* (UK Tour) and *Stick Man* (West End, UK Tour).

Casting procedures: Uses freelance casting directors. Scamp do not accept unsolicited CVs. Scamp consider applications from disabled actors to play characters with disabilities.

Scarlet Theatre

Studio 4, The Bull, 68 High Street, Barnet EN5 5SJ
tel 020-8441 9779 *fax* 020-8447 0075
email admin@scarlettheatre.co.uk
website www.scarlettheatre.co.uk
Director Gráinne Byrne

Production details: A touring theatre company founded in 1982 which stages between 2 and 6 productions each year. On average the company tours annually to 10 venues across the UK, Ireland and the rest of Europe, with anywhere between 2-10 actors working on each production. Recent productions include: *The Chair Women* (Riverside Studios and Traverse Theatre) and *The Wedding* (Southwark Playhouse).

Casting procedures: Casting is done in house and actors are welcome to write or email with their CVs and photographs. The company prefers not to receive showreels unless it has requested them.

Scene Three Creative

5 Gold Street, Stalbridge, Dorset DT10 2LX
tel (01843) 587950
email info@scenethreecreative.co.uk
website www.scenethreecreative.co.uk
Directors Philip Dart, Claudia Leaf

Production details: A creative production company making work for many different venues and communities.

Casting procedures: "We regret that we are unable to hold general auditions or see actors outside of designated casting periods. Agents' information services such as Spotlight are normally supplied with casting breakdowns."

Shakespeare at The Tobacco Factory

Raleigh Road, Southville, Bristol BS3 ITF
tel 0117-963 3054
email office@sattf.org.uk
website www.sattf.org.uk
Artistic Director Andrew Hilton

Production details: Established in 2000. 2 productions staged annually with 80 performances in Bristol. Up to 18 actors used in each production. Recent productions include: *Romeo and Juliet* and Sheridan's *A School for Scandal.*

Casting procedures: Casting breakdowns available via the website. Accepts electronic submissions (with CVs and photographs) from actors previously unknown to the company. Invitations to view individual actors' websites are also accepted. Actors writing to request inclusion should make contact in August. Rarely has the opportunity to cast disabled actors.

Shared Experience

Oxford Playhouse, 11-12 Beaumont Street, Oxford OX1 2LW
tel (01865) 305321
email admin@sharedexperience.org.uk
website www.sharedexperience.org.uk
Artistic Director Polly Teale

Production details: An award-winning theatre company founded during the 1970s, Shared Experience stages 2-3 productions annually and tours to different arts centres and theatres in the UK and abroad. In general 6-10 actors are involved in each production. Recent productions include: *Mermaid, Mary Shelley, The Caucasian Chalk Circle,, A Passage to India, Jane Eyre, Kindertransport* and *War and Peace.*

Casting procedures: Uses freelance casting directors. Advises that actors should contactthe office by phone to enquire about the current casting director. "Please do not send unsolicited mail." Offers TMA/Equity-approved contracts. Actively encourages applications from disabled actors and promotes the use of inclusive casting.

Simple8 Theatre Company

158 Princess Park Manor, Royal Drive, London N11 3FR
mobile (07710) 174717
email chris@simple8.co.uk
website www.simple8.co.uk
Simple8 are a collective. *Creatives* Chris Doyle, Sebastian Armesto, Emily Pennant-Rea, Dudley Hinton, Hannah Emanuel & Mat Wandless

Production details: Simple8 is a critically-acclaimed and award-winning ensemble based theatre company who specialise in creating innovative, bold new plays using large casts – all performed on a shoestring. Their approach is rooted in 'poor theatre', which focuses on the story and revolves around the ensemble, who create the atmosphere and setting without relying on extravagant lighting, scenery, props or sound. Simple8 have produced 6 productions to date, all at Arcola Theatre. Simple8 is an associate company of Shoreditch Town Hall.

Casting procedures: Uses freelance casting directors, but does not hold general auditions. Instead Simple8 recommend actors submit their details for consideration once they have seen a Simple8 production, attended a workshop, or introduced themselves in person. Welcomes both CVs and letters from actors previously unknown to the company and unsolicited CVs and photographs. These should be sent via email. Also welcomes invitations to view individual actors' websites and attend productions, but does not welcome showreels. Happy to consider disabled actors, though this is dependent on each individual project.

Sky Blue Theatre Company

14 Hayfield Avenue, Sawston, Cambridge CB22 3JZ
tel (01223) 529491 *mobile* (07850) 097520
email admin@skybluetheatre.com
website www.skybluetheatre.com
Directors Anne Bartram, Frances Brownlie, John Mitton

Production details: Founded in 2007. A Cambridge-based company touring schools, theatres and community venues with new plays, Shakespeare productions and workshops. Founded the Cambridge Theatre Challenge, an international playwriting competition. Works with young people through its own theatre school and with colleges developing skills in performing arts. Stages 5 productions annually, giving around 50 performances nationally. In general, 5 actors are involved in each production. Recent productions include: *Shakespeare Done Over*, *Cambridge Theatre Challenge* and *Pollyanna*.

Casting procedures: All casting is done in house. Holds general auditions, for which breakdowns are available via Casting Call Pro and the website. Welcomes letters (with CVs and photographs) from individual actors previously unknown to the company, sent by post or email. Does not accept showreels, but will consider invitations to view actors' websites and performances. Will consider applications from disabled actors for any role.

Small World Theatre

Canolfan Byd Bychan, Bath House Road, Cardigan, Ceredigion SA43 1JY
tel (01239) 615952
email info@smallworld.org.uk
website www.smallworld.org.uk
Director Ann Shrosbree *Artistic Director* Bill Hamblett *Administrator* Julie Evans *Marketing* Sam Vicary

Production details: Founded in 1979. Theatre and puppetry for children and adults, originally with environmental focus as well as theatre for development, touring theatre and theatre forum – now has small venue. Stages 4 productions annually, with around 50 performances in 30 venues (arts centres, theatres, outdoor, festival and educational venues). In general 4 actors are involved in each production.

Casting procedures: Uses in-house casting directors, and does not usually hold general auditions or advertise casting breakdowns. Will consider submissions (letters, CVs and photographs) from actors previously unknown to the company, sent by post or email, and invitations to view individuals' websites/performances, but cannot respond to all. No unsolicited showreels. Casts actors with disabilities in inclusive roles, and to play differently able roles.

Sole Purpose Productions

The Playhouse, Artillery Street, Derry, Londonderry BT48 6RG
tel 0044 (0) 28 7127 9918
email solepurpose@mac.com
website www.solepurpose.org
Artistic Director Patricia Byrne *Arts Administrator* Nicola Schnurr

Production details: Founded in 1997, Sole Purpose Productions create new theatre on social and public issues for working class and marginalised communities as well as mainstream audiences. Their productions aim to explore pertinent social issues and the dynamics of human relationships, in an attempt to promote good relations. Recent productions include: *The House* by Edie Shillue (a short play on human trafficking), *Don't Say A Word* by Patricia Byrne (a one-woman play on domestic violence) and *Pits and Perverts* by Micheal Kerrigan, script developed by Patricia Byrne (a play about the Lesbian and Gay community's involvement in the Miners' Strike). Each production consists of 4-5 actors and, on average, the company present 2-3 productions per year, touring to community venues and theatres.

Casting procedures: Holds general auditions at various times throughout the year and a casting breakdown is available via Sole Purpose's website when a production is coming up. Welcomes both CVs and letters from actors previously unknown to the Company and unsolicited CVs and photographs. Also welcomes invitations to view individual actor's websites and showreels. Promotes inclusive casting and welcomes applications from disabled actors to play characters with disabilities.

Spanner in the Works

95 Old Woolwich Road, London SE10 9PP
tel 020-7193 7995
email info@spannerintheworks.org.uk
website www.spannerintheworks.org.uk
Artistic Director Darren Rapier

Production details: Spanner in the Works produce plays and films, as well as running workshops in all media disciplines for a variety of clientele. The company produces films and books in partnership with Tualen Pictures and Tualen Press. Primarily, Spanner in the Works concentrate on stage productions and workshops. They have produced musicals, plays, short films and audio drama, as well as community theatre pieces. Recent productions include: *Riverscross* (online soap), *Blind Man's Bluff* (short film) and *Worlds Apart* (theatre).

Casting procedures: Uses in-house and freelance casting directors. Casting breakdowns are available, although this is dependent on the project. Will happily consider applications from disabled actors, but their inclusion is dependent on the nature of each individual project.

Sphinx Theatre Company

Ovalhouse, 52-54 Kennington Oval,
London SE11 5SW
020 7820 8899
email info@sphinxtheatre.co.uk
website www.sphinxtheatre.co.uk
Artistic Director Sue Parrish

Production details: Established 30 years ago, the company specialises in writing, directing and developing roles for women. Recent productions include: *Blame* by Judith Jones and Beatrix Campbell and *The Berlin Cabaret*.

Casting procedures: Casting breakdowns are available via email and/or postal application (with CVs and photographs). Offers Equity-approved contracts. Will consider applications from disabled actors to play characters with disabilities.

A Stage Kindly

7 Northiam, Cromer Street, London WC1H 8LB
mobile (07947) 074887, (07909) 884386
email mail@astagekindly.com
website www.astagekindly.com
Co-founders and Artistic Directors Giles Howe, Katy Lipson

Production details: Founded in 2008. Aims to enthuse about, advocate and help develop new musical theatre. Stages new-writing revues, feature-length and showcase presentations of new works, and offers services specific to writers creating new MT such as translation, appraisal, demos, etc. Also holds workshops for performers with a focus on new musicals. Recent productions include: UK premiere of *Ballets Russes*; preview showcase of *Soviet Zion*; and tour of international new-writing revue *Bravo*. Stages around 5 productions annually, with 25 performances in venues including theatres, bars, clubs, halls and arts centres. In general 6 actors are involved in each production.

Casting procedures: Audition information is posted on the website, as are casting breakdowns (also available from Casting Call Pro, Arts Jobs, etc.). Welcomes letters (with CVs and photographs) from actors previously unknown to the company, sent by post or email. Also accepts showreels and invitations to view individual actors' websites.

Ed Stephenson Productions

7 Hawthorn Road, Little Sutton, Cheshire CH66 1PR
tel 0151-339 6145
email roger@edstephensonproductions.co.uk
website www.edstephensonproductions.co.uk
Company Administrator Diane Barker

Production details: Founded in 2004. Stages on average 1 production every 1-2 years; has evolved from stage to film production. Recent films include: *A Quiet Night In* (2009), *The Weekend Hostage* (2011) and *A Matter of Principle* (2015).

Casting procedures: Uses in-house casting directors. Sometimes holds auditions. Uses casting agencies for auditioning. Welcomes letters (with CVs and photographs) from individual actors previously unknown to the company, sent by post or email. Accepts showreels and invitations to view individual actors' websites. Will consider applications from disabled actors where appropriate for the role. "Our contracts are heavily based on ITC/Equity contracts."

Suspect Culture

Kinning Park Complex, 40 Cornwall Street,
Glasgow G41 1AH
tel 0141-419 9666
email info@suspectculture.com
website www.suspectculture.com
Director Graham Eatough

Production details: Suspect Culture was formed in 1990 by Graham Eatough, David Greig and Nick Powell. Early productions include: *One Way Street* (1995), *Airport* (1996), *Timeless* (1997) and *Mainstream* (1999). The company is based in Glasgow and tours 1-2 productions throughout Scotland and internationally each year. Generally uses 2-6 actors on each production. Recent productions include: *8000m* (Tramway, Glasgow) and *One-Two* (Traverse, Edinburgh; Contact Theatre, Manchester; MAC, Birmingham; Tron, Glasgow; Byre Theatre, St Andrews; Lemon Tree, Northampton; Tolbooth, Stirling and Paisley Arts Centres).

"To us, a collaborative approach means giving text, design, music and performance equal weight in all our work. The director, writer, designer and composer are involved from the very beginning of each new idea, which is then developed through a long process of workshops and rehearsal before being presented to an audience. This emphasis on collaboration is reflected in the way we credit artists and assign authorship, which is always shared among the artistic team."

Casting procedures: Suspect Culture does not hold formal auditions, but rather open workshops which are by invitation. This gives the company a chance to meet practitioners it hasn't worked with before (and vice versa). The company welcomes letters, emails, showreels, invitations to view actors' websites, CVs and photographs from actors – but asks all applicants to gain a full understanding of Suspect's particular working methods before writing. Only rarely employs actors who have not seen at least some of Suspect's work.

TABS Productions

57 Chamberlain Place, London E17 6AZ
tel 020-8527 9266
email adrianmljames@aol.com
website www.tabsproductions.co.uk
Directors Adrian Lloyd-James, Karen Henson

Production details: Founded 15 years ago, the company stages approximately 6 productions each year totalling around 300 performances. It has produced No. 1 and middle-scale tours and has co-produced with repertory theatre companies. Generally tours to about 45 different arts centres, theatres and outdoor venues across the UK annually. The average cast size is 4-8 actors.

Casting procedures: Welcomes letters, CVs and photographs from actors previously unknown to the company, but does not accept emails or showreels. Actors should only write when a job has been advertised to agents. Occasionally offers Equity-approved contracts. Rarely (or never) has the opportunity to cast disabled actors.

Taking Flight Theatre Company

31 Brunswick Street, Canton, Cardiff CF11 9DB
tel 029-2022 6072
email takingflighttheatre@yahoo.co.uk
website www.takingflighttheatre.co.uk
Directors Beth House, Elise Davison

Production details: Established in 2007. Holds residential workshops with physically disabled adults. Accessible, professional promenade productions with integrated casts/support teams. Stages 1-2 productions annually, with around 30 performances in 20 outdoor venues across South Wales. In general 6-10 actors are involved in each production. Recent productions include: *Branwen's Starling* and *Twelfth Night.*

Casting procedures: Sometimes holds general auditions and actors may write at any time to request inclusion. Casting breakdowns are publicly available via the website, Equity Job Information Service and Casting Call Pro, as well as from the Disability Arts Cymru site. Welcomes letters (with CVs and photographs) from individual actors previously unknown to the company sent by post or email, as well as showreels and invitations to view individual actors' websites. Actively encourages applications from disabled actors and promotes the use of inclusive casting. "We are very eager to hear from disabled and/or sensory impaired actors."

Tamasha Theatre Company

RichMix, 35-47 Bethnal Green Road, London E1 6LA
tel 020-7749 0090 *fax* 020-7729 8906
email admin@tamasha.org.uk
website www.tamasha.org.uk
Artistic Directors Sudha Bhuchar and Fin Kennedy

Production details: Founded in 1989. Produces 'untold stories' in mainstream theatre venues. Stages 1-3 productions annually and gives approximately 60 performances during the course of the year. Tours annually to small- and mid-scale theatre venues in London and regionally In general 2-15 actors are involved in each production. Recent productions include: *The Arrival, Snookered, Wuthering Heights, The Trouble with Asian Men* and *Strictly Dandia.*

Casting procedures: Only holds auditions when casting for a specific production. Uses Spotlight and own files when inviting people to audition plus casting director on specific projects. Welcomes CVs and headshots by post at any time; these will be kept on file and looked at afresh during each casting process. Also runs professional artist development scheme: Tamasha Developing Artists – see website for details. Offers ITC/Equity-approved contracts.

Tara Arts Group

356 Garratt Lane, London SW18 4ES
tel 020-8333 4457 *fax* 020-8870 9540
email tara@tara-arts.com
website www.tara-arts.com
Artistic Director Jatinder Verma

Production details: "People, Words & Art: Connecting Worlds". Founded in 1977, the company's range of in-house and touring work spans European and Asian classics through to new plays, including plays for children. The company tours annually to England, Scotland and Wales, and has also toured Europe and the Far East. Recent productions include: *Macbeth, The Miser, Domestic Crusaders* and *Dick Whittington Goes Bollywood.* The renovated Tara Theatre, (opening late 2015), will be Britain's first multi-cultural theatre - its cross-culture architecture echoed by a diverse programme of classic and new plays produced by Tara and visiting companies - to inspire audiences and artists alike.

Theatr Genedlaethol Cymru

Y Llwyfan, College Road, Carmarthen SA31 3EQ
tel (01267) 233 882
email thgc@theatr.com
website www.theatr.com
Artistic Director Arwel Gruffydd *Associate Director* Sara Lloyd

Production details: Founded in 2003, Theatr Genedlaethol Cymru is the Welsh-language national theatre of Wales. Its work includes national tours, community projects and site-specific work. Recent productions include *Y Bont, Blodeuwedd, Y Negesydd* (*The Messenger*) and *Chwalfa.* Each production consists of 6 or more actors and, on average, the company present 5-7 productions per year. This equates to over 70 performances across the UK hosted at various venues, including arts centres, theatres and community spaces. Offers Equity-approved contracts negotiated through UK Theatre.

Casting procedures: Uses in-house casting directors, but does not hold general auditions. Welcomes both CVs and letters from actors previously unknown to the company and unsolicited CVs and photographs only when casting. These should be sent via email. Also welcomes invitations to view individual actors' websites, productions and showreels. Actively encourages applications from disabled actors.

Theatr Pena

19 Boverton Street, Cardiff CF23 5ES
mobile (07811) 439884
email info@theatrpena.co.uk
website www.theatrpena.co.uk
Artistic Director Erica Eirian *Producer* Ceri James

Production details: Founded in 2008, Theatr Pena is a project-funded company run by a group of professional theatre practitioners who came together to read Federico García Lorca's *The House of Bernarda Alba* and decided to stage a production. They are driven by a passion for classic and modern plays and their commitment to put women, particularly older women, centre stage. In 2011 they secured their first Arts Council of Wales project grant for a co-production with The Riverfront Theatre, Newport, in association with the Torch Theatre, Milford Haven. *The Maids* by Jean Genet was staged in both venues in 2012. Recent productions include: *The Killing of Sister George* by Frank Marcus (sping 2014); *The Royal Bed*, Sion Eirian's English language adaptation of the Welsh classic, *Siwan* by Saunders Lewis (spring 2015, Wales national tour).

Currently 1 production is staged per year. This consists of 3-4 actors and, on average, the company gives 10-30 performances annually. Next production (spring 2016 Wales national tour) *The Glass Menagerie* by Tennessee Williams.

Casting procedures: In-house casting directors, but does not hold general auditions. Company members offered first refusal of appropropriate roles. Welcomes letters (accompanied by CVs and headshots). Actively encourages applications from disabled actors and promotes the use of inclusive casting.

Theatre-Rites

Unit 206, E1 Business Centre, London E1 1DU
tel 020-7164 6196
email info@theatre-rites.co.uk
website www.theatre-rites.co.uk
Artistic Director Sue Buckmaster

Production details: Founded in 1995, Theatre-Rites is versatile in its approach, creating theatre shows which tour the UK and abroad and pieces set in unusual spaces such as an old tidal mill, a disused corner shop and an empty ward of a real working hospital. Theatre-Rites also creates interactive exhibitions and installations in galleries, museums and other public spaces. Drawing on a rich fusion of performance, installation art, puppetry, video and sound, Theatre-Rites creates work which stirs the imagination of children and adults alike. Recent productions include: *Rubbish*, *Bank On It*, *Mojo*, *Mischief* and *Paradise*.

Casting procedures: Welcomes letters (with CVs and photographs) from actors previously unknown to the company. Multi-disciplined performers are always very welcome. Offers ITC/Equity-approved contracts.

Theatre Absolute

Shop Front Theatre, 38 City Arcade, Coventry
mobile (07799) 292957
email info@theatreabsolute.co.uk
website www.theatreabsolute.co.uk
Artistic Director Chris O'Connell *Producer* Julia Negus

Production details: Founded in 1992, the company develops, produces and tours new plays. In 2009, Theatre Absolute opened the UK's first professional Shop Front Theatre in Coventry, West Midlands. Work includes performances, play readings, writing workshops, mentor support for actors and writers.

Casting procedures: Actors should consult the website for details of the next project.

Theatre Alibi

Emmanuel Hall, Emmanuel Road, Exeter EX4 1EJ
tel/fax (01392) 217315
email alibi@theatrealibi.co.uk
website www.theatrealibi.co.uk
Artistic Director Nikki Sved

Production details: Founded in 1982, the company creates new work for all ages that is physically and visually inventive and often enriched by other art forms including music, animation, film, puppetry, dance and photography. Stages 2 productions a year, with a total of around 130 performances. Tours theatres and arts centres as well as schools and community venues, the nature of the venue depending on the individual show. The company offers ITC/Equity-approved contracts and is an ITC Ethical Manager.

Recent productions include: *I Believe in Unicorns* (mid-scale national tour for 6-12 year olds); *Hammer and Tongs* (small-scale national tour of theatres and arts centres for adult audiences) and *Mucky Pup* (south-west tour for 5-11 year olds mainly to primary schools).

Casting procedures: Casts in house. For some productions publishes casting breakdowns. Welcomes letters and emails with CVs and photographs at any time of year. Also welcomes links to showreels and individual websites.

Theatre Broad

47 Carseview, Bannockburn, Stirling FK7 8HL
tel (01360) 440480
email info@theatrebroad.co.uk
email actors@theatrebroad.co.uk
website www.theatrebroad.co.uk
Artistic Director Carol Metcalf *Executive Director* Tangee Lenton

Production details: An innovative theatre company dedicated to providing regular, affordable, quality theatre to people in the Stirling area, then touring throughout the country. Aims to provide audiences with the opportunity to see the best available plays, from a broad range of styles, writers and cultures.

In addition to its mainstream productions, the company's award-winning Community Roots programme is in association with Forth Valley College, Stirling, Falkirk and Clackmannan. Disabled adult students appear in specially devised productions where they are supported in the rehearsal room and in performance by professional actors and practitioners.

Tours 2-4 projects annually, with around 20-40 performances at 6-12 venues in Stirling, Central Scotland, Dumfries and Aberdeenshire. Venues include mid-scale theatres, arts centres, village halls and art galleries. In general 2-15 actors go on tour, depending on the production. Recent productions include: A Scottish and Cumbria tour of Ira Levin's *Deathtrap*; *3 Stars and a Quest*: *Tron Labyrinth* (by Gareth Candy and Carol Metcalf); a Scottish tour of *J. M. Barrie: Peter Pan Man* (by Anne Stenhouse and J. M. Barrie); *When Santa Got Lost In Space* (a pantomime by Carol Metcalf); *Flights of Fancy* (by Anne Stenhouse); *Star Quest – The Musical* (by Mark Harvey and Carol Metcalf, a co-production with Forth Valley College) and *Table Manners* by Alan Ayckbourn.

Casting procedures: Casting is done in-house by the Artistic and Executive Directors, and actors may write at any time to request inclusion. Casting breakdowns are available from the website, Equity Job Information Service and Casting Call Pro. No hard copy submissions, but will accept CVs and photographs sent by email, as well as showreels and invitations to view individual actors' websites/other productions. Encourages applications from disabled performers and promotes the use of inclusive casting. Theatre Broad is a member of The Federation of Scottish Theatre.

Theatre Is

The Hat Factory, 65-67 Bute Street, Luton, Bedfordshire LU1 2EY
tel (01582) 481221 *fax* (01279) 506694
email info@theatreis.org
website www.theatreis.org

Production details: Established in 2006. Challenging and creating new models of live performance by, with and for young audiences across the East of England and beyond. 3 productions are staged annually touring East of England, London, Midlands, North West and Wales. 50 performances per year at an average of 20 venues. Types of venue include: arts centres, theatres, outdoor venues, educational and community venues. 4 actors are generally involved in each production. Actors are employed under ITC/Equity-approved contracts. Recent productions include: *Master Juba* (Hackney Empire, Norwich Playhouse); *Claytime* (New Wolsey Theatre, Lyric Hammersmith, Unicorn Theatre).

Casting procedures: Casting is done by an in-house casting director. Casting breakdowns are only available to agents via the Spotlight link. Does not welcome individual submissions from actors. Actively encourages applications from disabled actors and promotes the use of inclusive casting in new writing productions.

Theatre Lab Company

76 St Dunstan's Avenue, London W3 6QJ
mobile (07958) 4048806
email anastasia@theatrelab.co.uk
website www.theatrelab.co.uk
Director Anastasia Revi

Production details: Established in 1997. Stages 1 production annually, with around 20 performances in 3 theatres in the Midlands and South East, and abroad. In general 4-6 actors are involved in each production. Offers Equity-approved contracts as negotiated through ITC "when funded". Recent productions include *Velvet Scratch* (Prague Festival 2007; Edinburgh Festival 2007; Greek tour 2008; New York Fringe Festival 2008).

Casting procedures: Uses freelance casting directors. Holds general auditions and actors may write to request inclusion when advertised. Casting breakdowns are available from the website, by postal application (with sae) and in *The Stage*. Welcomes letters (with CVs and photographs) from individual actors previously unknown to the company, sent by post or email. Also welcomes showreels and invitations to view individual actors' websites. Will consider applications from disabled actors to play characters with disabilities.

Théâtre Sans Frontières

Queen's Hall, Beaumont Street, Hexham, Northumberland NE46 3LS
tel (01434) 603114 *fax* (01434) 607206
email info@tsf.org.uk
website www.tsf.org.uk
Artistic Directors Sarah Kemp (CEO), John Cobb

Production details: Founded in 1991. Set up by former students of Philippe Gaulier and Monika Pagneux. Specialises in physical theatre and stages texts in different languages for adults and children using international performers. Stages 2-3 productions annually with 60-100 performances in venues including arts centres, schools and theatres. In general 3-6 actors are involved in each production. Recent productions include: *Lipsynch* (co-produced with Robert Lepage and Ex Machina, toured internationally); *La Chanson du Retour* (with Sage Gateshead); *Canary Gold* (collaboration with Teatro Tamaska), Le Moulin Magique. *Heaven Eyes*, *Lorca: Amor en el Jardin*, and UK schools' tour *Contes Mauriciens* (for children aged 8 to 12 years).

Casting procedures: Sometimes holds general auditions. Actors may write at any time requesting inclusion. Casting breakdowns are available on request. Welcomes submissions (with CVs and photographs) sent by post or email. Invitations to view individual actors' websites are also accepted. "We are usually looking for actors who have languages other than English (especially French, Spanish or German), and who have a clear physical theatre training (i.e. Le Coq, Gaulier, Pagneux or Complicite)."

Theatre Set-up

12 Fairlawn Close, Southgate, London N14 4JX
website www.ts-u.co.uk
Charitable Director Wendy Macphee

This company has been taken over by the Festival Players **www.thefestivalplayers.org.uk.**

Theatre Without Walls

Forwood House, Forwood, Gloucestershire GL6 9AB
mobile (07962) 040441
email hello@theatrewithoutwalls.org
website www.theatrewithoutwalls.org
Directors Jason Maher, Genevieve Swift

Production details: Established in 2002. Award-winning theatre company specialising in forum, education and new writing. Productions represent only one-fifth of its output; also produces television and corporate films. 2 productions are staged annually with 60 performances per year, touring to 20 venues including arts centres, theatres and outdoor venues. Tours cover the UK, Ireland and Europe. 3 actors are involved in each production. Actors are employed under ITC/Equity-approved contracts. Recent productions include: *Don Quixote* (Banbury Mill); *The Hold* (Cheltenham Everyman) and *The Plant Hunters* (National Trust).

Casting procedures: "We cast mostly through agents and our own knowledge/word of mouth/ recommendations. We sometimes post casting information via Equity JIS and other 'freely available resources'. We never use casting services which actors have to pay for, except for Spotlight. Any information obtained via paid-for services has simply been copied from another source. Please don't send us any information (such as photos, CVs, showreels, etc.) unless we have requested it. We regularly hold actors' labs and often cast from them." Theatre Without Walls is a member of ITC and most of its work is undertaken using Equity contracts. Those working with vulnerable adults or children must have a current enhanced Criminal Record Bureau/Police Check and hold full insurance equal or greater than that provided by Equity for its members. Considers applications from disabled actors to play disabled characters.

See also the company's entry under *Role-play companies* on page 296.

Theatre Workshop

34 Hamilton Place, Edinburgh EH3 5AX
tel 0131-225 7942 *fax* 0131-220 0112
email afleming@twe.org.uk
website www.theatre-workshop.com
Artistic Director Robert Rae

Production details: Founded in 1965; stages 4 productions a year with around 60 performances across 2 theatre venues. Occasionally tours internationally. Employs an average of 5 actors on each production, using ITC/Equity-approved contracts. Recent productions include: *The Jasmine Road* (No Limits International Theatre Festival, Berlin) and *The Threepenny Opera* (Edinburgh Festival Theatre & Tramway, Glasgow).

Casting procedures: Casting breakdowns are available from the website and Equity Job Information Service. Welcomes letters and emails (with CVs and photographs) from individuals previously unknown to the company. Also happy to receive showreels and invitations to view individuals' websites. Encourages applications from disabled actors and promotes the use of inclusive casting. "Theatre Workshop casts both disabled and non-disabled actors in all our productions."

Third Party Productions Ltd

81 Braybrooke Road, Hastings, East Sussex TN34 1TF
tel (01424) 436149 *mobile* (07768) 694211/694212
email gleave@thirdparty.org.uk
website www.thirdparty.org.uk
Joint Artistic Directors Anthony Gleave, Nicholas Collett

Production details: Established in 1992. A UK and International touring theatre company. Work is usually based on classic plays which are deconstructed and re-imagined during the rehearsal process, and given a contemporary and experimental vitality. Currently working with John Wright – founder of Trestle Theatre and co-founder of Told By An Idiot – and co-producing work with French company BordCadre and Galician clown company Macquinaria Pesada. Stages 1-3 productions annually with around 40-120 performances at 30-90 venues of all types. In general 3-7 actors are involved in each production. Recent productions include: *Noggin the Nog* (based on the TV series created by Oliver Postgate and Peter Firmin), *The Tragicall History of Dr Faustus – A Damned Fine Play* (New Diorama, London), and *La Fausse Suivante/The False Servant* (Café de la Danse Paris and UK tour).

Casting procedures: Auditions by invitation only. May advertise for certain projects through various publications and websites. Welcomes unsolicited CVs and photographs, and invitations to view individual actors' websites, if sent by email only. Actively encourages applications from disabled actors when advertising for casting.

Tin Shed Theatre Company

46 Lennard Street, Newport, NP19 0EJ
mobile (07921) 366038 or (07511) 139773
email tinshedtheatre@gmx.com
website www.tinshedtheatrecompany.com
Company Directors Georgina Harris, Justin Cliffe, Antonio Rimola

Production details: Established in 2008. Specialises in devised theatre which lends itself to performance in unusual spaces. High-energy, high-impact work that focuses on many different genres. Also has an educational programme with an emphasis on the English curriculum.

Stages 1 production each year in the main house and 3 in the studio. Recent productions include: Brighton Fringe 2012, Edinburgh Fringe 2013 and national tour of *Dr Frankenstein's Travelling Freakshow*; *The Ritual*; *An Immersive* and Halloween Experience 2013.

Casting procedures: Uses freelance directors; actors may write at any time to request inclusion. Casting breakdowns are available from the website. Welcomes unsolicited approaches by post and email, and accepts showreels and invitations to view individual actors' websites/visit other productions. Encourages applications from disabled actors and promotes the use of inclusive casting.

Tinderbox Theatre Company

Imperial Buildings, 22 High Street, Belfast BT1 2BE
tel 028-9043 9313
email info@tinderbox.org.uk
website www.tinderbox.org.uk
Artistic Director Michael Duke

Production details: Founded in 1988. Produces, develops and stages new work which interrogates life in Northern Ireland. Stages 2-3 productions and tours to 12 different venues annually, including arts centres, theatres and site-specific locations in Ireland, England and Scotland. In general 6 actors are involved in each production. Recent productions include: *Lally the Scut* and *Summertime*.

Casting procedures: Sometimes holds general auditions. Welcomes letters (with CVs and photographs) and email submissions. Invitations to view individual actors' websites are also accepted. Offers ITC/Equity-approved contracts; only contributes to the Equity Pension Scheme for permanant staff. Encourages applications from disabled actors and promotes the use of inclusive casting.

Told by an Idiot

RADA Studios, 16 Chenies Street,
London WC1E 7EX
tel 020-7407 4123
email info@toldbyanidiot.org
website www.toldbyanidiot.org
Directors Hayley Carmichael, Paul Hunter

Production details: Founded in 1993, the company tours to theatres nationally and internationally.

Casting procedures: Freelance casting directors used on each production, check comapany website for details. Offers ITC/Equity contracts.

TOSG Gaelic Theatre Company

Sabhal Mor Ostaig, Sleat, Isle of Skye IV44 8RQ
tel (01471) 888542 *fax* (01471) 888542
email tosg@tosg.org
website www.tosg.org.uk
Artistic Director Simon Mackenzie

Production details: Founded in 1996. Professional Gaelic Theatre Company producing theatre for both adults and children. Also runs a new writing scheme. All productions are performed in Gaelic. Stages 2 productions annually and gives 50 performances per year. Tours to 30 different venues annually, including arts centres, theatres, educational and community venues in Scotland. In general 5 actors are involved in each production.

Casting procedures: Sometimes holds general auditions. Gaelic-speaking actors can write in May requesting inclusion. Welcomes letters (with CVs and photographs) but not email submissions. Invitations to view individual actors' websites are also accepted.

Trestle Theatre Company

Trestle Arts Base, Russet Drive, St Albans AL4 0JQ
tel (01727) 850950
email admin@trestle.org.uk
website www.trestle.org.uk
Artistic Director Emily Gray

Production details: Founded in 1981 as a touring theatre company, now also with a home venue (Trestle Arts Base), national workshop programme and a global business making and selling handcrafted theatre masks. Performers/facilitators used across all areas of the company. All projects concentrate on new, devised or commissioned work, incorporating text, physical theatre, dance and other movement forms, storytelling, puppetry, music and song. 1 small- to mid-scale tour annually, to 50 venues including arts centres and theatres in Britain, Europe and other international locations. In general 2-5 performers are involved in each project. Offers ITC/ Equity contracts.

Casting procedures: Rarely holds general auditions. Does not welcome on-spec CVs. Will consider invitations to see actors in shows if the performance style is relevant to the way in which Trestle works. If looking for suggestions, casting breakdowns will be posted on the website. Usually casts actors with strong physical/visual theatre acting training or experience. Actively encourages applications from disabled actors and promotes the use of inclusive casting.

Triangle Theatre Company

email office@triangletheatre.co.uk
website www.triangletheatre.co.uk
Joint Artistic Directors Carran Waterfield, Richard Talbot

Production details: Runs performances and talks for conferences, schools and colleges, and heritage sites as well as collaborations with academics and researchers contributing to the ongoing dissemination of Triangle's method of extended and immersive play with character, personal biography and history. Stages on average 1 major original production each year, including studio and site-specific situations. Studio work is actor-centred and scripted from lengthy, devised rehearsals. Site-specific work is experimental and participatory, and developed in partnership with universities and local authorities. Recent productions include: *The Last Women* (2009) and *Knickers and Vests* (part of the Cultural Olympiad to London 2010).

Winner of the UK Museums & Heritage Award for excellence, and the Roots & Wings Award for performance and interactive projects in response to museum collections. Also Fringe First and Independent Theatre Award Short List, Best Production/Actress, Festival of Experimental Theatre, Volgograd, Russia.

Casting procedures: Casting and contracts agreed by Artistic Directors. Triangle holds ensemble auditions and training workshops to develop material, generate ideas and employ associate artists. Actors are advised to consult the website for detailed information and to approach the company regarding specific, relevant projects. Does not welcome unsolicited submissions by post or by email, or showreels, but will accept invitations to view individual actors' websites. Offers independent contracts based on ITC. Actively encourages applications from disabled actors and promotes the use of inclusive casting.

Two's Company

244 Upland Road,London SE22 0DN
tel 020-8299 3714
email graham@2scompanytheatre.co.uk
website www.2scompanytheatre.co.uk
Artistic Director Tricia Thorns *Producer* Graham Cowley

Production details: Founded in 1999, Two's Company focus on presenting 'new plays of the past', forgotten plays from earlier times which depict events or people contemporary with them. For example, they have recently produced a series of plays about the First World War, originally written at the time. Other productions include: *The Cutting of the Cloth* and *What The Women Did* (Southwark Playhouse), and *London Wall* (Finborough Theatre and St James Theatre). Each production consists of 8-10 actors and, on average, the company present 1-2 productions per year. This equates to around 56 performances at 2 London venues, mainly small London theatres. Occasionally, a tour will go out to small theatres and arts centres.

Casting procedures: Occasionally uses freelance casting directors, but does not hold general auditions. Welcomes both CVs and letters from actors previously unknown to the company and unsolicited CVs and photographs only when casting. These should be sent via email. Also welcomes invitations to view individual actors' websites, but does not welcome showreels. Rarely has the opportunity to cast disabled actors.

TYPE (The Yellowchair Performance Experience)

89 Birchanger Lane, Birchanger, Bishop Stortford, Herts CM23 5QF
email contactTYPE@gmail.com
website www.wix.com/yellowchair/type
Key contact Hugh Allison

Production details: Aims to give new talent their first break on the UK Fringe (not limited to actors). Recent productions include: *A Midsummer Night's Dream, What Andrew Heard, The Bear.*

Casting procedures: Does not use freelance casting directors or hold general auditions. Actors may write in at any time. Casting breakdowns are usually available on CCP and at **mandy.com**. Welcomes letters (with CVs and photographs) from individual actors previously unknown to the company, sent by post. May cast disabled actors, depending on the role.

UK Arts International

6 Fort Crescent, Margate CT9 1HN
website www.ukarts.com

Production details: Mainly presents productions from overseas and tours them throughout the UK.

Casting procedures: Does not hold general auditions and does not welcome submissions from actors previously unknown to the company.

Unlimited Theatre

West Yorkshire Playhouse, Playhouse Square, Quarry Hill, Leeds LS2 7UP
tel 0113-213 7249
email unlimited@unlimited.org.uk
website www.unlimited.org.uk
Creative Director Jon Spooner

Production details: Founded in 1997. Creates work intended to "explore how personal experience can illuminate political debate, and which puts marginalised voices centre-stage". Stages 1-2 productions annually with 50-100 performances. Tours to 10-20 different venues each year, including arts centres and theatres throughout the UK (including Glasgow, Edinburgh and Belfast) and overseas. In general 4-6 actors are involved in each production. Recent productions include: *Money the Gameshow, Play Dough* and *Am I Dead Yet?*

Casting procedures: Sometimes holds general auditions. Welcomes responses to casting calls but not email submissions. Follow **@untheatre** on Twitter or sign up to newsletter for info on casting calls. "We are a small- to middle-scale organisation and only occasionally employ freelance actors. We are always interested in hearing from potential new collaborators." Offers ITC/Equity-approved contracts. Actively encourages applications from disabled actors and promotes the use of inclusive casting.

Unrestricted View

109 St Paul's Road, Islington, London N1 2NA
tel 020-7704 2001

email felicity@henandchickens.com
website www.unrestrictedview.co.uk
Artistic Directors Felicity Wren, James Wren *Theatre Manager* Mark Johnson

Production details: Unrestricted View produce new writing and comedy. Run by actors for actors, the company offer a safe, supportive space for creative people to work in. The theatre is also a cinema space. The theatre hosted 3 productions in 2014 and offers financial and professional support to 3 resident acting companies. Theatre productions are hosted on 3-week runs and comedy shows are hosted on an individual basis, with the theatre in use as a performance space 355 days per year. Recent productions include: *Get It Seen* (a month of feature films and shorts from independent producers – affliated with the BFI) and *A May's Plays* (a 15-year celebration of the theatre with 10 new 15-minute plays supplied by the company's sister theatre in New York City – The WorkShop Theater).

The main theatre space has 54 seats, which can be arranged in a number of different configurations. Hire-rates are as follows: £1,200 per week, or on a day-by-day basis of £120 (until 7.30pm) or £150 (until 9.30pm).

Casting Procedures: Uses in-house casting directors. A casting breakdown is available on Casting Call Pro and the website, with details of upcoming productions on Twitter and Facebook. Happy to consider applications from disabled actors.

Vanguard Productions

30 Coombe Rise, Findon Valley, Worthing, West Sussex BN14 0ED
tel 01903-872982
email vanguard.productions@ntlworld.com
website www.vanguardproductions.co.uk
Artistic Directors Nelson. E.Ward, Amaryllis Crooke

Production details: Founded in 1996, Vanguard take theatre and entertainment to areas of the community that are socially excluded. These include residential/ nursing homes, day centres, museums and village halls as well as smal-scale theatre venues. An outreach programme also exists for schools and colleges. Recent productions include: *Maxie: The Life of Max Miller*, *What A Swell Party* and *Magic Moments*. Each production contains 3-4 actors and Vanguard present 4 productions per year. This equates to 50-70 performances annually at venues across the south of England, including residential/nursing homes, day centres, museums, schools, colleges and art centres.

Casting procedures: Uses in-house casting directors and only holds general auditions periodically. The best time to contact regarding roles is during the summer for parts in the Christmas production. Casting breakdowns are put on Casting Call Pro and Equity job information service. Welcomes both CVs and letters from actors previously unknown to the Company and unsolicited CVs and photographs. These should be sent via email.

Volcano Theatre Company

229 High Street, Swansea SA1 1NY
tel (01792) 464790
email paul@volcanotheatre.co.uk
website www.volcanotheatre.co.uk
Directors Paul Davies, Fern Smith

Production details: Original theatrical productions and site-specific events. Small-scale national and international touring company based in Wales. Devised and collaborative work, physical theatre, new writing, adaptations/deconstructions of classics. Stages 2-4 productions and gives 50-80 performances each year. Venues include arts centres and theatres in the UK, Europe and worldwide. Usually 2-8 performers per production. Recent productions include: *i-witness*, *Dead Cat Bounce* and *A Few Little Drops*.

Casting procedures: There are no casting breakdowns. Performers are selected through workshops and invited auditions. Unsolicited admissions are read but not held on record.

Waking Exploits

15 Windsor House, Westgate Street, Cardiff CF10 1DG
email info@wakingexploits.co.uk
website www.wakingexploits.co.uk
Producer Iain Goosey *Associate Producer* Michael Salmon

Production details: Established in 2010. Produces high-quality, innovative work by contemporary playwrights from across the UK, in theatres and site-specific locations. Stages 1-2 productions each year, with 20-40 performances in 10-20 venues (England and Wales) including mid-scale arts centres and theatres. In general 5-10 actors are involved in each show. Recent productions include: *Serious Money* by Caryl Churchill and *Pornography* by Simon Stephens.

Casting procedures: Uses freelance casting director. General submissions from actors are encouraged only during casting period (published on the website). Breakdowns are displayed on the site and via Spotlight, Equity Job Information Service and Ideas Tap. Offers Equity TMA contracts. Does not welcome unsolicited approaches by post, but actors may email CVs, photographs, showreels and invitations to view websites or visit productions. Actively encourages applications from disabled actors and promotes the use of inclusive casting.

Walk the Plank

72 Broad Street, Salford, M6 5BZ
tel 0161-736 8964
email info@walktheplank.co.uk
website www.walktheplank.co.uk

Production details: Founded 2001, Walk the Plank are outdoor arts experts, who create events with mass appeal. Walk the Plank present over 10 productions per year, hosting outdoor productions at various locations across England and internationally. Recent production locations include: UK City of Culture – Londonderry, Manchester Day Parade and Hull's Freedom Festival.

Casting procedures: Uses in-house casting directors. Welcomes both CVs and letters from actors previously unknown to the company, but will not accept unsolicited CVs and photographs. Also welcomes showreels and invitations to view individual actor's websites or invitations to view specific productions. Actively encourages applications from disabled actors and promotes the use of inclusive casting.

Keith Whitall

25 Solway, Hailsham BN27 3HB
tel (01323) 844882
Director Keith Whitall

Production details: Founded in 2000. Produces revues, small-scale musicals and occasionally plays and one-person shows. Stages 2-3 productions annually with 20 or more performances in theatres in Brighton and the South East. So far has only toured to 1 arts centre. In general 9-10 actors are involved in each production. Recent productions include: *Broadway Calling*, *The Pleasure of Your Company* and *Noel Coward & Cole Porter Revisited.* Offers non-Equity contracts and does not subscribe to the Equity Pension Scheme.

Casting procedures: Sometimes holds general auditions. Actors may write at any time requesting inclusion. Casting breakdowns are usually made available to casting directors or actors seen in a production. Welcomes letters (with CVs and photographs) but not email submissions. "In my revues I usually use 3-4 experienced artistes plus new young artistes in whom I am especially interested." Musical theatre experience is preferable. Rarely has opportunity to cast disabled actors, but "possible in future depending on backstage access".

The Wrestling School

42 Durlston Road, London E5 8RR
tel 020-8442 4229
website www.thewrestlingschool.co.uk
Director Howard Barker

Production details: Founded in 1988. "Develops ways of presenting complex ideas in the theatre through the work of Howard Barker." Stages 1 production annually; in general 5-7 actors are involved in each production.

Casting procedures: Sometimes holds auditions. Welcomes letters when casting (with CVs and photographs) but not email submissions. Actors should telephone in late July, or consult the website, to find out if the company is casting.

Y Touring Theatre Company

One KX, 120 Cromer Street, London WC1B 8BS
tel 020-7520 3090
email d.jackson@ytouring.org.uk
website www.theatreofdebate.com
Artistic Director Nigel Townsend

Production details: Award-winning professional touring company for young people and adults. Produces 2 tours per year in the UK. Offers ITC/Equity-approved contracts and does not subscribe to the Equity Pension Scheme.

Casting procedures: Uses freelance casting directors and publishes casting breakdowns through Spotlight. Does not hold general auditions. Will accept CVs and photos at any time of year to be held on file for consideration. Please do not send showreels or unsolicited scripts. Will consider applications from disabled actors.

Yellow Earth Theatre

The Albany, Douglas Way, Deptford,
London SE8 4AG
tel 020-8694 6631 *fax* 020-7287 3141
email admin@yellowearth.org
website www.yellowearth.org
Artistic Director Kumiko Mendl

Production details: Yellow Earth Theatre was established by a group of British East Asian (BEA) performers in 1995. It develops and presents new theatre work by BEA artists. It engages new mainstream and BEA audiences in fresh, vibrant work that reflects the BEA experience and creates new opportunities for BEA actors, writers and directors. It has presented 22 high profile productions in London and on tour in the UK, including performances at the RSC, Barbican and Soho Theatres. It tours work nationally and shows are designed to tour easily. Detailed technical requiremetns are provided along with a touring stage manager. Yellow Earth is a member of ITC.

Casting procedures: Casts in-house. Sometimes holds general auditions. Welcomes emails with CVs and photographs from actors with East Asian heritage only. Accepts invitations to view individual actors' websites, but not showreels. Promotes the use of inclusive casting.

East Asian includes: Brunei, Burma, Cambodia, China, East Timor, Hong Kong, Indonesia, Japan, Laos, Malaysia, Mongolia, North Korea, Philippines, Singapore, South Korea, Taiwan, Thailand, Vietnam and their diasporas.

Starting your own theatre company

Pilar Ortí

The first question you should ask yourself before starting a theatre company is – do you really need to set up a company, or do you just want to put on a show? In order to put on a show you don't need to go through all the hassle of setting up a company. If you *do* want to set up a company – why? In some cases this might be as difficult a question to answer as, "Why do you want to act?", but it's worth having an idea of why you want to invest so much time and energy in setting up and running an organisation rather than looking for acting work. Whatever your answer, be honest with yourself. And the clearer you can be, the better, as your answers will affect the kind of organisation you end up creating.

Of course, many companies emerge after a group of actors produce a show together: at some point, someone decides that, as a company of people, you are worth keeping together. If this is the case, then you are ready to run a company of your own. But there are many ways of making theatre, as you well know, and the range of theatre produced is also vast. What kind of work do you want to do? At this point it is worth bearing in mind your 'artistic policy', and coming up with a couple of sentences that describe the work you do. I know that 'policy' sounds dry, but if you end up constituting yourself as a non-commercial organisation and applying to public funds (or trusts and foundations), you will need to learn a whole new vocabulary which seems to have little to do with your art. You should never lose sight of your artistic dreams and ambitions – but you may need to talk about them in terms of policy, objectives, qualitative evaluation, benefits, management structure, cultural diversity, contingency ... the list goes on and on. This article is meant to inspire you, not send you off to sleep, so don't despair: learn the language and then use it in a creative way that makes sense to you.

Allow yourself to dream

Long-term plans are necessary – so learn to dream. (Okay, give it a try in the first instance by putting on a show. Then, if you enjoy it, carry on!) Plans, of course, can change along the way: I suggest that you have an absolutely ambitious dream plan and a let's-try-and-see-what's-possible-now plan. Opportunities arise when you least expect them, and if you know where you are heading, you can grab them without letting them throw you off-course.

I view running a theatre company rather like directing a show: the more theatre you watch, the stronger the idea you will have of what *you* want the show to be, what is unique about it, and what you can realistically achieve. So if you, like me, trained as an actor or actress and suddenly find yourself running a company, seek advice and look at how others operate. If you consider how other people do things, you will be able to adapt the bits you like and which make sense to you. In a sector such as ours, it is not difficult to find those who are pleased to help – and the freshness of people just starting out reminds us all of how much can be achieved when we don't know our limitations.

Seek help

There is an awful lot of free/cheap advice out there. During the year in which we focused on building the administrative foundations for our company, my colleague and I talked to as many consultants, local authority officers, venue managers, etc. as we could. Some of these conversations came about through informal meetings; others, by taking part in official programmes. We found out what funders were really looking for, and what other companies were doing in our area; we learnt to draw up business plans with budgets covering three and five years; and we discovered what our strengths and weaknesses were, and what threats and opportunities exist 'out there'.

A word of warning: take *all* advice (including that which I am giving you now) with a pinch of salt, especially from those who hardly know you and your work. Follow your gut instinct. When we were in pre-production for *Antigone*, a business consultant suggested that we invite Funeral Services to advertise in our programme, "seeing as how they all die in the end". Mmm.

The best consultancies are those which have been carefully structured so that the consultant spends time with you, getting to know you and your plans, and then helps you find your own answers by providing their expertise. Arts & Business's 'Business in the Arts' programme is worth checking out, although you need to have a very definite idea of what you need help with. (To see what else Arts & Business do, check out their website, **www.aandb.org.uk**.)

Making it 'proper'

Once you have decided on the work you want to do and how you want to go about producing it, you will need to find a legal structure for your company. This shows outsiders that you are serious, and it also makes monetary transactions easier.

Forbidden's first show was produced in Edinburgh: the only 'proper' thing the company had was a bank account (and a name!). We then registered the name and became a limited company, and after our first London show, became a registered charity. This was a good idea as our income mainly comes from trusts and foundations (most of which require you to be a charity in order to receive their grants, for tax purposes); it also allows us to claim Gift Aid when we receive donations from individuals. (Gift Aid is great: the donor claims their donation as tax-deductible, and you receive an extra 23 per cent from the Inland Revenue.)

Setting up a charity still allows you to pursue your own artistic programme: making theatre for the public is considered to 'advance education', which is a charitable objective. So you can still run your company as a business, drawing salaries, etc. and making sure that any annual profits stay within the company.

Just like a limited company, a registered charity is governed by a Board. The main difference between the two set-ups is that those who sit on a charity's Board (the Trustees) do so on a voluntary basis. It therefore would make no sense for *you* to be part of the Board (although there is talk of a possible change in the law to allow Trustees to be remunerated for their work). This means that, in theory at least, you are putting the fate of your company in the hands of other people. So choose your Trustees very carefully, and try to include people who have some knowledge of legal matters and accountancy.

This set-up has worked for Forbidden, as we have been extremely lucky: we have managed to find experienced individuals with integrity and a passion for what we do. You might prefer a different kind of set-up which gives you more legal control: banks and Business Links offer free advice on the different options. If you want some focused advice and have a bit of cash to spare, you might attend the Independent Theatre Council's (ITC) seminar on 'Starting a Theatre Company'. And when you have a bit more cash, you might want to join the ITC – membership is bound to come in handy when questions on legal matters arise. (Have a look at the website, **www.itc-arts.org.uk**.)

Learn as you go along

Know your strengths and weaknesses. Setting up a theatre company will involve doing ten thousand things you might never have done before; however, a lot of it can be learnt along the way, and much of it is common sense. It won't take you long to discover those things you are useless at, and those that you absolutely hate. You then have two choices: do them anyway, or find someone else to do them for you/with you.

If there are more than two of you running the company, decide who will be in charge of what. Certain things, like fundraising, might be too daunting for one person to do on their own, but you can break it down into more manageable pieces. Someone might have a clearer head for numbers and can prepare the budget, and someone else can write the description of the show and why it will make a huge contribution to theatre in this country.

Let's talk about money

And seeing that I've come to fundraising, I shall dwell on it. You can't escape it. No matter how much your company grows, no matter how successful you are, no matter how large your staff is – if you are in charge, you will worry about it, so learn to enjoy it. I know that this sounds perverse, but fundraising applications are your chance to enthuse someone else about what you do. To tell them about your plans – about what you want to do and why you want to do it. Tell them how you want to make a difference; about *why* you think it's different; about how it will help you, and others, grow. And yes, you will need to learn some new vocabulary, and be able to distinguish between qualitative and quantitative evaluation, but it helps if you see this as a game with which you have to keep up. (At the last ITC annual general meeting, I found out that 'well-being' is a new way of convincing funders that theatre is necessary to people's lives!) What's really important is to convince funders that you really want to do the work, and that you want to do it well. (When I talk about funders, I am referring to anyone who might want to donate to or invest in your company. I have no experience of commercial deals, but I imagine that these work in a similar way: you find out what it is that people want in return for their money, and then convince them that you can provide it – as well as putting on a really good show.)

This is also where having long-term plans comes in handy: funding applications usually take between six weeks and three months to be assessed. Sometimes, even more: our first successful application for an Education Officer took more than one year from the date on which I sent it to the day the letter of acceptance came through. While I'm on the subject of those who will give you money – *nurture your relationships with them*. We have found that those trusts, foundations and individuals who are willing to help us out once, are likely to do so again.

I have also discovered that funding applications help you plan in detail how you are going to realise a production or a project. Good funding applications might come in useful even if you don't get the money – they will probably provide a good description of your plans, which you can then show others interested in your work. (For books and directories on fundraising, check out the Directory of Social Change's website, **www.dsc.org.uk**. They also have a small bookshop in Stephenson Way, near Euston Square in London NW1.)

Final words

I have left the most important thing until last. *Treat those working with you well, especially your actors.* Make working with you an enjoyable experience. If you hold auditions, make them worthwhile for those attending. When you are able to pay your personnel, pay them on time. Treat them like the professionals that they are. And when things go wrong, as they inevitably will, take responsibility for your company and make up for the hassle with a gesture, however small – custard creams work for me!

When I first started running Forbidden, I kept hearing that I should treat it like running a business. What I have discovered is that it is an exercise in people management. Forbidden exists because people have believed in our work and are willing to invest their time and money in what we do. Different organisations work in different ways: I hope these words have helped you find one that will work for you.

After running Forbidden Theatre Company as Artistic Director for seven years, Pilar now uses her people management skills to facilitate learning in leaders and in teams. She is director of Unusual Connections, a company which uses theatre-based training to deliver Leadership Programmes and Strategic Team-Away days. She also freelances as workshop leader and voice-over artist, and can be contated via **info@unusualconnections.co.uk**

Finding funding for projects

Sinead Mac Manus

Finding funding for projects is an essential part of the subsidised theatre scene. Unless you are working in the commercial sector, most theatre productions do not generate enough income to cover their costs. Fundraising provides the shortfall. The funding landscape in the UK is wide and varied, and can seem to the beginner to be an impossible terrain to navigate. However, as with most things, there are tricks of the trade that you can learn, and the process *does* get easier with practice.

Starting points

There are two good starting publications that I would recommend for fledging arts fundraisers: the first entitled 'Guide to Arts Funding in England', is an excellent overview of arts funding available to download for free from the Department for Culture, Media and Sport (DCMS) website (**www.culture.gov.uk**). Also recommended is Susan Forrester's and David Lloyd's *The Arts Funding Guide* published by the Directory of Social Change in 2002 (**www.dsc.org.uk**), which may be available in your local library. These guides take the user through the areas where you can find funding for projects, such as Government grants including Arts Council funding, Lottery funding, funding from your Local Authority, grants from charitable trusts and foundations, and bursaries.

Research, research, research

Successful fundraising is all about research, and matching available funds to your projects. If you approach fundraising creatively you should be able to adapt projects to available funds while still retaining your artistic integrity. So how do you discover what is out there? Get on the arts mailing lists to find out about new rounds of funds. Research the funding bodies and their criteria. Talk to your local Council about what funds they can offer you and your project. Find out what venues support new work with bursaries, or support in kind such as free space. Find out what trusts and foundations there are and who they give money to. Look up fundraising directories in your local library or one of the resource centres at organisations such as CIDA in east London (**www.cida.co.uk**), the Directory of Social Change (**www.dsc.org.uk**) or Arts and Business (**http://aandb.org.uk**).

The Funder Finder website (**www.funderfinder.org.uk**) features downloadable resources including a handy budget tool and grant application tool. Their cd-rom with details of hundreds of grants can be found in some resource centres or libraries for free use. They also have a free comprehensive advice pack on their website which has downloadable leaflets on areas such as budgeting, planning a funding strategy and tips for successful applications. The website also has a comprehensive A–Z list of trusts and foundations that have available funds.

It is important to research the funder that you are applying to, in order to find the 'essence' of the funder. This is essential so that you can match your projects to the relevant funder. For example, a Lottery Funding scheme such as Awards for All (**www.awardsforall.org.uk**) distributes public money for the benefit of local communities. Therefore any application to them must be for a project that demonstrates clear benefit to an identified community or body of people.

Similarly, the Arts Councils of England, Wales, Scotland and Northern Ireland all distribute public funds and have to be very open and transparent about how their funds are distributed.

Arts Council England (ACE) is the development and funding agency for the arts in England. You can apply to ACE as an individual for funding between £200 to £30,000. Organisations can receive up to £100,000. You can apply any time and there are no deadlines. A decision will be forthcoming within six weeks for grants under £5,000 and twelve weeks for grants over £5,000. ACE set aims every three years which form the basis of their grant-making policy, so it is important for applicants to think about how their project will fit into these aims. As with any funding body, building a relationship is paramount. Even before you approach ACE for funding, you should be inviting them to your productions and telling them about your projects. Full details of how to apply, including guidance notes, are on the website (**www.artscouncil.org.uk**).

The Arts Council of Wales (**www.artswales.org.uk**) has a similar funding system and structure to England, but there are regular funding deadlines throughout the year. Creative Scotland (formerly The Scottish Arts Council; **www.creativescotland.com**) has a slightly more complicated funding system with deadlines for different funding streams. The Arts Council of Northern Ireland (**www.artscouncil-ni.org**) has different funding schemes for individuals and organisations, and different closing dates for individual schemes.

In contrast to the Arts Councils in the UK, many charitable trusts and foundations only distribute funds to limited companies, and, in some cases, registered charities. Some can fund individuals, but they are not many. When applying to trusts and foundations, it is important to remember they were usually set up to address an issue or problem. You will need to identify what this is and ensure that your project addresses this.

Find out what you can about the funding body that you are applying to and what their funding priorities are. Make sure you fit into their guidelines and that you are eligible to apply. Remember that all funders have agendas – they do not give money away for nothing. For example, many Local Authority arts funding schemes usually look for local projects that impact on the community and have public benefit. View researching and applying for funding as you would looking for a job. You would not apply to a company if you did not think you were qualified. Similarly, you are wasting your time and theirs if you apply for funding that you are not eligible to get, e.g. your theatre company is not a registered charity, or they only fund work with older people and you work with children.

The proposal

An easy to read guide on writing funding proposals is Tim Cook's *Avoiding the Wastepaper Basket – A practical guide to applying to Grant Making Trusts* (LVSC, 1998). The book is written from the perspective of the funding body, and looks at examples of good and bad funding proposals.

If there is no application form, write a clear and concise (2 x A4 page) proposal. Write in plain English and do not use jargon. Find what the 'grain' of the funding body is. Do their work for them. Show in your funding application exactly how you meet their criteria and fit into their funding policy. Again to use the analogy of applying for a job, use the exact wording of the guidelines in your application when you are talking about your project, much in the way you would use the wording in the Person Specification when you are applying for a job. You can even highlight their criteria in bold or italics to make it stand out.

Follow the guidelines of the fund to the letter – supply all the information that they require but do not add in additional information if it is not requested. If you have something that you think may be of interest to them, mention in your application that this is available on request. Convey your enthusiasm and passion for your project and your belief in yourself and/or your company. Show how the project will be successful. Funders like to back winners.

When you are finished, show your finished application to a non-arts person and ask them to read it for clarity. If you do get a grant, remember to say thank you! Start to build a relationship with the funder and keep them updated on progress with the project. If you are not successful, ask for feedback from the funder on why.

Business sponsorship

Business sponsorship can be a useful way of raising funds for projects if you are not eligible to apply for grant project funding. Business sponsorship is where a company gives your organisation or project cash, or support in kind, in exchange for publicity for their product or service. It is important to remember that businesses will not give you money or support for nothing – they will require something in return. Sponsorship is essentially a commercial deal between yourself and the business, and therefore there should be a clear exchange of benefits, e.g. advertising benefit for the company and monetary benefit for the arts organisation, and there should be a value to the benefit given or received.

Arts & Business is the leading agency for bringing business and the arts together in the UK. Their website provides valuable information about building relationships between the arts and business, including details of investment schemes such as *Read* and *Invest.* They also publish an essential guide to business sponsorship entitled *Arts Business Sponsorship Manual,* which is included when you book on their Arts & Business Sponsorship Seminar – held regularly around the UK. The guide and other resources on sponsorship can also be read at their free resource centre in London (**http://aandb.org.uk**).

Income generation

An important part of finding funding for projects is generating your own income. Income can be earned or generated from a number of different sources: venues can pay you a fee or share the box office receipts of a production. They can also commission or co-produce a work. You can sell merchandise such as programmes, t-shirts or postcards at your events. You can generate income through education work including fees for workshops and residencies. Individuals can give you money for your projects (angels) or they can invest in your work and expect (or not!) a return. You can also raise funds through events ranging from theatre related events such as benefit performances and cabarets to 'fun' events such as sponsored walks to parachute jumps.

Creative thinking

When you are starting out, it can be difficult to see where you can obtain the money for projects. The Arts Council do prefer to fund artists or organisations with a track record, and therefore you may have to find alternative funding initially for your productions or projects. Trusts and foundations tend to only fund limited companies or registered charities, and so again this may not be an area of funding that you can tap into immediately.

Therefore it is important to think of ways of funding your work outside the traditional funding system. In many cases, this may mean that you have to fund your work yourself and hope that you can get a return on it, or at least break even. This is how the majority of companies fund their Edinburgh Fringe Festival run – by investing the money upfront in the hire of the venue, the accommodation and travel and the cost of the production and hoping that the take at the box office will cover these costs and give everyone involved in the production some wages. If you are using your own money to mount a production, you need to be able to assess what level of risk you are willing to accept and think of ways of lessening this risk. Examine your budget and see where you can reduce or cut costs. You could try to get free rehearsal space from a local school in exchange for workshops or use a local printer for your flyers in exchange for advertising in your programme. Consider sharing your venue with another company for a double bill (check that this is acceptable to the venue in advance) to halve the costs of the hire. Book a venue in your local area that you know so that you can at least invite friends and family to have a guaranteed audience. Ask friends and family to invest small amounts of money in your production. This can be done as a gift or on an investment and return basis e.g. an individual invests £100 and is guaranteed a return of £75 or an amount above £100, depending on how well the show does. Offer credits for purchase in the production as gifts – purchasers get credit in the publicity material, and an invitation to a performance.

There are many examples of artists and companies that have used creative ways to get their projects up and running. One company sold performances in the customer's sitting room on eBay for cash. Another company raised the money for a string of rural performances by doing a sponsored walk from venue to venue. Another company raised the money for a production by offering to do up a local community centre – they got free rehearsal space and a venue as part of the deal.

Remember that you are a creative individual! Use some of that creativity to think outside the box when it comes to finding money for projects.

Sinead Mac Manus has worked for a wide range of arts organisations, including Frantic Assembly, Tall Stories and Mimbre. She is currently a freelance creative business consultant and trainer, and has many years of experience working with and training creative entrepreneurs. She is the author of *eVolve Graduate Handbook: a practical guide to producing performance*, and founder of **StartaTheatreCompany.com** – an online guide to starting a performing arts company. Her activity in developing new business models around the idea of e-learning for creative entrepreneurs using web 2.0 tools and social media led her to be chosen this year as one of the Courvoisier: Future 500 to watch.

Pantomime

This section lists some of the major pantomime producers and some of the theatres and arts centres that produce their own pantomimes. These latter (often subsidised by a local authority) largely present touring and (sometimes) amateur productions. However, a number do mount their own professional pantomimes and it can be useful to look through the Theatres & Provincial/Touring section of *Contacts* to check which. Many have websites.

Another way of finding out is to check through the listings and reviews in *The Stage* every Christmas. (Also look at **www.its-behind-you.com** which lists forthcoming pantomimes.) Pantomimes in such theatres will often be directed by the resident director, and usually cannot afford the services of a casting director.

Some of these theatres occasionally produce their own shows throughout the year, especially as part of the work of their Education departments. Where possible we have included this information in each entry, but it is also worth visiting the theatre's website for further details.

PANTOMIME PRODUCERS

Chaplins Entertainment Ltd

Chaplins House, The Acorn Centre, Roebuck Road, Hainault, Essex IG6 3TU
tel 020-8501 2121
email enquiries@chaplinspantos.co.uk
website www.chaplinspantos.co.uk
Directors Mr J Holmes *Productions Manager* Jessica Djemil

Production details: A touring pantomime and theatre-in-education company which also works in film and television production. Stages 26 productions annually, performing in small theatres, schools, social clubs and community centres.

Casting procedures: Uses freelance casting directors and holds general auditions; actors requesting inclusion are asked to write from August until the end of October only. Casting breakdowns are publicly available from the website, by postal application (with sae), in *The Stage* and via Casting Call Pro. During the period specified, the company welcomes letters (with CVs and photographs) from individual actors previously unknown to them, sent by post or email, and will accept showreels and invitations to view individual actors' websites. Rarely or never has the opportunity to cast disabled actors.

Duggie Chapman Associates

Clifton House, 106 Clifton Drive, Blackpool FY4 1RR
tel (01253) 403177 *mobile* (07976) 925504
email info@duggiechapmanassociates.com
website www.duggiechapman.com
Director Duggie Chapman *Artiste Bookings* Kim Holmes

Production details: Established in 1970. Producers of pantomimes, concerts and plays. Annually produces 6 resident pantomimes in various locations throughout the UK, including Billingham (Forum Theatre), Bolton (Albert Halls) Barrow-in-Furness (Forum 28) and Preston Charter Theatre, plus tours.

Casting procedures: Casting is carried out by in-house casting director. Occasionally holds general auditions. For the pantos, actors should write from March onwards to request inclusion. Casting breakdowns are obtainable from *The Stage*. Accepts submissions (with CVs and photographs) from individual actors previously unknown to the company. Invitations to view showreels and individual actors' websites are welcomed. Rarely has the opportunity to cast disabled actors.

Evolution Productions

Little Statenborough House, Sandwich Road, Eastry, Kent CT13 0DH
tel/fax (01304) 615333
email emily@evolution-productions.co.uk
email paul@evolution-productions.co.uk
website www.evolution-productions.co.uk
Directors Emily Wood, Paul Hendy

Production details: Founded in 2004 and run by husband-and-wife team, Emily Wood and Paul Hendy. Produces pantomimes and occasional musicals (recently produced *Oliver!* at The Central Theatre, Chatham). Stages 5 pantomimes a year: The Marlowe Theatre, Canterbury; The Central Theatre, Chatham; Yvonne Arnaud Theatre, Guildford; Lyceum Theatre, Sheffield; and Gordon Craig Theatre, Stevenage. Offers non-Equity, in-house contracts ("Equity equivalent") and does not subscribe to the Equity Pension Scheme.

Casting procedures: Casts in-house – all casting enquiries should be addressed to Paul Hendy. Holds general auditions; the best time to write to request inclusion is March/May. Casting breakdowns are published via Spotlight and through agents. Welcomes letters (with CVs and photographs) and performance notices from actors previously unknown to the company, sent by post or email. Happy to receive appropriate showreels and invitations to view individual actors' websites. Will consider applications from disabled actors to play disabled characters.

Extravaganza Productions

Old Ferry House, 4 London Road, Boston,
Lincs PE21 8AA
tel (01205) 355978
email extravaganza@panto-mime.co.uk
website www.panto-mime.co.uk
Directors David Vickers, Richard Chandler

Production details: Established in 1995. Presenting Pantomimes for The Plaza, Stockport and Middlesborough Theatre. Number of productions staged annually varies.

Casting procedures: Casting is carried out in house; actors can write at any time to request inclusion. Submissions (with CVs and photographs) should be addressed to Richard Chandler, Casting Director. Also accepts invitations to view individual actors' websites, and showreels. Applications from disabled actors are considered to play disabled characters.

First Family Entertainment

Fortune Theatre, Russell Street, London WC2B 5HH
tel 020-7010 7890 *fax* 020-7010 7899
email casting@ffe-uk.com
website www.ffe-uk.com
Chief Executive Kevin Wood *Production Co-ordinator* Jamie Taylor

Production details: Produces large-scale pantomimes. Venues include: Theatre Royal, Brighton; Churchill Theatre, Bromley; The King's Theatre, Glasgow; Milton Keynes Theatre, Richmond Theatre, Regent Theatre, Stoke on Trent; New Wimbledon Theatre; New Victoria Theatre, Woking; Opera House, Manchester; Sunderland Empire. Offers Equity-approved contracts and subscribes to the Equity Pension Scheme.

Casting procedures: In-house casting director is Scott Mitchell. Does not hold general auditions: only write in response to a specific breakdown. Breakdowns are published in February on Castweb, CastNet and direct to agents. Welcomes letters (with CVs and photographs) from actors previously unknown to the company if sent by post, but not by email. ("Please do not phone!") Happy to receive appropriate showreels, invitations to view individual actors' websites and performance notices. Actively encourages applications from disabled actors and promotes the use of inclusive casting.

Paul Hammond Productions

271 Regent Street, London W1B 2ES
tel 020-7084 6378
email production@hftm.co.uk
website www.paulhammondproductions.com
Director Paul Hammond *Casting* Ruth Langridge

Production details: Produces 4 pantomimes annually: Victoria Theatre, Halifax; Hazlitt Theatre, Maidstone; Pavilion Theatre, Worthing; and Drayton Manor Big Top. Offers actors non-Equity contracts and does not subscribe to the Equity Pension Scheme.

Casting Procedures: Casts in house. Actors should write to or email Ruth Langridge (with CVs and photographs) between February and July. Casting breakdowns are published in *The Stage*, Castweb and Entsweb. Welcomes CVs and photographs from actors previously unknown to the company. Happy to receive appropriate showreels, invitations to view individual actors' websites and performance notices. Will consider applications from disabled actors to play disabled characters.

Hiss & Boo Theatre Company Ltd

1 Nyes Hill, Wineham Lane, Bolney,
West Sussex RH17 5SD
tel (01444) 881707
email email@hissboo.co.uk
website www.hissboo.co.uk
Artistic Director Ian Liston

Production details: Established in 1977. Pantomime producers also specialising in touring plays and revues in the UK and overseas. Actors are employed under UK Theatre Ltd/Equity-approved contracts. The company subscribes to the Equity Pension Scheme. See also entry under *Independent managements/theatre producers* on page 170.

Casting procedures: Casting is done in house. Casting breakdowns are only available to agents via Spotlight Interactive. Does not welcome unsolicited CVs and photographs by post or email. Rarely has the opportunity to cast disabled actors.

Paul Holman Associates

Morritt House, 58 Station Approach, South Ruislip,
Middlesex HA4 6SA
tel 020-8845 9408 *fax* 020-8839 3124
email enquiries@paulholmanassociates.co.uk
website www.paulholmanassociates.co.uk
Directors Paul Holman, Adrian Jeckells, John Ogle
Artistic Director/Associate Producer Lee Waddingham

Production details: Produces Pantomimes, Summer Seasons, Tours and other commercial projects. Stages between 10-15 productions annually. Venues where productions are staged include: Bridlington, Aylesbury (Civic), Catford (Broadway), Derby (Assembly Rooms), Leeds (Carriageworks), Newark (Palace), Redditch (Palace), Weston-super-mare (Playhouse). Summer Seasons: The Pier Theatre (Bournemouth), Princess Theatre (Hunstanton). Offers non-Equity (Variety) contracts and does not subscribe to the Equity Pension Scheme.

Casting procedures: Casting is done by in-house casting director. Occasionally hold general auditions; spring is the best time to write requesting auditions. Casting breakdowns are available on Castweb. Accepts submissions (with CVs and photographs) from individual actors previously unknown to the company, sent by post or email. Invitations to view showreels and to attend other productions are also accepted. Will consider applications from disabled actors to play disabled characters, but in practice rarely has the opportunity to cast them.

Imagine Theatre Ltd

2 Brandon House, Woodhams Road,
Middlemarch Business Park, Coventry CV3 4FX
tel 024-7630 7001
email casting@imaginetheatre.co.uk
website www.imaginetheatre.co.uk
Managing Director Stephen Boden *Business Director* Sarah Boden *Creative Director* Iain Lauchlan

Production details: Imagine Theatre (since 2009; formerly Wish Theatre) produces pantomimes and children's theatre for No. 1 tours, including *The Tweenies* and *Fun Song Factory*. Venues for pantomime include: Grand Pavilion, Porthcawl; Eden Court, Inverness; Victoria Theatre, Halifax; Belgrade Theatre, Coventry; Lyceum Theatre, Crewe; Palace Theatre, Kilmarnock; Town Hall, Loughborough; Roses Theatre, Tewksbury. Offers in-house contracts ("enhanced Equity") and does not subscribe to the Equity Pension Scheme.

Casting procedures: Casts mainly in house. Holds general auditions; actors should email the company in March-May to request inclusion. Casting breakdowns are not published except on Spotlight. Welcomes CVs and photgraphs from actors previously unknown to the company; prefers these to be emailed rather than posted. Will consider applications from disabled actors to play disabled characters. "Panto isn't a cop-out: it's a serious business. We use actors who can engage with the audience and have fun. It is really useful if actors can indicate their location/home town, which helps with accents and knowing if an individual is local to one of our pantomime venues. Please do not send showreels or invitations to view websites, as unfortunately we just don't have time to deal with them."

Owen Money Productions

4 Westgate Close, Porthcawl CF36 3NP
tel (07896) 258893
email owen.money@btinternet.com
Director Owen Money *Company Manager* Roger Bell

Production details: Established in 2000. Produces 3-4 family pantomimes a year, touring to 7-8 theatres and community venues around Wales between the end of November and the end of February. Also produces a Brian Rix-style 'adult' panto in April (2007 production was *Buttons Undone*). Offers non-Equity contracts and does not subscribe to the Equity Pension Scheme.

Casting procedures: Casts in-house. Casting notices are published in *The Stage*. Actors wishing to audition for the company should write (with CV and photograph) between November and January. Does not welcome unsolicited CVs and photographs by email. Happy to receive appropriate showreels and invitations to view individual actors' websites. Will consider applications from disabled actors to play disabled characters.

New Pantomime Productions

27 Shooters Road, Enfield, Middlesex EN2 8RJ
tel 020-8363 9920
email simonbarry@nppltd.freeserve.co.uk
Director Simon Barry

Production details: Produces pantomimes at 7 venues: Theatr Colwyn, Colwyn Bay; Brindley Arts Centre, Runcorn; Southport Theatre; Kings Theatre, Southsea; Princess Theatre, Torquay; Grand Opera House, York. Offers non-Equity contracts and does not subscribe to the Equity Pension Scheme.

Casting procedures: Casts in house. Holds general auditions; actors should write in July to request inclusion. Casting breakdowns are not publicly available. Welcomes emails only (with CVs and photographs) from actors previously unknown to the company. Does not welcome showreels or invitations to view individual actors' websites. "Make sure you're suitable for the job you're applying for. We have employed disabled actors – and not just to play disabled characters. So long as the actor is good, that's all that matters."

Pantoni Pantomimes

205 Bexhill Road, St Leonards on Sea,
East Sussex TN38 8BG
tel (01424) 443400 *fax* (01424) 714847
email david@pantoni.com
website www.pantoni.com
Directors David Lee and Rita Proctor

Produces pantomimes for the Doncaster Civic Theatre; Empire Theatre, Consett; New Floral Pavilion, New Brighton; The Leatherhead Theatre; Library Theatre, Luton; and Octagon Theatre, Yeovil.

Qdos Entertainment (Pantomimes) Ltd

2nd Floor, 161 Drury Lane, Covent Garden,
London WC2B 5PN
tel 020-7430 7900
email info@qdosentertainment.co.uk
website www.qdosentertainment.com
Casting Director/Producer Jonathan Kiley

Production details: The largest of the commercial pantomime producers with 24 pantomimes across the UK: His Majesty's, Aberdeen; Grand Opera House, Belfast; Hippodrome Theatre, Birmingham; The Alhambra, Bradford; New Theatre, Cardiff; The

Hawth, Crawley; Civic Theatre, Darlington; The Orchard, Dartford; Kings Theatre, Edinburgh; SECC Glasgow; White Rock, Hastings; Beck Theatre, Hayes; Wycombe Swan, High Wycombe; Hull New Theatre; Venue Cymru, Llandudno; Theatre Royal, Newcastle upon Tyne; Derngate Theatre, Northampton; Theatre Royal, Nottingham; Theatre Royal, Plymouth; Cliffs Pavilion, Southend; Mayflower Theatre, Southampton; Grand Theatre, Swansea; Wyvern Theatre, Swindon; Grand Theatre, Wolverhampton.

Casting procedures: Actors should send CVs and photographs by post to Jonathan Kiley in March (star-casting only in February). Welcomes performance notices. Send to: Qdos Entertainment (Pantomimes) Ltd, 2nd Floor, 161 Drury Lane, Covent Garden, London WC2B 5PN.

Spillers Pantomimes

The Old Post Office, Honey Tye, Leavenheath, Suffolk CO6 4NX
email bev.berridge@btinternet.com
Managing Director John Spillers *Casting* (Mr) Bev Berridge

Production details: Established 1989. Produces pantomimes for Alexandra Theatre, Bognor Regis; Epsom Playhouse; Woodville Hall Theatre, Gravesend; Motherwell Theatre; Majestic Theatre, Retford; Civic Theatre, Rotherham; The Music Hall, Shrewsbury; Pavilion Theatre, Weymouth. Offers actors non-Equity contracts and does not contribute to the Equity Pension Scheme.

Casting procedures: Casting is done in house. Holds general auditions. Best time for actors to write (with CV and photograph) to request inclusion is March/April. Casting breakdowns are published in *The Stage*. Welcomes CVs and photographs from actors previously unknown to the company, sent by post or email. Will consider applications from disabled actors to play disabled characters.

UK Productions

Brook House, Mint Street, Godalming, Surrey GU7 1HE
tel (01483) 423600
email mail@ukproductions.co.uk
website www.ukproductions.co.uk
Director Martin Dodd

Production details: Established 1995. Produces pantomimes, musicals and plays for No. 1 national and international touring. (See entry under *Independent managements/theatre producers* on page 175.) Offers non-Equity contracts.

Casting procedures: Casting is done in house. Does not hold open auditions. Casting breakdowns are distributed via Spotlight. Welcomes performance notices but not any other unsolicited form of correspondence. Will consider applications from disabled actors to play characters with disabilities.

IN-HOUSE PANTOMIMES

Buxton Opera House

Water Street, Buxton, Derbyshire SK17 6XN
tel (01298) 72050 *fax* (01298) 27563
email admin@boh.org.uk
website www.buxtonoperahouse.org.uk
*Chief Executive*Simon Glinn *Theatre Secretary* Pat Russell

Production details: A receiving theatre presenting around 450 performances each year including dance, comedy, children's shows, drama, musical concerts, pantomime and opera as well as Fringe Theatre and Community and Education Programme. Edwardian theatre designed by Frank Matcham, restored in 2001.

Casting procedures: Commissions Channel Theatre Company to produce its annual pantomimes. Philip Dart, Artistic Director of Channel Theatre, is responsible for casting. Please see the entry under *Middle and smaller-scale companies* on page 176.

Cambridge Arts Theatre

Programming & Production Department, 6 St Edwards Passage, Cambridge CB2 3PJ
tel (01223) 578903
email info@cambridgeartstheatre.com
website www.cambridgeartstheatre.com
Assistant to the Chief Executive Lucy Tregear

Production details: Seating capacity 665. A receiving theatre which presents a wide range of work, including children's theatre, music, dance and drama. Produces in-house panto annually.

Casting procedures: Engages a freelance director who, together with the producer and choreographer, is responsible for casting the panto. Actors should contact the theatre to request an audition for the pantomime in March/April. These submissions will be forwarded to the director, and marked for the attention of Sue Lowe. Actors are employed under Equity-approved contracts. Invitations to see actors in other productions are only welcomed from actors in whom the director has already shown interest. Will consider applications from disabled actors to play disabled characters.

The Capitol

North Street, Horsham, West Sussex
tel (01403) 756080 *fax* (01403) 756092
website www.thecapitolhorsham.com
General Manager Nick Mowat

Production details: Seating capacity 423. Produces a professional pantomime each year. Offers TMA/Equity-approved contracts.

Casting procedures: Uses in-house casting director. Optimum time to write requesting an audition is in spring/summer. Casting breakdowns are publicly available on the website, or by postal application (with sae). Accepts letters (with CVs and photographs) from individual actors previously unknown to the company, sent by post or email. Also welcomes invitations to view showreels and to attend other productions. Will consider applications from disabled actors to play disabled characters.

The Theatre, Chipping Norton

2 Spring Street, Chipping Norton, Oxfordshire OX7 5NL
tel (01608) 642349 *fax* (01608) 642324
email administration@chippingnortontheatre.com
website www.chippingnortontheatre.com
Director John Terry

Production details: The Theatre is a pivotal part of the artistic life of the area, and takes care to programme as diverse a range of performances – theatre, film, dance, comedy and opera – as possible. Its Community & Education programme takes film and opera out to village halls.

An intimate space, it seats 217 (including 4 wheelchair spaces) in either proscenium (end-on) or in-the-round configurations. While predominantly a receiving house, The Theatre produces an annual pantomime which runs for around 80 performances over the Christmas period, as well as occasional smaller ventures. Recent productions include: *Mother Goose* and *Puss in Boots*, new pantomimes by Simon Brett; and *Taste*, a new play which toured Normandy. The Theatre offers TMA/Equity-approved contracts and subscribes to the Equity Pension Scheme.

Casting procedures: Does not use casting directors. Welcomes unsolicited CVs and photographs from actors unknown to the company, as well as invitations to view actors' websites. Casting breakdowns for the pantomime are available March and September via Spotlight; this is the best time to write to request inclusion. Actively encourages applications from disabled actors, and promotes the use of inclusive casting.

City Varieties

Swan Street, Leeds LS1 6LW
tel 0113-391 7777 *fax* 0113-234 1800
email info@cityvarieties.co.uk
website www.cityvarieties.co.uk
General Manager Ian Sime

Production details: Seating capacity 531. Grade II* listed building, built in 1865. World-famous as the home of BBC TV's *Good Old Days*. Produces a professional pantomime each year, running from the end of November to mid-January. Also continues to produce *Good Old Days* music hall entertainment. Actors are employed under Equity-approved contracts and the theatre subscribes to the Equity Pension Scheme.

Casting procedures: Optimum time to write requesting an audition is between February and May. Accepts submissions (with CVs and photographs) from individual actors previously unknown to the company. Invitations to attend other productions are also welcome, depending on distance.

Connaught Theatre

Union Place, Worthing, West Sussex BN11 1LG
tel (01903) 231799
website www.worthingtheatres.co.uk
Admin Officer Rosie Gray

Production details: Seating capacity 506 with 6 wheelchair spaces. The Connaught Theatre was built in 1914, but was originally called the Picturedrome. For 20 years it was an early cinema, until 1935 when the Worthing Repertory Company outgrew its own premises and came into the venue, bringing with it the name Connaught Theatre.

Casting procedures: A receiving theatre, but from 2007 has been co-producing its annual panto with !!Link!! (see entry on page 0). Casting enquiries should be through Chris Lillicrap at The Proper Pantomime Company.

The Courtyard

The Courtyard Centre for the Arts, Edgar Street, Hereford HR4 9JR
tel (01432) 346500 *fax* (01432) 346349
email martyn.green@courtyard.org.uk
website www.courtyard.org.uk
Chief Executive Ian Archer

Production details: Seating capacity 436. The Courtyard opened in September 1998 and was the first Lottery-funded theatre to be built in England. It provides "an eclectic programme of work, from produced to received, and offers something for the whole community". Produces a professional pantomime each year, from the end of November to mid-January. Provides actors with Equity-approved contracts as negotiated through TMA.

Casting procedures: Uses in-house casting directors; actors may write in June to request an audition. Casting breakdowns are available from the website, or via CastNet and Castweb. Welcomes letters (with CVs and photographs) from individual actors previously unknown to the company, sent by post or email. Also accepts showreels and invitations to visit other productions. Actively encourages applications from disabled actors and promotes the use of inclusive casting.

Cumbernauld Theatre

Kildrum, Cumbernauld, Glasgow G67 2BN
tel (01236) 737235 *fax* (01236) 738408
email info@cumbernauldtheatre.co.uk
website www.cumbernauldtheatre.co.uk
Artistic Director Ed Robson

Production details: Established in 1978. A year-round producing theatre with a broad range of artist development and creative learning programmes. Produces a professional pantomime each year, together with other in-house plays, musicals and 'seasons'. Recent productions include: *The Wasp Factory* by Iain Banks.

Casting procedures: Casting is done by the Artistic Director. Auditions are held all year round; actors should obtain casting breakdowns from the website only. Welcomes letters (with CVs and photographs) from individual actors previously unknown to the company, sent by post or email. Will consider invitations to visit other productions, but requests that no showreels be submitted. Actively encourages applications from disabled actors and promotes the use of inclusive casting.

The Customs House Trust Ltd

Mill Dam, South Shields, Tyne & Wear NE33 1ES
tel 0191-454 1234 *fax* 0191-456 5979
email mail@customshouse.co.uk
website www.customshouse.co.uk
Executive Director Ray Spencer

Production details: Seating capacity 441. Established in 1994 as an arts centre, gallery, cinema and theatre. Produces approximately 6 in-house shows each year, and is a member of the North East Theatre Consortium. Stages a professional pantomime in early December which runs through to the first week in January, as well as new writing and occasional new musicals. Provides actors with Equity-approved contracts as negotiated through TMA.

Casting procedures: Uses both in-house and freelance casting directors. The pantomime is cast in June, and CVs are received all year. Welcomes letters (with CVs and photographs) from individual actors previously unknown to the compay, sent by post or email. Also accepts invitations to visit other productions. Advises actors to "find out about the venue via our website. Mention our work; it makes us feel important and makes you look as if you care!".

The Everyman Theatre

Regent Street, Cheltenham,
Gloucestershire GL50 1HQ
tel (01242) 572573 *fax* (01242) 224305
email admin@everymantheatre.org.uk
website www.everymantheatre.org.uk
Creative Director Paul Milton *Production Assistant* Deb Dovinson

Production details: Seating capacity: main house 668, studio 60. Built in 1891. A receiving theatre which presents a wide range of work, from stand-up comedy to children's theatre and including live music, dance and drama. Also works with many emerging and established theatre companies from Gloucestershire and beyond, creating partnerships and productions that are performed at the Everyman and on tour across the county. Produces in-house panto as well as promoting new writing.

Casting procedures: A freelance director is engaged to direct the panto. This director is responsible for the casting process and will choose how and where the casting breakdowns are made available. Actors should write in February to request auditions for the panto, as auditions are held in March and April. Submissions (photos and CVs) are welcomed from actors previously unknown to the company for both panto and new writing projects; these should be marked for the attention of Deb Dovinson. The Everyman also runs an Actor's Lab, providing professional training and opportunities to meet and work with established directors. The Everyman Theatre is an equal opportunities employer and gives due consideration to applications from all sectors of the community.

The Gatehouse

Eastgate Street, Stafford ST16 2LT
tel (01785) 253595
website www.staffordgatehousetheatre.co.uk
Artistic Programme Manager Derrick Gask

Production details: Celebrated its silver jubilee in 2007. A receiving theatre which presents a wide range of work, from stand-up comedy to children's theatre, and including live music, dance and drama. Usually produces its own in-house panto, with the occasional co-production.

Casting procedures: Casting is done by freelance casting directors. Breakdowns are available via Spotlight to agents only. Will consider applications from disabled actors to play disabled characters.

The Gatehouse also produces the Stafford Festival Shakespeare. See entry under *Festivals* on page 290.

Hackney Empire

291 Mare Street, London E8 1EJ
tel 020-8510 4500 *fax* 020-8510 4530
email susie.mckenna@hackneyempire.co.uk
website www.hackneyempire.co.uk
CEO Claire Middleton *Creative Director/Pantomime Director* Susie Mckenna

Production details: Grade II listed Frank Matcham theatre built in 1901. Recently renovated and refurbished. Provides a wide range of productions for the local community and London as a whole. Seating capacity is up to 1,280. Produces an immensely popular and critically acclaimed traditional pantomime, eschewing 'celebrities' in favour of the core elements of traditional pantomime: a well-conceived narrative line, spectacular sets and costumes, magical spectacle, music, dance and slapstick comedy. Offers TMA/Equity-approved contracts.

Casting procedures: Casting breakdowns are not publically available, but actors wishing to audition for the pantomime should contact Susie Mckenna, by post or email, in August/September. Happy to receive appropriate showreels and invitations to view individual actors' websites. Actively encourages applications from disabled actors and promotes the use of inclusive casting.

Kenneth More Theatre

Oakfield Road, Ilford, Essex IG1 1BT
tel 020-8553 4464 *fax* 020-8553 5476
email kmtheatre@aol.com
website www.kmtheatre.co.uk
General Manager and Artistic Director Steven Day

Production details: Seating capacity 358. The programme consists of visiting professional shows, the professional in-house panto production, and community theatre groups.

Casting procedures: Actors applying should have song and dance or previous experience. Submissions from ethnic minorities particularly welcome. Will consider invitations to see actors in other productions. Has employed disabled performers but the theatre building has a number of accessibility issues for disabled actors. "We will always consider young local performers."

macrobert

University of Stirling, Stirling FK9 4LA
tel (01786) 467155 *fax* (01786) 466600
email info@macrobert.org
website www.macrobert.org
Artistic Director & Chief Executive Liam Sinclair

Production details: A busy multi-venue arts centre seating 472, with particular emphasis on work with and for young people. Produces several professional shows per year, in November and December. Offers Equity-approved contracts as negotiated through TMA. Subscribes to the Equity Pension Scheme.

Casting procedures: Uses freelance and in-house casting directors; actors may write in April and May to request inclusion. Welcomes letters (with CVs and photographs) from individual actors previously unknown to the company, sent by post or by email. Accepts showreels and invitations to visit other productions. Rarely (or never) has the opportunity to cast disabled actors.

Millfield Theatre

Silver Street, Edmonton, London N18 1PJ
tel 020-8887 7301
website www.millfieldtheatre.co.uk
Arts Centre Manager and Producer Ralph Dartford

Production details: Produces panto in house. Has been a receiving theatre but is now starting to co-produce a couple of productions each year with partners such as Face Front Inclusive Theatre (**www.facefront.org**).

Casting procedures: Casting is done by liaising with show director and in-house producer. Breakdowns for the panto are sent out to agents via Spotlight Link. Contracts offered are negotiated directly with actors or their agents. Actors can write in May to request an audition for the panto, addressing their submission to Ralph Dartford. At present only welcomes submissions (with CVs and photographs) from actors previously unknown to the company at the time of casting the panto (May). As co-productions are still relatively new to the theatre, is considering developing the website to include a casting page. Will only view showreels if they have been requested. Welcomes invitations to see actors in other productions in the Greater London area. Will consider invitations to shows at The Edinburgh Festival. Encourages applications from disabled actors and promotes the use of inclusive casting.

Theatre Royal, Bury St Edmunds

Westgate Street, Bury St Edmunds, Suffolk IP33 1QR
email sharron.stowe@theatreroyal.org
website www.theatreroyal.org
Creative Producer Emily Slack

Production details: Seating capacity 358. Built in 1819, the theatre is the only surviving Regency theatre in the country. Produces an annual pantomime at Christmas and 2 other shows a year – a rural tour in the spring and an in-house production in the autumn, often from or about the Regency period. Offers non-Equity contracts.

Casting procedures: Casting breakdowns are published via Spotlight only. Actors wishing to be considered for the pantomime should write to the theatre in August. (The spring and autumn shows are cast in January/February and June/July respectively.) Only welcomes letters and emails (with CVs and photographs) from actors previously unknown to the company during these casting periods. Does not welcome showreels, but is happy to receive performance notices. Rarely or never has the opportunity to cast disabled actors.

Theatre Royal, Margate

Addington Street, Margate, Kent CT9 1PW
tel (01843) 292795 (Box Office)
and (01843) 296111 (Admin)
email pam.hardiman@yourleisure.uk.com
website www.theatreroyalmargate.com
Programme Manager Pam Hardiman

Production details: Seating capacity 465. A grade 2 star listed Georgian Theatre in the heart of Margate town presenting a year-round programme of mixed incoming professional and locally produced community work. Thriving youth theatre and strong relationships with local arts organisations and associate companies. Owned by Thanet District Council, managed by Your Leisure.

Theatre Royal, Norwich

Theatre Street, Norwich NR2 1RL
tel (01603) 598500 *fax* (01603) 598501
email j.walsh@theatreroyalnorwich.co.uk
website www.theatreroyalnorwich.co.uk
Programming Manager Jane Walsh

Seating capacity 1300. Produces an annual pantomime and is a receiving house for the rest of the year, so very little scope on casting. Actors wishing to audition for the pantomime should contact Jane Walsh **j.walsh@theatreroyalnorwich.co.uk** from March/April. Welcomes emails (with CVs and photographs) from actors not previously known to the company. Does not welcome showreels or performance notices. Will consider applications from disabled actors on the same basis as for non-disabled actors.

Theatre Royal, Nottingham

Theatre Square, Nottingham NG1 5ND
tel 0115-989 5500 *fax* 0115-950 3476
email enquiry@royalcentre-nottingham.co.uk
website www.royalcentre-nottingham.co.uk
Managing Director Mr Robert Sanderson

Production details: Seating capacity 1186. Pantomimes are produced by Qdos Entertainment; those produced in house are by its education-based Royal Company, which includes members of the community. Offers actors Equity-approved contracts but does not subscribe to the Equity Pension Scheme.

Casting procedures: Casts in house. Actors wishing to request an audition should contact Jimmy Ashworth in April/May. Casting breakdowns are not publicly available. Welcomes letters and emails (with CVs and photographs) from actors previously unknown to the company. Happy to receive appropriate showreels and performance notices. Actively encourages applications from disabled actors and promotes the use of inclusive casting.

Theatre Royal, Winchester

Jewry Street, Winchester, Hampshire SO23 8SB
tel (01962) 844600 *fax* (01962) 810277
website www.theatreroyalwinchester.co.uk
Director Mark Courtice

Production details: Seating capacity 400. A receiving theatre which presents a wide range of work, from stand-up comedy to children's theatre and including music, dance and classic plays. The theatre was re-opened in 2001 following a major refurbishment. Produces panto in house.

Casting procedures: Casting is done by the director of the show. Breakdowns are available publicly in mid June.

The art and craft of pantomime

Iain Lauchlan

Pantomime in the UK has naturally evolved; it has been altered enormously by many generations of performers and producers over the years – from its roots in Commedia dell'arte, which came to this country in the 17th century, to the modern panto we know and love today.

If you are a young actor trying to make your way in the business and you believe that panto is not for you (or indeed think it beneath you), then I suggest you look again at this very popular form of entertainment. I say this because when you get to know pantomime as an art form and become familiar with its challenges and traditions, I'm sure you will find a type of panto that will suit you as a performer.

In my experience, there are three main types of panto on offer in this country: the large-scale commercial panto; the 'rock and roll' panto; and the small- to mid-scale family panto.

Large-scale commercial pantomimes

These tend to be staged in 1000-seat-plus theatres by large commercial producers who use TV personalities to front them. They are more like large-scale light entertainment shows, which rely on a 'name' to sell tickets up front and then shoe-horn the celebrity's persona into the story.

Commercial pantomimes are very popular, but quality can range from poor to spectacular because the show is totally dependent on its star being able to do the job of playing the lead character – and it has to be said that some personalities are just not up to the 'live' challenge. The story also tends to be very thin and the supporting characters, who are normally played by jobbing actors, have a tough job driving the narrative because the shows tend to revolve around the personalities and speciality acts that are hired for their quirky entertainment value.

That said, whilst the quality of these shows tends to vary, there are several around the country that give the audience a really good, glitzy night out.

'Rock and roll' pantomime

These shows tend to be mid-scale and, as the name suggests, have a strong rock and roll element. They rely on actor musicians who can play the characters required for panto but also play an instrument. Although such pantos are often very entertaining and the rock and roll music uplifting, the characters and story tend to suffer a little: this is because all pantomime has three main elements which are equally important – music, story and routines. With music being such a key element in a rock and roll panto, the story may be altered and trimmed to fit more songs in, and the number of routines cut down to accommodate them.

The other issue with this style of panto is that scenery and props tend to be cut back, as there always has to be room for the drum kit or piano and guitars. This means fewer scene changes and does lead to a poorer visual experience. It also feels odd, to me, that the Dame or fairy, for example, suddenly picks up a saxophone or guitar to play for another character.

Traditional family panto

The third type of panto is the small- to mid-scale traditional family show, which is often performed in mid-scale theatres or community halls around the country. This is the model

I prefer, and I am responsible for 11 such pantos every season. For an actor, this type of pantomime offers the best opportunity to use a combination of storytelling, musical and comedy skills.

Some family pantos do use personalities, but because of limited budgets these tend to be jobbing actors who have made a name for themselves on TV or radio and are therefore able to play a story character – rather than diluting the narrative by over-using their TV persona.

The main elements you need in order to create a traditional family panto are:

1. **A strong story** – the foundation on which the entire panto is based. This strong narrative will serve the show well, as it provides a solid framework on which to hang the comedy routines, special effects and characters. It also offers something tangible that the audience members, young and old, can hold onto and follow while the fun and controlled anarchy unfolds onstage.
2. **A good cast.** The lead characters – whether they are Jack, Aladdin, Cinderella, Carabosse or Abanazar – must deliver the story whilst remaining clear, strong and rounded. Good three-dimensional characters will drive the narrative and allow the comedy personalities, like the Dame, Simple Simon, the squire or the baddie sidekick, to weave around the story and have the freedom to play the comedy.
3. **Great comedy routines.** Many traditional panto routines have been tried and tested over the years; some are rather dated and some a bit wordy, but all can be adjusted for today's audiences. The important ingredients of good comedy routines are slickness, clarity, surprise and good contact with the audience. The mirror routine, the wallpapering routine, the mop, or the busy bee can all be inserted into a pantomime to enhance the story.
4. **The music.** I am a great believer in a mix of covers and original songs written specially for the show. Audiences do like to know the songs, or at least to have heard them before; covers fulfil this need, but often fail to push the story on and develop it. Songs may be inserted because of their popularity but then have to be forced into the narrative, which may grind to a halt while the song is sung. If covers are used then they must be chosen wisely.

   Character songs written specially for the show may not be known by the audience, which can be a negative, but they are perfect for the moment and enhance the plot and punctuate the story. I like to give the baddies their own specially written song, if possible, so that they can use it to further build on their character and share their evil plans with the audience.

   The most difficult song to find is the panto opener. This needs to be an upbeat chorus number that sets the scene and opens the show with a huge burst of energy. It is really difficult to find a cover that will serve this function well, but equally it is one of the most difficult to write as often a new song will not have the impact of a well-known standard.
5. **Finally, the characters.** It is essential that these tell the story, fulfil the expectation of the audience and connect with them to sell the comedy and narrative.

In a traditional panto the Dame is key to both the plot and the comedy. 'She' is often a downtrodden mother who is doing her best against all the odds, and is played by a man in a frock. The Dame is completely different from an ugly sister; she is a good character and must be warm with a matronly quality. This character has to play off the Simple Simon character, who tends to be her youngest son and is a little slow but endearing and vulnerable. These two characters carry the bulk of the comedy routines, whilst Simple Simon has to be our link to the younger element in the audience.

The principal 'boy' or the hero should be played by a tall and shapely young woman who has a boyish quality and inner strength onstage. 'He' will have to drive the narrative through, whilst the comedy characters around him are causing chaos (albeit controlled and rehearsed chaos). It is traditional that this character will fall in love with the princess or principal girl, and will probably sing a ballad with her at some point in the show.

The panto baddie is essential to the story and is often set against the good fairy. This 'good versus bad' is another key element of panto and must be explored as the story develops. There are many different panto baddies; most of them male. Abanazar from Aladdin is the most evil of them all, followed closely by Carabosse, the evil fairy in Sleeping Beauty, and the wicked Queen in Snow White. There are also comedy baddies such as King Rat from Dick Whittington, the Demon King from Mother Goose, and the ugly sisters from Cinderella.

The good fairy can be played in many different ways, from straight traditional fairy to quirky fruit fairy or the 'cockney sparra' from Dick Whittington. She is always good and always on the side of the Dame, the principal boy and Simple Simon characters.

What does it take to succeed in pantomime?

Whatever part you may be asked to play in a panto, it should be an exhausting and uplifting experience, as it requires commitment, courage, skill and warmth to satisfy the many hundreds of thousands of audience members who pitch up to see a panto each year, expecting to be thoroughly entertained by one of our most loved and supported entertainment genres.

It's your choice: large-scale, glitzy, commercial panto with limited rehearsals but larger budgets? Rock and roll panto that will challenge your musical and acting skills? Or traditional mid-scale panto that tells a strong story and relies on tried-and-tested comedy routines? Whichever you may choose, make sure at the auditions that you are prepared to move and learn a short dance routine, and have a well-rehearsed song that shows off your voice. Do not learn one the night before! And remember, if you are asked to read for a part, that panto is a broad, larger-than-life genre of theatre which relies on audience contact. Make your performance big but light, and forge a connection with your audience.

Always keep in mind the 'three Cs': Clarity, Comedy and Contact.

Iain Lauchlan has been involved with children's television since 1980, when he became a presenter on *Playschool* for the following eight years. During this time he also presented *Fingermouse* and a selection of children's radio programmes. Iain later became the Producer of three of the daily *Playdays* programmes – *Why Bird Stop, Roundabout Stop*, and *Poppy Stop* – and has also run his own TV production company, which created children's programmes such as *The Tweenies, Boo, BB3B* and latterly *Jim Jam and Sunny*. During most of this time he has tried to keep his acting career going, and is now Creative Director for Imagine Theatre, producing 11 pantos each year and performing in one as the Dame.

English-language European theatre companies

This small section seems to be populated by companies set up by enthusiasts who have kept on going with very little subsidy – and sometimes with none at all. Although living away from home and isolated from auditions, it can be fun working for such companies. It is important to note that the work often involves educational projects and/or touring.

Dear Conjunction Theatre Company

6 Rue Arthur Rozier, 75019 Paris
tel (33) 1 4241 6965
email dearconjunction@wanadoo.fr
website www.dearconjunction-paris-theatre.com
Artistic Directors Leslie Clack, Patricia Kessler

Production details: Founded in 1991, this bilingual company is composed of professional actors, directors and writers who are resident in Paris and who present productions in both French and English. Past productions include: Pinter's *Ashes to Ashes* and *The Hothouse*; and *Someone Who'll Watch Over Me* by Frank McGuinness.

Casting procedures: Welcomes letters and emails (with CVs and photographs) from actors previously unknown to the company. Contact Leslie Clack for more information.

English Theatre Frankfurt

Kaiserstrasse 34, D-60329 Frankfurt
tel (49) 69 242 31615 *fax* (49) 69 242 31614
email mail@english-theatre.org
website www.english-theatre.org
Artistic and Executive Director Daniel John Nicolai

Production details: Founded in 1979. Presents contemporary plays, musicals and classics. 5 productions performed in the main house each year, totalling 260 performances.

Casting procedures: Uses London-based freelance casting directors. Does not hold general auditions. Actors should write in April to request inclusion. Casting breakdowns are only available via Spotlight.

The English Theatre of Hamburg

Lerchenfeld 14, 22081 Hamburg
tel (49) 40 227 7089 *fax* (49) 40 229 5040
email ethamburg@onlinehome.de
website www.englishtheatre.de
Contacts Robert Rumpf, Clifford Dean

Production details: Founded in 1976 by 2 Americans, Robert Rumpf and Clifford Dean, who originally trained and worked professionally in the USA. They share general management responsibilities, plan the artistic programme and direct productions. They hire a guest director for 1 production each year. Since 1981 the theatre has occupied its present premises at Mundsburg, 22081 Hamburg. Performs 8 times per week from September to June. A typical season at the English Theatre includes a classic American or British drama, a comedy and thriller or modern classic. Recent productions include: *Rose's Dilemma*, *Mrs Warren's Profession*, *The Importance of Being Earnest*, and *Reasons to be Pretty*. Also runs Education programmes.

Independent English Theatre Associazione Culturale

Via dell'Acquedotto Felice 36, 00178 Rome
tel (39) 349 6703331
email director@independentenglishtheatre.com
website www.independentenglishtheatre.com
Artistic Director Sandra Paternostro

Production details: A professional English-speaking theatre company based in Rome. Started producing its own work in 2011, with its first production: *Betrayal* by Harold Pinter.

Casting procedures: Uses in-house casting directors and is always happy to hear from English-speaking actors who have a base in Rome. Casting breakdowns are available via the website. Welcomes CVs and photographs if sent by email; will also accept showreels and invitations to view individual actors' websites if the actors are in Rome.

Light Nights – The Summer Theatre

Baldursgata 37, IS-101 Reykjavik
tel (354) 551 9181 *fax* (354) 551 5015
website www.lightnights.com
Artistic Director Kristín G Magnús

Production details: Runs a summer theatre show at the Idnó Theatre in Reykjavik. Previous productions have included: *Light Nights* and *On The Way to Heaven*.

Casting procedures: Sometimes holds general auditions. The best time to write requesting inclusion is February/March. Casting breakdowns are not publicly available. Welcomes letters (with CVs and photographs) from actors previously unknown to the company, but not via email. Does not welcome showreels, but is happy to receive invitations to view actors' websites. Offers non-Equity contracts; rarely (or never) has the opportunity to cast disabled actors.

London Toast Theatre

Kochsvej 18, DK 1850 Frederiksberg C. Denmark
tel (45) 3322 8686
email mail@londontoast.dk
website www.londontoast.dk
Managing Director Søren Hall

Production details: Founded in 1982. The largest English-speaking theatre company in Northern Europe. Presents theatre productions and provides corporate entertainment, stand-up comedy and Murder Mystery shows in Scandinavia and abroad. The company's voice-over bureau, 'Speaker's Corner', provides English and American voices for films and commercials. Recent productions include: *Dracula – A Pain in the Neck!* and *The Importance of Being Earnest.*

Merlin International Theatre

Gerlóczy Utca 4, Budapest 1052
tel 36 (1) 3179338 *fax* 36 (1) 2660904
email info@merlinszinhaz.hu
website www.szinhaz.hu/merlin/english
Director Laszlo Magacs *Associate Director* Emma Vidovsky

Production details: Founded in 1991; Hungary's first and currently its only international theatre. Recent productions include: *The Importance of Being Earnest*, *Don't Drink the Water*, *Stones in His Pockets* and *Twelfth Night.* Resident companies at the Merlin Theatre are the Atlantis Company, Junion Group and Madhouse.

Prague Shakespeare Festival

232/55 Belehradska, Prague 2, 120 00
tel (+420) 603 968 536
email info@pragueshakespeare.org
website www.pragueshakespeare.org
Artistic Director Guy Roberts

Production details: Founded in 2008. The Festival presents professional theatre productions, workshops, classes, lectures and other theatrical events, of the highest quality, conducted primarily in English by a multinational ensemble of professional theatre artists, with an emphasis on the plays of William Shakespeare. Stages 2-3 productions annually, and holds workshops and classes on an ongoing basis. Recent productions include: *As You Like It* and *King Lear* (in rotating repertory performed on the outdoor stage in Vysehrad, Prague, and on tour in Houston, Texas, USA).

Casting procedures: Casts in-house; check the website for annual casting and breakdowns. Welcomes approaches (with CVs and photographs) from actors by post and by email, and accepts showreels and invitations to view individual actors' websites. Actively encourages applications from disabled actors to play characters with disabilities, and promotes the use of inclusive casting.

Simply Theatre

8B Chemin des Couleuvres, 1295 Tannay, Switzerland
tel (41) 22 860 0518
email info@simplytheatre.com
website www.simplytheatre.com
Artistic Director Thomas Grafton

Production details: Founded in 2005. A professional English theatre for Switzerland and Continental Europe; and an English-speaking Drama Academy. Predominantly stages family-orientated theatre and shows for children.

Casting procedures: Holds general auditions. Casting breakdowns are available from Spotlight and Casting Call Pro.

Theatre From Oxford

BP 10, F-42750 St Denis de Cabanne, France
tel/fax 0790-544 4495
email fm.oxford@gmail.com
Artistic Director Robert Southam

Production details: Founded in 1984, the main aim for the past 20 years has been to introduce audiences on the continent to the best of theatre in English. The company has toured plays by Shakespeare, Shaw, Wilde, Willy Russell, Tennessee Williams and Arthur Miller, among others. Touring for 3 months from September to Christmas in 7 European countries, the company plays in anything from the best theatres to school gyms – but nearly always to full houses. Tours again in the spring to many of the same venues, providing theatre workshops. Half of the spectators are students; the other half, adult theatregoers. The company is shortly to have its own theatre in France.

Casting procedures: Actors are advised that the tours are enjoyable but demanding, and that the company seldom accepts anyone straight from drama school. Casts often include actors with RSC and RNT experience. Recently has been working with African, Asian and Latin American actors and writers, which has meant less work for British and American actors. Casting breakdowns are available by postal application (with sae) and actors are welcome to write letters or emails with their CVs and photographs. Showreels, however, are not welcomed. Offers non-Equity contracts. Will consider applications from disabled actors to play characters with disabilities.

Vienna's English Theatre

UK address: VM Theatre Productions Ltd,
16 The Street, Ash, Canterbury CT3 2HJ
tel (01304) 813330 *fax* (01304) 813330

email vanessa@vmtheatre.demon.co.uk
Theatre address: Josefsgasse 12, A-1080 Vienna
tel (0043) 1 402 1260 26 *fax* (0043) 1 405 4121 261
website www.englishtheatre.at

Production details: Founded in 1963; the oldest English-language theatre in continental Europe. Stages 5 shows each year in the main house and sends 6 Theatre-in-Education tours around the schools of Austria. The season runs from September to July each year.

Casting procedures: Casting breakdowns are occasionally posted on the website and actors may email the UK address above with their CV and photograph at anytime. Showreels are not accepted. "Contracts are especially written for us by Equity."

White Horse Theatre

Boerdenstrasse 17, 59494 Soest, Germany
tel (49) 2921 339339 *fax* (49) 2921 339336
email theatre@white-horse-theatre.eu
website www.white-horse-theatre.eu
Artistic Directors Peter Griffith and Michael Dray

Production details: Founded in 1978. Tours schools in Germany with occasional visits to neighbouring countries and to Japan and China. Contracts are for 10-11 months. 9 companies of 4 actors each perform 3 plays. Recent productions include: *The Glass Menagerie*, *Oliver Twist*, *Hamlet*, *Twelfth Night* and numerous plays for 14-16 year-olds, for 10-13 year-olds, and for primary school pupils.

Casting procedures: Does not use freelance casting directors. Holds general auditions; actors should write in April requesting inclusion. Casting breakdowns are available through the website, email application, Equity Job Information Service, CCP and *The Stage*. Welcomes postal and email enquiries from actors previously unknown to the company. Invitations to view individual actors' websites are also accepted. Contracts are approved by GDBA (the German equivalent of Equity). Rarely has the opportunity to cast disabled actors since "all our actors must take part in 3 different plays, and they must also cope with the rigours of touring".

A touring actor's survival guide

Maev Alexander

Touring is more tiring, harder work, more all-consuming and more relentless than playing in one house. In order to give your best to it and get the best from it, you need to be thoroughly organised and disciplined. The main differences are, of course, the travelling and the accommodation. If you arrange these well in advance, you're on your way to having a happy and rewarding experience and saving yourself angst and money.

Getting there

At the beginning of rehearsals, or even before, you'll be given a schedule of dates and venues and a sheaf of digs lists. Work out as early as you can how you will travel and where you will stay.

If you have your own transport you can plan your journeys on a week-by-week basis, pulling maps and route finders and estimated journey times off the Internet – if you have access – both to digs and to theatres. A good company manager will supply maps of town centres with the venue clearly marked. A satnav can be reassuring, but don't rely on it in big town centres – we had to hold the curtain for a leading lady in Sheffield when her instructions were impossible to follow in a new road layout, so it's a good idea to keep your map-reading skills honed. It's amazing how they improve when you *have* to find digs and theatres within a tight timeframe.

If you don't have your own transport, ask around the company and find out if anyone lives close enough to you, and is willing, to give you lifts. Make it clear that you will contribute to petrol costs, be punctual and not bring too much luggage. If you are using public transport, book as far in advance as you can: Apex (or the equivalent) on trains and low-budget airlines will save you huge amounts of money. The touring company will expect you to do this, and will calculate the amount they give you in fares as economically as possible. Be aware that fares are worked out from venue to venue, and not to your home and out again. Remember also that you may get stuck on a Saturday night if your show comes down after the last train, which is more likely than not; this may add to your accommodation expenses. It also eats into your only day off; most No. 1 tours play Monday to Saturday, running for a week in each venue.

The rule for fares and touring allowance is: outwith 15 miles of your permanent base to qualify for fares only, and 25 miles to qualify for touring allowance. This is calculated from postcode to postcode – not by the most convenient or quickest route. Equity has negotiated sharp rises in the level of touring allowance over the last few years, and this is now reasonable. It's meant to cover accommodation and living expenses – and if you're frugal and careful, it can. You have to balance the level of comfort and convenience with which you need to live happily with the budget on which you have to do it.

Finding the right digs

Digs lists cover hotels, guesthouses, self-contained flats, houses for sharing, B&Bs and rooms in private houses. They normally tell you the price (per night or per week), the type of accommodation, the facilities, the prohibitions (i.e. no smoking, no pets), the extras (TV, kettle in room) and the distance from the theatre. The headliners can probably afford to stay in hotels (and many hotels do deals for touring actors), but other ranks will have to juggle their priorities. If you can feel comfortable in a room in a private house, sharing a bathroom and having access to a kitchen, you can do so remarkably cheaply. If you can't do without an en suite or need to be self-contained, this will obviously be more expensive, and so on up the scale; but read the list carefully and you will find something that will tick most of your boxes without too much compromise. The people who do the letting are generally friends of the theatre in some way, and the standard of accommodation is usually pretty high. I have heard horror stories of rooms booked in hotels on last-minute websites – all-night disco music and overpowering 'room fragrancers'.

Start ringing the most promising-sounding digs as soon as possible, before everyone else does. Good options are places within a 15-minute walk (obviating cabs or long, lonely walks or parking problems), or a house or cottage that is further out, possibly in countryside, to share with fellow company members, both in terms of rent and transport. Beware of landlady-speak for 'a 15- to 20-minute walk' – some landladies clearly have seven-league boots! The level of rates varies from place to place: locations like Bath and Malvern tend to be more expensive across the board than, say, Southampton and Coventry. In big centres like Glasgow, Manchester, Birmingham and Leeds you will probably have to travel to the outskirts unless you can afford hotels.

When you've agreed terms with a landlord/lady, write to confirm the booking and the dates, and arrange to ring a couple of days in advance of the stay to negotiate a mutually convenient time to arrive (leave half an hour's leeway so you don't panic about getting lost). It's wise to at least drop off your luggage before the show so that you know you know where the place is, have keys and don't disturb anyone at a late hour – especially on the first night when there are likely to be drinks front-of-house afterwards. Sorting out digs gets easier the more you tour and the more contacts you acquire. If you're new to it, do ask experienced tourers – most actors are very generous about sharing the secrets of top digs. For future reference, keep records of where you've stayed and what it was like. Pay up front, and remember to leave keys when you leave; get a receipt and behave well enough for the landlord/lady to wish to stay on the digs list. You represent future tourers.

What to take

It's important to pack well. Travel as light as you can, and have as much of your luggage on wheels as possible. You need enough clothes for a week, or longer if you need to go straight to the next venue; keep it simple, remembering to have something warm and something cool (because this is Britain) and something smart for the first-night drinks often provided by the host management or friends of the theatre. A towelling robe doubles as a dressing gown and post-shower gear. Take comfortable, reasonably weatherproof shoes, since you'll spend a lot of time walking. Remember your phone charger (it's worth having a spare for touring), and a toothbrush charger and adapter in case there are no shaving points. It's also worth having an emergency kit containing plasters and painkillers and cold remedies. In most places towels are provided, but pack a hand towel just in case. Travel with a hottie in winter: the only miserable digs I've had were very smart but *freezing*. I complained – do complain; you're not paying to freeze. A pocket torch is useful for unfamiliar, unlit keyholes. Don't forget comforts like books or a radio or iPod.

If you have to be away from your base for extended periods, negotiate doing your laundry with the wardrobe department. If you're home on Sunday, it saves time and hassle if you've put what needs washing into a separate bag in your case so that repacking is straightforward and quick. I was told early in my career that no proper actor has less than three weeks' worth of underwear!

You can generally transport your make-up and other dressing-room necessities, comforts and amusements in a bag or box on the truck transporting the set and props, etc. This is not an automatic right, though, so check with your company manager. Some reasonably rigid receptacle is optimal to avoid breakage; label it clearly with the name of the production and your own name, and do not expect anyone else to lug it to or from your dressing room week by week. Pack it as soon as you can on Saturday night, and check where you can leave it so it's not in the way of the get-out.

Eating and drinking

It's easy to be lazy about eating sensibly on tour – financially and nutritionally. Even if there are cooking facilities in your digs, it's not always convenient to be there and it's tempting to eat out all the time or grab burgers. You're going to need all your energy, so make a point of eating healthily.

In most theatres you'll have access to a microwave and possibly a fridge: ring the stage door and check. They're often in the crew room, so ask if you may use them and be considerate about clearing up after yourself. Making an interesting dressing-room picnic is a worthy challenge even if everything has to be cold. Supermarkets do better and better ranges of salads and sushi. Invest in a mini kettle for your touring box and pack a plate, a mug and cutlery. Set yourself a daily budget for food and then you'll know if you can splash out on a restaurant meal.

It's also tempting to do a great deal more after-show drinking when you're away from home: it can feel as if you're living in a bubble, out of the real world. Ask yourself if you're getting jaded/broke, and limit alcohol to within sensible limits. (The same sense of not being quite in the real world can lead also to the most unlikely affairs: be discreet, whether it involves other people or yourself.)

Bonding and recreation

After-show company meals, weekly or fortnightly, are good bonding exercises providing you all get on. Remember that it's not only part of your job to get on, but also in your best interests. It's even more important in the living-in-each-others'-pockets world of touring to be a good company member; leave your troubles firmly at the stage door and don't moan or gossip. If there's someone you find tricky, keep out of their way. In my experience, touring companies bond well and form even more of a parallel family than usual.

That said, getting away by yourself for a time is restoring. Find the local Tourist Information Office and find out about places of interest and specialist shopping. There's bound to be something that appeals to you, even if you're not a galleries/museums/castles/cathedrals person (the ABC of touring is famously, "another bloody cathedral"). I am lucky – and not alone – in regarding touring as being paid to go sightseeing. Stage door, or your company manager, can tell you of gym and leisure facilities and often arrange temporary membership; they can also point you in the direction of the nearest supermarkets and best-value restaurants.

Sussing out the theatre

One of the interesting and rewarding things about touring is playing the same show in lots of different theatres – from 900-seaters to 2000-seaters; from raked stages to flat ones;

from Victorian to modern; from those with acres (seemingly) of orchestra pit to those where the front row is looking up your nose. You'll be called early in the first day of each new venue, generally at about 5 or 6pm, to walk the stage, get to know the backstage layout and take note of significant differences. The presence or lack of a rake may mean more or fewer steps on a staircase, for instance; furniture may be closer together or further apart; wing space may be tight; prop tables may be in different places; dressing rooms will be varying distances away and you may be sharing in one venue and by yourself in another. Take time to absorb these differences, test the acoustic and plan how you're going to accommodate any changes you personally will have to make. Discuss these changes too with anyone else they may affect. Bear in mind that the audiences are always different, as well: it's amazing that what makes people laugh or weep in Cardiff is not the same as what makes people laugh or weep in Hull.

Find out when stage door opens; most theatres allow you access to your dressing room from quite early in the day, which is useful for dumping shopping or 'nesting' when it's tipping with rain. A few don't open until much later, though, which is a great bore and makes it good to have digs close by.

Money matters

On a business level, keep a work diary and note down all your expenses (and mileages if you're driving). Have an envelope or plastic wallet in which to file all your receipts and payslips: it's easy to lose track of these when you're away from home.

Tax offices vary in what they will allow you to claim on tour. Travel and accommodation expenses above your allowances are OK, but some accept claims for all eating expenses (again over and above), some for restaurant/cafe receipts only, and some – including my own – clearly expect you not to eat at all.

Research a mobile phone tariff that will let you keep in touch with family and friends, and your agent, as cheaply as possible.

Finally ...

More and more of the available work involves touring at some level. You might just as well maximise your chances of having a good time and making a decent profit. Regard it as an adventure.

Maev Alexander trained at the Royal Scottish Academy of Music and Drama and has been working in theatre, television and radio for 40 years. She has performed in Rep all over the country, playing everything from Cleopatra to a French poodle, been a member of the RSC, and holds the record as the longest-serving Mollie in *The Mousetrap*. She has starred in two TV series and guested in many others, presented the Newsdesk on *That's Life*, and played in dozens of radio dramas. After completing her 7th No. 1 tour in as many years, and transferring the last but one – *A Man for All Seasons* – to the Theatre Royal Haymarket in 2006, she has filmed *Death Defying Acts* with Catherine Zeta Jones and Guy Pearce, and recorded the second series of *The Eliza Stories* for BBC Radio 4.

Editors' note There are a number of websites that can help you plan your journeys to and from the locations on your tour; they may also save you money. Here are some of the major ones:

• *Maps*: **www.streetmap.co.uk**, **www.multimap.com**, and **maps.google.co.uk**. If you have a mobile phone capable of web browsing, point it to **www.google.co.uk/mmp** to access Google Maps for Mobile. Rather cleverly, if you tell it where you are, it can even give you directions to all the nearest pubs. (If you're going to be using this a lot, check how much

Internet access you have on your call plan. Google does not charge you for the service, but you may find yourself with some hefty Internet usage bills if you're not careful.)

• *Driving*: **www.theaa.com** and **www.rac.co.uk** both offer route-planning and maps, as do Google Maps and Google Maps for Mobile (see above).

• *Trains*: **www.nationalrail.co.uk** for timetables and **www.thetrainline.com** for booking the cheapest tickets available. Also worth looking at **www.megatrain.com** to check for promotional fares. In addition to these, **www.traveline.org.uk** is a good way of exploring options (train, coach, plane, etc.) for getting to a location. And of course, the number that the 118 companies get the most requests for: National Rail Enquiries is **08457 48 49 50**; if it's not in your phone already, why not put it there now?

• *Coaches*: **www.nationalexpress.co.uk**, **www.citylink.co.uk** (Scotland), **www.megabus.com/uk** (which often has promotional fares), and **www.eurolines.com** (destinations around Europe). In addition there are some local companies offering low-cost services to major cities such as London, which a little research should uncover.

• *London Transport*: **journeyplanner.tfl.gov.uk** or, from your mobile, text 60835 (60TFL) with 'a to b' (where 'a' and 'b' are stations, stops or postcodes in London) to find out the best way – tube, train or bus – of getting to where you're going. For example: 'Clapham Junction to The Old Vic'. Common sense and some knowledge of the geography of London may need to be applied to the directions given: in this example the text service recommends a bus journey from Waterloo Station to The Old Vic – a walk of three minutes at most.

• *Flying*: **www.travelsupermarket.com** or **www.skyscanner.net** will search out all available flights to a given destination, sorted by price.

'Vanning it': the golden rules

Andrew Piper

Maev Alexander's article covers pretty much all you need to know about large-scale touring, and many of these principles carry over into small-scale touring too. However, the major difference between the two levels of touring is ... The Van.

On a large-scale (or No. 1) tour you are generally responsible for getting to the venue yourself, since these are often in large towns with good transport links. By contrast, much of the work of mid- and small-scale companies is done in venues rather more 'off the beaten track' (a.k.a. The Middle of Nowhere), and often with only one performance in each venue. Most of these companies will transport their actors around the country in a mini-bus, coach or van, which may also contain the set and lighting rig. Whereas the large-scale companies employ stage crew to do the get-ins and get-outs, on such productions it's often the actors and the stage manager who do everything.

'Vanning it' presents an additional set of challenges for the actor. If you don't get on with a fellow actor in a large-scale show, then you may be able to limit the amount of contact you have with them, other than your interaction on stage. If you're on a small-scale tour you will spend most of your waking hours in their company, so it's important that all company members work hard to keep a harmonious atmosphere. Van etiquette is similar to dressing-room etiquette – balancing your needs with the cast's collective needs, and the individual needs of cast members. You can never legislate for a happy company, but here are some of the 'Golden Rules' that will help enormously in that direction:

- *Pull your weight.* This kind of touring is very hard work – you may be travelling, doing a get-in, a show, and a get-out every day for several weeks or months, and slacking off is the one thing guaranteed to make you as popular as herpes. Don't dawdle in the get-out, either; being the cause of not getting to the pub in time for last orders will also not endear you to your colleagues.
- *Be punctual.* The call time is when the van *leaves*, not the time you start to leave your accommodation. Be sitting in your seat, bag stowed, ready to leave at least 5 minutes before the call time. As with almost anything in this business, you're wasting several people's time by keeping them waiting, so respect your fellow actors by being on time.
- *Music.* Bring a personal stereo or MP3 player; don't expect everyone in the van to like your taste in music. One stage manager I know resorted to telling the cast that the stereo had broken rather than sit through yet another argument about whose music to listen to. You might also want to consider a portable DVD player, either for the journeys (unless you're susceptible to travel sickness) or for something to do when you get to your accommodation. Check whether these would be covered by the company's insurance in case anything happened to them, and remember that very few pieces of electronic equipment are built to withstand the rigours of touring.
- *Mobile phones.* Keep conversations short, even (perhaps especially) with loved ones. There are few more irritating things to be forced to listen to than someone cooing to their lover for hours on end. If you're someone who gets a lot of calls, consider setting your phone to silent vibrate; there are only so many times one can listen to the Nokia tune before being overwhelmed by the urge to throw the offending phone out of the window.

• *Smoking. Never* smoke in the van, even if the windows are rolled down – it's inconsiderate, and most companies operate a no-smoking policy anyway. (Since the van is considered your workplace, it will also be covered by recent anti-smoking legislation.) Remember, too, that if you're puffing away seconds before climbing aboard then you will carry a strong smell of smoke with you into the van. Be considerate, too, about smelly food – curry, chips, fish, etc. – unless you're all tucking in.

• *Personal hygiene.* Important at all times in this business, but especially so when you're stuck in a confined space with the rest of the cast for what may be hours at a time, perhaps after a particularly physical show and/or get-out. Your fellow actors may be upfront enough to tell you if you're pongy – but don't rely on it. If someone else in the company is niffing, don't gossip behind their back: just tell them, in as direct and as kind a way as possible. Don't let it fester (in more senses than one!).

• *Games.* It's worth bringing a few travel games for when the conversation runs out, even if it's just a pack of playing cards – although not everyone will want to play at any given moment. A good book can help while away the time, although not everyone can read in a van without getting travelsick.

• *Sweets.* The 'tub of love'. It does wonders for morale if someone takes it upon themself to buy a big tub of sweets for the van.

• *Alcohol.* Check the company's policy. If it's permitted, then it's probably best that you either buy your own (sharing around if you desire) or join up with one or two other members of the cast. It's generally preferable not to have a kitty for the whole cast, because not everyone will want to drink the same stuff or the same quantities. If you are getting merry in the back of a van, be considerate to the driver: don't distract them (dangerous!) or be unreasonably raucous. S/he will have had a hard evening too, and tunelessly drunken renditions of football chants will hardly make the journey more pleasant. Remember that requests for toilet stops when everyone's tired and wants to get home may not be popular.

• *Make the most of solo time.* When you do get some time to yourself, make the most of it. Go for a walk, listen to music, read, exercise, meditate, call friends or just sit in a coffee shop and watch the world go by. Camaraderie and team spirit are important in this kind of work, but don't be afraid to take time for yourself when you need it.

• *Plan your meals.* You may be performing in some village hall miles from the nearest source of food, so be prepared. Sometimes – in village halls, especially – sandwiches are provided by the locals, but not always, so stock up before heading off for the day's performance, and keep an emergency supply of biscuits/fruit/pot noodles in your bag just in case. Make the most of the hotel or B&B breakfast.

• *Travel light.* Remember that you will be probably be checking into several different hotels or B&Bs a week, so only take with you what you can comfortably carry by yourself in one go. For ease of access when you want to find that one pair of socks or pants, wheeled suitcases or large hold-alls are preferable to rucksacks. While you may want to have more stuff back at your base, when you're on the road stick to one large bag and a day bag.

• *Finally, keep a sense of humour and a sense of perspective.* Not always the easiest thing to do on some jobs, but you're all in this together so have a good laugh at the absurdity of it all – it may just save your sanity.

Andrew Piper trained at Bristol Old Vic Theatre School. This piece was written in the van belonging to Northumberland Theatre Company (NTC) while he was playing Herbert Pocket, Uncle Pumblechook and Orlick in their production of *Great Expectations*.

Fringe theatres

Essentially, the idea of 'fringe theatre' began at the Edinburgh Festival more than half a century ago. It really started taking off (especially in London) in the late 1960s as an arena for 'alternative' and 'experimental' theatre. The 1990s saw a huge expansion in the number of venues being used, and a downturn in the exploration of theatre forms: the 'fringe' became more commercial and much more competitive – and not just in London and Edinburgh. Today, the terms 'alternative' and 'experimental' are far less frequently used, and the Fringe is now largely seen as a way for actors, directors and writers to showcase their work.

Casting for Fringe productions is usually advertised by one or more of the casting information services, and agents and casting directors do scout for new talent in them. However, it's highly unlikely that you will make any money from participating in such a production – you might end up with a net loss after deducting your expenses. Also agents and casting directors get blitzed with so many invitations that the chances of getting one of them to see you are not high. The only reasons for being in a Fringe production are (a) you might be 'seen'; (b) you fundamentally believe in the production's potential; and (c) it could help keep your acting-juices flowing. But you might find classes less time-consuming and possibly more beneficial.

The Edinburgh Fringe Festival

There is a real sense that every actor should try this 'Carnival of theatre' experience – 'the biggest theatrical lottery in the world' – at least once. You'll meet lots of new people, make contacts and it's a great few weeks, even if your own production doesn't hit the heights.

Good advice on mounting a production on the Edinburgh Fringe is available from the Festival Office (details below).

The listings that follow are restricted to the more 'established' venues, with performance spaces for hire. Some Fringe theatres only programme in work known to them.

Note If you are thinking of mounting a Fringe production and/or starting your own theatre company, start researching and planning well in advance. It is well worth consulting the Independent Theatre Council (ITC) – **www.itc-arts.org**.

UMBRELLA ORGANISATIONS

Edinburgh Festival Fringe

The Fringe Office, 180 High Street,
Edinburgh EH1 1QS
tel 0131-226 0026 *fax* 0131-226 0016
email admin@edfringe.com
website www.edfringe.com

The Edinburgh Fringe Festival started in 1947 and the Fringe Society was formed in 1959 to coordinate publicity and ticket sales, and offer a comprehensive information service both to performers and to audiences. It compiles information about venues, press and suppliers, and produces a series of publications designed to answer frequently asked questions. Its brochure contains details for Fringe venues and shows in Edinburgh. The office is open all year round and the staff are available to help by phone, email or personal appointment.

OffWestEnd.com

19 Eugene Cotter House, Beckway Street,
London SE17 1QS
website www.offwestend.com

A London UK theatre information and bookings site that makes it easy to find plays and performances in over 100 of London's innovative theatres outside the West End. Tickets are sold directly from these Off West End theatres, with no fees and no commission being charged.

Society of Independent Theatres (SIT)

website www.sitgb.org

The Society of Independent Theatres (SIT) is a recently established alliance of small independent theatres in London. "We welcome contact from all venue owners, venue managers and artistic directors of independent theatres. Although we are currently looking for members in London, we will eventually widen our catchment area to the rest of Great Britain and Northern Ireland. Our objectives are as follows:

• To raise the profile of small/independent/fringe/pub style venues within the theatre industry and with the general public.
• To encourage the development of the performing arts within independent venues.
• To exchange information on theatre companies and suppliers.
• To exchange ideas and proposals for marketing, promotion and audience development.
• To provide a better understanding of employment laws relevant to our sector of the industry.
• To liaise with Equity and other organisations over issues affecting our industry.

LONDON FRINGE VENUES

The Albany

Douglas Way, Deptford, London SE8 4AG
tel 020-8692 4446 *fax* 020-8469 2253
email boxoffice@thealbany.org.uk
website www.thealbany.org.uk
Chief Executive Gavin Barlow

Production details: A multi-use digital arts centre programming music, spoken word, dance, comedy and family shows. The Albany is an artistic and community resource with a fully equipped theatre space, studio theatre, café and rehearsal and meeting rooms for hire. Has a strong commitment to working collaboratively with the diverse communities of London and encouraging participation, especially by young people and disabled communities, in the arts. As well as programming performances, the centre provides seasonal participation programmes working with young people and is a social hub and facilitator for partnership working.

Seats 300 (500 standing); 2 secondary spaces seat 60 or 70. Performances also take place in the café – capacity 80. All spaces have fully configurable seating; there is also seating on the balcony. Shows usually run from 1 night to 2 weeks. Hire rates may be subsidised depending on community or charity status – see website for rates of different spaces. There is disabled access. Recent productions include: *Lipsticks and Lollipops* by Deafinitely Theatre; *A Warwickshire Testimony* by April de Angelis (Mountview Theatre School); and transfer from the Royal Court of *Gone Too Far!* by Olivier Award-winner Bola Agbaje.

Casting procedures: Does not produce in-house shows.

artsdepot

5 Nether Street, North Finchley, London N12 0GA
tel 020-8369 5455
email info@artsdepot.co.uk
website www.artsdepot.co.uk

The only professional arts venue in the London Borough of Barnet. Committed to providing a diverse range of high-quality visual and performance arts for everyone. artsdepot has brand new, state-of-the-art facilities in the form of the large Pentland Theatre, smaller Studio Theatre and Education Spaces, for the provision of drama, dance and visual arts, and a gallery, as well as an excellent café and bars.

Barons Court Theatre

The Curtain's Up, 28A Comeragh Rd,
West Kensington, London W14 9HR
tel 020-8932 4747
email londontheatre@gmail.com
Artistic Director Ron Phillips

A central London 62-seat theatre in the basement of the Curtain's Up public house and restaurant. Offers 1- to 5-week runs and can be booked up to 12 months in advance at a moderate rental. Also available for 1-day actors' showcases.

Battersea Arts Centre

Lavender Hill, London SW11 5TN
tel 020-7223 2223
email theaj@bac.org.uk
website www.bac.org.uk
Artistic Director David Jubb

Battersea Arts Centre's (BAC) mission is to inspire people to take creative risks to shape the future. Each year the organisation works with over 400 artists to develop new forms of theatre and connect with audiences and participants. The emphasis is on devised rather than script-based work. BAC is the original home and foremost pioneer of Scratch, a model that has transformed the way in which people make and experience theatre. Scratch is a shared space in which ideas are exchanged between artists and audiences as a way to develop the work. Finished shows are then performed throughout the building and often go on to stages across London, the UK and the world.

Work is rarely programmed on the strength of a proposal alone, and unsolicited scripts are not accepted. Instead they prefer to build up a relationship with artists over time. Typically, one of the producers might see a show or workshop by a company at another venue and then start a conversation. BAC welcomes enquiries and ask that they are told about any proposed project in good detail and why you are interested in the Centre. Performance notices are also welcome. Producers meet every week to go through all invitations and expressions of interest.

For more information visit **bac.org.uk/howweprogramme**. Contact Thea Jones (Project

Coordinator & Senior Assistant to the Artistic Director) with programming enquiries at (**theaj@bac.org.uk**).

Blue Elephant Theatre

59A Bethwin Road, Camberwell, London SE5 0XT
tel 020-7701 0100
email info@blueelephanttheatre.co.uk
website www.blueelephanttheatre.co.uk
Artistic Director Jasmine Cullingford

The only theatre in Camberwell. A vibrant arts venue aiming to nurture new and emerging artists across the performing arts. Promotes cross-artform work and all types of theatre, from physical and dance to new writing and classics.

Co-produces all shows and is particularly interested in supporting new and emerging London-based artists across the perfoming arts with work that complements the black-box performance space. Those interested in bringing a project to the Blue Elephant should submit a written proposal with suggested dates and a full background to Jasmine Cullingford.

The Bridewell Theatre

Bride Lane, Fleet Street, London EC4Y 8EQ
tel 020-7353 3331
website www.sbf.org.uk

The Bridewell Theatre is a versatile space, which provides both an atmospheric entertainment venue and an unique conference facility in the heart of the City. In addition to a 12x8m performance space, there is a modular tiered seating system that in standard configuration can accommodate a raked audience of 134 people. The theatre also offers dressing rooms with en suite amenities, as well as a box-office/reception area and a fully equipped bar. All areas of the theatre are accessible to disabled users via a lift.

The Broadway Studio Theatre

Catford, London SE6 4RU
tel 020-8314 9472
email martin@broadwaytheatre.org.uk
website www.broadwaytheatre.org.uk
Artistic Director Martin Costello

Originally opened in 1932, the venue is Grade II listed by English Heritage as a beautiful example of 1930s art deco architecture. There are 2 venues: the Main Theatre seats 800, and the Studio Theatre seats 100. "The Broadway Studio Theatre has extremely limited availability; please contact Martin Costello to check availability and prices."

Camden People's Theatre

58-60 Hampstead Road, London NW1 2PY
tel 020-7419 4841
email admin@cptheatre.co.uk
website www.cptheatre.co.uk

A central London space dedicated year round to supporting early-career artists making unconventional theatre. In particular, those whose work explores issues that matter to people now.

Canal Café Theatre

Delamere Terrace, Little Venice, London W2 6ND
tel 020-7289 6056 (Box Office): 020-7289 6054
email mail@canalcafetheatre.com
website www.canalcafetheatre.com

A comedy and new writing 60-seat theatre situated above the Bridge House pub in Little Venice. Home to NewsRevue.

Charing Cross Theatre (formerly New Players Theatre)

The Arches, Villiers Street, London WC2N 6NG
tel 020-7930 5868
website www.charingcrosstheatre.co.uk

The recently renovated New Players Theatre is a valuable addition to the London theatre scene and business community in the heart of the West End. Already a popular and well-known venue within the theatre, music and entertainment industries, the New Players now offers producers the opportunity to present a diverse and eclectic range of productions in an Off-Broadway-style, well-equipped, high-specification theatre, complete with on-site bars and a restaurant. It is also a distinctive setting for screenings, conference and corporate hires.

Chelsea Theatre

World's End Place, King's Road, London SW10 0DR
tel 020-7352 1967 *fax* 020-7352 2024
website www.chelseatheatre.org.uk

A 110-seat theatre which can be booked up to 6 months in advance. Particularly welcomes new writing.

The Cockpit

Gateforth Street, London NW8 8EH
tel 020-7258 2925
email mail@thecockpit.org.uk
website www.thecockpit.org.uk

Theatre seats 240 (60 seats on 4 sides) or 180 (60 seats on 3 sides) and should be booked 6 months in advance. Welcomes classics, foreign-language theatre and other niche market work.

The Courtyard Theatre

Bowling Green Walk, 40 Pitfield Street, London N1 6EU
tel/fax 020-7739 6868
email info@thecourtyard.org.uk
website www.thecourtyard.org.uk

Flexible seating arrangements, 2 theatres, rehearsal rooms.

Etcetera Theatre

Above the Oxford Arms, 265 Camden High Street, London NW1 7BU

tel 020-7482 4857 *fax* 020-7482 0378
email admin@etceteratheatre.com
website www.etceteratheatre.com

A black-box studio space with 42 raked seats, this intimate theatre is perfect for everything from new writing to comedy and cabaret all the way through to acoustic music. Open 7 days a week with an early and late slot. Available for one-off bookings as well as week runs and any number of shows in between. The Etcetera is also available during the day for rehearsals, auditions and workshops with rates starting from just £10 an hour.

Finborough Theatre

118 Finborough Road, London SW10 9ED
tel 020-7244 7439
email admin@finboroughtheatre.co.uk
website www.finboroughtheatre.co.uk
Artistic Director Neil McPherson

Founded in 1980, the Finborough is "one of London's leading new writing venues" (*Time Out*). It also presents rediscoveries of neglected work from 1800 onwards, music theatre and UK premières of foreign work, particularly from the US and Canada. The 50-seat theatre is sometimes available for hire: more information is available on the website.

See entry for Concordance, its resident company, under *Middle and smaller-scale companies* on page 183.

Hackney Empire Studio Theatre

291 Mare Street, London E8 1EJ
tel 020-8510 4500 *fax* 020-8510 4530
email info@hackneyempire.co.uk
website www.hackneyempire.co.uk
Chief Executive Claire Middleton *Creative Director* Susie Mckenna

80-seat studio attached to the historic, Grade II listed, Matcham-designed Hackney Empire. Contact Frank Sweeney for booking details.

Hen & Chickens Theatre

Above Hen & Chickens Theatre Bar,
109 St Paul's Road, Islington, London N1 2NA
tel 020-7704 2001
website www.unrestrictedview.co.uk

A 60-seat theatre welcoming new writing. Directly opposite Highbury and Islington station. Offers 3-to 4-week runs with Monday nights available separately.

The Jack Studio Theatre

410 Brockley Road, London SE4 2DH
tel 020-8291 1206
email admin@brockleyjack.co.uk
website www.brockleyjack.co.uk
Artistic Director Kate Bannister *Theatre Producer* Karl Swinyard

Production details: A vibrant performance space situated in South East London, offering a diverse theatre programme throughout the year. Home also to film, the Write Now Festivals, scratch nights, and the Jack Writers' Workshop. Provides high-quality, accessible and affordable productions for South London and beyond, with seasons of both innovative revivals and dynamic new writing. Comfortable cinema-style raked seating for 50; can be configured end-on or on 3 sides. The performing space is step-free and wheelchair accessible but the rehearsal room is not. Recent productions include: *No Rhyme*, *Rope*, *The Ghost Train*, *Brainville at Night* and *Around the World in 80 Days*.

Casting procedures: Produces in-house shows; uses both in-house and freelance casting directors. Casting is generally by invitation. Does not welcome unsolicited submissions from actors, but will accept invitations to view individual actors' websites and to visit other productions. Actively encourages applications from disabled actors and promotes the use of inclusive casting.

Jacksons Lane Theatre

269A Archway Road, London N6 5AA
tel 020-8340 5226
email kate@jacksonslane.org.uk
website www.jacksonslane.org.uk

Rooms are available for hire on a daily or hourly basis for private parties, rehearsals and performances. The Lavender Room seats up to 40; the Primrose Room seats up to 40; a multipurpose space seats up to 80; the Youth Space seats up to 25; and the Main Theatre seats 125-163.

Jermyn Street Theatre

16B Jermyn Street, London SW1Y 6ST
tel 020-7434 1443 (General Manager) and 020-7287 2875 (Box Office)
email info@jermynstreettheatre.co.uk
website www.jermynstreettheatre.co.uk
Artistic Director Anthony Biggs

Hire rates: Theatre seats 70, 5 rows facing, 2 rows on side. Stage space is 8 metres long x 4 metres deep x 3.5 metres high (to grid), 2 dressing rooms with fridges, sofas, microwaves, kettles, iron + ironing board. The theatre is air conditioned.

- Main Shows – Weekly rental is £2,950 (this includes get-in, fit-up time, technician operating/rigging, also operates sound as well as lights). A 30% non-refundable deposit is required when the contract is signed
- Showcases/Rehearsed Readings/Seminars – £90 per hour. Theatre is available on Tuesdays/Wednesdays/Thursdays between 10am and 3pm (includes technician)
- Sunday Nights (Cabaret Evenings) – £395 for the evening, available from 6.30pm on the night for 8pm show, includes rehearsal Friday before (includes technician)

King's Head Theatre

115 Upper Street, Islington, London N1 1QN
tel 020-7226 8561

website www.kingsheadtheatre.org
Artistic Director Adam Spreadbury-Maher

Famous for helping to launch the careers of many new writers, directors and actors including Stephen Berkoff, Anthony Sher and Victoria Wood. The theatre is situated at the back of a public house with flexible seating for up to 120.

The Landor Theatre

70 Landor Road, London SW9 9PH
tel 020-7737 7276
email info@landortheatre.co.uk
website www.landortheatre.co.uk

A 60-seat theatre situated above a public house.

Lion & Unicorn Theatre

42-44 Gaisford Street, Kentish Town,
London NW5 2ED
email info@giantolive.com
website www.giantolive.com and
www.lionandunicorntheatre.com

The Lion & Unicorn is the home of Giant Olive theatre company. Founded in 2008, the company has quickly developed a reputation for high-quality and imaginative theatre and dance. Giant Olive produces classical productions as well as supporting and developing new work and talent. "The Lion & Unicorn Theatre Space is available to hire at the 'Best Fringe Theatre Rates in London'. Giant Olive doesn't just offer a black box, they can provide full production support, with everything from rehearsal space to flyer and poster design. For prices and details, and to view the venue, please contact **info@giantolive.com**."

New Diorama Theatre

15-16 Triton Street, Regent's Place,
London NW1 3BF
tel 020-7916 5467
email hello@newdiorama.com
website www.newdiorama.com
Artistic and Executive Director David Byrne

New Diorama is an 80-seat theatre located in central London. "We host and support theatre companies, both emerging and established, presenting a variety of productions ranging from comedy to drama. We want to find and support the next generation of Complicites, Kneehighs, Headlongs whilst also offering a space to established companies wanting to work in intimate spaces."

Old Red Lion

418 St John Street, Islington, London EC1V 4NJ
tel 020-7833 3053 *fax* 020-7833 3053
website www.oldredliontheatre.co.uk
Artistic Director Nicholas Thompson

Founded in 1979, the Old Red Lion Theatre is a 60-seater Fringe theatre primarily dedicated to new writing. Companies wishing to hire the venue should post a script, some company information and a production proposal to the Artistic Director. Normally programmes 3 months ahead.

Oval House Theatre

52-54 Kennington Oval, London SE11 5SW
tel 020-7582 0080
email rachel.briscoe@OvalHouse.com
email rebecca.atkinson-lord@OvalHouse.com
website www.ovalhouse.com
Director Deborah Bestwick

Comprises 2 spaces; the downstairs theatre is a black box studio with semi-permanent rake seating, capacity 150. The upstairs theatre is an intimate black box studio with adjustable seating, capacity 50. Presents a diverse programme of work.

Pentameters

28 Heath Street, Hampstead NW3 6TE
tel 020-7435 3648
website www.pentameters.co.uk
Founder and Producer Léonie Scott-Matthews

Located in the heart of Hampstead village, among an abundance of cafés, restaurants, bars, pubs and shops and just a minute's walk from Hampstead tube. Aside from the choice of venues to have pre- or post-theatre drinks or dinner, Hampstead is also well-known for its artistic character, offering a supportive, interactive and thriving local community, making it an ideal spot to promote live theatre and creative arts events. To discuss requirements, please telephone Léonie Scott-Matthews directly on the above number: "Please leave a message, and we will respond."

Pleasance Theatre London

Carpenters Mews, North Road, London N7 9EF
tel 020-7619 6868 *fax* 020-7700 7366
email info@pleasance.co.uk
website www.pleasance.co.uk
Director Anthony Alderson

The Pleasance has 2 versatile spaces: the Mainhouse, seating just under 300; and the StageSpace, a new venue created to nurture the best in new theatre writing and emerging comedy talent, seating 54. The theatre also houses a number of rehearsal spaces, available for both short- and long-term rental.

Royal Academy of Dramatic Art (RADA)*

16 Chenies Street, London WC1E 7EX
tel 020-7908 4822
email bookings@radaenterprises.org

2 theatres and several rehersal spaces available for hire.

Rich Mix

35-47 Bethnal Green Road, London E1 6LA
tel 020-7613 7490 *fax* 020-7613 7499
email info@richmix.org.uk
website www.richmix.org.uk
Chief Executive Jane Earl

A 132,000 square foot flagship arts and cultural centre, boasting "the best in art, performance, fashion, design, music, dance, film, theatre and comedy – 5 floors of vibrant creativity and excellence".

Rosemary Branch Theatre

2 Shepperton Road, London N1 3DT
tel 020-7704 6665
email cecilia@rosemarybranch.co.uk
website www.rosemarybranch.co.uk
Co-Artistic Directors Cecilia Darker, Cleo Sylvestre

Under the same management since 1996, the theatre holds about 61 seats including a "royal box". Presents a diverse programme including opera, classics, new writing, puppetry and just about any genre you care to mention. Affordable rehearsal space available in the Pink Room as well as the theatre during the day. The theatre offers all visiting companies lots of support and goodwill. One-offs, part week and full week rentals all considered.

The Space

269 Westferry Road, London E14 3RS
tel 020-7515 7799
website www.space.org.uk
Centre Director Adam Hemming

A multi-arts centre on the Isle of Dogs, programming a mixture of theatre, music, comedy and dance. Converted from a 19th-century church, with stained-glass windows, a Steinway grand piano and flexible seating, the venue provides a uniquely atmospheric environment. The Space is also available for rehearsals and private hire.

Tabard Theatre

2 Bath Road, Turnham Green, London W4 1LW
tel 020-8995 6035
website www.tabardtheatre.co.uk
General Manager Simon Reilly

Situated within the Tabard building with own independent entrance, close to Turnham Green tube. Offers 3-4 week runs which are programmed 4-5 months ahead.

Theatre 503

The Latchmere, 503 Battersea Park Road, London SW11 3BW
tel 020-7229 8530 *fax* 020-7229 8140
email mail@theatre503.com
website www.theatre503.com
Artistic Director Paul Robinson

Situated above a public house, Theatre 503 aims to provide a venue for new playwrights, comedians and directors to develop their shows. It has a working relationship with television commissioners and producers, literary managers of established theatres and literary agents, and tries to offer a stepping-stone from Fringe to 'big' theatres.

Theatro Technis

26 Crowndale Road, London NW1 1TT
tel 020-7387 6617 *fax* 020-7383 2545
email info@theatrotechnis.com
website www.theatrotechnis.co.uk

Theatro Technis' ideas and policies are realised for anyone who is interested in the development of individuals and communities. The theatre maintains a balance between classic and contemporary work, and serves to embrace a variety of diverse artforms, ranging from theatre and dance to art, photography, music and film.

Toynbee Studios

28 Commercial Street, London E1 6AB
tel 020-7247 5102
email admin@artsadmin.co.uk
website www.artsadmin.co.uk/toynbee-studios

Toynbee Studios is run by Artsadmin for the development and presentation of new work. Toynbee Studios comprises a 280-seat theatre, rehearsal spaces, technical facilities, and the Arts Bar & Café, hosting rehearsals, meetings, performances and events throughout the year. Office facilities are also provided for a range of small arts organisations.

Toynbee Studios has 6 spaces for hire ranging from the intimate to larger high-spec dance and theatre studios. Requests for public events will be reviewed alongside Artsadmin's artistic policy. Spaces are usually hired daily/weekly Monday-Friday 10am-6pm. Occasional evening and weekend hires are available on request.

Artsadmin was founded in 1979 and has been based at Toynbee Studios since 1995. Artsadmin produces bold and inventive art, touring it to audiences across the UK and around the world. They also work to support artists at all stages of their careers with advice mentoring and bursaries.

Tristan Bates Theatre

The Actors Centre, 1A Tower Street, London WC2H 9NP
tel 020-7632 8010
email tbt@actorscentre.co.uk
website www.tristanbatestheatre.co.uk
Chief Executive Louise Coles *Creative Producers* Ben Monks, Will Young

The Tristan Bates Theatre (TBT) is an acclaimed, intimate studio theatre in the heart of the West End, with a commitment to showcasing and supporting the best new contemporary theatre and new writing alongside regional and international touring work. The artistic policy reflects the mission of the Actors Centre to provide a home for artists' continuing professional development, with the TBT providing a launchpad for performers to develop their craft and careers to the next step. Capacity: 68 seats.

Union Theatre

204 Union Street, Southwark, London SE1 0LX
tel 020-7261 9876 *fax* 020-7261 9876

email sasha@uniontheatre.freeserve.co.uk
website www.uniontheatre.freeserve.co.uk

Primarily a new writing venue, the theatre aims to present a diverse programme featuring the best new talent. Guest performances are supplemented by regular in-house productions. Normally offers 3-week runs.

Upstairs at the Gatehouse

The Gatehouse Pub, North Road, London N6 4BD
tel 020-8340 3477
email events@ovationproductions.com
website www.upstairsatthegatehouse.com
Directors John Plews, Katie Plews *Theatre Manager* Claire Thorn

Seats 132 (140 in cabaret style). See also the entry for Ovation Productions under *Middle and smaller-scale companies* on page 199.

White Bear Theatre

138 Kennington Park Road, London SE11 4DJ
tel 020-7793 9193
website www.whitebeartheatre.co.uk
Artistic Director Michael Kingsbury

An L-shaped studio space with seating for up to 50. Generally prefers new writing but occasionally accepts revivals.

Wimbledon Studio Theatre

In Wimbledon Theatre, 103 The Broadway, London SW19 1QG
tel 0870-060 6646 (Box Office)
tel 020-8545 7900 (Admin) *fax* 020-8543 6637
email sambain@theambassadors.com
website www.ambassadortickets.com/Wimbledon-Studio

A black box studio theatre with flexible seating for up to 80. Normally offers 1-2 week runs which are programmed 6 months ahead. The auditorium is wheelchair-accessible.

EDINBURGH FRINGE VENUES

Many of these venues are only available for hire during the Edinburgh Festival Fringe in August. For a full list of venues, see **www.edfringe.com/venues.**

Assembly Rooms

Assembly Theatre, 250 George Street, Edinburgh EH2 2LE
tel 0131-624 2442 *fax* 0131-624 7131
email info@assemblyrooms.com
website www.assemblyrooms.com

The Assembly Rooms have presented more than 1,000 productions featuring most of the major names in British comedy – as well as a huge array of theatre, dance and music events which have been seen by more than 1.5 million people over the last 20 years of the Edinburgh Festival Fringe. The daily programme runs from 11am to 3.30am with exhibitions, a café, 2 public bars and a club bar. Aims to programme a balance of theatre, comedy and new work.

Augustine's

Augustine United Church, 41 George IV Bridge, Edinburgh EH1 1EL
tel 0131-220 1677

During the rest of the year this venue is known as Augustine United Church. It is adapted during the Festival to house 2 performance spaces (the upper venue seats 110; the lower venue seats approximately 105). Programmes theatre, musicals, dance and children's theatre from the UK and elsewhere.

Bedlam Theatre

11B Bristo Place, Edinburgh EH1 1EZ
tel 0131-225 9873
email info@bedlamtheatre.co.uk
website www.bedlamtheatre.co.uk

A 90-seat black-box theatre in central Edinburgh housed in a neo-gothic church. The theatre is available for hire when not in use by the Edinburgh University Theatre Company.

C venues

(Administration Office): C venues Limited, 5 Alexandra Mansions, Chichele Road, London NW2 3AS
email info@cvenues.com
website www.cvenues.com

C venues programmes and hosts over 200 productions and events at the Edinburgh Fringe each August at multiple venue locations in central Edinburgh. Buildings include original Fringe venues from the first days of the Fringe and some of the newest venues on the Fringe. Alongside a broad theatre-based programme incorporating drama, new writing, physical theatre, musical theatre and children's theatre, C has developed a speciality programming immersive, interactive and site-specific theatre, and in hosting cabaret, circus theatre, performance art and cross-genre work. C's productions have come from and toured around the world, and have won Fringe First, Total Theatre and other awards. C venues is a founder member of Edinburgh's Associated Independent Venue Producers.

Greyfriars (Studios 1 and 2)

Greyfriars Kirk House, 86 Candlemaker Row, Edinburgh EH1 2QA

Studio 1 (upstairs, seats 60) and Studio 2 (seats around 40) are intimate spaces suited to 1- to 3-handers, storytelling or poetry. Applications should be made by February for hire during the Festival Fringe.

Hill Street Theatre

Hill Street Theatre, Universal Arts, 12 Edina Place, Edinburgh EH7 5RP
tel 0131-478 0195
email admin@universal-arts.co.uk

Presents a programme of well-known works alongside new writing, musicals, dance, mime and physical theatre. Theatrical production includes comic writing but not stand-up comedy. The main theatre seats 120 while the studio theatre is a more intimate space, seating a maximum of 60. Suited to 1-handers, the studio can accommodate up to 8 performers comfortably.

The Netherbow Scottish Storytelling Centre

43-45 High Street, Edinburgh EH1 1SR
tel 0131-556 9579
website www.scottishstorytellingcentre.co.uk

Intimate 100-seat theatre presenting drama, poetry, storytelling and puppetry events. Offers a strong programme of family shows. The whole building, being new-build from 2005, is very wheelchair-friendly both for the public and for actors.

The Pleasance

The Pleasance Courtyard: 60 The Pleasance, Edinburgh EH8 9TJ
The Pleasance Dome: 1 Bristo Square, Edinburgh EH8 9AL
The Pleasance Administration Office: Carpenters Mews, North Road, London N7 9EF
020 -7619 6868
website www.pleasance.co.uk

The Pleasance presents more than 220 shows across 2 sites and 23 venues during the 4 weeks of the Festival Fringe. With more than 500,000 visitors every year, it remains one of the most popular venues of the Fringe, offering a diverse mix of comedy, theatre, dance, music and everything in-between.

Traverse Theatre

10 Cambridge Street, Edinburgh EH1 2ED
email linda.crooks@traverse.co.uk
website www.traverse.co.uk
Executive Producer/Joint CEO Linda Crooks

Centre for new plays in Scotland. All-year-round venue in underground purpose-built theatre with 2 auditoria and off-site rehearsal facilities. Has staged many premieres, including work by David Greig, David Harrower, Rona Munro, Zinnie Harris and Gregory Burke.

The Underbelly

Edinburgh Permanent Office: 25 Greenside Place, Edinburgh EH1 3AA
tel 0131-622 6566 *fax* 0131-622 6576
email ed@smirnoffunderbelly.co.uk
website www.underbelly.co.uk
Venue Manager Ed Bartlam

Comprises 6 spaces over 4 floors with 3 bars. Venues cater for audiences of 60-200 with different seating configurations available. Programmes new writing, theatre, dance and comedy.

OTHER FRINGE LOCATIONS

Komedia

44-47 Gardner Street, Brighton BN1 1UN
tel (01273) 647101 *fax* (01273) 647102
email info@komedia.co.uk
website www.komedia.co.uk

Komedia host around 700 performances of comedy, music, cabaret and kids shows and club nights.

All taking place under one roof, Komedia incorporates two unique performance spaces with flexible set-ups and a kitchen serving freshly prepared food at most seated shows.

Komedia's programme features the international and national performers and includes a unique range of Komedia-grown resident shows such as the *Krater Comedy Club*, *Comic Boom* and *Bent Double*.

Sevenoaks Stag Theatre

London Road, Sevenoaks, Kent TN13 1ZZ
tel (01732) 451548
email enquiries@stagesevenoaks.co.uk

The theatre can seat up to 453 and has provision for wheelchair-users. Companies should book the space up to 6 months in advance. Programmes a wide range of theatre and dance events.

Watermans Arts Centre

40 High Street, Brentford, Middlesex TW8 0DS
tel 020-8847 5651 (1pm-9pm)
email info@watermans.org.uk
website www.watermans.org.uk

An arts venue comprising 236 plus 2 wheelchairs-seat theatre, 121-seat cinema (plus 3 wheelchairs), studio 1 (large), studio 2 (small), gallery, restaurant and bar, and river views of the Thames. Programmes across a range of different artforms including Asian arts, new media, children's theatre, cinema and participative arts. The studios have a nominal capacity of 80 and 30 seats respectively, but these spaces are mostly used for workshops, meetings and rehearsals.

To fringe, or not to fringe

Simon Dunmore

Although it is generally regarded as 'professional' work, there is a tendency in Fringe productions for professional standards (and facilities) to be somewhat lacking – and that is sometimes an understatement. Poor technical back-up, indifferent front-of-house arrangements and general unreliability are too often the case, almost inevitably damaging the quality of the final product.

Some potential problems to watch out for

- *The ego trip.* A number of productions are set up by individuals wanting a starring vehicle for themselves – much like the old actor-managers. It is generally better to avoid such enterprises unless you can be fairly sure that the central 'ego' will not be damaging to your contribution. Ask around for objective advice before accepting a part in such a production.
- *What else will you have to do?* Will you have to do other things – like paint the set, distribute posters, help with the get-in, and so on? You may think that you can make time to do things like this, but are you sure you want to be thus distracted in the last few days before opening night?
- *Is the script good enough?* There really is no point in doing a production that's flawed before it leaves the page.
- *Can you work well with the director?* This is a highly subjective judgement, but since you are not being properly paid, it is important that you feel as sure as you can be that it'll be a worthwhile experience.
- *Can you actually afford to do it?* There is no point in taking time out from paid work in order to rehearse and perform a Fringe production unless you really think that you'll get something out of the experience. (It can be worth asking if your rehearsal-calls can be arranged around your work commitments.) Also, check whether your participation will affect your benefits in any way.
- *Your agent.* If you have one, will s/he be happy for you to do the production?
- *Contracts.* In 2005, Equity published a set of guidelines (working hours, etc.) and a suggested contract for Fringe producers. This is not intended as an alternative to Equity's other agreements; rather, it is designed to help Fringe companies develop good employment practices. Some companies issue their own contracts; it is important to read these carefully and check with Equity if you have any doubts.
- *Will the production get reviews?* A good review equals good publicity – important for any production. Some productions in the most prestigious venues get reviewed in national newspapers. However, because there are so many productions at any one time, the press has strict rules (length of run, for instance) about what they will send reviewers to. It is important to note that the perceptiveness of some of the latter is somewhat shallow (that's not sour grapes; it's a fact).
- *Will the publicity and marketing be sufficient?* After the cost of hiring the venue, publicity and marketing represent the next major cost of a Fringe production. Too many productions try to skimp on these. In such a competitive environment, they are very, very important.
- *Does the venue have a good reputation?* It is much, much harder to get people into less prestigious ones.

• *Promises.* While enthusiasm for a project is wonderful, beware of promises when they seem over-the-top. Too much optimism can blind people to important practical realities.
• *Is it going to be properly organised?* There is far more to putting on a production than most actors realise (see below). Ask questions based on the above and, if you don't feel sufficiently satisfied, politely back away. There is no point in being miserable, as well as unpaid, for several weeks.
• *If I'm not being paid, can I not just pull out if something better comes along?* Legally, you can; morally and professionally it's an extremely dubious thing to do without the full understanding of your fellow participants – and you never know who, among them, might gain 'casting clout' in the future.

Setting up your own production

Too many people think that mounting a production is just a matter of getting a few friends together, borrowing some props and costumes, and getting on with it. What about the costs of hiring a venue, a rehearsal space, the publicity and marketing, the author's royalties (if still in copyright), and so on?

You may be lucky enough to get some, or even all, of these for free, or you might find a rich auntie. But however you fund the above essentials, you have got to do a lot of careful planning before rehearsals start. Will the playwright (and/or translator) allow you to do a production of the play in the first place? Just because a play is in print, it doesn't mean that anyone can perform it. Is the rehearsal room available for enough of the time? What is the deadline for getting the poster design to the printers, so that they can get the result back to you in time for the distributors to get them displayed in good time before opening night? And so on, and so on, and so on ... Oh, and it is essential to plan and budget with contingency in both time and money – there are always several things that take more time than you'd thought, and several things that cost more than you'd thought (or forgotten to budget for in the first place).

Doing it yourself is far more complex than most people realise, but can be incredibly satisfying if you succeed. For a technically simple production you probably need to find at least £5,000 – and that's without paying any of the participants. The chances of recouping this through the box office are very low; the average audience on the Fringe is about 30 per cent. A recent report stated that: "Theatres are among the most over-regulated businesses in the UK." Legal requirements like Health & Safety, VAT and performance rights cannot be neglected.

Note: For interesting discussion on the whole business of working for little or nothing, go to **http://actorsminimumwage.wordpress.com**.

Simon Dunmore has been directing productions for over 30 years – nearly 20 years as a resident director in regional theatres and, more recently, working freelance. In that time there have been over 200 productions (of all styles, colours, shapes and sizes) – recently: several Drama School Showcases, Maugham's *Home and Beauty* and new plays about sex, WB Yeats' up-and-down relationship with Maud Gonne, one set inside a pyramid and another about Bismarck. Past favourites include: *The Promise* (Alexei Arbuzov), *Antigone* (Jean Anouilh), a seven-handed version of *Antony & Cleopatra* and too many others to mention. He also teaches acting and has worked in many drama schools and other training establishments around the country. He has written several books: *An Actor's Guide to Getting Work* (fifth edition, 2012), the *Alternative Shakespeare Auditions* series and was formerly the Consultant Editor for *Actors' Yearbook*.

Edinburgh or bust: is it worth it?

Shane Dempsey

The Edinburgh Fringe was established in 1947 and has grown into one of the world's most renowned and diverse arts festivals. From its humble beginnings as an alternative to the Edinburgh International Festival, the Fringe has continued to increase and multiply, and, despite the growing costs to companies and performers alike, it still remains high on the agenda of many. The Fringe can be incredibly daunting and at times even crippling. My aim is not to shatter you, but to ensure that you are armed with as much knowledge as possible before you decide if it's worth it.

In 2009 there were 2098 shows performed in Edinburgh and an estimated 18,901 performers in 265 venues. These figures give you an idea of the level of competition for audiences during the three weeks of August. This is an aggressive and over-saturated market. In the Fringe environment, the efforts of many go unrewarded and often even unnoticed. So, can you break through with your production?

Evaluate your work honestly and realistically

The first thing to do is evaluate the production itself. Ask yourself, "What is the appeal of my particular production? What is it about my show that will make it stand out from the crowd? Do I have permission from the author or their estate to perform the piece? If so, what percentage of my overall income will this take, and what are the possibilities of extending this performance licence post-Edinburgh?"

If the piece is new writing or devised then there are fewer issues with performance rights, but it is crucial to discuss billing and authorship, as these can potentially cause problems later. Circumstances change, so with new work it is essential to secure written agreement over the intellectual copyright of the piece – and this also extends to directorial concepts and vision. Get it down on paper so you always know where you stand and can avoid or deal with any issues that may arise.

As well as fledgling companies taking new work to Edinburgh, the festival is also a testing ground for many established, heavyweight companies and producers. They have years of experience, and they have the economic power to invest large sums in PR and marketing. So ask yourself what will bring an audience to your venue, and why. The reality is that you are in direct competition with these established companies as well as with the other thousands who are newer to the game.

Choose the right venue

There are many venues associated with the Fringe. You need to be clear about the kind of work they are interested in programming; some are very specific as to their requirements, while others have a broader remit. Consider not only the price, but also the reputation and the location of a venue, as they vary considerably.

Your time slot is another point of negotiation: late evenings tend to be dominated by comedy, and a great deal of theatre now plays during the day and late afternoon. A general rule is that the more established venues have the best reputations and tend to charge significantly more for their services than smaller, up-and-coming venues. All venues will require you to sign a contract, and you need to be aware of the small print, as it has been known for companies to skim over this only to discover that they were not aware of all the terms and conditions.

Consider venue costs and other expenses

Many venues offer either a box-office split or ask for a flat fee. Almost all will require a deposit in advance. The average cost of mounting a production in Edinburgh is £8,000-10,000, and deposits will often be required months in advance – so unless you have access to sufficient funds, consider seriously if there is a more cost-effective way of getting your work out there.

And there are other expenses, including music performance rights, public liability insurance and VAT. Accommodation costs soar during the festival, and local landlords take advantage of the influx of artists and tourists, but if you're organised it is possible to secure a deal by booking early. Many companies choose to stay in Glasgow, which is an hour-long commute, but the time and energy required to do this needs to be weighed up against the convenience and cost of staying in Edinburgh.

What do you want from the experience?

Ask yourself early on what you want to achieve out of the experience. Too often this is not given enough thought, so that it is difficult, if not impossible, to achieve any significant outcomes. Remember that Edinburgh is a massive arts market, and that within any market you need to be specific about your audience – be it the general public or producers who can potentially remount your work post-Edinburgh.

If you want a London transfer, regional tour or international tour, target your promotions pack specifically to relevant individuals and always research their programming tastes. Invite them to the show, ensure that they are given complimentary tickets and try to set up a meeting after they have seen your work. Many international producers are seeking work that would be programmed two to three years after the festival, so you have to have a long-term plan for the production and ensure that it has the necessary factors that will support its longevity.

Network!

Many deals in Edinburgh are set up over late-night drinks and midnight meetings, often to fit in with the schedules of producers who are seeing work all day long. They can be fairly informal, but keeping your professional hat on is essential to any success. There are incredible opportunities to meet new people in Edinburgh, and there are numerous events specifically aimed towards networking, including the Producers' Breakfast.

In addition you can take part in a range of informal activities in which you can make connections that may lead to future work and collaborations. This is often triggered by seeing a company's work: the research trip I made recently to Russia to investigate ensemble practice has been greatly aided by contacts I met in Edinburgh. The key to any networking is to find the common links between you and the other practitioner, and then to develop them into a cohesive relationship. Be honest about what you do and why you do it, and people will usually respond positively.

Press officers have essential contacts with the media and could be a valuable asset to your production. They can not guarantee that your work will be reviewed, but having a person working on your behalf can give you a major advantage over the competition. If, like many companies, you are bringing the show to Edinburgh on a very tight budget, allocate one member of the company to be the designated press officer as this makes life a lot easier for all parties. Again, reputation means a lot in the world of the press and some papers will hold more influence than others. Target the ones that you believe will be interested in your work and be sure to read the reviews every day to get a flavour of what the festival has to offer.

Design, marketing, and word-of-mouth

In a market such as the Fringe, the role of good graphic design and web design is often overlooked, but it is essential to ensure that your work is seen – and seen at its best. Ensure that your production pack has strong imagery. The old cliché of a picture painting a thousand words still rings true, especially to overtired editors at the busiest time of their year. The array of flyers that are seen on the streets of Edinburgh is mind-boggling, but eye-catching design can really aid your marketing campaign.

Over and above marketing, however, is word-of-mouth – one of the key influences in persuading people to see your show. Such recommendations are difficult to achieve, and are dependent on your getting healthy, happy audiences early in your run. The majority of companies spend their days marketing their work, sending emails, chasing the press and leafleting: this is the Fringe, and if you're not prepared to do this to the point of exhaustion, stay at home!

For inclusion in the much-coveted Fringe Brochure you will be asked to submit 50 words of copy to describe your production. Keep it simple and clear, and remember that you are going to have to live with this for the life of your show in Edinburgh, so make sure it really sums your work up. It can be useful to have a quote in there from previous work – after all, everybody wants to see a show from a five-star company – but if it's not true, don't claim it to be so! Fabrication rarely, if ever, helps. The Fringe website provides comprehensive guidelines on producing work in Edinburgh: see **www.edfringe.com/take-part**. The information is there if you look for it, so take the time to investigate. It could save you much stress and money.

Dreams can come true ...

The likelihood of your company or show being picked up for a transfer or tour is extremely slim. The financial burden on companies is very high, and you have to weigh this up against the potential exposure and the possibility of gaining other work after the festival. There has been a recent rise in smaller fringe festivals happening outside of the main Fringe, partially in response to its overtly commercial nature. Notably, the Free Fringe and the Big Red Door are proving to be hugely popular and offer far better deals to the artists. Fragments' production of *The Bay* by Hannah Burke was performed at the Big Red Door, Te-Pooka; we also managed to be seen by representatives of the Traverse, Manchester International Festival, and were transferred into London's prestigious Theatre 503. So yes, dreams can come true ... but only after a serious amount of hard graft, and no little luck too.

Shane Dempsey trained as a director at E15 Acting School and runs Fragments, an international ensemble of theatre and video artists (fragments.ie). His work has been staged in Ireland, London, Scotland and Belgium. In 2008 he filmed the groundbreaking documentary *Mothers of Modern Ireland*. His production of *The Bay* toured extensively in 2009, and he is currently preparing to stage a new adaptation by Hannah Burke of Mikhail Bulgakov's *The Master & Margarita*. He has strong Russian connections, and was invited to observe rehearsals by Lev Dodin of the Maly Theatre of St Petersburg in Paris, November 2009 as well as observing acting workshops at GITIS and Vakhtangov Institute, Moscow 2010.

Open Book: fairer finances for fringe theatre

Piers Beckley

What is 'Open Book Theatre'?

Most fringe theatre productions don't make a profit. And as a large number of fringe productions offer only a profit-share as financial recompense for the actors performing in them, this can be a big problem.

Something that can be especially galling for an actor is to perform in front of a house filled with people, and still not receive any money at the end of the run because the production hasn't made a profit. But if half of those tickets are paper to fill the house in early shows in order to help word of mouth, then the number of people that you see in the audience may not give an accurate measure of how much money is actually coming in.

If the tickets were priced too low, or the producer failed to get a good deal on the advertising, or any number of other things, it's very easy for a production to make a loss. And without financial transparency throughout the process, there can always be the niggling suspicion that something, somewhere, has gone horribly wrong that need not have.

By its nature, fringe theatre will never have as much money to spend on props, print, advertising, design, or on actors as a fully professional production. But if a company can't provide the cold hard cash which we all desire, the very least that they can provide is transparency in recording what money goes in and comes out, so that everything is fair and above board, and is seen to be so.

Open Book Theatre is a new way of running the financial books for a fringe production, so that every member of the cast and crew can see the business of putting on a show. In an Open Book production, the budget is viewable by anyone involved – from first draft through to final income statements. This means that as well as knowing that they've been treated fairly throughout the entire process, everyone will be able to see how the production is doing – and, if all goes well, exactly how much of the profit-share pot they'll receive when the money comes in from the theatre.

Open Book Management is a set of techniques that have been used by companies across the world over the last 30 years. It's all about giving the people involved a stake in the outcome, and then giving them the tools to affect what that outcome is. In a business environment, the stake is most often shares in the company, while in Open Book Theatre (at least at the fringe level) it usually consists of a portion of the profit from the show.

What does Open Book Management involve?

Free access and exchange

There are three main points at the heart of an Open Book production:

- Free access to all financial information
- Regular updates on changes
- Listening to suggestions and implementing them

So how would you go about bringing this to life?

One of the easiest ways of sharing information is to use budget spreadsheets showing estimated outgoings and income, which are later updated as the real figures come in. These spreadsheets can be placed on a password-protected website, or emailed to the cast and crew every week to show exactly how much money has come in and gone out.

Because the budgets are available for all to see, as well as knowing exactly where the money has gone on advertising, design, print – all of the things that are necessary to a production, but which generally don't cross an actor's desk – then everyone involved can help suggest improvements.

Perhaps someone has a photographer friend who'll be able to take publicity shots in exchange for a credit or a lower fee. Or perhaps they will know a way to get the fabric needed by a costume designer more cheaply. If everyone knows the cost of the things that make up a production, and how those will affect the profits, then they can suggest ways to make things better for all.

As the financial spreadsheets are regularly updated throughout the show, then everyone involved can see the clock ticking towards breakeven – that magical moment when income from sales and advertising rises above what's been spent on the production, and everyone knows that they're going to be taking some money home with them. It's also nice to be able to celebrate when your production reaches a milestone – for example, when half-way to breaking even.

As well as making the budget documents visible to all, an Open Book production will ensure that all of the documents that are legally required are on display: the insurance schedule, health and safety policy, venue contract, and risk assessment documents. Seeing this information proves that you're dealing with a professional company and a professional production – not just one person's vanity project.

Fair profit-share: the 'tronc system'

In a fringe production, the final part of the Open Book story comes with the division of the profit-share pot. After all costs have been paid (and everyone will know what they are, because they can look at the income and expenditure of the show at any point throughout the production), then any gross profits can be divided between those who brought the show to life.

One way of doing this fairly and equitably is to use what's known as a tronc system, based on the tips system used in many bars and restaurants. In a tronc, everyone involved in the production is allocated a certain number of points depending upon their involvement. So the director and writer might have two points each, while each member of the ensemble cast has one point. It's important to be up front about how any profits will be divided – for example, if the star of the show is to receive more points than the other actors.

After the gross profit has been worked out, the value of each point can be derived by simply dividing the profit by the total number of points – and then everyone is paid that amount for each point that they have.

Control and visibility for everyone involved

Taken all together, these practices mean that everyone involved in a show can see exactly where the money flows from and to, and can be assured of the honesty and integrity of everybody involved in the process.

While some producers have been known to say that their books are open if the financial information for the production is published at the end of the show – or even the end of the year – that's not going to help the members of the production get involved. As well as the honesty of the system, Open Book Theatre relies on helping everyone to see the implications of creative decisions, and that means they need to be able to see what's going on throughout the course of production – not just take a look at a spreadsheet at the end.

The Open Book model, especially at the level of fringe theatre, shouldn't be seen as an attempt in any way to replace an Equity contract, which we would always recommend using. What Open Book Theatre should do, though, is provide some protection for actors working in those profit-share productions which currently are not in a position to use Equity contracts.

Running your productions on the Open Book model means more control and visibility for everyone involved, ensuring that you can be confident that things are under control – or, at least, as under control as they get.

Hopefully within ten years the question won't be, 'What is Open Book Theatre?', but rather, 'Why did we ever do things differently?'

Piers Beckley is a writer and producer. He's been a production manager, stage manager, project manager, line manager, extra, actor, web producer, copywriter, interviewer, sub-editor, video editor, and director. Writing credits include *The Treason Show, NewsRevue, Week Ending, Splendid, Spooks Interactive*, and acclaimed productions of *A Christmas Carol* and *Oliver Twist* for the Lion and Unicorn Theatre. He produced *The Just So Stories* and *Hans Christian Andersen's Fairy Tales* for Red Table at the Pleasance Theatre. You can generally find out what he's up to at his website **fatpigeons.com** or on Twitter as @piersb.

Children's, young people's and theatre in education

Paul Harman

Work in this very large sector of employment for actors in the UK varies greatly – both in the style of theatre created and presented, and in the wages and conditions offered by employers. Anyone taking work in the field should always be clear about the aims and status of their prospective employer.

Most producing theatres offer plays for young audiences as part of a season, and Christmas shows and pantomimes are mounted by a large number of receiving theatres and commercial touring companies. Some 200 independent touring companies regularly present original theatre productions, usually in schools, reaching a total audience of at least five million annually. Smaller touring companies may operate for profit, or as profit-share partnerships. Companies which are members of ITC (Independent Theatre Council) offer pay and conditions agreed with the performers' trade union, Equity.

Reality check

There is no official agency that collects reliable statistics or regulates the quality of what is offered. Your work may never be publicly reviewed – and it can be hard and demanding. Casts are often small, and living conditions on the road are sometimes difficult. The work may involve a lot of driving (if you are over 25 and insurable) as well as humping sets in and out of vans. However, the rewards for good-quality work conscientiously presented lie in the warmth of welcome from audiences and bookers alike, and a directness and openness of audience response which is often less evident at more formal, adult-orientated theatre events. In schools, you will perform in daylight, very close to children – so it helps if you like them. They can see every blemish on you, and you can see every reaction on a hundred faces.

You will need physical stamina; the ability to play many parts convincingly; and the facility to hit a peak of performance two or more times in a day, six days a week. You may need skill in playing a musical instrument. In addition, other aptitudes may be called upon. A play may be preceded or followed by workshop activity with young people – from 'hot-seating' in character to involving children in a performance. An understanding of drama education techniques is therefore an advantage, and experience of Youth Theatre useful.

What shows?

For good economic and marketing reasons, most theatre for children presented in larger houses is based on well-known stories by established authors, or on characters from TV shows. Companies may receive financial support from official agencies to present plays on health and social issues. Plays related to the National Curriculum, such as science topics, are in great demand from schools.

Theatre in Education (TIE) is a term commonly used to mean many kinds of theatre in schools. In the strict sense, TIE implies an extended theatre event, combining performance and participatory elements and designed to engage pupils in exploring their own knowledge, feelings and attitudes. This is quite a different process from explaining how magnets work, or presenting an account of an historical event. Very few companies nowadays can afford the time and staffing needed to support real TIE, but there are many opportunities to create and present challenging educational plays on a wide variety of subjects.

Independent touring companies receiving public subsidy from Arts Councils in England, Wales, Scotland and Northern Ireland generally aim to present original, commissioned drama. A small group of writers specialises in this field, addressing personal and social topics, from fear of the dark or the break-up of families to genetics and migration. This group of companies – whose aims are primarily artistic, rather than just to entertain or deliver educational messages – find like-minded companies in 70 countries through ASSITEJ (International Association of Theatre for Children and Young People). Overseas tours and international collaborations are increasing.

Above all, don't look upon this field as an easy step towards something else. Your first experiences may well be tough, but an apprenticeship served with a supportive company will open an area of work that you can return to with growing enjoyment and professional satisfaction.

Paul Harman has worked as an actor and director in professional theatre since 1963. He joined Belgrade Theatre in Education team in 1966, headed Education work at Liverpool Everyman from 1970, and founded Merseyside Young People's Theatre Company in 1978. In 1994 he became Artistic Director of CTC Theatre, Darlington and is now the Chair of TYA (Theatre for Young Audiences) – the UK Centre of ASSITEJ.

Children's, young people's and theatre-in-education companies

Notes:

• Some of the companies listed are members of the Independent Theatre Council (ITC) – **www.itc-arts.org.**

• The Criminal Records Bureau (CRB) is now called the Disclosure and Barring Service (DBS); CRB checks are now termed DBS checks.

Action Transport Theatre

Whitby Hall, Stanney Lane, Ellesmere Port, Cheshire CH65 9AE
tel 0151-357 2120 *fax* 0151-356 4057
email info@actiontransporttheatre.org
website www.actiontransporttheatre.org
Artistic Director Nina Hajiyianni

Production details: "A new writing company creating brave, collaborative theatre for, by and with young people." Stages 3 projects annually, with around 60 performances in 10 venues including schools, arts centres, theatres and community venues across the UK. In general 4-5 actors go on tour, playing to family (5+) and adult audiences. Incoming actors should have singing, musical instrument and physical theatre skills, and may be expected to lead workshops. Recent productions include: *My Mother Told Me Not to Stare, 10 Tiny Plays* and *Four for the Port.*

Casting procedures: Holds general auditions and actors may write at any time to request inclusion. Casting breakdowns are available from the website, by postal application (with sae), through Equity Job Information Service and Casting Call Pro, and in *The Stage.* Welcomes letters (with CVs and photographs) from individual actors previously unknown to the company, sent by post or email. Will consider invitations to view individual actors' websites. Offers Equity-approved contracts as negotiated through ITC. Actively encourages applications from disabled actors, and promotes the use of inclusive casting.

Actionwork Creative Arts

Ground Floor, 6 The Centre, Weston-super-Mare, North Somerset BS23 1US
mobile (01934) 815163
email admin@actionwork.com
website www.actionwork.com

Production details: Actionwork is a theatre and film company that seeks to promote empowerment and reduce bullying and violence in schools. They are committed to producing work through a number of different mediums in order to promote understanding of youth conflict and violence. 3 recent productions include: *Million a Week* (2013), *Out of the Box* (2013) and *Cyber Tears* (2014).

Each production consists of 3 actors and, on average, the company present 6-10 productions per year to audiences aged between 4 and 17. This equates to over 300 performances at over 150 venues across the UK, ranging from schools to community spaces, art centres and churches. Cast members are sometimes expected to lead workshops and activity sessions and it is advantageous for them to have a driving licence and some singing and dancing ability.

Casting procedures: Uses in-house casting directors and holds general auditions during September. Casting breakdowns are available through PCR and Bristol Online. Welcomes both CVs and letters from actors previously unknown to the company and unsolicited CVs and photographs. These should be sent via email. Also welcomes invitations to view individual actors' websites, but does not welcome showreels. Actively encourages applications from disabled actors.

Aesop's Touring Theatre Company

The Arches, 38 The Riding, Woking, Surrey GU21 5TA
tel (01483) 724633 *mobile* (07836) 731872
email info@aesopstheatre.co.uk
website www.aesopstheatre.co.uk
Director Karen Brooks

Production details: Established in 1999, a professional Theatre in Education company specialising in National Curriculum based plays for the nursery and primary age range. Tours extensively on a daily basis performing interactive plays and associated drama workshops. Plays are mostly performed in schools but also embrace theatres, community centres, village halls, arts centres and party venues. On average stages 300 performances each year, in 225 venues across London, in the Home Counties and further afield. 2 actors usually go on tour, plus occasionally a driver or stage manager. Applicants should be fit, versatile all-round actors and must have their own transport to easily reach bases in Weybridge or Woking, Surrey for very early morning starts. Applicants will be expected to drive the company estate car. A current DBS is essential.

Casting procedures: Auditions are held in May and actors may write in at any time: 'We reply to all enquiries'.

Ape Theatre Company

32 Brook Road, Epping, Essex CM16 7BT
tel (01992) 574843
email mail@apetheatrecompany.co.uk
website www.apetheatrecompany.co.uk
Artistic Director Matt Allen *Assistant Artistic Director* Andrew Mulquin

Production details: Established in 1980. Stages 4 projects annually, with 800 performances at the same number of schools and community venues nationwide. In general 4 actors go on tour with each project, playing to audiences aged 10+. Actors are sometimes expected to lead workshops and should hold a clean driving licence. Dance and physical theatre skills may be an advantage. Recent productions include: *Too Much Punch for Judy*, *Legal Weapon II*, *Pills, Thrills and Automobiles* and *Viscous Circle.*

Casting procedures: Holds general auditions, and actors are advised to write in July and November to request inclusion. Casting breakdowns are available by postal application (with sae), and via Equity Job Information Service. Welcomes letters (with CVs and photographs) from individual actors previously unknown to the company, sent by post and email, but does not accept unsolicited showreels or invitations to view actors' websites. Offers Equity-approved contracts as negotiated through ITC. Rarely or never has the opportunity to cast disabled actors.

Arty-Fact Theatre Co.

18 Weston Lane, Crewe CW2 5AN
tel 070-2096 2096 *fax* 070-2098 2098
email artyfact@talktalk.net
website www.arty-fact.co.uk
Artistic Director Yvonne Peacock *Co-director* Brian Twiddy

Production details: Has been performing in schools since 1993, running history workshops, original plays and classics. Performs 6-7 projects annually, with an average annual total of 500-600 performances in 200-300 schools across England. In general 2-4 actors go on tour and perform to audiences aged 7-18. Physical theatre skills and a driving licence are required. Actors may be expected to lead workshops. Recent productions include: *The Time Capsule 1914*, *A Christmas Box* and *Let's Eat Grandma.*

Casting procedures: Holds general auditions twice a year; actors are advised to write in April and July to request inclusion. Casting breakdowns are available via the website, Equity Job Information Service, and Castcall. Welcomes letters (with CVs and photographs) from individual actors previously unknown to the company sent by post or email.

Big Wheel Theatre in Education

PO Box 18221, London EC1R 4WJ
tel 020-7689 8670
email info@bigwheel.org.uk
website www.bigwheel.org.uk
Artistic Directors Roland Allen, Jeni Williams

Production details: Since 1984 has developed interactive theatre for use in education and training in the UK and abroad. Normally tours 15 projects each year, with an average annual total of 500 performances and 250 different venues. Venues include schools, universities, conferences and training centres across the UK and Europe. In general 2 actors go on tour and play to audiences aged 7 upwards. Actors are required to hold a driving licence and to lead workshops. Experience in teaching or training is also useful. Recent productions include: *Introduction to Shakespeare*, a gameshow-based interactive workshop; *Breakfast with Big Wheel*, a show to teach English abroad; *Go! Go! Go!*, a show about sustainable transport; and shows in French and Spanish: *Voulez Vous?!* and *Siesta Fiesta!* Also presents a variety of workshops for the NHS and university postgrads about communication, service improvement, and presentation skills.

Casting procedures: Sometimes holds general auditions; actors may write at any time requesting inclusion. "Best to have a good look at the website. Particularly interested in performers with fluent French and Spanish."

Big Wooden Horse (UK) Ltd

30 Northfield Road, London W13 9SY
tel 020-8567 8431
email info@bigwoodenhorse.com
website www.bigwoodenhorse.com
Artistic Director Adam Bampton-Smith

Production details: Aims to present high-quality theatre to younger audiences across the UK and to represent the best of British theatre craft abroad. Strives both to entertain and to inform young people, drawing from different cultures and traditions. On average 3 actors tour 3 projects annually, with 400 performances at around 80 venues including arts centres and theatres in the UK, US, Canada and the Far East. Audiences range from 2 to 8 years. Recent productions include: *Aliens Love Underpants*, *STUCK*, *The Way Back Home*, *Don't Let the Pigeon Drive the Bus!* and *The Night Before Christmas*.

Casting procedures: Casting breakdowns are available from Spotlight, Castnet and Castcall. Welcomes approaches from actors previously unknown to the company, sent by email only.

Bitesize Theatre Company

8 Green Meadows, New Broughton,
Wrexham LL11 6SG
tel (01978) 358320 *fax* (01978) 756308
email casting@bitesizetheatre.co.uk
website www.bitesizetheatre.co.uk
Artistic Director Linda Griffiths

Production details: Founded in 1992, the company strives to provide high-quality, entertaining theatrical productions for young people, from children's classics to Shakespeare and pantomime to new works. Also runs Theatre in Education projects and bespoke workshops across the UK. The company performs in schools and community venues across the Northwest. Rehearsals take place in North Wales. Between 3-6 actors work on each show and play to audiences aged 3-19 years. Actors are required to be able to sing, dance and drive and may also be expected to participate in workshops. Recent productions include: *Robin Hood*, *Aladdin*, *Macbeth – The Tortured Mind*, *Red Riding Hood* and *Where There's a Will There's a Play*.

Casting procedures: The company holds general auditions; actors requesting inclusion in these should write in July. Casting breakdowns are available from *The Stage* and Castcall. Happy to receive email enquiries to **casting@bitesizetheatre.co.uk**. Mainly takes actors from recognised drama schools; actors aged over 25 years are preferred for jobs requiring driving. All employees must pass a DBS (Disclosure and Barring Service) check for work with children. Offers non-Equity contracts. Actively encourages applications from disabled actors and promotes the use of inclusive casting.

Blue Moon Theatre Company

20 Sandpiper Road, Blakespool Park, Bridgewater, Somerset TA6 5QU
tel (01278) 458253
email info@bluemoontheatre.co.uk
website www.bluemoontheatre.co.uk
Company Manager Steve Apelt *Artistic Director* Kerrie Seymour *Writer* Mark Scott-Ison

Production details: A producing "fun-packed" children's theatre with lots of participation and involvement – mainly incorporating workshops and after-show discussions. Stages on average 2-3 projects annually. In general 4 actors go on tour, staging around 50 performances for young audiences at 40 UK venues including schools, arts centres, theatres, outdoor and community venues. Singing and physical theatre skills are required, as well as a clean driving licence.

Casting procedures: Sometimes holds general auditions, with casting breakdowns publicly available. Welcomes letters (with CVs and photographs) from individual actors previously unknown to the company, sent by post or email. Also welcomes showreels, and invitations to view individual actors' websites. Offers Equity-approved contracts. Actively encourages applications from disabled actors and promotes the use of inclusive casting.

Blue Star Productions

7-8 Shaldon Mansions, 132 Charing Cross Road, London WC2H 0LA
tel 020-7836 6220/4128 *fax* 020-7836 2949
email Hopkinstacey@aol.com

Production details: Blue Star Productions specialises in first-class children's musicals and Songbook Concerts. These shows tour theatres nationally. They include 8-10 performers, beautiful costumes and scenery, and always feature 'live' music. Recent productions include: *The Wonderful Wizard of Oz*, *The Adventures of Pinocchio*, *Tales from the Jungle Book*, *Alice in Wonderland*, *Snow White and the Seven Dwarfs* and many others. Songbook Concerts include at least 4 singers, depending on venue and finance. One-man shows include: *Life Upon the Very Wicked*

Stage, an audience with Barrie Stacey. Barrie Stacey and Blue Star Productions were voted Best Children's Show Producer of the Year 2009 and 2010 at the *Encore Magazine* Theatre Awards.

Casting procedures: All casting is done in-house through Blue Star Associates, also at the above address. Holds general auditions annually, or for specific productions. Welcomes letters with CVs and photographs, and also email submissions.

Box Clever Theatre Company

@ The Oval House Theatre, 52-54 Kennington Oval, London SE11 5SW
tel 020-7793 0040 *fax* 020-7357 8188
email admin@boxclevertheatre.com
website www.boxclevertheatre.com
Artistic Director Michael Wicherek

Production details: Founded in 1996, the company produces contemporary theatre for young people: new plays, contemporary adaptations of classic texts, and issue-based and educational work. 6 major national tours are staged each year with an average annual total of approximately 600 performances in 500 different venues. The company performs to more than 60,000 young people every year. Venues include arts centres, theatres, and educational and community venues nationwide. Approximately 3 actors are involved in each production. Recent productions include: *Time for the Good Looking Boy* (for theatres); *The Buzz, Driving Ms Daisy, The Hate Plays* and *Boxed Macbeth* (for secondary schools); and *Car Story* for primary schools.

Casting procedures: Does not use freelance casting directors. Casting breakdowns are available via Equity Job Information Service and the website (normally June/July and October/November). Welcomes submissions (with CVs and photographs) from actors previously unknown to the company if sent by post and if in response to casting breakdowns only. Advises actors that the company receives a huge response to advertisements, and is therefore unable to return photographs or respond in writing to applicants not invited to audition. Non-Equity contracts "in line with ITC". Considers applications from disabled actors to play characters with disabilities.

Brief Candle Theatre

Oaker View, Wenslees, Darley Bridge, Matlock, Derbyshire DE4 2JZ
tel (01629) 735576
email office@briefcandle.co.uk
website www.briefcandle.co.uk
Artistic Director David Shimwell *Writer/Director* Paul Whitfield

Production details: Established in 2002. Produces high-quality Theatre in Education and theatre for young people and family audiences. On average performs 5 projects each year, with 450 performances in 100 venues including schools, colleges, theatres, community venues and occasionally outdoor performances and festivals. Areas covered: Derbyshire, South Yorkshire, Lincolnshire and Wigan. On average 4 actors go on tour, playing to audiences aged 11 to adult. "We seek to work with actors who are committed to working with young people, and who have the skills required to build fast, effective working relationships with company and audience." Actors may be required to lead workshops. Recent productions include: *The Tower* – a play looking at domestic abuse and power in relationships; *Tight* – a play for 14 year-olds, looking at use and misuse of alcohol; *An Evening with Mallet and Ming* – a dark comedy for adults and older children, set in a Victorian Music Hall; and *No Place for Dreams* – a family show for the Edinburgh Festival.

Casting procedures: Holds general auditions and actors may write in at any time; the company keeps all submissions for consideration. Casting details are available via Spotlight Link and from the website. Prefers email applications. An approved Manager member of the ITC; all contracts are ITC Equity-approved. Encourages applications from all actors, regardless of ability or disability, and promotes the use of inclusive casting.

C&T

University College Worcester, Henwick Grove, Worcester WR2 6AJ
tel (01905) 855436
email info@candt.org
website www.candt.org
Artistic Director Paul Sutton

Production details: Founded in 1988. A theatre company incorporating performance, learning and digital media. Works in schools, colleges and universities in the UK and across Europe. Normally tours 2-3 projects each year with an average annual total of 50-100 performances at 50-100 different venues. In general 2-3 actors go on tour and play to audiences aged 5-65. Dance/physical theatre skills, proficiency with computers and digital media, and a driving licence are required. Actors are also expected to lead workshops. Recent productions include: *Living Newspaper.com*, a docu-drama project online for schools.

Casting procedures: Sometimes holds general auditions; actors should write in September requesting inclusion. Accepts submissions (with CVs and photographs) from actors previously unknown to the company sent by post or email. Will also accept showreels and invitations to view individual actors' websites.

Cahoots NI

109-113 Royal Avenue, Belfast BT1 1FF
tel 028-9043 4349

email info@cahootsni.com
website www.cahootsni.com
Artistic Director Paul Bosco McEaney

Production details: Creates world-class, inspirational theatre for children aged 4 to 11 years. Aims to "expand the imagination of children, and to stimulate their artistic creativity through the visual potential of theatre and the age-old popularity of music, magic and illusion". On average tours 3 productions to schools, special schools, respite centres, councils, arts centres and theatres both nationally and internationally. 4-8 actors go on tour, performing to audiences aged 4-11. Actors should have singing, musical instrument, physical theatre, circus and magic skills, and are sometimes required to lead workshops. Recent projects include: *Egg, The Incredible Book Eating Boy, A Spell of Cold Weather, Leon and the Place Between, The Snail and the Whale* and *The Musician.*

Casting procedures: Sometimes holds general auditions; actors may write at any time to request inclusion. Welcomes letters (with CVs and photographs) from actors previously unknown to the company sent by post or email, and is happy to receive showreels. Does not welcome invitations to view individual actors' websites. Actively encourages applications from disabled actors, and promotes the use of inclusive casting.

Cambridge Touring Theatre

29 Worts Causeway, Cambridge CB1 8RJ
email info@cambridgetouringtheatre.co.uk
Director Rosie Humphreys

Production details: Founded in 2002. A family fun touring theatre. Stages 1 production each year, with 50 performances in 50 theatres and outdoor venues in the South, South East and East of England. In general 5 actors go on tour, playing to audiences aged 2-12 and their families. Incoming actors will be required to lead workshops; some singing, dance and driving ability is an advantage. Recent productions include: *Alice in Wonderland, Robin Hood, Wind in the Willows,* and *Sword in the Stone.*

Casting procedures: Casting breakdowns are available via the website, Spotlight, postal application with sae, and Casting Call Pro. Welcomes letters (with CVs and photographs) from individual actors previously unknown to the company.

Changing Faces Theatre Company

PO Box 57877, London SE26 9AN
tel 020-8776 8706 *fax* 020-8778 4079
email info@changingfacestheatre.com
website www.changingfacestheatre.com
Artistic Director Nicholas Kessler

Production details: A not-for-profit theatre company that is young, vibrant and ready to bring the highest quality of interactive, literacy-based theatre and workshops to primary-aged children. With classroom experience, a passion for language, a little bit of glue and a lot of imagination, Changing Faces was formed as a direct response to the challenges of teaching literacy in the classroom in the 21st Century. On average stages 6-10 projects per year, with around 300 performances and 250 workshops in 100-150 schools, community venues, theatres and libraries in London and the South East. In general, 2 actors perform an interactive, audience-actor collaborative show and /or workshop, working with audiences aged 4-11. Musical instrument, vocal and physical theatre skills are required, as is a clean driving licence. Puppetry, workshop skillls and classroom experience are an advantage.

Casting procedures: Sometimes holds general auditions. Casting breakdowns are available via Spotlight. Rarely or never has the opportunity to cast disabled actors.

The Children's Touring Partnership

2nd Floor, National House, 60-66 Wardour Street, London W1F 0TA
tel 020-7292 8896
email info@childrenstouringpartnership.com
website www.childrenstouringpartnership.com

Production details: Established in 2010. Stages 1-2 productions annually, with around 60 performances in 12 large and mid-scale theatres UK-wide. In general 12 actors are involved in each production. Recent productions include: *Goodnight Mister Tom* and *Swallows & Amazons.*

Casting procedures: Uses freelance casting directors. Does not welcome unsolicited approaches from actors previously unknown to the company, but will consider visiting other productions, and accepts invitations to view actors' websites. Actively encourages applications from disabled actors.

Clwyd Theatr Cymru Theatre for Young People / Theatr ar gyfer Bobl Ifanc

Raikes Lane, Mold, Flintshire CH7 1YA
tel 01352-701 575
email ctctyp@clwyd-theatr-cymru.co.uk
email youngclwyd@clwyd-theatr-cymru.co.uk
website www.ctctyp.co.uk
Artistic Director Tim Baker *Producer* Anne Plenderleith *Administrator* Nerys Edwards

Production details: Founded in 1997, Clwyd Theatr Cymru strives to provide creative and unique arts experiences for children and young people. Their recent productions include: *Portrait of The Artist as a Young Dog, Sky Hawk* and *Humbug!* Each production consists of 4 actors and performers are asked to have some singing and dancing ability, as well as proficiency with a musical instrument. Performers are sometimes expected to lead workshops. The company presents up to 5 productions per year,

Theatre

equating to around 110 performances annually. These are held at various venues, ranging from schools to theatres, community spaces and arts centres, to audiences of childen, young people and their families.

Casting procedures: Uses a freelance casting director. Offers Equity-approved contracts negotiated through TMA and subscribes to Equity Pension Scheme.

Creaking Door Productions

Rhys Jones House, St Peter's School, Harefield, Lympstone, Devon EX8 5AU
tel (01395) 264877
email office@creakingdoor.co.uk
website www.creakingdoor.co.uk
Artistic Director Tom Sherman

Production details: Established in 2005. Specialises in small-scale children's theatre productions in schools and venues throughout the South West; in 2010 the company implemented its new Education Programme. Stages 2-4 productions annually with around 40 performances. In general 2-4 actors go on tour, playing to audiences aged 4 to 13, plus family audiences. Incoming actors should have singing and good basic movement skills, as well as a current driving licence. Actors may be expected to lead workshops. Recent productions include: *Cindarella*; *The Life and Times of Isambard Kingdom Brunel*; KS2 History workshops – *From Time to Time*; *Just So Stories*; *Frogs, Kings and Golden Wings*; *Tales of Bread and Golden Thread* and *Beauty and the Beast.*

Casting procedures: Sometimes holds general auditions; actors may write in July and October to request inclusion. Casting breakdowns are available from the website, via Equity, and from Theatre Bristol and Theatre Devon. Welcomes letters (with CVs and photographs) from individual actors previously unknown to the company, sent by post only. Rarely or never has the opportunity to cast disabled actors.

Cwmni Theatr Arad Goch

Stryd Y Baddon, Aberystwyth, Ceredigion SY23 2NN
tel (01970) 617998 *fax* (01970) 611223
email post@aradgoch.org
website www.aradgoch.cymru
Artistic Director Jeremy Turner

Production details: Founded in 1989. Main focus of work is theatre. Normally tours 6 projects each year with an average annual total of 150 performances and more than 100 different venues. Venues include schools, theatres and community venues across Wales and occasionally abroad. In general 3-6 actors go on tour and play to audiences of all ages. Singing ability, proficiency with a musical instrument, fluency in Welsh and a driving licence are required. Actors may also be expected to lead workshops. Recent productions include: *SXTO*, a performance for secondary school pupils written by Bethan Gwanas; *Cysgu'n Brysur*, an ambitious, large-scale musical drama; *Lleuad yn Olau*, a stage adaptation of one of the best known Welsh language books for children; *Hola!*, the story of Welsh emigration to Patagonia 150 years ago; *Mwnci ar Dan*, a challenging play for young people by Sara Moore Williams; *Innocent as Strawberries*, a play based on the work of Dylan Thomas in collaboration with the National Library of Wales. The company also performed works from their repertoire at various venues on Europe. Offers ITC/Equity-approved contracts and does not subscribe to the Equity Pension Scheme.

Casting procedures: Sometimes holds general auditions; actors requesting inclusion should write before the start of the academic year. Accepts submissions (with CVs and photographs) from actors previously unknown to the company sent by post or email. Will also accept showreels and invitations to view individual actors' websites. Will consider applications from disabled actors to play disabled characters.

Daylight Theatre

66 Middle Street, Stroud, Gloucestershire GL5 1EA
tel (01453) 763808
website www.daylighttheatre.co.uk
Artistic Director Hugh Young *Key personnel* Roger Burfield

Production details: Founded in 1977. Tours educational theatre into schools. Topics have included drugs, HIV/AIDS, Shakespeare, history and mythology, and have been linked to the National Curriculum. Normally tours 7 projects each year with an average annual total of 200 performances and 150 different venues. Venues include schools (mainly primary but some secondary), arts centres and theatres across the UK, Germany and Luxembourg. In general 2-3 actors go on tour and play to audiences aged 4-18. Actors are required to hold a driving licence and may also be expected to lead workshops. Recent productions include: *Can You Take It?* – drugs, alcohol and tobacco education for 9-11 year-olds; *A Midsummer Night's Dream* and *Macbeth* for Key Stage 2 level; and *Ghostcliff Grange*, a World War II drama, also for Key Stage 2.

Casting procedures: Advises that the company rarely needs new actors.

Fevered Sleep

c/o Young Vic, 66 The Cut, London SE1 8LZ
tel 020-7922 2988
email admin@feveredsleep.co.uk
website www.feveredsleep.co.uk
Artistic Directors David Harradine and Samantha Butler

Production details: Established in 1996. Creates original performances, installations, films, books and digital art for adults and for children. Fearless about experimentation and passionate about research, develops projects that challenge people to rethink their relationships with each other and with the world. Work appears in very diverse places across the UK and beyond, from thatres, galleries and cinemas, to parks, beaches and schools, and the spaces of everyday life; in people's homes, on phones, online. "Whatever we make and wherever it's experienced we're driven by an ambition to present otstanding and transformative art."

Tours 3 projects annually, in around 15 venues (theatres, arts centres, galleries, and site-specific) in the UK, internationally and in London. In general, 2-4 performers go on tour, playing to audiences aged 3-7 and 17+. Incoming artists may be expected to lead workshops, and may require dance, physical theatre and/or musical instrument skills, depending on the project. Recent productions include: *Dusk*, *Brilliant*, *An Infinite Line: Brighton*, and *Stilled.*

Casting procedures: Sometimes holds general auditions, artists may write at any time. Welcomes CVs by email only from individual performers previously unknown to the company, sent by post or email, as well as invitations to view individual artists' websites – but prefers not to receive showreels. Offers Equity-approved contracts as negotiated through ITC. Will consider applications from disabled actors "in line with our equal opportunities policy".

Freshwater Theatre Company

Channelsea House, Canning Road, Abbey Lane, London E15 3ND
tel 0844-800 2870
email info@freshwatertheatre.co.uk
website www.freshwatertheatre.co.uk
Directors Helen Wood, Carol Tagg

Production details: Established in 1996 with the aim of offering high-quality, affordable, innovative drama opportunites to primary school children and teachers. Now also offers workshops for secondary schools. Runs workshops and storytelling sessions addressing a range of curriculum areas including history, geography, Shakespeare, citizenship, multicultural studies, maths, science, cross-curricular and modern foreign languages and the needs of early years pupils. Also runs drama in-service training courses for teachers. Does not tour, but provides around 45 types of sessions all year round at nurseries, schools, libraries and community venues in Greater London, South West, Essex, the West Midlands conurbation, and Greater Manchester. Around 60 freelance facilitators work with audiences aged 3 to 12. Relevant experience is required, and actors are expected to lead workshops. Recent workshops include: *Mary Seacole*, *The Three Musketeers*, and *Great Fire of London.*

Casting procedures: Holds general auditions once a year; actors may write in at any time. Welcomes letters (with CVs and photographs) sent by post or email, but only from experienced workshop facilitators. Does not accept showreels or invitations to view individual actors' websites. "We only engage dedicated, experienced workshop leaders to undertake our drama sessions, and will only consider those who can provide regular and ongoing availability within the areas we cover."

Gazebo Theatre in Education Company

Bilston Town Hall, Church Street, Bilston, West Midlands WV14 0AP
tel (01902) 497222 *fax* (01902) 497244
email admin@gazebotie.org
website www.gazebotie.org
Artistic Director Michael O'Hara *Strategic Director* Pamela Cole-Hudson

Production details: Founded in 1979. Normally tours 3-5 projects each year plus workshops, with an average annual total of 300 performances and 250 different venues; these are mainly schools and community venues in the West Midlands and South Shropshire. In general between 1 and 3 actors go on tour and play to audiences aged 4-25. Musical ability and movement skills are sometimes required, as is a driving licence. Actors may also be expected to lead workshops. Recent productions include: *Billy No Mates!* (Special Needs); *If you see a crocodile* (Nursery & Reception); *Presents from the Past* (KS2); *Doing our Bit* (KS3).

Casting procedures: Casting breakdowns are sometimes available by postal application (with sae) or through Equity Job Information Service. The company website will also show details of auditions and artists opportunities. Accepts submissions (with CVs and photographs) from actors previously unknown to the company if sent by post. Open auditions take place over the summer months. Will accept invitations to view individual actors' websites. Does not welcome unsolicited emails. Offers non-Equity contracts. Actively encourages applications from disabled actors and promotes the use of inclusive casting.

Gibber Theatre Ltd

The Old Library, 2A Woodleigh Road, Whitley Bay, NE25 8ET
tel 0191-252 2039 *fax* 0191-252 4833
email hello@wearegibber.com
website www.wearegibber.com
Artistic Directors Victoria Blackburn, Tim Watt

Production details: Founded in 1999. An educational theatre company specialising in drama-based experiential learning programmes for young people of all ages. The company has built a reputation for making a difference in education, by delivering high-quality presentation, performance, workshop, road show and special events. On average performs 10 projects each year, with approximately 300 performances in 250-300 schools across the UK. Also tours to outdoor and community venues, hospitals and theatres. In general 3-4 actors go on tour, playing to audiences aged 5 to 18+. Actors may be required to lead workshops, and should have singing and physical theatre skills as well as a driving licence. Recent productions include: bespoke performances and workshops for London Learning Skills Council (Year 10 careers tour exploring post-16 learning and voluntary opportunities); and Newcastle Healthy Schools (KS4 tobacco education tour with a focus on tobacco-industry tactics).

Casting procedures: Sometimes holds general auditions; actors may write at any time. Casting breakdowns are available from *The Stage* and Casting Call Pro. Welcomes letters (with CVs and photographs) from actors previously unknown to the company, sent by post or email. Accepts showreels and invitations to view individual actors' websites. Will consider applications from disabled actors to play characters with disabilities.

Greenwich & Lewisham Young People's Theatre (GLYPT)

The Tramshed, 51–53 Woolwich New Road, Woolwich, SE18 6ES
tel 020-8854 1316
email info@glypt.co.uk
website www.glypt.co.uk
Artistic Director Jeremy James *Education Officer* Claire Newby.

Production details: GLYPT creates theatre for, with and by young people. It runs Youth Theatre workshops for 8-21 year-olds, and specialist programmes for young people with learning difficulties. The company also runs a comprehensive programme of workshops for young refugees and new arrivals. Tours 2 productions a year to young audiences across South East London and beyond; these visit schools as Theatre in Education programmes, and also play at community and arts centres and at theatres. The work explores current and provoking issues that affect the lives of young audiences, and offers a platform for aesthetic and educational debate. Recent productions have included: *The Inquiry*, *Mud City*, *SK8 Angel* and *Master Juba*.

Casting procedures: Operates the ITC/Equity contract and works with actors committed to the young people's theatre sector. "We actively encourage applications from disabled actors and promote the use of inclusive casting." Welcomes letters and emails (with CVs) from actors and skilled workshop facilitators.

Half Moon Young People's Theatre

43 Whitehorse Road, London E1 0ND
tel 020-7265 8138 *fax* 020-7709 8914
email admin@halfmoon.org.uk
website www.halfmoon.org.uk
Director Chris Elwell

Production details: Established in 1990, Half Moon is a local organisation with a national remit, based in Tower Hamlets, East London. The company gives young people from birth to 18 (25 for disabled young people) an opportunity to experience the best in young people's theatre, both as a participant and as an audience member. Half Moon tours its own productions nationally, as well as a portfolio of work through its producing arm "Half Moon presents" to venues including theatres, libraries, schools, community spaces and festivals. The portfolio covers a range of work from artists and companies drawn from all the genres of theatre, spoken word, new writing and dance, reflecting the UK's contemporary, diverse communities. Half Moon has ethical status with ITC and offers ITC/Equity-spproved contracts.

Casting procedures: Casting breakdowns are available through the company's website, circulated to agents and through Spotlight. Actively encourages applications from disabled actors and promotes the use of inclusive casting.

Hopscotch Theatre Company

2nd Floor, 7 Water Row, Glasgow G51 3UW
tel 0141-440 2025 *fax* 0141-440 2025
email info@hopscotchtheatre.com
website www.hopscotchtheatre.com
Artistic Director Ross Stenhouse

Production details: Founded in 1988. A Theatre in Education company touring 4 productions each year to primary schools with an average annual total of 520 performances. Venues include schools, arts centres, theatres and community venues across Scotland. In general 4 actors go on tour and play to audiences aged 5-12 years. Singing ability and some proficiency with a musical instrument would be beneficial, but are not necessary. Recent productions include: *Brand New Andrew & Fair Trade Fred*, *The Life & Times of Robert Burns* and *Tam O' Shanter*.

Casting procedures: Accepts CVs, photographs and covering letter from actors previously unknown to the company sent by post or email. Will also accept showreels. Offers non-Equity contracts. Rarely (or never) has the opportunity to cast disabled actors.

In Toto Theatre Company

97 Upper Ground, London SE1 9PR
tel 020-7261 9187
email sarah@in-tototheatre.co.uk
website www.in-tototheatre.co.uk
Artistic Director Sarah Carter *Associate Director* Lennie Charles

Production details: Founded in 1989 and became a charity in 2000. Provides inclusive theatre for all ages using a combination of puppetry, live music, storytelling and dance. Specialises in creating 'total theatre' by, with and for young audiences – "a highly visual musical style of theatre approach which is inclusive and accessible to a wide range of ages and abilities". Also runs participatory arts activities for families, children and young adults to make their own performance. Has completed 7 projects to date with an average of 50 performances in up to 30 venues (schools, community venues and outdoor festivals, including site-specific). On average 2-3 performers/actors tour in the company's small-scale productions devised for age groups from 18 months upwards. An additional skill is usually required of actors; playing a musical instrument and puppetry are especially valued.

Casting procedures: Does not hold general auditions. Will accept email enquiries, but unsolicited letters by post are not welcomed. Sometimes advertises casting breakdowns via Arts Jobs or Equity information line. Rather than showreels, prefers to receive links to actors' websites by email. Offers Equity-approved contracts through ITC. Actively encourages applications from disabled actors and promotes the use of inclusive casting.

"We usually recruit artists with an interest and proven experience in making theatre collaboratively, with an interdisciplinary approach. Being able to facilitate workshops is a very important requirement, and those with a background in arts therapy, social work, education or working with special needs, in addition to professional performance or visual arts training, are far more likely to be considered."

Jack Drum Arts

St Cuthberts Centre Crook, Church Hill, Crook, County Durham DL15 9DN
tel/fax (01388) 765002
email info@jackdrum.co.uk
website www.jackdrum.co.uk
Co-Directors Paddy Burton, Helen Ward, Julie Ward

Production details: Founded in 1986. Delivers a strong programme of participatory arts for all sectors of the community, often linked to the production of touring theatre. Historically, toured 2 theatre projects annually with an average annual total of 40 performances at up to 40 different venues, including schools, arts centres, theatres, outdoor venues and community venues across the UK and abroad, with a focus on rural touring and schools. In general, productions involve 3-4 actors, playing to audiences of pre-school age and upwards. Singing ability, proficiency with a musical instrument and a driving licence are required for some shows. Actors may also be expected to lead workshops.

Recent productions include: 3 new shows for young audiences created as part of Children & the Arts START scheme, and a co-production with Mad Alice Theatre Company of a play for family audiences inspired by the Lindisfarne Gospels and the stories of the Northern Saints. Other projects include large-scale community play productions, which are created with local communities working in tandem with professional practitioners and film/media projects.

For the First World War commemoration the company is looking to retour its adult production *Set in Stone* by David Napthine, which was originally created in 1999 to coincide with the Millennium Pardon Campaign and is mentioned in Hansard.

Casting procedures: Accepts submissions (with CVs and photographs) from actors with a North East connection. "We like to know who is around in the North East, especially if based in County Durham. Can help access local networks and professional development." Offers Equity and non-Equity contracts. Rarely (or never) has the opportunity to cast disabled actors, but would be interested in developing projects which can make this possible. Particularly interested in actors who have BSL skills.

Kazzum

Oxford House, Derbyshire Street, London E2 6HG
tel 020-7749 1123
email info@kazzum.org
website www.kazzum.org
Artistic Director Daryl Beeton

Production details: Established in 1989. "We create playful theatre and participative arts activities for young people, using art forms that reflect diverse cultural influences." Stages 1-2 productions each year, with around 40-70 performances in 30 arts centres, theatres, and outdoor and community venues across the UK. In general 3 actors go on tour, playing to audiences aged 4-8 and 10+. Incoming actors should have singing, musical instrument, dance and physical theatre skills and may be expected to lead workshops. Recent productions include: *The Boy Who Grew Flowers, Hunt, The Sorcerer's Apprentice,* and *Beginning with Blobs.*

Casting procedures: Actors may write in March through to May to request inclusion. Casting breakdowns are available from the website, through Equity Job Information Service and Arts Jobs. Welcomes letters (with CVs and photographs) from individual actors previously unknown to the company, sent by post or email. Also accepts showreels and invitations to view individual actors' websites. Offers Equity-approved contracts as negotiated through ITC. Actively encourages applications from disabled actors, and promotes the use of inclusive casting.

Kinetic Theatre Company

Suite H, The Jubilee Centre, 10-12 Lombard Road, London SW19 3TZ
tel 020-8286 2613
email sarah@kinetictheatre.co.uk
website www.kinetictheatre.co.uk
Producer/Writer Graham Scott *Artistic Directors* James Austin-Harvey (Casting Director), Bridget Lambert, Rachel Hickson, Julie Kinsella, Andy Byron

Production details: Established in 1988. One of the country's most prominent Theatre in Education companies. Performs plays geared to the National Curriculum for Science, to schools and theatres througout the UK. Has 9 shows, 4 of which are on the road at any one time. All shows are self-contained musical comedies, all being very different in style. On average performs 12 tours every year with around 900 performances in 600 venues in England, Scotland, Wales and Northern Ireland. All shows are 2-handers, and actors play to audiences aged 5 to 12. Actors require reasonable singing and dancing skills and a driving licence is essential. Recent productions include: *The Hospital Force*, *Down to Earth*, *Lady Cecily's Sound Box*, and *Robin & the Withering Wood.*

Casting procedures: Does not hold general auditions; lets actors know when to write in, via the usual casting breakdown sites. Casting breakdowns are widely available: consult the website for full details. Contracts are based on Equity/ITC guidelines for small-scale touring. Will consider applications from actors with disabilities to play characters with disabilities. "We cast for our productions 3 times a year, usually around February, June and October, and we always put out castings for our workshop-style auditions. We cannot consider applications outside these times and due to limited space do not hold details on file. Please do not send unsolicited CVs/ photos as it will just waste your money. We recommend that actors check the auditions page on our website for general information on when auditions are coming up, and also for more detailed information to prepare for our auditions."

Krazy Kat Theatre Company

173 Hartington Road, Brighton BN2 3PA
tel (01273) 692552
email krazykattheatre@ntlworld.com
website www.krazykattheatre.co.uk
Artistic Director Kinny Gardner

Production details: A children's theatre company founded in 1982, specialising in highly visual forms of theatre that are accessible to Deaf children. Normally tours 2 projects each year with an average annual total of 50 performances and 35 venues. Venues include schools, arts centres, theatres, outdoor venues and community centres throughout UK. In general 2 actors and a technician go on tour and play to audiences aged 3-7. Singing ability, physical theatre skills, British sign language and a driving licence are required. Actors may also be expected to lead workshops. Recent productions include: *A (Midsummer Night's) Dream,Petrushka*, *The Pied Piper*, a Victorian *Mikado*and *The Very Magic Flute.*

Casting procedures: Sometimes holds general auditions; actors can write at any time requesting inclusion. Accepts submissions (with CVs and photographs) from actors previously unknown to the company if sent by post. Does not welcome unsolicited emails. Will also accept invitations to view individual actors' websites. Offers non-Equity contracts but at Equity and ITC rates. Actively encourages applications from disabled actors and promotes the use of inclusive casting.

The London Bus Theatre Company

37 Chestnut Close, Hockley, Essex SS5 5EQ
tel (01208) 814514 *fax* (01208) 814514
email kathy@londonbustheatre.co.uk
website www.londonbustheatre.co.uk
Principal Chris Turner

Production details: One of the most respected theatre-in-education companies in the UK, supported by the National Theatre, Arts Council, National Lottery, police and private companies as well as the Home Office. Provides innovative workshops on the subjects of drugs, bullying, anti-social behaviour, alcohol, domestic abuse, job interview techniques and knife crime. Also provides schools and colleges with the celebrated 'Kick It – Bullying', 'Kick It – Smoking' and 'Kick It – Binge Drinking' DVD series. In 2008 the company produced the award-winning 'Nutter' anti-bullying DVD. Stages an average of 20 projects each year, with approximately 200 performances in 200 venues including leisure centres, colleges and youth detention centres all over England. In general 6 actors go on tour and play to audiences aged 8-18. Actors may be expected to lead workshops and should possess singing, dance, and physical theatre skills as well as holding a driving licence. Recent productions incude: *2 Smart* (Essex police/ Essex FM tour of Essex theatres in 2008): and *Nutter* (tour of schools 2008, Arts Council project 2008). Also produced the feature film *Angels vs Bullies* 2009-2012 and is now shooting second feature film *Oil City Rockers.*

Casting procedures: Holds general auditions and actors may write in at any time. Welcomes letters (with CVs and photographs) from individual actors previously unknown to the company, sent by post or email. Accepts showreels and will consider invitiations to view individual actors' websites. Considers applications from disabled actors to play characters with disabilities.

Loudmouth Education & Training

The Friends' Institute, 220 Moseley Road, Highgate, Birmingham B12 0DG
tel 0121-446 4880 *fax* 0121-440 3940
email info@loudmouth.co.uk
website www.loudmouth.co.uk
Company Directors Chris Cowan, Eleanor Vale

Production details: Founded in 1994. Supplies interactive education and training programmes for young people on personal, social and health education issues, and accessible training for adults to aid personal and professional development. On average 4 teams of 2 actors tour 14 projects around 600 UK venues each year; venues include schools, colleges, community venues and youth centres.

Actors are expected to lead workshops and must have a full driving licence. Recent productions include: *Trust Me* – an interactive theatre programme focusing on STIs, contraception and unplanned pregnancy.

Casting procedures: Holds general auditions. Welcomes letters with CVs and photographs from individual actors previously unknown to the company. Will accept unsolicited CVs and photographs sent by email. Does not welcome showreels or invitations to view individual actors' websites. Rarely or never has the opportunity to cast disabled actors.

M6 Theatre Company

Studio Theatre, Hamer County Primary School, Albert Royds Street, Rochdale OL16 2SU
tel (01706) 355898 *fax* (01706) 712601
website www.m6theatre.co.uk
Artistic Producer Dorothy Wood

Production details: M6 Theatre Company specalises in producing and touring high-quality, accessible and emotionally engaging theatre for young audiences. Founded in 1977, the company tours 3-5 productions each year, through approximately 300 performances/ workshops. Touring venues include theatres, schools, festivals, prisons and early years settings across the North West and nationally. Cast sizes are generally 2-4; actors may be expected to participate in workshops accompanying productions. Recent productions have included: *One Little Word* (a sensitive and moving production for children aged 3+ exploring friendship and conflict resolution, underscored with original music and with only 1 spoken word); *Sunflowers and Sheds* (a heart-warming tale of friendship, family and fun on the allotment, for ages 5+ and anyone who's ever made a friend); *Mavis Sparkle* – touring Spring 2013 (this delightful new production mixes illusion, animation and laughter to discover the magic and wonder in the universe, each other and ourselves – ages 5+). M6 also creates and delivers an exciting participatory programme of creative, free time; theatre-arts based workshops and sharing events – ACT NOW! A diverse range of young people from Rochdale (8-18s) participate in and lead activities at M6's purpose-built Studio Theatre and at a range of outreach community settings in Rochdale. ACT NOW! is an ambitious extension of M6's participatory workshop programme, building on proven successful experience, practice and partnerships. Participants' involvement and achievements will be shared with the local community regularly throughout the 3-year project (Big Lottery Reaching Communities funded) and will culminate in a high-profile showcase event/Youth Theatre Festival in 2014.

Casting procedures: Accepts submissions (with CVs and photographs) from actors previously unknown to the company. Unfortunately the company is unable to return photos. Actor contracts are ITC/ Equity-approved.

Magic Carpet Theatre

18 Church Street, Sutton on Hull, East Yorkshire HU7 4TS
tel (01482) 709939
email jon@magiccarpettheatre.com
website www.magiccarpettheatre.com
Artistic Director Jon Marshall

Production details: Professional touring children's theatre company presenting shows and workshops in the UK and abroad. Tours 3-4 productions annually, with around 250 performances in 250 venues including schools, arts and community venues, and festivals. In general 3 actors go on tour, playing to audiences aged 5-11. Actors may be expected to lead workshops. Recent productions include: *Mr Albert's Big Finish; The Wizard of Castle Magic* and *Magic Circus.*

Casting procedures: Does not hold general auditions; actors may write in the autumn to request inclusion. Advises actors to "ring us rather than sending CVs, etc., to see when we are casting".

MakeBelieve Arts

The Deptford Mission, 1 Creek Road, London SE8 3BT
tel 020-8691 3803 *fax* 020-8691 3880
email info@makebelievearts.co.uk
website www.makebelievearts.co.uk
Artistic Director Trisha Lee

Production details: Established in 2002 and gained charitable status in 2006. A leading provider of high-quality arts and education programmes, for Foundation Stage, Primary and Secondary School pupils and their parents and teachers. Based in South London but works in other boroughs and counties across the UK. In general 4-6 actors stage 1 project a year, with around 100 performances at 50 schools. Skills required depend on the production, and actors may be asked to lead workshops. Recent productions include: *The Woman Who Cooked Everything, Gulliver's Travels, Giant Tours* and *Journey to the Centre of the Brain.*

Casting procedures: Holds general auditions. Casting breakdowns are available from the website and in *The Stage.* Welcomes letters (with CVs and photographs) from individual actors previously unknown to the company, sent by post or email. Does not however accept showreels or invitations to view individual actors' websites. Offers Equity-approved contracts negotiated through ITC. Rarely has the opportunity to cast disabled actors.

Moby Duck

12 Reservoir Retreat, Birmingham B16 9EH
tel/fax 0121-242 0400
email info@moby-duck.co.uk
website www.moby-duck.com
Artistic Director Guy Hutchins

Production details: Founded in 1999. Performs 2 projects annually, with more than 50 performances at the same number of schools, arts centres, theatres and community venues across all regions. In general 3-4 actors go on tour, playing to audiences aged 4 to 80. Requires actors to have "an understanding of the other cultures we work in". Actors may be expected to lead workshops. Singing, musical instrument, dance and physical theatre skills are an advantage, and actors should hold a clean driving licence. For details of recent productions, see the website.

Casting procedures: Sometimes holds general auditions, and actors may write at any time to request inclusion. Welcomes letters (with CVs and photographs) from individual actors previously unknown to the company, sent by post or email. Also welcomes showreels and invitations to view individual actors' websites. Offers Equity-approved contracts as negotiated through ITC. Rarely or never has the opportunity to cast disabled actors.

Newfound Theatre Company

mobile (07753) 237209
email newfoundtheatre@gmail.com
website www.newfoundtheatre.co.uk

Production details: Theatre in Education company touring/performing several projects each year, with around 200 performances annually to schools in London and the North West. In general, 3 actors go on tour playing to audiences aged 5 to 16. Actors are sometimes expected to lead workshops. Recent productions include: *Making Monologues*, *Rewind* and *Thinspiration*.

Casting procedures: Uses in-house casting directors; does not hold general auditions. Casting breakdowns are available via Casting Call Pro. Welcomes unsolicited CVs and photographs from actors previously unknown to the company if sent by email; also accepts invitations to view individual actors' websites. Encourages applications from disabled actors and promotes the use of inclusive casting.

Nimble Fish

30 Wilton Square, London N1 3DW
mobile (07939) 522518
email getnimble@nimble-fish.co.uk
website www.nimble-fish.co.uk
Directors Samatha Holdsworth, Greg Klerkx

Production details: "An evolving collective of creative individuals who actively pursue collaborations with disadvantaged communities to foster positive social change." Performs 1 project annually with around 13 peformances in 14 venues, including schools, outdoor and community venues, and other site-specific venues in London, the South East and Edinburgh. Around 3-6 actors go on tour performing to adult audiences. Actors may be expected to lead workshops. Recent productions include: *The Container* (winner of a 2007 Edinburgh Fringe First and a 2007 Amnesty International Freedom of Expression Award) and *Einstein's Dreams*. Current productions in development include *The Trial of Wernher von Braun*.

Casting procedures: Sometimes holds general auditions. Does not welcome unsolicited approaches from individuals not previously known to the company. Offers Equity-approved contracts via ITC. Actively encourages applications from disabled actors and promotes the use of inclusive casting.

Nottingham Playhouse Roundabout TIE

Nottingham Playhouse, Wellington Circus, Nottingham NG1 5AF
tel 0115-947 4361
email enquiry@nottinghamplayhouse.co.uk
website www.nottinghamplayhouse.co.uk

Production details: Part of Learning & Participation Department at Nottingham Playhouse, and established in 1973, Roundabout creates 1-2 small-scale productions per year. These are performed mostly in East Midlands schools, with some performances in small theatre venues – including own studio at Nottingham Playhouse. Employs 3-6 actors each year, on contracts usually lasting from 6 to 12 weeks. Actors are usually multi-skilled. Singing and physical theatre are essential for many of the productions, and actors often have workshop skills and/or play a musical instrument as well. A driving licence is helpful. The company has a specialism in creating theatre for young people with profound learning difficulties and autism, and Makaton signing skills are very welcome for these productions.

Casting procedures: Casting, which is inclusive in every sense, is carried out by the director of the production, usually in collaboration with the Playhouse's Casting Director, Sooki McShane. Welcomes CVs by email or permanent web link, marked for the attention of the Associate Director. Offers ITC/Equity contracts.

Oily Cart Company

Smallwood School Annexe, Smallwood Road, London SW17 0TW
tel 020-8672 6329 *fax* 020-8672 0792
email oilies@oilycart.org.uk
website www.oilycart.org.uk
Artistic Director Tim Webb

Production details: One of the leading theatre companies in the UK, creating highly interactive multi-sensory performances for the very young (6 months to 6 years) and for young people (aged 3-19) with Profound or Multiple Learning Disabilities (PMLD) or an Autistic Spectrum Disorder (ASD). Tours national and international venues like theatres and arts centres with early years shows, and takes its special-needs work to special schools around the UK. Recent productions include: *Baby Balloon* for audiences aged 6 months to 2 years; *If All The World*

Were Paper; *Blue* and *Pool Piece* – an interactive hydrotherapy pool show for young people with PMLD or ASD.

Casting procedures: Casting breakdowns are available on the website **www.oilycart.org.uk** and the Arts Jobs website **www.artsjobs.org.uk.** Offers ITC/ Equity-approved contracts. Actively encourages applications from disabled actors and promotes the use of inclusive casting.

Onatti Productions Ltd

The Old Chapel, Yorkley Slade, Yorkley, Gloucestershire GL15 4SB
tel (01594) 562033 *fax* 0870-164 3629
email info@onatti.co.uk
website www.onatti.co.uk

Produces foreign-language productions performed at Primary and Secondary schools throughout the UK, France and Spain. Plays are produced in French, German, Spanish and English; all are written by the company and used as an exciting way of promoting and enhancing languages in schools. Onatti produces around 8 tours each year. Employs native foreign actors for contracts from 3 to 10 months. Actors are sourced from the UK and Europe.

Passe-Partout

13 Stanford Avenue, Brighton BN1 6AD
tel (01273) 557595
email p@sse-partout.com
Artistic Director Michele Young

Production details: Founded in 1986. "Theatre for social change – assisting people to have a voice about an issue which concerns them." Normally tours 3 projects each year, with an average annual total of 20 performances and 20 different venues including schools, outdoor centres, community venues and office spaces in the UK and abroad. In general 4 actors go on tour and play to audiences of all ages. Any additional skills that actors may have will be put to use. Actors may also be expected to lead workshops. Recent projects include: *Anti-bullying Strategy Development* (prisons, UK); *Social Capital* (various schools, Europe); *Street Children* (Nairobi, Kenya); *Bio-diversity* (Toulouse, France) and *Silkworm Journey* (France). Has an alliance with Inedit Films to produce 3-minute dramas (fact-based) for educational purposes.

Casting procedures: "We cast from the group of people who have proposed an issue they want to take forward. We sometimes build-in 1 or 2 people from outside that group who have interest and energy."

Pied Piper Theatre Company

1 Lilian Place, Coxcombe Lane, Chiddingfold GU8 4QA
tel (01428) 684022
email twpiedpiper@aol.com
email info@piedpipertheatre.co.uk
website www.piedpipertheatre.co.uk
Artistic Director Tina Williams *Associate Director* Nicola Sangster

Production details: Founded in 1984, Pied Piper creates exciting, high quality and magical plays for children. Works in schools, theatres and arts centres specialising in new writing or new adaptations of favourite stories or books. Funded by Arts Council South East. ITC/Equity contracts.

Pilot Theatre

York Theatre Royal, St Leonard's Place, York YO1 7HD
tel (01904) 635755
email info@pilot-theatre.com
website www.pilot-theatre.com
Artistic Director Marcus Romer

Production details: A national mid-scale touring company producing a programme of education resources for young people. Stages on average 3-6 projects annually, with 150 performances in 20 arts centres and theatres across the UK. In general 6-10 actors go on tour, playing to audiences aged 11-25. Actors are sometimes expected to lead workshops.

Casting procedures: Actors may write in May and August to request inclusion. Casting breakdowns are available on the website or via Spotlight. Welcomes unsolicited CVs and photographs if submitted by email. Also accepts showreels and will consider invitations to view individual actors' websites. Offers Equity-approved contracts as negotiated through TMA/ITC. Actively encourages applications by disabled actors and promotes the use of inclusive casting.

The Play House

c/o Birmingham Repertory Theatre, Centenary Square, Broad Street, Birmingham B1 2EP
tel 0121-265 4425 *fax* 0121-233 0652
email info@theplayhouse.org.uk
website www.theplayhouse.org.uk
General Manager Sarah-Jane Watkinson *Head of Programmes* Juliet Fry

Production details: Established in 1986. An educational theatre charity that uses uses participatory theatre and drama to stimulate and support the language and learning of children and young people. Best known for its *Language Alive!* theatre-in-education tours, which bring the curriculum to life for 3-11 year olds and a range of issue-based projects as well as INSET and CPD for teachers. Tours an average of 15-20 projects annually, with around 1,000 performances in 60-70 schools, outdoor and other venues in the West Midlands. In general 2-3 actors go on tour, performing to young audiences aged 3-18. Skills required vary according to the project and a clean driving licence is required. Actors may be expected to lead workshops.

Casting procedures: Sometimes holds general auditions; actors should write in when these are advertised. Rarely or never has the opportunity to cast disabled actors.

Playbox Theatre (Generator)

The Dream Factory, Shelly Avenue,
Warwick CV34 6LE
tel (01926) 419555 *fax* (01926) 411429
email stewart@playboxtheatre.com
website www.playboxtheatre.com
Artistic Director Stewart McGill *Directors* Emily Quash, Mary King

Production details: Established in 1986, Generator is the professional acting company of Playbox Theatre, reworking classic drama for contemporary audiences. 2 productions staged annually, touring nationally to arts centres, theatres, outdoor venues and educational venues. Based in Warwick. Up to 12 actors used in each production. Offers Equity approved contracts. Recent productions include: *A Doll's House* and *Henry VI – The Wars of the Roses.*

Casting procedures: Accepts submissions (with CVs and photographs) from actors previously unknown to the company sent by post or by email. Actively encourages applications from disabled actors and promotes the use of inclusive casting.

Playtime Theatre Company

18 Bennell's Avenue, Whitstable, Kent CT5 2HP
tel (01227) 266272 *fax* (01227) 266648
email Playtime@dircon.co.uk
website www.playtimetheatre.co.uk
Artistic Director Nicholas Champion

Production details: Established in 1983 with the aim of bringing imaginative and innovative professional theatre and workshops to children and young people. Has grown to become "one of the leading children's theatre companies in the South East", and tours both nationally and internationally. Normally tours 2-4 projects each year with an average annual total of 200 performances and 190 venues. Venues include schools, arts centres, theatres, community venues and festivals. Tours have covered the South East, Yorkshire and various countries in Europe and the Middle East. In general 2-4 actors go on tour and play to targeted audiences of 5-7, 4-11, 7-11, 9-13 and 14+. Actors are expected to offer 1-2 additional skills. Singing ability, proficiency with a musical instrument, physical theatre, puppetry and mime skills and a driving licence are all useful. Actors may also be expected to lead workshops. Recent productions include:*The Jackdaw*, a history play set during the Napoleonic Wars; *TUI*, a road and cycle safety play and *A Silent Song*, a WW1 play looking at pacifism.

Casting procedures: Holds general auditions; actors should write in August requesting inclusion. Casting breakdowns are available through the website, postal application (with sae), Equity Job Information Service, *The Stage* and, Casting Call Pro Castcall. Welcomes submissions (with CVs and photographs) from actors previously unknown to the company sent by post or email. Also accepts showreels and invitations to view individual actors' websites (if actor is shown performing). Advises actors to: "Be truthful. Tell us about the things that make you stand out. Tell us briefly why you want to work in children's theatre and why you like touring. Seriously consider the implications of living away from your base for months on end!" Offers non-Equity contracts. Will consider applications from disabled actors to play characters with disabilities.

Polka Theatre

240 The Broadway, Wimbledon, London SW19 1SB
tel 020-8545 8320 *fax* 020-8545 8365
email stephen@polkatheatre.com
website www.polkatheatre.com
Artistic Director Peter Glanville

Production details: Established in 1979. A theatre for children aged 0-14. 6 productions staged annually with 700-800 performances per year. The following skills are required from actors: singing, musical instruments, dance, puppetry and physical theatre. Offers TMA/Equity contracts.

Casting procedures: Casting breakdowns sometimes available. Actors are invited for specific shows. Accepts submissions (with CVs and photographs) from actors previously unknown to the company if sent by post, but not by email. Showreels and invitations to view individual actors' websites are also accepted. Actively encourages applications from disabled actors and promotes the use of inclusive casting. "Find out in advance what we're doing, come and visit Polka and see the work."

Pop-Up Theatre

27A Brewery Road, London N7 9PU
tel 020-7609 3339 *fax* 020-7609 2284
website www.pop-up.co.uk
Artistic Director Michael Dalton

Production details: Founded in 1982. Produces and tours theatre for young people to an annual audience of more than 25,000 across theatres, arts centres, schools and nurseries both in the UK and overseas. Normally tours 3 projects each year, with an average annual total of 150 performances at 75 different venues. In general 2-4 actors go on tour and play to audiences aged under 11.

Casting procedures: Accepts submissions (with CVs and photographs) from actors previously unknown to the company sent by post or email. Also accepts invitations to view individual actors' websites. Offers ITC\Equity-approved contracts. Actively encourages applications from disabled actors and promotes the use of inclusive casting.

Q20 Theatre

Creative Arts Hub, Dockfield Road, Shipley,
West Yorks BD17 7AD

01274 221360
email info@q20theatre.co.uk
website www.q20theatre.co.uk
Artistic Director John Lambert

Production details: Tours in excess of 10 projects each year with an average annual total of 350+ performances. Venues include outdoor venues, corporate workspaces and shopping centres throughout the UK. In general 2 or more actors go on tour and play to audiences of all ages. Singing ability and dance/physical theatre skills are required. Recent productions include: *Duelling Wizards* for National Media Museum; 'Snail Sex' Show for Natural History Museum; *Get Thinking About Your Drinking* for NHS Kirklees; *Mother Goose* at Metrocentre.

Casting procedures: Does not hold general auditions – auditions are for specific productions only. Will accept submissions (with CVs and photographs) from actors previously unknown to the company, preferably by email. Will also accept invitations to view individual actors' websites.

Quantum Theatre

The Old Button Factory, 1-11 Bannockburn Road, Plumstead SE18 1ET
tel/fax 020-8317 9000
email office@quantumtheatre.co.uk
website www.quantumtheatre.co.uk
Artistic Directors Michael Whitmore, Jessica Selous

Established in 1993. 15 productions performed annually. National touring productions visit schools, arts centres, theatres and outdoor venues. Casting breakdowns available. Holds general auditions. Accepts submissions (with CVs and photographs) from actors previously unknown to the company – email idea. Showreels, voicereels and invitations to view individual actors' websites are also accepted. Operates own contracts based on TMA Equity terms and conditions.

Quicksilver Theatre

The New Diorama Theatre, 15-16 Triton Street, Regents Place, London NW1 3BF
tel 020-7419 2000
email talktous@quicksilvertheatre.org
website www.quicksilvertheatre.co.uk
Artistic Directors Guy Holland, Carey English

Production details: Founded in 1977, Quicksilver, since 2008, produces 1 new production every 2 years, which is presented at a London venue as well as at partner venues around the UK, mostly small- and middle-scale. Cast numbers change from production to production and vary between 1 and 5. Most of the work is aimed at young audiences, and skills required from actors vary depending on need; may include the playing of musical instruments, singing, puppeteering and dance. Actors may also be expected to lead workshops, as Quicksilver has in recent years expanded its artistic and education projects involving participation by children. Recent productons include *Winter's Tale* (2007, adapted by None Shepphard); *Water Colours* (2007); *Primary Voices* (2007 and 2009, a playwriting project with children and professional actors; and *Ladidada* (2008 and 2010, a co-production between Quicksilver and Indefinite Articles).

Casting procedures: Casting breakdowns are available through the website, by postal application (with sae), and as advertisements in *The Stage*. Accepts submissions (with CVs and photographs) from actors previously unknown to the company sent by post or email. Will also accept showreels and invitations to view individual actors' websites.

Replay Theatre Company

Skainos Square, 239 Newtownards Road, Belfast BT4 1AF
tel 028-9045 4562 *fax* 028-9045 0572
email info@replaytheatreco.org
website www.replaytheatreco.org
Artistic Director Anna Newell

Production details: "Founded in 1988, Replay aims to produce high-quality theatre and related activities that entertain, educate and stimulate children and young people." Normally tours 3 projects each year with an average annual total of 100 performances. Venues include schools, arts centres, theatres and community venues in Northern Ireland and occasionally the Republic of Ireland. In general 4 actors go on tour and play to audiences aged 3-18. Recent productions include: *Macbeth*, a site-specific production at the Crumlin Road Gaol; and *New Kid* by Dennis Foon for children 8-11 years.

Casting procedures: Sometimes holds general auditions; casting breakdowns are available through the news section of the website. Accepts submissions (with CVs and photographs) from actors previously unknown to the company sent by post or email. Will also accept invitations to view individual actors' websites.

S4K International Ltd

Oxted Production Office, PO Box 287, Oxted, Surrey RH8 8BX
tel (01883) 723444 *fax* (01342) 893754
email carolyn@s4kinternational.com
website www.s4kinternationalcom
Producer and Director Julian Chenery *Producer* Carolyn Chenery

Production details: S4K International produces 4 musical theatre productions, including Shakespeare 4 Kidz shows, each year. Performances are now touring mainly to the Middle East and play to 500,000+ students and children each year. Between 6 to 13 actors go on tour and play to audiences aged 5 upwards. S4K now uses mainly actor/musicians with strong singing ability and dance/physical theatre skills. Recent productions include: *The Snow Queen*; *Aladdin*; *Pinocchio*; *S4K's Romeo and Juliet*; *S4K's Hamlet*; *S4K's A Midsummer Night's Dream* and *S4K's Macbeth.*

Casting procedures: Holds general auditions throughout the year. Casting breakdowns are available through the website and Spotlight. Accepts submissions (with CVs and photographs) from actors previously unknown to the company sent by post or email. Will also accept showreels and invitations to view individual actors' websites.

Scene Productions

55 Langborough Road, Wokingham,
Berks RG40 2BU
email info@sceneproductions.co.uk
website www.sceneproductions.co.uk
Artistic Directors Katharine Hurst, Kelly Taylor-Smith

Production details: Founded in 2004. Specialises in exploring new and imaginative ways of examining political contexts and social relationships, using storytelling, audience interaction, mime, puppetry and multimedia. Stages 2 projects annually, with around 80 performances in the same number of schools, arts centres and theatres. In general 3-4 actors go on tour, playing to audiences aged 17+. Requires singing and physical theatre skills from incoming actors, who should hold a driving licence and may be asked to lead workshops. "You should be a good all-rounder who can cope with the pressures of small-scale touring." Recent productions include: *Fear and Misery of the Third Reich*, *The Threepenny Opera*, *The Good Person of Szechwan* (all by Brecht) and *The Other Side*, a devised production which premiered at the 2009 Edinburgh Festival.

Casting procedures: Sometimes holds general auditions and actors may write in May to request inclusion. Welcomes letters (with CVs and photographs) from actors previously unknown to the company, sent by post or email. Does not accept showreels, but will consider invitations to view individual actors' websites. Rarely (or never) has the opportunity to cast disabled actors.

Sixth Sense Theatre for Young People

c/o The Wyvern Theatre, Theatre Square,
Swindon SN1 1QN
tel (01793) 614864 *fax* (01793) 616715
email sstc@dircon.co.uk
website www.sixthsensetyp.co.uk
Artistic Director Benedict Eccles *Education and Outreach Leader* Laura Barnes

Production details: Founded in 1986. Tours to schools and small-scale venues in the South and South West, and increasingly nationally. Receives funding from Swindon Borough Council and Arts Council England, South West, and has an "excellent reputation in the region". Normally tours 3 projects each year with an average annual total of 150 performances across 90 venues. Venues include schools, arts centres and community venues. In general 3-5 actors go on tour and play to audiences aged 5-18. Singing ability, proficiency with a musical instrument, dance skills and a driving licence may be required. Actors are usually expected to lead workshops. Recent productions include: *Bob the Man on the Moon* (2012) and *Splosh!* (2012).

Casting procedures: Accepts submissions (with CVs and photographs) from actors previously unknown to the company sent by post or email. Will also accept invitations to view individual actors' websites. Issues ITC/Equity contracts for 5- to 10-week tours. "Happy to receive actors' details but can't always respond. Please don't chase us; if we're interested we'll contact you."

Sky Blue Theatre Company

14 Hayfield Avenue, Sawston, Cambridge CB22 3JZ
tel (01223) 529491 *mobile* (07850) 097520
email admin@skybluetheatre.com
website www.skybluetheatre.com
Directors Anne Bartram, Frances Brownlie, John Mitton

Production details: Founded in 2007. A Cambridge-based company touring schools, theatres and community venues with new plays, Shakespeare productions and workshops. Founded the Cambridge Theatre Challenge, an international playwriting competition. Works with young people through its own theatre school and with colleges developing skills in performing arts. Stages 6 productions for young people's theatre and TIE annually, giving around 100 performances in 40 venues nationally. In general, 4 actors go on tour, playing to audiences aged 7 to 18. Actors are sometimes expected to lead workshops. Recent productions include: *Much Ado About Nothing*, *Real Love – A New Musical*, and *Romeo and Juliet* workshops.

Casting procedures: All casting is done in house. Holds general auditions, for which breakdowns are available via Casting Call Pro and the website. Welcomes letters (with CVs and photographs) from individual actors previously unknown to the company, sent by post or email. Does not accept showreels, but will consider invitations to view actors' websites and performances. Will consider applications from disabled actors for any role.

Small World Theatre

Canolfan Byd Bychan, Bath House Road, Cardigan,
Ceredigion SA43 1JY
tel (01239) 615952
email info@smallworld.org.uk
website www.smallworld.org.uk
Director Ann Shrosbree *Artistic Director* Bill Hamblett

Production details: Founded in 1979. Theatre and puppetry for children and adults, originally with environmental focus as well as theatre for development, touring theatre and theatre forum – now has small venue. Stages 3-4 projects annually, with on average 55 performances in 12 venues, mostly in Wales but also in the West Country and internationally. Venues include schools, arts centres, theatres, outdoor spaces, community venues, festivals, universities and touring circuits. In general 3-4 actors go on tour, playing to audiences aged 4 to 90. Actors are generally expected to lead workshops. Additional skills such as puppetry, mime, street skills, singing, musical instrument and physical theatre are beneficial, and a driving licence plus knowledge of the Welsh language useful. Recent productions include: *Tales of the Taiga* and *One Way Street.*

Casting procedures: Uses in-house casting directors, and does not usually hold general auditions or advertise casting breakdowns. Will consider submissions (letters, CVs and photographs) from actors previously unknown to the company, sent by post or email, and invitations to view individuals' websites/performances, but cannot respond to all. No unsolicited showreels. Casts actors with disabilities in inclusive roles and to play differently able roles.

Solomon Theatre Company

Penny Black, High Street, Damerham,
Fordingbridge, Hants SP6 3EU
tel (01725) 518670
email office@solomon-theatre.co.uk
website www.solomontheatre.co.uk
Artistic Director Mark Hyde

Production details: Founded in 2003. Specialises in communicating messages that result in crime reduction, improved community safety and the promotion of healthy schools and healthy lifestyles. Has performed award-winning plays to tens of thousands of people in schools and community locations across the country, as well as producing films and support material for national programmes. Performs around 7 projects annually in more than 300 venues, including schools, theatres and community venues in the South West, South East, Midlands, Wales and Northern Ireland. On average 12 actors go on tour, performing to audiences aged 12-16 to over 60. Actors must have a driving licence and may be required to lead workshops. Recent projects include: *Last Orders* (alcohol education); *Trickster* (burglary education); *Gemma's Wardrobe* (drugs education) and *Power of Love* (domestic violence education).

Casting procedures: Holds general auditions; actors may write in July, November and April to request inclusion. Welcomes letters (with CVs and photographs) from actors previously unknown to the company sent by post or email. Also welcomes showreels and invitations to view individual actors' websites. Does not offer Equity-approved contracts but does offer Equity rates. Will consider applications from disabled actors to play characters with disabilities.

Spare Tyre Theatre Company

Unit 3.22, Canterbury Court, 1-3 Brixton Road,
London SW9 6DE
tel/fax 020-7061 6454
email info@sparetyre.org
website www.sparetyre.org
Artistic Director Arti Prashar

Production details:

• Work with older people: a company of artists aged 60+, outreach workshops for older people, and interactive storytelling for people with dementia.
• Work with people with learning disabilities: a company of artists with learning disabilities.
• Work with women who have experienced violence.

Primarily covers the London area. Skills required from actors include workshop-leading and facilitation skills, experience of working with community groups and a sensitivity to, and understanding of, relevant issues.

Casting procedures: Casting breakdowns are published and on the website. Unsolicited approaches at other times – including CVs, showreels and invitations to view individuals' websites – are discouraged. Offers ITC/Equity-approved contracts. Actively encourages applications from disabled actors and promotes the use of inclusive casting.

Splendid Productions

The Dairy, 5 Marischal Road, London SE13 5LE
tel 020-8318 6469 *fax* 0871-750 2166
email info@splendidproductions.co.uk
website www.splendidproductions.co.uk
Artistic Director Kerry Frampton

Production details: Founded in 2003. A theatre company and an education company creating "challenging, vibrant theatre for young people". Also provides expert training in all areas of drama, from practitioner theory to presentation skills. In the last 12 years the company has gained an excellent reputation for the inventiveness of its performances and the clarity of its teaching. Tours 1 main project per year (September through to March), staging on average 130 performances in 130 venues across England and Wales, including schools, arts centres and theatres. 3 actors go on tour, playing to audiences aged 13 years and beyond. Actors require singing skills, strong physicality and a driving licence; workshop-leading experience is desirable. Recent productions include: *Medea, The Trial, Dr Faustus, Woyzeck, Good Woman of Szechuan, Antigone, Animal Farm* and *The Resistible Rise of Arturo Ui.*

Casting procedures: Does not hold general auditions. Actors may write during April/June to request inclusion. Welcomes letters (with CVs and photographs) from actors previously unknown to the company, sent by post or email. Does not accept showreels but is happy to receive links to individual actors' websites. Will consider applications from disabled actors to play characters with disabilities. "We work hard and are very passionate about working with young people. You need to be flexible, approachable and keen to create good theatre in education. Look at our website to see what we do before getting in touch."

StopWatch Theatre Company

Unit 318 Solent Business Centre,
Millbrook Road West, Southampton SO15 0HW
email info@stopwatchtheatre.com
website www.stopwatchtheatre.com
Artistic Director Adrian New

Production details: Established in 1990. A theatre-in-education company specialising in safety and health programmes. Stages 6 productions annually, with around 800 performances in 700 schools UK-wide. In general 4 actors go on tour, playing to audiences aged 5-16. Actors are expected to lead workshops, and driving is an advantage but not essential. Recent productions include: *Chicken!*, *Arson About*, *Footsteps the Movie*, and *The Road Race.*

Casting procedures: Holds general auditions; actors may write in June and October to request inclusion. Casting breakdowns are available from Equity Job Information Service and Casting Call Pro. Welcomes letters (with CVs and photographs) from individual actors previously unknown to the company, sent by post or email, and will consider invitations to view individual actors' websites. Rarely, or never, has the opportunity to cast actors with disabilities. "We always look favourably on those who have done some research and are evidently committed to working in quality theatre in education."

The Take Away Theatre Company

10 Millbank Street, Dalrymple, Ayrshire KA6 6FE
tel 0800-158 3840
email admin@takeawaytheatre.co.uk
website www.takeawaytheatre.co.uk
Artistic Director Lee O'Driscoll

Production details: Founded in 2007. A theatre-in-education company delivering "high-impact and dynamic drama projects in schools and other venues throughout the UK". Tours 9 projects annually with 270 performances at schools, arts centres, theatres and community venues. In general 4 actors go on tour, playing to audiences aged 1 to 101. Actors may be expected to lead workshops and should hold a current driving licence; singing, musical instrument, dance and physical theatre skills are an advantage. Recent productions include: *The Jungle Book*, *Scotland (an' a' that)*, *The Wind in the Willows* and *Hansel and Gretel.*

Casting procedures: Sometimes holds general auditions; actors may write at any time to request inclusion. Casting breakdowns are available via the website, by postal application (with sae), and from Casting Call Pro and CastNet. Welcomes letters (with CVs and photographs) from individual actors previously unknown to the company, sent by post or email. Also accepts showreels and invitations to view individual actors' websites. Will consider applications from disabled actors to play characters with disabilities.

Tall Stories Theatre Company

Jacksons Lane, 269a Archway Road, London N6 5AA
tel 020-8348 0080
email info@tallstories.org.uk
website www.tallstories.org.uk
Artistic Directors Olivia Jacobs, Toby Mitchell
Producer Lucy Wood *Projects Manager* Charlotte Lund, *Production Assistant* Natalia Scorer

Production details: Founded in 1997, Tall Stories creates entertaining and imaginative performances for audiences of all ages, with their productions characterised by a blend of storytelling, music and laughs. Recent productions include: *The Gruffalo* (UK and international tours, West End), *The Snail and the Whale* (UK and international tours, West End) and *Emily Brown and the Thing* (UK tour). Performers are expected to have good singing and devising abilities, whilst experience of physical theatre and the ability to play an instrument is desirable. Performers may be expected to lead workshops, but training will be given. Each production consists of 3-4 actors and, on average, the company undertakes 2 UK and 3-4 international tours per year. This equates to over 1,500 performances at around 650 venues, ranging from schools and arts centres to West End theatres.

Casting procedures: Tall Stories holds 1-2 workshop auditions a year for up to 30 actors. Actors can send in a CV at any point during the year for consideration. Casting breakdowns are generaly posted on Spotlight, but the company prefers to invite actors via agent recommendations or those that have directly written to them. Offers contracts based on ITC guidelines. Welcomes applications from disabled actors and promotes inclusive casting.

Ten Ten Theatre

PO Box 49063, New Southgate, London N11 1YU
tel 0845-388 3162 *fax* 0845-388 3167
email office@tententheatre.co.uk
email casting@tententheatre.co.uk
website www.tententheatre.co.uk
Artistic Director Martin O'Brien

Production details: Established in 2006. Specialises in young people's theatre in primary schools, secondary schools, young offender institutions and the local community. Stages 4-6 productions annually with around 400 performances in 200 schools, arts centres, theatres and community venues across England, Scotland and Wales. In general 2-4 actors go on tour, playing to audiences aged 5 to 21. Actors may be expected to lead workshops. Recent productions include: a 6-month tour of secondary schools with 3 separate plays; and a 1-week residency at Feltham Young Offender Institution.

Casting procedures: Does not hold general auditions; actors may write at any time to request inclusion. Casting breakdowns are available from the website or via Equity Job Information Service and Spotlight. Welcomes letters (with CVs and photographs) from individual actors previously unknown to the company, sent by post or email, and will accept showreels and invitations to view individual actors' websites. Offers Equity approved contracts as negotiated through ITC. Will consider applications from disabled actors to play characters with disabilities. "Please view our website to look at our projects and ethos before sending details."

Theatr Iolo

The Old School Building, Cefn Road,
Cardiff CF14 3HS
tel 029-2061 3782 *fax* 029-2052 2225
email admin@theatriolo.com
website www.theatriolo.com
Artistic Director Kevin Lewis

Production details: "Formed in 1987, Theatr Iolo aims to produce and programme the best of live theatre, making it widely accessible to children and young people in Cardiff and the Vale of Glamorgan to stir the imagination, inspire the heart and challenge the mind. Theatr Iolo works alongside teachers and advisers to enhance teaching and learning across the curriculum." Normally tours 5 projects each year with an average annual total of 150 performances across 120 venues. Venues include schools, arts centres and theatres in Wales and occasionally England, and international festivals. Cast sizes vary, playing to audiences aged 3-18. Singing ability, proficiency with a musical instrument, dance/physical theatre skills and a driving licence are frequently required. Actors may also be expected to lead workshops. Recent productions include: *Grimm Tales* by Carol Ann Dufy; *Lenny* by Francis Monty (trans. Paul Harman) and *Under the Carpet* by Sarah Argent.

Casting procedures: Sometimes holds general auditions; actors should write in June requesting inclusion. Casting breakdowns are available through Equity Job Information Service. Accepts submissions (with CVs and photographs) from actors previously unknown to the company if sent by post. Emails are also welcome, as long as the file is not too big. Offers ITC/Equity-approved contracts. Actively encourages applications from disabled actors and promotes the use of inclusive casting.

Theatr na nÓg

Unit 3, Millands Road Industrial Estate,
Neath SA11 1NJ
tel (01639) 641771 *fax* (01639) 647941
email drama@theatr-nanog.co.uk
website www.theatr-nanog.co.uk
Artistic Director Geinor Styles

Production details: Theatr na nÓg was established in 1982 to produce theatre for a wide spectrum of audiences throughout Wales in a variety of venues and locations, in both languages. "The literal translation of Theatr na nÓg is theatre of eternal youth and this encapslutates the ethos of the company by creating theatre that has the power to excite and engage audiences of all ages." The company is a regular provider of main stage work throughout the country and continues to expand its portfolio of venues. Theatr na nÓg continues to evolve from being a company that solely produces work for schools to being recognised by the Arts Council of Wales as one of their producing theatre companies that will be encouraged to produce work to a variety of audiences throughout Wales and beyond. Theatr na nÓg is now an Associate Company to the Wales Millennium Centre. This enables it to produce new work for a broad range of audiences, and to raise its profile on the international stage.

Casting procedures: Although most casting goes through Spotlight and casting agents, Theatr na nÓg still holds general auditions (depending on the project); actors may write at any time requesting inclusion. Acceps submissions (with CVs and photographs) from actors previously unknown to the company sent bu post or email. Will also accept invitations to view individual actors' websites.

Theatre-Rites

Unit 206, E1 Business Centre,
3-15 Whitechapel Road, London SW9 0XZ
tel 020-7164 6196 *fax* 020-7928 4347
email info@theatre-rites.co.uk
website www.theatre-rites.co.uk
Artistic Director Sue Buckmaster

Production details: Committed to creating challenging productions which push the boundaries of theatrical form by experimenting to combine different artistic disciplines. Highly imaginative visual experiences for families to share together. Stages 2 productions annually, with around 45 performances in 12 arts centres and theatres across all English regions, in Scotland and internationally. In general 5-8 actors go on tour, playing to audiences of various ages, often 5+. Actors are sometimes expected to lead workshops; singing, musical instrument, dance, physical theatre and puppetry skills may all be advantageous, depending on the project. Recent productions include: *Bank On It* – site specific; *Rubbish* – puppetry; *Mischief* – dance theatre; *Hang On* – circus collaboration and *Salt* – site specific.

Casting procedures: Sometimes holds general auditions; actors may write at any time to request inclusion. Casting breakdowns are available via the website and Spotlight. Welcomes letters (with CVs and photographs) from individual actors previously unknown to the company, sent by post or email. Also welcomes showreels and invitations to view individual actors' websites. Offers Equity-approved contracts as negotiated through ITC. Actively encourages applications from disabled actors, and promotes the use of inclusive casting. "The work is devised and often physical, so we frequently look for performers with previous experience of this kind."

Theatre Centre

Shoreditch Town Hall, 380 Old Street,
London EC1V 9LT
tel 020-7729 3066 *fax* 020-7739 9741
email admin@theatre-centre.co.uk
website www.theatre-centre.co.uk
Artistic Director Natalie Wilson

Production details: Theatre Centre has been bringing the art of play-making to children and young people across England since 1953. It continues as a leading new writing company for young audiences, creating performances at the cutting edge of the theatre industry. The company is renowned for its collaborative practice between writers and young people in making Theatre Centre's critically acclaimed work, which stretches the imagination, critical thinking and skills of children and young people wherever they live. The company tours 2-3 projects each year with an average annual total of 100 performances across 70 different schools and venues. Normally 3-4 actors go on tour and play to targeted groups aged 4-18. Singing ability, proficiency with a musical instrument and dance/physical theatre skills may be required. An affinity with new writing and touring audiences is an advantage. Offers TMA/Equity-approved contracts and subscribes to the Equity Pension Scheme.

Casting procedures: Casting breakdowns are available through the website, Spotlight and agents.

Theatre Company Blah Blah Blah!

Roundhay Road Resource Centre,
233-237 Roundhay Road, Leeds LS8 4HS
tel 0113-380 5646
email info@blahs.co.uk
website www.blahs.co.uk
Artistic Director Deborah Pakkar-Hull

Production details: A Leeds-based Theatre in Education company, founded in 1985, which specialises in participatory theatre for children and young people training teachers to integrate drama into their practice. Tours 2 performances each year – regionally, nationally and internationally. In general 3-4 actors go on tour and play to audiences aged 5 upwards. Proficiency with a musical instrument, dance/physical theatre skills and a driving licence are all potentially useful. Experience of TIE work is desirable as actors are expected to lead participatory elements in the performance. Recent tours to schools and colleges include: *Rummage!* (a collaboration with The Play House, Birmingham), *The Raft of the Medusa* and *Messerschmitt vs Spitfire* – a love story (in partnership with the Theaterhaus Ensemble of Frankfurt). Also CPD/Coaching and interactive story-making work with primary schools. Offers ITC/Equity-approved contracts and does not subscribe to the Equity Pension Scheme.

Casting procedures: Holds general auditions for major tour each summer. Accepts submissions (with CVs and photographs) from actors previously unknown to the company throughout the year, as details are kept on file. Will also accept invitations to view individual actors' websites. "We are particularly interested in hearing from people with both acting and facilitation skills."

Theatre Exchange Ltd

114 Station Road East, Oxted, Surrey RH8 0QA
tel (01883) 724599
email theatreexchange@tandridgetrust.co.uk
website www.theatre-exchange.org.uk
Artistic Director Katy Potter *Associate Director* Andrew Mulquin

Production details: An educational theatre company focusing on the creative exchange between young people, artists and those who work with young people. Works on up to 21 projects each year, with an average annual total of 650 performances across 400 different venues. Venues include schools, arts centres, theatres and community venues across the South East of England. In general 6 actors go on tour and play to audiences aged 4-13. Interest in and some experience of working with young people is necessary; a driving licence is also useful. Actors are also expected to lead workshops. Recent productions include: *Only a Game?*, *Our June's Midsummer*, *Luverly Jubilee* and *The Greeks.*

Casting procedures: Holds general auditions; actors requesting inclusion should write between May and July. Casting breakdowns are available by postal application (with sae), on Equity Job Information Service and through advertisements in *The Stage.* Accepts submissions (with CVs and photographs) from actors previously unknown to the company sent by post or email. Will also accept invitations to view individual actors' websites. "Please send a letter detailing why you are interested in working with young people, along with your CV."

Theatre Hullabaloo

The Meeting Rooms, 5 Skinnergate, Darlington,
County Durham DL3 7NB
tel (01325) 352004
email info@theatrehullabaloo.org.uk
website www.theatrehullabaloo.org.uk
Creative Producer Miranda Thain

Production details: Founded in 1979. A specialist producer of theatre for young audiences. Tours regionally, nationally and internationally for audiences aged 3 to 16 years. Recent productions include: *My Mother Told Me Not to Stare*, a deliciously dark operetta for everyone aged 8 and above and *Five* – a contemporary dance installation for 3-5 year-olds (also touring in Ontario).

Casting procedures: General auditions are sometimes held; actors are advised to write in the autumn to request inclusion. Welcomes letters (with CVs and photographs) from individual actors previously unknown to the company, sent by post or email. Also accepts showreels and invitations to view individual actors' websites. Offers Equity-approved contracts as negotiated through ITC.

Tin Shed Theatre Company

46 Lennard Street, Newport NP19 0EJ
mobile (07921) 366038 or (07511) 139773
email tinshedtheatre@gmx.com
website www.tinshedtheatrecompany.com
Company Directors Georgina Harris, Justin Cliffe, Antonio Rimola

Production details: Established in 2008. Specialises in devised theatre which lends itself to performance in unusual spaces. High-energy, high-impact work that focuses on many different genres.

Tours 1 project annually, with around 30 performances in 20 venues, including schools, arts centres and theatres. In general 7 actors go on tour, performing to audiences aged 11 to 16. Actors are required to lead workshops. Recent productions include *Of Mice and Men* by John Steinbeck.

Casting procedures: Uses freelance directors, actors may write at any time to request inclusion. Casting breakdowns are available from the website. Welcomes unsolicited approaches by post and email, and accepts showreels and invitations to view individual actors' websites/visit other productions. Encourages applications from disabled actors and promotes the use of inclusive casting.

Travelling Light Theatre Company

Barton Hill Settlement, 43 Ducie Road, Barton Hill, Bristol BS5 0AX
tel 0117-377 3166 *fax* 0117-377 3167
minicom 0117-377 3168
email info@travellinglighttheatre.org.uk
website www.travellinglighttheatre.org.uk
Artistic Producer Jude Merrill; *General Manager* Dienka Hines

Production details: Since 1984 the company has produced innovative and inspiring work for young audiences using live music, visual and physical performance in its work. Produces on average 2 tours each year with an average annual total of 200+ perfomances across 50+ different venues, and at least one Christmas show with an extended run. Venues include theatres, arts centres, community venues and festivals across the UK, as well as local schools. Target audiences vary form 0-adult. Casts are usually 1-5 actors.

Singing ability, proficiency with a musical instrument and physical theatre skills are often required and most plays are devised with the cast. Recent touring productions include: *How Cold My Toes* (for age 2+); *Strictly Balti* (age 11+); and *Sammy and the Snow Leopard* (age 5+). Most recent Christmas show was *101 Dalmatians*, co-produced with Tobacco Factory Theatres.

Casting procedures: Casting breakdowns are available through Equity Job Information Service and Spotlight. Accepts submissions (with CVs and photographs) from actors previously unknown to the company only if sent by post. Does not welcome unsolicited emails. Will also accept invitations to view individual actors' websites.

Unicorn Theatre

147 Tooley Street, London SE1 2HZ
tel 020-7645 0500 *fax* 020-7645 0550
email admin@unicorntheatre.com
website www.unicorntheatre.com

Production details: The Unicorn Theatre was founded by Caryl Jenner as a touring company in 1947, with a commitment to giving children a valuable and often first-ever experience of quality theatre, and a philosophy that "the best of theatre for children should be judged on the same high standards of writing, directing, acting and design as the best of adult theatre".

Today, the Unicorn is the national home of theatre for children and young people. Its purpose-built premises at London Bridge contains 2 theatres, 4 floors of public spaces and 2 rehearsal studios dedicated to producing and presenting work for and about audiences aged up to 21. It is an Arts Council National Portfolio Organisation. Offers TMA and ITC/Equity-approved contracts and subscribes to the Equity Pension Scheme.

Casting procedures: Generally by invitation via agent, but will read CVs and photographs from actors previously unknown to the company if sent by email.

Whirlwind Theatre for Children

The Kings House, Phoenix Street, Lancaster LA1 1DD
tel (01524) 812480
email enquiries@whirlwindtheatre.org.uk
website www.whirlwindtheatre.org.uk
Artistic Directors Myette Godwyn, Mike Whalley
Associate Artistic Director Alistair Ganley *Patron* David Wood OBE

Production details: Formed in 2000 to produce a community play for the Museum of Cannock Chase in association with Illyria Theatre Company and a South of England tour of a music-based show for children age 5-10 – *Goldie Locks and the Three Bears.* The company has close ties with the Palm Court Theatre Orchestra, and productions are period-music-based with physical and visual performance aimed at the 4-10 year age-group. Whirlwind runs a performance summer school; also has a Saturday youth theatre club and a programme of workshops.

Normally undertakes 2-3 projects each year with a total of around 150 performances. Venues include churches, arts centres, fields, schools, theatres, outdoor and community venues across England. In general 3 actors go on tour and play to audiences aged 4 upwards. Actors must be proficient in workshop-leading for this age-group; will also need singing, dance/physical theatre skills and preferably the ability to play an instrument to a high standard. A driving licence is also required and actors must be prepared to help with get-ins and get-outs. Whirlwind Theatre has a strong Christian ethos, and most rehearsals and community work are carried out at King's Community Church in Lancaster. Although the company welcomes applications from actors of all beliefs and backgrounds, they should feel at ease with this when applying. Recent productions include: *King's New Clothes* (TIE) and *Hamish Bear and Storytelling Magpie* (TIE) and *Toad of Toad Hall* (summer-school production in Ryelands Park, Lancaster).

Casting procedures: Sometimes holds general auditions; these are always held in Lancaster. Welcomes letters and emails (with CVs and photographs) from actors previously unknown to the company. All actors are required to be DBS checked.

Wizard Theatre

Blenheim Villa, Burr Street, Harwell,
Oxfordshire OX11 0DT
tel 0800-583 2373
email info@wizardtheatre.co.uk
website www.wizardtheatre.co.uk
Artistic Director Leon Hamilton *Associate Producer* Oliver Gray

Production details: Established in 2002. Performs in schools, theatres and conferences across the country. Message-based shows are commissioned annually. Works with various organisations, from the Met Police to Drug Action teams. The winter show tours in theatres: 2015's production is *Pinocchio.*

Stages 7+ projects annually, with more than 600 performances in 400 venues across London, the Home counties and Shropshire. In general 2-3 actors go on tour, playing to audiences aged 4-18. Actors may be required to lead workshops. Good singing, musical instrument, driving and stage combat skills are useful. Recent productions include: *The Wind in the Willows, Choices* and *On the Right Road.* We are always looking for excellent facilitators and drama teachers.

Casting procedures: Sometimes holds general auditions; actors are welcome to write in at any time. Casting breakdowns are available via Casting Call Pro and on the Equity Job Information Service. Welcomes unsolicited approaches by actors by post or email. Also accepts showreels and will consider invitations to view individual actors' websites. Does not offer Equity-approved contracts: "Usually we pay well above Equity rates." Rarely or never has the opportunity to cast disabled actors.

Young Shakespeare Company

213 Fox Lane, Southgate, London N13 4BB
tel 020-8368 4828
email youngshakespeare@mac.com
website www.youngshakespeare.org.uk
Artistic Directors Christopher Geelan and Sarah Gordon

Production details: One of the longest-established and most respected educational theatre companies in the UK. Currently performs Shakespeare to more than 100,000 young people each year, working in schools and theatres to provide a year-round programme of performances and workshops. On average stages 10 productions each year, with around 1,000 performances in theatres and schools throughout England. In general, 5 actors per show perform to audiences aged 6-16. Actors may be expected to lead workshops. Recent productions include: *Twelfth Night, Romeo and Juliet, Macbeth, The Tempest, Hamlet* and *A Midsummer Night's Dream.*

Casting procedures: Holds auditions every June for autumn season and every November for spring season. Casting breakdowns are available via Spotlight link. Also welcomes emails from individual actors previously unknown to the company.

Casting calendar

Many companies are happy to receive CVs and photographs from actors at any time of the year, but some – such as those listed below – have a regular, annual schedule of casting and as such are most receptive to approaches in certain months. The table below shows the best time to approach companies, and gives information about whether their casting breakdowns are published on their website; whether they will send out breakdowns on receipt of a sae; where they publish their breakdowns (other than via the Spotlight Link); and in what section of this book their details may be found. ('JIS' is the Equity Job Information Service. Details for most of the casting breakdown services can be found under *Spotlight, casting directories and information services* on page 381.)

Read the company's entry carefully before contacting them, to ensure that you are not wasting either their time or yours by making an inappropriate submission. The letters in brackets after the company name indicate the section in which their details may be found.
Euro = *English-language European theatre companies* (page 235)
IHP = *In-house pantomimes* (page 227)
IM = *Independent managements/theatre producers* (page 167)
MSS = *Middle and smaller-scale companies* (page 176)
PP = *Pantomime producers* (page 224)
PT = *Producing theatres* (page 132)
YP = *Children's, young people's and theatre in education* (page 261)

COMPANY	BREAKDOWNS PUBLISHED
January	
The Derek Grant Organisation (IM)	
Imagine Musical Theatre (IM)	Website, CastNet, Castweb, Spotlight, Stage Castings
Louche Theatre (MSS)	Website
Midland Actors Theatre (MSS)	JIS
Nick Brooke (IM)	Website, Post
January/February	
Theatre Royal, Bury St Edmunds (PT)	Spotlight
February	
The Capitol, Horsham (IHP)	Spotlight
First Family Entertainment (PP)	Castweb, CastNet
Jasperian Theatre Company (MSS)	CastNet
Kinetic Theatre Company (YP)	Website
February-July	
Paul Hammond Productions (PP)	The Stage, Castweb, Entsweb
March	
Andy Barnes Productions (IM)	Spotlight
Duggie Chapman Associates (PP)	The Stage
The Original Theatre Company (MSS)	Website, Post, Spotlight
Theatre Royal Chipping Norton (IHP)	Spotlight
Shakespeare 4 Kidz (YP)	The Stage, Website

March/April	
HOME Theatre, Manchester (PT)	Spotlight
Spillers Pantomimes (PP)	The Stage
March-May	
Evolution Productions (PP)	Spotlight
Imagine Theatre (PP)	Spotlight
Kazzum (YP)	Website, JIS, Arts Jobs
Spring	
The Capitol (IHP)	Website, Post
Paul Holman Associates (PP)	Castweb
Theatre Centre (YP)	Website, Spotlight
April	
Arty-Fact Theatre Company (YP)	JIS, Website
English Theatre Frankfurt (Euro)	Spotlight
White Horse Theatre, Germany (Euro)	JIS, The Stage, Website
April/May	
The Theatre, Chipping Norton (IHP)	Spotlight
May	
20 Stories High Theatre Company (MSS)	JIS, Website
Frantic Theatre Company (MSS)	JIS, Post, The Stage
May/June	
Nick Brooke (IM)	Website, Post
May-July	
Greenwich Theatre (PT)	Website
Hiss and Boo Theatre Company (PP)	Spotlight
Theatre Exchange Ltd (YP)	Post, JIS, The Stage
June	
The Courtyard (IHP)	Website, CastNet, Castweb
Imagine Musical Theatre (IM)	Website, JIS, CastNet, Castweb
Jasperian Theatre Company (MSS)	CastNet
Kinetic Theatre Company (YP)	Website
Midland Actors Theatre (MSS)	JIS
StopWatch Theatre Company (YP)	JIS, CCP
Theatr Iolo (YP)	JIS
Theatre Royal, Winchester (IHP)	Email
Torch Theatre, Milford Haven (PT)	Post, JIS, Website
Young Shakespeare Company (YP)	Spotlight
June/July	
Box Clever Theatre Company (YP)	JIS, Website
Imagine Musical Theatre (IM)	Website, CastNet, Castweb, Spotlight, Stage Castings
MANACTCO (MSS)	JIS, CCP
Theatre Royal, Bury St Edmunds (PT)	Spotlight
Theatre Royal, Margate (IHP)	JIS, Castnet
July	
ApeTheatre Company (YP)	Post, JIS
Arty-Fact Theatre Company (YP)	JIS, Website
Bitesize Theatre Company (YP)	The Stage, Castcall
Creaking Door Productions (YP)	Website, JIS
Pitlochry Festival Theatre (PT)	Spotlight, via Agents
The Original Theatre Company (MSS)	Website, Post, Spotlight
The Wrestling School (MSS)	Website, Phone

August

Actors of Dionysus (MSS)	Spotlight, Website
Playtime Theatre Company (YP)	Post, JIS, The Stage, Castcall
Theatre Royal, Bury St Edmunds (IHP)	Spotlight

August-October

Chaplins Ltd (PP)	Website, The Stage, CCP

September

Andy Barnes Productions (IM)	Spotlight
Jasperian Theatre Company (MSS)	CastNet
Nick Brooke Ltd	Post
NTC Touring Company (MSS)	Post, Website
Open Clasp Theatre Company (MSS)	Website, Post
Theatre Royal Chpping Norton (IHP)	Spotlight

October

Creaking Door Productions (YP)	Website, JIS
Imagine Musical Theatre (IM)	Website, JIS, CastNet, Castweb
Kinetic Theatre Company (YP)	Website
Pitlochry Festival Theatre (PT)	Spotlight, via Agents
StopWatch Theatre Company (YP)	JIS, CCP

October/November

Box Clever Theatre Company (YP)	Post, JIS
Imagine Musical Theatre (IM)	Website, CastNet, Castweb, Spotlight, Stage Castings
Shakespeare at The Tobacco Factory (MSS)	Website

November

Ape Theatre Company (YP)	Post, JIS
Frantic Theatre Company (MSS)	JIS, Post, The Stage
Owen Money Productions (PP)	The Stage
Young Shakespeare Company (YP)	Spotlight

December

Playtime Theatre Company (YP)	Spotlight, JIS, CCP
Shakespeare at The Tobacco Factory (MSS)	Website

Festivals

These are populated by all kinds of companies listed in previous sections. Some are hired-in by a festival's organisers; others 'hire' space in order to participate – the latter predominate at the most famous festival of all, in Edinburgh. Participation in a festival can be enormous fun, and a great opportunity to meet other actors and see other productions. However, the chances of such a production transferring, let alone making money, are limited.

UMBRELLA ORGANISATIONS

British Arts Festivals Association (BAFA)

1 Goodwins Court, London WC2N 4LL
tel 020-7240 4532
email info@artsfestivals.co.uk
website www.artsfestivals.co.uk

Provides information and a professional network for the festivals movement in the UK, working to promote the profile and status of arts festivals. As well as the arts festivals website, which catalogues festivals in the UK and provides links to festivals in Europe, BAFA also publishes a free Calendar and Directory of the 100+ festival members in print, and produces an advance festivals press pack each January. Members have the opportunity to attend BAFA conferences, training courses and focus meetings. Membership is open to all arts festivals in the UK and associate membership to other arts organisations. Does not promote individual artists, companies or tours.

The European Festivals Association

General Secretariat, Kleine Gentstraat 46, B-9051 Gent, Belgium
email info@efa-aef.eu
website www.efa-aef.eu

The European Festivals Association is the umbrella organisation for festivals across Europe and beyond. The oldest cultural network in Europe, it was founded in Geneva, Switzerland, in 1952 as a joint initiative of the eminent conductor Igor Markevitch and the great philosopher Denis de Rougemeont. Since its foundation, the Association has grown from 15 festivals into a dynamic network representing more than 100 music, dance, theatre and multidisciplinary festivals, national festival associations and cultural organisations from 40 countries.

UK ARTS FESTIVALS

24:7 Theatre Festival

Astley & Byrom House, 21-23 Quay Street, Manchester M3 3JD
tel/fax 0845-408 4101
email info@247theatrefestival.co.uk
website www.247theatrefestival.co.uk

An annual festival of new writing based in Manchester. The festival operates an adjudication process, and then invites selected writers to participate. All submitted scripts must be under 60 minutes, original, never performed before and capable of being staged in non-theatre spaces. Venues are selected to provide the best combination of technical facilities and audience experience, with reasonable production costs. Participation fees are subsidised to allow both experienced theatre companies and first-time solo writers to take part. The festival seeks to provide opportunities for emerging actors, directors and technicians to showcase their talents in the invited productions, and arranges events before and during the week in order to encourage new networks and collaborations to be forged.

Arundel Festival

tel (01903) 883474
email arundelfestival@btopenworld.com
website www.arundelfestival.co.uk

For 10 days each August, the market town of Arundel is host to a multi-arts festival which began in 1977. Street theatre and a festival Fringe are regular features, as are concerts, exhibitions, fireworks and jazz. The festival culminates in an open-air production of a Shakespeare play in the grounds of Arundel Castle. Each production is led by a cast of experienced professional actors, and extended with members of the local community, who work with the professionals throughout the 6-week rehearsal period.

Barbican

Barbican Centre, Silk Street, London EC2Y 8DS
tel 020-7628 3351
email theatre@barbican.org.uk
website www.barbican.org.uk/bite

Since its first programme in 1998, the Barbican Theatre and Dance programme has presented some of the most significant artists and innovative companies from around the world, including Robert

Wilson, Cate Blanchett with Sydney Theatre Company, Pina Bausch, Cheek by Jowl, Peter Brook, Ivo van Hove with Toneelgroep Amsterdam, Ninagawa Company, Complicite and many more.

Belfast Festival at Queens

Ulster Bank Belfast Festival at Queens,
8 Fitzwilliam Street, Belfast BT9 6AW
email n.murphy@qub.ac.uk
website www.belfastfestival.com
Festival Director Shan McAnena

Founded in 1963, the Belfast Festival is an annual 3-week international arts festival held in October and November each year. The largest festival of its kind in Ireland, it covers all artforms including theatre, dance, classical music, literature, jazz, comedy, visual arts, folk music and popular music, attracting more than 50,000 visitors. Theatre performances in 2004 included: the Belfast Theatre Company's production of *A Most Notorious Woman*; Theatre Royal Bath's production of *Blithe Spirit* with Penelope Keith. Artists wishing to participate in the festival should submit a written proposal to the address listed above.

Birmingham ArtsFest

Events Section, Birmingham City Council,
Alexander Stadium, Walsall Road, Perry Barr,
Birmingham B42 2LR
tel 0121-464 5678
email artsfest@birmingham.gov.uk
website www.artsfest.org.uk

ArtsFest is one of the UK's largest free arts festivals and is held in venues across Birmingham for 2 days in September. It programmes a range of free performances including theatre, jazz, opera and dance events. Street theatre also features heavily, with musicians, jugglers, visual artists and stand-up comedians all presenting their work outside. There are also a variety of workshops on offer, ranging from screenwriting to Bollywood dancing. *Note*: Because of the need for budget cuts, the future of this festival is uncertain.

Brighton Festival

email info@brightonfestival.org
website www.brightonfestival.org

Founded in 1967. For 3 weeks in May, there are more than 300,000 attendances at 800 separate arts events taking place in venues across Brighton and Hove. Artists from a number of different countries are represented in theatre, dance, music, opera, books, events and outdoor spectaculars.

Running alongside Brighton Festival, Brighton Festival Fringe (previously called 'the Open') has been in existence for 37 years, and is the biggest in England, showcasing a variety of artforms and activities. Applicants for the Fringe should first read the 'How to be in Brighton Festival Fringe' document available on the website, and then register online.

Canterbury Festival

8 Orange Street, Canterbury, Kent CT1 2JA
tel (01227) 452853
email info@canterburyfestival.co.uk
website www.canterburyfestival.co.uk

Founded in 1929, the Canterbury Festival takes place over 2 weeks in October. The festival features music, dance, drama, opera, science, community events, talks, walks and visual arts. The Marlowe and Gulbenkian Theatres in Canterbury and the Theatre Royal in Margate are host to major dance, drama and opera companies. Many small professional and amateur companies perform in the smaller venues and present a wide variety of drama and dance during the 2 weeks of the festival. Theatre companies that have appeared at the festival include the Royal Shakespeare Company, the National Theatre, Spymonkey, Ridiculusmus, Trestle Theatre, Shared Experience and Yellow Earth Theatre.

Dumfries and Galloway Arts Festival

Gracefield Arts Centre, 28 Edinburgh Road,
Dumfries DG1 1JQ
tel (01387) 260447
email info@dgartsfestival.org.uk
website www.dgartsfestival.org.uk

Established in 1979. Scotland's largest rural Arts Festival – runs for 10 days in May. The festival programme includes a wide range of events covering music – classical, jazz and folk – dance, theatre, literary and children's. Events take place in a range of venues throughout the region.

Edinburgh Festival Fringe Society

Edinburgh Festival Fringe Society, 180 High Street,
Edinburgh EH1 1QS
tel 0131-226 0026 *fax* 0131-226 0016
email admin@edfringe.com
website www.edfringe.com

The Fringe began in 1947, when 8 theatre companies decided to perform uninvited alongside the first Edinburgh International Festival. It is now the largest arts festival on the planet, with over 45,000 performances of over 2,800 shows in more than 250 venues across Edinburgh each August. The Fringe is still entirely open-access and anyone who wants to bring a show can do so.

The Fringe Society was formed in 1959 to provide a comprehensive information service both to performers and to audiences. You can contact the Society year round with general questions and advice on how to take part.

Edinburgh International Festival

The Hub, Castlehill, Edinburgh EH1 2NE
tel 0131-473 2001 *fax* 0131-473 2003
email eif@eif.co.uk
website www.eif.co.uk

Founded in 1947, the Edinburgh International Festival is an annual event held over 3 weeks in

August, using venues across the city. With music, opera, classical music and dance, the festival is recognised as one of the world's most important celebrations of the performing arts. Also offers a programme of year-round education and outreach activities. Performance at the Edinburgh International Festival is by invitation only, issued by the Festival Director.

Fierce Festival

Unit 57, 27 Colmore Road, Birmingham B3 2EW
email contact@wearefierce.org
website www.wearefierce.org

Annual festival of performances and events in theatres, bars, clubs, galleries and public spaces across Birmingham and the West Midlands. The festival used to take place in the spring, but has moved to October for the next editions in 2013 and 2014.

Grassington Festival

The Festival Office, Grassington Festival, Grassington, North Yorkshire BD23 5AT
tel (01756) 752691
email katebeard@grassington-festival.org.uk
website www.grassington-festival.org.uk
Festival Director Kate Beard

An annual multi-disciplinary festival featuring contemporary and classical music, theatre, poetry and film, and taking place in the last 2 weeks of July.

Greenwich and Docklands International Festival (GDIF)

The Borough Hall, Royal Hill, London SE10 8RE
tel 020-8305 1818 *fax* 020-8305 1188
email admin@festival.org
website www.festival.org

Taking place over the 4 weekends of July, the Greenwich and Docklands International Festival programmes multi-disciplinary arts events around East London each summer. As well as programming large-scale, visually impressive work, the festival places emphasis on educational projects and participatory arts.

High Tide Festival

High Tide Festival Theatre, 24A St John Street, London EC1M 4AY
tel 020-7566 9765
email info@hightide.org.uk
website www.hightide.org.uk
Artistic Director Steven Atkinson

Founded in 2007, High Tide is a new writing theatre company committed to discovering, producing and championing emerging playwrights. It produces an annual festival of new work in Suffolk each year, following which it works with its partners to present work nationally and internationally.

Hotbed: Cambridge New Writing Theatre Festival

Cambridge Junction, Clifton Road, Cambridge CB1 7GX
tel (01223) 403361
email office@menagerie.uk.com
website www.menagerietheatre.co.uk

Produced by: Menagerie Theatre Company

Following the success of the original Hotbed 2002, Menagerie Theatre Company (**www.menagerietheatre.co.uk**) and Cambridge Junction (**www.junction.co.uk**) joined forces to present Hotbed 2004 and 2006, Cambridge's New Writing Theatre Festival. Over 3 weeks in July, venues around Cambridge – including CB2, Cambridge Drama Centre and Cambridge Arts Theatre's Playroom – hosted a variety of new plays by a selection of regional and national writers. Productions ranged from 15-minute lunchtime shorts to full evening performances, with a selection of workshops, talks, masterclasses and seminars also included in the programme.

In 2014/2015, the festival will present opportunities both for writers and for actors to get involved. Writing opportunities are advertised on the Menagerie website (**www.menagerie.uk.com**). A repertory company based around the members of Menagerie Theatre Company supports the festival, and actors are welcome to audition for the company a few months in advance. For further information about the next Hotbed and how to get involved, contact Paul Bourne at **office@menagerie.uk.com**.

Lichfield Festival

7 The Close, Lichfield, Staffordshire WS13 7LD
tel (01543) 306270
email info@lichfieldfestival.org
website www.lichfieldfestival.org
Festival Manager Peter Bacon

Annual 10-day multi-arts festival in early July, Literature Festival in September/October, plus occasional seasonal events.

London International Festival of Theatre (LIFT)

Trinity Buoy Wharf, 64 Orchard Place, London E14 0JW
email info@liftfestival.com
website www.liftfestival.com
Artistic Director Mark Ball

Started in 1981, LIFT is a biennial summer festival introducing some of the world's most exciting artists and theatre-makers to London. LIFT events have been staged in more than 30 London venues as well as in a number of site-specific venues such as streets, disused buildings, the river, parks and open spaces.

Also runs developmental and educational programmes exploring the nature of exchange and creativity for a range of audiences including schoolchildren and industry leaders.

London International Mime Festival

Somerset House (South Wing), Strand, London WC2R 1LA

tel 020-7637 5661
email direction@mimelondon.com
website www.mimelondon.com
Directors Joseph Seelig, Helen Lannaghan

Founded in 1977 by Joseph Seelig and Nola Rae, the London International Mime Festival presents contemporary visual theatre. Events are non-text based and can include circus theatre, puppetry, mask, mime, clown and visual theatre. Most work will be either a UK or a London premiere.

The festival takes place each January with the deadline for submissions in early June. Participation is by invitation only. To be considered, email Helen Lannaghan and Joseph Seelig at the address above.

Ludlow Festival

email info@ludlowfestival.co.uk
website www.ludlowfestival.co.uk

Running for more than 45 years, the Ludlow Festival takes places over 2-3 weeks in June/July with a range of music, theatre and exhibitions on offer. Each year it features open-air Shakespeare productions which are staged in the grounds of Ludlow Castle.

Manchester International Festival (MIF)

Blackfriars House, Parsonage, Manchester M3 2JA
tel 0161-817 4500 *fax* 0161-839 2662
email info@mif.co.uk
website www.mif.co.uk

Manchester International Festival (MIF) is a biennial leading festival of original, new work, created by a wide range of major international artists. The first festival took place in June-July 2007; the fifth edition will take place in July 2015. Strengthening Manchester's reputation as a leading cultural city, the Festival features work across all art-forms, including MIF Creative, a programme of innovative community-based commissions.

The Mayor's Thames Festival

website www.thamesfestival.org

The Mayor's Thames Festival is a free annual event that takes place on and around the River Thames between Westminster and Southwark Bridges. Using the river as a powerful unifying symbol for the whole of London, one of the festival's main aims is to enable more collaborations between artists and community groups. Over 1 weekend in September it programmes events such as night carnivals, fireworks spectaculars, mass choirs, music stages, a range of participatory activities, and both artist-led and river-orientated events.

Merseyside International Street Festival

tel 0151-709 3334 *fax* 0151-709 4994
email info@brouhaha.uk.com
website www.brouhaha.uk.com

Established in 1990, the Merseyside International Street Festival brings a mix of dance, drama, acrobatics, music, comedy, puppetry and street theatre to around 30,000 spectators in Liverpool each July/August.

Minack Theatre Summer Festival

Porthcurno, Penzance, Cornwall TR19 6JU
tel (01736) 810694 *fax* (01736) 810779
email info@minack.com
website www.minack.com

Founded in 1932. An annual, 20-week summer season of plays, musicals and opera held at Minack's unique open-air theatre carved into the Cornish cliffside. Created in 1932 by Rowena Cade and her gardener Billy Rawlings, the Minack lends itself to large-cast plays. Most companies involved are amateur, although approximately 3 each year are professional.

Pulse Fringe Festival

c/o The New Wolsey Theatre, Civic Drive, Ipswich IP1 2AS
website www.pulsefringe.com

Founded in 2000, Pulse Fringe is "a bright snapshot of contemporary theatre and performance, comprising finished shows, work in progress and new ideas". The festival brings an exciting blend of artists embracing a wide variety of performance arts to Ipswich, offering a unique opportunity to see a wide range of top-quality, emotionally charged and entertaining work and innovative thinking.

Stafford Festival Shakespeare

c/o Gatehouse Theatre, Eastgate Street, Stafford ST16 2LT
tel (01785) 253595
website www.staffordfestivalshakespeare.co.uk
Artistic Programme Manager Derrick Gask

As well as an annual pantomime, The Gatehouse Theatre, generally a receiving house, produces the Stafford Festival Shakespeare, an open-air production at Stafford Castle every summer. Casting breakdowns for The Festival Shakespeare are sent out in January and casting is done by freelance casting directors; rehearsals start in June. Photos and CVs sent to the theatre by actors wishing to be considered for audition will be forwarded to the casting director. Invitations to see actors in other productions are welcomed and should be addressed to Derrick Gask. Will consider applications from disabled actors to play disabled characters.

See entry under *In-house pantomimes* on page 229 for details of the annual pantomime.

The Sunday Times National Student Drama Festival (NSDF)

Woolyard, 54 Bermondsey High Street, London SE1 3UD

tel 020 7036 9027
email info@nsdf.org.uk
website www.nsdf.org.uk
Director Michael Brazier *General Manager* Chris Wootton *Adminstrator* Sarah Georgeson

For over 50 years, NSDF has been at the heart of the British Theatre. NSDF selects and presents work created by young people and empowers and inspires young talent – providing masterclasses, workshops and year-round practical advice from experienced professionals including a core team of selectors.

The NSDF has a remarkable alumni including Olivia Vinall, Ruth Wilson, Alex Jennings, Lucy Prebble, Simon Russell Beale, Meera Syal, Kate Mellor, Steve Pemberton and many, many more.

For all information, please visit the website. NSDF is an Arts Council England National Portfolio Organisation.

Role-play companies

Actors have long used their craft in promotional areas like selling products and services over the phone and in department stores; work opportunities in these fields are advertised in *The Stage*. More recently, the idea of using theatre skills deeper inside the world of business (and the service professions, like medicine) has grown considerably. Essentially, the high level of co-operation ('interactivity') and the excitement, creativity and inspirational power of good theatre is being grasped by hierarchies 'outside the proscenium arch'. Role-play practitioners today are using techniques evolved by the Theatre in Education movement in the 1960s and 70s – but with far better-paying 'customers'.

The established companies – mostly created by actors – have built up a great deal of expertise in this new world, and do not take on new 'role-players' lightly. It is therefore especially important to research each individual company's *modus operandi* before spending time and money in contacting them. However, this is a world well worth exploring as an exciting and lucrative alternative area of work.

aardvark productions ltd

Withywinds, Mill Hill, Edenbridge TN8 5DQ
tel 0800-3285 766
email info@aardvarkproductions.biz
website www.aardvarkproductions.biz
Directors Daniel Kerry, Angela Youngs

Production details: Formed in 1991, aardvark creates themed events for corporate and private clients. They also supply historical characters to museums, country houses and schools for education and entertainment as well as performing murder mysteries for any kind of event.

Casting procedures: Uses in-house casting directors, but only holds auditions as and when people apply. Welcomes both CVs and letters from actors previously unknown to the company and unsolicited CVs and photographs. Also welcomes invitations to view individual actor's websites and showreels. Happy to consider disabled actors for all roles. However, a lot of their roles would be difficult to manage for those with disabilities. Currently, there are 4 actors with differing disabilities working for aardvark.

Repliefor2016

Acting Out Ltd

Regal Chambers, Cavendish Street,
Chesterfield S40 1UY
tel (01246) 520014 *mobile* (07852) 320788
fax (01246) 558396
email acting.out@btinternet.com
website www.acting-out.co.uk
Artistic Director Claire Ashcroft, BA (Hons)

Company's work: Supplies professional role-play actors for training for all kinds of staff, from medical and legal to bar staff and corporate training. All actors must have professional role-play experience. Clients include: NHS Trust and the National Trust.

Recruitment procedures: Periodically extends its actor-base, monthly to annually, via agents, websites and Equity. Welcomes letters (with CVs and photographs) from actors previously unknown to the company sent by post or email; is happy to receive showreels and invitations to view individual actors' websites. Will consider applications from disabled actors to play characters with disabilities.

Activation

Riverside House, Feltham Avenue, Hampton Court, Surrey KT8 9BJ
tel 020-8783 9494 *fax* 020-8783 9345
email info@activation.co.uk
website www.activation.co.uk
Director Paul Gilmore

Company's work: A leading provider of bespoke interactive training. Services include forum theatre, role-play, scriptwriting and performance and the design and delivery of training programmes. Incoming actors are trained by the company, according to the requirements of the project. Strong acting and listening skills are required of all the actors. Recent clients include: Diageo, Barclays and Lloyds TSB.

Recruitment procedures: Periodically extends its actor-base, often by word-of-mouth but also using the Internet. Welcomes letters (with CVs and photographs) from actors previously unknown to the company if sent by post, but not by email. Does not welcome showreels, but is happy to receive invitations to view individuals' websites. Will consider applications from disabled actors to play characters with disabilities.

Actors in Industry Ltd (Aii Training)

Talbert House, 52A Borough High Street, London SE1 1XN
tel 020-7234 9600 *fax* 020-7357 0915
email enquiries@actorsinindustry.com
website www.actorsinindustry.com
Directors Bill Cashmore, Carry Clubb, Roger Ayres, Lorraine Brunning

Company's work: Established in 1992. "We are the foremost interactive training company in the UK, using role-play, facilitation and interactive training and coaching to create meaningful skills improvement and behavioural change for individuals and organisations." Requires incoming recruits to possess a good knowledge of business, giving feedback, and the ability to understand the perspective of delegates on training programmes. Provides training for associates in the form of an induction, group workshops and one-to-one sessions. Recent clients include: PWC, Amey, Linklaters, Astellas, Barclays, Lilly, Kraft, Johnson & Johnson, RBS, IBM, Jones Lang Lasalle, Mercer and Ernst & Young.

Recruitment procedures: Interviews twice yearly, and recruits via emailed/posted CVs (business and role playing) and covering letter. Advises recruits to be honest about experience; over-elaboration will be discovered very quickly. When submitting files with an application, please make sure that all file names contain the name of the applicant, e.g. NOT roleplay CV but John Smith rolepaly CV.

Adhoc Actors

3rd Floor, 47 Newton Street, Northern Quarter, Manchester M1 1FT
tel 0161-2360 618
email info@adhocactors.co.uk
website www.adhocactors.co.uk
Director Rodney Paulden *Artistic Director* Guy Hepworth

Company's work: Found in 2005, Adhoc Actors have worked mainly in the public and private sector business for the last 9 years. They have provided training, writing, drama, entertainment and educational workshops to a number of different organisations. The company requires its actors and performers to have excellent feedback skills and experience of working in corporate role-play. However, there is a thorough briefing before any job is undertaken. Clients include: Merseyside Police, North Yorkshire Police (PB Commnit) and The Co-operative Bank (Breathe POD).

Recruitment procedures: Uses in-house casting directors but does not hold general auditions. Casting breakdowns are available from the Equity JIS and CCP websites. Welcomes letters (with CVs and photographs) from individual actors previously unknown to the company and unsolicited CVs with photographs, sent by email. Will consider invitations to view individual actors' websites and performance notices. Also welcomes showreels. Will consider applications from disabled actors to play characters with disabilities

AKT Productions

262 Waterloo Road, London SE1 8RQ
tel 020-7620 0843
email info@aktproductions.co.uk
website www.aktproductions.co.uk
Directors Tim Bannerman, Andy Powrie

Company's work: Established in 1996. Provider of theatre-based learning resources, developing quality learning and development programmes. Incoming actors are expected to have experience of corporate role-play. Clients include: KPMG, Rolls Royce, BG, Shell and BP. Actor-base is extended every 8-12 months via recommendations and applications.

Recruitment procedures: Accepts submissions (with CVs and photographs) from actors previously unknown to the company. Prefers CVs and photographs sent via email. Invitations to view individual actors' websites are also accepted. Applications from disabled actors are considered.

Apropos Productions Ltd

53 Greek Street, London W1D 3DR
tel 020-7739 2857 *fax* 020-7739 3852
email info@aproposltd.com
website www.aproposltd.com
Director Paul Dubois

Company's work: Established in 2004. First feature film completes post-production August 2015, *Dark Signal* (executive producer Neil Marshall). Short films: *The Juror, X-Why* and *Cocktail*. Web series: award-winning web series: *A Quick Fortune* and *Le Method* (2016). Script events include *My German Roots are Showing* at the Arcola Theatre, London, starring Miriam Margolyes.

Provides training for local, national and international clients. Key focus is on Organisational Behaviour. Training is provided for incoming actors. Corporate experience is useful but not essential. Actor-base is extended annually through agents, the website and Equity Job Information Service. Clients include: SKANKSA, Sony Computer Entertainment, House of Commons, UBM and the Discovery Network.

Recruitment procedures: Accepts submissions (with CVs and photographs) from actors previously unknown to the company. Disabled actors regularly form part of its teams and are actively encouraged to apply.

Michael Browne Associates Ltd

The Cloisters, 168C Station Road, Lower Stondon, Beds SG16 6JQ
tel/fax (01462) 812483
email enquiries@mba-roleplay.co.uk
website www.mba-roleplay.co.uk
Directors Michael Browne, Angie Smith

Company's work: Established in 1997. Holds an extensive database of more than 750 professional, corporate actors. Works closely with clients to cast, devise, manage and interpret events and assessments to inform, challenge, develop, assess and train. Will provide training for incoming actors on particular clients' material as and when required. Actors should have professional drama training and experience in the corporate world using role-play for assessment, training and development. Clients include: MoD, KPMG, Nationwide, NHSBT, UKTI, FCA, RBS, DVLA and Open University.

Recruitment procedures: Periodically extends its actor-base when required "via interview/workshop after personal application and recommendation". Welcomes letters (with CVs and photographs) from actors previously unknown to the company, sent by post or email. Accepts showreels and invitations to view individual actors' websites. Will consider applications from disabled actors for specific projects.

CentreStage Partnership

South Hill Park, Ringmead, Bracknell,
Berkshire RG12 7PA
tel (01344) 304305
email info@cstage.co.uk
website www.cstage.co.uk
Contact Pippa Shepherd

Company's work: A leading development consultancy specialising in the use of drama to enhance learning.

Recruitment procedures: In the first instance, actors should send a CV outlining their acting and business experience, along with a recent photograph and covering letter, to Pippa Shepherd via **info@cstage.co.uk**.

Characters

12 Stillness Road, Honor Oak Park,
London SE23 1NG
tel 020-8856 4005 *mobile* (07710) 493483
website www.characters.uk.com
Contact Catherine Hamilton

Company's work: A well-established role-play company with 14 years' experience. Owned by Catherine Hamilton, whose background combines a professional acting career with community health experience. Initially, the company focused on working with police forces and social services departments. It has now begun to expand into the NHS and private sector, more than doubling its client base.

CragRats

Vine Court, Chalkpit Lane, Dorking, Surrey RH4 1AJ
tel (08444) 774100
email enquiries@cragrats.com
website www.cragrats.com
Managing Director Will Akerman

Company's work: A theatrical communications company founded in 1989; specialises in corporate training, TIE and issue-based theatre nationwide. Events draw on a unique mix of live theatre, dynamic workshops, e-learning, video and inspirational ambassadors with evey element supported by in-depth research. Employs 500 actors per year. Project managers and facilitators are trained in-house. Clients include: ASDA, NHS, British Airways, Learning & Skills Councils, and the Royal Bank of Scotland.

Recruitment procedures: Extends its actor-base each month. Recruits actors through the website and through agents, Equity Job Information Service and advertisements in *The Stage*. Welcomes submissions (with CVs and photographs) by post or email from actors with at least 3 years of training at an approved drama school. "We regularly recruit actors aged 21-60. Please contact us. All rehearsals are Yorkshire-based, though work can be anywhere in the UK."

Cragrats are now part of the Speakeasy4schools family: **www.speakeasy4schools.com**.

Dramanon

email info@dramanon.co.uk
website www.dramanon.co.uk
Directors Steven Brough, Melanie Nicholson

Company's work: A leading provider of live and multi-media training in business in teh UK and beyond. Uses a blend of forum theatre and role play bespoke to each client. In operation for more than 15 years. The company has built up a large client base including the public sector, together with professional business sectors such as law firms, retail, construction, financial and pharmaceutical companies. Dramanon has expanded its activities to providing conference input and now offers full DVD production and company TV material.

Dramatrain Ltd

7 Fines Road, Medomsley,
County Durham DH8 6QR
mobile (07595) 220255 (Chas);
(07595) 219951 (Diggy)
email info@dramatrain.co.uk
website www.dramatrain.co.uk
Directors Chas Thomason, Diggy Wilson

Company's work: Established in 1994. Interpersonal and management skills development, using forum theatre. Provides incoming actors with in-house and on-the-job training; work experience and life skills required. Clients include: BP, Conoco, Rolls Royce and the NHS.

Recruitment procedures: Periodically extends its actor-base as needed, through personal recommendation and via the website. Welcomes letters (with CVs and photographs) from actors previously unknown to the company, sent by post or email. Welcomes showreels and invitations to view individual actors' websites. Will consider applications from disabled actors for specific projects.

Frank Partners

website www.frankpartners.co.uk
Key personnel Neil Bett, Anna Carus-Wilson

Company's work: "We work in a variety of ways, including role-play, forum theatre, facilitation, games, coaching, making films ... in fact, any kind of creative, bespoke intervention from fronting conferences (at Deloitte) to enabling creative, strategic thinking (at BBC Worldwide)."

Instant Wit

6 Worrall Place, Worrall Road, Clifton, Bristol BS8 2WP
tel (0117) 974 5734 *mobile* (07808) 960826
email info@instantwit.co.uk
website www.instantwit.co.uk
Directors Chris Grimes, Stephanie Weston

Company's work: "A quick-fire comedy improvisation show packed full of sketches, gags, songs, surreal situations, flying packets of 'Instant Whip' and prizes! The show is completely improvised and shaped around audience suggestions. Because of this, each show is unique and takes the form that you – the audience – want it to take."

Interact

138 Southwark Bridge Road, London SE1 0DG
tel 020-7793 7744 *fax* 020-7793 7755
email info@interact.eu.com
website www.interact.eu.com
Directors Derek Hollis, Ian Jessup *Company Administrator* Jamie Wright

Company's work: Founded in 1996, the company brings theatre skills to Training, Development and Assessment, using the abilities of professional actors, writers, directors and facilitators. Role-play constitutes just 30% of output. Provides incoming actors with training in the form of a briefing for basic role-play, rehearsal and guidance for complex work. Offers facilitators specific training in running projects. Clients include: Disney, The Royal College of General Practitioners, Allianz, Prudential.

Recruitment procedures: Periodically extends its actor-base. Recruits actors through the website, agents, Equity Job Information Service, Spotlight and direct contact. Fluency, confidence and strong acting and improvisation skills are required. Business and forum theatre experience can also be an advantage. Prefers email (with CVs and photographs). Advises actors that: "Those with previous experience are most likely to be invited to a workshop/audition."

Maynard Leigh Associates (MLA)

3 Bath Place, Rivington Street, London EC2A 3DR
tel 020-7033 2370
email info@maynardleigh.co.uk
website www.maynardleigh.co.uk

Company's work: MLA is essentially a community of about 25 people who share common values, are committed to their own and other people's personal growth, and are passionate about their work affecting an increasing number of individuals and organisations. Associates are required to be expert workshop leaders with an interest in the psychological aspects of human potential development. Clients include: Aviva, DHL, Hewlett Packard, Ernst & Young, BBC TV, Barclays and Visa.

Recruitment procedures: All new consultants and leaders go through a rigorous and lengthy process, regardless of their professional experience. It can take up to 18 months of participation in Maynard Leigh activities before being allowed to represent the consultancy with clients. There are regular personal development sessions. As Maynard Leigh invests heavily in its existing associates, its pace of growth is limited. Professional actors with a good working knowledge of business and corporate life should submit their details by email.

Pearlcatchers Ltd

Claremont House, 70-72 Alma Road, Windsor SL4 3EZ
tel (01753) 670187 *fax* (01753) 830855
email enquiries@pearlcatchers.co.uk
website www.pearlcatchers.co.uk
Director Sharon M Young *Key personnel* Melanie Wright (Business Operations Manager), Karen Hanley (Business Development Manager)

Company's work: An event and training consultancy offering a fresh approach to learning, team-building and conferences. Provides actors with opportunities to shadow at events, and offers regular training afternoons and briefing sessions. Requires business skills/knowledge and prior experience in role-playing and forum theatre. Clients include: AWE, BT, Tesco, London Underground, Cisco, BUPA, DVLA and the RAF.

Recruitment procedures: Extends its actor base every 2 years, recruiting via *The Stage*. Welcomes letters (with CVs and photographs) from individual actors previously unknown to the company, sent by post or email. Does not accept showreels or invitations to view individual actors' websites. Considers applications from disabled actors for specific projects.

The Performance Business

78 Oatlands Drive, Weybridge, Surrey KT13 9HT
tel (01932) 888885
email info@theperformance.biz
website www.theperformance.biz
Directors Michael McNulty, Lucy Windsor

Company's work: Provides incoming actors with personal assessments and one-to-one coaching. Requires excellent feedback skills and experience of working in business. Clients include: organisations in the financial, pharmaceutical, engineering, and manufacturing & public sectors.

Recruitment procedures: Periodically extends its actor-base, recruiting via the website and CastNet. Welcomes letters (with CVs and photographs) from individual actors previously unknown to the company, sent by post or email. Will consider invitations to view individual actors' websites. Actively encourages applications from disabled actors and promotes the use of inclusive casting.

Role-Players NGA

tel 0207-394 3221 *mobile* (07984) 471512
email info@role-players.co.uk
website www.role-players.co.uk
Proprietor Nick Gasson

Company's work: Established in 2003. Provider of professional actors as corporate role-players to the industry, in both the private and public sector. Incoming actors are expected to have experience of corporate role-play. Clients include accountancy and law firms, property development companies and management consultancies.

Recruitment procedures: Applications are accepted throughout the year, but mostly through personal recommendation from the company's existing actor list, and through potential actors applying having seen their website. Prefers CVs and photographs sent via email and does accept unsolicitied CVs and photographs via the same method. Invitations to view individual actors' websites are also accepted.

Roleplay UK

Suite 453 South Bank House, Black Prince Road, London SE1 7SJ
tel (0333) 121 3003
email actors@roleplayuk.com
website www.roleplayuk.com
Director James Larter *Creative Director* Andy Blair

Company's work: Established in 1994. Drama-led communications and training. Provides training for incoming actors in the form of workshops.

Recruitment procedures: Periodically extends its actor-base every 6 months or every year, depending on demand. Recruits via Equity Job Information Service. Does not welcome unsolicited approaches by individuals unknown to the company, but actively encourages applications from disabled actors and promotes the use of inclusive training.

Simpatico UK Ltd

63 Petworth Road, London N12 9HE
mobile (07759) 085132
email admin@simpaticouk.com
website www.simpaticouk.com
Managing Director Amanda J. Band

Company's work: Founded in 2003. Focuses on medical role-play. Specialising in communication skills.

Steps Drama Learning Development

Suite 10, Baden Place, Cosby Row, London SE1 1YW
tel 020-7403 9000 *fax* 020-7403 0909
email mail@stepsdrama.com
website www.stepsdrama.com
Account Managers Robbie Swales, Simon Thomson, Mark Shillabeer, Gary Bates, Caitlin Morrow, Jack Rebaldi

Company's work: Founded in 1990, the company supplies training to a wide variety of corporate companies through the use of drama. The work includes role-play, forum workshops and drama facilitation. Incoming actors receive training in the areas of feedback skills, forum workshops, coordinator workshops, facilitation skills and 'train the trainer'. Clients include: Network Rail, BaE Systems, and Virgin Active.

Recruitment procedures: Extends its actor-base on a needs basis. Actors should submit their CV via the website; they should have excellent improvisation skills and be able to present themselves realistically as part of the business world in both their dress and language. Requires actors to behave in a professional manner both in their dealings with Steps and with its clients. Must be organised, reliable and good team players.

Theatre&

25 Queen Square Business Park, Huddersfield Road, Honley, West Yorkshire HD9 6QZ
tel (01484) 664078 *fax* (01484) 660079
email cmitchell@theatreand.com
website www.theatreand.com
Directors Kath Hirst, Russell Watters *Casting and Service Delivery Manager* Clare Mitchell

Company's work: Founded in 2005. An innovative training, development and creative presentation company working all over the UK. Designs and develops a variety of learning and communications interventions, which incorporate drama-based training techniques in order to deliver the client's desired outcomes. Live Drama training focuses on public and private sector organisations; Educational Presentations work within the education sector, delivering issue-based information to schools. Offers some training to incoming actors, who should ideally possess some touring or corporate training experience, strong improvisation skills, and the ability to use a variety of accents. Clients include a range of public- and private-sector organisations.

Recruitment procedures: Regularly holds auditions to increase its database of actors, and employs up to 100 actors per year. Contract lengths range from a week to 6 months. "Please send your CV and a photo along with a covering letter detailing why you think you are a suitable candidate. We are unable to respond to everyone, but will be in touch to invite you to audition if you are successful." Accepts showreels and invitations to view individual actors' websites, and will consider applications from disabled actors for specific projects.

Theatre Without Walls

Forwood House, Forwood, Gloucesterhire GL6 9AB
mobile (07962) 040441

email hello@theatrewithoutwalls.org.uk
website www.theatrewithoutwalls.org.uk
Directors Genevieve Swift, Jason Maher

Company's work: Established in 2002. Award-winning producing theatre company with an active training/corporate wing, working in the public and private sector. Also produces television and corporate films. Clients include: National Trust, Gloucestershire Local Authority, Apollo, BBC and The Prince's Trust. Training is provided for incoming actors in the form of workshops and rehearsals in forum, role-play and interactive drama. Incoming actors require good improvisational skills.

Recruitment procedures: Actors are recruited through agents and Equity Job Information Service. Disabled actors regularly form part of the team and are actively encouraged to apply. See also the company's entry under *Middle and smaller-scale companies* on page 211.

Trainerpool

Hartham Park, Corsham, Wiltshire SN13 0RP
tel 0845-2302 880
email info@trainerpool.co.uk
website www.trainerpool.co.uk
Director Andy Collett

Company's work: Provides corporate training, workshops, coaching, facilitation, roleplay, events and speakers and presenters for corporate events. Requires actors to have prior knowledge and experience of corporate roleplay work. Clients include: BMW, Hill Group and RSM International.

Recruitment procedures: Extends its actor-base on a quarterly basis, recruiting via direct approach and word-of-mouth. Welcomes letters (with CV and photograph) from individual actors previously unknown to the company, sent by email. Also welcomes showreels. Happy to receive unsolicited CVs and photographs via the same method. Will consider performance notices and invitations to view individual actors' websites. Does not generally recruit disabled actors unless this is specifically required for a role by a client.

Wizard Theatre

Blenheim Villa, Burr Street, Harwell,
Oxfordshire OX11 0DT
tel 0800-583 2373
email info@wizardtheatre.co.uk
website www.wizardtheatre.co.uk
Artistic Director Leon Hamilton *Associate Producer* Oliver Gray

Production details: Established in 2002. Performs in schools, theatres and conferences across the country. Message-based shows are commissioned annually. Works with various organisations, from the Met Police to Drug Action teams. The winter show tours in theatres: 2015's production is *Pinocchio*.

Stages 1-2 productions in the Studio each year. Also works in TIE, Theatre in Business and Role Play. Recent productions include: *Ali Baba & the Forty Thieves*, *The Wind in The Willows*, *Choices* and *On the Right Road*.

Casting procedures: Sometimes holds general auditions; actors are welcome to write in at any time. Casting breakdowns are available via Casting Call Pro and on the Equity Job Information Service. Welcomes unsolicited approaches by actors by post or email. Also accepts showreels and will consider invitations to view individual actors' websites. Does not offer Equity-approved contracts: "Usually we pay well above Equity rates." Rarely or never has the opportunity to cast disabled actors.

Professional role-playing

Robbie Swales

In 1992 an actor rang me and asked if I would do a job with him, which he had been offered through another actor. The job was to do a role-play with some accountants. I said, "What's role-play?" My friend explained that I had to role-play a demotivated worker, and that the purpose of the role-play was to help the accountants learn how to motivate members of their team. I did the job and enjoyed it. Since then – my first experience of role-play – this area of work for actors has expanded enormously. Although there are still networks of individual actors gaining role-play assignments, the bulk of the work for actors is provided by drama-based training companies, which provide organisations with role-players and actor/facilitators.

So why has this sector grown, and why is there a need for drama-based training companies, rather than individual actors applying directly to the end-user to offer their acting skills?

Trainers and developers within organisations have discovered that when they deliver behavioural skills training, an experiential interactive session provides better learning opportunities for the participants than the traditional talk-and-chalk approach. Because actors can put different behaviours on and take them off like a coat, they have become a valuable resource to the trainers; they make the sessions lively, interesting, interactive and memorable. Participants remember the learning, and then go on to use the skills in the workplace. Training and development in the workplace is only carried out if a company or organisation believes that it will improve efficiency, and therefore productivity. The use of actors for training is no exception; they help to make the behaviour of people in organisations more effective.

Drama-based training companies are what one might call one-stop shops. If an organisation, such as a high street bank, wants to employ actors to role-play on a series of development centres, the training department in the bank will find it easier to approach a role-play company. The trainer from the bank can explain their needs, check how that role-play company guarantees the quality of their actors, and then negotiate a fee. The role-play company can book the actors, brief them appropriately, and arrange for them to be in the right place at the right time.

The field of drama-based training is growing more and more sophisticated, and some of these companies are becoming more like consultancies, with entire interactive theatre programmes being researched, designed, written, rehearsed and delivered by the drama-based company. For such companies to be effective at this type of work, they need a core team of full-time staff, while maintaining a freelance team of actors trained in the appropriate skills whom they can employ on a project-by-project basis.

There are, very broadly, two types of role-play work: role-playing one-to-one with a participant; and role-playing with another actor in front of an audience, with whom the actors then interact. Most role-play work is improvised; however, there are some types of interactive theatre which kick off the session with a scripted scene, before the actors then start improvising the suggestions of the audience.

One-to-one role-play

The range of work performing one-to-one role-play with a participant requires different levels of skill from the actor. An example of the simplest type of role-play is improvising a patient for an assessment centre, where no feedback is required from the actor to the participant. The Royal College of Anaesthetists requires candidates for their anaesthetist qualifying exams to role-play with a simulated patient (an actor), so that the communications and empathetic skills of the candidate can be assessed. The role-play lasts about five minutes and is not complex.

An example of a one-to-one role-play at the more challenging end of the scale would be role-playing a Senior Tax Manager being interviewed for a job. It is important to remember that an actor is used, primarily, to display different types of behaviour (e.g. being nervous, arrogant, aggressive, etc.). However, for the actor to be a convincing Senior Tax Manager for a behavioural role-play, they need to have an overall grasp of what the job entails, and they may need to throw in a few technical phrases to add reality to the situation. This kind of role-play requires a day of training for the actor, so that they can learn about the role of the Tax Manager, memorise a few key technical words and phrases and rehearse the role-play encounter.

Actors are also required to give each participant with whom they role-play some high-quality feedback about their performance. At this highly sophisticated level of role-play, being able to deliver such feedback is an essential skill. Remember to frame the feedback with affirmative and supportive language.

The skills required to be a good one-to-one role-player are: the ability to go into character instantly; the ability to improvise well; the ability to understand and interpret the brief; the ability to memorise some technical terms; the ability to adjust your performance in relation to the quality of the input from the participant; and the ability to give feedback that is communicated sensitively and is useful to the participant.

Delivering an interactive theatre session

This technique has been used in schools by Theatre in Education companies for many years, and is now being used increasingly in the workplace. There are many different variations in the way that interactive theatre, or forum theatre, is delivered, but the principle is quite simple. Actors playing a scene will break out from that scene and talk to the audience, in character, asking for advice. This advice is then taken back into the scene by the actor and played out to see if it is effective.

Many aspects of development and learning can be addressed via interactive theatre: managing difficult conversations; feedback skills; diversity awareness; assertiveness skills; customer service; influencing skills; leadership; performance management; coaching; recruitment; and employment law awareness.

The skills necessary for performing high-quality forum theatre are: good improvisational skills; the ability to gain a thorough understanding of the objectives of the programme; being an able facilitator in order to confidently handle the responses from the audience; and the ability to hang onto a character while improvising and facilitating.

Applying for work

There are many different types of role-play/drama-based training companies. When we created Steps in 1992, we were one of only a handful of role-play companies; I have now lost count of the number of similar organisations! They all have different cultures and different ways of approaching the work, and each individual company's style probably reflects the personalities of their creators. Some companies may only provide actors to do one-to-one role-play, while others may concentrate on providing interactive theatre. Companies may have a large database of actors; others may have a small pool of actors who work on a fairly regular basis.

My advice would be to browse through the websites of the companies listed and get a feel of what they all claim to be offering. Find out from other actors who have worked in this area about their experiences. Ask them what they think of the company who employed them. At Steps we look at all actor CVs that we receive, and run audition workshops as, and when, we need to select new actors onto our team.

Role-playing for learning is no less a professional activity than professional acting. Punctuality, wearing the appropriate business/work clothes, maintaining confidentiality, interacting in an exemplary way with clients and participants, and working effectively as a member of a high-performance team with fellow role-players, are all behaviours that are required during a role-play assignment.

Being a role-player is a fascinating way for an actor to use their skills in between acting assignments while maintaining an income. Also, from the feedback I have received from role-players, the benefits are not only one-way: actors can learn a great deal from the organisations in which they role-play. The work they do can build their confidence and help them to discover new ways of managing their own careers.

Robbie Swales attended the Bristol Old Vic Theatre School from 1968 to 1970. During the 1970s he acted in Rep, toured and appeared in the West End; during the 1980s he made most of his income from TV commercials. In 1994 Robbie joined Steps – Drama Learning Development, and is now one of six directors who manage the company. In 2002 and 2003 Steps was one of the hundred fastest-growing inner-city companies in the UK, appearing on the HM Treasury-sponsored Inner City 100 Index.

Media
Introduction

The last few decades have seen incredibly rapid advancements in recording technology, computers, digital media and the Internet. There has also been an enormous growth in the principal broadcasting companies contracting-out much of their output; this in turn has led to an increase in the number of independent companies employing actors. (There are also companies whose output does not include drama – these have not been included in the listings.)

Most film and television companies use casting directors (usually freelance), and it's usually a waste of time and money writing to anyone else unless you have a personal contact. It is worth remembering that many companies do work for businesses – training and promotional films, for instance.

Student films may be a somewhat poor relation to Hollywood blockbusters, in terms of pay (if any) and exposure, but they can provide useful experiences, be a good addition to your CV, and have the potential to lead onto something that is properly paid and much more prestigious. Extracts from such a film could also be useful for your showreel.

Casting for radio is much more akin to that for theatre, although often without the use of a casting director.

Countdown to 'Action!'

Edward Hicks

The shooting process will vary slightly from production to production, and will present different challenges. But the one element that is certain – be it multi-camera studio or single-camera location – is the waiting. It's hardly surprising that actors have a reputation for story-swapping; it helps to pass the time! However, as actors spend the day unable to fully relax, in a permanent state of standby ready for 'Action', the waiting can be strangely tiring.

The average shooting day is long, and even though a finished shot lasts seconds on-screen, setting up a shot and lighting takes hours. If the sequence involves stunts, special-effects, animals or supporting artistes, it can take several days. For the actor, this means intense moments of concentrated activity (lasting minutes) followed by long periods of waiting (lasting hours). This balance between being relaxed, yet at the same time remaining focused and energised, can be difficult to achieve. Then, when things fall behind schedule (which inevitably they do), the pressure to get it right intensifies – making it even harder to relax.

A small role in an episode of a long-running television programme can frequently be far more nerve-racking than a larger part. I've often seen actors sitting around all day waiting to do a few lines, only to discover that their little scene is to be covered in one shot ... which is to be the last shot of the day. The director knows that the crew (who have worked flat-out all day) must finish on time, as there's no money in the budget for overtime; a good 1st AD won't be shy about reminding the director of this. So with only ten minutes to get the scene in the can, you're frantically called to the set (not a good moment to leave a jacket or prop in your dressing room!); you're introduced to the 1st AD (the person responsible for keeping the director on schedule); you do a rough block with the director, followed by final make-up and wardrobe checks; then someone screams "turn over", the board is read out and the director yells "Action!" Suddenly, with all eyes on you (not to mention a camera), the pressure to get it right first time is enormous. This kind of scenario may sound extreme, but every actor will experience it.

Every production will be slightly different, but the countdown to a standard shoot (if such a thing exists) will probably be as follows.

Firstly, the audition. Remember that getting one is an achievement in itself – so make the most of it. It's hard to get seen for TV and films, and even if you don't land this job, the audition may lead to others. Nearly all castings are handled by a casting director who liaises with the agents and assembles various actors to meet the director. These castings are more like an interview than an audition, involving a brief chat followed by a reading. Arrive early, as you may find a couple of pages waiting for you at reception. Don't be surprised if you only get to read the scene a couple of times; that's quite normal, and the casting director usually reads the other roles. It will probably be filmed and may only last ten minutes or so.

Having been cast, you'll be sent a script (possibly a revised draft) and a schedule. Read them both carefully. The schedule is an important document and should help to answer a lot of your questions. At the very least, it will contain a call sheet with details of where you need to be and when; most are far more detailed than that, and include cast lists, crew lists, phone numbers, maps, directions to locations, travel arrangements, health and safety regulations, etc. Check that your contact details are correct and that the dates on the schedule are the dates you were booked for. It's rare for them to be wrong, but it's always best to check as you may start work before your contract arrives. Your agent would have the original booking dates from when the company first checked your availability.

Next you'll receive several phone calls. Firstly, one from the 2nd AD or a production assistant confirming your call. If you have any questions that the schedule can't answer, this is the time to ask. For instance, if by this stage you've not received a script, mention it. They listed me as the wrong character on a schedule once and when I mentioned it to the 2nd AD, it turned out that some of the lines and my character's name had been changed. Nobody had told me and I had learnt the wrong role. Luckily, I still had time to learn the right one! Then, you'll probably get calls from someone in the Costume and Make-up departments. Depending on the scale of the production they may arrange fittings and make-up tests. Either way, make sure you know all your measurements for Costume, including hat and glove sizes. (Incidentally, it's not uncommon in TV for you not to try on your costume until you arrive for the shoot – so give them your real sizes, not the sizes you wish to be!) Also, if your hair is different from your Spotlight photo, tell them, as they might be making decisions based on it.

While waiting for your shooting day to come around, work on your script; familiarise yourself with the lines and characters. Any work you do at home that better prepares you before the shoot could prove useful, especially as less and less time is allocated for rehearsing on set. Don't forget to work on the standby scenes too; these are scenes that are held in reserve in case the schedule is changed at the last minute. They'll be on the call sheet listed as standby scenes or wet weather scenes. You'll probably then hear nothing until a day or two before you start, when they'll ring to confirm your call.

When you arrive at the unit base, the first person you'll meet will most likely be the 2nd AD who, among other things, is responsible for your whereabouts during the shoot. Make sure that they, or someone else, knows where you are at all times: 2nd ADs are full of stories about wandering actors bringing shoots to a grinding halt because they decided to look around a location. Remember, you'll end up looking foolish – but the 2nd AD gets the blame.

Having arrived at the unit base or the studios, and provided the shoot is running to schedule, you'll be shown to a dressing room or green room. If the schedule has been changed (it often is), you'll be taken straight to Costume and Make-up. If on location, the unit base will either be a building or various trailers and trucks. You'll probably be left on your own, as most people will be shooting somewhere else, but there may be other actors around (and if on location, catering people and various drivers). However, at some point you'll be collected and taken to Costume and Make-up. First thing in the morning, these places are a hive of activity, so look out for the other actors in your first scene that day. The chances are that some of them will be in Make-up at the same time as you.

Depending on the size of the production, you may have your own make-up artist and your own dresser, who will be responsible for your costumes. As you will end up spending a lot of time with these people, they'll be a large factor towards your enjoyment of the shoot. I know one director who judges the mood of his cast and crew by the atmosphere in the Wardrobe, Make-up and Catering trailers.

Once you are in costume and have been to Make-up, you'll probably get sent back to your dressing room or trailer. How long you spend waiting to be called will depend on how well they are sticking to the schedule ... and how you pass the time is up to you. Every actor I've met has their own way (I know of one actor who used to spend his time trying to write sitcom scripts, and ended up becoming a very successful writer). Some actors (but not all!) like to get together and run lines, which is great if you are inexperienced as it can help calm the nerves. However, the important thing to remember is that you have to be ready, so that whenever you are called to the set, you are able to do the best you can when the director yells, "Action!"

Every actor knows that work generates work. So no matter how small your role is, never forget that you've been given an opportunity many other actors would relish. I can't think of a more exciting place than a film set full of talented technicians and actors, who are all pulling together to create something. So make the most of it and enjoy it, because if you're lucky, you can work in some amazing places with some incredibly talented people.

Edward Hicks is currently Head of Film, TV and Radio at RADA – a post sponsored by Warner Bros. He has directed numerous Shorts, commercials and promos, is a graduate and former governor of LFS, has various film projects in development, and has written articles on screen acting in addition to being a regular contributor to *Actors and Performers Yearbook*. Ed has taught at various Drama Schools including East 15, where in 2001 he created the first media-based acting course to gain NCDT (now Drama UK) accreditation. Under the name Edward Rawle-Hicks he started his professional career as a child actor (from the age of ten), appearing at the RSC, in the West End and in numerous commercials, films and television projects.

Television companies

These almost always use casting directors who, in turn, will circulate casting breakdowns to agents they trust. However, a carefully timed (and crafted) submission from an individual can occasionally excite interest.

BBC NETWORK TELEVISION

BBC (Drama Production)

Lighthouse Building, Media Village, 201 Wood Lane, London W12 7QT
tel 020-8743 8000
BBC Elstree, Neptune House, Clarendon Road, Borehamwood WD6 1JF
website www.bbc.co.uk/drama
Director, Drama Production Nicolas Brown *Controller, Series & Serials* Kate Harwood *Head of Production* Susie Liddell *Creative Director, Drama Production* Katie McAleese *Casting Directors* Rowland Beckley, Ben Cogan, John Cannon, Stephen Moore, Liz Stoll *Casting Executive* Janet Crampsie

Note that while most of these senior programme makers are based at Wood Lane, many BBC Casting Directors are based at the Elstree site.

Casting information: The BBC no longer has a central casting department. Casting advisers are appointed to each specific programme as required. Output includes: *Casualty*, *Holby City*, *Doctors*, *EastEnders* and much else. The various programmes' casting departments will accept letters from actors previously unknown to them (with CVs, photographs, showreels and performance notices); however, actors are advised that while casting personnel are on the lookout for new talent and do attend shows, they are extremely busy and tend to use agents while casting. See the Casting directors section on page 51 for more information.

Birmingham

BBC Birmingham TV Drama Village, Archibald House, 1059 Bristol Road, Selly Oak, Birmingham B29 6LT
tel 0121-432 8888
website www.bbc.co.uk/birmingham
Executive Producer Birmingham Drama Will Trotter

Manchester

New Broadcasting House, Oxford Road, Manchester M60 1SJ
tel 0161-200 2020
website www.bbc.co.uk/manchester
Editor, Entertainment and Features Helen Bullough

BBC Northern Ireland

BBC Broadcasting House, Ormeau Avenue, Belfast BT2 8HQ
tel 028-9033 8000
website www.bbc.co.uk/ni
Head of Drama Stephen Wright

BBC Northern Ireland produces a broad spectrum of radio and TV programmes, both for the BBC's networks and for its home audience. Output includes news and current affairs, documentaries, education, entertainment, sport, music, Irish-language and religious programmes. It also has a thriving drama department which reads unsolicited scripts across all genres, i.e. single, serials, series, feature films and the short-film scheme Northern Lights, which is aimed at new talent from within Northern Ireland.

In addition to making network radio programmes, broadcasting on BBC Radio 1, 2, 3, 4, and 5 Live and BBC World Service, BBC Northern Ireland also makes programmes for its local radio listeners.

BBC Scotland

40 Pacific Quay, Glasgow G51 1DA
tel 0141-339 8844
website www.bbc.co.uk/scotland
Head of Drama, Television Christopher Aird *Head of Drama, Radio* Bruce Young

BBC Scotland is the BBC's most varied production centre outside London, providing BBC TV and radio networks and BBC World Service with pivotal drama, comedy, entertainment, children's, leisure, documentaries, religion, education, arts, music, special events news, current affairs and political coverage. Internet development is also a key element of production activity.

In addition to making network output, more than 850 hours of TV programming per year are transmitted on BBC1 Scotland and BBC2 Scotland. BBC Radio Scotland is the country's only national radio station, and is on air 18 hours a day, 7 days a week. Local programmes are also broadcast on Radio Scotland's FM frequency in the Northern Isles, and there are daily local bulletins for listeners in the Highlands, Grampian, Borders, and the South West. BBC Radio Nan Gaidheal provides a Gaelic service on a separate FM frequency for around 40 hours a week.

The BBC Scotland offices are wheelchair accessible.

BBC Wales

BBC Broadcasting House, Llandaff, Cardiff CF5 2YQ
tel 029-203 22000
website www.bbc.co.uk/wales
Head of Drama Faith Penhale

BBC Wales provides a range of services in both English and Welsh, on radio, television and online.

The Drama department produces programmes for local and network BBC television channels and local and network radio stations. Notable recent successes of the department include *Doctor Who*, *Torchwood*, *The Sarah Jane Adventures*, *Life on Mars* and *Ashes to Ashes* for television, and the serialised and single dramas for radio, *The Wooden Overcoat*, *Investigating Mr Thomas* and *Solo Behind the Iron Curtain*.

INDEPENDENT TELEVISION

ITV (**www.itv.com**) is the biggest commercial television network in the UK. It is made up of a network of 15 different regional licences, each with its own set of obligations and conditions designed to reflect the particular character of their region and the interests of their viewers. Eleven of the licences in England and Wales are owned by ITV Plc (**www.itvplc.com**), formed in 2004 following the merger of Carlton and Granada. SMG owns the two Scottish licences, Scottish Television and Grampian; UTV and Channel Television own the licences for Northern Ireland and the Channel Islands respectively.

Note: Many companies commission from independents, so don't have casting departments.

Channel Television

The Television Centre, St Helier, Jersey JE1 3ZD
tel (01534) 816816 *fax* (01534) 816777
website www.channelonline.tv

Provides programmes for the Channel Islands during the whole week, relating mainly to Channel Islands news, events and current affairs. Does not produce any in-house drama.

ITV Yorkshire (YTV)

The Television Centre, Leeds LS3 1JS
tel 0113-243 8283 *fax* 0113-244 5107
website www.itv.com/yorkshire
Casting Director Faye Styring

Established in 1968, YTV is one of the biggest ITV companies. Following the new Communications Act and the merger of Granada and Carlton, it is part of the new single ITV plc which began life on 2nd February 2004.

YTV continues to produce a range of drama and light entertainment programmes, including: *A Touch of Frost*; *Emmerdale* (shown on the network every weekday night) and *Heartbeat* – ITV1's most popular long-running drama series. In 2003 a new sister programme, *The Royal*, attracted 11.3 million viewers and a 41.3% share of the television audience. In addition to its drama series, YTV has made a number of one-off dramas for the ITV network, including: *Booze Cruise* and *Brides in the Bath*. With an audience of 9.7 million viewers and a 44% audience share, *Booze Cruise* ranked as the best performing Single Drama from any channel for the whole of 2003.

The Casting Department generally works through agents, but will accept submissions (with CVs and photographs) from actors previously unknown to the company if sent by post. As the Department is very busy it cannot guarantee to acknowledge all submissions, but advises actors to enclose an sae for a quicker response. Prefers not to be contacted by telephone or email.

ITV Tyne Tees & ITV Border

Television House, The Watermark, Gateshead, Tyne and Wear NE11 9SZ
tel 0844-881 0100
website www.itv.com/tynetees; www.itv.com/border

Broadcasts to the North of England 7 days a week, 24 hours a day.

ITV Wales & ITV West

ITV Wales, The Television Centre, Culverhouse Cross, Cardiff CF5 6XJ
tel 0844-881 0100
ITV West, Television Centre, Bath Road, Bristol BS4 3HG
tel 0844-881 2345
website www.itv.com/wales; www.itv.com/west

Provides programmes for Wales and the West of England during the whole week. Produces programmes for home and international sales.

The ITV West Television Workshop, aimed at young people (up to 26), offers experience in the performance and production skills required for TV, film, theatre and radio. See **www.itvworkshop.co.uk** for more information.

ITV Meridian

Forum One, Solent Business Park, Whiteley, Hants PO15 7PA
tel (08448) 812000
website www.itv.com/meridian

The ITV franchise-holder for the South and South East coast of England. Does not produce any in-house drama.

ITV Central

Gas Street, Birmingham B1 2JT
tel 0121-643 9898 *fax* 0121-643 4897
website www.itv.com/central

Provides ITV programmes for the East, West and South Midlands every day.

ITV Anglia

Anglia House, Norwich NR1 3JG
tel 0844-881 6900 *fax* 0844-556 3931
website www.itv.com/anglia

Provides programmes for the East of England, daytime discussion programmes, documentaries and factual programmes for UK and international broadcasters. Does not produce any in-house drama.

ITV London

South Bank, London SE1 9LT
tel 020-7827 7000
website www.itv.com/london

See ITV Yorkshire and ITV Granada for casting contacts.

ITV Granada

Granada Television Centre, Manchester M60 9EA
tel 0161-832 7211
email casting@itv.com
website www.itv.com/granada
Casting Director Gennie Radliffe

The ITV franchise-holder for the North West of England. Produces programmes across a broad range for both its region and the ITV network.

Welcomes submissions (with CVs and photographs) from actors previously unknown to the company sent by post or email. As the Casting Department is extremely busy, it cannot guarantee to respond to all submissions. Advises actors to call to find out what projects are being cast, and to send in their details as and when appropriate.

SKY Satellite Television British SKY Broadcasting Ltd (BSKYB)

Sky Entertainment, NHC1, Grant Way, Isleworth, Middlesex TW7 5QD
tel 020-7705 3000
email bskybpress@bskyb.com
website www.sky.com/corporate
Chief Executive Jeremy Darroch *Head of Entertainment* Stuart Murphy *Head of Drama* Anne Mensah *Drama Senior Commissioning Editor* Cameron Roach *Executive Producers* Jo McClellan, Lizzie Gray *Drama Head of Development* Beverley Booker *Drama Development Executive* Danny Takhar *Drama Development Coordinator* Daniel Walker

Casting procedures: BSkyB does not have its own casting department, but uses freelance casting directors, for example, Michelle Guish (*Moonfleet*).

STV Productions

STV Central, Pacific Quay, Glasgow G51 1PQ
tel 0141-300 0300
STV North, Television Centre, Graigshaw Business Park, West Tullos, Aberdeen AB12 3QH
tel (01224) 848848
website www.stv.tv
Head of Drama Eric Coulter

STV Productions (formerly SMG Productions) is the television production arm of STV Group Plc, and incorporates Ginger Productions. Its client list includes all terrestrial networks and major satellite and cable channels. Output includes drama, factual/ factual entertainment, entertainment and children's programming.

The Drama Department has more than 20 years' experience of producing network drama for ITV1. Credits include: *Taggart*, *Dr Finlay*, *Rebus* and *Goodbye Mr Chips*. The Drama team is based at Glasgow offices. Casting procedures differ from project to project; generally uses independent casting directors, but also accepts letters from actors 'on spec' (with CVs and photographs). Where appropriate these will be passed on to a relevant programme or project.

UTV

Havelock House, Ormeau Road, Belfast BT7 1EB
tel 028-9032 8122 *fax* 028-9024 6695
email info@u.tv
website www.u.tv

Provides programmes for Northern Ireland. All drama is produced by the ITV network.

Casting for television

Janie Frazer

There are now many casting directors working in television, and each will have their own way of working. This is my own viewpoint and may not be shared by others, but I hope it may be helpful.

I came into casting by way of the theatre. When I was a schoolgirl I fell in love with the theatre and, being good at English, thought perhaps I could become a drama critic. However, some wise person suggested that before writing about the theatre I should work within it, and so I managed to get a job – at first unpaid, sweeping the stage and as a dresser, and subsequently as an ASM and then handling publicity for the Citizens Theatre Glasgow. I had also been involved in the big auditions held at the start of each season for the Citizens, and had come to realise that the actors were the thing that interested me most about the theatre. Subsequently I moved to London and incessantly badgered LWT for a job as a casting assistant, which finally transpired. I have worked there, through several mergers which have resulted in the company currently known as ITV, for many years. I have cast for all types of television productions; mainly drama, comedy drama and situation comedy, but also sketch comedy, factual drama, hidden camera, animation (voice-over), and various others programmes which defy definition.

Each production has its own specificity, but there are basic requirements that apply to all of them.

The script

This is the first principle and the foundation for everything else, even though the script may change beyond recognition during the process of getting the production to the screen. The script contains the characters, their descriptions, and the dialogue; from this, in consultation with the director and producer, I will put together a list of suggested actors for the roles.

Casting for television carries with it certain commercial considerations. The casting of the main characters is often crucial to a programme getting commissioned in the first place, since in commercial television the advertisers need to be assured of getting a specific audience for the programmes around and within which they buy advertising space. This is the reason for the often-heard grumble that the same well-known faces crop up again and again, and the reason for it is that they have good form – i.e., the programmes they appear in produce good viewing figures, which is what both ITV and the BBC are striving to maintain.

Beyond the 'name' casting, the casting for other roles involves interpreting the director's vision, style, ideas and the tone of the piece, to come up with suggestions that will best express the way in which the director wants to portray the material. Therefore, the same script may elicit different suggestions from me, according to the individual director.

Suggestions for actors

How do I arrive at these? I have many lists, and many files, sorted in an idiosyncratic fashion over the years and added to constantly after seeing actors' work on stage and screen. Also there is *Spotlight*, which is the casting director's invaluable and indispensable tool. If there was only one piece of advice I could offer to an actor, it would be to appear in *Spotlight*, and to keep one's entry accurate and up to date. I now use *Spotlight* almost exclusively via the Internet, as the information contained on the website is wonderfully comprehensive and well organised, and allows me to do cross-reference searching (e.g. for a 30-year-old Punjabi speaker with a Manchester accent) which is extremely swift and useful. The information contained on the site does however rely entirely on the input of the actors who subscribe to *Spotlight*, and it is therefore very important that they keep their credits and personal details current.

Also and most importantly, their photographs. To state the crashingly obvious, television is a visual medium. It's vital that an actor's photograph is up to date and actually looks like them. Vanity should not be the issue, as television requires all types and ages to be portrayed; moreover, an inaccurate photograph can be misleading and time-wasting. Spotlight's website has now progressed to offer audio and video clips of each actor, and I have found that these can be really useful to play to a director when discussing casting. Therefore, I would strongly recommend that actors make full use of all the opportunities offered by *Spotlight* to show their wares.

Via the Spotlight Link I am also able to send out a breakdown of characters to the agents, who then relay back their suggestions, which I can order, prioritise and follow up. I will discuss with the director and producer the various suggestions we have made between us, and those that have come from agents; I will then arrange casting sessions for the various roles.

Getting in touch

I would love to be able to say that receiving letters with photos and CVs, or emails with all those attachments, is always a boon – but I'm afraid it's not usually the case. More useful is to be notified of actors' forthcoming performances: even if it's not always possible to cover these, it's good to know what work you are doing, and one may ask other casting directors if they have seen you in the piece.

Showreels can be useful to view as examples of an actor's work, but tend not to be so significant if they arrive unsolicited – there are simply not enough hours in the day to watch everything that is sent in. I find I am most likely to watch them if they are directly relevant to a current project (for instance, if I am looking for young Northern actors, or working on a sketch comedy show, I will select to watch those that might fall into the relevant categories).

When you are called for audition

Almost invariably now, casting sessions for television dramas and comedy are video-taped. This allows for greater scrutiny of the actor, and assessment of their presence on screen away from the social context of the audition. It does not mean that the actor has had to produce a flawless reading, but many things emerge from watching an actor on screen which may have been missed during the live reading. The camera is sensitive to minute changes in thought-processes and expression as the actor is being filmed in close-up; this is something the actor needs to bear in mind during a television casting audition – that the performance will be watched at close hand, and therefore a loud voice and large expressions will convey considerable impact and may need to be scaled down.

Whatever an actor's looks, the most important feature on screen is the eyes. The people casting the programme need to see yours. Therefore, it will help enormously if you are able to absorb, familiarise yourself with, or, best of all, learn the scene so that you are able to raise your eyes from the script. Almost all 'sides' or scenes for reading will have been emailed to your agent or yourself prior to audition. Make sure you have an email address. Acquaint yourself with script formats such as Final Draft (at the time of writing, a free download for viewing scripts in Final Draft format is available from the website **www.finaldraft.com**). If you wear glasses, print the scene in a large font so that you can still read it if at the casting they would prefer to see you without glasses.

Other basic things to bear in mind are to arrive on time; make sure you know the specific whereabouts of the casting venue, and how long it is likely to take you to get there. You may be unavoidably kept waiting, in which case make sure you let the casting director know if you have another appointment you need to attend. If you can, do some prior research, both about the project, and also about the producer and director of the programme. You can find out about their previous work via the IMDb website, **www.imdb.com** – and since they will after all be looking at your CV, they may be impressed and flattered if you also know something about theirs.

Spend some time thinking about the material you've seen, so you have something to say about it. Many actors would be surprised at how much their observations have contributed to the final version of the script. In television as in film, time is money. Pre-production periods have been reduced to the minimum, which means that there is often very little time for rehearsal once shooting begins. Directors often therefore use the casting process to try out ways in which they would like to scenes to play – this can be rewarding for the actor, and useful even if they do not finally land the part; often directors keep their interview lists, and bear actors in mind whom they've liked but who haven't been quite right for the part in question.

If you look good, I look good

Sometimes actors view casting interviews as an exam, or as some sort of test they have to pass. However, there is at least one person in the room who is completely on your side – the casting director. The casting director's reputation relies on the calibre of the actors invited for interview, and if the actors aren't up to it then the casting director is the one who's on the line. Therefore, by getting you in for audition, the casting director is demonstrating faith in your ability and rightness for the part.

Know your value

Everyone has their own USP – their unique selling point. Even if you are Mr/s Ordinary, then that's it. It's valuable. Get to know what it is that is most intriguing about you, and play to your strengths. Ask your colleagues for constructive criticism and listen to it. Emphasise your strengths and don't pretend to be what you are not. Whereas the theatre can thrive on disguise and artifice, the camera takes no hostages and is ruthless in its exposure.

Did you get it?

If you got the part, then congratulations! But an actor is often confused as well as disappointed about not getting a part. They will ask: should I have done it like this, dressed like that, what did I do wrong? It's hard to explain to an actor that the choice is not dependent on something they did or didn't do, but often is the result of someone else being more right for the part than they are. This is a nebulous assessment which I can appreciate is very unsatisfactory to hear, but it is nevertheless the truth. Those actors who have ever been on the other side of the casting process often remark how they now understand what this means, but it doesn't help much with the feeling of frustration. One can only suggest that, by the law of averages, eventually the part will come up for which you are the most right; that you've done pretty well to get the interview in the first place; that the director may well have clocked you for the future – and that the whole experience stands you in good stead.

For most of her professional life **Janie Frazer** worked as a casting director for ITV Productions, the programme-making division of ITV. She is now working freelance. Janie's career in casting has covered all the genres of single drama, drama series, continuing drama, factual drama, comedy drama, situation comedy, single comedy and sketch comedy. Amongst the many productions she has cast are *Spaced*, the cult comedy series with Simon Pegg; *Coronation Street*, Britain's longest-running soap; and *Blue Murder*, the detective series starring Caroline Quentin.

Auditioning for camera

Nancy Bishop

'The camera is your friend' is the first lesson I teach in my courses on auditioning for camera. The ironic truth is that many theatre actors who feel perfectly comfortable performing in front of thousands of people become timid in front of a small piece of electrical equipment. The antidote to camera fear is to practise on screen as often as possible. Own a camera, use it, grow comfortable with the lens, love it – and it will love you back.

What's the difference between auditioning for film and auditioning for theatre?

In theatre, you are often asked perform a prepared monologue, while in film, you read from 'sides' (short scenes from the actual screenplay.) In theatre, you can find yourself reading with another actor, while in film you might end up reading with a talentless casting director.

Actors are deluded in thinking that if they were actually on location, with all of the props and sets, it would be easier than acting in an empty casting studio. ("If I had the actual laser gun then I could act it so much better.") But acting in a dull audition room or in front of a green screen in a film studio is not so different from acting during Shakespeare's time. The Globe didn't have elaborate sets, which is why characters say obvious lines such as, "Well, this is the Forest of Arden." There was no forest on stage ... just a wooden O. So the actors had to use their imagination.

It's the same now. When you're doing a horror film, the oozy monster doesn't perform with you. He's created by a computer geek later on. *Actors must use their imagination.* This includes imagining that you have a brilliant scene partner to play off, even when you only have a casting assistant in a bad sweater.

What can I expect at an on-camera audition?

Slating and introduction

Your first audition is likely to be a screening process, or 'pre-read'. Often the director will not be there, so the casting director will need to 'slate' – which means slipping a name card in front of camera and asking you to turn both profiles. Yes, it feels like a prison shot, and every casting director has heard that joke before.

Next the casting director may ask you to introduce yourself, for the benefit of the absent director. For some reason, this trips up a lot of actors. They feel perfectly comfortable playing some one *else*, but when they have to be *themselves* for a few minutes they stumble around. The introduction, however, may be the most interesting part for the casters. We want to see who you *really* are, your personality. It's the alchemy between the actor's unique energy and the screenwriter's written word that creates the character.

It's best to have some kind of pithy introduction semi-rehearsed so that you don't corpse for camera when the casting director asks you to introduce yourself. Remember that it's all about spin. This is your opportunity to sell yourself for the role. Be enthusiastic and be yourself. Here are a few examples of good and poor introductions.

If you already have professional credits:

• Poor spin: "I had a tiny role on *Inglorious Bastards*. I waited on set forever and I think my line didn't make it to the final cut."

• Good spin: "I had a great time working with Quentin Tarantino on my last project."

If you are new to the business:

• Poor spin: "I haven't really played any big roles before. I'm just out of drama school."

• Good spin: "I'm just out of drama school and can't wait to land my first job. I really like this project. I've always wanted to work on a World War II film."

These are the kind of personal details you might include in an introduction (such things humanise you; it's interesting to us if you're a mother, if you like to travel, etc.):

• "I just celebrated my daughter's third birthday;"

• "I just got back from a fascinating trip to India;"

• "I work part time in a homeless shelter."

It's better not to include such comments as "I'm working as a temp in an office right now and I hate it." This tells us that you're not really a professional. True, you might have to work a day job to support yourself, but you don't have to emphasise it.

How do I best play to camera?

You should ask the camera operator about frame size. It's a perfectly professional question. What does the camera see? Is it wide, medium or close? If it's a close-up, you're wasting your energy with hand gestures. Be careful not to pop out of frame, and calibrate the performance in your face, where the camera will detect inner monologue.

Calibrating a performance to frame size can be one of the trickiest parts of screen acting. Often the actor's fear is that the camera will amplify their performance so that they will appear to be over-acting. In my screen-acting courses, actors sometimes become discouraged when they watch the play-back and realise that they haven't hit the right level; they see themselves either popping out of the screen, or plagued by the opposite problem which I call *dead face* – when a performance is boring and dead. Nice house but nobody is home.

Theatre actors often fall prey to dead face because great screen actors create the illusion, to the unstudied eye, that they are 'doing nothing'. It's a great misnomer. In a close-up, the actor becomes a talking head, and the only thing that matters is the information communicated by the face. Therefore the performance may have to be even intensified in the eyes and face. The antidote to dead face is an active and ever-changing inner monologue. The camera photographs thought and it loves to watch a character thinking.

This is true of acting in any medium, but in screen acting, listening and reacting become more than half of the performance. One of the most common mistakes in an audition is when an actor reads along with his or her scene partner's lines rather than truly listening and reacting in the moment.

Where do I look? Directly into camera?

The answer is no. Unless specifically asked, you only look directly into camera when you are introducing yourself. There are exceptions, like in the mock-documentary genre. In the US TV series *Modern Family*, for example, the characters speak directly into camera as if questioned by an imaginary interviewer. It's the modern form of Shakespeare's soliloquy; the character speaks his/her thoughts out loud to the audience. That is the exception, not the rule. Most film and TV genres still assume the removal of the fourth-wall type of realism, wherein the characters go about their lives, not knowing that they are being observed.

The best place to focus is somewhere near the lens. This will give the viewer a three-quarter view of your face. You want to be as generous as possible about playing towards the camera. We won't cast you if we can't see you. Placing an off-screen reference on the floor will only bring your eyes down. Hopefully the casting director will help you with this by placing the reader directly next to the lens. But if not, you can focus on a fixed point, rather than on the reader. Know your best side for photography and play accordingly.

How can I prepare for a project when I only have a few pages of text?

You can ask for information. The casting director should provide a summary, but if they don't, then ask for information or ask to read the script. Sometimes it's available and sometimes not, but a question never hurts. If you can't get the script, then you need to make decisions about the pages according to the information you have. If the script wasn't available to you, then it wasn't available to other actors either, and you have an even playing field. Start with the basic Stanislavski questions:

- *Who am I?*
- *Where am I?*
- *Who am I talking to?*
- *What do I want?*

I also encourage actors to add:

- *What are the stakes?* Make the stakes as high as possible, and this will drive the dynamics of the performance.

Answering these questions is one of the basic tenets of acting, yet many actors (even experienced ones) forget to do this for an audition, and they find themselves floating in a sea of too many possibilities. Anchor yourself in the 'W' questions; this will guide your performance.

In order for actors to develop their onscreen skills and comfort level, they must practise. Screen acting is like driving a car. No one gets in a car the first time and just drives. You have to learn how to give the car gas and ease up on the clutch so that the car doesn't jerk. This is why I encourage actors to own a camera, practise with it and take on-camera courses. Modern smart phones with cameras are equally useful for practice and self-filmed auditions, which are increasingly prevalent.

Last of all, I always advise actors to have fun and enjoy the process. If you're enjoying yourself, then so will we, the casters. Love the camera – it will love you back.

"*Good actors are good because of the things they can tell us without talking.*" Cedric Hardwicke

Nancy Bishop is an Emmy-award nominated CSA casting director who casts from Prague. She has cast large-scale studio pictures such as *Mission Impossible IV* and *Prince Caspian*. She also coaches actors and teaches master classes on audition technique throughout Europe and the US. She is the author of Methuen's *Secrets from the Casting Couch*.

Self-taping auditions

Ros Hubbard

Time is the enemy! When we set up Hubbard Casting in London in 1976, we had much more time and money (!) available to us. Now with film budgets under far more pressure there are more and more time constrictions. We have been forced to come up with a solution to actors being considered all over the world for parts: self-taping. The positive development that has influenced the simultaneous growth in numbers of actors to be considered for any one role is that there is much more of an international focus. Films have been enhanced by the growth of international audiences and their taste for more broadly based stories with multinational casts, so there is a greater chance of more actors being considered. The facility of self-taping cuts out so much delay caused by booking a live audition, when wanting to take a first look at an actor.

Once I have accepted your agent's recommendation that you be considered for a role, self-tapes allow me to see your acting even if you are working in a different country or elsewhere in the UK, on a theatre job, another film shoot, or even on holiday. Several well-known actors self-taped behind their agent's backs for *The Lord of the Rings* and *The Hobbit*. It is worth chancing your luck by submitting unsolicited self-tapes. I do look at these, but make sure you are brilliant, if you want to catch and hold my attention. However you cannot ring to see if they have arrived, as casting directors do not have the time to respond to such requests. Similarly, if you have been rejected from an arranged submission, you just have to accept it. Do not attempt to open a dialogue about it. You may be called to a live meeting from self-tapes but actors are rarely cast directly from them. Sam Underwood is one of the exceptions we have just cast at the time of writing (summer, 2014).

Now, I may actually physically meet only three to five actors per character, but I like to be inundated by possibilities, and will publicise my search anywhere I think I may discover a new talent. But this itself can demand a big investment of hours, weeks, months. For a film with ten speaking characters, I can watch up to 600 actors on tape. Recently, I was thrilled to be asked to cast John Carney's (director of *Once*) *Sing Street*. With two Irish mid-teens at the centre of the film, my nets would have needed to be cast wide and deep for one of my favourite challenges: hunting the unknown. Regrettably, calculating existing commitments, I knew I could not afford to employ my usual tactics and had to decline the offer, because it would have involved a huge amount of internet searches and self-tapes.

Much of what I have to say about making self-tapes may seem plain common sense, but each piece of advice I give here is based on scores of bad examples seen in the thousands of self-tapes sent to Hubbards in the very few years in which self-taping has become the most prevalent form of first-level audition.

1. The simplest way of self-taping is on an iPhone – it is also very effective. Laptops' sound reproduction is not so good. You can enhance the quality of the filming by using a camera placed on a tripod, but a friend filming you on an iPhone should really be quite sufficient. You should use a closed room, not the corner of a hall or passageway, which is more likely to pick up extraneous noise. If shooting for an American show, try to hire a room at Spotlight. They will put the video on a link for you.

2. Be off-book! No paper should be in view. Margie Haber in LA says you do not need to be off-book in the US, but you would have to be amazing not to be. She runs workshops in on-book auditions, but US auditions can be as many as up to seven a day, so it is impossible to learn that many for one day. You should allow at least one night to prepare. Form a group of actor friends to read in during preparation and filming, so you can support each other and know that at least one of them will always be available to work with you.

3. Remember to have the phone/camera mic as close to you as possible: a foot between your legs is ideal. We embarrass ourselves and the actors ramming the camera and mic close up, but it is the difference between being heard and not being heard. Casting offices are as noisy as chip shops. All four members of the Hubbard family have at least their associate caster working with them at any one time. In the summer of 2014 Amy Hubbard was casting the fourth series of *Homeland* and had just finished *24*, so had a team of ten assistants whirling around the office. The actor on the tape needs to be heard above all that racket. It does not matter if your recording level sounds unnaturally loud – it can always be lowered.

4. Shoot from an angle that shows more of you, with your head and chest occupying the centre of the image – keep it close. It's your soul they are after. A director may later call for an actor to reshoot the scene as full length. Try to shoot in daylight, but *don't sit in front of windows or all we will see is your silhouette.* Filming on camcorders in electronic light is much less effective. Keep your eyes level with the camera. Looking down on the floor or the script will kill the opportunity. Do not look directly at the camera. You should look at your just-off-camera scene partner. If the scene demands physical contact, then you can use a certain amount of movement. Some part of the partner can be visible, but just indicate the action, do not try to be sensational. American casters never use any actors to read in – so your partner can sound very flat and you have to really energise yourself. Do not use any props apart from a cup or a cigarette. There should be no people in the background, or any children or pets anywhere in the field of vision. Do not use too much make-up. Electronic signals are hard and make-up makes you look hard and older.

5. If your tape has been solicited and sides have been sent to you to record, you will be handicapped in doing thorough character preparation, if you are not sent the script or given any other guidance. It never harms to ask for a synopsis of the whole story. You don't have to shoot the whole scene. It will be clearly said to your agent or you how much dialogue is required. I am likely to edit tapes before forwarding them to the director. Don't use showreel material in place of a self-tape, but they are a useful addition. Your showreels should only consist of clips from your films and TV productions. Do not use personally manufactured scenes. Look at other actors' showreels before choosing your own selection. There should not be too many other actors in the clips, especially actors, who look like you – very confusing for us old dears!

6. Do not try charming the casting director by using moody talk or blathering on about what you are doing at the moment. Never bring your fears into an audition, live or recorded. Leave them on a coat hook before you enter the room or screen. Your spoken introduction on tape should simply give your full name, height, your agent's details or whether you are representing yourself, the title of the scene and your availability for a

live meeting and the shoot dates. If an accent is required for the scene, use it for your introduction as well, even if it is less than technically perfect because the effort made will impact positively on your performance. Do not read out the stage directions. Do not underscore the tape with music.

7. You must discipline yourself to closely examine the tape. In the first place you may have forgotten something essential. Ask a friend or friends to give their honest opinion of how well your tape serves the scene, and trust it. This will help you avoid subjective judgements such as choosing the tape most flattering of your general appearance, as opposed to what suits the character best. You can send two versions, especially if the scene is short. Do not announce differences between the two takes. Be subtle in your introductory explanation for sending two. In live auditions, I will always listen to an actor, who feels they have not done themselves justice, and would like to rerun their audition. But it is not always possible to get you back and there have been many occasions when an actor has thought that they read badly and got the part – you are your own worst critic!

8. Use a watermark app on your phone to protect the copyright of your self-tape. You may be the next big thing within two to three years, but in any case do not put your self-tapes on YouTube: that would be even more silly. Also, the script is not your property or the public's. You are in a position of trust. The producers can decide against you no matter how good you are for indiscreet behaviour with scripts. I have seen uploads on YouTube before I can get it out to the director and that is where it ends for you.

9. Do not use an ordinary attachment to email your tapes because their downloading time clogs up our inboxes and slows up the casting process even more. Use web transfer services, e.g. Hightail, WeTransfer or Vimeo. Label your file with your name and the character you are playing.

Good luck with your careers!

Ros Hubbard was born in Dublin and ran a model agency there in the late 1960s. She moved to London and became 'Queen of the Commercials', at which point her husband, John, joined her as a casting director. They went on to cast a myriad of films and TV dramas. The company expanded to include both their daughter Amy and son Dan. Ros and John now live in London but they call their real home Dingle, in Co. Kerry, Ireland.

Are you ready for Pilot Season?

Brendan Thomas

It has been suggested that the exodus of British actors, especially young British actors, to Los Angeles each spring is somewhat akin to the 1840/50s Californian Gold Rush. They come to participate in the casting frenzy of Pilot Season. The surge is understandable as the quantity and quality of UK actors in leading roles in American features and TV series appears to be on an ever-rising tide. Despite this increasing visibility of UK actors on American screens, I would advise others against hoping for great outcomes from purely speculative trips to the US before their careers have gained any momentum. However, if such visits are thought of as largely gaining knowledge for the future combined with aspects of a vacation, there is much to be learned if you come with as much information about the American industry as possible. An initial trip could be very useful in determining how difficult your personal negotiation of the increasingly fierce border regulations would be, as well as giving you the opportunity of discovering how compatible you are with life in Los Angeles.

The internet has transformed pilot season in numerous ways. One of those ways is self-taping for auditions. This is used if an actor cannot make an audition, or is out of town etc. A casting director will review the tapes and, if there is interest, pass it along to producers/ studio/ network. If there is further interest, you may be asked to fly out to test for the role, or in some cases, they will use your original self-tape. You can participate in American pilot season virtually anywhere in the world. For initial contact with a US manager, I would recommend a discussion over Skype. Most managers are very amenable to these.

There are a number of different temporary visas that could cover your investigative trip/ participation in Pilot Season. Obviously you would not be receiving a fee for auditioning, but the nature of Pilot Season is such that you could be filming within weeks. The audition process could range from three auditions a day to radio silence for a week, you really never know how busy you will be. There are also circumstances where you could be under consideration for several pilots. If you are one of the lucky ones to do so you can only continue as a series regular in one. Most roles are already made as offers to known actors so the wider auditioning process is one for insurance/ back-up in case offered roles are not accepted. This may seem dispiriting but there is a chance that the offered actor's deal may not work out for all sorts of different reasons, leaving room for the newcomer.

The commitment to screen test is really a very heavy one as effectively you will have agreed in advance to film the full series, if you are accepted to test for the pilot. A series can continue for up to seven years, so you have to know that you are legally available, which means having more than a temporary visa. While it is possible to audition for most series regular roles without the appropriate visa (productions will often sponsor if they like the actor enough) there is not time, normally, to sort your paperwork out between accepting a role and filming. This may feel like Catch 22 territory. You will require a **O-1B** visa petition (as an individual with an extraordinary ability in the arts or extraordinary achievement in the motion picture or television industry) to be filed at least 60 days before you wish to enter the US to avoid delays in the visa processing. This will permit you to accept most roles: star, regular, recurring or guest star, but certain networks in some cases can demand Green Card (permanent residency) status. It is important to note that any entertainer or artist cannot file for a visa on her/his own behalf – your visa application must be lodged by your sponsor or petitioner. The O-1B filing entity must be an employer (the actual production company/ network/ studio that is offering you work), or a US agent or Management company located in the US – meaning they must be an organization or entity that has an American address and an IRS (Internal Revenue Service) Employer tax number. A blanket 0-1B visa, which lasts for three years, costs on average about $5,000. A Green Card can cost up to twice that amount.

Beware of companies that offer to act as a 'middle man' to help secure visas. They say the folk who made the most money in the Gold Rush were the ones selling the shovels. These 'middle men' are charging an unnecessary fee to help secure a visa which is easily done by contacting an American lawyer, and his/her paralegal. Some of these legal services are advertised on the web, but if you are operating without ready access to an American agent or manager, it would probably be safer to take a recommendation from an actor friend who has been through the process.

Pilot Season has served not only as the core mechanism for the American television networks' collective market research for programming their subsequent year's drama productions, but as a huge actor job-seeking convention. It has incorporated the advent of the cable channels joining the process and, so far, the explosion of online streaming companies such as Hulu, Amazon and Netflix's expansion into production of original drama television: Netflix's *House of Cards* being the most prominent example so far, while in June 2015 Netflix announced it would be making its first feature film, *War Machine*, starring Brad Pitt. An increasing number of pilots are being made outside the January–March box with many going year round. Aside from stand-alone pilots, there are many shows that are straight to series, meaning there will be ten episodes set to air as opposed to shooting a one-episode pilot and seeing how that rates.

It is already common practice for shows to engage casting directors in other countries, alongside their lead home casting director, especially as more and more drama is shot abroad or elsewhere in the US. There can be a casting director in Los Angeles, New York, Ireland, London and Canada (Vancouver/Toronto) all for the same series. The magnetism of American television has grown over the last decade, attracting top writers, directors and actors. There is no longer a stigma for marquee actors to do television. Everything is material driven as opposed to where it will be shown or viewed.

For the lone UK actor venturing into Pilot Season without the direct support of a single representative, or even one audition in place, there is a lot of casting information to be gleaned free of charge on the web from the sites of the trade journals such as *Variety.* American agents and managers (and some UK agents) have access to each network's comprehensive grid of the pilots they are seeking to cast, so it is possible to align all the grids and gain an overview of all the roles available. These grids contain far more detail than the related articles that appear in the trade journals. They are used and reorganized differently at each agency, however, they all contain the vital information about projects throughout all stages of development. They show all the elements to each show: network; studio; producers; length of the episode; shoot dates being aimed for; location; number of episodes; logline; the writer, director, actors attached; executives at network/ studio; roles: type, description status; and are updated at each stage of the process.

Having identified a number of roles you think match your casting profile, it is possible to submit your profile to the casting directors through *Breakdown Express*'s Actors Access, part of *Breakdown Services*: a near equivalent to the interactive casting services of the UK's *Spotlight*, but without its link to a comprehensive actor directory. Individual agencies and personal managements can organize all data relating to their clients' acting credits, diaries (including upcoming auditions, rehearsal calls and filming schedules) and vital statistics, on *Breakdown Services* but they cannot access files of *any* other agencies/managements or those of *any* individual actors, who are not their own clients.

Breakdown Services introduced Actors Access via its website to stem illegal trading of *Breakdown Express*'s casting information between represented and unrepresented actors. The latter are able to receive the same breakdowns that agencies/ managements do. However, casting offices have the option to have *Breakdown Services* release their breakdowns strictly to agents/ managers only. The option to release breakdowns to Actors Access is not made clear, so most if not all of the big project breakdowns go straight to agents/ managers and bypass the actors. Nevertheless you should be able to obtain enough information from sources in the public realm (e.g. deducing there would be a role to match your profile from a plot summary), you can research the casting director's address and make a submission via postal services. You may not receive any response to your submitted CV/ resume and/or tape, or you may be asked to go back on tape incorporating the casting director's notes. A manager would monitor your tapes for you, weeding out ineffective material. This reflects the distinction between the roles of the American agents and managers. While both categories submit their joint clients for castings, the agents deal with booking of meetings and contracts, while the manager works more closely with her/his clients, shaping careers and strategies, forming the basis of decision making for accepting roles. As with any American casting, if your tape is successful you will be asked over for a film test, if you are not already in situ for Pilot Season. Your flight will be paid for and you will receive a $60 per diem. The flights used to be booked "business" class until the recent SAG (Screen Actors Guild) agreement rolled the status back to "coach", though this is subject to variation from case to case.

Signing up to a seven-year deal may appear to be the key to Hollywood from where you stand at the moment, but could become a dreary, unfulfilling commitment, which entraps you from taking much more creatively fulfilling and perhaps more lucrative opportunities over those years. On the other hand, you might not be filming continuously. It is possible to combine filming different series on both sides of the Atlantic, for example O.T. Fabengle shot the first series of *Looking* (San Francisco) alongside (but not clashing specific shoot dates) *The Interceptor* (UK) hopping back and forth across the Atlantic in two incredibly diverse roles. However the chances are your best opportunities elsewhere would arise exactly across your annual commitment to an American series.

From the point of view of general experience, auditioning in America is likely to up your game. It is very, very tough over here. There is a massive amount of competition for roles. Preparation is vital but you often don't get a lot of time to prepare your sides, nevertheless the expectation to be entirely off book is universal here, while not always the case in the UK. Your American accent needs to be 100 per cent in place. Expect blunt criticism if it is not right. Some casting directors have advised, if you are meeting producers etc. in the casting, that you should come into the room speaking in an American accent, otherwise, if you come in speaking in your own accent, and then switch, their attention is focused on what's not right with the accent rather than focusing on the work. Ultimately the choice is yours, but you may need to decide what lessens the odds against you getting the job. See a reputable dialect coach. There are many – generally actors trying to supplement their income – who are not suitably qualified. On the positive side you may sometimes have up to three castings a day in different parts of LA which often entails a lot of driving across often busy freeways. A full driving licence is essential.

Having digested all this information you may feel more secure about striking out alone for next year's Pilot Season, but here is one final warning: the overall chance factor will be against you, but is higher in some years and unpredictable. Which way will the dice fall for you?

Brendan Thomas is one of a number of managers at **Untitled Entertainment** which is led by two partners and has offices on both coasts repping actors, writers and directors. Brendan comes to the UK three or four times a year combining seeing his UK clients in theatre performances or on film/ TV sets and locations, including elsewhere in Europe, while maintaining face-to-face contact with their UK agents.

Working in a soap

Susan Penhaligon

I had never been in a soap. When I started back in the seventies, doing a soap was seen to be a bit downmarket and selling out. If you wanted to be considered a 'serious actor' you avoided them like the plague – a bit grand maybe, but that was the perceived wisdom then. Now, all that has changed. With the nature of TV – reality shows, multi channel choices, repeats – most actors today would be very happy to get a few episodes, or even a long-term engagement on a prime time terrestrial channel performing in front of an audience of ten million. For an established actor like me, it's a chance to let everyone know I'm not dead! And for a young actor it can be a fantastic way of upping your profile and introducing yourself (let alone earning some money to put in the bank). When the call came for me to get on the train to Leeds to audition for *Emmerdale* I was both delighted and very nervous. I was lucky, and got the part and a six-month contract which was then extended for another six months. The work process was completely new to me and after thirty years in the business it was a challenge. My observations are obviously personal and about *Emmerdale*; another actor might have a different view. Hopefully the following will be useful to you.

Auditioning often means you have to travel to either Leeds or Manchester, or if it's *EastEnders*, to Elstree. Make sure you arrive on time. This is very important as it tells the casting director you are punctual and reliable (very important for soap schedules). I went by train to Leeds which allowed me to look at the script on the way up.

Do try to learn the scenes they send you and to go in with confidence. Different actors have different methods: I convince myself I don't want the job, as apparently producers and directors feel uneasy if someone is needy and desperate! Sometimes you are handed the script when you arrive, so try and get there early to pick up the pages, take them away and learn as much as you can. This shows you can learn lines quickly, a useful tool for soap acting. Often, if it's going to be a long-term contract, they will give you an emotional scene and a funny scene and it can be hard to do these without preparation. I focus on the lines and the emotion, trying to make the lines come off the page, but don't be surprised if you come away thinking you've done badly. Its part of the process. If you get the part, the ability to learn quickly and focus emotion without much discussion will be very handy.

Don't worry about accommodation. Most TV companies have lists of hotels and B&Bs for your initial weeks. If you are going to be a long-term character you might want to rent a flat or, after you get settled, share with another actor. At the *Emmerdale* studios there is a noticeboard outside the actors' Green Room where people advertise rooms and flat sharing.

I found most of the regulars on *Emmerdale* had moved within commuting distance and had families. This can make you feel a bit lonely. After a day's work they go back to their cosy homes while you sit in a hotel room. But the young actors on the show had a great social life and I found most people to be extremely friendly and welcoming. Given time, you find a life for yourself. It's a help if you know friends in the area whom you can visit and who are not in the show, so you can debrief. It's not a good idea to let off steam with people you are working with. Tread carefully to begin with. Keep your own counsel.

A word of warning: when I was in *Emmerdale*, the way expenses were paid was changed after much consultation between Equity and management. The result was that individual expenses are now paid on top of your fee – the flat-rate expenses for everyone became redundant. Your agent needs to sort this out for you. Also I found that the expenses were sent a few weeks after I had to pay my rent, so be prepared to have those funds available or have your agent arrange an advance.

You will probably be asked to go on a costume trip with the costume supervisor before you start. I would advise that you have a good idea of how you would like the character to look, particularly if you are on a long contract, as the bulk of your wardrobe will be bought at the beginning (obviously if you are involved in a wedding scene or special occasion, another shopping trip will be done). In fact I would go as far as having a chat with the producer about how you see the character and what they have planned for you.

A good producer will suggest that you go to them if you have any problems. Be bold about doing this, it's important. I foolishly didn't clarify some issues I had, and for me there was always a grey area about where my character came from, what social band she belonged to and how she fitted in with the three main regulars – the family she joined. *And* I never discussed with the producer what kind of clothes she wore.

This also goes for later on, when you might feel strongly about a speech change or story line you're not sure about. The names and extension numbers of the script editors are in the Green Room, and they don't mind if you ring to discuss any lines you feel don't work.

The layout of the *Emmerdale* studios is a bit like a factory! The management are on top, the workers are on the shop floor, so it's easy to get to see someone. I'm sure it's true for the other soaps.

I have to say that my first day passed in a flurry of nerves, meeting people, attempting to remember names, constantly changing costume and trying to figure out which camera was on me. Most of the soaps do what they call a multicamera set-up, i.e. you have four cameras recording the scene at the same time. If this is a new experience for you, it can be a bit nerve-wracking – but don't worry. Actually you don't have to know which camera is on you, and if the director needs you to be aware for whatever reason, he will make a point of telling you on the appropriate line. Eventually it becomes like second nature; you kind of see the red light going on in the corner of your eye and it won't throw you. On location you will only have, at most, two cameras – it's easier.

In the studio, which is more like a warehouse, the different sets are lined up side by side. This is very confusing for a beginner, and it's easy to get lost. Even after a year, I could still be found wandering aimlessly around muttering, "Where's the Woolpack?" Try not to feel a fool just because the long-termers know exactly where they are going. I used to follow the herd, but sometimes ended up in the wrong set! The runners (or third assistant directors), who give you the morning calls, will tell you the number of the next scene and come and get you when you are needed on set. They are wonderful. They're young and keen; anything you need to know – ask them.

Emmerdale does three blocks of four scripts every fortnight. You may be involved in four or five episodes, but no more than eight, over two blocks. Each block has its own crew, A/Ds and director. There are three units working at all times, but you will only be involved with two units. One unit is usually out at the *Emmerdale* village, the other in the studio, and during the day you will be taxied between the two. Most soaps do between 20 and 30 scenes a day (*Emmerdale* tries to do 38). You won't be involved in all those scenes, but you could do up to 20.

Your scenes will be out of sequence and in different blocks, so you might be changing your costume from scene to scene (when you start, it's best to ask the costume department after each scene if you need to change). This sounds simple, but I found that when I had a lot to do, the speed at which you finish a scene, rush back to your dressing room, change and then rush back to the studio can be very confusing at first. The costume department will choose your clothes for the scenes and are on the ball with continuity. They are usually willing to bring you something else out of your wardrobe if you are unhappy, but generally it's best to wear what they have chosen for you; otherwise you can spend the whole day discussing or even arguing, and it's not worth it.

I did find the make-up and costume departments, production team and crew amazing. They worked the longest hours of anybody, with professionalism and good humour. And the latter is one of the essential ingredients to creating a happy work atmosphere. Particularly in the hot-house environment of a soap!

This brings me on to another important problem: how to divide up your script. I found that every actor had their own method. Some of them had large folders with each filming day, date and episode cross-referenced with the director's name and a short break-down of the story order. (People called the blocks by the director's name.)

I found my own way, which was to put the scenes together in a daily shooting order with the day and date at the top. I made sure I read the episode thoroughly before I split it up, hoping I would remember the story order on the set. I did come a cropper once, forgetting that in a scene I had shot the week before I was tearful and vengeful, only to be too sunny and smiley in the following scene. A pitfall of shooting out of sequence. Some of the directors are very good at reminding you of the story order. The regulars seem to have an uncanny ability to make every scene work as well as it can with the minimal amount of effort and worry about story order.

The changing nature of soap storylines has no logic. To begin with it's frustrating, particularly if you've been lucky enough to work in an environment where all the right questions are asked about your character's motivations and behaviour. I advise you to give all that up; there just isn't time. A soap is about narrative, so your lines are taking the story forward (not necessarily revealing anything about your character). This is why people are always seen in the same sort of costume or hat – it identifies them (if you start off carrying a dog you'll probably carry the dog in every scene!).

Unlike a play, or an episode of *Casualty*, there is no beginning, middle and end. You step onto the roller-coaster and you go with it until you leave. I found if you play the emotion in the scene for what it is, as real and as truthfully as possible, without thinking about what has happened to the character in the past or what's coming up in the future, it saves you a lot of angst and time trying to talk to the director about your motivation while the first assistant is looking at her watch, making 'got to GET ON' noises. The shooting schedules are such that directors rarely have time to discuss the scenes in depth (although there are exceptions) and a lot of the time the scenes can't take too much analysing.

Obviously if the only line you have all week is, "Pull us another pint, Val," then there's not much you can do except arrive on time, be friendly, have a laugh and know your words.

If you have a short stint in the soap then you might only work with one director, but if it's a year or so you can work with a lot more. I found this to be the single most confusing part of being in a soap. After years of working on productions where you build a relationship with a director, acknowledging that they are team leader, taking notes from them, trying to collectively put their vision on the stage or screen, I discovered that in a soap this is all topsy turvy. Directors come and go. They do a block at a time, which will involve three or four storylines, then go away to edit while the story machine rolls on with another director. There are often first-time directors and you will know more about your character than they do. If a director has been away for six months on other jobs, they can't possibly catch up on all the story lines – so you end up explaining that no, you can't get in the car and drive out of the village because two episodes ago you lost your licence. Having said that, I worked with some very good directors who did a lot of other TV work, so it's best you understand that they can be as frustrated as you. For both of you it's the nature of the format that describes your working methods.

A typical day would be getting up at 6am, either driving yourself to the studio or paying for a taxi (if you are on location, a studio car will pick you up). You arrive in your dressing room to put on costume, then into make-up to be ready on set for 8am. You might work through the day until 7pm (not necessarily in every scene). So you wait either in your dressing room or in the Green Room to be called. The A/Ds don't like you to leave the building or location. Such is the nature of schedules that you can have one scene first thing in the morning and five more starting at 6pm – be prepared for this. I used to take a book; some actors spend the time learning their lines. I always preferred to learn my lines the night before, even if I got in late. And a word on learning: don't over learn, it's not like a play. And learn to learn quickly. It's quite possible that you could be given a new piece of script just before going into the studio ... this happens, and there are always rewrites. Don't feel bad about drying on set either. Everyone does it. Obviously if you dry all the time people will get fed up with you. But I discovered that fluffing and drying is very much part of a day's work.

More than likely you will have blocks out when you can get home. I had a month out when I came back from Leeds to London. On top of that you are entitled to two weeks' holiday a year. At Emmerdale the blocks are posted up on a notice board with the episode numbers running along the top and the characters involved listed down the side, so you can have some idea of your work pattern. But, not only did I need a degree to understand this schedule, I also found that it changed, so don't take it as gospel. There is always a friendly soul nearby to explain everything to you but don't expect to be told. Ask, ask, ask would be my motto. *Nobody sits you down and says this is how it all works.* Including when the canteen opens and shuts. Find out to avoid disappointment! (The canteen is subsidised, by the way, so really OK food is very cheap.)

Although most people know how to behave, just a little word. Too much ego is frowned on. Without losing your own identity, it's common sense that you should acknowledge there are actors who have been doing the show much longer than you. A modicum of humility is appreciated, along with a bit of respect. They will respect you in return. Being able to laugh or make people laugh is at a premium. I had a day when I had 18 scenes and by mid-afternoon I couldn't remember my own name. So a bit of banter relieves the pressure.

Believe me, it's hard work doing a soap. It's not a doddle, like a friend of mine suggested. The days can be long with a lot of scenes to remember, or very tedious, when you have little or no storyline and you are needed for a non-speaking background appearance. You can be playing high emotions one minute and a lighter moment the next, and there is very little feedback apart from 'that's fine, next scene'. There's no audience to clap you and producers are busy people, so they can't be on the studio floor the whole time telling actors how good they are. Don't expect it. If it happens, and it can, be happy. I found that it was the other actors who encouraged me. They were kind and supportive, a lovely crowd.

Now, there is that thing called FAME. After about six months, depending on your story lines and the success of your character, you will be noticing people looking oddly at you on the train, or someone comes up and says, "Didn't I meet you on holiday in The Himalayas last year?" Six months on and the general public think they know you. They'll call you by your soap name, ask for your autograph and generally be pleased to see you.

Along with all this good feeling comes publicity. If you are young and good looking, the soap publicity machine will want to use you. It's part of the job – but if you feel adamant that you don't want the readers of *Heat* magazine to know what underpants you wear, then don't do it. I personally think there is a way of doing the publicity while keeping your private life intact, but be careful. If you become a successful soap actor you have to watch your back. There will always be a photographer when you least expect it, or a member of the public will snap you staggering legless out of a club. There is nothing wrong with getting your name known; the problem with a soap is that you become known as your character. That's ok if you are happy to stay in the show for as long as they'll have you, but if you have ambitions to play other parts, it can take time to erase the memory of the character you played. Of course there are some actors who come out of soaps and do very well. But there are more young actors who seem to fall by the wayside. And some, sadly, hardly work at all. If you do go down the celebrity route, I would say go for it big time. Make sure your *own name* is printed large in the paper and in people's minds.

And please, please don't believe your own publicity. It's a fickle game. If it's decided that your character has run its course, they will write you out and the publicity stops. So keep your feet on the ground, however famous the attention makes you feel.

And there's something else. If you are good in your part and show you are serious about the process of acting, people take notice; the word goes around. You can be in a soap and still be rated as a good actor. Sometimes you'll get the chance to play a well-written scene with substance so you can show what you're made of. I found that the actors in *Emmerdale* worked hard to keep the standard of acting high, sometimes against all odds. They cared about it and wanted it to do well in the ratings.

I had a wonderful year and I learnt a lot. That's very satisfying when you've been working for as long as I have.

Susan Penhaligon's first appearance in theatre was playing Juliet in *Romeo and Juliet* at the Connaught Theatre, Worthing. Since then stage appearances include two seasons with the Royal Exchange Theatre (Manchester) and parts in productions at the Nuffield Theatre (Southampton), Birmingham Rep and the Palace Theatre (Watford). In the West End her appearances include Natasha in *The Three Sisters*, a leading role in Richard Harris' *The Maintenance Men*, and Annie in *The Real Thing*. She has appeared many times on television; early work included *The Taming of the Shrew*, *Doctor Who*, *Upstairs Downstairs*, *Tales of the Unexpected* and *Dracula* with Louis Jordan. She is best known to viewers as Pru in *Bouquet of Barbed Wire* and as Judi Dench's sister in *A Fine Romance*. Among other film parts Susan played Mae Rose Cottage in the movie of *Under Milk Wood* and appeared in Paul Verhoven's film *Survival Run*. She has published her first collection of poems in collaboration with Sara Kestelman, called *Two Hander* (Do-Not Press).

The world of children's television

Iain Lauchlan

What are the special skills you need for this murky world of children's TV? Well, to answer that I would have to divide my reply into three sections: children's drama, children's presenting, and animation voice-over work.

Children's drama has to be tackled like an adult drama. You have to commit to the part, find and play the truth of the part, and be sure to play the relationships with the other characters in a believable and truthful way. Children are not a separate race; they are just like little adults with less experience. They tend to like the same things – good quality storytelling and characters that entertain.

Children's drama is like any other kind of drama. You need to be able to act, audition well and be handy with a pen and paper to write to the producers and commissioning editors. There is so little drama done for children that you need to be sending letters to these people constantly, as they need to be reminded of your existence. The truth of the matter is that there is no money around for big children's drama productions anymore: as a result, the producers never get to know many actors, so you need to keep writing to them.

There is a move to increase the drama output by the BBC and by Channel 5 for children, so hopefully the possibility of doing a drama may increase.

Children's presenting is another story altogether. Not every actor can present ... it's a different skill. Some actors master it easily, and some have great difficulty. If you are an actor that likes pantomime and enjoys breaking the fourth wall to contact the audience directly, then the chances are you will enjoy presenting.

Finally the voice-over artiste. There are many opportunities in this field, as voices are always required for animation characters, puppet characters and costume characters.

As an actor it can be a very enjoyable experience exploring what your voice can do. I often get voice CDs sent to me that only explore the different accents that an actor can do, but it is important to explore the different qualities of voice you can achieve, because these are the artistes that get the work.

You must explore how high a voice you can sustain, how low you can go, how odd you can make it. Where in your mouth, throat or nose you can place the voice so that you can switch voices when asked to in a session.

I find that if you study pictures of characters from children's books and give them the voice you think suits them, then you can begin to expand the limits you have set on your voice. It will amaze you the different qualities of voice you can achieve without falling back on accents.

There are many animations made every year in this country, and they all need voices. Once you have settled on some crazy voices as well as a selection of normal ones, then get them down on a clear CD. Not a tape done in your living room, as these are painful to listen to when you are searching regularly. And get them out there. Send them to everyone. Tell people you exist and that you have a very useful collection of voices.

Here are three 'C's' which are important to remember when acting, presenting and performing voices for children– whether it is in the theatre, recording studio or in a TV studio... **Commitment, Contact and Communication.**

Firstly you must **commit** to whatever age range you are presenting to or acting for. This means getting to know your audience, whether it be pre-school, 7-10 year-olds, 10-12 year-olds, or teenagers. Each age range needs to be spoken to in a way that is not condescending, that is truthful and that seems to treat them as older than they are. All children are aspirational and will only engage with a presenter, actor or programme if they feel that it caters for older children as well.

Contact is the most important aspect of presenting and acting. Particularly presenting. You have to commit to the audience and let your performance either cross the footlights or drive its way down the lens of the camera, to contact and connect with your young audience. Many actors are more comfortable with their performance staying within the fourth wall and allowing the audience to have a passive experience enjoying the relationships, together with the twists and turns in the plot.

Presenters must contact the audience directly and have a dialogue with them. The experience must be an active one from the audience's point of view, and is a commitment by the presenter to the audience with a similar commitment back to the presenter. If I can mention the actor in the pantomime again, this is a half-way house for a character like Idle Jack. Although he is playing a character and telling a story, his performance will not be complete until he has an audience and builds a rapport with them. The audience is the final member of the cast. This is also true for a presenter.

If you are performing with others on stage, then the process of communication must be an imaginary triangle that begins with you and travels to the other presenter via the audience. This is just as important if you are having a dialogue on stage between two presenters. It is essential that you have contact with your audience at all times. This contact is most important when presenting to a pre-school audience. There must be a trust, a respect and an entertaining rapport built up that should never falter.

Communication is therefore a key factor in performing to children. If you are not communicating – be it dialogue, a song or a comedy routine – then the audience will not be engaged and will get bored. They will either chat if they are in a theatre, or walk away from the screen if they are in a cinema. Children will give a very honest response.

If you feel that you are one of those actors that could be a successful presenter, then how do you break into the world of children's television?

There are many types of children's programming, like animations, live action with costume characters, live action with presenters, documentaries, game shows and magazine programmes. Some of them do not require presenters, but others do – and ask presenters to offer information, facts, link songs and comedy routines. Experience as an actor will come in very useful when required to do these things, and should be played up when writing for work. Time spent as a Holiday Camp host is also invaluable; you experience at first hand the reaction children have to you and to your material. When I audition for presenters or costume characters, I often see Red Coats.

How do they know I exist?

It is the old story here yet again. You must write to the producers who make children's programmes and tell them you exist. This will be all of the major children's broadcasters like BBC, ITV, Channel 5 and Nickelodeon, plus many of the Independent Production Companies that now produce a large percentage of children's programming for the above broadcasters.

You must tell them you are around and what you are capable of – and keep telling them. Every time they are casting for their latest production your letter must be on their desk, otherwise they will not think about you. A good clear CV with relevant information including your height, age, weight, experience and skills, together with a professional-looking letter showing clearly your contact details and a good, truthful photograph, is all that is required. I am not a great lover of showreels as they often show the limitations of the artist rather than their true capabilities. They are also way too expensive to produce.

Yes, there is a children's TV world out there, and it is possible to break into it. The advice you must keep in mind at all times is this: make sure that people know about you and what you can do. Don't just tell them – *keep* telling them.

Start collecting a list of production companies and who runs them. They keep changing, so keep up to date with them. *Contacts* should be able to provide you with the broadcasters information, and PACT should have a list of Independent Producers. Good luck!

Iain Lauchlan has been involved with children's television since 1980, when he became a presenter on *Playschool* for the following eight years. During this time he also presented *Fingermouse* and a selection of children's radio programmes. Iain later became the Producer of three of the daily *Playdays* programmes – *Why Bird Stop*, *Roundabout Stop*, and *Poppy Stop* – and has also run his own TV production company, which created children's programmes such as *The Tweenies*, *Boo*, *BB3B* and latterly *Jim Jam and Sunny*. During most of this time he has tried to keep his acting career going, and is now Creative Director for Imagine Theatre, producing 11 pantos each year and performing in one as the Dame.

Independent film, video and TV production companies

Companies in this field start up and close down all the time, and it is very important to have a proper contract if offered work with an independent. If in doubt, check with Equity.

Absolutely Productions

Unit 19, 77 Beak Street, London W1F 9DB
email info@absolutely-uk.com
website www.absolutely.biz
Managing Directors Gordon Kennedy, Chris Pye

Founded in 1988. Produces scripted drama and comedy for radio, TV and film, and Factual and Factual Entertainment shows for TV and radio. Recent credits include: *The Very Bits of Armstrong and Miller* (C4), *The Go Betweenies* (BBC Radio 4), and *Red Letter Day* (BBC 1 Wales).

Actaeon Films Ltd

50 Gracefield Gardens, London, SW16 2ST
tel 020-8769 3339 *fax* 0870-134 7980
email info@actaeonfilms.com
website www.actaeonfilms.com
Company Director/Producer Daniel Cormack *Producer* Matt Gunner *Head of Development* Becky Connell

Production details: A London-based production company established in 2004 to develop and produce theatrical motion pictures, both drama and comedy. Recent productions include: the Tiscali Award-winning *Amelia and Michael* (35mm, 2007) starring Anthony Head; the UK Film Council completion-funded *A Fitting Tribute* (HD/Super 8mm, 2007); and the micro-short comedy *Nightwalking* (HD, 2008) starring Raquel Cassidy.

Casting procedures: Uses freelance casting directors. Offers PACT/Equity approved contracts and does not subscribe to the Equity Pension Scheme. Actively encourages applications from disabled actors and promotes the use of inclusive casting. "We welcome invitations to showcases, screenings and theatrical productions and will view showreels, but we don't advise sending CVs/headshots unless in relevant response to a current casting call."

Anglo-Fortunato Films Ltd

170 Popes Lane, London W5 4NJ
tel 020-8932 7676 *fax* 020-8932 7491
email anglofortunato@aol.com
Contact Luciano Celentino (Managing Director)

Produces action drama, comedy and psychological thrillers. Offers Equity-approved contracts and does not subscribe to the Equity Pension Scheme. Actively encourages applications from disabled actors.

Avalon Television Ltd

4A Exmoor Street, London W10 6BD
tel 020-7598 8000 *fax* 020-7598 7313
website www.avalonuk.com
Joint Managing Directors Jon Thoday, Richard Allen-Turner *Director* Rob Aslett

Production details: TV, film and radio company producing drama, comedy and documentaries. Recent credits include: *The Frank Skinner Show, Shane, Harry Hill's TV Burp*, and *The Sketch Show.*

Casting procedures: Always casts through freelance casting directors and does not issue public casting breakdowns. Does not welcome unsolicited contact of any kind from actors previously unknown to the company. Offers Equity-approved contracts.

Bentley Productions

Pinewood Studios, Pinewood Road, Iver, Bucks SL0 0NH
tel (01753) 656594 *fax* (01753) 652638
website www.all3media.com/companies.php
Managing Director Jo Wright

Specialises in high-quality drama, and has completed productions for both ITV1 and BBC1, including *Midsomer Murders.* Bentley followed the success of *Midsomer Murders* with an action thriller for ITV1, *Ultimate Force.*

Big Bear Films

48 Priory Road, Richmond, Surrey TW9 3DH
tel 020-8332 9765 *fax* 020-8332 9765
email office@bigbearfilms.co.uk
website www.bigbearfilms.co.uk
Producer/Director Marcus Mortimer

Production details: Established in 1998. Makes comedy, drama, and factual entertainment programmes for all networks. Recent productions include: *My Hero* (BBC1), *Get A Grip* (ITV with Ben Elton), *Strange* (BBC1), and *The Hairy Bikers Cookbook* (BBC2).

Casting procedures: Casting is done by freelance casting directors Tracey Gillham and Sara Crowe. Actors are employed under Equity-approved contracts. Actively encourages applications from disabled actors. "Please come to auditions with some knowledge of the part and the production."

Big Red Button Ltd

91 Brick Lane, London E1 6QL
email hello@bigredbutton.tv
website www.bigredbutton.tv
Key personnel John Burns, Pier Van Tijn, Sagar Shah

Production details: Established in 2002. Specialises in short films and music videos. Works in live action, puppetry and animation. Also employs actors in drama, comedy and commercials.

Casting procedures: Holds general auditions and actors can write to request inclusion at anytime. Casting breakdowns are available on the website. Does not offer Equity-approved contracts. Rarely has the opportunity to cast disabled actors.

Blakeway Productions

6 Anglers Lane, London NW5 3DG
tel 020-7428 3100 *fax* 020-7284 0626
email admin@blakeway.tv
website www.blakeway.co.uk

Established in 1994. In 2004 the company was bought by Ten Alps PLC and in 2007 it merged with 3BM Television and Ten Alps TV, bringing together strong track records of successful production across the genres of documentaries, docu-dramas, current affairs and factual entertainment formats.

Has produced more than 200 hours of prestigious programming for the BBC, Channel 4, More 4, ITV1 and Five in the UK, and leading US broadcasters including PBS, National Geographic, HBO, The History Channel and Discovery. Recent hits include: the Emmy-nominated docu-drama *9/11: The Twin Towers*, a co-production with Dangerous Films for BBC1 and Discovery; *The Clinton Years* for Radio 4 and the BAFTA-winning docu-drama *Nuremberg: Goering's Last Stand* for Channel 4 and The History Channel.

Bryant Whittle Ltd

49 Federation Road, Abbey Wood, London SE2 0JT
tel 020-8311 8752
email info@bryantwhittle.com
website www.bryantwhittle.com
Directors John Bryant, Amanda Whittle

Production details: An independent production company working in feature-film production, with a slate of live action and CGI animated movies. Also offers a script-editing service. Employs actors in drama and voice-over.

Casting procedures: Uses freelance casting directors, and actors may write at any time to request inclusion; details will be kept on file. Offers Equity-approved contracts.

Cactus TV

1 St Luke's Avenue, London SW4 7LG
tel 020-7091 4900 *fax* 020-7091 4901
email touch.us@cactustv.co.uk
website www.cactustv.co.uk
Joint Managing Directors Amanda Ross, Simon Ross

Specalises in broad-based entertainment, features and chat shows. Since its inception in 1994 Cactus has produced 41 distinct titles in the UK, for 10 different channels.

Carlton Television Productions

35-38 Portman Square, London W1H 0NU
tel 020-7486 6688 *fax* 020-7486 1132
Director of Programmes Steve Hewlett

Comprises Carlton Television Productions, Planet 24 and Action Time. Makes drama programmes for all UK major broadcasters (ITV, BBC, Channel 4, Channel 5 and Sky) and regional programmes for Carlton Central, Carlton London and Carlton Westcountry.

Carnival Film & Television Ltd

55 New Oxford Street, London WC1A 1BS
tel 020-3618 6600
email info@carnivalfilms.co.uk
website www.carnivalfilms.co.uk
Managing Director Gareth Neame

Production details: Founded in 1978. Works mainly in TV production, creating drama with a popular and international feel. Employs actors for drama. Commissioned by major UK broadcasters including BBC, Channel 4 and ITV. Has received various prestigious awards/nominations, including Oscars, BAFTAs, Golden Globes and Emmys. Recent credits include: *Whitechapel*, *Downton Abbey*, *Hollow Crown* and *Dracula*.

Casting procedures: Uses freelance casting directors, does not deal directly with actors. Offers PACT/ Equity contracts. Will consider casting disabled actors to play disabled characters.

Celador Films Ltd

39 Long Acre, London WC2E 9LG
tel 020-7845 6800 *fax* 020-7845 1147
email mdavies@celador.co.uk
website www.celador.co.uk
Chairman Paul Smith *Managing Director* Christian Colson

Develops and produces high-quality, commercially viable feature films across all genres. Film credits include: *Dirty, Pretty Things*; *Separate Lies* and *The Descent*. All projects are commissioned and developed in-house. Christian Colson is responsible for the commissioning, development and production of all projects presented to the company. Unsolicited scripts are not accepted.

Works also in television and radio. TV output is mostly non-fiction and light entertainment – e.g. *Who Wants to be a Millionaire?* and *You Are What You Eat* – although the company produced the sitcom, *All About Me*, starring Jasper Carrott and Meera Syal.

"The company is developing a number of other projects, including a further Neil Marshall project for production; BAFTA-winner Adrian Hodges' adaptation of Claire Tomalin's Whitbread Award-winning biography of Samuel Pepys, *The Unequalled Self*; *Farang*, a low-budget road movie set in Thailand – a collaboration with writer Richard Cottan and director Peter Webber; an original screenplay from Paul Webb, based on events following the accession of Lyndon Baines Johnson to the United States presidency in the aftermath of Kennedy's assassination and *Big Deal*, a comedy about a hapless English journalist attempting to navigate the shark-infested waters of the international poker circuit."

Celtic Films

1st Floor, 24/25 New Bond Street, London W1S 2RR
tel 020-7727 6049
website www.celticfilms.co.uk

Production details: Established in 1986, Celtic Films has acted as a co-producer for 15 feature-length episodes of *Sharpe* for ITV, and for the award-winning *The Girl from Rio*.

Casting procedures: Accepts submissions (with CVs and photographs) from actors previously unknown to the company if sent by email. Showreels, voicereels and invitations to view individual actors' websites are also accepted. Offers Equity-approved contracts. Will consider applications from disabled actors to play characters with disabilities.

Coastal Productions

c/o 16 The Plantations, Wynyard Woods, Wynyard, Teesside TS22 5SN
tel (01740) 661025
email coastalproductions@msn.com
website www.coastalproductions.co.uk

Created in 1997 by Sandra Jobling and Robson Green with the aim of making feature films and TV dramas in the North East of England – and supporting local young people wanting to get into the industry. The company's many production and co-production credits include: *Take Me*, *Blind Ambition*, *The Last Musketeer*, *Touching Evil*, *Close and True*, *Grafters 1 & 2*, *Rhinoceros*, *Hereafter*, *Unconditional Love*, *Rocketman*, *Wire in the Blood* and *Place of Execution*.

Collingwood & Co.

10-14 Crown Street, London W3 8SB
tel 020-8993 3666 *fax* 020-8993 9595
email info@collingwoodandco.co.uk
website www.collingwoodandco.co.uk
Head of Development Helen Stroud

Founded in 1988. Animation series and specials for children. Does not deal directly with actors: prefers to deal with agents.

The Comedy Unit

The Comedy Unit, Unit D,
Glasgow North Trading Estate, 24 Craigmont Street, Glasgow G20 9BT
tel 0141-305 6666 *fax* 0141-305 6600
email info@comedyunit.co.uk
website www.comedyunit.co.uk
Managing Director Rab Christie

Produces some of Scotland's best-loved television and radio shows, as well as a range of programmes for transmission across network and satellite channels. Formed in 1996, became part of the RDF Media Group in 2006 and part of the Zodiak Media Group in 2010.

Company Pictures

New London House, 172 Drury Lane (2nd Floor), London WC2B 5QR
tel 020-7380 3900 *fax* 020-7831 5601
email enquiries@companypictures.co.uk
website www.companypictures.co.uk
Managing Director John Yorke

Does not accept unsolicited submissions. Proposals should be submitted through agents.

Cowboy Films

40 Langham Street, London W1W 7AS
tel 020-7580 2982
email info@cowboyfilms.co.uk
email charles@cowboyfilms.co.uk
website www.cowboyfilms.co.uk
Managing Director Charles Steel

Until recently, Cowboy Films represented a range of top-quality commercial and music video directors, and also worked on feature films such as *The Hole* and *Goodbye Charlie Bright*. Sister company Crossroads Films in the US has taken over the roster of music video and commercial projects, while Cowboy continues to work on features. Kevin Macdonald's *The Last King of Scotland* is the company's most recent project.

Dalton Films Ltd

127 Hamilton Terrace, London NW8 9QR
tel 020-7328 6169 *fax* 020-7624 4420

Production details: Established in 1987. Working mainly in film drama. Recent credits include: *Oscar and Lucinda*, *Country Life* and *Madame Sousatzka*.

Casting procedures: Casting is carried out by freelance casting directors. Actors should only make contact in response to announcements in the trade press – does not welcome any form of unsolicited communication from actors. "Do not waste time or postage until a film is actively being cast or being developed." Rarely or never has the opportunity to cast disabled actors.

Don Productions Ltd

2 Foskett Mews, Shackwell Lane, London E8 2BZ
tel 020-7254 0044 *fax* 020-9227 3283
email london@donproductions.com
website www.donproductions.com
Director Donald Harding

Japanese/English bilingual TV and media production company based in London. Produces TV drama, documentaries, news and sports programmes. Clients include: Japan Broadcasting Corporation, Nippon Television and Channel 4. Recent work includes: *The Life of Charles Darwin.*

The Drama House

email jack@dramahouse.co.uk
website www.dramahouse.co.uk
Chairman/Chief Executive Jack Emery

Produces drama and drama-documentaries for film and TV. Recent credits include: *Inquisition* for Channel 5, one of the first HD drama shoots – starring Derek Jacobi; also *Breaking the Code*, *Witness Against Hitler*, *Little White Lies* and *Suffer the Little Children.* Commissioned by major UK broadcasters: BBCTV, Channel 4 and C5. Also international PBS and HBO. Winner of many international and national awards. Hopes that high-profile work will encourage writers and other professionals to come to the Drama House.

Ecosse Films Ltd

Brigade House, 8 Parsons Green, London SW6 4TN
tel 020-7371 0290 *fax* 020-7736 3436
email info@ecossefilms.com
website www.ecossefilms.com
Director Douglas Rae *Head of Drama* Robert Bernstein

Founded in 1988. Works mainly in TV and feature film production and employs actors in dramas and comedies. Recent credits include: *Mrs Brown*, *Nowhere Boy* and *Wuthering Heights.* Uses freelance casting directors and does not deal directly with actors.

Extra Digit Ltd

PO Box 71676, London NW3 9TX
website www.extradigit.com

Production details: Founded in 2002. Works in film and television and employs actors in drama, comedy and documentary. Recent credits include: *Somewhere*, starring Hugh Cornwell, and *Life is a Circus*, starring Steve Ryland.

Casting procedures: Occasionally uses freelance casting directors. Welcomes approaches by actors by post only, with CVs and photographs. Will accept showreels if these do not require a response. Has no equal opportunities policy: "If you can do the part better than anyone else, you get the job – regardless."

Eye Film and Television

Room F7, Epic Studios, 112-114 Magdalen Street, Norwich NR3 1JD
tel 0845-621 1133
email production@eyefilmandtv.co.uk
website www.eyefilmandtv.co.uk
Managing Director Charlie Gauvain

Independent producers of film and TV drama and documentaries. Also produces corporate, commercial, education and training material. Clients include: BBC, ITV1/Anglia, Channel 4, Five and First Take Films. Recent credits include: *The Secret of Eel Island* and *POV.*

The Farnham Film Company

34 Burnt Hill Road, Lower Bourne, Farnham GU10 3LZ
tel (01252) 710313
email info@farnfilm.com
website www.farnfilm.com
Key personnel Ian Lewis, Melloney Roffe

Production details: Areas of work include film, TV, video, documentaries and corporate. Recent productions include: *Children of the Lake*, *The Chef's Apprentice*, and *Mona the Vampire.*

Casting procedures: Casting breakdowns are available via the website. Offers Equity contracts. Does not welcome unsolicited CVs. Actively encourages applications from disabled actors and promotes the use of inclusive casting.

Feelgood Fiction Ltd

49 Goldhawk Road, London W12 8QP
tel 020-8746 2535 *fax* 020-8740 6177
email feelgood@feelgoodfiction.co.uk
website www.feelgoodfiction.co.uk
Managing Director Philip Clarke *Drama Producer* Laurence Bowen

Producers of film and TV drama.

Flashback Television Ltd

mobile (07952) 090884
email mailbox@flashbacktv.co.uk
website www.flashbacktelevision.com
Managing Director Taylor Downing *Creative Director* David Edgar

Flashback Television has been in continuous production since 1982 and is one of the top-rated production companies in the UK. The company has a reputation for the quality of its work, for high visual standards and powerful story-telling. Flashback produces factual, factual entertainment and drama programming for broadcasters in the UK and around the world. In the UK Flashback has worked for all the other major British broadcasters including the BBC, Channel Four, ITV, Five and BSkyB. Recent credits include *Nigella's Christmas Kitchen* (BBC), *Married to the Prime Minister* (C4), *Secrets of the Classroom* (C4) and *Beau Brummell: This Charming Man* (BBC). Flashback also produces many hours of programming each year for the UK Government-backed channel Teachers' TV.

Flashback has a long track record of production in the international market. For over a decade the company has been producing series direct for North American broadcasters Arts & Entertainment

Television Networks and Discovery. They have also co-produced several major projects with FR2 in France. Recent credits include *The Lost Evidence* (The History Channel), *Superhomes* (Discovery), *Top Tens* (Discovery), and *Weaponology* (Discovery).

Flashback also produces interactive material including the website *History Quest* for Channel 4 Learning, and educational podcasts for the British Council.

Flashback Television is based in London and Bristol. More information can be found at **www.flashbacktelevision.com.**

Focus Films Ltd

30 Avenue Close, Avenue Road, London NW8 6BY
07785 398604
email focus@focusfilms.co.uk
website www.focusfilms.co.uk
Development Producer Adam Polonsky *Executive Producer* David Pupkewitz

An independent feature film development and production company founded in 1982 by David Pupkewitz and Marsha Levin. Early successes with TV documentaries and dramas preceded a transition to feature films in the 1990s. Recent productions include: *51st State* with Robert Carlyle and Samuel L. Jackson; *Master Harold & the Boys* with Ving Rhames and Freddie Highmore; *Chemical Wedding* with Simon Callow and *Crimetime* with Stephen Baldwin and Pete Postlethwaite. Upcoming projects include: *Tainted*, *Leroy Purcell* and Barry.

Focus Productions Ltd

4 Leopold Road, Bristol BS6 5BS
tel 0117-230 9726
email martinweitz@focusproductions.co.uk
website www.focusproductions.co.uk
Directors Ralph Maddern, Martin Weitz

Production details: Established 1993. Specialises in TV features and documentaries. Employs actors in TV, radio and film; also for presentation and voice-overs. Recent credits include: *The Real Rain Man* (C5), *Painting the Mind* (C4), *The Piano Player* (C5) and *Vivaldi's Fantasia* (film).

Casting procedures: Holds general auditions. Actors are advised to apply requesting inclusion at any time. Casting breakdowns are available by telephone. Welcomes letters (with CVs and photograph) from actors previously unknown to the company if sent by post, but not by email. Also accepts invitations to view individual actors' websites. Offers Equity-approved contracts. Rarely has the opportunity to cast disabled actors.

Mark Forstater Productions Ltd

11 Keslake Road, London NW6 6DJ
tel 020-8933 5475

Works in film and TV production.

FremantleMedia

1 Stephen Street, London W1T 1AL
tel 020-7691 6000 *fax* 020-7691 6100
website www.fremantlemedia.com

FremantleMedia is one of the largest creators, producers and distributors of television brands in the world. It is responsible for much entertainment, drama, serial drama, factual entertainment and kids and family programming, with capabilities that extend from content creation to licensing, digital and branded entertainment, gaming and home entertainment.

The FremantleMedia Group (which includes FremantleMedia International, FremantleMedia Digital & Branded Entertainment, FremantleMedia Kids & Family Entertainment, FremantleMedia North America, UFA, FremantleMedia UK, FremantleMedia Australia, Ludia, @radical.media and Original Productions, among others) has operations in 28 countries, creating over 10,000 hours of programming a year, across more than 45 formats and airing 300 programmes a year worldwide.

Fremantle's brands include: *Idols, Got Talent* (co-produced with Syco in the UK and the US), *The X Factor* (co-produced with Syco in the UK), *Take Me Out, Hole In The Wall, Family Feud, Gute Zeiten Schlechte Zeite, Wentworth, Neighbours, Generation War, Grand Designs, Tree Fu Tom* and *Strange Hill High, Munchies* (with VICE Media) and *Full Time Devils.*

Funny Face Films Ltd

8A Warwick Road, Hampton Wick, Surrey KT1 4DW
Director Steven Drew

Production details: Works mainly in film/video.

Casting procedures: Uses in-house casting director. Sometimes holds general auditions. Welcomes letters (with CVs and photographs) from actors previously unknown to the company, sent by post or email. Accepts showreels and will consider invitations to view individual actors' websites. Will consider applications from disabled actors to play characters with disabilities.

G2 Entertainment Ltd

Unit 7, Whiffens Farm, Clement Street, Hextable, Kent BR8 7PQ
tel (01322) 666077
email jules@g2ent.co.uk
website www.g2ent.co.uk
Producer Steve Gammond; *Director* Jules Gammond.

Founded in 1990. Sport and special interest production company.

Galleon Films Ltd

50 Openshaw Road, London SE2 0TE
tel 020-8310 7276
email alice@galleontheatre.co.uk
website www.galleonfilms.co.uk
Chief Executive Alice De Sousa

Production details: An independent film and drama production company.

Casting procedures: Uses freelance casting directors and sometimes holds general auditions. Casting breakdowns are publicly available via all actor-accessible publications and the website. Does not welcome unsolicited letters and CVs or showreels, but will consider invitations to view individual actors' websites. Actors are employed under Equity-approved contracts.

Handle and Spout Ltd

Suite 14, Centre House, Wood Lane,
London W12 7SB
tel 020-7100 2758
email info@handleandspout.com
website www.handleandspout.com
Key contact Paul Shuttleworth *Head of Production* Loretta Cocchi *Development Producer* Jill Kinnaird

Production details: Handle and Spout is a BAFTA-nominated television production company with bases in London and Leeds. Established in 2006 by former BBC executives, Paul Shuttleworth and Loretta Cocchi, to date the company has completed over 50 hours of television and radio broadcasting for the BBC, ITV and Turner Networks.

Comprised of people who have built careers working on children's classics such as *Blue Peter*, *Live & Kicking* and *Record Breakers*, Handle and Spout's specialism lies in making content for children. In addition, team members bring a wealth of experience in working on more mainstream flagship productions such as *The One Show*, *Come Dine With Me* and *How Do You Solve a Problem Like Maria?* The company is currently looking to build on its growing relationship with the commercial sector and is actively working with advertisers to bring new AFP concepts to air. Alongside the core business of television production, Handle and Spout offers consultancy to other broadcasters and production companies, as well as a full range of corporate video services.

Casting procedures: Employs actors in drama, comedy, children's TV, presentation and voice-overs. Recent credits include: *Harry & Toto*, *Farm Camp*, *Go And . . .* Welcomes submissions by post and email, and accepts showreels and invitations to view individual actors' websites. Strives to be an equal opportunities employer and has signed up to the PACT Diversity pledge.

Handstand Productions

13 Hope Street, Liverpool L1 9BQ
tel 0151-708 7441 *fax* 0151-709 3515
email info@handstand-uk.com
website www.handstand-uk.com
Producer Han Duijvendak *Producer* Nicholas Stanley

Working almost exclusively in documentary, film, TV and video production. Rarely requires actors, so please do not submit anything unless a specific casting requirement has been made available on the website.

Hat Trick Productions Ltd

33 Oval Road, London NW1 7EA
tel 020-7184 7777 *fax* 020-7184 7778
email reception@hattrick.com
website www.hattrick.co.uk
Managing Director Jimmy Mulville

Founded in 1986, Hat Trick Productions is one of the UK's most successful independent production companies working in situation and drama comedy series and light entertainment shows. Recent credits include: *The Kumars at No. 42*, *Worst Week of my Life*, *Have I Got News for You* and *Room 101*.

Heavy Entertainment Ltd

111 Wardour Street, London W1F 0UH
tel 020-7494 1000 *fax* 020-7494 1100
email info@heavy-entertainment.com
website www.heavy-entertainment.com
Directors Davy Nougarede, David Roper

Production details: Established in 1992. Audio, video and web producers. Areas of work include drama, corporate, commercials, audiobooks and actor showreels (audio and video). Offers Equity-approved contracts.

Casting procedures: Welcomes showreels and voicereels (via agents only), and invitations to view individual actors' websites.

HuRica Productions

89 Birchanger Lane, Birchanger, Bishop Stortford, Herts CM23 5QF
mobile (07941) 236871
email HuRicaProductions@gmail.com
website www.wix.com/HuRica/HuRicaProductions
Director Hugh Allison

Production details: Established in 2010. A company founded on the ethos that "Art Is What You Make It". Works in radio and film. Recent credits include: *The Chronicles of Banania* (radio series aired on Radio North), *Call On Me* (short film) and *Shared Accommodation* (short film).

Casting procedures: Does not use freelance casting directors or hold general auditions.

Hurricane Films Ltd

17 Hope Street, Liverpool L1 9BQ
tel 0151-707 9700 *fax* 0151-707 9149
email sol@hurricanefilms.co.uk
website www.hurricanefilms.net
Managing Director Solon Papadopoulos

Founded in 2000, produces single films and documentary series from original ideas. Recent credits include: *Warship* (in association with Granada TV); *Comm-Raid on the Potemkin* (FilmFour); and *Wrecked* (BBC2).

J I Productions

90 Hainault Avenue, Giffard Park, Milton Keynes, Buckinghamshire MK14 5PE
mobile (07732) 476409
email jasonimpey@live.com
website www.jasonimpey.co.uk
Director Jason Impey

Production details: Works mainly in film, making feature horror films. Also employs actors in the fields of drama, comedy and documentary. Recent credits include: *Twink, More Sex, Lies and Depravity, Boys Behind Bars, Lustful Desires* and *Sex, Lies and Depravity* (all feature films).

Casting procedures: Uses freelance casting directors and holds general auditions; actors may write in at any time requesting inclusion. Casting breakdowns available via postal application with sae. Welcomes letters (with CVs and photographs) from individual actors previously unknown to the company, sent by post or email. Also accepts showreels and invitations to view individual actors' websites. Actively encourages applications from disabled actors and promotes the use of inclusive casting. "Always on the lookout for new talent."

Kelpie Media

The Executive Suite, 44 Washington Street, Glasgow G3 8AZ
tel 0800-840 2815
email info@kelpiemedia.com
website www.kelpiemedia.com

Independent production company that produces a range of broadcast and corporate/commercial work, from computer-animated children's programmes to documentaries in the Middle East and low-budget feature films. Credits include: BAFTA-nominated animation, *Cannonman*; Grierson Award-winning documentary, *And So Goodbye*; and large-scale corporate work for global clients such as Shell and the UK Government.

Left Bank Pictures

33 Foley Street, London W1W 7TL
tel 020-7612 3299, 020-7612 3132
email info@leftbankpictures.co.uk
website www.leftbankpictures.co.uk
Chief Executive Andy Harries

An independent television and film production company founded in July 2007 by Andy Harries and Marigo Kehoe, and named "Best Independent Production Company" at the Broadcast Awards in 2011. "We continue to work with the UK's leading writing, directing and onscreen talent to produce bold, innovative feature films, television dramas and cutting-edge comedy. We also pride ourselves on nurturing and championing exciting new talent set to create the hits of tomorrow."

Lexitricity Ltd

15-25 Vereker Road, West Kensington, London W14 9JU
tel 0870-840 4466
email alexandra@lexitricity.com
email production@lexitricity.com

Founded in 2006. An independent production company making short films, music promos, documentaries and actors' showreels. Comprises a writer, director, producer and storyboard artist, teamed up with an experienced professional crew employed on a freelance basis. Work includes experience on feature films, BBC dramas and documentaries as well as award-winning short films. Will take clients through the entire production process, from concept and storyboard to a creative shoot and edit. Works closely with photographers, illustrators and graphic artists to produce original marketing material including flyers, posters and DVD cover designs.

LWT and United Productions

London TV Centre, Upper Ground, London SE1 9LT
tel 020-7620 1620
Controller of Drama Michele Buck

Founded in 1996. Producers of TV and film.

Maya Vision International Ltd

3rd Floor, 6 Kinghorn Street, London EC1A 7HW
tel 020-7796 4842 *fax* 020-7796 4580
email info@mayavisionint.com
website www.mayavisionint.com
Producer/Director Rebecca Dobbs *Producer* Sally Thomas *Writer* Michael Wood

Maya Vision International is an independent film and television production company, founded in 1983. Since then it has won many awards, and become renowned for making work of the highest quality.

Specialising in producing "original, landmark documentaries, features and drama for film and television", Maya Vision has developed a unique style, making some of history's great stories accessible to a wider public.

Working alongside many broadcasters and funders, including the BBC, ITV, Channel 4, Five, PBS, UK Film Council and Arts Council England. Maya Vision's acclaimed catalogue has been screened in more than 140 territories worldwide. Since 2002 the company has been managing the UK Film Festval's successful Short Film Completion Fund, and has helped support nearly 60 titles that have gone on to win more than 150 awards and appeared in at least as many festivals worldwide. See the website for how to apply for funds.

Met Film Production

Ealing Studios, Ealing Green, London W5 5EP
tel 020-8280 9127 *fax* 020-8280 9111
email mfp@metfilm.co.uk
website www.metfilmproduction.co.uk
Managing Director Jonny Persey *Directors* Paul Morrison, Jerry Rothwell *Producers* Stewart le Maréchal, Al Morrow

Enterprise dedicated to the development and production of feature films for national and international audiences. Also produces short films. The company has a number of feature films in development.

Recent credits include: *Deep Water, Wondrous Oblivion* and *Soloman & Gaenor*. Upcoming work includes: *Heavy Load* and *The Pied Piper of Hutzovina*.

NFD Productions Ltd

21 Low Street, South Milford, Leeds LS25 5AR
tel/fax (01977) 681949
email alyson@nfdproductions.com
website www.nfdproductions.com
Director Alyson Connew

Production details: Production company producing feature films specialising in 3D, children and teenage programmes specialising in 3D, and commercials.

Casting procedures: Please send CVs to **alyson@northernfilmanddrrama.com**. We do require a minimum of 4 featured/named roles in either a film or TV series.

On Screen Productions Ltd

Ashborne House, 33 Bridge Street, Chepstow NP16 5GA
tel (01291) 636300 *fax* (01291) 636301
email action@OnScreenProductions.com
website www.OnScreenProductions.com
Director and Producer Richard Cobourne *Producer and Director* Alison King *Assistant Producer and Production Manager* Esther Prosser

Production details: Established in 1992. Creative, business-led, integrated visual communications company producing the full range of broadcast and non-broadcast TV, video, TV commercials, interactive media, training, live events, conferences, exhibitions etc. Frequently uses actors across many of its productions – the majority of which are non-broadcast (60% for Health and Pharmaceutical companies).

Casting procedures: Casting is done by freelance casting directors as needed, or in-house by Joe Allansen. Accepts submissions (with CVs and photographs) from individual actors previously unknown to the company if sent by post or email (postal submissions are preferred). Invitations to view showreels and individual actors' websites are also accepted. Deals in 'buy out' contracts (except broadcast and theatrical). "We do not discriminate either positively or negatively against disabled actors."

OVC Media Ltd

88 Berkeley Court, Baker Street, London NW1 5ND
tel 020-7402 9111 *fax* 020-7723 3044
email eliot@ovcmedia.com
website www.ovcmedia.com
Director Joanne Cohen

Production details: Established in 1982. Areas of work include TV, film, video and documentary production. Recent credits include: *History of the World Cup, African Odyssey* and *My Matisse*.

Casting procedures: Accepts submissions (with CVs and photographs) from actors previously unknown to the company if sent by post, but not by email. Showreels, voicereels and invitations to view individual actors' websites are also accepted. Offers Equity approved contracts and does not subscribe to the Equity Pension Scheme. Will consider submissions from disabled actors to play disabled characters.

Park Village Ltd

1 Park Village East, Regents Park, London NW1 7PX
tel 020-7387 8077 *fax* 020-7388 3051
email peter.ryan@parkvillage.co.uk
website www.parkvillage.co.uk
Producer Pete Ryan

Established in 1972. Commercials production company working mainly in commercials and content/interactive. Casting is done by freelance casting directors. Recent credits include Marks & Spencer Food. Actors are employed under Equity-approved contracts. Will consider applications from disabled actors to play disabled characters.

Picture Palace Films Ltd

13 Egbert Street, London NW1 8LJ
tel 020-7586 8763 *fax* 020-7586 9048
email info@picturepalace.com
website www.picturepalace.com
Producer and Chief Executive Malcom Craddock

Founded in 1972. Works mainly in feature films and TV drama production. Recent credits include: *Sharpe's Peril, Sharpe's Challenge, Frances Tuesday* and *Extremely Dangerous* (all ITV); *Rebel Heart* (BBC); *A Life for a Life* (*The True Story of Stefan Kizko*) and the *Sharpe* series.

Pinball London Ltd

20 Attneave Street, London WC1X 0DX
tel 0845-273 3893
email info@pinballonline.co.uk
website www.pinballonline.co.uk
Director Paula Vaccaro

Production details: Founded in 2009. Independent film production company assembled by creative and business entertainment industry professionals with a common goal of producing independent auteur-oriented films. Film is main area of work, but may do music promos, TV and Internet content. Recent credits include: *A Day in Two Lives* (short); *Margo & Max* (long feature); and Perempay & Dee feat. Shola Ama (DJPLAY music video).

Casting procedures: Uses freelance casting directors. Sometimes holds general auditions; actors may write at any time to request inclusion. Only accepts postal submissions, which *must* include CV, professional actor's reel on DVD, and headshot photos.

Red Rose Chain

Gippeswyk Hall, Gippeswyk Avenue, Ipswich, Suffolk IP2 9AF
tel (01473) 603388 *fax* (01473) 601102
email info@redrosechain.com
website www.redrosechain.co.uk
Director Joanna Carrick *Key personnel* David Newborn (*Producer*), Jimmy Grimes (*Designer*)

Production details: Established in 1997, a theatre and film company that focuses on tackling challenging subjects such as domestic violence, teenage pregnancy and child abuse. As well as being screened at international festivals and winning a number of awards, the company's films – which are used in 50% of UK schools – aim to raise awareness and train health and social care professionals and young people. Recent productions include: *Valentine's Day*, *Friday Night Shirt* and *Walking Away*.

Casting procedures: Sometimes holds general auditions: actors may write in Jan/Feb to request inclusion, but are asked to "please check the website regularly for information regarding upcoming film or theatre work". Welcomes letters (with CVs and photographs) from actors previously unknown to the company sent by post, but not by email. Accepts showreels but prefers not to receive invitations to view individual actors' websites. Actively encourages applications from disabled actors and promotes the use of inclusive casting.

The Reel Thing Ltd

20 The Chase, Coulsdon, Surrey CR5 2EG
tel 020-8660 9609
email info@reelthing.tv
website www.reelthing.tv
Key personnel Frazer Ashford, Chris Day

Production details: Established in 2001. Specialising in corporate and business TV production. Working the UK and worldwide for small, local clients and large multinationals. Recent credits include: *Fire Safety* (Homebase Ltd) and *Lake Avalon* (US).

Casting procedures: Does not welcome unsolicited CVs. Offers non-Equity contracts and does not subscribe to the Equity Pension Scheme. Actively encourages applications from disabled actors and promotes the use of inclusive casting.

Replay Film & New Media

25 Museum Street, London WC1 1ST
tel 020-7637 0473
email solutions@replayfilms.co.uk
website www.replayfilms.co.uk
Directors Dave Young, Stuart Slade

Production details: Established in 1990. Activities include: drama, documentary, corporate, e-learning, training, consultancy. Involved in all aspects of film and new media, web design, working mainly in TV, video and computer media production.

Casting procedures: Casting breakdowns are available publicly on the website and Castweb. Invitations to view individual actors' websites are accepted.

September Films

22 Glenthorne Road, London W6 0NG
tel 020-8563 9393 *fax* 020-8741 7214
email september@septemberfilms.com
website www.septemberfilms.com
Chairman David Green

September Films is a leading UK independent television and film production company with offices in London and Los Angeles. It was founded in 1992 by feature film director David Green, who devised the groundbreaking *Hollywood Women* series that launched the company. Having produced over 1,000 hours of primetime television during the last 13 years, September is an established specialist in factual entertainment, features, reality programming and entertainment formats.

Sightline

Guildford, Surrey GU3 1DQ
tel (01483) 813311 *fax* (01483) 813317
email keith@sightline.co.uk
website www.sightline.co.uk
Director Keith Thomas

Production details: Fully resourced. Long-established video and interactive media production company specialising in corporate and training videos, media for the Web, and interactive CD Roms and DVDs. Employs actors in corporate work and TV commercials.

Casting procedures: Welcomes letters (with CVs and photographs) from actors previously unknown to the company – please send by email, not by post. Invitations to view individual actors' websites are welcome.

Sixteen Films

2nd Floor, 187 Wardour Street, London W1F 8ZB
tel 020-7734 0168 *fax* 020-7439 4196
website www.sixteenfilms.co.uk
Director Ken Loach *Producer* Rebecca O'Brien

Sixteen Films was set up by Ken Loach and Rebecca O'Brien following the dissolution of Parallax Pictures in Spring 2002. They are joined by Paul Laverty as Associate Director.

Speakeasy Productions Ltd

5th Floor, 28 St John's Square, London EC1M 4DN
tel 020-7336 6066
email info@speak.co.uk
website www.speak.co.uk
Company Directors Jonathan Young, Shona Johnstone, Jeremy Hewitt

Production details: Corporate media production company and event management company based in London and Perth. Works mainly in video production, employing actors in documentary, corporate, and commercials. Occasionally holds general auditions. Recent clients include: Royal Bank of Scotland, Lloyds Group, BAE Systems, Food Standards Agency and the NHS.

Casting procedures: Accepts submissions (with CVs and photographs) from actors previously unknown to the company. Will also accept CVs and photographs sent via email. Invitations to view showreels and individual actors' websites are also accepted. Promotes inclusive casting and applications from disabled actors are considered.

Spellbound Productions Ltd

90 Cowdenbeath Path, Islington, London N1 0LG
tel 020-7713 8066 *fax* 020-7713 8066
email phspellbound@hotmail.com
Producer Paul Harris

Small independent production company specialising in feature films and drama for television. Curent projects in development include: 2 animated features, a drama series and other "genre" pieces.

Stagescreen Productions

Suite 92, One Prescot Street, London E1 8RL
tel/fax 020-7481 4810
website www.stagescreenproductions.com
Director Jeffrey Taylor *Development Executive* John Segal

Founded in 1986, Stagescreen is a film and TV production company with offices in London and Los Angeles. Recent credits include: *What's Cooking*, directed by Gurinder Chadha (Lionsgate); *Alexander the Great* directed by Jalal Merhi (ProSeiben) and *Jekyll*, directed by Douglas Mackinnon and Matt Lipsey (BBC). Forthcoming work includes *Young Cleopatra.*

Offers PACT/Equity-approved contracts and does not subscribe to the Equity Pension Scheme. Will consider applications from disabled actors to play disabled characters.

Talkback Thames

20-21 Newman Street, London W1T 1PG
tel 020-7861 8000 *fax* 020-7861 8001
website www.talkbackthames.tv

Founded in 1981. Produces TV situation comedies and comedy dramas, features and straight drama. Credits include: *Property Ladder*, *Jamie's Kitchen*, *Smack the Pony*, *The 11 O' Clock Show* and *Da Ali G Show*. TalkBack is part of the FremantleMedia Group. (See the entry for FremantleMedia under *Independent film, video and TV production companies* on page 334).

Tiger Aspect Productions

4th Floor, Shepherds Building Central, London W14 0EE
tel 020-7434 6700 *fax* 020-7544 1665
email general@tigeraspect.co.uk
website www.tigeraspect.co.uk
Head of Drama Will Gould

Founded in 1993. Produces TV drama with the aim of "investing in and working with the leading writers, performers and programme-makers to produce original, creative and successful programming". Credits include: *Ripper Street* (BBC1), *Public Enemies* (BBC1), *Prisoners' Wives* (BBC1), *Robin Hood* (BBC1), *White Girl* (BBC2), *Secret Diary of A Call Girl* (ITV2), *Teachers* (C4), *Omagh* (C4) and *Playing the Field* (BBC1).

Trafalgar 1 Limited

153 Burnham Towers, Fellows Road, London NW3 3JN
tel 020-7722 7789 *fax* 020-7483 0662
email t1ltd@blueyonder.co.uk

Production details: Established 1985. Produces feature films, music videos, documentaries and short films. Recent productions include: *Rough Cut and Ready Dubbed* and *Art of the Critic.*

Casting procedures: Welcomes letters (with CVs and photographs) from actors previously unknown to the company sent by email. Showreels, voicereels and invitations to view individual actors' websites are also accepted. Offers Equity-approved contracts.

Twenty Twenty Television

85 Gray's Inn Road, London WC1X 8TX
tel 020-7284 2020 *fax* 020-7284 1810
email triciawilson@twentytwenty.tv
website www.twentytwenty.tv
Creative Director Meredith Chambers *Director of Programmes* Lisa Edwards *Head of Casting* Jonny Francis

Twenty Twenty Television is one of the UK's leading independent television production companies, making award-winning documentaries, hard-hitting current affairs, popular drama and attention-grabbing living history series. Its recent primetime children's shows are also bringing success in an exciting and challenging genre. *The Choir* won a 2007 BAFTA Award; the series *That'll Teach 'Em* won an Indie Award and was nominated for a British Academy Award; the *Lads Army* series gained the Royal Television Society primetime features award as well as a BAFTA nomination and the international factual hit *Brat Camp* brought home an International Emmy from New York in November 2004.

Formed in 1982 by 'hands-on' programme-makers, Twenty Twenty Television has always grown organically. Its industry-wide reputation for quality, intelligence and rigour was built in factual programmes. Twenty Twenty remains truly independent and is still run by creative and enthusiastic programme-makers. Its work has been broadcast by networks around the world including the BBC, CBBC, ITV, Channels 4 and Five in the UK, and ABC, The Discovery Channel, Turner Original Productions, Sundance Channel, CNN, The Arts and Entertainment Channel and WGBH in the USA.

Video Enterprises

12 Barbers Wood Road, High Wycombe, Bucks HP12 4EP
tel (01494) 534144 *mobile* (07831) 875216
email videoenterprises@ntlworld.com
website www.videoenterprises.co.uk
Director Maurice R. Fleisher

Video Enterprises is a UK-based video production and crewing company specialising in broadcast, corporate, industrial, theatrical and social events programme-making.

Walsh Bros Ltd

29 Trafalgar Grove, London SE10 9TB
tel 020-8858 6870 *mobile* (07879) 816426
email info@walshbros.co.uk
website www.walshbros.co.uk

Double BAFTA- and Grierson-nominated film company. Productions range from television series and dramas for BBC like *Sofa Surfers*, Channel 4's *Don't Make Me Angry* and feature film productions *Monarch* and *Toryboy: The Movie*. The BBC documentary series *Headhunting the Homeless* was shortlisted for the Grierson Awards.

Wilder Films

21 Little Portland Street, London W1W 8BT
tel 020-7631 3417 *fax* 020-7636 4439
email molliebishop@wilderfilms.co.uk
website www.wilderfilms.co.uk
Managing Director Richard Batty

Production details: Established in 2003. Works mainly in film and video production, especially corporate, brand and short films, and commercials.

Casting procedures: Uses in-house and freelance casting directors and holds general auditions – but "will look for people if needed". Does not welcome unsolicited approaches but may accept invitations to view individual actors' websites.

Working Title Films

26 Aybrook Street, London W1U 4AN
tel 020-7307 3000 *fax* 020-7307 3003
website www.workingtitlefilms.com
Chairmen Tim Bevan, Eric Fellner *President* Liza Chasin *President UK Production* Debra Hayward

Recent films include *Atonement* (with James McAvoy, Keira Knightly, Romola Garai, Saoirse Ronan and Vanessa Redgrave) and *The Golden Age* (with Cate Blanchett and Geoffrey Rush, who reprise the roles they orginated in the award-winning *Elizabeth*, joined this time by Clive Owen).

World Productions Ltd

101 Finsbury Pavement, London EC2A 1RS
tel 020-3002 3113
email enquiries@world-productions.com
website www.world-productions.com
Creative Director Simon Heath, *Managing Director* Roderick Seligman, *Head of Drama* Jake Lushington, *Head of Development* Kirstie MacDonald, *Development Producer* Priscilla Parish, *Script Editor/ Producer* Gwen Gorst, *Production Assistant* Freddie à Brassard

Produces TV drama features, series and serials. Recent credits include: *Line of Duty* (BBC2), *The Bletchley Circle* (ITV), *The Great Train Robbery* (BBC1) and *The Fear* (C4).

Film schools

Although the work is minimally paid (if at all), it is well worth contacting film schools for casting consideration. Despite the fact that you'll often find yourself in the hands of a director with no idea about actors and acting, the potential of gaining something from the experience is possibly greater than that of participating in a Fringe theatre production – and the end result could contain material worthy of use in a showreel. Some schools keep files of actors' CVs and photographs for students to refer to when casting.

Castings for many low- or non-paid films are advertised on Shooting People (**www.shootingpeople.org**) – see entry on page 466.

The Arts University College at Bournemouth

Wallisdown, Poole, Dorset BG12 5HH
tel (01202) 363049
website www.aub.ac.uk
Key contact David Munns

Students do not only consider local actors for their short films. Actors are generally offered their expenses and a DVD copy. Welcomes enquiries (containing CV, photograph and covering letter) from new actors; actors' details are kept on file.

Brighton Film School

The Brighton Forum, 95 Ditchling Road, Brighton BN1 4ST
tel (01273) 602070
email info@brightonfilmschool.org.uk
website www.brightonfilmschool.org.uk
Head of School Gary Barber *Creative Director* Carol Harrison

Film-industry-recognised. Provides training in all aspects of motion-picture production: screenwriting, directing, cinematography, editing and production management. More than 30 student short films are made each year; students generally recruit actors through Shooting People (**www.shootingpeople.org**). There is no formal agreement with Equity. Students do not only consider local actors. Actors are generally offered their expenses and a DVD copy. Welcomes enquiries (containing photograph and 1-page CV) from new actors if sent by post.

London College of Communication

Elephant and Castle, London SE1 6SB
tel 020-7514 7935 *fax* 020-7514 6843
email info@lcc.arts.ac.uk
website www.lcc.arts.ac.uk
Course Director Emily Caston

A long-established film and television course with both BA and FdA programmes. Students work on 16mm, video and HD, and cast for projects throughout the year. Letters and CVs are welcome. Expenses only are offered, but a copy of finished work is supplied for showreels.

London Film Academy

52A Walham Grove, Fulham, London SW6 1QR
020-7386 7711 020-7381 6116
email info@londonfilmacademy.com
website www.londonfilmacademy.com
Joint Principals and Founders Daisy Gili, Anna MacDonald

Specialises in professional full-time film training. Students make a series of short graduation films and commercials using both professional and non professional actors. Students train in all areas of filmmaking.

"Students use agents, casting directors, and various Internet websites and paper casting publications to recruit actors". Accepts submissions (with CVs and photographs) from actors previously unknown to them. Actors' details are kept on file for student reference and actors are contacted directly. Payment to actors depends on the individual project budgets. Expenses will usually be paid and the actor will receive a copy of the showreel.

The London Film School

24 Shelton Street, London WC2H 9UB
tel 020-7240 0161 *fax* 020-7240 0167
email c.bright@lfs.org.uk
website www.lfs.org.uk
Director Dr Jane Roscoe

London Film School offers a 2-year MA course in the art and technique of filmmaking, with approximately 120-130 student short films being made each year. Students generally recruit actors through Spotlight, Star Now, and Talent Circle. Expenses and a DVD copy of the film are normally offered to actors cast in student films. "The school welcomes enquiries from actors (with CVs and photographs), but asks that students use websites such as Spotlight and CastingCall Pro to recruit their actors. We also have a 1-year MA Screenwriting Course".

National Film and Television School

Beaconsfield Studios, Station Road,
Beaconsfield HP9 1LG
tel (01494) 671234 *fax* (01494) 674042
email info@nfts.co.uk
website www.nfts.co.uk

Offers 2-year MA courses including Cinematography, Composing, Directing, Animation, Directing Documentary, Directing Fiction, Editing, Producing, Producing and Directing Television Entertainment, Production Design, Screenwriting, Sound Design, SFX/VFX and DPP. Also diplomas in Sound Recording and Production Management. Students generally recruit actors through casting directors and Spotlight, but files are kept by **casting@nfts.co.uk**. Has a formal agreement with Equity. Welcomes enquiries (with CVs and photographs) from new actors, which should be marked for the attention of **casting@nfts.co.uk**. Actors' details are held on file. Actors are also required throughout the year for workshops and files are kept for this purpose. Graduation projects are cast by external casting directors.

Newport Film School

University of South Wales, City Campus, Newport, Gwent, Wales NP20 2BP
tel (03455) 760101
email philip.cowan@southwales.ac.uk
website http://courses.southwales.ac.uk/courses/1393-ba-hons-film
Head of Film School Philip Cowan

A recognised Welsh national institution for the production and development of the audiovisual culture of Wales, through training, education and postgraduate research. On average 60-80 student short films are made each year. Students generally recruit actors through agents, casting directors, Equity Job Information Service and public notices at the Royal Welsh College of Music and Drama. There is no formal agreement with Equity. Actors' details are held on file. Welcomes enquiries (with CV, photograph and covering letter) from new actors. Students at BA and MA level increasingly work in production groupings, and cast professionally. "As the main centre for film education and training in Wales, we seek, encourage and support the casting of professional actors wherever possible."

University of the Creative Arts

Falkner Road, Farnham GU9 7DS
tel (01252) 722441
email cbarwell@ucreative.ac.uk
email swelsford@ucreative.ac.uk
website ucreative.ac.uk
Head of Film, Media and Performing Arts Sarah Jeans

Film Production at Farnham is accredited by the BKKSTS, the International Moving Image Society. The course offers students the opportunity to work on 16mm film and HD formats on both fiction and documentary. Students can specialise from the second year in directing, producing, screenwriting, cinematography, editing, sound and production design. Over a 100 short films are produced every year. The Television Production course based at Maidstone Studios offers students the opportunity to study in a live working studio environment. Actors are recruited through online casting sites such as Casting Call Pro and Stage Castings.

University of Westminster

University of Westminster, Watford Road, Northwick Park, Harrow, Middlesex HA1 3TP
email P.S.Hort@westminster.ac.uk
website www.westminster.ac.uk/courses/subjects/television-film-and-moving-image
Course Director Peter Hort

Westminster Film School

Makes around 40 short films per year, from 3 minutes to 20 minutes in length, on 16mm film and high definition digital video. Films regularly win prizes at international and UK film festivals, notably the 2012 Student Academy Award. Expenses and DVD copy of the film to actors. Welcomes letters (including CV and photograph) from actors previously unknown to the school.

The essentials of screen acting

Mel Churcher

The first question I always ask when I run a film acting workshop is, "What are the differences between screen acting and theatre acting?" The first and most fundamental difference is always the last one that actors tell me, and yet it is the most crucial.

In theatre, there is an audience. In film, there is no audience.

It sounds so simple and obvious, but this awareness has a deep and subtle effect on your work. When you perform for the stage, you are always sharing with the people out there in the darkness, even if it is a tiny space with an audience of one. Even in the most intimate production, there is live interplay between you and the audience – the watchers and the watched.

In film, you do your work surrounded by technicians, but they are not your audience. They are there to do their own important tasks and, apart from making sure that their aspect of the work is as good as they can get it, most have little interest in, or knowledge about, what you are doing. In fact only a few key people like the director, the producer, script supervisor, sound crew and dialogue coach are wearing headphones to hear what you are saying!

Certainly, the camera isn't your audience. It is an inanimate object that is there to record your secret life. You need to open yourself up to being minutely scrutinised by it, but you share with it at your peril: once you start to 'show' to it, you will be perceived as false.

In other words, you have to believe that this weird world full of cameras, microphones and people is a form of real life. You have to believe that there is no one there but the other characters who also inhabit this strange reality. You have to think extremely hard at every moment and trust that the camera sees that. And it will. Martin Scorsese calls it 'the physic strength of the lens'. Thinking is enough, and you have to trust it. You must never 'show' us what you are thinking. If you do that, we won't believe you are living this real life that we are privileged to observe from our safe position in the darkened cinema or from the corner of our sofa. That explains why it would be possible to move a close-up of a good actor from one film situation to another. The camera can see you thinking – but it doesn't know what you are thinking. You can test this out. Look around you in the tube and watch someone closely who is just sitting and thinking. Now, in your imagination, try putting them into different situations. Perhaps they are looking at a loved one, worrying about a bill or thinking about a hidden secret. You will see how, in life, they could be in any of those scenarios and yet look the same. Of course, I don't mean you should be consciously deadpan. We can see emotion when you feel and think. Your eyes literally shine with all the thoughts that light them up. Too often, this light dims when an actor is speaking learned text. You need all the thoughts, memories and pictures in your head to be as specific and extra-ordinary as they are in life, but not 'acted'.

One day you hope that an audience will see the assembled jigsaw of your film flickering on a screen, but that audience has nothing to do with your work at the time of shooting.

The next most important difference between screen and live work is that a film is shot out of order. You may bury your lover before you've met them or murder your boss before you've interviewed for the job. Each scene is done from many different angles (or set-ups).

The bigger the production, the more of these set-ups there will be. Then each set-up can involve many takes, and each take needs to be fresh and spontaneous. So film takes tremendous imagination and focus, not to mention stamina.

You also need to know where you are in the story. You, as the role, can only live in the moment, but you, as the actor, need to know exactly where you are in the story. How long ago did you hurt your knee? Do you know about that affair yet? Exactly how drunk are you?

I have a quick tip for this. Take a pack of filing cards. Now write a card for each scene you are in, including the ones where you don't have any dialogue. Write the scene number at the top of the card. Then put down where you've come from and, at the bottom of the card, put where you're going to. Write who is in the scene with you and what you know or feel about them at this time. For example, is this before or after you're pregnant? Do you know about the robbery yet? Then put down anything else that's important – I'm feeling hungry, I've just run a mile, it's a heat wave, etc. Now tie all your cards together and you have a flickbook of your journey through the film.

Now when they pick you up at 5am and tell you you're not doing scene 32 but scene 64 because the set blew down in the night, you won't spend the next hour in a panic, thumbing through the script trying to find out where you are in the story and how bad your limp is!

You don't need to write down your dialogue – that's in your script. Why can't you write these notes there too? Because, in a big film, that script will change a dozen times and you'll end up with a rainbow-coloured script of re-writes. You'll never have the energy to keep transferring your notes. Also, it is bulkier than your little carry-around flickbook. And doing this work really makes sure you read the script thoroughly!

Of course the technology makes filming so different from live theatre. It comes hard to realise that no matter how well you act, if the camera doesn't see it, it doesn't exist. There's only one reality, and that's what ends up on the screen. That means hitting your mark, or you'll be out of focus; watching your continuity, or the shot can't be used; having to be closer than you want to be to your partner, because the camera, with its two-dimensional nature, changes spatial relationships; and enduring long hours of waiting for that technology to work properly.

You need tremendous, specific imagination. You may have to imagine strange alien creatures whilst staring at a blue or green screen, Your partner may not be able to be in your eye-line for your close-ups. And you need to be thinking the whole time and visualising what you talk about.

Which brings me to rehearsal. There's not much rehearsal for film – well, not as we know it in theatre. If you're very lucky, there may be a few weeks of pre-production, but it is unusual for all the cast to attend at the same time. You'll have a script reading of sorts (where everyone will want to change the text), and meetings with the director. You'll have costume fittings, make-up tests, horse-riding, sword-fighting and dialect coaching where applicable. But, until you arrive on that set for shooting, you may never have rehearsed with, or even met, the person you are going to play the scene with.

And yet you do need to do a tremendous amount of preparation before you get to that stage. But it must be the right kind. Beware of imposing a 'character', as the camera will read it as overdone and false. You really do need to 'inhabit' the role. It needs to be you 'as if' you were in that situation or living in that time. And that 'as if' could mean a complete change of physicality, depending on the life you've led in the role. You might be a medieval peasant who digs the ground or an astronaut who has trained for a weightless environment. So 'Who am I?' and 'Where am I?' will take the life you've led and the period into account. But you have to reach it organically through research, work and specific imagination.

Now you need to ask. 'What do I want? Your needs must be powerful and strong. You may not show those needs to the other people in the story (that's sub-text), but strong needs must drive you.

Beware of deciding how you get what you want. If you plot a course or decide how to play the scene, you will not be open to react in the moment. And you don't know what the other people will bring to the scene yet. Until you have that short but valuable rehearsal on set before shooting, you need to stay open to all possibilities.

What you can also do on your own or with a willing partner is to improvise scenes that fill in the gaps. You can't break up with someone till you've met and loved them. So if your only scene is a divorce, improvise your first meeting at home. Or imagine waking up and thinking of them the morning after the first date. Act out stories you're going to tell in the dialogue so that you've already lived through the events and have powerful specific pictures in your head when you come to tell them on the screen.

You are a unique and exciting human being – don't let your character be less engaging than you are!

So keep open, really listen, think hard and react in the moment. And also sit back. This sounds silly, but nerves and a desire to please will often make you crane forward. Good actors are comfortable in their own skins and we are drawn to people who show a little 'attitude'. We shy away from people who are needy, insecure or sorry for themselves.

Find out the size of the shot from the camera crew so that you can work out technical problems and know how much you can move to stay in shot.

Remember to warm up. Your breathing should be relaxed and centred. Make sure you're releasing your abdominal area as you breathe in and not holding it tight and breathing high up in your upper chest. When you are relaxed, you will feel your stomach gently moving away from you as you breathe in and flattening back as you breathe out. You need to make sure that you continue to breathe like this when, with the excitement of shooting, adrenalin is pumping round your body. This will keep you relaxed and your face clear. It will put you in touch with your feelings, so that you don't 'push' emotions. If your face keeps screwing up or overworking, it is a sure sign that you are not centred and you're manufacturing emotion. The breathing work will also help to keep your voice warm and resonant. You only need to use the level of voice you'd need in life, but don't choose a half-whispered sound that doesn't carry any emotional life and will mean you'll need to record it again in post-production because no-one could hear you! This is an expensive business and it is much harder to re-find your performance months later, standing in a recording studio, trying to match your lip-movements to your image on screen.

Finally, forget anything you've ever heard about theatre work being big and screen work being small. Films and TV plays are about extreme situations, emotions or characters. How can that be small? If you are truly rooted in truth, you can be as big as you'll need to be (allowing for the technical aspect of where you can move in a close-up). If the director says it's too big, then sure thing, you're sharing or manufacturing or signalling what you want us to feel and it's not too big – it's just not truthful.

Mel Churcher was an actor for many years but now works as a director and international acting and voice coach. Her theatre voice work includes The Royal Shakespeare Company, Shakespeare's Globe and The Open Air Theatre, Regent's Park, where she was resident voice and text coach from 1996 to 2007. Mel has coached on dozens of major movies, including *The Lady*, *The Door*, *Control*, *The Count of Monte Cristo*, *King Arthur*, *The Fifth Element*, *The Hole*, *Lara Croft: Tomb Raider*, *Tristan & Isolde* and *Danny the Dog/Unleashed*. She runs regular film acting workshops in London and abroad. She has an MA in Performing Arts (Mddx), and Voice Studies (CSSD). She has written two books. Her first, which is now required reading for many drama schools and universities, is entitled *Acting for Film: Truth 24 Times a Second* (Virgin Books); her latest book is called *A Screen Acting Workshop* + DVD (Nick Hern Books). **www.melchurcher.com**

Fringe film: low-budget shorts, student films and web-based work

Edward Hicks

A challenging and changing environment

Fringe theatre is familiar to most actors as an area for potential work that may be low-paid, but which can give you the chance to experiment and/or stretch yourself more than you might in commercial theatre. The equivalent is happening in screen work, with a growing area of possible opportunities that splits into two categories: Short films (including Student films), and web-based work. It is to this new and expanding area of potential screen work that I am referring, under the umbrella title of 'fringe film'. Is it time to take this work more seriously, or is it just another example of how actors are poorly paid and sadly exploited?

With filmmaking equipment being more accessible than ever before (even phones now have cameras), more and more people are 'Shooting'. The days of needing to hire expensive equipment and a huge crew to make a film are now behind us, thanks to digital technology. A reasonable digital camera from your local high street, and a computer with an editing program (some even come with free editing software), are all you need to shoot and edit a film that could be of sufficiently high technical quality to be broadcast (provided the filmmakers know what they are doing!). But remember, just because a person can use a computer does not mean they can write a novel. The technology may have opened the doors to more filmmakers, but the abilities and artistic choices of everyone involved in the project, and how the equipment is used, are – and always will be – the most important factors.

Thus this changing environment of 'fringe film' presents a dilemma for the professional actor. On the one hand, there is more potential screen work out there; on the other, the quality of this work varies hugely. In the past, some of this work was seen as being a little amateur, not taken too seriously and perhaps considered not really appropriate work for the professional actor. However, it could also be argued that just as fringe theatre may not be as well paid as the more traditional commercial theatre, it can still prove a worthwhile commitment for an actor to take on – after all, a few West End shows started on the fringe. There is also a popular misconception that this area of work is expenses-only and unpaid, whereas in reality that is not always the case.

Short films

Film schools and websites such as Shooting People (**www.shootingpeople.org**) are a good place to start finding work in Shorts. Although the majority are Student films listed under the Lo/No Budget category (usually meaning expenses-only), don't presume that the film will be rubbish. The script is all-important, and I'm often amazed by the creative ideas of young filmmakers who are desperate to make their films despite the lack of funds.

It's also worth noting that despite the new HD technology, some of the best-regarded film schools shoot some films on 35mm (celluloid), which is far more expensive; they see it as fundamental to the film training. These films can provide a fantastic opportunity for an actor to experience being surrounded by expensive equipment and a large crew – an opportunity that might not present itself with projects that are shot digitally. And there's always the additional chance that the student director you work with today will be a successful feature-film director tomorrow.

However, be under no illusion. The vast majority of Shorts (and indeed web-based work) will be expenses-only, and therefore as a professional actor you need to consider carefully if working for free is something that you wish to do and/or promote. Some actors argue that working for free should not be allowed, and that actors are being unfairly treated – taken advantage of, in fact. I can understand this point or view, since nobody wishes to see anyone being exploited. That said, it is a reality of the world we live in that there are budding, often very talented, filmmakers out there who are also struggling and failing to secure funding. Funding for film is extremely competitive, and can be a simple matter of a particular film or filmmaker not fitting one single criterion. They are then left with no choice but to fund the film themselves – which goes some way to explaining the lack of money available with which to pay crew and actors. Simply put, for some projects, paying both actors and crew can mean that the Short does not get made. For more advice on this, and with any specific queries or concerns, contact Equity (**www.equity.org.uk**).

So don't rule out an expenses-only Short if the project provides you with an exciting challenge: an opportunity to stretch yourself and experiment, gain more experience on camera, make material for a showreel, and forge new contacts. One advantage of Shorts is that the shooting process is quick (not just for budgetary reasons) – often only taking a few days. Therefore your time commitment is minimal, and you can squeeze it around any castings that may come up. Most people working in this area will try to accommodate you (especially if they are not paying you), because they understand that, just like them, you have to earn a living and can't turn down a casting or a paid job. I've known several actors who have even managed to work on a Short during the day while performing in the theatre at night, as the shooting schedule was designed around the performance times.

There is a huge international film festival circuit for Short films, which caters to every level – from the more established and respected events that include a Short film section, to festivals that are aimed purely at Shorts. It's not unusual for some of the better Shorts that win prizes at the biggest festivals to end up being broadcast on television. However, if the filmmakers claim they are submitting the Short to Cannes as an incentive to get you on board, remember that *submitting* a film to a festival does not mean that it will automatically be accepted.

Make sure you fully understand what it is you are getting involved in, and, if the filmmakers are new and you don't know them, do some research (consult IMDb, the International Movie Database; browse via various search engines; talk to fellow actors and so on). You could ask to see examples of the director's work, find out if any of his or her films have ever been selected for a festival, and then research the festivals (there are some that take anything and everything!).

I would also recommend that you always ask to see the script before a meeting, especially if they are not paying you. The best advice I ever heard given to actors about Shorts was, "*If the script and project do not excite you, walk away.*" Remember, if you commit to a project like this, you have a responsibility to take it as seriously as you would anything else you do, regardless of salary. If your professionalism is not reciprocated by the people you are working with, word will soon spread – and you cannot afford to be tarnished by the wrong kind of association.

Bear in mind too that not all Shorts will be Student films, expenses-only or made by the DIY filmmaker. Some will have competed for funding, and the criteria for gaining funds may include paying a fee to the actors and crew. It's not uncommon for Shorts to win funding, provided this is matched by the production company – and some film schools have been known to pay a token fee to the actors. Peter *'Lord of the Rings'* Jackson made a Short in order to test a new type of camera; directors often make a Short in order to help gain funding for a feature film project. Shorts at this level are more likely to be funded, and to have an established production company on board to produce them, as well as a casting director to cast them.

Web-based work

You only have to look at the number of Shorts, commercials, virals (web content that is aimed at triggering an online following which builds its own momentum as it spreads – a commercial of sorts) that are posted on sites like YouTube to see how the web has become a huge growth area for screen work. However, it also highlights how quality standards can vary massively. At one end of the scale are huge, multinational companies with budgets to match, employing production companies to make virals, commercials and Short films; and at the other is the DIY filmmaker filming his dog on a skateboard. Just as with the Short film market, do your research, make sure you know what you are getting involved in, and check with Equity.

Advertising agencies continue to look for less traditional outlets for their work, and the web is becoming an important area for them – which in turn means more potential screen roles for actors. I know one actor who has been able to establish himself as a cabaret act, based on a character that he originally helped to create for a web-based advertising campaign. More recently, too, web-based TV shows have started to spring up: projects that are made exclusively for the web and not broadcast on traditional TV. The first web-based soap was sold not long ago to a TV network, having established a large initial following on the Internet. With more and more of the population now watching TV over the web rather than on traditional TV sets, this phenomenon looks set to grow and grow over the next few years; actors will need to be especially careful as to what they sign in terms of agreements over future sales.

So, if you're a new actor who has just left drama school and wants more screen experience, or a more experienced actor keen to stretch yourself, this growth area I refer to as 'Fringe Film' might be worth considering. However, like all new growth areas, approach with caution. Despite people's best efforts and intentions, quality is never guaranteed. You must be realistic about what it is you are doing – and be honest with yourself about why.

Edward Hicks is currently Head of Film, TV and Radio at RADA – a post sponsored by Warner Bros. He has directed numerous Shorts, commercials and promos, is a graduate and former governor of LFS, has various film projects in development, and has written articles on screen acting in addition to being a regular contributor to *Actors and Performers Yearbook*. Ed has taught at various Drama Schools including East 15, where in 2001 he created the first media-based acting course to gain NCDT (now Drama UK) accreditation. Under the name Edward Rawle-Hicks he started his professional career as a child actor (from the age of ten), appearing at the RSC, the West End and in numerous commercials, film and television projects.

Actors and gamesters: Video games are very good news for the actor

Mark Estdale

And the reason is a simple one. Games need actors. From voice performances to motion and full performance capture, games require actors of all ages, accents and nationalities. There is a significant demand, and the need is growing. What's more, an actor working on a game will be paid more for a few hours in session than they would for a week labouring on the West End.

Games have also changed the way we are entertained. As a medium they bring together two strands of human leisure: the active nature of playing and interacting, and the passive engagement of being an audience. The essence of the video game experience is choice and consequence. Games today embrace every genre, educate and amuse. And it's no exaggeration to say games are also transforming the way we inform and live our lives. They're in the classroom, and they're in your phone, your watch, your car's dashboard design and your workplace. Games are never far away when you go online. They are everywhere, they are here to stay, and they are brimming with performances.

So how does an actor get started in acting for games?

Games present actors with two core avenues down which work can be found: motion and performance capture presents one option, while voice acting provides another opportunity. And it happens that the UK boasts some of the world's most well-known motion capture studios.

Training resources like The Mocap Vaults are the perfect place to start a journey into the rapidly expanding world of motion capture. Since the technique was first truly brought to public attention with Andy Serkis's captivating performance as Gollum in Peter Jackson's *Lord of the Rings*, motion capture has grown into a global industry serving hundreds of games and films every year. As the technology advances it is becoming more cost accessible, putting it in reach of ever more creators. And so it is that the trend is not going to slow down. Anything but, in fact. Motion capture is increasingly a bedrock of many of today's most famed entertainment properties. The film *Avatar* and the acclaimed game *The Last of Us* are great examples of this type of work.

For voice acting, the story is a similar one. Ultimately, the demand is high and growing.

But a game script is unlike any other, in equal parts an opportunity and a challenge any actor should relish. The mapping to allow for player choice and consequence can make a script huge and complex. As such, a game with hundreds of characters and 300,000 lines of dialogue isn't unusual.

Imagine any play, TV or film script as a piece of string with a beginning and an end. Pull the ends and you have a straight line. A game script, by comparison, could be like a detailed map of London, including sewer, water and gas pipes. Now make it 3D, then muss it up, and remember your performance is in a virtual environment. There's no set, and no audience, and potentially no other actors around to perform against. Recording for games is a challenge. The skill is in being true the moment, however it is presented to you.

To be cast for a game, the first obvious thing is to be open to taking part in casting and letting your acting and voice agent know that you are available and keen to work with games. Some agents still choose to remain blissfully unaware of this $90 billion global industry.

Second, make sure you have a pertinent showreel. The ideal reel is a dramatic character reel with real characters and perfect accents. If you approach the reel as if it were a film casting which is to be shot in close up, you'll be in the right space: real and intimate. And remember, if you are casting for an accented role, the person evaluating you will be the neighbour of the role being cast. Have no other voice on the reel than yours, and don't use music or sound effects. Additionally, remember that you may be required to keep in character consistently for weeks in the studio, so don't include performances you cannot sustain. The most common showreel error in this field is to think of games as 'playful' and go pantomime or cartoon. Heightened performances are usually the most efficient path to rejection here.

When casting for a game at OMUK I think like an MI6 officer selecting an agent to work undercover. If the candidate can be someone else, in an alien environment, and never attract suspicion, they have potential. Undercover agents have no script, and there's no scene rehearsal. Only character preparation can carry them through when their lives are at stake. In games your life isn't on the line, fortunately, but the same skills are needed. Being true to character whatever is thrown at you is essential.

There's plenty else that can help you too. Valuable acting skills that are beneficial to voice acting in most games are great sight reading, radio drama, ADR and improv experience. Motion and full performance capture – that latter combining movement with voice recording – are staged theatrically. They require precise physical performances where screen, theatre and clowning skills come into play.

If you're still unsure what the games industry can offer you, here's a few statistics.

The UK has the largest games development community in Europe, with the most recent study indicating over 1,900 games development companies are based here, employing almost 10,000 creative staff. Data from the UCAS web portal for undergraduates demonstrate that there are now 315 specialist video games degree courses in the UK.

And the audience may surprise you. There are more gamers today older than 50 than there are those aged under 18. The average player is in their 30s, and 49 per cent of players are women. And violent crime rates have gone down as game sales have increased. That may or may not be related, but games today are too diverse and established to be the hotbed of aggressive stimulation some headlines might have you believe.

The games industry is growing at an extraordinary rate too. It already effortlessly eclipses Hollywood in the US. Almost nine out of ten game companies began operations in the 2000s or the 2010s. And between 2011 and 2013, the number of games companies grew at 22 per cent per year, while current estimates indicate the global industry will pass $100 billion in value by 2017. In 2014 alone, games contributed £1.7 billion to the UK games industry, according to figures from NESTA.

There's a lot of games, and they need actors. Actors, meanwhile, need to recognise the games opportunity, and be willing to re-appropriate their skills and open their minds. It's already happening, of course, but the closer games and actors become, the better it is for both.

Originally an actor, **Mark Estdale** founded **Outsource Media Ltd** (**OMUK**) in 1996. It is the UK's largest independent production company providing voice casting and recording of video games. Mark also coaches actors for working with games. **OMUK** has produced audio content for over 600 titles including titles nominated for eighteen BAFTA Game Awards since 2004.

Radio and audio book companies

Unlike in the visual media, many radio directors have their roots in theatre and will go to stage productions to inform their future casting. And, unlike their visual media counterparts, they have a far greater understanding of actors and acting, and are far more open to casting against obvious physical type.

The BBC has by far and away the biggest radio drama output, and also uses actors to read poetry, narrations and stories. Some of this 'output' is made in-house; a good proportion is contracted out to independent companies. This is one area of work that doesn't very often use casting directors. It is a good idea to listen to radio drama in order to become aware of its ways – you won't hear much swearing, for instance. Also see 'Voice-over agents' (page 100) and 'Showreel and voice-demo companies' (page 416); some of the latter have excellent advice on making a voice demo on their websites.

BBC Radio Drama

Broadcasting House, Portland Place,
London W1A 1AA
tel 020-7580 4468
website www.bbc.co.uk/soundstart
Head of Radio Drama Alison Hindell *Production Executive and Radio Drama Company* Rebecca Wilmshurst

BBC Radio Drama Department is the biggest producer of drama on radio in the world. It provides more than 700 hours of drama a year for Radio 3, Radio 4, BBC World Service, BBC7 and the BBC Asian Network. Plays are broadcast every day of the week and can be heard at any time, either on air or on the website. An audience of about half a million people is listening every time a play is aired. Output includes: *Westway* (drama set in a London health centre); *The Archers* (countryside soap opera); the Friday and Saturday plays (thrillers, mysteries and love stories); afternoon plays, classic serials, Woman's Hour Drama (weekday drama serial); play of the week (from around the world); book of the week (non-fiction) and book at bedtime (fiction, including modern classics).

The Radio Drama Company was founded in 1940 as the BBC Repertory Company, and is still frequently referred to as The Rep. The company's focus allows new acting talent to work alongside established actors in a variety of radio productions. Actors joining the RDC have already worked with many eminent artists such as Julia Mackenzie, Derek Jacobi, Richard Griffiths, Cheryl Campbell, Anna Massey and Daniel Day-Lewis.

Past members of the company have included Stephen Tompkinson, Alex Jennings, Adjoa Andoh, Norman Bird, Emma Fielding, Anthony Daniels, Ben Onwukwe, Joanna Monro, Ann Beach, Janet Maw, Suzanna Hamilton and Carolyn Pickles.

The RDC does not use freelance casting directors and casting breakdowns are not publicly available. Sometimes holds general auditions, and actors can write at any time requesting inclusion. Welcomes postal submissions from individual actors previously unknown to the company, but does not accept email enquiries. Voice demos and invitations to view individual actors' websites are also accepted. More information can be found under 'FAQs' at **www.bbc.co.uk/soundstart**

The Norman Beaton Fellowship is part of BBC Radio Drama's commitment to place integrated casting at the heart of its output. The NBF aims to provide access to BBC Radio Drama for talented actors from non-traditional training backgrounds, and particularly those from minority ethnic backgrounds who are currently under-represented in radio drama.

The Radio Drama Company will also be forging links with theatre companies all over Britain to help develop and nurture new talent for both radio and the stage and to find new NBF bursary winners. Consult the website for information about the next Norman Beaton Fellowship and for details of eligibility requirements.

The Carleton Hobbs Bursary is aimed at students graduating from accredited drama courses across the country. Looks for distinctive, versatile radio voices to form the next season's Radio Drama Company. It aims to recruit 4-6 winners annually. Students will be seen through an audition process, from which an equal mix of men and women will be selected. Winners receive a 6-month binding contract as members of the Radio Drama Company. Up to 4 runners-up will be engaged as freelance actors in one-off productions.

Belfast

BBC Broadcasting House, Ormeau Avenue, Belfast BT2 8HQ

tel 028-9033 8000
website www.bbc.co.uk/ni
Executive Producer Radio Drama Gemma McMullan

Birmingham
BBC Birmingham TV Drama Village, Archibald House, 1059 Bristol Road, Selly Oak, Birmingham B29 6LT
tel 0121-432 8888
website www.bbc.co.uk/birmingham
Editors, Radio Drama Jessica Dromgoole, Sean O'Connor (*The Archers*)

Cardiff
BBC Broadcasting House, Llandaff, Cardiff CF5 2YQ
tel 03703 500 700
website www.bbc.co.uk/wales
Senior Producer, Radio Drama Kate McAll

Glasgow
40 Pacic Quay, Glasgow G51 1DA
tel 0141-339 8844
website www.bbc.co.uk/scotland
Head of Drama, Radio Bruce Young

Manchester
New Broadcasting House, Oxford Road, Manchester M60 1SJ
tel 0161-200 2020
website www.bbc.co.uk/manchester
Executive Producer, Radio Drama North Susan Roberts

INDEPENDENT RADIO COMPANIES

Above the Title Productions
50 Lisson Street, London NW1 5DF
tel 020-7453 1600 *fax* 020-7723 6132
email mail@abovethetitle.com
website www.abovethetitle.com
Senior Producer Brian King *Producer* Matt Willis

Production details: Founded in 1998, Above the Title Productions has made over 500 hours of radio programming covering a range of genres, from comedy to factual programmes, drama, discussion programmes, and music and the arts. See the website for detailed programme credits.

Casting procedures: All casting is done through agents; direct contact with actors is not welcomed. Is no longer able to accept voice demos and CVs, as the company has received such a large number of applications in the past.

Art and Adventure Ltd
5 Darling Road, London SE4 1YQ
tel/fax 020-8692 0145
email rogerjameselsgood@gmail.com
website www.artandadventure.org
Creative Director Roger James Elsgood

Production details: A production company specialising in making high-production-value, location-recorded long-form drama for BBC Radio 3 and 4 with international casts and directors. Recent work includes: *The Two Gentlemen of Valasna* and *The Mrichhakatikaa* for Radio 3, both recorded entirely on location in India; *To the Wedding* for Radio 3 – a collaboration with Complicite; *Shooting Stars*, for Radio 3 (directed by Mike Hodges and starring Michael Gambon, Michael Sheen and Clive Owen); *King Trash*, the second play in Mike Hodges' radio trilogy and *Inferno* with Corin Redgrave, Alex Jennings and Laurie Anderson.

Casting procedures: The company is always happy to receive submissions and voice demos from actors, and auditions as necessary. It sometimes offers Equity contracts. Actively encourages applications from disabled actors and promotes the use of inclusive casting. Art and Adventure Ltd is actively working with actors with south Asian and Middle Eastern heritage and welcomes creative relationships accordingly.

The Bunbury Banter Theatre Company CIC
Office 34, 67-68 Hatton Garden, London EC1N 8JY
tel 020-3137 7994
email info@bunbanter.com
website www.bunbanter.com
Artistic Director Ali Anderson-Dyer *Creative Producer* Philip Anderson-Dyer

Production details: Founded in 2006; broadcasts audio plays across the globe. Has a strong education background, and dabbles in theatrical work. In 2008 the company reached the final of the Channel 4 Talent Awards and in 2012 was nominated for a Radio Academy Award. In 2013 the company won a British Public Radio Award for best short drama. Works very collaboratively on a mixture of audio and stage projects. Incoming actors need regional dialects, strong and accurate accents and versatility.

Casting procedures: Casting breakdowns are released via all the usual sites, social media and the company website. Welcomes submissions from individual actors previously unknown to the company, upon receiving a voicereel. Also welcomes email submissions and voice demos, preferably with a lot of variety. The company is completely opposed to discrimination in any form.

The Comedy Unit
Glasgow TV & Film Studio, Craigmont Street, Glasgow G20 9BT
tel 0141-305 6666 *fax* 0141-305 6600
email info@comedyunit.co.uk
website www.comedyunit.co.uk
Managing Director Rab Christie

Production details: Founded in 1996. Works in TV and radio productions – has produced approximately 30 hours of TV and 25 hours of radio. Areas of work include drama, sitcoms, comedy and other light entertainment. Recent drama credits include: *Ronan the Amphibian* and *Coming Home.*

Casting procedures: Sometimes holds general auditions. Actors can write at any time requesting inclusion. Submissions from actors previously unknown to the company are accepted, sent by post or email. Voice demos and invitations to view individual actors' websites are also accepted.

CSA Word

6A Archway Mews, 241A Putney Bridge Road, London SW15 2PE
tel 020-8871 0220 *fax* 020-8877 0712
email info@csaword.co.uk
website www.csaword.co.uk
Key personnel Victoria Williams, Clive Stanhope

Production details: Founded in 1991. Producer of audiobooks, drama, readings, feature programmes and documentaries for BBC Radios 4, 2 and BBC World Service.

Casting procedures: Does not hold general auditions, as the company tends to use agents for casting. Invitations to view individual actors' websites are accepted. Equity contracts are not used, "but we usually pay above Equity minimum." Happy to consider disabled actors. "We work mainly in speech, audio and radio work, so there is rarely an issue with regard to physical disability."

Culture Wise

1 Chiswick Staithe, London W4 3TP
website www.culturewise.org
Key personnel Mukti Jain Campion, Chris Eldon Lee

Production details: Founded in 1988. Areas of work include TV and radio documentaries.

Casting procedures: Does not hold general auditions. Invitations to view individual actors' websites are accepted. The company rarely employs actors, as the primary focus is on factual output: actors are generally used for short readings only, within a feature programme.

Curtains for Radio/Curtains for Pictures

1-3 Middle Row, London W10 5AT
tel 020-8964 0111
email contactus@curtainsforradio.co.uk
website www.curtainsforradio.co.uk
Producers/Directors Andrew McGibbon, Jonathan Ruffle, Nick Romero

Production details: Established in 2001. Specialises in comedy, comedy drama, some drama, comedy archive, music, and arts in film, television and radio. The ability to perform in foreign languages, regional dialects and singing are among the skills required by actors. Records/films 1 production play annually. Recent titles include: *Wheeler's Fortune* (2003), *Wheeler's Wonder* (2004), I *Was Morrissey's Drummer* (2005), *Reality Is An Illusion Caused By Lack Of N. F. Simpson* (2007), *The Cornwell Estate* – 2 series (2009-2011), *Rory Bremner's International Satirists* (2010), *With Nobbs On* (2012) and *The Pickerskill Reports* – 4 series (2005-2013).

Casting procedures: Casting is carried out by freelance casting director Rachel Freck and others. Accepts submissions from actors previously unknown to the company. Voice demos and invitations to view individual actors' websites are also accepted. "Voice demos should only be sent on a CD that can be played in any CD player." Online links to film reels are preferred to DVDs. Voice-over artists are employed under Equity-approved contracts. Actively encourages applications from disabled actors.

Falling Tree Productions (formerly Alan Hall Associates)

318 New Cross Road, New Cross, London SE14 6AF
tel 020-8320 2219
email info@fallingtree.co.uk
website www.fallingtree.co.uk
Executive Director Alan Hall

Production details: Founded in 1998, Falling Tree Productions is an independent supplier to BBC Network Radio (3 and 4 principally) and foreign broadcasters, crafting documentaries and music feature productions. Winner of the Sony Gold in 2004 feature category, and previously, in the music feature category. Has also been awarded the Prix Italia (twice) and the Prix Bohemia. The company has employed actors in documentaries, music features, anthology programmes and museum guides. Recent credits include: *Song on the Death of Children, Brahms' Beard* and *Something Understood.*

Casting procedures: Will accept submissions (written or emailed) and voicereels from actors previously unknown to the company. Welcomes invitations to view actors' websites. Advises that actors are used mainly for readings in radio productions, but also in the production of numerous voice-overs for museum and art gallery audioguides.

Fiction Factory Productions Ltd

4 Chevening Rd, London SE10 0LB
tel 020-8853 5100
email production@fictionfactory.co.uk
website www.fictionfactory.co.uk
Key personnel John Taylor

Production details: Founded in 1993. Makes radio drama and features for the BBC. Areas of work include drama, documentaries, light entertainment and voice-overs. Recent drama credits include: Kafka's *The Castle* and Michael Butt's *Chronicles of Ait: Stay With Me* both for BBC Radio 4..

Casting procedures: Does not hold general auditions. Submissions from actors previously unknown to the company are accepted if sent by post. Voice demos are also accepted. Does not welcome email submissions or invitations to view individual actors' websites. "It is helpful if showreels contain material appropriate to the kind of work sought; for example, corporate voice-overs or radio advertisements don't necessarily show off acting skills."

Heavy Entertainment Ltd

111 Wardour Street, London W1F 0UH
tel 020-7494 1000 *fax* 020-7494 1100
email info@heavy-entertainment.com
website www.heavy-entertainment.com
Directors Davy Nougarede, David Roper

Production details: Established in 1992. Audio, video and web producers. Areas of work include drama, corporate, commercials, audiobooks and actor showreels (audio and video). Offers Equity-approved contracts.

Casting procedures: Welcomes showreels and voicereels (via agents only), and invitations to view individual actors' websites.

HuRica Productions

89 Birchanger Lane, Birchanger, Bishop Stortford, Herts CM23 5QF
mobile (07941) 236871
email HuRicaProductions@gmail.com
website www.wix.com/HuRica/HuRicaProductions
Producer/Director Hugh Allison

Established in 2010. A company founded on the ethos that "art is what you make it." Works in radio and film. Recent credits include: *The Chronicles of Banania* (Radio Series aired on Radio North), *Call On Me* (short film) and *Shared Accommodation* (short film). Does not use freelance casting directors or hold general auditions.

Ladbroke Productions

17 Leicester Road, East Croydon, Surrey CR0 6EB
mobile (07590) 555458
email neilgardner@ladbrokeradio.com
website www.ladbrokeradio.com
Producers/Directors Neil Gardner, Richard Bannerman, Neil Rosser, Adam Fowler, Anna Scott-Brown *Assistant Producer* Anna Van Dieken

Production details: Founded in 1975, Ladbroke Productions produces for all BBC networks in many genres, including drama, documentaries, music, light entertainment and features. Its studio and production facilities are also used by BBC Drama, BBC Readings and BBC Factual Learning. Actors are mainly employed by the company in its drama and documentary production. Recent credits include: *Sitting in Limbo* (BBC World Service) and *In the Company of Men* (BBC Radio 3).

Casting procedures: Will accept unsolicited submissions (written or emailed), voice demos and invitations to view actors' websites. April and September are generally better months to write.

Note Ladbroke Productions will soon join with their audiobook production sister company, Ladbroke Audio, to form one enterprise, focusing on the audiobook and archive sales and production market. They will no longer be pitching for BBC radio work.

Loftus Media Ltd

2A Aldine Street, London W12 8AN
tel 020-8740 4666
email office@loftusmedia.co.uk
website www.loftusmedia.co.uk
Director Joanne Coombs

Production details: Small award-winning audio and radio production company based in West London, specialising in features, documentaries and readings for BBC Radio. Requires plain narration and poetry from actors. Records several audiobooks a year. Recent titles include: *Disability: A New History for Radio 4.*

Casting procedures: Accepts submissions from individual actors previously unknown to the company. Will also accept submissions sent via email. Straight narration is preferred on voice demos and should be sent as an MP3. Actors are employed under Equity-approved contracts. Applications from disabled actors are welcomed.

Pennine Productions LLP

17 Crimicar Lane, Sheffield S10 4FA
tel 0161-427 1460
email janet@pennine.biz
website www.pennine.biz
Key contact Janet Graves

Production details: Founded in 2000. Has made documentaries and features for BBC Radio 4 since 2001, and programmes for BBC Radio 3 since 2004. Has produced book readings for Radio 4 since 2005. Broadcasts northern, national and international stories. Main areas of work include documentaries and readings. Recent credits include: *Israel in East Africa*, *When Jesus Rode into Bristol* and *Land of the Oval Ball* (all Radio 4). Offers Equity-approved contracts and does not subscribe to the Equity Pension Scheme.

Casting procedures: "We only welcome unsolicited approaches from actors with significant broadcast experience, particularly of book readings – or other audiobook productions. We are too small to be useful to actors trying to break into the network radio or TV." Happy to consider applications from disabled actors: "radio experience is the over-riding concern".

Pier Productions

8 St George's Place, Brighton BN1 4GB
tel (01273) 691401 *fax* (01273) 693658
website www.pierproductionsltd.co.uk
Managing Director Peter Hoare

Production details: Founded in 1993, an award-winning Brighton-based company and a significant supplier of factual and drama productions to BBC Radio 4. The company employs actors for drama productions and is keen to work with talent located in Brighton and the surrounding area.

Casting procedures: Does not hold general auditions. Submissions from actors are accepted by post and email, but invitations to view individual actors' websites are not welcomed. It must be emphasised that opportunities in radio drama are limited and that the company does not use the services of voice-over artists.

So Radio Ltd

1 Boundary Row, London SE1 8GN
tel 020-7960 2000 *fax* 020-7960 2095
email info@sotelevision.co.uk
website www.sotelevision.co.uk
Producer/Director Graham Stuart

Production details: Founded in 2003 as the radio arm of So Television Ltd. Recent credits include: *Don't Make Me Laugh with David Baddiel* and *It's that Jo Caulfield Again* for BBC Radio 4. The company has employed actors mainly for light entertainment productions.

Casting procedures: Does not accept unsolicited written submissions. As the company is small it cannot promise to reply to all enquiries. Offers Equity-approved contracts (where applicable). Actively encourages applications from disabled actors and promotes the use of inclusive casting.

Lou Stein Associates Ltd

email info@loustein.co.uk
Producer/Director Lou Stein *Co-Director* Deirdre Gribbin

Production details: Lou Stein founded the Gate Theatre, Notting Hill, and was Artistic Director of the Palace Theatre, Watford. Lou Stein Associates was formed in 2002 to continue Lou's interest in new work, adaptations, music theatre and media. Employs actors for drama programmes. Recent drama credits include: *My Month with Carmen* (starring Miriam Colon and Julian Glover); *Embers* (adapted by Lou Stein from the novel by Sandor Marai and starring Patrick Stewart); *The Possessed* (written and directed by Lou Stein from the Dostoevsky novel, starring Paul McGann); *Performances* by Brian Friel (Wilton's Music Hall, starring Henry Goodman and Rosamund Pike) and *Crossing the Sea* (a new opera by Deirdre Gribbin).

Casting procedures: Voice demos and invitations to view individual actors' websites are accepted, but actors are requested to email in first instance. Please note that no reply will be given unless the actor is suitable for immediate casting. Names will be retained on file. Offers Equity-approved contracts. Actively encourages applications from disabled actors and promotes the use of inclusive casting.

Tempest Productions Ltd

6 Woodend Drive, Airdrie ML6 7EA
tel (01236) 768795
email info@tempestproductions.co.uk
website www.tempestproductions.co.uk
Producer/Director Dominic Reynolds

Production details: Records around 4 plays in a year. Is interested in good actors who can portray a range of different accents. Recent titles include: *The Meeting* (BBC Radio Drama) and *The Mighty Jungle* (BBC Radio Sitcom).

Casting procedures: Uses freelance casting directors (EH7 Casting – Morag Arbuthnot; Kathleen Crawford). Will consider approaches from individual actors previously unknown to the company, but stresses that, as a small unit, it is difficult to manage these. Welcomes invitations to view actors' websites. Offers Equity-approved contracts. Welcomes all actors from every walk of life, regardless of race, disability or creed.

Tintinna Ltd

Summerfield, Bristol Road, Bristol BS40 8UB
tel (01275) 333128
email tintinna@aol.com
Directors Ian and Sandy Bell

Production details: Founded in 1998. Produces a variety of output, formerly factual documentaries including history, lifestyle and human interest but more recently business-related work.

Casting procedures: Does not hold general auditions. Submissions from actors previously unknown to the company are accepted if sent by post. Voice demos are also accepted. Does not welcome email submissions or invitations to view individual actors' websites.

Unique

50 Lisson Street, London NW1 5DF
Executive Producer: Drama and Entertainment Frank Stirling

Production details: Produces drama, documentaries, comedy and light entertainment for radio. Recent drama credits include: *Zazie* (World Service), *A Confidential Agent, Fragile!* (Radio 4), *Professor Bernhardi, Bajazet* (Radio 3), and *Something Understood* (poetry and prose readings for Radio 4).

Casting procedures: Submissions from actors previously unknown to the company are accepted, sent by post or email. Voicereels are also accepted. Does not welcome invitations to view individual actors' websites. Advises actors to "include radio work on demo". "We regret that we cannot reply to all submissions, but your details will be kept on file."

Whistledown Productions

8A Ayres Street, London SE1 0AS
tel 020-7407 8001
email davidprest@whistledown.net
website www.whistledown.net
Producers/Directors David Prest, Katherine Godfrey, Kevin Dawson

Production details: Founded in 1998. One of the largest independent suppliers to BBC Radio, with a background in features and landmark documentaries, as well as programme strands such as Radio 4's *The Reunion*. Also has custom-built studio available for commercial hire.

The Wireless Theatre Company

11A Bolton Gardens, London SW5 0AL
mobile (07931) 168911 / (07787) 141403
email info@wirelesstheatrecompany.co.uk
website www.wirelesstheatre.co.uk
Artistic Director Mariele Runacre Temple *Executive Producer* Cherry Cookson *Producer* Jack Bowman

Production details: An online audio theatre company founded in 2007 to bring original and exciting audio drama to the 'iPod Generation'. Provides original radio plays, comedy, stories, sketches and more to be downloaded from the website. The company has worked with more than 300 actors, including Stephen Fry, Brian Blessed, Lionel Blair, Linda Robson, Prunella Scales, Timothy West, Richard O'Brien, Nicholas Parsons and Mary Tamm. In 2011 the company won Best Entertainment Producer and Best Online Platform at the Radio Academy Awards.

The company is very keen to hear from versatile actors with a large range of accents and vocal styles. Experience is not essential, but does prefer some sort of audio sample from actors when applying. Records a minimum of 1 new play each month, as well as 3 live recordings a year at the Leicester Square Theatre's Main House. Recent titles include: *We Are The BBC* starring Stephen Fry, *Gino Lives* starring Linda Robson, *Life At Death's Door* starring Brian Blessed and *Stage Fright* starring Abi Titmuss.

Casting procedures: Uses freelance casting directors (regularly, Leoni Kibbey). Advertises casting through CCP, but once an actor has worked for WTC they become part of the company and are used frequently. Also casts through Facebook and Twitter. Welcomes submissions by email, at **casting@wirelesstheatre.co.uk**, and all details are kept on file. Prefers applications with voicereels: simple, definitely without long musical introductions (rarely will listen to more than 2 minutes of any voicereel) and with 1 example of natural accent and some other, shorter samples of accents or voices. Welcomes invitations to view individual actors' websites. Contracts are made using Equity guidelines and frequently uses disabled actors and crew.

AUDIO BOOKS

Barefoot Audio Books Ltd

123 Walcot Street, Bath BA1 5BG
Director Tessa Strickland *Group Project Manager* Emma Parkin

Production details: Recent titles include: *Mrs Moon, Animal Boogie* and *Tales of Wisdom and Wonder*.

Casting procedures: Does not use freelance casting directors. Accepts submissions from actors previously unknown to the company if sent by post, but does not welcome email enquiries. Voice demos and invitations to view individual actors' websites are also accepted. Singing ability is required from actors, and Caribbean and African voices are needed in particular.

HarperCollins Audio

77-85 Fulham Palace Road, London W6 8JB
tel 020-8307 4444 *fax* 020-8307 4517
email enquiries@harpercollins.co.uk
website www.harpercollins.co.uk
Director Rosalie George *Editorial/Production Manager* Nicola Townsend *Director of Audio* Jo Forshaw *Content Producer* Tanya Brennand-Roper

Production details: Has produced more than 1,000 titles for both children and adults over the last 15 years. Work spans all genres including crime, comedy, literary fiction, mass market fiction, non-fiction, poetry and classics. Recent titles include: *Brick Lane* by Monica Ali; *Sharpe's Havoc* by Bernard Cornwell and *Lovers and Liars* by Josephine Cox. Foreign languages and regional dialect skills are required from actors.

Casting procedures: Does not use freelance casting directors. Advises actors to make contact by email or telephone, or preferably through an agent. Also accepts invitations to view individual actors' websites.

Isis Audio Books

7 Centremead, Osney Mead, Oxford OX2 0ES
tel (01865) 250333 *fax* (01865) 790358
email studio@isis-publishing.co.uk
website www.isis-publishing.co.uk
Audio Production Manager Catherine Thompson

Production details: Founded in 1975. Publishes unabridged audiobooks. Recent titles include: *The Shepheard's Crown* by Terry Pratchett; *H is for Hawk* by Helen Macdonald and *Perfidia* by James Ellroy.

Casting procedures: Does not use freelance casting directors. Accepts submissions from actors with proven audiobook experience if sent by post or email, but does not welcome telephone enquiries. Actors should have a range of voices and good sight-reading ability. Offers non-Equity contracts and does not subscribe to the Equity Pension Scheme. Actively encourages applications from disabled actors and promotes the use of inclusive casting.

Macmillan Audio Books

20 New Wharf Road, London N1 9RR
Audio Publisher Alison Muirden *Audio Editorial Coordinator* Rebecca Folkard-Ward

Casting procedures: Casts in-house. Accepts submissions from actors previously unknown to the company if sent by post, but does not welcome email enquiries. Voice demos are also accepted. Does not offer Equity contracts or subscribe to the Equity Pension Scheme. Will consider applications from disabled actors to play disabled characters.

Naxos AudioBooks

5 Wyllyotts Plaace, Potters Bar, Herts EN6 2JD
tel (01707) 653326
email info@naxosaudiobooks.com
*Producer/Director*Anthony Anderson

Production details: Founded in 1994. Produces classic fiction, modern fiction, non-fiction, drama, poetry and children's classics for CD and download. Recent titles include: *The Decline and Fall of the Roman Empire, Remembrance of Things Past, Middlemarch* and *Julius Caesar*. Regional dialect skills are required from actors. Accepts voice demos from agents.

Orion Audio Books

Orion Publishing Group, Carmelite House,
50 Victoria Embankment, London EC4Y 0DZ
tel 020-3122 6876 *fax* 020-7379 6158
email audio@orionbooks.co.uk
website www.orionbooks.co.uk
Audio Publisher Pandora White

Production details: Established in 1996, Orion Audio draws mainly on the Orion Group imprints to create their audio list, with notable authors such as Ian Rankin, Maeve Binchy, Michael Palin, Michael Connelly, Linwood Barclay, Joe Abercrombie and Patrick Rothfuss. Orion is now firmly established in the digital download market and produces 150-200 unabridged audiobooks a year, across all genres.

Casting procedures: Casts in-house. Useful skills include regional dialects and occasionally singing ability. Welcomes submissions and voice demos from actors previously unknown to the company. Offers Equity-approved contracts. Happy to receive submissions from disabled and non-disabled actors with the right skills for the job.

Random House Audio Books

20 Vauxhall Bridge Road, London SW1V 2SA
tel 020-7840 8400 *fax* 020-7834 2509
email jlewis@randomhouse.co.uk
Audio Publisher Videl Bar-Kar *Commissioning Editor* Jenni Lewis *Assistant Editor* Ania Duggan

Production details: Created in 1991, the Audio Books division of Random House publishes writers such as James Patterson, Andy McNab, Lee Child, Ian McEwan and Kathy Reichs.

Casting procedures: Uses freelance casting directors. Accepts submissions from actors previously unknown to the company, sent by post. Voice demos and invitations to view individual actors' websites are also accepted.

TalkingPEN books

Global House, 303 Ballards Lane, London N12 8NP
tel 020-8445 5123 *fax* 020-8446 7745
email info@talkingpen.co.uk
website www.talkingpen.co.uk
Producers/Directors R Dutta, DM Chatterji, Henriette Barkow

Production details: Established in 2002. Produces audiobooks, e-books, TalkingPEN books and posters. The ability to perform in foreign languages, singing and storytelling are often required of actors. Records 20 audiobooks annually. Recent titles include: *Hansel and Gretel, Jill and the Beanstalk* and *English Terms Explained.*

Casting procedures: Accepts submissions from actors previously unknown to them. Voice demos and invitations to view individual actors' website are also accepted; voice demos should include short storytelling in English or other language(s). Actively encourages applications from disabled actors.

Acting for radio

Gordon House

I remember once, in a burst of evangelical enthusiasm at having decided never to touch a cigarette again, upbraiding a distinguished member of the Radio Drama Company for her constant disappearances to the Green Room to light up. (Nowadays, of course, all BBC Green rooms are smoke-free, and your poor cigarette-smoking actor has to shiver in the car park.) "My dear man," she wheezed grandly. "The only reason you employ me on the wireless is because of my nicotine-nourished, port-soaked larynx. Living badly has made me the radio actress I am today!"

Well – it's a point of view. Just as the camera relishes certain skin textures, so the microphone may embellish the actor or actress who has lived a little – resulting in, shall we say, an idiosyncratic oesophagus. But as a way of getting a radio part, it's not a course of action I'd recommend. Radio simply doesn't pay enough to sustain a life of alcoholic debauchery.

So how do you get into radio? "It's a closed shop," moaned one actor to me the other day. "You hear the same names, time and again – and there's no way of breaking into this magic circle." I personally have worked with well over 800 actors, so it can't be that much of a closed shop ... although it's true that given the ruthless time constraints of the medium (a 60-minute play will be rehearsed and recorded in two days), there's a natural tendency for producers to work with those actors whom they know can 'deliver' quickly. There's no joy to be had in the seventh take of a difficult scene when your nervous newcomer is finally coming to grips with the ambiguities of his or her character, as well as the technical demands of this strange new medium, while everyone else's performances have long-since peaked and are now beginning to sound tired and lacklustre.

But that said, new writers and new actors are the lifeblood of the medium. And what do you need to be a good actor on radio? It's simple. You need to be a good actor. If you're successful in the theatre, in film, on TV – then of course you can be successful on radio. A good actor is a good actor. It obviously helps if your voice doesn't sound like a creaking door (given that creaking doors are a staple diet of many a radio play), and the medium has no place for prima donnas. With every producer sparingly counting his or her loose change, there's no such happy luxury as a radio 'extra'; so if you're cast as Hamlet, you can also expect to do your fair share of off-mic mumbling in Claudius' court. And if that doesn't appeal, don't do radio.

You also have to be prepared to work fast and make almost instant decisions. Over the years I've worked with a few actors whom I admire hugely; whom I've seen – in other media – give performances of rare charm and intelligence; but who in radio have simply been unable to 'come off the page' – make the character they're playing sound truthful and real. Of course this may simply be attributed to the crass inadequacy of the director. But for some actors the sheer speed at which they have to make decisions about character, motivation, sub-text and so forth is incredibly daunting. And then there's the physical absurdity of much of what they have to do: "How the xxx do you expect me to be 'truthful' when I'm carrying a xxxing great script in my left hand, a glass of water, masquerading as gin, in my right, and you want me to walk through a carpet of scrunched-up audio tape and pretend it's a meadow," shrieked one despairing actor to me a couple of years ago.

And yet that's exactly what we expect – truth. There's no medium as unforgiving for exposing over-acting or over-emoting (or worse – simple 'reading'). A radio play – and particularly a contemporary, naturalistic play – should make listeners feel that they are eavesdropping on real conversation. It's a medium that may owe much to theatre for providing it with great writing and acting talent (though the reverse is equally true), but the technique of radio acting is far closer to that of film than of theatre. "Less is more! Less is more!" as my erstwhile colleague, Martin Jenkins, one of Radio Drama's finest practitioners, used to impress on his casts. (It was Martin, incidentally, who uttered the memorable phrase: "Good Luck – Please!" before the umpteenth take of one particularly stressful scene.)

How do you bring yourself to the attention of radio producers? Well – there's no denying the fact that a lovingly crafted CD arriving on your desk just as you're in the process of casting your next play, and can't for the life of you think who you can get to play the embittered Glaswegian ex-shipbuilder who's contemplating a sex change, can make all the difference. But choose the pieces you record with care – and keep them short. If varied accents are not a speciality, there's no point in doing all sorts of varied accents. Obviously, it's a great asset to be master – or mistress – of many different voices, this being a medium where 'doubling' and 'trebling' is done with impunity. But a CD where the truthfulness of most of your extracts is undone by your game, but doomed, attempt to do a passable Geordie, won't help anyone. Many years ago I remember auditioning Jeremy Sinden for a part. "What accents do you do?" I asked him. "I do two actually," he said. "I do posh. And I do very posh." Well a mere two accents didn't stop Jeremy getting a load of work in every medium – including radio – in his all-too-brief, but exhilarating, career.

Having recorded your tape or (preferably) CD, you can, of course, circulate it to every producer who's ever made a radio play. But my advice would be to be a little more discerning. Listen to some radio plays (a great way of determining for yourself what works and what doesn't) and note the names of the producers whose productions particularly appeal to you. You can then write a personal note to them – you know the kind: "I must say, Mr House, I really enjoyed your fascinating and unusual interpretation of *Hedda Gabler* on Radio 3 last night, and incidentally Hedda is a part I've always yearned to play myself,"(etc.). I'm not saying it will get you a part, but producers are as vain as the next person (I should know) and it may well make them more inclined to slip your CD into the CD player, on the basis that anyone with such discerning judgement as yours must be worth hearing.

Radio is a fantastic and hugely under-rated medium, and actors, by and large, love working for it. It can also be the stepping-stone to fame and fortune. For many years we've been running our own radio bursary scheme for accredited drama schools – the Carleton Hobbs Competition (named after one of the great 20th century radio actors) – and the role-call of actors who have been winners, from Richard Griffiths to Stephen Tompkinson, from Nerys Hughes to Emma Fielding, is hugely impressive. Our new bursary scheme, the Norman Beaton Fellowship, for actors who didn't go to an accredited drama school, is also providing us with some excellent new talent. Details of both these schemes can be found on the BBC website.

And of course we producers don't simply wait to receive your CDs, but are constantly on the lookout for new and exciting talent from wherever we can find it. You may not need to approach us – we may approach you! As World Service Drama producers, Hilary Norrish and myself gave a young actor called Ewan MacGregor his first two professional jobs, having seen him in a drama school showcase. And Ewan – if you ever get to read this – where are the invitations to those glamorous film previews you promised you'd send us when you were famous? Remember – it was radio that gave you your first break!

Gordon House is the former Head of the BBC Radio Drama Department. He joined the BBC as a studio manager in 1972, working in Children's Television and Radio Sport before becoming a drama director. For 14 years he headed the small BBC World Service Drama team, during which time the Unit won more than 30 national and international awards. In 1998 Gordon won the Writers' Guild Special Prize for services for his work with new writers, and has twice won the Sony Drama Award. He is a founder member of The Worldplay Group, a radio association of drama directors from broadcasting stations around the world, which initiates a yearly season of international radios dramas broadcast on BBC World Service, ABC, CBC, RTE, Radio New Zealand and Radio Television Hong Kong.

Media festivals

These are geared towards showcasing directors, rather than actors. However, they can be useful places to network, learn and (if your film is short-listed) to gain extra exposure.

Belfast Film Festival

The Exchange Place, 23 Donegal Street,
Belfast BT1 2FF
tel 028-9032 5913 *fax* 028-9032 5911
email info@belfastfilmfestival.org
website www.belfastfilmfestival.org

Normally held in March/April each year, the Belfast Film Festival brings the best of independent, world, local and classic cinema to screens across Belfast. In addition there are panel discussions, workshops, music events and a series of related club events in venues across the city.

Candidates may submit features, shorts, animation and documentaries for inclusion in the festival. The deadline for submissions is normally early December. While all categories will be considered for screening, the only competitive category is the Irish short film. To be eligible for the £1,000 Kodak Short Film Prize, films must have been shot in Ireland during the previous year and last no longer than 20 minutes.

BFI London Film Festival

BFI South Bank, London SE1 8XT
tel 020-7815 1322 or 020-7815 1323
fax 020-7633 0786
website www.bfi.org.uk/lff

The BFI London Film Festival is Europe's largest public film event, screening an average of 280 films from 60 countries in October/November each year. Leading figures in the film industry present their work at the festival, and the programme is supported by a number of interviews, industry and public forums, lectures, education events, Gala films and special screenings promoting the best in cinema across the world.

Bradford International Film Festival

National Media Museum, Bradford BD1 1NQ
tel (01274) 203308
email biffenquiries@nationalmediamuseum.org.uk
website www.nationalmediamuseum.org.uk/bradfordinternationalfilmfestival
Directors Tom Vincent, Neil Young

Held each year in March, the Bradford Film Festival presents a number of special guests, tributes, screentalk interviews, masterclasses, spotlights, the Crash symposium and the Widescreen weekend, over a 15-day period.

Features, shorts, documentaries and experimental work submitted for competition must have been completed during the previous 2 years.

Cambridge Film Festival

Arts Picture House, 38-39 St Andrew's Street,
Cambridge CB2 3AR
tel (01223) 500082 *fax* (01223) 462555
email info@cambridgefilmfestival.org.uk
website www.cambridgefilmfestival.org.uk

Established in 1977, the festival was relaunched in 2001 after a 5-year hiatus, and now runs for 10 days in July. Aiming to screen the best of current international cinema and to rediscover neglected films of the past, it also runs a programme for children, supported by events and workshops, and organises free outdoor screenings and touring events across the Eastern region. The festival is attended by many actors and directors and is complemented by parties, receptions, drive-in movies and educational events. Recent visitors include Cate Blanchett, Richard Harris, Timothy Spall and Joel Schumacher.

Directors such as Peter Greenaway, Patrice Chereau, Philip Kaufman and Francesco Rosi have also presented work at the festival, and many acclaimed films – including *Reservoir Dogs*, *Intimacy*, *Bowling for Columbine*, *Goodbye Lenin!* and *La Haine* – received their UK premiere in Cambridge.

Celtic Media Festival

249 West George Street, Glasgow G2 4QE
tel 0141-302 1737
email info@celticmediafestival.co.uk
website www.celticmediafestival.co.uk

The Celtic Media Festival celebrates the cultures and languages of Cornwall, Brittany, Ireland, Scotland and Wales in film and in television broadcasting. Awards include: Short Drama Award, Drama Feature Award and Drama Series Award. The festival is attended by producers, directors, commissioning editors, film executives, media students, distributors and schedulers.

Chichester International Film Festival

Chichester Cinema at New Park, New Park Road,
Chichester PO19 7XY
tel (01243) 786650 *fax* (01243) 790235
email info@chichestercinema.org
website www.chichestercinema.org/film-festival
Director Roger Gibson

An 18-day festival in August/September presenting more than 70 feature films, Q&As with visiting directors, and related talks. More than half the films shown are previews and premieres; the remainder form retrospectives on important contributors to the film world.

Encounters (Short Film and Animation Festival)

Watershed Media Centre, 1 Canon's Road, Harbourside, Bristol BS1 5TX
tel 0117-929 9188 *fax* 0117-952 8888
email info@encounters-festival.org.uk
website www.encounters-festival.org.uk

Encounters is an international short film and animation festival which runs in Bristol for 1 week in September and promotes new talent in the film industry. Encounters provide a meeting place for emerging talent, those in the industry and new audiences. It enjoys excellent links with the prestigious BAFTAs, Cartoon D'Or and European Film Awards. It is a qualifying festival for the Academy Awards. With screenings of diverse new shorts from around the world, alongside special guests and events, parties, awards, seminars, masterclasses and focus sessions, the festival offers insights and advice from industry professionals about every aspect of film. For advice about submitting your work, visit the website.

Foyle Film Festival

The Nerve Centre, 7-8 Magazine Street, Derry-Londonderry BT48 6HJ
tel 028-7137 3456 *tel* 020-7126 0562
email bernie@nerve-centre.org.uk
website www.foylefilmfestival.org
Festival Director and Programmer Ms Bernie McLaughlin

Established in 1987, the annual Foyle Film Festival is the flagship project of the multi-media Nerve Centre. For 9 days in November, the Foyle Film Festival capitalises on all the technical expertise of the Nerve Centre to produce a unique programme of film, music, digital technologies, and education. The festival is themed and delivers a programme of art house cinema: international and local premieres, foreign language, documentaries, classic film, industry workshops, presentations, outreach events, as well as a stand-alone education programme which is curriculum focused, and targets all local primary and secondary schools, colleges, and universities.

The festival competition has received Oscar recognition for its Light In Motion (LIM) Film Awards. Foyle Film Festival is renowned for attracting top industry professionals to the city, with past guests including high-profile names such as: Julie Christie, Neil Jordan, Wim Wenders, Kenneth Branagh, Jenny Agutter, Julien Temple, Christiane Kubrick, Andrew Eaton, Brenda Blethyn, Roddy Doyle, Irvine Welsh, Stephen Frears, Ronan Bennett, Jimmy McGovern, Rob Coleman, Sam Taylor-Wood, Kate Adie, Jonathan Rhys Meyers, Cillian Murphy, Ardal O'Hanlon and Dervla Kirwan.

Leeds International Film Festival

Town Hall, The Headrow, Leeds LS1 3AD
tel 0113-247 8398
email filmfestival@leeds.gov.uk
website www.leedsfilm.com
Director Chris Fell

Leeds International Film Festival has been presenting extensive programmes of new and unseen cinema from around the world since 1987, supported by a number of events and workshops for those wanting to get into film and TV. The Yorkshire Short Film Competition highlights emerging new filmmaking talents in the Yorkshire region, while the Louis Le Prince International Short Film Competition promotes some of the best fiction completed around the world in the last year. The key features of the festival include UK Film Week, an annual showcase of emerging talent; Film Festival Fringe, where the bars and clubs of Leeds host human rights films, music documentaries and special events; the Main Programme; and Unique Retrospectives.

The festival is complemented by the Leeds Children's and Young People's Film Festival held in April each year, with an award for National Young Filmmaker of the Year.

London Independent Film Festival (LIFF)

Studio 160, 77 Beak Street, London W1F 9DB
email info@londonindependent.org
website www.liff.org
Festival Director Erich Schultz

The London Independent Film Festival is the premier event for micro-budget and no-budget films in the UK. LIFF offers a fantastic opportunity for indie filmmakers to showcase their achievements, with spaces reserved for first- and second-time filmmakers and for films that have been overlooked by other events. LIFF presents the best of low-budget filmmaking from around the world and mixes it with relevant industry discussions and targeted social networking events. LIFF's audience is London's sizeable independent filmmaking community; it's an indie film festival for indie filmmakers.

London Lesbian & Gay Film Festival

c/o BFI Southbank, Belvedere Road, South Bank, Waterloo, London SE1 8XT
tel 020-7928 3535 or 020-7928 3232 (Box Office)
website www.bfi.org.uk/llgff
Festival Programmers Jason Barker, Michael Blyth, Nazmia Jamal, Brian Robinson, Emma Smart

The London Lesbian and Gay Film Festival presents the best of British and international Queer Cinema in all its forms – mainstream and avant garde. Features and shorts are complemented by discussions and interviews with writers and filmmakers. The London run of the festival is based at the BFI Southbank (formerly known as the National Film Theatre), with other screenings taking place in Leicester Square. Following this run in March and April, it continues on tour around the UK until the autumn. See the website for programme details, including the tour schedule, or contact the BFI box office for a brochure of the London run.

Manchester International Short Film Festival

Kinofilm, 42 Edge Street, Manchester M4 1HN
tel 0161-288 2494 *fax* 0161-281 1374
email john.kino@good.co.uk
website www.kinofilm.org.uk
Director John Wojowski

British New Wave and an International Panorama of film provide the main focus to the festival, with a regional showcase, 'Made up North', aimed at promoting films from local and regional filmmakers. Education and Professional Development events are also hosted by the festival and are presented by external curators and organisations.

The festival is open for film submissions each year from January to June, with shortlisted entries being screened at the festival itself in October. Short films on any theme, subject or category and made on any format are eligible, as long as they run no longer than 20 minutes and have been made within the 18 months prior to the festival. The Kinofilm Awards acknowledge outstanding achievements in short film, with awards in many categories. Rules, regulations and application forms are available on the website.

Raindance Film Festival Ltd

10 Craven Street, London WC2N 5PE
tel 020-7930 3412
email info@raindance.co.uk
website www.raindance.org
Producer Julian Chapelle

Running for 2 weeks at the end of September and early October, Raindance is the UK's largest independent film festival and is committed to screening the boldest, most innovative and challenging films from the UK and from around the world. Weighted heavily towards new talent, the festival offers more than 100 features (many of which are directorial debuts), 20 shorts programmes and a wide range of events, workshops and parties.

Rushes Soho Shorts Festival

66 Old Compton Street, London W1D 4UH
tel 020-7851 6207
email info@sohoshorts.com
website www.sohoshorts.com

Taking place for 1 week in July/August, shortlisted films are screened free of charge throughout Soho's cafes, bars and cinemas, as well as other special events and screenings being held. In addition, Vue cinemas around the country will also be holding screenings throughout that week. The festival culminates in an awards cremony with winners being announced in the following categories: Short Film, Newcomer, Animation, Music Video, and Title Sequence & Idents. Patrons of the festival include BAFTA and the Directors' Guild of Great Britain.

Films for submission should be no longer than 12 minutes, and should have been produced in the 12 months prior to the deadline.

UK Jewish Film Festival

5.09 Clerkenwell Workshops,
27-31 Clerkenwell Close, London EC1R 0AT
tel 020-3176 0048
website www.ukjewishfilm.org

Established in 1997, the festival is committed to showing a wide variety of films which celebrate the diversity of Jewish cultures and identity, and which reach both Jewish and wider audiences. In addition to film screenings there are education projects and talks with directors. The UK Jewish Film Festival Short Film Fund offers a grant of up to £15,000 for the production of a short film or video (drama, animation or factual) of a Jewish theme and with a significance both to Jewish and to general public audiences. For application details, consult the website.

Disabled actors
Introduction

This section brings together companies and organisations of specific interest to disabled actors. It should also be noted that (a) some agents and companies now welcome enquiries from disabled actors (see listings), and (b) many drama schools have detail on their disability admissions policies on their websites.

In addition, disabled Equity members can add their details to the *Disability Register*, which is published by Spotlight. Casting directors looking for disabled actors can search this register via the Spotlight website.

Note The UK Government recognised BSL as an official language in March 2003, and the Editor acknowledges that many deaf people consider themselves to be members of a linguistic and cultural minority – Deaf with a capital 'D' – rather than disabled people. For the sake of simplicity, however, this book uses a broad definition of disability to encompass Deaf people (although an individual entry will retain the distinction if present in the material provided to us by that company).

The Editor would like to thank Silvie Fisch (of The National Disability Arts Forum) and the staff of Graeae Theatre Company for their help in compiling this section.

TRAINING

Apart from the training offered by drama schools, a number of theatre companies and organisations operate training schemes or courses for disabled actors. Many of these schemes are relatively short – a few days or weeks – but Lawnmower's Liberdade, Chickenshed's BTEC National Diploma and Mind the Gap's Staging Change operate over a longer term. Shorter courses are run by (among others) Birds of Paradise, Candoco, and Oily Cart. (Details for all the theatre companies listed here can be found in the *Sources of work* section below.)

SOURCES OF WORK

Amici Dance Theatre Company

Turtle Key Arts, Ladbroke Hall, 79 Barbly Road, London W10 6AZ
tel 020-8964 5060 *fax* 020-8964 4080
email tkas@amicidance.org
website www.amicidance.org
Artistic Director Wolfgang Stange

Dance theatre company integrating disabled and non-disabled artists and performers.

Anjali Dance Company

The Mill Arts Centre, Spiceball Park, Banbury, Oxfordshire OX16 8QE
tel/fax (01295) 251909
email info@anjali.co.uk
email education@anjali.co.uk
website www.anjali.co.uk
Artistic Director Nicole Thomson

Production details: A professional contemporary dance company. All Anjali's dancers have a learning disability. The company produces and tours performances, and undertakes Educational and Outreach work; it is one of the first of its kind in the world. It aims to show that disability is no barrier to creativity. Stages 1-2 productions a year with up to 10 performances over 6-8 venues around the country, such as the Mill Arts Centre (Banbury), Stratford Circus (London), and the Pegasus Theatre (Oxford).

Casting procedures: Casts in-house, does not issue casting breakdowns, and welcomes letters (but not emails) from individuals previously unknown to the company. Welcomes invitations to view individuals' websites, but not showreels.

Apropos Productions Ltd

53 Greek Street, London W1D 3DR
tel 020-7739 2857 *fax* 020-7739 3852
email info@aproposltd.com
website www.aproposltd.com
Director Paul Dubois

Company's work: Established in 2004. First feature film completes post-production August 2015, *Dark Signal* (executive producer Neil Marshall). Short films: *The Juror, X-Why* and *Cocktail*. Web series: award-winning web series: *A Quick Fortune* and *Le Method* (2016). Script events include *My German Roots are Showing* at the Arcola Theatre, London, starring Miriam Margolyes.

Provides training for local, national and international clients. Key focus is on Organisational Behaviour. Training is provided for incoming actors. Corporate experience is useful but not essential. Actor-base is extended annually through agents, the website and Equity Job Information Service. Clients include: SKANKSA, Sony Computer Entertainment, House of Commons, UBM and the Discovery Network.

Recruitment procedures: Accepts submissions (with CVs and photographs) from actors previously unknown to the company. Disabled actors regularly form part of its teams and are actively encouraged to apply.

art+power

Centre Gate, Colston Avenue, Bristol BS1 4TR
tel 0117-317 8099
email info@artandpower.com
website www.artandpower.com
Key contact David Richmond

Bristol-based organisation that uses the arts to empower disabled people and build a more equal, inclusive and creative society. art+power produces theatre, dance and live art projects.

Birds of Paradise Theatre Company

The Old Sheriff Court, 105 Brusnwick Street, Glasgow G1 1TF
tel 0141-339 1155
email all@birdsofparadisetheatre.co.uk
website www.birdsofparadisetheatre.co.uk
Artistic Directors Robert Softley Gale, Garry Robson

Birds of Paradise is a force for change in Scottish theatre, creating world class projects and performances that place disabled artists centre stage.

We exist to:

• increase the representation of professional deaf and disabled artists and performers in Scottish theatre - by working with exciting and skilled disabled and non-disabled artists and leading a national debate on inclusive theatre practice and issues around deaf and disability arts;

• to create world class performances and projects that embody the aesthetics of access - by becoming acknowledged leaders in the practical application of the aesthetics of access in Scotland;

• to nurture the next generation of deaf and disabled performers and artists - by introducing young deaf and disabled people to theatre.

Previous productions include: *Crazy Jane* by Nicola McCartney; *Wendy Hoose* by Johnny McKnight; *The Farce of Circumstance* by Tom Lannon; *The Resistible Rise of Arturo Ui* by Bertolt Brecht; *Tongues* by Sam Shephard and Joseph Chaikin; *Working Legs* by Alistair Gray; *Playing for Keeps* by Archie Hind; *Merman* by Susan McClymont and Dave Buchanan; *Twelve Black Candles* by Des Dillon; *The Irish Giant* by Garry Robson; *Brazil 12 Scotland 0* by Ian Stephen; *Mouth of Silence* by Gerry Loose and *Beneath YouSpider Girls are Everywhere!* by Kathy McKean. Birds of Paradise Theatre Company in association with The Citizens' Theatre produced *Offshore* by Alan Wilkins, directed by Morven Gregor, in September 2008.

Candoco Dance Company

2T Leroy House, 436 Essex Road, London N1 3QP
tel 020-7704 6845
email info@candoco.co.uk
website www.candoco.co.uk
Artistic Co-Directors Stine Nilsen, Pedro Machado

Candoco Dance Company is a leading contemporary dance company of disabled and non-disabled dancers. By producing creatively ambitious dance performances, the company aims to push the boundaries of contemporary dance and to broaden people's perception of what dance is and who can dance.

Candoco was founded in 1991, and through its performances and education work has developed into the world's leading exponent of inclusive dance practice. The company regularly commissions artists and choreographers to create new dance work that tours nationally and internationally. It also runs a variety of training courses, residencies and workshops, and Cando2 – Candoco's Youth Dance Company.

Chickenshed Theatre

Chase Side, Southgate, London N14 4PE
tel 020-8351 6161 (181001 020 8292 9222 Typetalk)
website www.chickenshed.org.uk
Executive Management Jo Collins MBE, Gill Dodge, Paul Morrall, Louise Perry

A theatre company that makes beautiful and inspirational theatre, working on the basis that *everyone* should be included regardless of their background, age or ability."Our vision is a society that celebrates diversity and enables every individual to flourish." In addition the company runs:

• An inclusive theatre education workshop programme for nearly 700 members from the ages of 5 upwards

• 3 nationally accredited education courses
• Community Outreach projects
• A growing number of satellite 'sheds' including 2 in Russia
• Training in inclusive practice through workshops and seminars for a range of professionals from the fields of education, social services and health

Dark Horse

Lawrence Batley Theatre, Queen's Street, Huddersfield HD1 2SP
tel (01484) 484441 *fax* (01484) 484443
email info@darkhorsetheatre.co.uk
website www.darkhorsetheatre.co.uk
Artistic Director Vanessa Brooks

Production details: Established in 2000. Production company exploring a range of projects that include actors with learning disabilities and promote inclusive working practices. Approximately 1 production per year touring to 10-15 venues, including arts centres and theatres in Yorkshire, the North West and internationally. Roughly 5-8 actors are used in each production.

Casting procedures: Occasionally uses freelance casting directors. Does not welcome unsolicited CVs. Actively encourages applications from disabled actors and promotes the use of inclusive casting. Offers Equity-approved contracts.

Deafinitely Theatre

Unit 20, Deane House Studios, 27 Greenwood Place, London NW5 1LB
tel 020-7424 7360
email paula@deafinitelytheatre.co.uk
website www.deafinitelytheatre.co.uk

Artistic Director Paula Garfield *Executive Director* Mark Sands

Founded in 2002 to produce performance ideas by Deaf people. All the company's work is Deaf-led but is accessible to hearing people as well. The company runs projects and workshops for Deaf people and colleges in writing, acting and technical theatre. Recent productions include: *Dysfunction* (Soho Theatre); *Children of a Greater God* (Jackson's Lane); *Motherland* (Jackson's Lane) and *Two Chairs* (Oval House).

Graeae Theatre Company

Bradbury Studios, 138 Kingsland Road, London E2 8DY
tel 020-7613 6900 *fax* 020-7613 6919
email info@graeae.org
website www.graeae.org
Artistic Director Jenny Sealey

Production details: Founded in 1980. Produces theatre made by disabled people (actors, directors and other theatre practitioners) with physical and sensory impairments. Stages 3 productions annually and gives 70 performances at 50 venues each year. Venues include arts centres and theatres in England, Scotland, Wales and Ireland. 3-6 actors are involved in each production. Recent productions include: national tour of *Blasted* by Sarah Kane and *Whiter Than Snow* by Mike Kenny, which was a co-production with Birmingham Rep. Graeae and New Wolsey Theatre co-produced *Flower Girls* by Richard Cameron in autumn 2007, and Graeae co-produced a new play in spring 2008 with with Suspect Culture.

Casting procedures: Sometimes holds general auditions. Welcomes postal or email submissions (with CVs and photographs) from actors with physical and sensory impairments. Also accepts showreels and invitations to view individual actors' websites. Offers ITC/Equity-approved contracts.

Into The Scene is a new Arts Council England initiative led by Graeae. Works with leading drama schools on inclusive practice to encourage drama schools to recruit more disabled actors onto their training courses.

Scene Change is a Graeae initiative working with venues, drama schools and colleges, offering taster workshops to encourage more young people to apply to drama schools.

The company offers Continued Professional Development workshops for actors. Past workshops have included Comedy Acting with director Gordon Anderson (ATC/Catherine Tate), and Singing with Barb Jungr.

Grid (part of Inter-Action MK)

The Old Rectory, Waterside, Peartree Bridge, Milton Keynes MK6 3EJ
tel (01908) 678514
email info@interactionmk.org.uk
website www.interactionmk.org.uk
Project Manager Hannah Kitchen

Inspired by the work of Chicken Shed Theatre Company (see page 368), Shed MK runs various inclusive performance projects – among them, youth theatre projects for 7-11 and 12-16 year-olds.

Hijinx Theatre

Wales Millennium Centre, Bute Place, Cardiff CF10 5AL
tel 029-2030 0331
email info@hijinx.org.uk
website www.hijinx.org.uk
Artistic Director Ben Pettitt-Wade

Production details: Founded in 1981, the company stages professional theatre performed by actors with and without learning disabilities; tours to theatres, festivals and communities in the UK and Europe.

Offers ITC/Equity-approved contracts and does not subscribe to the Equity Pension Scheme.

Casting procedures: Shows are cast by the Artistic Director. Welcomes letters, CVs and photographs from actors previously unknown to the company.

Welcomes applications from disabled and non-disabled actors.

IMPACT Theatre

IMPACT Community Arts Centre,
Ealing Central Sports Ground,
Horsenden Lane South, Perivale UB6 8GP
tel/fax 020-8997 8979
email info@impacttheatre.co
website www.impacttheatre.co
Artistic Director Kim Mughan FRSA

IMPACT (IMagine, Perform And Create Together) Theatre was founded in 1999. It was set up by and for adults with learning disabilities. While not a professional company, IMPACT helps to develop skills of performance and self-expression for its actors, musicians and dancers. IMPACT Theatre stages original productions featuring up to 60 performers with learning disabilities. In addition to the disability arts that IMPACT has become known for in West London, it is now embarking on innovative inclusive arts work.

Krazy Kat Theatre Company

173 Hartington Road, Brighton BN2 3PA
tel (01273) 692552
email krazykattheatre@ntlworld.com
website www.krazykattheatre.co.uk
Artistic Director Kinny Gardner

Production details: A children's theatre company founded in 1982, specialising in highly visual forms of theatre that are accessible to Deaf children. Normally tours 2 projects each year with an average annual total of 50 performances and 35 venues. Venues include schools, arts centres, theatres, outdoor venues and community centres throughout UK. In general 2 actors and a technician go on tour and play to audiences aged 3-7. Singing ability, physical theatre skills, British sign language and a driving licence are required. Actors may also be expected to lead workshops. Recent productions include: *A (Midsummer Night's) Dream,Petrushka*, *The Pied Piper*, a Victorian *Mikado*and *The Very Magic Flute.*

Casting procedures: Sometimes holds general auditions; actors can write at any time requesting inclusion. Accepts submissions (with CVs and photographs) from actors previously unknown to the company if sent by post. Does not welcome unsolicited emails. Will also accept invitations to view individual actors' websites. Offers non-Equity contracts but at Equity and ITC rates. Actively encourages applications from disabled actors and promotes the use of inclusive casting.

Lawnmowers Independent Theatre Company

Swinburn House, Swinburn Street,
Gateshead NE8 1AX
tel/fax 0191-478 9200
email info@thelawnmowers.co.uk
website www.thelawnmowers.co.uk
Arts Director Geraldine Ling

Theatre company addressing issues of concern for people with learning difficulties, often with an international dimension. Uses theatre and drama as a means for people with learning difficulties to explore and develop ideas, and help plan and take control of their futures.

Magpie Dance

The Churchill Theatre, High Street,
Bromley BR1 1HA
tel 020-8290 6633
email info@magpiedance.org.uk
website www.magpiedance.org.uk
Artistic Director Avril Hitman

Magpie Dance is a company for people with learning disabilities. Based in Bromley, Magpie can also deliver workshops to any region in the UK. With an emphasis on ability rather than disability, the company has a national reputation for its exciting approach to inclusive dance.

Mind the Gap

Mind the Gap Studios Bradford, Silk Warehouse,
Patent Street, Bradford BD9 4SA
tel (01274) 487390 *fax* (01274) 493973
email arts@mind-the-gap.org.uk
website www.mind-the-gap.org.uk
Artistic Director Tim Wheeler

Production details: Founded in 1988, Mind the Gap is a theatre company with a belief in quality, equality and inclusion, and a mission to dismantle barriers to artistic excellence so that learning-disabled and non-learning-disabled actors can appear as equals. The company has 5 main areas of activity:

• National Touring: in 2000, Mind the Gap progressed from devised work to adaptations of well-known texts. In recent years the company has produced: *Of Mice and Men* (2000 and 2005); *Dr Jekyll and Mr Hyde* (2001); *Pygmalion* (2002); *Don Quixote* (2003 – collaboration with Northern Stage) and *Cyrano* (2004). Total audiences for the 2005 tour were approximately 6,700
• Learning & Skills: each year Mind the Gap runs a full-time accredited training course for people with learning disabilities. In addition, as part of the DaDA awards scheme, the company runs Staging Change – a residential, nationally recruited training course for people with learning disabilities, working in partnership with 5 of the country's leading mainstream drama schools
• Acting Company: comprising 7 learning-disabled graduates of Mind the Gap's training courses who work on National Touring productions and their own programme of local and regional performance work and workshops
• Outreach: each year, Mind the Gap's Outreach programme works with 300 young learning-disabled

people from West Yorkshire on short-term drama training and performance projects
• Advocacy: Mind the Gap advocates for people who are traditionally excluded or marginalised from mainstream practices. Mind the Gap is also commissioned to do a variety of performance projects: e.g. *Finding their Feet* – a production commissioned by Bradford School of Health Studies; and *Inside Knowledge* – commissioned by Tonic as part of a consultation to provide guidance for the design of a new cancer care centre in Leeds

Stages 1 or 2 national tours annually (25-30 performances each), 1 large-scale regional performance project (3-6 performances) and 1 or 2 regional schools tours (12 performances). The national tour visits 15-20 venues. In 2005 these included West Yorkshire Playhouse; The Theatre, Chipping Norton; Ustinov Studio, Bath; Norwich Playhouse; Rose Theatre, Ormskirk; New Vic, Newcastle-under-Lyme and Jackson's Lane Theatre, London. 3-5 actors are involved in the national tour, up to 7 actors in the schools tour, and over 20 performers in the regional performance project.

Casting procedures: Casts in-house. When seeking to recruit an actor from outside the core company, the company contacts agents, and advertises in *The Stage* and on its website. Casting breakdowns are available on request. Welcomes letters (with CVs and photographs) as well as showreels and invitations to view individuals' websites, "although we do not often employ actors who are not known to us. For national touring work we rarely cast outside our core Acting Company, but we do keep on record details which have been sent to us. We are particularly interested in hearing from disabled artists." Offers TMA/Equity-approved contracts.

Oily Cart Company

Smallwood School Annexe, Smallwood Road, London SW17 0TW
tel 020-8672 6329 *fax* 020-8672 0792
email oilies@oilycart.org.uk
website www.oilycart.org.uk
Artistic Director Tim Webb

Production details: One of the leading theatre companies in the UK, creating highly interactive multi-sensory performances for the very young (6 months to 6 years) and for young people (aged 3-19) with Profound or Multiple Learning Disabilities (PMLD) or an Autistic Spectrum Disorder (ASD). Tours national and international venues like theatres and arts centres with early years shows, and takes its special-needs work to special schools around the UK. Recent productions include: *Baby Balloon* for audiences aged 6 months to 2 years; *If All The World Were Paper*; *Blue* and *Pool Piece* – an interactive hydrotherapy pool show for young people with PMLD or ASD.

Casting procedures: Casting breakdowns are available on the website **www.oilycart.org.uk** and the Arts Jobs website **www.artsjobs.org.uk.** Offers ITC/Equity-approved contracts. Actively encourages applications from disabled actors and promotes the use of inclusive casting.

Salamanda Tandem

52 Albert Road, Nottingham NG2 5GS
tel/fax 0845-293 2989
email info@salamanda-tandem.org
website www.salamanda-tandem.org
Artistic Director Isabel Jones

Producer of contemporary art works, creative environments and sensory performances, where people can choose to observe or become part of the artwork itself. Works with a wide spectrum of people, and in particular people with disabilities. Strong advocate for ethical practice in arts and health. Publishes articles and conducts training and professional education.

Spare Tyre Theatre Company

Unit 3.22, Canterbury Court, 1-3 Brixton Road, London SW9 6DE
tel/fax 020-7061 6454
email info@sparetyre.org
website www.sparetyre.org
Artistic Director Arti Prashar

Production details:

• Work with older people: a company of artists aged 60+, outreach workshops for older people, and interactive storytelling for people with dementia.
• Work with people with learning disabilities: a company of artists with learning disabilities.
• Work with women who have experienced violence.

Primarily covers the London area. Skills required from actors include workshop-leading and facilitation skills, experience of working with community groups and a sensitivity to, and understanding of, relevant issues.

Casting procedures: Casting breakdowns are published and on the website. Unsolicited approaches at other times – including CVs, showreels and invitations to view individuals' websites – are discouraged. Offers ITC/Equity-approved contracts. Actively encourages applications from disabled actors and promotes the use of inclusive casting.

StopGAP Dance Company

Farnham Maltings, Bridge Square, Farnham, Surrey GU9 7QR
tel (01252) 718664
email vicki@stopgap.uk.com
website www.stopgap.uk.com
Artistic Director Vicki Balaam

A vibrant integrated dance company that includes disabled and non-disabled dancers. It challenges traditional notions about dance by using each dancer's physical and intellectual potential as a starting point for creating new work. "We work from a philosophy of physical, psychological and social integration. In so doing, we recognise and celebrate individuality and the differences between people, while continually seeking artistic and technical excellence in all that we do."

Theatre Without Walls

Forwood House, Forwood, Gloucesterhire GL6 9AB
mobile (07962) 040441
email hello@theatrewithoutwalls.org.uk
website www.theatrewithoutwalls.org.uk
Directors Genevieve Swift, Jason Maher

Company's work: Established in 2002. Award-winning producing theatre company with an active training/corporate wing, working in the public and private sector. Also produces television and corporate films. Clients include: National Trust, Gloucestershire Local Authority, Apollo, BBC and The Prince's Trust. Training is provided for incoming actors in the form of workshops and rehearsals in forum, role-play and interactive drama. Incoming actors require good improvisational skills.

Recruitment procedures: Actors are recruited through agents and Equity Job Information Service. Disabled actors regularly form part of the team and are actively encouraged to apply. See also the company's entry under *Middle and smaller-scale companies* on page 211.

Theatre Workshop

34 Hamilton Place, Edinburgh EH3 5AX
tel 0131-225 7942 *fax* 0131-220 0112
email afleming@twe.org.uk
website www.theatre-workshop.com
Artistic Director Robert Rae

Production details: Founded in 1965; stages 4 productions a year with around 60 performances across 2 theatre venues. Occasionally tours internationally. Employs an average of 5 actors on each production, using ITC/Equity-approved contracts. Recent productions include: *The Jasmine Road* (No Limits International Theatre Festival, Berlin) and *The Threepenny Opera* (Edinburgh Festival Theatre & Tramway, Glasgow).

Casting procedures: Casting breakdowns are available from the website and Equity Job Information Service. Welcomes letters and emails (with CVs and photographs) from individuals previously unknown to the company. Also happy to receive showreels and invitations to view individuals' websites. Encourages applications from disabled actors and promotes the use of inclusive casting. "Theatre Workshop casts both disabled and non-disabled actors in all our productions."

Touchdown Dance

Waterside Arts Centre, Sale M33 7ZF
tel 0161-912 5760 *fax*
email info@touchdowndance.co.uk
website www.touchdowndance.co.uk
Director Katy Dymoke

Touchdown Dance provides dance workshops for visually impaired and sighted people of all ages and ability, ranging from 'jam' weekends to more intensive courses.

Louise Dyson at VisABLE People

PO Box 80, Droitwich WR9 0ZE
tel (01386) 555 170 *mobile* (01905) 776631
email louise@visablepeople.com
website www.visablepeople.com
Agent Louise Dyson

Production details: Founded in 1994, VisABLE is the UK's first agency representing only disabled people for professional engagements. It represents artistes with a wide range of impairments and in every age group, including children. 2 agents represent around 150 artistes in all areas of acting, including presenting.

Casting procedures: Does not welcome performance notices: "Sorry, usually no time to get out and see them; existing clients only." Happy to receive other enquiries (with CVs and photographs) from disabled actors via website only. Showreels should always be accompanied by an sae for return. Also happy to receive invitations to view individual actors' websites. Recommends the photographer Simon Donnelly. *Commission*: 10%-17.5% (commercials: 20%).

Wolf + Water

Beaford Centre, Beaford, Winkleigh EX19 8LU
tel (01805) 625533
email office@wolfandwater.org
website www.wolfandwater.org
Co-founders Steve Newton, Philip Robinson

Since establishing itself independently in 1991, after 3 years as the Beaford Centre's 'Common Sense Project', Wolf + Water Arts Company has brought its creative and therapeutic approaches to a wide variety of groups locally, nationally and internationally. These groups have included people with learning difficulties; people with mental health issues; people in conflict situations; offenders; communities; young people at risk; children with life-threatening illnesses and their families and staff groups working with all the above. The company produces original topical performances for conferences and for tour, and provides a wide range of training courses for those wishing to use drama and arts techniques in special-needs situations. Work has taken the company throughout the UK, the Republic of Ireland, Scandinavia, the Middle East and the Balkans.

ARTS ORGANISATIONS

Ableize Arts

website www.ableize.com/disabled-arts

A selection of disabled arts sites, from theatre and dance to visual arts. The Ableize site also features links, from accommodation and travel to support groups and employment and benefits. A fantastic, wide-ranging site.

Arcadea

2nd Floor, Commercial Union House,
39 Pilgrim Street, Newcastle NE1 6QE
tel 0191-222 0708 *mobile* (07932) 304241
email info@arcadea.org
website www.arcadea.org

Arcadea aims to promote the artistic and cultural equality of disabled people in the North East region, serving Co. Durham, Northumberland, Tees Valley and Tyne & Wear.

Artlink Central

Cowane Centre, Cowane Street, Stirling FK8 1JP
tel (01786) 450971 *fax* (01786) 465958
email info@artlinkcentral.org
website www.artlinkcentral.org

Established in February 1988, Artlink Central is a registered charity founded in the belief that involvement in the arts is life-enhancing and should be available to all. It enables a wide range of disabled and/or marginalised people to work with experienced professional artists on high-quality arts projects in the Stirling, Falkirk and Clackmannanshire areas of Central Scotland.

Artlink Edinburgh

13A Spittal Street, Edinburgh
tel 0131-229 3555 *fax* 0131-228 5257
website www.artlinkedinburgh.co.uk

As Artlink Central, but based in Edinburgh and the Lothians.

Artsline

c/o 21 Pine Court, Wood Lodge Gardens,
Bromley BR1 2WA
tel fax minicom
email admin@artsline.org.uk
website www.artsline.org.uk

Founded in 1981 with the aim of increasing disabled people's participation in the arts, and to provide them with accurate information about access to arts and cultural events in London. In collaboration with the London Disability Arts Forum, it began producing *Disability Arts in London* (*DAIL*) magazine in 1986, and now provides a newly launched access database with details for arts and entertainment venues across London, including: theatres, cinemas, museums, art centres, tourist attractions, comedy, music venues and selected restaurants. For details of other publications, projects and services available, consult the website.

Carousel

Community Base, 113 Queens Road,
Brighton BN1 3XG
tel (01273) 234734 *fax* (01273) 234735
email enquiries@carousel.org.uk
website www.carousel.org.uk
Artistic Director Mark Richardson *Executive Director* Liz Hall

Carousel was founded in 1982, and operates primarily in the South East of England. It is a Brighton-based arts organisation that works with people who have learning disabilities. Among its projects are the High Spin Dance Company and the Oskabright Film Festival.

DaDaFest

The Bluecoat, School Lane, Liverpool L1 3BX
tel 0151-707 1733 *fax* 0151-708 9355
email info@dadafest.co.uk
website www.dadafest.co.uk
Artistic Director Ruth Gould

DaDa-Disability & Deaf Arts is a disability arts organisation. It aims to facilitate the active participation of disabled and Deaf people in all aspects of the arts and creative industries and to promote and celebrate disability and Deaf arts and culture. Based in Liverpool city centre, the company's work covers the whole of the North West and the UK, as well as operating on an international scale.

Disability Arts Cymru

Sbectrwm, Bwlch Road, Fairwater, Cardiff CF5 3EF
tel 029-2055 1040 *textphone* 029-2055 1040
fax 029-2055 1036
email post@dacymru.com
website www.dacymru.com
Director Maggie Hampton

Disability Arts Cymru is the only organisation in Wales providing Disability Equality Training (DET) specifically for arts providers; it lists among its clients the Arts Council of Wales and the Royal Welsh College of Music and Drama. A number of documents are available from its excellent website, which offer advice on a range of subjects including access issues for touring companies. In June 2006 the company ran 'The Unusual Stage School', a free 11-day course aimed at disabled would-be actors living in Wales.

Disability Arts Online

9 Jew Street, Brighton BN1 1UT
mobile (07941) 1824458
email info@disabilityartsonline.org.uk
website www.disabilityarts.org

Aims to assist the professional development of disabled and Deaf writers and artists, working across all art forms.

Diverse City

3 Manwell Drive, Swanage, Dorset BH19 2RB
tel (07795) 247216
website www.DiverseCity.org.uk

Advocates for and delivers diversity and equality of opportunity in culture and learning.

First Movement

Level Centre, Old Station Close, Rowsley, Derbyshire DE4 2EL
tel (01629) 734848
email fmt@first-movement.org.uk
website www.first-movement.org.uk

First Movement is an experimental arts organisation developing projects which uniquely reflect the experiences, choices and abilities of groups of people with severe and profound learning disabilities. Runs a performance company called Spiral.

Northern Ireland Arts & Disability Forum

Cathedral Quarter Managed Workspace, 109-113 Royal Avenue, Belfast BT1 1FF
tel 028-90 239 450
email info@adf.ie
website www.adf.ie
Chief Executive Officer Chris Ledger

A non-profit-making voluntary organisation that aims to provide:

- Information to disabled people and organisations – both inside and outside the arts sector
- A body that advocates on behalf of disabled people in the arts sector
- A networking, developmental and coordinating body
- A body that identifies and fills gaps in training provisions for disabled people working in the arts
- A focus for campaigning

Also runs a gallery to exhibit the work of disabled artists.

Prism Arts

Carlisle Business Interaction Centre, 4-5 Paternoster Row, Carlisle, Cumbria CA3 8TT
tel (01228) 888630
email office@prismarts.org.uk
website www.prismarts.org.uk
Director Catherine Coulthard

Promotes diverse access to creative arts activities in Cumbria. Runs Studio Theatre for learning-disabled performers.

Shape

Deane House Studios, 27 Greenwood Place, London NW5 1LB
tel 020-7424 7344 *fax* 0845-521 3458
email info@shapearts.org.uk
website www.shapearts.org.uk

Shape's mission is to provide skills, opportunities and support for disabled artists, individuals and cultural organisations and to help build a more inclusive cultural sector.

Zinc Arts

Great Stony, High Street, Chipping Ongar, Essex CM5 0AD
tel (01277) 365626
email info@zincarts.org.uk
website www.zincarts.org.uk
Director Dan Burman, Sonia Cakebread, Lyann Kennedy

Zinc Arts work with people of all ages and abilities, but specialise in working with children, young people and adults who are disabled, learning disabled or are mental health service users. Zinc Arts provides beneficial inclusive opportunities for people to engage with the arts; creatively, educationally and vocationally. Zinc Arts Centre offers an inclusive environment with meeting/training rooms, studio theatre, conferencing and performance facilities, as well as contemporary en-suite accommodation.

RIGHTS, ADVICE AND SUPPORT

Business Disability Forum

Nutmeg House, 60 Gainsford Street, London SE1 2NY
tel 020-7403 3020 *fax* 020-7403 0404
minicom 020-7403 0040
email enquiries@businessdisabilityforum.org.uk
website http://businessdisabilityforum.org.uk

The leading employers' organisation focused on disability as it affects business. Funded and managed by more than 400 members, the Forum works to make it easier for companies to recruit and retain disabled employees and to serve disabled customers. Umbrella organisation for the Broadcasting & Creative Industries Disability Network (BCIDN), a forum for the UK's major broadcasters to explore and address disability as it relates to the media industry. It is advised by a panel of associates – 14 disabled people with considerable media experience who work in different areas of broadcasting and the media in general.

Directgov

website www.direct.gov.uk/disability

The government's Public Services portal, with links to information and advice on employment, home and housing options, financial support, health, education and training, rights and obligations, transport, travel and holidays, leisure and recreation and caring for someone.

Equality and Human Rights Commission

England: Freepost RRLL-GHUX-CTRX, Arndale House, Arndale Centre, Manchester M4 3AQ
tel 0845-604 6610 *textphone* 0845-604 6620
fax 0845-604 6630
email englandhelpline@equalityhumanrights.com
website www.equalityhumanrights.com

Having taken over from the Disability Rights Commission in 2007, the Equality and Human Rights Commission's role is to:

• Ensure that people are aware of their rights and how to use them
• Work with employers, service providers and organisations to help them develop best practice
• Work with policymakers, lawyers and the government to make sure that social policy and the law promote equality
• Use its powers to enforce the laws that are already in place

Wales
Freepost RRLR-UEYB-UYZL, 3rd Floor, 3 Callaghan Square, Cardiff CF10 5BT
tel 0845-604 8810 *textphone* 0845-604 5520
fax 0845-604 5530
email waleshelpline@equalityhumanrights.com

Scotland
Freepost RRLL-GYLB-UJTA, The Optima Building, 58 Robertson Street, Glasgow G2 8DU
tel 0845-604 5510 or 0845-604 5520/0845-604 5530
email scotlandhelpline@equalityhumanrights.com
(The helplines are open Monday-Friday 8am-6pm.)

Ouch!

website www.bbc.co.uk/ouch

The BBC's online disability magazine, including weblogs, message board and a monthly podcast.

Skill: National Bureau for Students with Disabilities

Skill closed on April 4th 2011. Following a period of financial difficulty, Skill's Board of Trustees decided it was no longer viable to keep the charity open. Although Skill will not be returning in its previous form, Disability Alliance (**www.disabilityalliance.org**) has been supported by the Department for Business, Innovation and Skills to fill part of the gap. Some parts of the Skill website (**www.skill.org.uk**) will continue to be hosted as a free information archive to disabled people, parents and key advisers.

Opportunities for disabled actors

Jamie Beddard

The plethora of journeys and experiences of disabled performers over the past 30 years has ranged from the lonely, demoralising, and depressing to the downright bizarre. The barriers encountered far outreach the regular obstacles preventing non-disabled actors from learning, and plying their trade. Performance attributes of technique, voice, improvisation and movement seem distant concepts when you cannot get through the doors of drama school, producers baulk at the idea of employing disabled performers, and most training and employment opportunities are based around strict notions of 'the classical actor'. This is altogether surprising in the creative industries, which should surely celebrate uniqueness, individuality and diversity. However, where once black actors were denied access to stage and screen, so those with different bodies have fought similar battles for opportunity, acknowledgement and representation. This, against a backdrop in which esteemed, non-disabled actors regularly pick up Oscars for their touching portrayal of characters with disability: Daniel Day Lewis in *My Left Foot*; Jamie Foxx in *Ray*; John Voight in *Coming Home*; Tom Hanks in *Forrest Gump* – there's a long list, and they are one-dimensional replications of impediments, far outweighing any considerations around full and meaningful characterisations. Authenticity has been a label seldom attached to the portrayal of disability in the mainstream.

Personal anecdotes are perhaps best served by exploring the issues faced by disabled performers, as, until recently, there have been no formal routes of progression into the industry. Those few who have made the periphery have tended to have random and short-lived paths, based around such indeterminates as maverick directors, word of mouth or, as in my particular case, luck. The groundbreaking film *Skalligrigg* – a road movie in which a rag tag of disabled characters take to the road on a mythical quest – threw my staid career path into chaos, and levered a window (previously boarded up!) into performance. In the absence of disabled actors, many first-timers with no experience were suddenly thrust onto a film set; I thought the sound-boom was a cheap prop! 'Rough diamonds' probably most accurately described those of us fortunate enough to get such a break, and, for me, the film opened up a completely new, and exciting, world. A mixture of bluff, wide-eyed enthusiasm and no little begging had to suffice in the absence of any formal training.

This 'new and exciting world' was also populated by baffling and disheartening prejudices, and initial enthusiasm soon became tinged with disappointment and anger. A casting director for *Eastenders* once informed me that a disabled character – played by a disabled actor, heaven forbid! – would place the programme in the realm of freak show. So much for diverse communities and gritty realism! This attitude is unfortunately still painfully prevalent, and theatre directors are worried that their audiences will be put off by seeing a disabled person on stage.

I contacted Graeae Theatre Company – a company that had been going since the early 1980s, and was run by, and for, actors with sensory and physical disabilities. Graeae had become accustomed to (and was hardened by) irksome battles against prevalent prejudices and barriers. I found a group of like-minded individuals who were challenging these ridiculous, outdated and offensive attitudes, and were determined to pursue careers considered impractical and unrealistic. They were developing, writing and performing theatre as does any small-scale company; sometimes very good, and sometimes not so good. However, the normal critical faculties brought to bear on other companies seemed strangely absent from assessment of Graeae's work, with emphasis on the 'oh so strange impairments' rather than art. The *Independent*, when reviewing Graeae's 2002 production – *Peeling* – came up with such helpful insights as, "Beaty is four feet tall; Coral has tiny limbs and a torso about the same size as her head." Apart from gross inaccuracies, the obvious offence to the individual actors involved and the banality of such revelations, what relevance has this to the art? Hopefully, the paying public didn't recoil in shock at this assembled collection of bizarre physical specimens!

I always yearned for a bad – rather than ignorant, ill informed and avoiding – review, because this would suggest a considered judgement based on the same criteria as any other performer. Undoubtedly, I have been involved in a few 'turkeys', and they should be recognised as such! However, fascination with individual impediment always seems the central tenet of any assessment of performance. Perhaps it would be interesting to apply such criteria to the wider acting fraternity – solely judging Woody Allen on his glasses, Tom Hanks on his stature, or Kenneth Williams on his nasal inflection.

Over the years, the profile of Graeae, and of disabled performers in general, has grown, and there has been a gradual acceptance that it is no longer acceptable to marginalise their talents, aspirations and contributions. In many ways the Arts have lagged behind society in taking the first steps towards embracing and committing to diversity. Although, there has, in many quarters, been a genuine will to broaden participation, the stick of the Disability Discrimination Act has been instrumental in initiating fundamental appraisal and change. The possibility of legal challenges has shaken many organisations, venues and makers from their comfy inertia. Even tokenism is preferable to apartheid!

Drama schools, in particular, have found the concept of students with disability difficult to grasp, but the introduction of the Dance & Drama Awards (DaDAs) has started the process of drama schools thinking not only about the physical access to their buildings, but also about the attitudinal access, and ways to promote inclusive teaching. This is very exciting, and will no doubt pave the way for young disabled people to go through mainstream training rather than be reliant on Graeae.

While the process of change will take time (especially the attitudinal aspect), Graeae has had to respond to the obvious demand by setting up the training course in conjunction with London Metropolitan University. This course offers all the elements found in drama schools, and provides the skills, disciplines and training that were denied people of my age. Lack of sufficiently trained and experienced disabled actors has long been an excuse for the 'cripping up' of non-disabled actors, while training providers continually stress the unlikelihood of disabled graduates sustaining careers in the industry. A classic chicken-and-egg situation, in which aspirant disabled performers are denied entrance at all levels. However, the percentage of those who have graduated through Missing Piece, and have gone into the industry, compares favourably with other drama schools, and Graeae is frequently approached by casting directors looking for disabled talent. So, young people with disabilities do share the same aspirations as any others; there is an increasing demand for such actors; and the institutions are failing to shoulder responsibility.

Missing Piece is fulfilling this vacuum, and has now been running since 2000. The nine-month (September to May) intensive training allows disabled students to work with a wide range of theatre practitioners – both specialist and mainstream. The course can act as a foundation course to further education or drama school – access and will permitting! – or, as is often the case, a direct gateway into the industry. Academic and practical elements of performance are covered, and opportunities for showcasing and touring afforded. Recent years have culminated in professional touring productions of *Mother Courage* and *George Dandin*, and many relationships have been brokered between Graeae's performers and directors, producers and casting directors. There is a crossover with the Performing Arts degree at London Metropolitan, with disabled performers working alongside, and in collaboration with, tutors and students at the University. As well as the main Missing Piece course, Graeae run a series of taster workshops throughout the year for prospective actors.

So strides are being made by Graeae, and by other companies; the excuses and barriers preventing inclusion are slowly being dismantled. There are viable careers for those with the talent, determination and thick skin when necessary.

BBC has set up a talent fund for disabled actors to try and address dated attitudes, and to encourage writers to write storylines which are not always hospital-based or about the whole 'disability thing'!

However the failure of mainstream films such as *Inside I'm Dancing*, which continue to propagate stereotypes and exclusion – with all the main disabled characters played by non-disabled actors – will hopefully mark a sea-change in attitudes and imaginations among creators. The existing, and perspective, body of talent out there no longer allows for petty excuses or wilful misrepresentation. Disabled people, like any others, can make good, bad or indifferent performers, and should be judged as such. However, we have a right to expect the same opportunities, treatments and prospects as all. Banging the door down has become boring – just let us in. It's not rocket science!

Jamie Beddard is an actor, writer and director. Involved with Graeae since 1991, he was Associate Director of the company for some years. He is currently working as a freelance director and co-editor of *DAIL* magazine. Graeae productions 2006/7 include *Blasted* by Sarah Kane, touring March to May; *Once Beyond These Walls, A Girl* by Richard Cameron, touring October to November; and *Whiter Than Snow* by Mike Kenny – a co-production with Birmingham Rep, touring February to April 2007. For full details, visit the website **www.graeae.org**. For information on Missing Piece, contact: **ellie@graeae.org**.

Resources
Introduction

This section covers those practical items (and sources of more detailed help and advice) that are, to the actor, what tools and a first-aid kit are to a carpenter. Some may be irrelevant to you – for instance, you may feel as though you could never have the organisational skills to set up your own company. Others are essential to all actors: good photographs, for example. Whatever your needs, time taken to formulate clearly your requirements before approaching any of the contacts listed below will be time well spent.

Equity

Equity is the only Trade Union to represent performers and people working creatively across the entire spectrum of arts and entertainment, both live and recorded. The main function of Equity is to negotiate minimum terms and conditions of employment throughout the whole world of entertainment, and to endeavour to ensure that these take account of social and economic changes. We look to the future as well, negotiating agreements to embrace the new and emerging technologies which affect performers – so satellite, digital television, new media and so on are all covered, as are the more traditional areas. We also work at national level by lobbying government and other bodies on issues of paramount importance to the membership. In addition we operate at an international level through the Federation of International Artists which Equity helped to establish, the International Committee for Artistic Freedom, and through agreements with sister unions overseas.

As well as these core activities, Equity strives to provide a wide range of services for members so that they are eligible for a whole host of benefits which are continually being revised and developed. These include helplines, job information, insurance cover, members' pension scheme, charities and others. (For more information, visit the Equity website **www.equity.org.uk**. For details of Equity's Job Information Service, see entry under Spotlight, casting directories and information services.)

Equity

Head Office, Guild House, Upper St Martins Lane, London WC2H 9EG
tel 020-7379 6000 *fax* 020-7379 7001
email info@equity.org.uk
website www.equity.org.uk

See www.equity.org.uk/contact-us/equity-helpdesks for specific helpdesk telephone numbers.

Regional offices:

Midlands
Office 1, Steeple House, Percy Street, Coventry CV1 3BY
tel (02476) 553612
email midlands@equity.org.uk

North East
The Workstation, 15 Paternoster Row, Sheffield S1 2BX
tel 0114-275 9746
email northeastengland@equity.org.uk

North West and Isle of Man
Express Networks, 1 George Leigh Street, Manchester M4 5DL
tel 0161-244 5995 *fax* 0161-244 5971
email northwestengland@equity.org.uk

Scotland and Northern Ireland
114 Union Street, Glasgow G1 3QQ
tel 0141-248 2472 *fax* 0141-248 2473
email scotland@equity.org.uk
email northernireland@equity.org.uk

South East
Guild House, Upper St Martins Lane, London WC2H 9EG
tel 020-7670 0229 *fax* 020-7379 7001
email southeastengland@equity.org.uk

Wales and South West England
Transport House, 1 Cathedral Road, Cardiff CF1 9SD
tel 029-2039 7971 *fax* 029-2023 0754
email wales@equity.org.uk
email southwestengland@equity.org.uk

Spotlight, casting directories and information services

Spotlight is a fundamental part of the fabric of the acting profession and it is essential to have an entry. (It is a false economy not to have one.) The growth of the Internet has seen a rise in companies offering similar services – usually for a lower subscription. Once again it is important to research thoroughly the value to you of investing in one of these. As well as trying to assess whether such an investment will really enhance your visibility to employers, an essential part of that research is to read the 'small print' properly.

With some exceptions (major musicals, for instance), many employers do not openly advertise the properly paid acting work they have to offer. It's simpler to contact agents whom they know and trust for casting suggestions. This limits the number of submissions, largely prevents time-wasting via unsuitable applicants, and goes some way towards ensuring that those suggested for consideration are really suitable for the parts available. Consequently, the time required to consider all the CVs and photographs submitted is contained within reasonable limits. It can take a day's work to go through a thousand submissions to select whom to interview; it can take another day's work to interview just 30 of these.

Casting information services – often allied to Internet casting directories – glean their information from all kinds of sources. The important thing to remember is that some of the information about 'properly paid acting work' is of a second-hand nature – that is, it was not sent directly to them in the first instance. Consequently, it is important to research reputations for accuracy (and 'up-to-dateness') before committing your funds to such companies. However, many Fringe production and student film opportunities are directly advertised in such publications and such opportunities might lead on to 'properly paid acting work'.

Actors Centre

1A Tower Street, London WC2H 9NP
email reception@actorscentre.co.uk
website www.actorscentre.co.uk
Head of Creative Programming Michael John

Details of casting information services: The Actors Centre offers a Central London venue, in partnership with the Tristan Bates Theatre, and provides an opportunity to network with other actors and industry professionals. It has established contacts within the industry and offers professional development courses including workshops and masterclasses. It also offers a range of 'Get Into' courses for non-members interested in acting for stage, screen, TV presenting and the drama school audition circuit. For more details on membership, see the website.

ArtsJobs

website www.artsjobs.org.uk

Freely advertises a range of opportunities within the arts sector, including positions that require specialist knowledge and skills, and unskilled positions at arts organisations.

Castcall

106 Wilsden Avenue, Luton LU1 5HR
tel (01582) 456213
email info@castcall.co.uk
website www.castcall.co.uk

Details of casting information services: Established in 1986. The service is available by email, to professional actors with regular updates throughout the week. Charges from £10 per month. Actors can put subscriptions on hold if required and to resume when appropriate. Also offers general advice and free image scanning.

Sources of casting breakdowns include: Crocodile Casting, Mark Summers, Pippa Ailion, Heather March, Hannah Birkett, Sharon Lawrence, Tree Petts, Nicci Topping, Beverley Keogh, Debbie O'Brien, David Graham, Louise Kiely, Belinda King, Natasha

Gane and many production companies in theatre, video, film and TV.

Casting Call Pro

131-132 Upper Street London N1 1QP
tel 020-7288 7404
email info@castingcallpro.com
website www.castingcallpro.com/uk

Details of casting information services: Established in 2004, CCP is one of the UK's leading casting directories, designed with the actor in mind. Featuring over 40,000 professional members, the site is updated daily with a wide range of casting breakdowns including film roles, theatre tours, corporate work, and commercials. CCP also provides a wealth of resources for actors, including a directory of photographers, agents and employers, and a lively forum. All members have an entirely free profile in the online directory, which is used by thousands of employers. Additionally CCP offers a Premium Service with a wider range of features. To discover more about the benefits of using Casting Call Pro as well as current subscription rates and latest updates to the service, please visit the website at **www.castingcallpro.com/uk**

Casting Networks

website www.castingnetworks.co.uk

Details of casting information services: Casting Networks is one of the biggest casting websites in the USA, but has only recently opened up in the UK. Like others, it offers casting professionals a means to distribute breakdowns and receive submissions, but Casting Networks also provides a very different suite of tools for streamlining, simplifying and facilitating the subsequent casting process: straightforward actor check-in; integration of audition video-recording into online casting tools; software for handling the scheduling and arranging of auditions – these are just a few examples.

Casting Networks is a commitment-free site, where actors have the choice to pay if and when they find value in the services on offer – this equates to no mandatory yearly upfront payment. If and when you choose to pay, payments are made monthly and operate as various ad-ons. The Media Hosting ad-on, for example, allows you to add, delete and update your videos as much as you wish. Anything you upload can also be attached to your CV, meaning you or your agent can tailor your CV for a job in just a few clicks.

"Casting Networks continuously improves the casting process through the application of innovative solutions, cutting-edge technologies, and superior customer support, making a career in the entertainment and advertising industries more efficient, accessible, and fun for everyone involved."

CastNet Ltd

tel 0333 800 0250 (local rate)
email admin@castnet.co.uk
website www.castnet.co.uk
Key contact Fran Gillett

Details of casting information services: Established in 1997. The information service is only available online, with casting information circulated to members by email and uploaded to the website throughout the day. Casting information is tailored to the exact requirements of the actor; if an actor is not interested in working in certain areas, such as student films or TIE, they will not be sent details of those projects. Information is also filtered according to the skills and physical characteristics of actors. When suitable casting opportunities do arise, CastNet will send actors free text messages and emails. Actors may make a submission for any project via the website; CastNet will then send their CV, headshot and a covering letter to the casting director.

All reproductions of photos and postage costs are included in the subscription charge. Sends a weekly summary report by email, detailing every production for which actors have been submitted. CastNet receives casting breakdowns from a range of clients including Fringe theatre, mainstream films and TV.

Details of actors' Internet directories: All actors must meet the following criteria to be included: have graduated from an NCDT (now Drama UK) accredited course; have a minimum of 3 professional theatre, film or acting credits (does not include extra or drama school work); be able to use 1 UK-based accent to a 'native' standard; have full membership of Equity (or be eligible); have a professionally taken publicity photograph; and be at least 18 years old at the time of application.

Admits new members daily. CastNet has more than 4,000 casting professionals registered on the site, and supports the casting of around 2,500 productions each year. Actors' CVs are included on the website, with instant messaging facility for casting directors to contact them by email or text message. Will also include photos, showreels and voicereels at no extra charge. All members receive a free personal website which they can tailor to their own needs and preferences, from a wide range of designs and styles. Anyone can access the online directory. Members' online details are updated daily. For details of current clients (both actors and casting professionals), consult the website.

The weekly subscription rate varies depending on the pricing plan selected and includes all the services listed above.

See also the entry for CastNet Websites under *Showreel, voicereel and website services* on page 417.

Castweb

7 St Luke's Avenue, London SW4 7LG
tel 020-7720 9002
email info@castweb.co.uk
website www.castweb.co.uk
Key contact Patrick Warrington

Details of casting information services: Established in 1999. A daily information service is available online, with casting breakdowns circulated to subscribers throughout the day. Subscription starts at £19.95 per month. Castweb has circulated casting opportunities for over 3,000 production companies and casting directors and subscription is strictly for the use of professional actors and established agents only. It is now received by more than 1,000 agents across Europe, as well as over 400 in the UK. At just 44p per day, it remains the essential source of casting opportunities for professional performers and agents in the UK.

Dramanic

website www.dramanic.com

Dramanic, developed in 2009, is an online resource for professional actors only, helping them find work opportunities at theatre companies in London and other major towns and cities throughout the UK. "Anyone new to the business will find that keeping tabs on different theatre companies is challenging and time-consuming, and marrying that with your normal lives leaves you no time to effectively find acting work. Dramanic takes all the hassle out of that by alerting you when opportunities arise at the hundreds of theatre companies in our system. We cover a huge variety of theatre companies, big and small, touring and non-touring, and arts council – or otherwise – funded companies. The good news for actors is that such companies would usually pay Equity/ITC minimum wages."

Other features include:

- Casting calendar – know what theatre companies are casting well in advance
- Theatre company research profiles, giving you up-to-date information about company personnel and actor-relevant news
- Contact details of UK actor agents, personal managers and casting directors updated throughout the year
- Swap plays/books with other dramanic.com users
- Look for casual employment in between acting jobs

Equity Job Information Service (JIS)

Guild House, Upper St Martin's Lane,
London WC2H 9EG
website www.equity.org.uk

Details of casting information services: It is available free of charge to all full Equity members. The service provides details of job opportunities in the wide range of fields in which Equity members work. Users of the service can search for jobs in acting, singing, dance, variety, light entertainment and circus and in non-performance work such as stage management. All the work listed is at least reasonably paid (although not necessarily at full Equity-agreed rates), thoroughly checked for accuracy and the job-providers checked for their record of fair treatment of employees.

Internet Movie Database (IMDb)

website www.imdb.com

This is not just a comprehensive database of film and television around the world, but also an opportunity for actors to post their photos and CVs ('resumés') for a fee (currently, $15.95 per month) if they have a profile of work listed there. Once you've subscribed, you also have access to a huge international contact database of people and companies, and the facility to track film and television projects from development to post-production.

Mandy.com

website www.mandy.com

Posts casting calls for actors for film. See entry under *Publications, libraries, references and booksellers* on page 464.

The Page UK

website www.thepageuk.com

The Page UK is a new directory, which aims to be "the most advanced casting service in the UK". Actors can add media and information direct to each role included in their CVs, painting a far clearer picture of their suitability for a particular role. You must meet one of the following requirements to become a member:

- Be represented by a talent agency/agent
- Be a current member of Equity
- Have trained at a Drama UK accredited drama school

Shooting People

email contact@shootingpeople.org
website www.shootingpeople.org
Co-founders Cath LeCouteur, Jess Search *Casting Editor* Andrew Robertson

Shooting People allows thousands of people working in independent film to exchange information via a range of daily email bulletins, including a daily UK Casting Bulletin. This allows actors to discuss their craft and receive casting calls from directors, producers and casting directors. Shooting People's overall membership is currently more than 38,000. Actors can create a public casting profile as well as getting significant discounts off key film products and services.

Full membership costs £35 per year and entitles users to a range of other services. See entry under *Publications, libraries, references and booksellers* on page 466 for further details.

Spotlight

Head Office, 7 Leicester Place, London WC2H 7RJ
tel 020-7437 7631 *fax* 020-7437 5881
email info@spotlight.com
website www.spotlight.com

Spotlight was founded in 1927 and has since become world-famous for its casting directories. Today more than 30,000 performers appear in the book and Internet versions of Spotlight, including actors and actresses, child artists, presenters, dancers and stunt artists. As the industry's leading casting resource, Spotlight is used by TV, film, radio and theatrical companies throughout the UK, and many worldwide. Its Internet casting services have become an essential communication tool, uniting actors, agents and production professionals more quickly and easily than ever before.

Membership of Spotlight means that a performer is promoted to casting opportunities in a number of ways. Firstly, each artist has a photo and contact details in the Spotlight Directories, which are printed once per year. Their details are also held on an Artists' Records telephone database, so that casting/production professionals know immediately where to call when they want to get in touch.

Additionally, every performer is promoted on Spotlight Interactive (**www.spotlight.com**) – the online version of Spotlight. Here, casting professionals can search performers' details according to very specific criteria. For example: "Show me all actors with black hair, aged 35-40, who can speak French and play the guitar." In 2006, the Spotlight website received over 1 million artist searches, and actor CVs were viewed a total of 5,753,312 times.

Performers can upload showreels, voice-clips and additional photos to enhance their online CVs, which is a far quicker and more cost-effective way of promoting themselves than sending out endless copies to casting directors and agents in the post. Artists are also issued with a pair of unique PIN numbers which allow them to access their CV whenever they wish – keeping credits and skills up-to-date – and to email a link to their Spotlight CV to others.

Spotlight is also used on a daily basis by production professionals sending out casting briefs to agents. In 2006, a weekly average of 160 casting breakdowns was sent out via Spotlight link, with more than 33,370 artists submitted weekly for an average of 541 individual roles, spanning a wide variety of TV, film, theatre, radio and commercial work. This makes Spotlight by far the busiest casting service in the UK. Spotlight also offers a job information service which goes directly to artists themselves: see the website for the latest details.

Spotlight also publishes *Contacts* every November. This is a directory of companies and individuals working across TV, film, stage and radio.

To join Spotlight, visit the website **www.spotlight.com**, call 020-7437 7631, or email **info@spotlight.com** for application forms. Entry is strictly limited to professionally trained and/or professionally experienced performers, and applications are always vetted.

The Stage

47 Bermondsey Street, London SE1 3XT
tel 020-7403 1818
and (01858) 438895 (Subscriptions)
email newsdesk@thestage.co.uk
website www.thestage.co.uk
Managing Director Hugh Comerford *Acting Editor* Alistair Smith

Online and weekly print publication for the entertainment industry. Established in 1880. Advice, news, reviews, features and recruitment for theatre, entertainment, opera, dance, TV, radio, backstage and technical, management, education and training. *The Stage* is also available on iPad, Android, Kindle and other tablet devices. *The Stage* Castings, the company's online casting service (**www.thestage.co.uk/castings**), offers access to hundreds of jobs for all kinds of performers.

Talent Circle

website www.talentcircle.org

Details of casting information services: Established in 2003. Provides a free online casting information service and resource where emails are circulated to members on a daily basis.

Details of actors' Internet directories: Directory is open to all actors free of charge and is publicly accessible. Casting directors can select level of experience required at sign-up, as no minimum criteria are demanded of members. Members can update their own entry (to include photograph, voice sample and CV) at any time.

To Be Seen

website www.tobeseen.co.uk

To Be Seen is an online community for the entertainment industry, with 2 membership options:

• Basic (free): a unique web page for your photos and showreel
• Premium (£5.99, £6.99 or £7.99 per month): the benefits of a Basic membership, plus the facility to apply for as many jobs as you like and be searchable in the directory

There are no set-up fees or extra hidden charges; you can stay a member as long as you like, upgrading or downgrading your account at any time.

'Point me in the right direction': navigating the casting services

Isabelle Farah

The hardest battle for an actor has always been, and will always be, "Where do I find my next job?" The growth of the Internet has meant that it is now much easier to find out what's being cast where, when, how and by whom. However, with a multitude of sites offering casting services, it's hard to determine which ones will work best for you.

The industry is ever-changing, and such sites will pop up and fade into insignificance with relative frequency – though some have proved their longevity. In March 2013, PCR, a long-time stalwart, and in my experience a source of good breakdowns, sadly folded.

Different services will, of course, suit different actors. Some gear themselves more towards certain media, while some cover all areas with varying degrees of success. I'm afraid there's simply no denying that Spotlight is the market leader, and has been so forever; others have made their mark, though, and clearly have reasonable success. I believe, though I hate to say it, that you cannot be an actor without Spotlight. It's expensive, yes, and it can feel like a lot of money with little (or no) payback, particularly if you don't have an agent. Bear in mind that in the US there is no single market leader, so that actors are required to pay for several similar services – therefore while the situation here in the UK is not ideal, it's definitely not the worst. My own experience as a member of a co-operative agency corroborates this.

I think it's important to remember that acting is your profession – the craft by which you want to make your living. While I accept that I may have to make money doing something else in between acting jobs, and am not going to be employed by Stephen Spielberg straight after graduating from drama school, if I am paying for a casting service, I should expect to get paid work from it.

Many of the services listed below have other features included in the cost, but I have looked solely at their capacity as a casting resource.

Actors Centre

Cost: Actors Membership: £50/6 months and £75/year Associate Membership: £40/year

The Actors Centre offers a Central London venue, in partnership with the Tristan Bates Theatre, where you can network with other actors and industry professionals. It has established contacts within the industry and offers professional development courses including workshops and masterclasses. It also offers 'getting into acting' workshops for non-members.

Casting Call Pro

Cost: £17/month or £130/year (+VAT) if you want access to paid jobs

CCP is like Marmite: some actors I know swear by it, while others think it's a waste of time. I sit somewhere between the two. There are some good, paid jobs and plenty of (sometimes questionable) unpaid opportunities, including interesting small-scale tours, commercial work, short films and voiceovers. The jobs here are not going to make you a household name, but you can make money from lower-profile ones and build your CV without an agent using CCP. There are also some options for free upgrade by working in their offices, or building their database of plays and companies remotely. They recently developed a mobile site, which is functional, and has certainly made applying on-the-go a little easier. With paid membership you can upload up to 20 headshots and 20 voice/showreels at no extra cost.

Casting Networks

Cost: £10 registration and £10/month with photos and multimedia

Casting Networks is a recent import from across the pond. Its functions are actor-friendly and it does have a mobile site. There are some translation issues – it would be helpful if measurements and sizes could be given in British rather than American formats. But the site works. Breakdowns do come through here from certain casting directors – most often for commercials and short films – but generally not exclusively to Casting Networks, and I have found most duplicated on the other big sites. The plus side of this site for the unrepresented actor is that such breakdowns, as far as I can tell, go to all actors rather than through a filtering system as exists on Spotlight. There is some hype surrounding Casting Networks, and I wonder whether the rumours are true about casting directors being given iPads in return for promotion.

CastWeb

Cost: £19.95/month or £159.95/year (inc. VAT)

CastWeb works in the form of emails, rather than a website and boards. There is no filtering system, so you may get several messages in a day, which may or may not be relevant. A small advantage is that the emails often include the Casting Director's contact details: I have found this useful in building my own records. The work they have is mainly commercial, with occasional fringe/touring theatre work, and stills photography shoots.

CastNet

Cost: £6.50/week

There's a variety of work here, but, like many of these services, the good stuff tends to be duplicated elsewhere. You'll find a large proportion of low-paid and unpaid parts in short films and music videos, some of them only listed here. You can stop or suspend your subscription, but this is by far the most expensive of the services reviewed.

Dramanic

Cost: £11.99/month or £99.99/year

Most of the work here is in theatre, including some regional touring with small but well-known companies on top of the mainstream West End/Off-West End stuff. Rather than advertising jobs as and when casting directors list them, Dramanic gives you as many details as they have about upcoming theatre projects, as well as the contact details of the Casting Director pretty soon after a project has been announced. Ideal, I suppose for a cash-rich, time-poor actor! Most jobs listed appear to pay Equity/ITC rates, and all bring some payment. Dramanic takes out a lot of the research hassle involved in writing letters – but as a letter will almost always be needed, this is no quick-fix solution to getting a job.

Mandy

Cost: £24.00 + VAT/year to sign up for weekly email alerts

This site is no piece of art, but it's easy enough to navigate. Mandy is predominantly known as a resource for finding film and TV production staff, and the acting casting calls are also mainly in TV and film – though I have seen some theatre jobs listed for little pay. You can pay to receive alerts or look at the 'casting' section of the website for free.

Shooting People

Cost: £10.95/month, £39.95/year (£24.95/year for students)

Shooting People is by far the most user-friendly of the services listed in this article, with a helpfully put-together website and social network-esque tagging features. I have seen an increase in the amount of traffic here, though most of it is still low/no pay/student films. These tend to only be listed here, and the yearly subscription rate is good value.

Spotlight

Cost: £186/year

Spotlight is where the breakdowns are. I don't think any other service gets as many from as wide a pool of good casting directors through their sites, let alone exclusive to their sites. The website does need updating. It's not awful by any means, but it's not mobile friendly, making it difficult to use for those without agents and/or working from a smartphone. Many features (search functions on the Link board, etc.) are not available to actors. With some pushing, Spotlight will change things that need to be changed. They recently made it free for actors to upload show- and voicereels to their pages, which is excellent news. If you want to be in something, it's probably cast here, and your chance of making your money back is far higher here than anywhere else.

Talent Circle

Cost: Free

You receive a daily bulletin email with casting calls and other industry jobs, and boards for both on the website. There aren't many breakdowns coming through here, and very few of these jobs seem to be paid at all.

The Page UK

Cost: Currently free, but will be moving to a pay model once the casting section of the website has launched

A pretty website which is easy to use, with uploads included in the (already cheap) cost. The Page UK is advertised as a marketing resource rather than a casting service, so not many breakdowns come through here, few of them are paid, and most of them were duplicated on other websites.

To Be Seen

Cost: £5.99, £6.99 or £7.99/month

There is work here, and things I did not see in other places. However, not much of it was paid, and, as people with no experience can also register for a profile, there are adverts for extras and talent shows, etc. amidst the acting breakdowns.

With a cost totalling over £1,200/year, not including registration or joining fees, it would be impossible for many actors to subscribe to all of these services. From a business perspective, the best way to decide which service to use would probably be to check how much money month-on-month you make back from each one. However, I'm not sure an artist's success can be measured by money alone, and it may be easier to work out over time which ones get you the most auditions. As with most aspects of your career, you will probably need to adapt or change tactics quite often – if a site is not working for you, then try something else for a while.

Isabelle Farah trained at Drama Studio London, graduating in 2011. She is has since worked in theatre, film, and radio (and a call centre). For updates about her career or what she ate for breakfast, you can find her on twitter @is_ab_el_le.

Marketing and the Internet: maintaining your online presence

Nancy Bishop

Where do you go when you want find something? To the Internet. Casting directors do the same. Today, casting happens quickly and initially online: casting directors post their breakdowns on search engines, such as Spotlight, and agents submit actor suggestions electronically. As a casting director, I receive hundreds of submissions in the first hour after a breakdown is posted. Only moments after an actor auditions, I pop the clip on a site that shares it with production. Any actor in these times must have an Internet presence 24/7, so that casters anywhere anytime have the information to cast you.

If I can immediately access an actor's showreel online, during a brain-storming session with a director, he's that much closer to the job. When the director can see your work at the click of a button, he's more likely to short-list you for a role. Yes, it is your agent's job to market you, but by getting your own materials online you're giving them the tools they need to help you book the job.

I suggest a three-pronged strategy to boost your Internet presence:

1) Register on the major quality casting sites, and search engines.
2) Construct and maintain a website that uniquely markets you.
3) Be Google-able and YouTube-able.

1. Casting sites and search engines

The most ubiquitous entertainment website is the Internet Movie Data Base (**www.imdb.com**). Serious actors exploit all of the possibilities that it offers. Once you have professional film or TV credits, join its professional sister site, IMDb Pro, which allows you to insert contact details so that professionals can find you, and you can find them.

Keeping your material updated on IMDB is also essential; you can do it yourself. Although it costs, posting your headshot on IMDB is a solid investment. A director may see an actor in a film, but not know the name of the role he played. With your photo posted, there's no doubt.

In the UK, Spotlight membership is essential, as it is the first and last website that many casting directors use. My pet peeve, when using Spotlight, is when actors don't include a showreel. By all means, use all of the options available to you: CV, reel, photo gallery, voice clips. If I don't know your work, I will most definitely want to see tape on you.

Suggested websites:

Spotlight (www.spotlight.com)
Casting Call Pro (www.castingcallpro.com)
Cast Web (www.castweb.co.uk)
Shooting People (www.shootingpeople.org)

2. A website

A website, properly designed, is a worthwhile investment. The actor search engines are necessary, but not enough; there are directors who are looking outside the box. A website enables you to uniquely brand and market yourself because you can control the content and presentation. Make sure that your pages are designed to strategically market you as a professional actor, not as a vanity site. The central questions in a marketing campaign are:

1. What do you do?
2. Who are your customers?
3. Why do they buy from you?

Let these marketing questions guide the content of your website.

What do you do? You're a professional actor. Don't confuse your viewers with too many images or superfluous interests. If you are expert in something that enhances your acting, such as singing, horse-back riding, or dance, then devote some space to it. But make sure it's not too prominent or it will look like you're a singer who acts, rather than an actor who sings.

Who are your customers? They are casting directors, producers, directors. Figure out what information they would need to cast you. Ensure your site's usability for all customers by testing it on different systems and browsers like Mac and PC, Firefox and Outlook.

Why should they buy from you? This is a good question. Why should they cast you? What are you selling? Since YOU are the product, identify your image and the range of roles that you play. Through your own personal style you will reflect, on the site, what you have to offer, how you look, what your experience is, how you've trained. "All things spring from the client's identity," claims web designer Deborah Dewitt, "which incorporates logo, fonts, colours, graphics, photos and layout – all of these combine to visually represent their offering, personality and communication style." An effective actor's website will include the following:

Home page

The home page features the actor's one main headshot. Don't muddle it with multiple images; they're for the gallery. Change the content on your home page often; announce news, like a new show, or snippets of good reviews on the front page. Not only will this keep us up to date but it will make your site easier for search engines to find.

Menu items

CV – hone down your résumé to the most impressive selected credits, rather than bombarding your viewers with everything you've done since secondary school. Provide a downloadable PDF version with contact info, so casting directors can print it.

Biography (optional) – this is a short prose section that includes where you were born and how you've got to where you are. It is a way to emphasise your background, and what makes you unique. If you witnessed 9/11, or lived in the wilds of Borneo, for example, that could inform your experience for a given role.

Gallery – here's a chance to show the range of roles you can play and to offer additional information. Make sure the images are truly representative of you and what you look like now. Supplement your headshot with a wider shot, so we can see your wonderfully round, or modestly slim, frame. If your main headshot is quite serious, consider including a comedic photo. A variety of production stills are helpful but be selective about what images you choose: web expert Ellen Treanor Strasman notes that "The average visit time per page is less than one minute, so people won't look at that many photos. The rule of lists is that people will look at the first three and the last one." So put the strongest photos in these positions.

Showreel – don't miss this part. There is no substitute for the moving picture. Some actors separate their work by project, showing a few clips from each. Others divide their clips by type – for example, comedy, drama, action – and make mini-reels. Ordinary showreels with a variety of clips should be no longer than 2-3 minutes. Start the reel and each clip with your image so we know exactly who we should be watching. If you have clips in different languages, separate them.
Other sections that you might include are:
Voice-over – if you do voice work, and have a voicereel, include it.
Blog – this is an opportunity to express, in journal form, your own notes on projects or work. Keep it professional. Political blogging or personal information can go on a separate site. If you use Facebook, keep two separate accounts; one for business and one for personal.
Links – link your page to a professional search engine, your agency or a project you're working on, and ask them to link back to you. The more links there are to your site, the more traffic you'll get, which will push your site further up in the search engines.

3. Be Google-able and YouTube-able

If you are not already famous, no one will know to Google your name. So how will casting directors find you? If you're shopping on the Internet for roses in Prague, what do you Google? "Roses, Prague." If I'm looking for an actor who can juggle, what will I type in? "Actor, juggler."

Google needs text and key words in order to index and find your site. Think about your specific skills and what makes you unique. Use these as keys words that link to other pages on your webpage. Keep the important keywords towards the top of the page; this will help casters find you. If you have a special marketing point, you can even name your website accordingly – for example, www.kenchu.karateactor.com or www.kiwi-actor-in-london.com.

Name your video clips specifically as well, such as "Ken Chu, Karate fight" and load it onto YouTube. I love it when I can type an actor's name into YouTube and immediately a showreel or clip surfaces. I can then paste the link into an email and send it as a suggestion to a director.

The Internet has changed the way casting happens. It allows casting directors to sweep the far corners of the earth for talent at the click of a button. I recently cast a film with actors from four different countries, and never left my office to do it. The director was in South Africa, and interviewed actors on Skype, as the budget didn't allow him to meet them in person. Maintain an online presence and be ready to put your audition on tape and upload it for us to view. Don't be a technophobe and throw away the many wonderful possibilities that the Internet offers.

Nancy Bishop is a Casting Society (CSA) casting director, who casts from her base in Prague. She is also the chair of the Prague Film School Acting Department, and the author of Methuen Drama's *Secrets from the Casting Couch*. For more information see **www.nancybishopcasting.com**

Photographers and repro companies

Good photographs (and quality reproductions of same) are an essential part of an actor's professional armoury and there is absolutely no point in trying to scrimp on them. ('A picture is worth a thousand words.')

Your photograph is a silent, static, two-dimensional representation of vocal, mobile, three-dimensional you. It should be of your head down to your shoulders, reasonably stylish and well produced without necessarily being too glamorous. It should look natural and have life, energy and personality – especially in the eyes, the most important part of your face. Your photo should say, 'Here I am; I know who I am; I'm OK with who I am.' Also, it is very important that your photograph really looks like you when you arrive for interview.

Crucial to the final result is finding a good photographer (a) who understands the world that the end result is intended for and (b) with whom you can work well. In the listings that follow, you'll find a wide range of prices and deals. It is important to research as many of these as possible, without making cost your prime consideration. Ask friends, teachers and your agent (if you have one) for recommendations, and check through *Spotlight* and websites to see samples of work. Read the details under each listing to get a 'feel' for who might produce the 'goods' for you. Once you have a shortlist of possibilities, phone each with appropriate questions (what to wear, studio or natural light, and so forth) in order to get a sense of how well you might be able to work with him/her. Only *after* you've done all this research should cost be a consideration. Even then, a cheap deal could mean that the photographer will spend much less time, and take fewer photographs, than a more expensive one. You might be lucky with the former, but you'll enhance your chances of getting really good results with the latter.

Note: Allow plenty of time for this research. Also, bear in mind that as the deadline for *Spotlight* gets nearer, photographers become increasingly busy and it becomes more difficult to book a session.

Copyright

Under the Copyright, Designs & Patents Act 1988, the photographer owns the copyright on any new photograph, even though you've already paid for the original. That means that you have to obtain his/her permission to have new photographs reproduced in *Spotlight* or anywhere else. Your photographer may be happy to approve such reproduction, but may not be so happy about any cropping or other alterations: you must get permission if you intend to do this. The other important new legal requirement is that your photographer must be credited on any reproduction of the original. Some of the repro companies are now doing this as a matter of course.

Repros

You could get subsequent, high-quality reproductions done by your photographer or by someone else nominated by him/her. However, these will be expensive. The specialist repro companies can do this significantly more cheaply with minimal loss of quality. Once again, check with others about the quality (and service and reliability) of individual companies before taking costs into consideration. It is also useful to overestimate the number of copies you might need over the lifetime (generally, about two years) of your chosen photograph – because (a) you'll almost always find that you underestimate that number in the first place, and (b) you can take advantage of cheaper unit costs.

Note: It is often preferable to send a 10x8in (25x20cm) photograph for submissions; however, good-quality 'jpegs' (around 400 pixels wide) inserted into your CV are becoming increasingly acceptable. If you're planning to email a CV containing your photograph, make sure that the total document size is not more than about 200kb, or you'll end up clogging up the casting director's mailbox. (Most image-editing software will have a menu option to allow you to reduce the image size if required.)

It is important to check the current charges of each photographer (and repro company) that interests you, as some will change during the lifetime of this edition.

Abacus Photography

38 Drakes Avenue, Devizes, Wilts SN10 5AZ
tel (01380) 829943 *mobile* (07966) 551909
email nick@abacus-photography.co.uk
website www.abacus-photography.co.uk

Services & rates: Prices start from £75 in a fully equipped studio. Images supplied on disc so you can make your own prints economically, or email them to casting agents. Discounts available for group bookings.

Established in 1992.

Vincent Abbey

6 Lynton Road, Chorlton, Manchester M21 9NQ
tel 0161-860 6794
email vabbey@yahoo.com
website www.vincentabbey.co.uk

Services & rates: Established in 1995. Charges £90 for a photoshoot, which includes approximately 100 shots and 3 touched up images on CD. Additional images are £8 each. Shoots take place at home studio. Has taken publicity photos for over 2,000 actors.

The Actor's One-Stop Shop

2b Dale View Crescent, Chingford, London E4 6PQ
tel 020-8888 7006 and (07894) 152 651
email info@actorsonestopshop.com
website www.actorsone-stopshop.com

Services & rates: Market leaders in showreels both edited from existing material and filmed. Edited from existing material have a flat rate of £140 or £40 per hour when reels are updated. Filmed scenes can be made from just £110 a scene and includes scripts, location, direction and the hire of professional actors opposite. There are a variety of different packages available.

Stuart Allen

mobile (07776) 258829
email info@stuartallenphotos.com
website www.stuartallenphotos.com

Services & rates: Charges £150 for a digital photo shoot which includes 360-500+ images, your own website for proof viewing the whole shoot with email links to you and your agent, contact sheets emailed to you as Adobe PDF files, updated contact sheets emailed to you as you narrow down your selection, cost of retouching 4 images, photos prepared for Spotlight, Casting Call Pro and CastNet, images emailed to Spotlight, Casting Call Pro and CastNet (if applicable). Shoot taken in natural light and typically lasts 2-3+ hours. All the images can be in b&w and/or colour. "The photos are captured in uncompressed high resolution 'raw' format so as to give you the best possible quality and maximum control over the final image. This is the digital equivalent of a negative. It is superior to the other smaller and lower quality digital formats."

Film shoots also available at £130 for 2 36exp films and contact sheets. Competitive print service available. Offers full advice on clothing, makeup and hair.

Areas that are covered in the UK for headshots are London, Bath, Bristol, Brighton, Cardiff, Cheltenham, Guilford, Oxford, Warwick and Winchester. If you do not live near one of these cities please check on availability.

Work portfolio: Stuart studied photography at Salisbury College of Art and Design. Since then he has worked in numerous spheres of the entertainment industry, shooting headshots of actors for almost a decade. His work can be seen on his website, Casting Call Pro website and *Contacts*. Please check website for latest prices.

AM-London Photography

2 The People's Hall, 2 Olaf Street, London W11 4BE
mobile (07974) 188105
email studio@am-london.com
website www.am-london.com

Services & rates: Offers 3 types of headshot session; please see details below:

• 1.5-hr Actors Headshot Session at £340 inc. VAT. The package includes: 1.5-hour shoot – in the studio and a range of natural light (outdoor) shots. Variety of headshot styles. Full-length/character/commercial

shots (optional). 200+ edited images supplied colour and black & white in high res. 6 retouched 10x8in prints
• 1-hour Actors Headshot Session at £270 inc. VAT. The package includes: 1-hour shoot – studio shots and natural light (outdoor) shots. Variety of headshots. 150+ edited headshots supplied colour and black & white in high res. 4 retouched 10x8in prints
• 40-min Actors Headshot Session at £200 inc. VAT. The package includes: 40-min shoot – studio only. Variety of headshots. 100+ edited headshots supplied in colour and black & white in high res. 2 retouched 10x8in prints

"With all sessions we make sure that you get lots of variety. This means using different lighting set-ups, different backdrops and a number of outfit changes. Each individual set-up will be described and discussed with you in detail. This process allows for you to develop natural reactions and expressions to the different set-ups, altering the mood and intensity as we move through them. The longer session allows time for some additional shots that you may need, e.g. full-length or more commercial shots. After the session we send you a link to download all your high res. images in colour and black & white. These are yours to keep. You then get back to us with your selection. These are retouched and printed 10x8in and sent out to you along with your retouched digital files."

Matt Anker

London
mobile (07835) 241835
email matt@mattanker.com
website www.mattanker.com

Services & rates: Charges £300 inc. VAT for a photo shoot. Takes 300-350 shots and will provide a complete set in colour and black and white on disc. Discounted rate for students is £240 inc. VAT. All photography is digital. Simple re-touching of final choice of shots included. The shoot takes place at a home studio and on location. Has taken publicity shots for around 100+ actors.

Simon Annand

mobile (07884) 446776
email simonannand@blueyonder.co.uk
website www.simonannand.com
established 1986

Services and rates: Charges £350 for a photo shoot, which includes approximately 350-400 shots. Concessionary rate of £310 available for students and the unemployed. The whole session on disc is taken away on the day; after the actor chooses 6 images, Simon will make a second disc with these choices fully photoshopped in colour/b&w. High-end digital cameras are used. Photos are usually taken at home studio with natural light, but can be taken outside if preferred – will travel if necessary. Home studio is wheelchair-accessible.

Work portfolio: With 30 years' experience, has taken publicity shots for around 2,500 actors. Clients include: Eddie Redmayne, Claire Foy, Benedict Cumberbatch, Tamla Kari, Dan Stevens, Jane Asher, Vicky McClure and Clemency Burton-Hill. Advises actors: "There is no time-limit for the session; I see one person a day. Please bring 6-8 different tops and previous photos to discuss." Author of *The Half*; has worked for the NT, RSC and Royal Court amongst many others.

Ric Bacon

30 Fortis Green Road, Muswell Hill,
London N10 3HN
mobile (07970) 970799
website www.ricbacon.co.uk

Services & rates: Charges £280 for a photo shoot which includes photographer's fee, processing of 2 b&w 36exps, 6x4in print of every shot (rather than a contact sheet) and all negatives. Offers reduced rates to students. Shoots in a very relaxed manner, in natural light or studio and offers advice on all aspects including clothing and make-up. Prints are ready to view in 1 hour and will be reviewed with the client, offering advice on selection of images for self-promotion if needed. Happy to look at old photographs of the client that they particularly like or dislike. Works with film or digital.

Work portfolio: Established in 1999. Photographs can be viewed on the website and has a comprehensive portfolio at Spotlight's offices. Has taken publicity shots for around 500 actors.

david bailie photography

tel 0207-460 1105
email davidbailie@davidbailie.co.uk
website http://davidbailie.photium.com

Services & rates: Photographer since 2007. Charges £180 (inc. VAT). Quote ACTORS HANDBOOK for 20% discount. Special discount for students. 2-hour shoot consisting of approx. 120 shots with all contacts saved to disc. Each shoot also includes 4 8x10in or A4 prints, with additional ones available at £15 each. Offers this package at a special rate of £145 (inc. VAT) to actors and £95 (inc. VAT) to students. Uses studio in Kensington and outdoor location for shoots. Only the outdoor location is wheelchair accessible.

Work portfolio: Examples of work can be seen on the website. Has taken photographs for many actors, among them Kevin McNally, Nick Bartlett, Mackenzie Crook, Chris Adamson, Dermot Kelly, Katrina Vasiliev and Patricia Merrick. See also YouTube channel www.youtube.com/user/mdebailes/feed?activity_view=3 - search for mdebailes.

Sophie Baker

tel 020-8340 3850
email sophiebaker@totalise.co.uk

Services & rates: A photographer since 1972 initially

working in theatre front-of-house – National Theatre, Royal Shakespeare Theatre and many West End shows; no relation to Chris. Rate is £160 for unlimited digital shots and 4 10x8in printed enlargements. Student rates are £100 for solo sitting and £150 for a shared sitting. Photographs taken in natural light in studio overlooking Hampstead Heath and outside in the park.

Work portfolio: "As a former student at the Central School of Speech and Drama (after the 1st year I realised that 'acting' wasn't for me – I would be happier behind the camera) I am aware of the discomfort and tensions the sitter can feel so I attempt to empathise and look to make the subject feel as comfortable as possible. The sessions are therefore relaxed and tailored to create a calm atmosphere. I have seen many directors and casting agents looking through books of photographs and therefore aim for a 'bright-eyed and bushy-tailed look' but not to over-glamorise. It is important that a portrait photo attracts the eye of the director but it must be an honest reflection of the sitter. I suggest the client has a good night's sleep beforehand and comes with a mixture of tops and necklines. It is not easy to dictate what will work over the phone."

Taken photographs for as many as 14,000 actors, among them Judi Dench, Ian Holm, Nigel Hawthorne, Ben Whitrow, Hugh Bonneville, Jane Horrocks, Rachel Weisz and John Lynch. "As I have been working for over 35 years the list is long. Over a period of 25 years I was also a film stills photographer working with Ken Loach, Stephen Frears, Louis Malle, Denys Arcand, Atom Egoyan to name a few but now prefer working on my own and not at the dictate of crazy film scheduling hours."

Paul Barrass

Unit 6, Ellingfort Road, London E8 3PA
mobile (07973) 265931
email paul@paulbarrass.co.uk
website www.paulbarrass.co.uk

Services & rates: Session price is £120. Includes 4 10x8in prints. Special student rate of £100. All photography is digital. Photos can be taken either in the studio or outdoors. All locations have wheelchair access. Images are viewed during the photo session on a monitor. Has photographed in excess of 1,000 actors.

Pete Bartlett Photography

Notting Hill, London W11 1PJ
mobile (07971) 653994
email info@petebartlett.com
website www.petebartlett.com

Services & rates: Photographer since 2004. Charges £235 for photo shoot, which includes 150-200 digital photographs. Prints from each session are available through Blaze Image, please ask for details upon arrival. A student rate of £195 for a shoot is also available. Uses studio and outdoor location (although neither are wheelchair-accessible).

Work portfolio: Examples of work can be seen on the website. Has taken photographs for around 2,000 actors; recent clients include: Elliot Knight (*Sinbad*), Jeff and Matt Postlethwaite (*Peaky Blinders*), Matt Milne (*Downton Abbey*), Jo Brand (*Getting On*), Ian Hislop (*Have I Got News For You*) plus many of London's top agents such as Williams Bulldog and Middleweek Newton. "I give you 100% to get that killer set of headshots. Please check out my website, drop me an email and we can begin the process today."

Helen Bartlett Photography

Based in London
tel 0345-603 1373
email info@helenbartlett.co.uk
website www.helenbartlett.co.uk/headshots

Services & rates: "I specialise in black and white portraits that reflect who you are and show you at your very best. All pictures are taken on location – we will go for a walk outdoors, finding interesting backgrounds and the best natural light. I work hard to ensure that your portrait session is a fun and enjoyable experience. There is no presure to 'smile for the camera'; by chatting and enjoying ourselves, the smiles come naturally and, over the course of the shoot, we will capture a variety of different moods in your set of images. Headshot sessions start at £295 which includes the session, a web gallery of images to choose from and 3 high-resolution digital files for your own printing.

Richard Battye

Birmingham
mobile (07860) 824101
email info@riverstudio.co.uk
website www.richardbattye.com

Services & rates: Charges from £95 for a photoshoot, which includes 30-60 shots with the best 5 edited. 10x8in prints are charged at £9 each. Special packages are available, please call to discuss. Digital photography offered at commercial/advertising rates. Shoots take place at studio and elsewhere, most locations are wheelchair accessible.

Work portfolio: Established in 1990. Has taken publicity shots for around 180 actors. Recent clients include: Birmingham Theatre School, self-employed actors, Sharon Foster Productions and Birmingham Royal Ballet.

Jonathan Bean

mobile (07763) 814587
email mail@beanphoto.co.uk
website www.beanphoto.co.uk

Services & rates: Established 2004. Offers a digital service only and charges £75 for a photo shoot, which includes shoot, editing, online contact sheet and choice of selected hi-res files or 10x8in prints. Additional prints or files may be purchased.A discounted 10% rate is available to students. Shoots are either outdoors (on location) or indoors at client's home or chosen venue. Wheelchair-accessible rooms can also be hired (for £15).

Work portfolio: Examples of work can be seen on the website. Portfolio includes many actors, writers and muscians, among them Blake Morrison and John Hegley. "My aim is to make you comfortable and relaxed for natural-looking, great portrait photos that show you at your best."

A Beautiful Image Photography & Design (Debal Bagachi)

31 Church Walk, Brentford, Middlesex TW8 8DB
tel 020-8568 2122 *mobile* (07956) 861698
email debal@abeautifulimage.com
website www.abeautifulimage.com

Services & rates: Charges £150 for a photo shoot which includes photographer's fee, studio and equipment costs, processing of 2 b&w 36exps, contact sheets and 2 10x8in prints (either hand- or digitally printed). Occasionally offers 10% discount for clients sharing a shoot. Digital photography is also available at the same rate; images can be supplied on CD-ROM. Also able to provide website and print publicity. Advises actors to keep make-up simple for b&w photography and wear unfussy, unpatterned tops with simple necklines.

Work portfolio: Established in 1994. Photographs can be viewed on the website and at Spotlight's offices. Has taken publicity shots for around 50 actors. Recent clients include: Elizabeth Alexander, Patrick Regis, Fiona Marchant and Diane Cracknell.

Misha von Bennigsen Photography

Harberton Road, London N19 3JR
tel 020-7263 8862
email misha@mishaheadshots.com
website www.mishaheadshots.com

Established in 2009. Charges £180 for a photo shoot, which includes unlimited shots. Prints are charged from 77p each. Student price £120. Offers digital photography at the same rates. Photos are taken outdoors, at wheelchair-accessible locations. Has taken publicity shots for around 30 actors. Recent clients include: Abby Leamon, Polly Banwell, Michelle Miller, Howard Corlett, David Loughlin.

Georgina Bolton King

1st Floor Flat, 51 Sherriff Road, West Hampstead, London NW6 2AS
mobile (07780) 866082
email georginaboltonking@gmail.com
website www.boltonkingphotography.com

Services & rates: Charges £80 for a photoshoot (digital only), which includes around 150 shots. 10x8in prints are charged extra, at £10 each. 10% discount for actors/students. Shoots take place at a home studio, in the client's home or in an outdoor location which is wheelchair accessible.

Work portfolio: Established in 2010. Has taken publicity photos for 200 actors. For details of recent clients, please search at **www.castingcallpro.com/uk/psearch.php**. Advises actors: "Wear neutral make-up. Bring a simple black top (preferably V-necked) and a white top."

Nev Brewer Photography

mobile (07967) 993458
email nevbrewer@gmail.com
website www.nevbrewerphotography.co.uk

Services & rates: Photographer for actors and performers since 2013. Offers several photo shoot packages:

• The Theydon Shoot £175 (3+ hours) — For actors who have no time pressures and want a portfolio of both studio lit and natural light images.
• The Classic "Outdoor" £145 (2+ hour) — For actors who have limited time at their disposal and/or want naturally-lit headshots.
• The Classic "Studio" £145 (2+ hours) — For actors who prefer studio-lit images or for those who want to be less dependent of the vagaries of the weather for their headshot session.

All prices include a relaxed pre-shoot discussion. Contact sheets will be supplied within 24 hours and usually 2 to 3 hours after the shoot. Retouched images are supplied in both colour and b&w within a week. These will be in web-ready and print-ready formats. The Theydon Shoot includes up to 300 shots with 4 retouches, The Classic options include up to 200 shots and 3 retouches. Additional images can be retouched at £15 per image. Discounts are available to students. Call or visit the website for more details. The Theydon Shoot includes a studio shoot and natural light shots taken on the local village green.

Work portfolio: Examples of work can be seen on the website. Has taken photographs for around 70 actors to date, among them Paul Beech, Grace Cookey-Gam and Alex Freeborn. "Prior to the headshot session I send out information with recommendations on how best to prepare for the session, what clothing to bring etc. I work hard to ensure that every actor gets a range of great headshots and has a really enjoyable experience."

Marc Broussely

South West London
mobile (07738) 920225
email info@10x8headshots.com
website www.10x8headshots.com

Services & rates: Established in 2008. Charges £180 for a photo shoot at home studio: this includes 4 retouched shots and the whole session delivered in high-res. digital files. Optional 10x8in prints are extra at £20 each. Student price is £160.

Sheila Burnett

email sheila@sheilaburnett.com
website www.sheilaburnett-headshots.com

Services & rates: Charges between £180 and £280 for a photo shoot. Includes 100 proofs in b&w and colour plus 4-6 10x8in images also saved to disc. Offers digital photography. Photos taken in studio or on location if preferred. Works with 170 actors per year including Imelda Staunton, Catherine Tate, David Soul, Paul Freeman, Jon Culshaw, Simon Pegg, Anita Harris, Jackie Clune, Caroline Quentin and Helen Lederer.

"Appointments can be made either online or by phone. I always advise on what is good to bring. I'm open to any questions and happy to have a chat about what it is you want to achieve. My sessions always start with a 10-minute warm-up, this is mainly for me to adjust the lights and find the best position for you. Working indoors makes it possible for you to freshen up upon arrival and to change outfits, apply make-up etc., and, for the boys, to shave mid-session if you want. The outdoor part of the session is 2 minutes away in a large garden; these shots are very compatible with the studio shots and are included in all sessions (weather permitting)." Visit the website for further details.

Will C

Pygar Cottage, 31 Oxford Street, Exning, Newmarket, Suffolk CB8 7EW
tel (01638) 577535 *mobile* (07712) 669953
email billy_snapper@hotmail.com
website www.specialelitepicturelibrary.com
website www.theukphotographerexhibition.co.uk
website www.billysnapper.com

Services & rates: Established in 1968. £160 includes 80 colour, 80 b&w and 2 high-res. CDs with all photos at 14 million pixels, delivered to the client in the studio. All photos are seen at the moment of taking on a large screen. Make-up and hair can be provided in full attendance for the whole photo session for £80. Prints are obtained from an independent printer for £5 (b&w) and £7 (colour). Majority of photos taken in studio (home studio), other location prices are available on request. No wheelchair access to studio.

Work portfolio: Has photographed approximately 6,500 performers, including Dame Judi Dench, Will Young, Charles Dance. Advice: "Neutral colours for clothes, no patterns, simplicity."

Jon Campling Headshots

206 Ellison Road, London SW16 5DJ
tel 020-8679 8671 *mobile* (07941) 421101
email photo@joncampling.com
website www.joncamplingheadshots.com

Services & rates: Established in 2004. All photography is digital. £100 includes online contact sheet, CD of all images in full resolution, and full digital correction of 4 images, only payable if client uses the images. Uses instant, full-size preview at session. Happy to give free advice via email or telephone. Prints of images are available at £1.99 each or 99p if order of 20 or more of each. Photos are taken in home studio. No wheelchair access.

Work portfolio: Has photographed over 150 actors. Clients include: Shenna Ellis, Dominic Cazenove and Charlotte Graham. "I am an actor myself . . . I advise a simple approach to make-up and clothing."

Charlie Carter

mobile (07989) 389493
email charlie@charliecarter.com
website www.charliecarter.com

Services & rates: Established in 1998. Digital – colour and b&w. Charges £400 for photo shoot including web gallery and 4 Spotlight-ready jpgs and prints. Sessions are in a home studio on the 2nd floor, so not wheelchair-accessible.

Work portfolio: Examples of work can be viewed on my website, www.charliecarter.com, my Charlie Carter Photography Facebook page and at Spotlight's offices. Clients include: Kenneth Branagh, Simon Russell Beale, Philip Franks Tom Hollander, Roger Allam, Emily Blunt, Isla Blair, Jemma Redgrave, Jamie Glover, Tom Mison, Cush Jumbo, Chloe Pirrie, Sarah MacRae, Eve Best, Harry Enfield, Eleanor Bron, Martin Shaw, Joanna Van der Ham, Kerry Condon, Jasmine Hyde, Paul McEwan, Serena Evans and Charlie Condou – as well as agents The Artists Partnership, The Richard Stone Partnership, Rebecca Blond Associates, Conway van Gelder Grant, Independent, United, Markham & Froggatt and many others.

"However lovely a photograph is, it has to work. It has to look like you *and* be accurate to your casting - somehow tell the casting directors who to expect will walk through their door. The way I work is totally collaborative – we talk about your casting and what your range is. We look at how you see yourself. We do it together. I suggest you prepare for it as you would for a significant interview by making sure yo do what is necessary to look and feel your best."

Andrew Chapman

198 Western Road, Sheffield S10 1LF
tel (0114) 266 3579 *mobile* (07779) 861921
email andrew@chapmanphotographer.eclipse.co.uk
website www.andrewsphotos.co.uk

Services & rates: Charges from £125 for a photo shoot, which includes all photography and computer labour charges, studio and equipment costs. The session includes 100+ photos, b&w and/or colour) which are transferred to the computer; you may select any or all images and these are written to a CD for you to take away for immediate use. Prints and contacts are available (e.g. a 10x8in is £15) if required, but in most cases images are emailed directly to Spotlight and for repros. Also gives clients a 'release note' so that photos can be used for PR, repros, agents, Spotlight etc.

Black and bright colours work well in b&w, and higher necklines are usually better than low: "I always advise people on an individual basis. Ideally, allow about 2 hours for the session."

Work portfolio: Has more than 3,500 actors on database as well as singers, dancers, models, martial artists and others. Clients are from agents across the country; they include: Philippa Howell, Sharron Ashcroft, Jane Hollowood, Liberty Management, David Daly, Direct Line and Act One. "Qualified member of BIPP, SWPP, BPPA with over 25 years' experience."

John Clark Photo Digital

tel 020-8854 4069
email info@johnclarkphotography.com
website www.johnclarkphotography.com

Services & rates: Charges £145 per hour for digital photography.

Work portfolio: Established in 1982. Photographs and advice can be found on the website. Has taken publicity shots for around 500-600 actors. Recent clients include: actors represented by Roger Carey Associates, Collis Management, Crawfords, Rossmore and Langford Associates.

John Cooper Photography

Unit 2, Kelvin Trading Estate, Eastvale Place, Yorkhill, Glasgow
tel 0141-334 7815 *mobile* (07803) 929091
email studio@johncooperphotography.com
website www.johncooperphotography.com

Services & rates: Offers 2 packages at £210 and £280 (all photography is digital). Fee includes 4 or 8 shots, depending on the package, with a 10x8in print of each selected image. Can offer student discount for multiple bookings. Shoots take place at own studio, which is wheelchair accessible, plus options for other locations.

Work portfolio: Established in 2005. Has taken publicity photos for hundreds of actors. Recent clients include: Billy Boyd (*Lord of the Rings Trilogy*), Mark Cox (BBC's *Chewin' The Fat* and *Still Game*), Katrina Bryan (*Taggart* and Children's BBC), Des Clarke (SMTV Live and Capital Radio), Pamela Byrne (BBC River City), Claire Knight (BBC River City). Advises actors: "I think a lot of actors' headshots are very intense and serious looking – because it's easy to do. I help my clients produce contemporary publicity images, with energy and personality, which make a real difference to their casting opportunities."

Ruth Crafer

Highbury, North London
mobile (07974) 088460
email ruth.crafer@mac.com
website www.ruthcrafer.co.uk

Services & rates: Photographer since 1993. Charges £300 (inc VAT) per session. Each session lasts 60-90 minutes and the client will end up with 60-80 final images in both colour and b&w. The 5 best images will then be retouched where necessary and high-res. images (in both colour and b&w) will be sent to the client for immediate use. A student rate of £250 (inc. VAT) is also available. Photo shoots take place at Ruth's studio in Highbury.

Work portfolio: Examples of work can be seen on the website. Has taken photographs for hundreds of actors over 12 years. "I aim to provide a relaxed and enjoyable session that is a collaboration between the photographer and sitter. This is very important as actors only get one chance to catch the attention of casting directors and directors, which an only be achieved with an arresting, engaging, confident image."

CW Photos

Southampton
tel (02380) 732550
email cwp@cwphotos.co.uk
website www.cwphotos.co.uk

Services & rates: Charges from £55 for a photo shoot, which includes fees, studio, processing and prints (2 selected from 40 taken). An option of either 10x8in prints or files on CD. Special packages for actors (including students) include a 10-image portfolio disc from £125 (headshots, 3/4 length, full length, different backgrounds and lighting, and 10 selected finished images from 100 taken). Other packages are available to suit all budgets. All locations are possible: the main studio is wheelchair-accessible.

Work portfolio: Established in 1990. Has photographed more than 100 productions and taken publicity shots for more than 60 actors. Clients include: Ros Liddiard, Steven Fawell, Susannah Steadman, James Norton and Joanna Russel. Each client gets a personal assessment and recommendation.

James Davies Photography

London
mobile (07716) 515170
email mail@jamesdaviesheadshots.com
website www.jamesdaviesheadshots.com

Services & rates: Charges £200 for a photoshoot (£165 student rate; special package for those quoting *Actors' and Performers' Yearbook*). Fee includes unlimited shots with no time limit, plus 3 high-res., retouched 10x8in images on a CD. All sessions are digital. Shoots take place in a studio, and at a private outdoor location which is wheelchair accessible.

Work portfolio: Established in 2007. Has taken publicity photos for around 200 actors. Recent clients include: Jenny Eclair, Amy Lennox, Melissa Suffield, Lauren Samuels, Stephanie Fearon and Robert O'Neil. "I take headshots alongside a career as an agent with a busy theatrical agency. I deal with actors and actresses, as well as casting directors on a daily basis and know exactly what they look for in a headshot."

Nicholas Dawkes Photography

London W10
mobile (07787) 111997
email studio@nicholasdawkesphotography.co.uk
website www.nicholasdawkesphotography.co.uk

Services & rates: Prices start at £255 for headshots. Includes a full consultation, 2-3 hour session, with both outdoor and studio shots available. Up to 200-300 pictures taken, with full review of images on a large screen. Same-day uploading of images in colour and b&w on private client area, with email links to the client and their agent. Retouching 4 images included in price.

"Before becoming a full-time photographer I worked as an actor in television, film and theatre, which, unlike a lot of photographers, gives me an in-depth understanding of the creative industry. The aim of my sessions is to not put pressure on you to 'perform'; I want you relaxed and comfortable. Only then can we capture some life in the image."

DF: Photographer/arc172 Ltd

Studio 33, North 6 Flr, New England House,
New England Street, Brighton BN1 4GH
mobile (07958) 272333
email david@arc172.com
website www.arc172.com (videos: www.youtube.com/arc172tv photos: www.arc172.zenfolio.com)
Photographer David Fernandes

Has worked as a photographer since 1995 and has taken photographs for roughly 500 actors. Charges £85 for a photo shoot including 2 10x8in prints, shooting digitally. Special 'shared sitting' rates are available to students. Works in a studio, outdoors or in the client's home. Shoots and edits actors' showreels; please phone for prices. The studio is not wheelchair-accessible. Advises clients to "bring a selection of tops with different necklines. Not too 'fussy'. A black top always works well".

Mike Eddowes

mobile (07970) 141005
email mike@photo-publicity.co.uk
website www.theatre-photography.co.uk

Services & rates: Services offered include headshots and theatre production photography. Cost of portrait photoshoots is £190. This includes 6 10x8in prints plus CD with up to 50 images in both high-res. (for making prints) and also low-res. for emails, websites or agents. Special discount of £25 is offered to clients who mention *Actors' and Performers' Yearbook*. Studios in Kennington (near Waterloo, South London) and also in Hampshire for clients based in the south near Bournemouth and Southampton.

"Don't wear too much make-up; bring clothes which are you as yourself (not dressing up!); and have an early night before the photography session. Try and build a relationship with a photographer and stick with him or her. Don't get a keen amateur friend to try and take your photos – acting is a very tough career and you need all the help you can get!"

Sean Ellis

5 Meadow Road, Claygate, Esher, Surrey KT10 0RZ
mobile (07702) 381258
email sean@seanellis.co.uk
website www.seanellis.co.uk

Services & rates: Photographer since 1986. Charges £150 for a 2-3-hour photo shoot including 200 shots. All images will be supplied on disc or via email in low-res. format from which 3 can be chosen to be enhanced/retouched and supplied in high-res. digital format. Additional images will be charged at £25 per image. Bespoke 10x8in prints can be supplied at £30 per print. If a large print run is required, this can be arranged at a more economical price. Sean uses a purpose-built studio at his home.

Work portfolio: Examples of work can be seen on the website. Has taken photographs for hundreds of actors, almost all of them have been have been for the Buttercup Agency website and their Spotlight entries. "Bring your upbeat, positive self with a clear idea of what you want and we'll do the rest together!"

Elliott Franks Photography Services

PO Box 29801, London SW19 1WW
tel 020-8544 0156 *mobile* (07802) 537220
email elliottfrankse@gmail.com
website www.elliottfranks.com

Services & rates: Charges £250 for a 2-hour photo shoot either on location or in the studio.

Work portfolio: Established in 1997. Photographs can be viewed on the website and at the Spotlight offices. Has taken publicity shots for more than 800 actors. Elliott Franks is one of the UK's leading performing arts press photographers.

Adrian Gibb

44A Wallbutton Road, Brockley, London SE4 2NX
tel 020-76396215
email adriangibb@gmail.com
website www.adriangibb.co.uk

Established in 1995. Specialises in headshots/portraits for actors. Charges actors £100 and students £60 for a photo shoot. Digital photo session includes 100-200 images. Price includes 4 b&w 10x8in prints and a CD disc of images. Works at home in studio and/or garden. Studio is wheelchair accessible. Has taken publicity shots for 60-100 actors, including Tamara Beckwith and Sophie Monk.

Chris Giles

5 Waldron Avenue, Brighton, East Sussex BN1 9EF
mobile (07525) 752823
email studio@chrisgilesphotography.com
website http://chrisgilesphotography.com

Services & rates: Charges £50-200 for a photoshoot, depending on number of images. Fee includes 80-180 images, usually shot in medium-format digital. Shoots take place at the studio or in the grounds. Home visits are available at extra cost.

Work portfolio: Has taken publicity shots for around 300 actors. Clients include: Tessa Cushan, Verity L. Jones, Gary Phoenix, Katie Green, Alice Christian and Derek Horsham. Advises actors: "Always try to work with nice people, as they tend to rub off on you."

James Gill

6 Hanover Gardens, London SE11 5TL
tel 020-7735 5632

Services & rates: Charges £85 for a photo shoot which includes photographer's fee, studio and equipment costs, processing of 1 b&w 36exps, contact sheet and 2 10x8in (25x20cm) prints. Increases to £130 for 2 rolls and 4 10x8in prints. Extra 10x8in prints are priced at £12.50 each. Advises actors to keep it simple. Will take photos of actors as they wish to be presented and will take all the time necessary.

Work portfolio: Established in 1992. Photographs can be viewed at Spotlight's offices. Has taken publicity shots for around 500 actors and in addition has more than 40 years' experience of working in theatres, both in casting and as company manager.

Nick Gregan Photography

Unit 3, 10A Ellingfort Road, London Fields, London E8 3PA
tel 020-8533 3003 *mobile* (07774) 421878
email info@nickgregan.com
website www.nickgregan.com

Services & rates: Charges £249 for a 2-hour photo shoot, which includes fees, studio (around 300 shots are taken), 3 retouched images and a CD of all saved images in colour and b&w. Students are offered a discount price of £175 on production of a valid student card. Also offers digital photography, for which the same rates apply. Photos are taken in a studio or outdoor location and both are wheelchair-accessible.

Work portfolio: Established in 1992. Has taken publicity photos for more than 3,000 clients, including Paul Danan, Lucinda Rhodes and Jenny Powell. "My website offers '7 secrets to a great headshot' – check it out for loads of useful information."

Charles Griffin Photography

PO Box 36, Deeside, Chester CH5 3WP
tel (01244) 535252
email studio@charlesgriffinphotography.co.uk
website www.charlesgriffinphotography.co.uk

Services & rates: Photographer since 1993. Charges £149 for photo shoot, which includes processing of 2 12exps medium-format (high-quality) rolls, contact sheets and 2 10x8in prints. (Offers this service at £92.83 if client mentions *Actors' and Performers' Yearbook* when booking a 2-hour session. Student rates are also available – telephone or email for information.) Digital service also available at the same rates, although an extra charge is made to provide the images on CD. Uses studio and outdoor location (both wheelchair accessible).

Work portfolio: Examples of work can be seen on the website. Has taken photographs for around 250 actors, among them Raquel Lee, Gemma Gray, Sam Gratton and Paul Draw. "Sessions are conducted in a relaxed atmosphere: I will shoot images of actors as they wish. Clients should bring a variety of plain tops: those with high neckline or v-neck in red, grey or black are most useful."

Claire Grogan

18 Calverley Grove, London N19 3LG
tel 020-7272 1845 *mobile* (07932) 635381
email claire@clairegrogan.co.uk
website www.clairegrogan.co.uk

Services & rates: Actors headshots charges – film or digital: £290 for full photo shoot, 2 roll b&w 36exps contact sheets and 4 10x8s plus retouched jpegs (prints on film shoot only). This shoot can be either outdoors, studio or combination of both and either b&w film or colour/b&w digital. Also offers 1 roll 36 exps and 2 10x8s/jpegs studio shoot, film or digital for £195. Special rates for full-time drama students, CCP members and newcomers, phone for details. Offers full advice and help with clothing and make-up. Sessions last approx 3.5 hours in a relaxed environment. Studio and private outdoor space. Time and facilities for changing clothes/hair/make-up or shaving during shoot. Specialises in capturing shots that really reflect the actor's personality and casting potential, also special TLC for those who normally find having their headshots done difficult.

Work portfolio: Established in 1991. Photographs can be viewed on the website and at Spotlight offices. Takes around 400 publicity shots for actors each year and is recommended by many agents and casting directors. Clients include: Steve McFadden, Lindsey Coulson, Stephen Tompkinson, Heather Peace, Nicola Blackman, Ben Richards, Debbie Arnold, Chris Walker, Caroline O'Neill, Phil Whitchurch, Tiffany Chapman, Philip Brown, Frances Tomelty,

Martin Freeman, Gillian Bevan, Shobna Gulati, John Altman, Marilyn Cutts and Simon Bowman.

Brendan Harrington

Newry, Northern Ireland
mobile (07850) 001075
email b.harrington@pobroadband.co.uk
website www.brendanharringtonphotography.co.uk

Services & rates: Charges approximately £70 for a 2-hour session (around 150-225 shots). Fee includes 3 finished images at high res.; small quantities of hand prints are available at £5 each if required. Shoots take place mainly in the studio, which is wheelchair accessible. Emails web galleries to clients for their final image selection.

Work portfolio: Established more than 25 years ago. Has taken publicity photos for thousands of actors: clients include most Dublin agents as well as Casting Call Pro and Spotlight.

HCK Photography

Based in London
tel 020-7112 8499 (Studio)
email info@hckphotography.co.uk
website www.hckphotography.co.uk, www.actorsheadshotslondon.org.uk

Services & rates: Established in 2007. Specialises in headshots and publicity photography. Charges from £150 for a photoshoot; call friendly staff for more information. Offers student discounts. Studio based. First 10 to mention Actors' and Performers' Yearbook 2016 receive £50 discount.

Work portfolio: Has taken publicity photos for many actors. Recent clients include: Shane Rangi and Kiran Shah.

Headshot Photography by Lynn Herrick

The Studio, 9A Sylvester Road, London N2 8HN
tel 020-8349 3632
email lynnherrick@gmail.com
website www.headshotslondon.co.uk

Services & rates: Charges £80-175 for a photoshoot, which includes 25-60 images. 10x8in prints are available at extra cost. Work takes place in the studio and attached garden. Has taken publicity photos for around 300 actors.

Jamie Hughes Photography

mobile (07850) 122977
email jamie@jamiehughesphotography.com
website www.jamiehughesphotography.com/headshots

Services & rates: Charges £285 for a bespoke photo shoot lasting up to 2 hours in a relaxed atmosphere. Over 300 images are shot with the best supplied on CD to take away, plus retouching and processing of 3 10x8in prints and digital originals. Additional prints (including retouching) are available for £15 each. Uses a studio and outdoor location, both of which are wheelchair accessible. Please see website for examples.

Remy Hunter

Flat 2, 9 Belsize Park, London NW3 4ES
tel 020-7431 8055 *mobile* (07766) 760724
email remy@remyhunterphotography.com
website www.remyhunter.co.uk

Services & rates: Established in 2003. Charges £190 and £140 for a 4-hour and 2-hour actors' session respectively. Includes 80 digital shots taken for 4-hour session and 40 shots for 2-hour session. Also includes CD of all shots given to client at end of session and a further CD of 6 high res. images for 4-hour session and 4 images for 2-hour session. Student discount available as follows: £150 for a 4-hour session and £120 for a 2-hour session. Shared sessions available for half of the above prices per person. Also includes 2 CDs. Studio and outdoor shots available during same session. Free retouching of images where necessary. Uses a studio that is not accessible to wheelchair users.

Work portfolio: Has taken photographs for roughly 500 actors, including (with Spotlight PIN in brackets): Freya Dominic (2211-8979-4470), Gemma Harvey (0615-5643-5877), Julie Pollin (0459-1206-3661) and Jonathan Grace (aka James Dillinger – 2517-8940-4373). Advises clients to "bring a range of tops with varying necklines. Black tends to come out best, so a couple of black tops are a good idea. For make-up bring what you'd wear from day to day".

David James Photography

mobile (07808) 597362
email info@davidjamesphotos.com
website www.davidjamesphotos.com

Established 2001. Charges £230 for photoshoot including processing of 2 36exps b&w films and 4 10x8in prints. Also offers digital shoot at the same price. Uses studio, outdoor locations and client's own home for the shoot; the studio is not accessible for wheelchair users. Has taken photographs for around 200 actors including clients of Independent, PFD and Markham & Froggatt.

Nick James

39 Autumn Street, London E3
mobile (07961) 122030
email nick@nickjamesphotography.co.uk
website www.nickjamesphotography.co.uk

Services & rates: Photographer since 2005. Digital service only. Charges £390 for photoshoot, which includes processing of 800 shots taken with 400 taken on contact sheets and 2 images retouched. Student rate available at £350 per session. A 2 hour session is also available for £280. Does not provide prints, but extra photographs are available at £35. Uses studio natural and flash and outdoor location (both wheelchair accessible).

Work portfolio: Examples of work can be seen on the website.

Matt Jamie

North East and London
mobile (07976) 890643
email photos@mattjamie.co.uk
website www.mattjamie.co.uk/portraits

Services & rates: Established in 2000. Digital photography. Cost of photoshoot is £160 (Newcastle) or £210 (London). This includes a studio and outdoor session with well over 200 images taken (viewable on camera during the shoot and then on an online gallery same day), with 3 finalised images in high-res. sent via email. Further images may be purchased any time. Offers 100% satisfaction promise. If you're not happy with the result the shoot fee will be refunded. Special packages include student and group discounts. Will travel to outdoor locations selected by client. Local outdoor locations used are wheelchair accessible. Studio sessions at drama schools can also be arranged.

Work portfolio: Examples of photography can be seen online. Has photographed hundreds of actors, including commissions from Ambassador Theatre Group, WhatsOnStage.com, TheatreMAD and *Theatregoer Magazine* to photograph stars including Kevin Spacey, Kristin Scott Thomas, Patrick Swayze and John Barrowman. Matt also works as an actor and film maker, so understands the requirements of the shot and the pressures involved. He offers a relaxed, informal shoot which can take as long as you need. You can bring a variety of different clothes, wigs, friends or anything else you might want with you to make you feel confident on the shoot.

JK Photography

17 Delamere Road, West Wimbledon,
London SW20 8PS
tel 020-8946 9549 *mobile* (07816) 825578
email jkph0t0@yahoo.com
website www.jk-photography.net

Services & rates: Established in 1997. Sessions start at £160 (studio & outdoor). Includes professional make-up artist and all of your images in high-res. in b&w and colour on disc.

Work portfolio: Has photographed over 500 actors with 15 years of industry experiance. "Our creative team will ensure a relaxed session amd images that are a true representation of your casting needs."

Neil Kendall Photography

19 Oakfield Court, Haslemere Road, London N8 9RA
tel 020-8340 4214 *mobile* (07776) 198332
email mondo.nez@virgin.net
website www.neilkendallphotography.co.uk

Services & rates: Charges £135 for a photo shoot which includes photographer's fee, studio and equipment costs, processing of 3 b&w 36exps, contact sheets and 2 10x8in prints. Uses both studio and natural light.

Work portfolio: Photographs can be viewed on the website. Has taken publicity shots for around 30-35 actors. Recent clients include: Vanessa Earl, Peter Ackyroyd, Graham Norton and Liberty X.

Jack Ladenburg Photography

mobile (07932) 053743
email info@jackladenburg.co.uk
website www.jackladenburg.co.uk

Services & rates: Established in 2006. Only digital photography. Cost of photo shoot is £205. Includes 6 digital images with basic retouching. Student discount of £30; further discounts for group bookings. Includes high and low res versions of each image. Photos taken in studio or outdoor locations.

Work portfolio: Portfolio is available to view at Spotlight's offices. Has photographed approximately 400 actors. Recent clients include: Roger Moore, Hattie Morahan, Julian Rhind-Tutt, Nicholas Day, Tara Summers and Katherine Tozer. "I place a big emphasis on making sure that my clients are happy and relaxed before we start the shoot, and that they enjoy themselves on the day. I never rush through a session and always devote either a morning or an afternoon to one shoot. I don't set a limit on how many photos I'll take in a session, and make sure we concentrate on the casting needs of each actor."

Carole Latimer

113 Ledbury Road, Notting Hill, London W11 2AQ
tel 020-7727 9371
email carole@carolelatimer.com
website www.carolelatimer.com

Services & rates: Professional photographer for over 25 years. Charge for actors' headshots is £350 inc. VAT (student rate is £300). An electronic contact sheet is provided and up to 5 chosen images are put on to a CD. Photographs are taken in a studio and occasionally outdoor locations. The studio does not have wheelchair access.

Work portfolio: Has provided publicity photos for approximately 2,000 actors, including: Kate O'Mara, Alistair McGowan, Maureen Lipman, Zoe Lucker, and clients from the following agencies: Independent, Conway Van Gelder Grant, Narrow Road. "No large patterns. If it's a b&w shoot, bring at least one black top. Always bring a selection of tops so I have a choice. I have an exceptional daylight studio with full lighting equipment. Good facilities for make-up."

Steve Lawton

134 Randolph Avenue, Maida Vale, London W9 1PG
mobile (07973) 307487
email stevelawton2@msn.com
website www.stevelawton.com

Services & rates: Charges £280 for a photoshoot, which includes A3 contact sheets; CD of all shots in colour and b&w; and 4 touched-up 10x8in prints. The same package is offered to students at the reduced price of £260. Additional 10x8in prints are priced at £15 each. A traditional b&w film service is also available. Advises clients not to bring patterned tops; fitted t-shirts and v-necks in blue, grey or black are most effective.

Work portfolio: Established in 2001. Has taken photographs for more than 3,000 actors and is recommended by Curtis Brown, Independent Talent Group, United Agents, Lou Coulson, Jorg Betts, Shane Collins, International Artists and Bronia Buchanan, amongst others. A full portfolio and price information is available on the website.

LB Photography

36 Nutley Lane, Reigate, Surrey RH2 9HS
tel (01737) 224578 *mobile* (07885) 966192
email lb@lisabowerman.com
website www.lisabowerman.com

Services & rates: Working actress and photographer for 30 years. Charges £190 for a photo shoot (£170 student rate). No VAT chargeable. Includes 40-50 shots, taken in natural light. Price also includes a choice of 7 high-res. and re-touched images, in colour and in addition b&w conversions. Based near Redhill in Surrey – about 30 mins' train journey from Victoria – and the the client can be picked up at station. If the weather's bad the shoot can be rearranged for a different day. For portfolio and more details, visit website.

Pete Le May

mobile (07703) 649246
email pete@petelemay.co.uk
website www.petelemay.co.uk/headshots

Services & rates: Based in London and established in 2002. Typically charges £250 (£200 for students) for a session lasting 2-3 hours, a disc of all the photographs – allowing you to make as many prints as you want – and minor retouching of your favourite 6 images. All photography is digital, allowing us to review and discuss photos during the session. Photos are taken using natural light, both indoors and outdoors. Visit the website for full details and examples of recent work.

Leejay Photography

London N13
mobile (07590) 463428
email leejay@leejayphotography.com
website www.leejayphotography.com

Services & rates: Charges £119 for a digital photoshoot, which includes 500 shots with the best 200 images sent to client. 10x8in prints are available at £15 each. Student price is £99. Shoots take place at own studio as well as outdoors.

Work portfolio: Established in 2011. Has taken publicity shots for around 150 actors. Recent clients include: Nick Julian (Independent Talent Group), Lisa Kerr (Conway Van Gelder Grant), Kim Ensor (K Talent), Annabel Lloyd (International Theatre Collective). Advises actors: "I trained as an actor and feel in most cases it takes an actor to take a great actors' headshot."

Murray Lenton

2 Toll Bar Barn, High Hesket, Near Carlisle, Cumbria CA4 OHR
tel (01697) 475442 *mobile* (07941) 427458
email murray.lenton@btinternet.com

Services & rates: Digital or film as required. Rates to be discussed at time of booking.

Work portfolio: Established as a general photographer in 1983, and as a theatre photographer in 1997. Recent clients include: Tamsin Greig, Simon Dormandy, Luke Sorba and Wild Girls.

James Looker Photography

mobile (07973) 566537
email james@jameslookerphotography.com
website www.jameslookerphotography.com

Services & rates: Photographer since 2000. Charges from £270 for a 2-hour session, which includes 120+ headshots supplied as high-res. digital colour and b&w files. From these, 3 will be retouched and cropped to 10x8in/300dpi. Student rate is £220 or £150 per student if 3 book the same session. Uses studio at home for shoots, although is happy to arrange a different location to meet each individual client's needs.

Work portfolio: Examples of work can be seen on the website. Has taken photographs for over 500 actors, muscians, directors and performers, among them Mike Leigh, Jarvis Cocker, Kanye West and Adrian Simpson. "Clients should bring a variety of outfits for their shoot."

MAD Photography

200 Gladbeck Way, Enfield EN2 7HS
tel 020-8363 4182 *mobile* (07949) 581909
email mad.photo@onetel.net
website www.mad-photography.co.uk

Services & rates: Charges £220 for actors' photoshoot which includes photographer's fee, studio and location shoot, 150 proofs contact sheets emailed same day and 4 high-res. images on disc. Offers discounted rate of £160 to students (includes as above, but with 3 images on disc); also offers student shared shoots at £95 each (includes as above, but with 75 proofs contact sheets and 2 images on disc). Extra 10x8in prints are priced at £20 each and images on disc are £20. "Hair and make-up should be natural. Bring 4 tops in any colours: one v-neck, one collar, one t-shirt and one jacket. No white!"

Work portfolio: Established in 1997. Photographs can be viewed on the website and in *Contacts* and on

Casting Call Pro. Has taken publicity shots for over 6,000 actors and student actors. Clients include: Shane Richie, Michelle Ryan, Susan Penhaligon, Michael Knowles, Jessica Wallace, John Partridge, Tom Law, Belinda Owusu, Janie Dee and Phoebe Thomas.

Raymondo Marcus

Marlow, Buckinghamshire
mobile (07831) 649 000
email r.marcus@raymondomarcus.co.uk
website www.raymondomarcus.co.uk

Services & rates: Photographer since 2009. Minimum charge £250 (no VAT) full usage licence included. Photoshoot at Spotlight Leicester Square, studio in High Wycombe, or location of your choosing. If location is more than 20 miles from Marlow, travel costs will be added to overall fee. Images guaranteed siutable for Spotlight and to meet agree requirements. Testimonials from show business subjects provided on request.

Work portfolio: Examples of work can be seen on his website. Has taken photographs for a number of different actors and actresses, among them Suzanne Kendall, Laura Waddell (*Saving Mr Banks*), Shirley Anne Field, Jo Brand, Emma Thompson, Valerie Leon, Henry Jameson, Claudia Schiffer and Daniel Craig. "I have a good understanding that to generate casting calls is to present you as well as possible but so that there should be no surprises for casting directors i.e. quality images with no reliance on airbrushing."

Kirsten McTernan Photography & Design

Cardiff
mobile (07791) 524551
email kirsten@kirstenmcternan.co.uk
website www.kirstenmcternan.co.uk

Services & rates: Charges £75 for headshots (digital photography only, approximately 50 images); fee includes 2 high-res. digital images, with options to purchase others. Shoots can take place in studio or at an outdoor location.

Work portfolio: Established in 2005. Theatre and portrait photographer working exclusively within the arts community. Has taken publicity photos for over 300 actors. Recent clients include: Regan and Rimmer, Emptage Hallett, Boom Talent and David Chance.

John Need

Studio 147, 1 Summerhall, Edinburgh EH9 1QE
mobile (07756) 178947
email pics@johnneed.co.uk
website www.johnneed.co.uk

Services & rates: Charges £125 (+ VAT) for a photoshoot, which includes 200-250 shots. Prints are optional at £15 each. Only shoots digital. Shoots take place at own studio which is wheelchair accessible.

Work portfolio: Established in 2008. Has taken publicity shots for around 400 actors, a collection of which can been viewed on the website. Advises actors: "I know that getting photos right for media is a high priority for any performer. Whether you're in the biz or trying to get into it, get in touch, as I've shot hundreds of actors, presenters and DJs. First impressions count, so give casting directors what they're after – you!"

Paul J Need Photography

5 Metro Business Centre, Kangley Bridge Road, London SE26 5AQ
tel (07860) 305327
email pauljneed@hotmail.com
website www.pauljneed.co.uk
Photographer Paul J. Need

Services & rates: Charges £80 for a photoshoot. Photographer has a background in theatre, film, concert and television lighting, as well as teaching lighting design at RADA. Offers digital photography.

Claire Newman-Williams

mobile (07963) 967444
email claire@clairenewmanwilliams.com
website www.clairenewmanwilliamsheadshots.com

Services & rates: Claire is a fine art and portrait photographer who has worked with actors for 17 years in both the US and the UK, beginning in 1999. Charges £340 for a 3-hour+ photoshoot. All photographs are digital and each session includes unlimited shots edited down to 150 pictures on contact sheets. 2 10x8in retouched digital images are included as part of the session and further copies are available at £30 each. Student rate is also available at £340. Full details about headshot sessions can be seen on the website. Uses a studio for each photo shoot, though this is not wheelchair accessible.

Work portfolio: Has taken photographs for around 2,500 actors, among them Stephen Fry, Tom Hiddleston, Joanna Page, Ben Barnes, Richard Armitage and Kerry Ellis.

Michael Pollard Photographer

Manchester-based
tel 0161-456 7470 *mobile* (07800) 989457
email info@michaelpollard.co.uk
website www.michaelpollard.co.uk

Services & rates: Charges £110 for at least 100 shots to the contact sheet, including the first 5 images chosen in both colour and b&w. Additional images are charged at £10 each, either to CD or print. The shoot is unhurried and relaxed and generally lasts up to 2 hours; the shoot can be both outdoors in natural light and in a studio environment to give the widest variety of images possible. As many shots as necessary are taken, which are later carefully edited down to give the actor the very best and most varied images. Sets of colour contact sheets are then emailed to the actor and can be sent to their agent also.

"Actors can bring a number of tops ranging from lighter to darker tones. Tops should be simple and comfortable with generally a round- or V-neck, though more character-based shots are now also taken which may involve a wider variety of clothing and styling. Hair generally needs to be tidy but avoid going to the hairdresser the day before to have it cut or styled. For women, make-up should be simple and sparing, avoiding lip liner or lipstick that is too dark or too red. For men, they can arrive with a beard or stubble and shave part way through. The key is to keep things simple and natural and to be positive and be prepared. Think how you want to look and how you don't want to look. Enjoy it and be yourself!"

Work portfolio: Established in 1982 (1993 for actors). Photographs can be viewed on the website. Has taken publicity shots for around 4,000 actors. Recent clients include: Darren Day Lucy-Jo Hudson, Vicky Entwistle, Lee Otway, Peter Armitage.

Will Polley

Unit 2C, 81-85 Wharf Road, Pinxton,
Notts NG16 6LH
tel (01773) 776379 *mobile* (07766) 274205
email info@polleyphotography.com
website www.polleyphotography.com

Services & rates: Photoshoots from £89 for a 30-minute session with 1 digital image retouched in high-res. in colour, b&w and low-res. for web or email. Choose from 5 images (not retouched) selected from all taken at the shoot and viewed on laptop at end of session, image emailed. Prints charged at extra. Special packages and student discounts available, please enquire for more information. Shoots take place at studio and some on location.

Work portfolio: Established in 2005. Recent clients include: Neil Ashley, Darren Richardson and Peter Adcock.

David Price Photography

78 Luke Street, London EC2A 4PY
mobile (07950) 542494
email info@davidpricephotography.co.uk
website www.davidpricephotography.co.uk

Services & rates: One of London's leading headshot specialist photographers since 2003, offering a personal session tailored to your needs as a performer. All sessions at my own studio in Hackney, East London. See website for full details. Prices start from £170.

Work portfolio: See website for full details.

Ben Rector

mobile (07770) 467791
email ben@benrector.com
website www.benrector.com

Please view my updated portfolio at **www.benrector.com**.

Mat Ricardo

Based in South East London
mobile (07743) 494675
email MatRicardo@hotmail.co.uk
website www.MatRicardoPhotography.com

Services & rates: Charges £200 for a photoshoot, which takes 1-3 hours. Also offers digital photography at the same rates. Shoot takes place at a studio, on location, or at a mobile studio.

Work portfolio: Established in 2009. Has taken publicity shots for around 20 actors. Clients include Jenny Eclair, Barry Cryer, Richard Herring and numerous comedy, variety and burlesque performers.

Davey Ross

Central London
mobile (07956) 302894
email davixuk@hotmail.com
website www.davidrossphotography.com

Services & rates: Photographer since 1982. Davey is happy to discuss specific pricing over the phone, and charges a student rate of £300. Uses a studio, or is happy to arrange an outdoor location or travel to client's home.

Work portfolio: Examples of work can be seen on the website. Has taken photographs for hundreds of actors, among them Anne Stafford, Fiona Cuskelly and Christopher Sciueref.

Scott Rylander

South East London
mobile (07775) 785250
email contact@scottrylander.com
website www.scottrylander.com

Services & rates: Digital only. Charges £170 for headshots (£150 for students) and from £200 (£180 for students) for publicity stills (e.g. for websites), depending on requirements. Stage advertising and production photography also offered: rates negotiable. Fee for headshots includes a sub-selection of 60-100 unretouched shots, and 3 retouches; for publicity stills the fee covers 5-8 retouches, depending on requirements and the nature of the job, plus sub-selection as necessary for the shoot. For 10x8in prints, recommends that clients use one of the several London printers who can offer far more competitive rates for actors. Shoots take place at a studio or outdoor location, or (for publicity stills) wherever is agreed with the customer.

Work portfolio: Established in 2010. Has taken photographs for around 80 actors. Headshot clients include: Actors Direct Associates, Alliston & Foster and Jessica Carney Associates. Clients for production and stage advertising include: English National Opera and Tarento Productions Ltd. Advises actors: "With many actors setting up their own websites and building their presence on Facebook, the types of photos they need are changing. Headshots will always be hugely important for casting, and my approach is to focus on your personality, not to make everyone look the same. But creative publicity stills – shot with more freedom for you to wear different clothes and do different things – are becoming just as necessary. I take a very relaxed approach to both: we take as long as we need until we have the right look for you."

Martin Saint Photography

London
tel 020-8503 3159 *mobile* (07912) 091318
email info@martinsaint.com
website www.martinsaint.com

Services & rates: Charges £150 for a photoshoot, which includes 200-300 shots (all digital). Discount of £30 available for students. Photographs are taken at a home studio and/or outdoor location – only the latter is wheelchair accessible.

Work portfolio: Has taken publicity photos for approx. 50 actors, please see website for further details. Recent clients include: Sarah McKendrick, Lawrence Stubbings, Elle G Lewys, Alexandra Hathaway and Jessica Hughes.

Robin Savage Photography

North London
mobile (07901) 927597
email contact@robinsavage.co.uk
website www.robinsavage.co.uk

Services & rates: A London-based actors' photographer. Shoots a maximum of 2 headshot sessions a day from a private studio in north London. Shoots using both daylight and studio, and a session results in around 250 proofs from which a choice of 4 images can be made for retouching. Current rate is £230 (£200 for students). Get in touch to book a session or for more information.

Howard Sayer Photography

tel 020-8123 0251 or (07860) 559891
email howard@howardsayer.com
website www.howardsayer.com

Services & rates: Casting headshots £195 (inc. VAT) for 90-minute sitting; includes images posted to web gallery for viewing and high-res. download. Studio in Surrey able to travel to client location (supplement applies).

Karen Scott Photography

London
mobile (07958) 975950
email info@karenscottphotography.com
website www.karenscottphotography.com

Services & rates: Charges £175 for Actors Headshot Shoot – unlimited images are taken during a relaxed and unhurried shoot (with outfit changes as necessary) and then edited to 100 proofs. All proofs are b&w and colour and cropped to 10x8in. High quality contact sheets of the proofs are then emailed to you, after which your chosen 10 images are fully finished including contrast and tonal adjustments and retouching. The 100 proofs and the finished 10 images in colour and b&w are saved to DVD as high-res. printable files. Outdoor or indoor locations are possible using natural light. Student rates are available.

Work portfolio: Portfolio of images can be viewed on the website, please check for details of contemporary shoots for models, dancers, musicians, etc. Production, publicity and live shoots are also possible – check website for details.

Catherine Shakespeare Lane

The Monsell Stores, 43 Monsell Road,
London N4 2EF
tel 020-7226 7694
email catherineshakespeare.lane@gmail.com
website www.csl-art.co.uk

Services & rates: Charges £390 for a photoshoot which includes photographer's fee, studio and equipment costs, processing of 2 b&w 36exps, contact sheets and 4 10x8in prints. Offers a student package for £270 (1 roll of 36 and 2 10x8in prints). In special circumstances this package is also available to non-students for £280. Uses natural light inside and favours a natural look. "My aim is to show my clients at their most interesting."

Work portfolio: Established in 1975. Photographs can be viewed at Spotlight's offices and in *Contacts*. Has taken publicity shots for more than 2,000 actors.

Michael Shelford

London Bridge
mobile (07753) 610784
website www.shelfordheadshots.com

Services & rates: Charges £230 for a photoshoot, which includes as many images as needed, but usually 200-400. Special price for students £200. Shoots take place inside (home) and outside, both of which are wheelchair accessible.

Work portfolio: Has taken publicity photos for 200-plus actors. Recent clients include: David Adjala (Independent Talent Group), James McGregor (Curtis Brown), Nick Hendrix (Ken McReddie), Daniel Ings (The Rights House), James Rastall (Rebecca Blond), Antonia Thomas (Curtis Brown), Theo James (Markham & Froggatt), Ruth Kearney (Roxanne Vacca) and Shazid Latif (Lou Coulson).

Shot By Sodium

Leeds
tel (0113) 238 1011
email info@shotbysodium.com
website www.shotbysodium.com/headshots

Services & rates: Charges £175 for a photoshoot, which includes 50 images to view – 5 final retouched files supplied. 10x8in prints are charged at £10 for 1, £5 for 10+. Shoots take place at a studio location, which is wheelchair accessible.

Work portfolio: Established in 2009. Has taken publicity photos for around 160 actors. Recent clients include: Paul Fox, Liam Rooke, Natashia Mattocks, Tonicha Lawrence Agency and Northern Spirit Creative. "Our philosophy is that your photo is the single most important tool you have as an actor to market yourself. Forget dirty brick walls, a zillion outfit changes and awkward poses. Our headshots concentrate on one simple goal: to make you look like you, on a really good day."

Alan Sill Photography

43 Surtees Road, Peterlee, County Durham SR8 5HA
tel 0191-518 1677 *mobile* (07977) 141809
email alansillphotography@hotmail.co.uk
website www.alansillphotography.com

Established in 1990. Charges £90 for a photoshoot, which includes as many shots as it takes to complete the assignment. Prints are charged at £20. 20% discount for students with a valid student union card. Rates for digital photography are the same. Works on location, at the client's home or at a home studio, which is wheelchair accessible. Member of the National Union of Journalists.

Peter Simpkin

Apartment 13, Stefan House, London N21 3RF
email petersimpkin@aol.com
website www.petersimpkin.co.uk

Services & rates: Charges £350 for a photoshoot which includes photography fee, studio and equipment costs, processing of 3 contact sheets with a minimum of 100 shots, and 6 10x8in prints (also supplied with a CD). Student price is £300.

Work portfolio: Photographs can be viewed on the website. Has taken publicity shots for thousands of actors. Recent clients include actors represented by most leading agents and many students from the big 10 drama schools.

Rosie Still

391 Sidcup Road, London SE9 4EU
tel 020-8857 6920 *mobile* (07597) 946252
email contact@rosiestillphotography.co.uk
website www.rosiestillphotography.co.uk£

Services & rates: A professional photographer for 40 years. Charges a special price for actors of £190 (normally £240) to be photographed in 4 tops, or £145 (normally £180) to be photographed in 2 tops. This includes session fee, a change of top and the entire shoot (minus any unflattering ones!) on CD (all cropped to 10x8in) in both colour and b&w as large, high-res. Spotlight-ready jpegs and also smaller websize jpegs (for fast email/Facebook, Twitter, etc.). For prices of sessions including more outfits, or full-body shots, please check out the Acting page of the website. Also offers a special reduction for students of £120 (normally £150) to be photographed in 2 tops, which includes all of the above. Takes as many shots as are necessary, depending on the client's needs. All sessions are carried out in own South London studio, approx. 15 minutes' train journey from London Bridge station and with parking spaces directly outside. The studio is wheelchair accessible.

Work portfolio: Portfolio includes many famous actors, presenters, musicians and pop stars from the 70s onwards. Examples of work and testimonials can be seen on the website. "Ladies should keep make-up to the minimum as if going out for the evening, nothing heavier. Men should wear none at all. My priority is to finish a shoot with the client 100% satisfied with their results."

Faye Thomas Photographer

Camden/Highgate, North London
tel 020-7684 6465 *mobile* (07813) 449229
email faye@fayethomas.com
website www.fayethomas.com

Services & rates: Charges £290 for a photoshoot (all digital). On average 450-750 high-res. photos are provided on DVD; includes 3 retouched digital copies (does not do prints). Student rate is £280; more details of additional packages are available from the website. Rates subject to change. Shoots take place in an outdoor location or studio – neither is wheelchair accessible. Advance booking recommended.

Work portfolio: Established in 2005. Recommended by many of the top London agencies. High-profile clients include: Joseph Morgan, Jonathan Slinger (Curtis Brown Group); Michelle Dockery, Shaun Evans, Samantha Spiro, Ruth Gemmell, Georgie Henley, Morven Christie (Hamilton Hodell); Ramin Karimloo, Michelle Fairley, Hannah New (CAM); Alex Hassell, Emily Beecham (United Agents); Elliot Cowan, Rupert Friend, Pippa Nixon, Alex Waldmann (Independent Talent Group); Tom Riley, Tuppence Middleton, Olivia Hallinan (Conway Van Gelder Grant); Al Weaver (Julian Belfrage). Recent work and updates can be seen on **www.facebook.com/fayethomasphotography**.

TM Photography & Design

Suites 14 & 15, Marlborough Business Centre, 96 George Lane, South Woodford, London E18 1AD
tel 020-8530 4382
email info@tmphotography.co.uk
website www.tmphotography.co.uk

Services & rates: Established in 1995. All photography is digital. Cost of photoshoot is £70. The cost includes a 10x8in print which can be taken away on the day of the shoot. Images can be viewed by the client as they are taken. Images are loaded on to a private webpage to be viewed. Orders can be placed online. Student photoshoot is discounted at £40. Photos taken in studio or outdoor locations or client's home. Studio is wheelchair accessible.

Work portfolio: Has photographed approximately 3,000 actors, walk-ons and background artists. Has photographed many of the clients of Allsorts Agency, Ray Knight, G2 and Guys & Dolls. Actors photographed include: Fraser Hines and Antonia Okonma. Photoshoots can be booked at short notice. Also offers repro service and promotional products such as websites, model cards and CV creation.

Steve Ullathorne

London
tel (07961) 380969
email steve@steveullathorne.com
website www.steveullathorne.com

Services & rates: Charges £250 for a digital photo shoot; this covers all fees, studio costs and contact sheet. Will offer a discount to students, negotiable at the time of booking. All clients receive an online contact sheet with a web address that they can pass on to their agent. Prior to the shoot, clothing and locations will be discussed with the client on the telephone. All photos are retouched in Photoshop to remove any blemishes plus any other light retouching required by the actor. Email proofs are sent of each chosen image. Rather than specifying a number of images, prices are dictated by duration of the shoot, which is 2 hours. Actors usually end up with more than 100 shots to choose from, in colour and b&w.

Work portfolio: Please see website for samples. Agency recommendations include: Brown, Simcocks and Andrews, RBM, PBJ, Noel Gay, Troika, DAA and Q Talent.

Vanessa Valentine Photography

mobile (07904) 059541
website www.vanessavalentinephotography.com

Services & rates: Headshots. Based in London and Manchester. Please see the website for more details.

Luke Varley

mobile (07711) 183631
email luke@lukevarley.com
website www.lukevarley.com
website www.headshotsbylukevarley.com

Services & rates: Established in 2004. Charges £250 for a photo shoot (£225 for students and returning clients), which includes approximately 130 shots and 4 retouched high-res. files for printing and web use. Shoots take place in a studio that is not wheelchair accessible.

Work portfolio: Has taken publicity photos for several hundred actors, including for the following agencies: 42, Troika, and Cole Kitchenn. He also shoots production, press and unit stills for film, TV and theatre.

Ana Verastegui Photography

mobile (07818) 067557
email anaphotography@me.com

Services & rates: Charges £170 for a photo shoot, which includes approximately 150 shots and 3 10x8in prints. Student rate is £140. Also offers digital photography at the same rates. Shoots take place mainly outdoors in wheelchair accessible locations.

Work portfolio: Established in 2008. Has taken publicity photos for over 100 actors. Clients include: Cordelia Bugeja, Polly Maberly, and Hannah Melbourn.

Vincenzo Photography

tel 020-8372 0428 *mobile* (07962) 338289
email info@vincenzophotography.com
website www.vincenzophotography.com

Services & rates: Photographer since 2000. Charges £230 for a 2-hour photoshoot, which includes 8 high-res. digital files, 4 each in b&w and colour. Offers a student rate of £200 per session. Uses a studio with garden for external shots or is happy to arrange another location of a client's choosing.

Work portfolio: Examples of work can be seen on the website. Has taken photographs for many actors, among them Ken Stott, Hayley Atwell and Paul Nicholas.

Philip Wade

88 Englefield Road, London N1 3LG
tel 020-7226 3088 *mobile* (07956) 599691
email pix@philipwade.com
website www.philipwade.com

Services & rates: Spotlight package £125 (includes around 200 images). 10x8in prints are charged at £10 each. Digital photography only. Shoots take place in own studio, and at an outdoor location which is wheelchair accessible.

Work portfolio: Has taken publicity shots for hundreds of actors. Recent clients include: PHM, Abacus, Imperium, Shepherd Management and Sandra Boyce.

Caroline Webster

North London
mobile (07867) 653019
email caroline@carolinewebster.co.uk
website www.carolinewebster.co.uk

Services & rates: Established in 2009. Charges £150 for studio or outdoors shoot, and £200 for both studio and outdoors shoot. Approximately 100 digital shots are taken, and final photos provided in colour and b&w, as high-quality jpegs on disc. Offers a student rate of £120 for a studio or outdoors shoot, and £150 for both.

Work portfolio: Has taken publicity photos for over 1,000 actor clients, including Maureen Beattie, Paul Merton, Geraldine Fitzgerald and Kate Duchene.

Michael Wharley Photography

Waterloo, London, Zone 1
mobile (07961) 068759
email michaelwharley@michaelwharley.com
website www.michaelwharley.com

Services & rates: Established in 2006. Shoots in digital, featuring studio-lit and outdoor, colour and b&w shooting as standard. Range of packages to suit all budgets: Basic (1.5hr): £250; Standard (2.5hr): £350; American (2.5hr+): £350. Between 150 and 450 photos taken. Photos supplied in industry-standard web- and print-optimised formats. Up to 15% student discounts. See website for full details of packages and approach.

Work portfolio: Has taken hundreds of photos for each edition of Spotlight – 'Top Theatre Photographer' (*The Stage*). Works for actors and agencies across the spectrum of the industry. Recent clients have been represented by agencies such as United, Angel & Francis, Curtis Brown and Felix de Wolfe, studied at drama schools like RADA and Central, and worked on high-profile film, theatre and TV projects. Also writes regularly on headshot and digital trends in the acting industry (see **www.wharleywords.co.uk**).

Alex Winn Photography

Studio 6B, The Electricians Shop,
Trinity Buoy Wharf, 64 Orchard Place,
London E14 0JW
tel 020-3432 4408 *mobile* 07816 317038
website www.alexwinn.com

Services & rates: Photographer since 2006. Offers 3 packages priced between £175-£200 for sessions starting at 1.5hrs up to 3.5hrs. Depending on package selected, they include either 2, 4 or 6 professionally retouched images delivered via digital download and most include two 10 x 8in prints. Contact sheets are made available online 24 hours after each session in both b&w and colour. All sessions are shot and delivered digitally. Studio and outdoor location (both wheelchair-accessible).

Work portfolio: Examples of work can be seen on the website. Has taken photographs for several hundred actors, among them Elizabeth Carling (Curtis Brown), Claire Hope-Ashitey (United Agents), Martin Jenson (Simon & How), James Farrar (Cole Kitchenn), Olly Yellop (A&J Management), Michael Rivers (Marcus & McCrimmon) and Wil Johnson (CAM). "I operate in a relaxed but professional way to ensure that everyone can feel as comfortable as possible in front of the camera. I think good headshots are the result of a collaboration between myself and the actors I work with so each session is tailored accordingly."

Robert Workman

Studio 32, West Kensington Mansions,
Beaumont Crescent, London W14 9PF
tel 020-7385 5442
email bob@robertworkman.demon.co.uk
website www.robertworkman.demon.co.uk

Services & rates: Casting portrait session £250, which includes the session with portraits taken both in the studio and outside in a nearby park, a web gallery of the results, the client's choice of 5 retouched 10x8in prints, and a CD of jpegs ready for digital submissions to casting directors and Spotlight online.

Work portfolio: Photographs can be viewed on the website or in a portfolio kept in Spotlight's offices. Has been taking around 200 publicity shots for actors every year for nearly 30 years.

REPRO COMPANIES

Denbry Repros trading as Studio 57 Ltd

6 The Old Chapel, 69 Primrose Hill,
Kings Langley WD4 8HX
tel (01442) 242411
email info@denbryrepros.com
website www.denbryrepros.com

Please refer to the website for current details and prices. Other services include a studio for casting photography, downloading images from the Internet and supplying images on CD in colour or b&w.

Denman Repros

Burgess House, Main Street, Farnsfield,
Nottinghamshire NG22 8EFF
tel (01623) 882272 *fax* (01623) 882272

Initial scan of a 10x8in print is free. Can also work with CDs, negatives and transparencies.

Repros of a b&w 10x8in are priced as follows: £48 for 100, £64 for 250 and £88 for 500.

Repros of a b&w postcard print are priced as follows: £34 for 100, £39 for 250 and £64 for 500.

Note: Please ring for latest prices for colour repros.

Faces Prints

10 Avondale Road, Carlton, Nottingham NG4 1AF
tel (0115) 847 5640 *fax* 0115-847 5640
email facesprints@ntlworld.com

Initial scan is free.

Repros of b&w 10x8in are priced as follows: £28 for 25, £43 for 50, £56 for 100, £73 for 200, £85 for 250 and £99 for 500.

Repros of a b&w postcard print are priced as follows: £22 for 25, £32 for 50, £37 for 100, £49 for 200, £59 for 250 and £85 for 500.

Will also provide a free gloss on quantity of 25, free photo retouch, free design on 'z-cards', and email proofing and free name/caption insertion.

Image Photographic

Horizon House, Azalea Drive, Swanley,
Kent BR8 8HY

tel 020-7602 1190
email digital@imagephotographic.com
website www.imagephotographic.com

Initial scan or negative £7.50.

Repros of a b&w 10x8in are priced as follows:
£30 for 25, £50 for 50, £70 for 75, £90 for 100

Repros of a b&w 'real' postcard are priced as follows:
£27.50 for 25, £47 for 50, £68 for 75, £85 for 100

See website for other options and pricings.

Moorfields Photographic

2 Old Hall Street, Liverpool L3 9RQ
tel 0151-236 1611
email info@moorfieldsphoto.com
website www.moorfieldsphoto.com

Established in 1981. Please refer to the website for full details.

Profile Prints

Unit 2, Plot 1A, Rospeath Industrial Estate, Crowlas TR20 8DU
tel (01736) 741222 *fax* (01736) 741255
email sales@courtwood.co.uk
website www.courtwood.co.uk

One-off charge of £2.75 for negative from email, CD or original. All media accepted.

Repros of 10x8in b&w or colour are priced as follows:
£29.75 for 24, £52.25 for 50, and £94.25 for 100.

Credit card-sized self-adhesive 'minis' (great for CVs):
£13 for 50, and £18.25 for 100.

Produces all sizes, postcards and z-cards. Prices include P&P and VAT.

Visualeyes Imaging Services

F167 Riverside Business Centre, Bendon Valley, London SW18 4UQ
tel 020-8875 8811
email imaging@visualeyes.co.uk
website www.visualeyes.co.uk

Dedicated reproduction of performers' photographic headshots. Free postage. Print sizes: 6x4in; 10x8in; 12x8in (A4); 16x12in (A3). *Other services include*: retouching, captioning, online ordering. Standard or 5-day economy service. Multi-run print discount and individual student or group discounts available. See website for details.

Getting the most from your photographs

Angus Deuchar

When searching for actors, most casting directors or directors start with a pile of photographs. Their time is limited, so they really only want to see the people who stand a chance of being right for a part – and the picture will be a vital part of their decision-making process. It's important therefore, to ensure that the photographs you use are as good as they can possibly be.

Have a flick through *Spotlight*. As well as being compulsive entertainment for any actor, it can be a great way to decide what works and what doesn't. If *you* were the casting director, who would (and wouldn't) you see? Try it for different types of production: a musical, a Shakespeare play, a TV drama. You may be surprised at the assumptions you make based on the photographs.

I'm going to look at what makes a good actor's photograph; help you think through how to choose a photographer; and discuss how you can get the best results from a photo session. Here is a list of, in my opinion, some important qualities to look for in a good headshot. It should be:

- **Honest.** This to me is the key to a good actor's photograph. Decisions at interviews are often largely made in the first few seconds, so it's important that the person who walks through the door is the person they saw in the photograph. If an actor looks different in some way, the interviewer's first reaction may well be disappointment. Which can't be a good start!
- **Well lit.** The face and hair should be well lit. If there are excessively bright areas or shadows on the face, the photo is probably not doing the actor any favours.
- **In focus.**
- **A good connection with the eyes.** These are possibly the most important feature, as these are what we generally look at first. We make a connection with the eyes. They should be well lit, in focus, looking *at* the camera and not squinting. They should also be 'alive' and not glazed over.
- **Well framed.** Ideally just head and shoulders. Not too close up, as it can look a bit overbearing. Likewise, not too far away as the face becomes too small.
- **Nothing 'tricksy'.** No fake hand-gestures, and certainly no props!

Can't I just get my friend to take some pictures in the back garden? Well, you could (in fact, some do). But what kind of image of yourself would that portray? You can always see such pictures in *Spotlight* – the actor looking awkward, squinting into the sunlight or the picture out of focus. Again, if you were the casting director, would you consider that actor to be serious? There's no point in cutting costs here. Decent photographs can more than pay for themselves.

Finding a photographer

Assuming you've decided to employ a photographer, how do you find the right one? Professional photographers are not all alike. Some who may be fantastic at, say, press or fashion, may not be good at actors' portraits. It's important that the photographer knows the business of Acting. There are countless listings of specialist actors' photographers – in publications like this one; as adverts in *Contacts*; or on posters in The Actors Centre; but the style of photographs, and the ability of the photographers, are as varied as the prices and packages. It is therefore essential to check out their work for yourself. Have a look at their website if they have one, or at least try to see several different examples of their work.

Don't make a choice based solely on price. The amount a photographer charges is not necessarily an indication of how good (or bad) they are. Wherever possible, make your decision about a photographer based mostly on the *work* they produce, rather than how much they charge. It's important ultimately that you get the best possible photographs.

Find out the following:

• **Studio or natural light?** Studio light is easier to standardise and can be used at any time of the day or night and during any weather. It can be made to flatter someone, but won't necessarily show what they will look like in 'real life'. I prefer natural light, as I believe it to be generally more honest. Good natural light can still show someone at their best, but it won't deceive. It can also be more relaxing for the subject to be outside for the session. Casting directors often prefer natural light as it gives a better indication of who is actually going to walk through the door.

• **Film or digital?** Digital technology has moved on to such an extent that the quality of either format is comparable. Digital tends to produce a cleaner, less grainy image *and* you can check the results as you go along. It is essential however, that whoever is preparing the final photograph knows how to convert the image into a good-quality black and white print, with decent contrast and without loss of detail. This takes a reasonable amount of skill and know-how.

• **How much do they charge?** Does that include VAT? If relevant, you may want to ask about concessions for students.

• **How many photos do I get?** Find out how many photos will actually be taken at the session and how many different, finished 8x10 prints you can choose.

• **How will I view my proofs?** Some photographers will put your proofs onto a website enabling you to view them blown up on the screen. You may prefer a paper contact sheet, which, although much smaller to view, is more portable. If you want both, you may need to pay extra – so ask.

• **How long until I see my proofs?** Websites can often be published the same day as the session, while a paper contact will usually need to be produced and posted, so will take a few days. Some photographers will show you pictures on a computer straight away. This can be useful as a guide, but you probably shouldn't try to make final decisions without a bit of time to think.

• **How long will it take until I get my finished prints?** Try to get an indication of how long you should expect to wait after placing your final order. Hopefully, no more than a few days.

• **Do I get a CD?** As well as the prints, a few electronic versions of the final photos are extremely useful. They can be used on a website, to send a submission via email, to send to Spotlight, to print out yourself, or to act as the master-copy for your 'repros'. Find out if the photographer will provide you with a few different versions on a CD, and if it's included in the price.

The session itself

Here are some important things to prepare before – or think about during – your photo session.

• **Your 'look'.** Do you want to appear neutral or as a particular 'type'? For instance, earrings (on men especially) or other piercings, may limit you to modern or even 'alternative' characters. A formal jacket might suggest a business person or MP. Any of these looks may be fine, as they can make you 'ideal' for a particular type of role – but it's likely that that's all you'll ever be seen for while using that photograph! You decide – it really depends upon how you are marketing yourself.

• **Make-up and hair.** Preferably little or no make-up, but certainly no more than you would wear normally, day to day. Some photographers provide a 'hair and make-up' service but I would strongly discourage actors from using this. Don't confuse actors' portraits with having a glamorous photo to stick on top of the piano! If someone else prepares you, you're unlikely to look like the 'normal' you and it may be difficult to recreate that look in the future. Likewise, if you're planning to get a new hairstyle before your session, do so several days in advance to give you a chance to get used to it.

• **What to wear.** Concentrate on the neckline. Wear something you feel comfortable in, but avoid distracting patterns or logos. Most colours are fine, and black often works well. Bright white can affect the exposure so is less helpful. A jacket of some sort for some of the photos can often work well. Jewellery can be distracting so is usually best avoided.

• **Facial expression.** A big smile is often great for musicals or front-of-house pictures, but for other casting purposes it can seem a little over the top. Any kind of 'emoting' can seem over-earnest or, worse, corny. I tend to favour a good neutral expression with 'spark' behind the eyes. A kind of a relaxed, open look with the smallest hint of a smile.

Ultimately, photographs play an important part in helping you get a foot in the door. But once you've been called for the interview, it's over to you.

Angus Deuchar trained as an actor, during which time he subsidised his grant by taking photographs of his fellow students. When he left drama school in 1987 he soon realised that this was an ideal way to make a living between jobs! He pursued both careers for the first seven years, but has continued with just the photography since then. A website showing examples of his work can be seen at **www.actorsphotos.co.uk**.

Making money from your voice

Marina Caldarone

Clichés and misconceptions abound! 'It's a closed shop'; 'agents won't take you on in this climate'; 'you need an agent to stand any chance of getting work'; 'it's impossible to get into radio drama'; 'audio book recording is really badly paid'; and, the best one, 'you can earn a fortune making voiceovers'. That last bit can be true, incidentally, but it's far from the full story. The voiceover industry seems to be booming; there are more voiceover agencies appearing every year. But only a select few actors are lucky enough to make a living solely through their voiceover work: more likely, the latter supplements the former.

So, it doesn't matter what you look like, it's what you can sound like, it's about your ability to lift the text from the page, to bring it to life, often without rehearsal.

The following is a Users' Guide to debunking some of the myths, and setting the record straight on how to make money from your voice.

A glossary

A **Voiceover CD** or **Voicereel** is the full version of your recording, generally averaging 6-10 tracks in length, each track lasting anything from a 20-second commercial to a 90-second piece of documentary narration. It should be professionally edited to include music and effects where appropriate; it should not be a series of dry recordings of you reading, but rather should play to your strengths. It should *not* include 'everything' you think should go on – the reel itself needs to be about diversity within your natural range, not about you showing every accent you can do. Focus on the different colours and weights and drives within your natural voice.

The reel needs to include some factual material/documentary commercials and maybe fiction/audio book too – and I think, though this is a moot point, a drama track also. This should be delivered to you post-recording in two formats – an audio CD which you can copy and play on your computer/car stereo/CD player, and a data CD, so that the audio (mp3 files) can be sent electronically, as individual tracks.

The **Voice-clip** is a 'best of' compilation of excerpts of your full CD (sometimes called a 'megamix', or 'montage'). This should be delivered to you in the same two formats as the voicereel. Voice-clips are (usually) 2 x 1-minute in length (one clip being all commercial excerpts, and the other covering everything else), or 1 x 2-minute maximum compilation of the whole CD.

Copyright clearance does not need to be obtained for any of the material used, as it is for 'critical review' purposes only. So just tick the box that Spotlight asks you to check to confirm that you have clearance; it's often a formality.

Copy is the script. This can be emailed to you before the recording – although it may not be, if it is still being worked on.

A **Contacts Brochure** is something that all voiceover CD production companies should offer you, at no additional cost. It lists hundreds of potential employers, from the studios that make commercials, to advertising agencies, to Independent Radio Drama production companies.

A **Rate Card** specifies what each voiceover artist charges for the work. There is a minimum rate set by Equity; however, the rates aren't always adhered to. And some voiceover agents, in an attempt to get their client the job, will undercut that rate. It's not difficult to see where this leads to – fees spiralling lower for all.

The **Basic Studio Fee (BSF)** is what each voiceover agent will set for their clients. Most rates start at around £200 an hour.

The **Buyout Fee** is a variable based on many other criteria, such as distribution, whether there is web usage, global coverage, amount of airtime and whether the campaign is local or national.

The most commonly asked questions – answered

If I make a voicereel, will I get work?

Without a voicereel which can be sent by email, and which can be uploaded onto your Spotlight page, it is unlikely that you will get work. There is certain amount you can do to promote your voice, even without a voiceover agent; with your voice-clip costing nothing to send, this just takes application and energy – and time, of course. You can appreciate that a CV is great to back up your CD, but it won't replace it if you are looking for audio work.

So how do I select a company to make my CD?

Do your research, check out their credentials and their website. Listen to examples of their work, some of which should be online. Do they provide a Producer/Director, or just an engineer, and what is the quality of their edit? Who are their previous clients? Look at testimonials. All companies will recycle the same scripts, but to what extent? They should be able to tell you. If it looks too good to be true, it generally is.

How do different companies make the CDs?

Each company will have a house style, of sorts. For example, do you want an opening spot where you introduce yourself? For many companies, that is now old-fashioned, whilst for others it's a feature. The first voices we hear on both clips should be the ones that are closest to your natural voice; that is undisputed. Some companies, at very little cost, will just make a voice-clip for you, but you will have no full CD recorded to back those clips up. Others will invite you on to their website for you to select your own choice of material from their online archive, adjusting that choice on the recording day if it isn't quite right for you. Some will have a chat with you on the phone, get the measure of your voice and email you relevant material; others will meet you for a one-on-one consultation before the recording day, go through scripts and make a selection for you to take away and prep. Some companies keep you in studio from the start of the record through the edit to the mastering, so you walk away with the CD; others keep you in studio just for the recording and will send you the fully edited CD soon after.

What should I expect to pay to have a voicereel made?

Anything from £130 for just a voice-clip to £500 for the full CD with added extras (each company's website should give clear information about what you get for whatever rate).

I am interested in animation – what then?

An animation reel is very different. It comprises lots of different voices, heavily edited with effects and music to pack a punch. It might be that you make an animation track on your regular CD: this could be, say, 12 different 4-second-average sentences (these don't have to be connected but should be funny, caricature-ish and extreme, rather than just good accents). You would need more time to record this, so there would be an extra cost, otherwise you could include a couple of character voices in one of your commercials.

I have an existing CD, but it's a bit tired and old fashioned. What should I do?

Upgrade it. But check out whether there is anything there you can recycle before getting rid of it all. Send it to the company you are making the CD with; they will listen to it and recommend whether there is anything there you could keep for the new voice-clip.

What do I do if my agent doesn't represent clients for voiceover?

You go hunting for a specific voiceover agent. Always start with your regular agent, as they may have a specific connection with a particular voiceover agent, so you're approaching them by personal recommendation, which is always good.

How do I approach voiceover agents about representation?

Research who they currently have on their books. Your opening gambit, with your voice-clips and CV attached, should be that you note they don't already represent anyone like you. Do not approach anyone who has 'your voice' already. Chase them for a response, carefully, after a few weeks/a month with maybe one other email – but do not hound them, it will backfire.

So I've got a job for a commercial, what does the employer expect?

For you to be efficient, precise, imaginative, and *quick to take and interpret direction into a new reading*. To be positive, upbeat, someone who won't let their irritation show when asked to repeat the same sentence 30 times, with the only direction being, 'Can you try something different?' Someone who will be fine about running a little over the studio booking. If that really is an issue, take it up with your agent, after the booking; they will know how and whether to act on it. Studio etiquette is paramount, this can't be overstated.

Should I include a Radio Drama track?

Being a really strong actor does not mean you will necessarily be a good voiceover. The skills are quite different. The pay rates are different, the representation is different, and your 'regular' agent would put you forward for it, not your voiceover agent. So in spite of some agents saying that there is no need for the actor to have any drama on the CD, this feels like a wasted opportunity. You need to play to your natural casting, as long as it offers an alternative take on your voice.

Marina Caldarone is a Director with Crying Out Loud (**www.cryingoutloud.co.uk**), a company that has been making voiceover CDs for actors since 1999. She is a Radio Drama Producer, a Theatre Director and Acting Coach and is co-author with Maggie Lloyd Williams of the bestselling *Actions – An Actors' Thesaurus*. She has been a tutor in actor training since 1984, which makes her older than she would care to admit to.

Showreel, voicereel and website services

The rapid developments in recording and computer technologies have seen an explosion of such actor-marketing tools over the last decade. There has also been a significant increase in the amount of (sometimes contradictory) advice offered on content, length, and so on. Much of this 'advice' is available on individual service-providers' websites, where you can usually find samples of their work.

Voicereels (also known as 'voice demos' and, sometimes confusingly, 'showreels') have been around for several decades, and a good one could attract the attention of a voice agent. However, the world of voice-overs is hard to break into and so a quality-produced 'reel' is very important. Showreels (applied to videoed performances) are a more recent innovation and are not yet quite the 'norm' – some agents and casting directors insist on seeing you perform live. However, a good one might just tip the balance in your favour.

Personal websites (for actors) are becoming more popular, but are still far from being essential. After all, you should already have a 'web presence' via Spotlight's website – and, possibly, elsewhere.

If you intend to travel down these routes, check the details (including pricing) of each possible company and the quality of their work. You should also assess whether the financial investment(s) involved could produce sufficient return. These additional 'calling cards' need to be of broadcast quality and professionally packaged to have any impact. As with photographers, it is very important to research as thoroughly as possible before committing your meagre funds. Is there a real possibility that one (or more) will enhance your chances of acting work?

Note: It is very important that you have permission from the copyright-holders of any material that you intend to use, and some companies will help with this. It is also important to check the current charges of each company that interests you, as some will change during the lifetime of this edition.

Accent Bank

420 Falcon Wharf, 34 Lombard Road,
London SW11 3RF
tel 020-7223 5160
email enquiries@accentbank.co.uk
website www.accentbank.co.uk
Director Lisa Paterson

A voice-over portal distributed to an international market. Acts as a shop window for experienced voice-over talent specialising in authentic regional and international voices. "Accent Bank provides bespoke one-on-one coaching and workshops for those new to the business. We pride ourselves on a very personal service, using the best coaches and directors, original material and excellent production facilities to bring out the best in your voice. For more information, or to have a chat, contact us by phone or email."

Actor Showreels

97B Central Hill, London SE19 1BY
tel (07853) 637965
email post@actorshowreels.co.uk
website www.actorshowreels.co.uk
Key contact Hugh Montini Lee

Showreel services: The actor works with an editor to select the material from pre-existing clips. The edited material is uploaded online, so that the actor's agent can also view the edit. The editing/upload process continues until the actor is totally satisfied with the final edit. The average duration of a showreel is 3.5 minutes. Average cost per showreel is £175. Recent clients have included: Claire Goose (Independent), Gina Bellman (Independent), Tulisa (Cole Kitchenn), Kerry Ellis (Cole Kitchenn), Colin Salmon (Curtis Brown) and Jennifer Hennessy (Curtis Brown).

Actors Apparel

London based – travels to clients
mobile (07738) 876295, (07877) 142823
email contact@actorsapparel.com
website www.actorsapparel.com

Showreel services: Established in 2010. Charges £780 for a Popular Showreel, £980 for an Exclusive Showreel. Tailor-made showreels; originally written scenes tailored to client's brief. HD footage, montage clips, editing and high-quality sound. Online links and hard copies included. Charges £50 per hour for producing a showreel from existing material only. Popular Showreel includes 3 free hard copies, Exclusive Showreel includes 6 free hard copies. Both packages include online conversion for Spotlight and Casting Call Pro. Editing from existing material, £50 per hour. Average showreel duration is 3-5 minutes. Discounts offered for dual bookings. Please see website brochure for more details and special offers. Also offers Short Film Packages. Recent clients include: Max Fowler (Eamonn Bedford Associates), Katie Redford (Red Canyon Management), Verity Hewlitt (Hoxton Street Casting), Nick Lavelle (SCA Management), Cherice Mckenzie-Cook (Top Talent Agency), Thea Cantell (Sandra Boyce Management), Katie Redford (Red Canyon Management), Max Fowler (Macfarlane Chard Associates) and Carla Nicholls (Lynda Ronan Personal Management).

The Actor's One-Stop Shop

First Floor, Above the Gate Pub, Station Road, London N22 7SS
tel 020-8888 7006 *fax* 020-8888 9666
email info@actorsonestopshop.com
website www.actorsonestopshop.com
established 1997

Showreel services: Offers broadcast-quality, professionally packaged reels. Scenes are crafted like film/TV excerpts rather than being 'audition pieces'. Actors can choose either monologue or dialogue scenes, in any combination they wish. A single scene (monologue) reel costs £310 (including final copy in box DVD presentation).

Also edits reels from past work at a cost of £60 per hour; clients sit-in on the edit and receive the finished product the same day. Price includes full archiving of material so that the reel can be easily and affordably updated in the future. The company also supplies 'streamed' copies for agency and Spotlight websites.

Recommended by several agents, Spotlight and Casting Call Pro. See website for reel samples.

Bolt Tight Showreels

Based in South East London
mobile (07533) 353836
email info@samanthabolter.com
website www.vimeo.com/bolt
Key contact Samantha Bolter

Showreel services: Established in 2004. Charges £100 per showreel edit (which includes 1 DVD copy, Internet files and DVD cover). Motto is the '3 M's' - "no Montage, no Monologues to camera and no longer than 3 Minutes!" £400 daily fee to shoot scenes (price can be split between actors; roughly 2-3 scenes can be shot in a day. Price negotiable for updates to existing reel(s). Packages offered: 20% off edit (total £80) and shoot price (total £320 per day) for students, recent graduates and Equity members. Also see Bolt Tight's Facebook page (**BoltTightReels**) or follow the company on Twitter (**@BoltTightReels**).

Does not supply scripts though will happily give advice on how/what to pick. Rehearsal and direction given on day of shoot. Professional directors, sound and camera operators on every shoot (all on IMDb, please contact for details). Editing equipment is portable to locations within London or Brighton. Recent clients include: Russell Floyd, Kimberley Adams and Brad Glen.

CastNet Ltd

20 Sparrows Herne, Bushey, Hertfordshire WD23 1FU
tel 020-8420 4209 *fax* 020 8421 9666
email support@castnetwebsites.co.uk
website www.castnetwebsites.co.uk
Key Contact Fran Gillett

Founded in 2007, CastNet Websites offer affordable and adaptable website building services, designed specifically for UK performers.

Website services: Offers a basic website building service which is free, but standard templates start from £2 per week or £7.45 per month. Premium templates start from £4 per week or £17.45 per month. Standard packages include hosting and domain name registration, email addresses, search engine optimisation and a facility for clients to update their own site. Premium templates include integrated blog, Twitter feed, unlimited video and audio clips, visitor statistics and private document storage. Recent clients include Will Wollen (Steve Nealon Associates), Morven Macbeth (Regan Rimmer Management) and Sophie Cartman (MSFT Management).

See also the entry for CastNet Ltd under *Spotlight, casting directories and information services* on page 382.

Ben Crowe

25 Holmes Avenue, Brighton BN3 7LB
mobile (07952) 784911
email bencrowe@hotmail.co.uk
Key contact Ben Crowe

Charges £65 for producing a voicereel from scratch (or £55 with Spotlight card, and for students). Includes 2 additional CD copies. Average duration of the reel is 60-90 minutes. "Select 4 30-second speeches for Spotlight voice clips."

Crying Out Loud Productions

Chester House (1:04), 1-3 Brixton Road,
London SW9 6DE
mobile Simon: (07809) 549887;
mobile Marina: (07946) 533108
email simon@cryingoutloud.co.uk
website www.cryingoutloud.co.uk
Key contacts Simon Cryer, Marina Caldarone

Voicereel services: Established in 1999. Charges from £315 to produce a bespoke voicereel from scratch; this includes a face-to-face consultation with Marina Caldarone to select material, studio time with both producer and director, full editing and production, 2 x 1-minute megamixes for Spotlight, a 2-year archive, a Master Audio CD and a data CD containing MP3 files and Contacts Brochure. There are no hidden costs.

Clients will record a selection of material consisting of commercials, narrative, documentary and dramas as well as any other content they may wish to add.

Both Simon Cryer and Marina Calderone are practitioners in the industry working in radio commercials and radio drama. Recent clients have included: Charles (Lord) Brocket, Andrew Castle, Sky TV, Elizabeth Norman (the voice of BT 1571), the Disasters Emergency Committee (DEC), Ubisoft, Sally Gunnell OBE, Magnum, Intel and Sky News Radio.

Cut Glass Productions

Studio 185, 181-187 Queens Crescent, Camden,
London NW5 4DS
tel 020-7267 2339
email info@cutglassproductions.com
website www.cutglassproductions.com
Producer Phil Corran

Voicereel services: Three package options:

• £210 'Revive' – created for artists who wish to update or make changes to an existing showreel.
• £250 'Create' – for actors/artists who need a completely new reel. A lot of support and advice is given to beginners. Includes script consultation and 4 hours' studio time.
• £350 'Raw Talent' – this package is for complete newcomers to the voice industry who feel they are going to need the freedom of unlimited time in the studio.

Once each actor's showreel expectations are established, there is a detailed pre-consultation by phone – this enables Cut Glass to get to know you and select material suitable for your playing age/range. Cut Glass doesn't recycle scripts – each piece (4-5 commercials, 2 narrations or documentaries, maybe an animation/story piece) will be unique to you. There is also a detailed consultation on the day to discuss selected material. The recording session itself is a creative experience in terms of ideas and performance, with Phil Corran directing and producing the session. You will be guided throughout the production and go home with your mastered reel and 1 extra copy. Showreels are around 4 mins long, with an option to produce a 90-second punchy 'montage' which sits at the beginning of your reel and can be emailed to casting directors as an MP3 or used on Spotlight.

As well as specialising in creating high-quality voice-over showreels, Cut Glass is a digital voice-over production studio and creative voice agency. As such, the company has a diverse range of clients – both professional voice-over jobs and showreel customers – and works with animation/computer games companies, corporates, the BBC and independent production companies. It regularly produces audio guides and comedy podcasts, and produces showreels for other agencies as well as its own. See the website for examples of 'montages' of the agency's showreels.

Advice to beginners: As voice-over agents, Cut Glass recommends that your showreel be no longer than around 4 mins; any longer and you will have lost the casting director/agent's attention. Talk to people who work in the voice industry, and listen to recommendations. It's so important to get your showreel production spot-on, because it's your one chance to showcase your vocal talent.

Opus Productions Ltd

9A Coverdale Road, London W12 8JJ
tel 020-8743 3910 *fax* 020-8749 4537
website www.opusproductions.co.uk
Key personnel Claire Bidwell, Neil Wilkes

Established in 1999. Works mainly in computer media production. Specialises in video and audio encoding, DVD authoring, video editing, graphic design and website design. Will edit, produce and encode video and DVD showreels for actors.

Pelinor

Harberton Road, London N19 3JR
tel 020-7263 8862
email support@pelinor.com
website www.pelinor.com
Key contact Misha von Bennigsen

Showreel services: Established in 2003. Charges £150 for producing a showreel with existing material only, which includes 1 DVD; extra copies are charged from £1. Average duration of a showreel is 3 minutes. Offers 10% off for CCP and TAG members. Recent clients include: Samantha Robinson (Curtis Brown), Margo Stilley (Curtis Brown), Dave Berry (Troika) and Sharon Duce (JAA).

Website services: Charges £450 for designing and setting up a basic website (£360 for existing clients). Offers a bespoke 'from scratch' design. Package includes hosting and domain name registration, email addresses, search engine optimisation, and facility for clients to update their own site. Updates charged at £40 per hour. Material is usually selected from existing headshots, biographies/CVs, publicity stills, showreels and voicereels.

Quulzz

mobile (07900) 133303
website http://quulzz.blogspot.co.uk

Showreel and voicereel services: Quulzz specialise in showreel and voicereel work. Packages: £80 per showreel previous materials edit. £60 students or recent graduates. Can select to pay £20 an hour if they do not want a package, but need a tweak. Quulzz welcome a phone call to discuss the best package for each individual if a bespoke reel from scratch is required. Both showreel and voicereel packages include a free DVD of their content and free link upload. The average length of a showreel or voicereel is 3 minutes.

Other services are available, including DVD/file transferring and reel tweaking. Please see the website for more details. "Quulzz's priority is to keep its clients pleased."

The Reel Deal Showreel Co.

6 Charlotte Road, Wallington, Surrey SM6 9AX
tel 020-8647 1235
email info@thereel-deal.co.uk
website www.thereel-deal.co.uk
established 2003

Showreel services: Has 2 rates for editing a showreel: £199 for a full day's editing, which includes 2 free hours in the first year to update the reel, and 2 free DVDs; or the hourly rate of £35 for actors who don't have a lot of material. A discount of 15% is offered if you mention this publication when booking your edit. Clients include: James McAvoy, Rory Kinnear, Rula Lenska, Shane Richie and Shobna Gulati, among others.

Replay Film & New Media

25 Museum Street, London WC1 1ST
tel 020-7637 0473
email solutions@replayfilms.co.uk
website www.replayfilms.com
established 1991

Showreel services: Although Replay can record presentations and performances from scratch, for most clients the task is to produce a carefully constructed compilation of highlights from existing TV and film performances. Advises that the correct selection and juxtaposition of these clips is essential, and it is therefore vital that clients sit in on the editing process to ensure that they are happy with the final result. Most showreels last 4-7 minutes. Will supply scripts if requested, but does not organise for copyright clearance.

As most showreels take around 4 hours to edit, Replay has put together the following package for a fixed fee: up to 4 hours in the edit studio with the editor (digitising existing clips from VHS, capturing digitised clips onto an Avid editing suite, editing the captured clips and inserting titles where required). The digital master will be archived at 2 sites. Exact prices are available on application only. Discounted rates are available to actors, presenters, students and non-commercial theatre companies. Overtime (anything over 4 hours) is charged at approximately 50% of the commercial editing rate.

Recent clients include: Donald Standen, Julian Hanshaw, Justine Waddel, Michael Mears, Patsy Kensit, Shared Experience Theatre Company and Vicky Johnson.

Round Island

London
tel 020-7112 8458
email mail@roundisland.net (Showreels)
email voice@roundisland.net (Voicereels)
website www.roundisland.net
Key contact Ben Miller

Showreel services: Established in 2002. Charges £150 for producing a showreel working with existing material. This includes a DVD copy plus Spotlight and CCP upload. Extra copies are chargeable; a full price list is available from the website. The edit normally takes 3 hours. Recommends that showreels should last no more than 3 minutes. Actors Guild members are eligible for a special rate of £115. Clients' work is saved, so updates are easy, and actors work with the editor on the day of the edit.

Voicereel services: Charges £285 for producing a commercial voicereel from scratch; the price for a commercial and radio drama voicereel is £385. Option to purchase CDs at £25 for 10 custom-printed copies. The average duration of a voicereel is approximately 4 minutes, with 90-second compilations included for Spotlight/CCP etc. "We guide the artist through the entire process with expert direction, production and career advice. Our testimonials on our site and from our many clients support our belief that we are London's most bespoke service."

Website services: Charges £30 upwards for designing and setting up a basic website. Offers both a bespoke 'from scratch' design and a template service. Email addresses are not included in the package, but can be set up for the actor. Basic hosting starts at £5 a year, and search engine optimisation is offered on each website. Updates are charged at £30 per hour: the client may do these updates for themselves and the price to facilitate this depends on the requirements of the site.

The Showreel Ltd

Soho Recording Studios, 22-24 Torrington Place, London WC1E 7HJ
tel 020-7043 8660
email info@theshowreel.com
website www.theshowreel.com

Showreel services overview:

• Get started in voiceovers with our Beginner's Workshop
• One-to-one personal training plans
• Agents demos
• Spotlight demos
• Graduate packs and deals
• Update your existing demo and get more and more ...

For other services, please visit the website.

Showreelz.com

28 Eastbury Grove, Chiswick, London W4 2JZ
mobile (07885) 253477
email brad@showreelz.com
website www.showreelz.com
established 1998

Showreel services: Showreelz.com has been editing showreels for performers since 1999. The company is based in Chiswick, London W4. Editing rates are £75 for the first two hours and then £30 per hour for additional time.

Recent clients include: Ricci Harnett, Tamer Hassan, Rosemary Ashe, Justine Glenton, Isabel Losada, JC Mac, Eugene Washington, Abbin Galeya, Satnam Bhogul and Amy Darcy. Online payment now accepted. Offers a 15% discount on editing to actors mentioning this publication.

Voicereel services: Supplies scripts for actors to use if desired. Total cost approx. £120 to produce a voicereel from scratch. This includes the company fee, studio and equipment costs, recording and editing of material and 2 CD copies. Rates are set at £75 for the first 2 hours. Normally produces voicereels lasting 2-3 minutes. Will offer a 10% discount to actors quoting this publication. Recent clients include: Kelsey Cameron, Kal Mansoor, David Lee, Brian Scoltock and Eugene Washington.

Signalize Ltd

Based in Hampshire and Gloucestershire
mobile (07816) 411341
email showreels@signalize.tv
website www.signalizecorporatevideo.com
Key contact Vicky Stone

Showreel services: Established in 2004. Charges £600 for producing a showreel from scratch (includes fees, studio and equipment costs, recording and editing of new material, etc.). Working with existing material only, the fee is £300. Price includes 5 copies on DVD; the usual duration of a showreel is 1.5 to 3 minutes. Special packages may be negotiated individually. New material is selected via a process of review, consultation, trial edit, and final review. Supplies scripts and organises copyright clearances. Recent clients include: Deborah Moore, Jane Lehrer Associates, Claire Broomby, Charlotte Thomson, Casting Call Pro and Burnett Granger Crowther.

Details of voicereel services: Charges £400 for producing a voicereel from scratch; working from existing material the fee is £200. Includes 5 CD copies. Duration, packages and selection/recording process as above.

Advises actors: "You can't compensate for lack of quality with additional quantity."

Silver-Tongued Productions

tel 020-8309 0659
email contactus@silver-tongued.co.uk
website www.silver-tongued.co.uk

Voicereel services: A small independent company recording high-quality voicereels at a competitive price. They guide you through the whole process of recording your voicereel, from choosing scripts to directing you during the recording session, making it as simple and as easy as possible. Their voicereels are truly bespoke, so are as individual as you are. Visit the website for full details of services.

Silvertip Films Ltd

8 Quadrum Park, Old Portsmouth Road, Guildford, Surrey GU3 1LU
tel (01483) 407533 *mobile* (07786) 331502
email info@silvertipfilms.co.uk
website www.silvertipfilms.co.uk
Key Contact Geoff Cockwill

Showreel services: Established in 2005.

Shoot and Edit 1 is £360 inc VAT + any expenses – this is a half day shooting 3 scenes, either monologue or duologue and editing the scenes for the reel plus any existing material you have.

Shoot and Edit 2 is £600 inc. VAT + any expenses. This is as above but a full day shooting up to 5 scenes plus editing, including any existing material.

Editing existing material only is £180 inc. VAT + any expenses. This is a half-day edit and includes transfer of existing material on DVD or from online and editing the reel either using either notes or direct input from the client. The reel is sent to the client for approval and any reasonable changes will be made where possible.

A discount of 10% is available to readers of *Actors and Performers Yearbook*. Packages include reel in web HD format, HD data file and a DVD or BluRay copy. Additional copies at £1.50 (inc. P&P). Silvertip also upload the reel to their YouTube channel and CCP page. The average length of a showreel is 3-4 minutes

Silvertip's previous clients include: Alexis Peterman (United Artists), Dar Dash (Hobsons), Heather Skermer (Red Hot Entertainment) and Libby Gore (Imperium Management).

Small Screen Showreels

17 Knole Road, Crayford, London DA1 3JN
tel 020-8816 8896

email info@smallscreenshowreels.co.uk
website www.smallscreenshowreels.co.uk
Key contact Anthony Holmes

Showreel and voicereel editing service for talent with existing footage. Clients include: Andrew Sachs, David Jason and Cas Anvar. Charges £50 per hour (no minimum charge). Showreel provided as a digital file for direct upload to Spotlight or other casting websites. DVDs also available – up to 10 copies £3 each. Able to record material broadcast on television on request, and to download/record material from websites such as YouTube or iPlayer (where client has permission to do so). Showreel material archived for easier updates. Average duration of a showreel is 3 minutes. Spotlight members, or those who quote *Actors and Performers Yearbook* when booking, will receive a 10% discount. Also offers assistance with selection of material for existing footage if required. Does not record voicereels, but is able to edit existing ones if required.

SonicPond Studio

70 Mildmay Grove South, Islington, London N1 4PJ
tel 020-7690 8561
email martin@sonicpond.co.uk
website www.sonicpond.co.uk
Key contact Martin Fisher

Showreel services: Editing of existing material only. Charges £200 (£180 for students) to edit a showreel from existing material, uploaded directly to Spotlight for you. The average duration of a showreel is 3-4 minutes. Clients include: Annie Cooper (Felix de Wolfe); Zoe Lister (*Hollyoaks*) and Sid Owen (*EastEnders*). Advises actors: "Don't worry that you may not have enough material; you most likely do. Less is truly more with showreels. Also, don't wait for that copy of the student film you have been waiting to be sent; think of the reel as an organic growing thing which you will add to and change for the whole of your career. Just get it started."

Voicereel services: Supplies scripts for actors to use if desired. Charges £325 to produce a voicereel from scratch; working from existing material the rate is £45 per hour. 2 CDs are included in the package, with extra copies charged at £2 each. Nine pieces recorded, commercial and narrative, with a 90-second montage included. Students: £295 for a full voicereel. Voice clients include: Bob Golding (Hobsons); Nicholas Keith (Yakety Yak); Kellie Bright (Sue Terry Voices); Sam & Mark (Harvey Voices); Ronan Vibert (Harvey Voices) and James Alexandrou (Earache). Advises actors: "Don't worry about the pieces, we will work together to find you the best material. It's much more about finding the tone for each piece, and material that suits you perfectly, rather than the best copy. In the meantime, listen to as much voice-over as possible, and think about why any particular voice is used for any piece."

Sound

Sound, Pembroke House, 7, Brunswick Square, Bristol BS2 8PE
tel 0117-9245 853
email kenwheeler@mac.com
website www.soundat7.com
Key Contact Ken Wheeler

Voicereel services: Established in 1987. Charges £300 (+ VAT) to produce a bespoke voicereel from scratch.This includes a pre-production meeting to select material suitable for the artist and they will be provided with copies for familiarisation and rehearsal before any recording takes place. Sound are happy to provide scripts and organise copyright clearance issues. Editing existing material will cost £110 (+ VAT).The average length of a voicereel is 15 minutes and CD copies of the final recording are available for purchase at 75p each.

Sound's recent clients include: Jaguar, Virgin Media, DFS, Really Useful Theatres Group and Stihl.

Sounds Wilde

Wood Green, London N22
mobile (07930) 689132
email kirsty@soundswilde.com
website www.soundswilde.com
Key contact Kirsty Gillmore

Voicereel services: Established in 2010.

Standard Voicereel Package: £225 inc. VAT (clients record 2 x 1min mixes, commercial and narrative, with copies of all recordings).

Student and Graduate Voicereel Service: £95 inc. VAT (clients record up to 5 individual pieces (commercials, documentary, narrative and drama, which are mixed into a 90-second master montage, with copies of all recording).

Extra CD copies can be provided on request at £2 per copy. Charges £40 per hour for producing a voicereel working from existing material and for recording/ mixing individual clips. Supplies bespoke scripts appropriate to a client's voice type, ascertained at an initial personal consultation; no scripts are reused.

Recent clients include: Marc Warren (*Hustle*, *The Musketeers*); Helen George (*Call the Midwife*); Jill Winternitz (*Once* and *Dirty Dancing*, West End); Will Merrick (*Skins*, *About Time*). Advises clients: "Come prepared for your voicereel session – be familiar with the material you'll be recording, fully warmed up and ready to work hard. Your voicereel producer will offer any direction you need, but don't be afraid to ask questions or add your own input. Only include character voices and varying accents if you are 100% comfortable with them."

Take Five

37 Beak Street, London W1F
tel 020-7287 2120 *fax* 020-7287 3035
email info@takefivestudio.com
website www.takefivestudio.com
Key contact Charlie Lort-Phillips
established 1995

Showreel services: Charges £70 per hour for filming and £45 per hour for editing (this includes all studio and equipment costs). VHS copies are priced at £6 each, DVDs at £13 each and CDs at £6 each. Discounts are offered for bigger quantities.

A script consultation is held with each actor, preferably 7 days prior to filming. Scenes can be shot in the studio or on location, and benefit from professional direction, lighting and cameramen. Most showreels last around 5 minutes. The company advises actors who are sending in existing material only to cue scenes on the tape or to have the timecodes written down to speed up the capturing process.

Recent clients include: Siobhan Hewlett (Hamilton Hodell), Harry Eden (Independent), Lee Ingleby (Conway van Gelder Grant) and Tim Barlow (Paul Becker).

Twitch Films

22 Grove End Gardens, 18 Abbey Road,
London NW8 9LL
tel 020-7266 0946
email post@twitchfilms.co.uk
website www.twitchfilms.co.uk

Established in 2006; offices are fully wheelchair accessible. Working with existing material, charges a flat fee of £200, which includes editing, design of DVD interface and discprint, 10 professionally printed and packaged DVDs, digital files for use on the Internet, websites and for emailing and full archiving. For shorter edits and updates the hourly rate is £40; additional discs can be ordered from £2.50 each, depending on quantity. The average duration of a showreel is 3-5 minutes.

"We advise recording material from scratch only in exceptional circumstances, primarily when an aspect of the actor's range, which would be key to their castability, is under-represented in their existing footage. We do not provide scripts, but will give detailed advice on what scripts may be appropriate, and assist in making the selection." Recent clients include: Darren Boyd and Eleanor Matsuura (Amanda Howard Associates); Colin Salmon (GMM); Jane Perry (Andrew Manson Personal Management); Kevork Malikyan (United Agents) and Trevor White (Price Gardner Management).

Ken Wheeler

28 Wellington Terrace, Clevedon,
North Somerset BS21 7PT
tel (01275) 879799
email kenwheeler@mac.com
website www.soundat7.com

Established in 1987. Supplies scripts. Recent clients include: Virgin, Asda, DFS, Sainburys, Parampara, Jaguar, The Co-Op, Alfa Romeo, Scholastic Education and Bristol City Council.

Voicereel services: Normal hourly rate is £100. For an inclusive cost of £350, including direction, recording, editing and mixing, we will produce a voicereel from scratch. During a pre-production meeting, scripts (commercials, corporate, narration, prose and poetry) will be selected that are suited to the particular voice to provide a varied and balanced reel.

Effective and affordable digital marketing

Benjamin Warren

Like it or not, digital marketing is becoming not just important, but in some cases vital to a successful acting career. You need to keep up, but you don't have to spend a lot of money to do so. As technology evolves, the methods used when casting are getting faster and faster, so that having a quality representation of yourself online really can make the difference between getting the role or not.

You are not only an actor, you are a business, and you need to present yourself like one. The industry sees you as a product. Casting directors and agents talk about you in terms of type. Don't see this as a negative, though – there is plenty of opportunity to show you're unique – it's just their way of processing the vast number of actors out there. Work with them and package your product professionally, and you will without a doubt improve your chances.

There are many companies out there that can help you achieve effective and affordable digital marketing, but by following these simple pointers you can not only create the right digital marketing for you, but also avoid paying any more than you need to.

Showreels

First and foremost, these should be short and fancy-free: 'no frills' does not have to mean 'no good'. Actors all too often make choices based on what *they* like. That's fine if you plan to be the only one to watch your showreel, but you're missing the point if you want it to be a useful marketing tool.

Many casting directors and agents use showreels regularly to assess suitability. If you sat down with them and watched 20 actors' showreels, you would soon agree that they should be short; that every clip should tell the viewer something new; and that the first 30 seconds are by far the most important. You don't have to start a scene at the beginning or finish it at the end – in fact, lifting out key sections from a scene can mean that you keep your viewer's interest. Your face should be the first face we see – and the last. The scene should also be cut (where necessary) to focus the scene on you and your performance.

Another consideration is the montage. Actors tend to like montages, as do some agents, but these can all too often contain repeated information and, even with the right music track, get the showreel off to a slow start. Ultimately, a casting director or agent wants to watch you acting and interacting – a good scene, focused on you and showing them what you do well. If you have a casting director about to press play on your showreel, why delay giving them what they really want? If you simply feel you have to have a montage, put it at the end as an outro. That way it will annoy no one. I'm not saying that montages should never be used; they do have their place – for example, if you have a lot of work, they can be a good way of showing images from scenes you don't have time to include. Likewise, if, say, your casting bracket includes 'barrister/doctor/vicar' but the films where you played such roles are not suitable to include as scenes, lifting 2-3 seconds for a short montage might be useful. That way the casting bracket has been covered but the integrity of the scenes has not been compromised.

A common misconception is that a showreel needs to be lots of clips edited into one piece of footage. This is not the case. In fact, depending on your needs, it might be better for you to separate out your scenes into separate clips. This can sometimes simplify the editing process. You can upload up to four clips onto Spotlight, and more on other sites, so the viewer can pick and choose exactly what they want to watch. You could also split your work into categories: for example, Film, TV Drama, Commercials, and Corporate.

As computers get more and more powerful, and we become more proficient in using them, you may find you can do some simple editing yourself. Depending on the job, this might be fine for you – but please bear in mind that just because you can, it doesn't mean you should. Many people can edit, but only a few can cut showreels correctly. In paying for an editor, you are paying for experience, understanding of the business, and (very importantly) an objective eye. Another advantage of using a reputable showreel company is that they will be able to provide you with versions rendered correctly for all the industry sites, and ensure that you are not losing quality when transferring footage from DVD or VHS.

Voicereels

There are now many ways of utilising your voice in the profession, and if you are successful it can provide a very good income. However, it's a misconception that any actor is automatically a voice-over artist. Voice-over work is a specific branch of the industry and therefore requires specific skills.

First and foremost you need a detailed understanding of your own voice. It's not all about how many accents you can do; it's about what you can do with *your* voice and *your* accent. You need to know what your strengths are and understand the limitations of your voice so that you can target the industry specifically – therefore increasing your chances in an already crowded market.

Once you have established this, then consider the difference between drama and commercial reels. They are two distinct areas and therefore require totally different products. The world of radio and audio books won't be interested in your commercial or corporate tracks, and vice-versa. Know what part of the industry you are looking to break into and produce your reel accordingly.

When it comes to sourcing pieces, I would always advise using original material where possible. Every voice is unique so the same script will not suit everyone. Flicking through a folder of previously used scripts just does not make sense. Some companies will provide scripts that have never been used before; others will show you how to go about finding or even creating your own. Again, you need to 'know your voice'. Once you know this you will be able to determine what kind of products you could be employed to advertise or the range of parts you could realistically play in radio drama. You may be surprised – in a medium where your looks are totally irrelevant, you might discover a whole new casting bracket! If you simply don't know where to start, there are some great one-off classes available which are an inexpensive way to explore the possibilities of your voice before you pay out for a voicereel.

Finally, understand what represents good value for money. If you are seriously looking to break into the voice industry, and seeking a regular income from it, then you will need to plan and produce demos that are specifically tailored to your specific skills.

Websites

There is a fine line between what is necessary and what is not when it comes to actors' websites. Personally I believe that they are only really useful as a place to store all your necessary professional information – laid-out and designed on your terms, so that it can be accessed around the world at the click of a button without the need for PINs or passwords, etc. On the whole, individual websites are not used to search for actors; the casting directories do this already.

Many actors may choose not to have a website because they already have all their personal information on their Spotlight (or similar) CV. This is true – if you are already paying for online services, make sure first of all that you are utilising these. However, a personal site means you can dictate its limits. You can have your information displayed exactly as you want the world to see it. You can upload as many individual showreel scenes and voice clips as you want. You can have them displayed (and this is especially important when it comes to video) at the size and quality you want. You can include press pages, where you detail recent reviews, and design a gallery around your needs.

I always think sites work best when written in the third person. When actors sell themselves in the first person, there is a fine line between self-promotion and self-indulgence. Less is almost always more; let the review, photograph or reel do the work. And it doesn't need to be a big site – a single page can be sufficient. This means you can get online without breaking the bank and dictate exactly how your professional information is displayed.

In conclusion ...

Getting up to speed with digital marketing does not have to cost the earth. Know what you are after and how best to sell yourself at any given moment. Then research and locate a company that can advise you accordingly, and can create products which will offer you really useful tools, specifically tailored for your acting career. There is a product and price for everyone: you don't have to put up with the generic, or pay over the odds. And always keep your eyes open for discounts. Sites like **www.actorsguild.co.uk** offer discounts to their members for headshots, showreels, voicereels, websites and plenty more – you can literally save hundreds of pounds as you achieve the online profile that is right for you.

Benjamin Warren trained as an actor at East 15, graduating in 2002. Career highlights since then include playing leads in the West End, at the Royal Exchange and on many UK tours; working for BBC and ITV on the small screen and on film, playing opposite the late Susannah York. Eight years ago he founded Round Island after being underwhelmed by the services on offer when it comes to marketing yourself as an actor. Round Island produces showreels, voicereels and websites for actors at every level. For more information, visit **www.roundisland.net**.

Digital wellbeing for actors

Essentially, digital wellbeing is using the web to work better, not longer; making smart digital choices that work for you. Here, Sinead Mac Manus looks at some of the ways in which you can harness the power of the social web without suffering the burnout.

Getting a web presence

Having a dedicated web presence is increasingly important for any freelance actor. Your personal website can act as a central place on the web for potential employers or collaborators to find you. With free platforms such as WordPress[1], Posterous[2] or Flavors[3], it's never been easier to raise your profile online.

Your domain name

The first step before choosing a web platform is to register your own domain name. Even if you never use it, for the cost of a few pounds each year it is worth owning your own .com and retaining control of your name online. Use a site such as Netnames[4] to search for your professional name and check that it is available. 123-reg[5] is a company with a good reputation for domain name management in the UK, or you can buy your domain name with your web hosting package (see below).

Now you have your domain name secured, how can you build your web presence?

Building a WordPress site

WordPress's easy-to-use and powerful Content Management System (CMS) makes it perfect for freelance artists wanting to create their own website. The platform is free to install and adapt; the only expenses incurred are registering a domain name and paying for web hosting. The CMS of WordPress is easy to get to grips with: in fact, anyone at ease with Microsoft Word will be able to publish a website using WordPress.

Before you start building your site, have a think about what content you want on it. Suggested pages could be Biography, Photography, Credits, Reviews and Contact Me. With WordPress you can easily add a blog to your website with updates of your work.

For a practical step-by-step guide to using WordPress to build your web presence, do read my two-part series on WordPress written for the London Theatre Blog[6]. Part One covers the basics, and Part Two goes into more detail about design, themes, widgets and plug-ins.

Zen Tip: Use a WordPress approved web hosting service to install the WordPress software in one click, rather than going through the complicated manual process.

Do I need a blog?

Blogging can be a great way of building your personal brand as an actor. Through text, images, video or sound, you can demonstrate, reflect and comment on your artistic process. Writing a blog is also a powerful learning tool, promoting critical and analytical thinking, as well as being a powerful audience development and marketing tool.

Microblogging platforms such as Posterous[2] and Tumblr[7] are simple and free ways of starting a blog. Easier to set up than a WordPress blog, these platforms really come into their own when blogging on the go; perfect for freelance actors on tour. Both platforms allow you to post snippets of text, photos, quotes, links, dialogues, audio, video and slideshows from the web or direct from your smart phone.

For a look at the multimedia capabilities of Posterous in action, go to my blog *From Apps to Zen.*[8]

Zen Tip: Use the scheduling feature of Posterous or Tumblr to queue your posts for autoposting during busy tour periods.

Other platforms

Flavors[3] is a relative newcomer to the platform scene, but a fantastic way of creating a personal portal for all your online content in minutes. Simply register your Flavors name (or use you own custom domain), design your layout and background, and then add your choice of 30 social websites. You can pull in tweets from your Twitter Feed, your Wall activity from your Facebook Page, videos from YouTube or Vimeo, posts from your Posterous, Tumblr or WordPress blogs, or photos from Flickr or Instagram[9].

Have a look at some of the wonderfully creative sites on the Flavors' Directory[10] for inspiration.

Zen Tip: Use the Promote tab to add a Search Engine Optimised (SEO)[11] title and description of your page to ensure you are easily found in the search engines.

Using social media

There is a wide range of social media networks and platforms that you can use to communicate and connect with people in the creative industries. Social networks such as Facebook and Twitter, as well as multimedia platforms such as YouTube and Flickr, can help you market yourself, raise your profile and connect with potential employers.

Getting started on social media is relatively easy as the entry barriers are low, both technologically and financially. Social media also harnesses the most highly prized of the marketing methods: word of mouth. It allows you to exponentially expand your marketing potential and reach many more potential audience members or clients than you could using solely an offline approach.

All good so far … But if social media is so effective and easy to use, why isn't every artist jumping on board?

The number one reason why creative people do not get engaged with social media is lack of time, and specifically a fear that if they do engage, it will eat up large chunks of an already busy day. Questions to consider are: do you have the time to plan how you are going to use social media in your work? Do you have the time to set up profiles and start connecting with people? Do you have the time to maintain your online presences and maximise the return from these sites?

I think social media has a bad reputation for being a source of time-wasting. Many of us are guilty of having spent too much time on Facebook or YouTube when we could have been doing something more productive! However, social media does not have to be an unnecessary drain on your time. Rebecca Coleman, a Canadian PR consultant in the performing arts, has written an excellent guide to getting started in social media[12]. She recommends that artists create a Social Networking Marketing Plan, outlining what they want to achieve with social media; what platforms and tools they will focus on; and lastly, how much time they are going to dedicate to being online. Think of social media like email: a brilliant innovation which, when used strategically, can enhance your business and increase opportunity. Of the social media-savvy people I know, many deliberately limit their time online to one or two hours a day for this very reason.

LinkedIn

My first recommendation would be to set up a LinkedIn[13] profile for your professional name. LinkedIn is a popular social networking site for professionals, featuring high in the search engine rankings, so you can use it as an opportunity to shine.

Setting up a LinkedIn profile is easy. A great profile picture is essential, and an easy one for actors – you can use one of your headshots.

Next, add a juicy-sounding headline that highlights your talents, e.g. "Freelance Actor, Facilitator & Workshop Leader specialising in Site-Specific Theatre". Add Current and Past employments, bearing in mind that LinkedIn lists these in order of start date with the latest position appearing at the top. Claim your 'vanity' URL, i.e. http://uk.linkedin.com/in/yourname by clicking on the Edit link beside it.

Spend some time writing a Summary for your profile. Have a search for other actors on LinkedIn for inspiration. Highlight any noteworthy achievements or credits. Use the Specialities section to summarise any particular talents or skills that you have, e.g. workshop facilitating, fluent Spanish speaker, trained ballet dancer, mask skills, etc.

Recommendations on LinkedIn are a powerful example of what's called 'social proof' – proof to your potential clients that others have already gone before and had a positive experience working with you. No one wants to be the guinea pig!

Now you are ready to start connecting. Use the Add Connections button to find people through your email contacts or through LinkedIn's recommendations. I make a point of connecting on LinkedIn with people I meet socially or at networking events to keep them in my network.

LinkedIn can be a great way of getting introductions to a particular person, e.g. a director or agent that you want to connect with. The more you build your network on LinkedIn, the more likely it is that someone in your network might know them and can provide an introduction.

Twitter

Twitter is one of those social networking sites that divides opinion. To the Twitterarti, it's a way of keeping abreast of what's going on in their industry as well as a way to connect and boost their online profile. To everyone else, it seems like a complete waste of time! But its reach is growing exponentially.

Once you have set up a Twitter account by registering a Twitter name and posting some information about yourself, you can start 'tweeting'. Other users can choose to 'follow' your tweets – they are called 'followers', and you can search for and follow others using the Find People tab. The best way to learn how to use Twitter is to use it: get an account, search for people you think are interesting to follow, and watch and learn how people interact. The Arts Council England digital strategy programme AmbITion has a free Twitter for Beginners ebook[14] on their website, which is a great guide to getting started.

For me, the number one strategic use of Twitter is the constant sharing of valuable information. Following others in your industry or sector allows you to have a network at your fingertips to share ideas and conversations, to find answers or to keep updated on great blog posts and resources. The beauty of Twitter is the brevity of the medium. No essay-style blog posts here, just up-to-date, relevant and interesting conversation that can be skimmed through in minutes. Andrew Girvan[15] on his blog has a great article on 129 people to follow in theatre, crossing venues, companies, news feeds and commentators, and is a good place to start to build your Twitter community.

Zen Tip: Use a free Twitter application such as Tweetdeck[16] to provide a one-stop shop dashboard for managing all your social media use.

Video sharing

The practical application of being able to upload and share video on the web to someone working in theatre is fairly self-explanatory. With video cameras built into almost everything, it's inexpensive to make high-quality videos to showcase your talents.

There are many different video hosting and sharing sites, but a handful do stand out from the rest. YouTube[17] is the world's most popular video sharing site, and it is easy to see why. The site is free to use and, once you have set up an account, videos are easy to upload either singly or in batches. YouTube videos, now that the company is owned by Google, also rate highly in the Google search engine, and therefore clever tagging of your videos can help potential customers and audiences find your work. Another good video sharing site is Vimeo,[18] which features a lot of content from creative people.

The mobile office

An actor's life is sometimes a nomadic one, and therefore it is essential to be able to access your email and important documents wherever you go. I find a combination of Gmail[19] as my email client and file storing and sharing site Dropbox[20] fulfils all my needs when I am away from the office for any period of time.

Using Gmail on your smart phone can mean that you don't need to travel with a laptop and you can process your emails on the go. Similarly, with Dropbox, you can access all your important documents for reading, forwarding or printing direct from your smart phone.

Final thoughts

The social web can provide many benefits to the jobbing actor. It can provide an online showcase for your work, connect you to potential clients, and be used to manage your work.

With mobile computing so readily available, the social web is not going to go away. The smart actor can use these free tools to promote her/himself above the rest of the bunch.

[1]http://wordpress.org; [2]https://posterous.com; [3]http://flavors.me; [4]http://www.netnames.co.uk; [5]http://www.123-reg.co.uk; [6]http://www.londontheatreblog.co.uk/category/articles; [7]http://www.tumblr.com; [8]http://www.fromappstozen.com; [9]http://instagr.am; [10]http://flavors.me/directory; [11]http://en.wikipedia.org/wiki/Search_engine_optimization; [12]http://www.rebeccacoleman.ca; [13]https://www.linkedin.com; [14]http://www.getambition.com/resources/twitter-for-beginners; [15]http://andrewgirvan.com/100-theatre-people-to-follow-on-twitter; [16]http://www.tweetdeck.com; [17]http://www.youtube.com; [18]http://vimeo.com; [19]www.gmail.com; [20]www.dropbox.com

Sinead Mac Manus is founder of 8fold (**www.eightfold.org**), a digital well-being company that helps busy people work better. She writes about mindful 21st-century working at her blog *From Apps to Zen* (**www.fromappstozen.com**) and is the author of *From Apps to Zen: 26+ Ideas for Building a Business with Balance*. Sinead has worked for, consulted and provided training for organisations as diverse as the Independent Street Arts Network, London Metropolitan University, CreativeCapital and the Anne Peaker Centre for Arts in Criminal Justice. Sinead's activity in developing new business models around the idea of e-learning for creative entrepreneurs, using web 2.0 tools and social media, led her to be selected in 2009 as one of the Courvoisier: Future 500 to watch.

Performers careers advice service

Give your career the attention it deserves, with this invaluable advice from Beverley Hills, one of only three Equity-accredited performance careers advisers in the country.

As an actress, I'm lucky to have carved for myself what has been termed a 'freelance portfolio career'. This means that I do several freelance jobs in between performing.

My own journey in the Arts began working backstage at the Birmingham Rep, moving on to dressing at the RSC, then designing Opera in Italy, before becoming a jazz singer and finally an actress. I am also a commissioned writer with a Masters Degree, which gives me knowledge of Higher and Further Education opportunities, plus the funding issues that face freelancers. Experiencing all these different backgrounds at first-hand gives me a wider than average skills-base when it comes to my work as an accredited careers adviser.

What is the service, and who is it for?

The Performers Careers Advice Service was piloted by Equity and Skillset, and is now fully supported by Equity. It is an advice service that is available to all performers, regardless of their area of specialism. You might be a circus performer, dancer, actor, singer, variety performer, DJ, VJ (Video Jockey) or burlesque stripper – anything you can do in front of an audience is termed 'performance' (steady now!), and as a performer you are eligible to benefit from the service.

The service is available to everyone, no matter what their level of experience or expertise. I have advised new entrants, returners, and those who simply feel that their career is stuck in a rut. My clients have included those at the very top of their game: big TV and film celebrities, who perhaps need no help to find work, but instead are trying to rediscover their passion for performing.

How does it work?

There are three accredited advisers (two in London and one in the North West) who offer the service on a freelance basis. All three of us are working practitioners with a wealth of shared experience, covering stage, TV, radio and theatre, plus our own specialisms – so we're not stuck behind a dusty computer terminal looking at stats and telling you how to do your job; we're out there in the field, working ourselves as we gather vital practical information about the wonderful, ever-changing business of performing. Furthermore, we're experienced in the age-old problem of how to survive when you're not working!

After contacting one of us directly (our biographies and email addresses can be found at **www.creativeskillset.org/careers/services/access_careers_advisors**), you will be sent an online application form to complete. This gives us an idea of where you are in your career, and what you would like to achieve. A number of performers are returners, having been out of the business for a while for whatever reason; some people haven't worked for a spell, or need to know how to find an agent; and some are seeking permission to leave the business. Whatever your position, as your adviser I will help facilitate movement or change.

After I receive your completed application form, I will do some research into how best to help your achieve your goals. You will then be invited to attend a one-to-one session. My sessions take place in London and last for 60 minutes. During the session together we devise a tailormade action plan, which is specifically designed to encourage progression. Subsequent to this initial meeting there is a follow-up service, where you have the opportunity to see the same adviser for the sake of continuity, or to talk to another in order to get a fresh perspective. Once you've seen an adviser you can also take advantage of the free email service for any questions that may subsequently spring up. There's no need to feel isolated any longer, which is a common trait in our business. You are fully supported for as long as you want to be.

The wonderful thing about being an accredited adviser is that I have privileged access to the profession, with links to casting directors, agents, directors, producers, etc. that are usually denied the working actor. I can ask direct questions, and pass on information to you, the client, 'from the horse's mouth'. I can tell it like it actually is, rather than reverting to mere speculation or outdated hearsay.

What if I change my mind?

Occasionally, performers do change their minds between filling out an application form and meeting me – and that's fine. Often, simply writing down your list of goals can help clarify the muddy waters. It's hard for performers to talk rationally about their careers: spouses and agents have heard it all before, and other actors are probably in the same boat. It can all end up with a collective moan down the pub, which may be therapeutic but is not necessarily productive! Our service is objective, confidential and based in extensive experience. We look honestly at your career and give you up-to-date advice about CVs, photos, agents, marketing and all the other elements involved in being a performer.

But does the service work?

That depends on how much effort you think your career is worth. Last time my acting work was once again thin on the ground, I took a long, hard and *objective* look at myself as a performer, and noted where I could make some changes (some of the same changes I also encourage my clients to make, by the way). It took a year to fully make all the adjustments, which included some classes, a revamp of my marketing strategies and, most of all, a significant weight loss. Did it work? Put it this way: I got my first theatre job in a long time, playing Shirley Valentine at The Garrick, which sold out every night and broke all box office records.

What will it cost me?

The current prices are:

- For a 60-minute session: £40
- For a 60-minute follow-up session: £35

How can I apply?

You can find the advisers' full biographies and contact details at www.creativeskillset.org/careers/services/access_careers_advisors/. Otherwise, visit **www.equity.org.uk** – and give your career a boost.

Beverley Hills has a wide-ranging portfolio career as an actress, voice-over artiste, TV presenter and writer, Equity careers adviser and workshop leader, Skillset course accreditor and workshop leader, NCDT (now Drama UK) performance reviewer, ITC trainer and University/Drama School lecturer. She was recently appointed Creative Adviser for the Westminster-based charity 'Dream Arts'. For more information, visit **www.beverleyhills.co.uk**.

The five steps to successful networking

Shaun Prendergast

There are two qualities required to become successful in this business. One is talent, the other the willingness to learn about the business of being an actor. Networking daunts most of us, but it is essential in acting, where the normal career pattern consists of short-term contracts for a variety of employers, interspersed with meetings which may bear fruit in the future. Once you have met and worked with someone, chances are you'll do it again and again. But networking is how you initially meet new people, and meeting people for the first time is how you get that first, all-important job with them. Nothing will get you work like personal contacts – people thinking of you *before* they go to the casting directories.

But of course, you hate networking. A lot of people feel like this even in the commercial world, but the problem is exacerbated in the arts, where there is a lingering feeling that an actor who approaches their career with a strategy is somehow compromising their artistic standards. This is amateurish rubbish. It matters hugely in this business who you know, not because it is ruled by nepotism, but because personal recommendation lies at the heart of all casting. Basically, no-one recommends you for a job unless they've seen your work themselves, or met you in person. Contacts are all, so follow these five simple networking rules and you'll gain in confidence, form a wider circle of contacts and get more work.

1. Be charmed, not charming

Remember, everyone you meet while networking is also networking too – and is probably as ambivalent about it as you are. Where most actors slip up is in thinking that networking is about selling themselves as performers to strangers, without the comfort of a character to hide behind. It isn't, and once you acknowledge this, you'll relax.

Of course, you must be positive about your talents, but you don't need to 'perform' in any way – just be yourself. Successful networkers know that networking isn't just about making other people interested in you; it's about you being interested in them. People like to be able to make a personal recommendation, because it increases their own status as someone who possesses a wide circle of contacts. But you will only spring to mind if they've had some form of comfortable contact with you. The surest way of making someone uncomfortable is to foist yourself or your career details on them without first establishing a bond between you. So listen rather than speak.

And as you listen, you'll be gaining a deeper understanding of how the business works: who runs theatres or TV departments, who commissions, how finance is raised, how a series is created, what a film storyboard is. The value of this is simple – the more you know, the better you'll be able to appreciate what your own role is. You'll also be ahead of the game when it comes to understanding changes in direction within the industry, and be able to plan your strategy accordingly. Remember, your career is *your* responsibility – not your agent's (they are part of your strategy, not the sum of it). You are only as good as your contacts. So you must cultivate contacts in every aspect of the business, because they in turn will provide you with more contacts.

2. Be businesslike

Adopting the right tone when you communicate is essential, as are correct spelling and grammar – no text-speak or slang. And don't fall for the 'make your message stand out by adding a poem/petal/aphorism' school of thought. Such devices make you look like a needy child, not a fellow professional. Keep messages brief, polite, businesslike and to the point.

You will meet thousands of contacts throughout your career, and forget most of them, unless you keep a record. Create a contacts file on your computer, and a profile for each person you have ever met in the business – every fellow student, tutor, playwright, actor, director, etc.; what they look like, where you met them and so on. Add new people every week, and update once a month. I'm not talking about stalking here, just creating an *aide memoire* for the future.

Has the casting director called you in before? Have you appeared in or studied other work by the author? Checking this stuff means you don't insult someone by forgetting them – which can easily happen – and it also gives you something to talk about, should you be asked. It helps enormously to know a director's work – have you seen a production of theirs you can talk about?

You need business cards, good quality, giving your agent or contact details. You also need really good photos, which actually look like you. Join social networking sites (such as Facebook) and become allied to as many theatre, film and TV organisations as you can. Create a Wikipedia entry, and update it. Create links to favourable reviews of your work or the shows you are in. Check if any film or TV work you do is included in an IMBD rating, and update it. Get excellent showreels and a website. Work at it. This is not school, where it's cool to do as little as possible; this is the business where graft counts. To stay in the game for the long term, it's important to remember to cultivate contacts in the generation before you as well as the established figures you meet. In ten years' time the fresh-faced wunderkind you vaguely remember could be producing a movie with you in it – if they know who you are.

3. Start with those you know

You already have a network. The people you train with are your most valuable asset – there is a bond there which may survive a lifetime, so stay in contact and share those contacts. This is not just a matter of swapping names, it's about going to see people in shows, meeting casting directors and writers and theatre directors, and then keeping a log of those you've met.

If you hear of a job going for someone you know, tell them. If you can recommend them, even better. Like for you, these initial contacts will gradually widen their own circles of contact and influence. Some of the people you share grotty flats with and see at old school reunions will end up running the very companies you're both desperately trying to get work with now. Staying in contact with each other and promoting each other throughout your careers is essential.

4. Never turn down an invitation

Most actors tend to isolate themselves when they're not working, and then reconnect when they are. But it is impossible to tell when you will make a valuable contact – and for that reason you must go to any gathering you can, to learn, and to network. This is especially true of something you've actually been invited to, and can gain entry for free!

Get out there, and meet people in the flesh. Go to first nights, to talks, to festivals. If you are invited to a play reading, be there, and stay and talk afterwards. Somewhere out there are people who could employ you, and would do so if they know you existed. Go find them.

5. Be the first to keep in touch

If you go to see a show you like, send a message of thanks to the director. Again, keep messages brief (two lines is good), businesslike and positive. If you get a casting, ditto: a short message of thanks to the director, producer and casting director. Let people know if you have a show on – send emails to everyone on your contact list.

One of the best ways you can increase your profile is to create new work and get it seen. This is where the Internet is in its infancy and where the rules change by the week. Where once the only chance of spreading the word was by persuading people to see you in Rep or Fringe shows, this is now no longer the case. YouTube, podcasts and whatever other forms of self-broadcasting come along next are incredibly effective methods of establishing a profile cheaply and getting it to a wider audience. Learn to use them. Write your own stuff (or persuade someone else to write it for you) and get it out there.

Finally, a word of warning. These five rules are not to be applied sometime, or next week, or when you feel like it. If you are serious about this career, they should be applied now, today, every day. Tomorrow depends on it.

Shaun Prendergast is an award-winning actor and writer. Recent acting work includes Mr Boo in *The Rise and Fall of Little Voice* in the West End (directed by Terry Johnson), Detective Superintendant Mike Evans in *Collision* for ITV (directed by Mark Evans), and Heinrich in the feature film *Fast Track No Limits* (directed by Axel Sand). His writing credits include *Eastenders, Roman Mysteries* and *The Lightning Kid* (all BBC), and *Rocket Man* (ITV Coastal).

Accountants

Alexander & Co.

17 St Ann's Square, Manchester M2 7PW
tel 0161-832 4841 *fax* 0161-832 2539
email nikim@alexander.co.uk
website www.alexander.co.uk
Accountants John Evans, Stephen Verber

Established in 1976. Charges start at £250 depending on complexity. Supports clients via meetings, phone calls and email and written correspondence. Can provide document or spreadsheet templates as required, all of which are Windows compatible. Clients include 20 actors and entertainment industry professionals; the firm is recommended by Equity. "Our tax experts can give strategic planning advice to ensure that you make the most of the opportunities within the current tax system and an introduction to further specialist advice as and when required."

Alexander James & Co.

Upper Deck, Admirals Quarters, Portsmouth Road, Thames Ditton, Surrey KT7 0XA
tel 020-8398 4447 *fax* 020-8398 9989
email Andrew.Nicholson@alexanderjames.co.uk
website www.alexanderjames.co.uk
Accountant Andrew Nicholson

Established in 1991. Fees vary according to complexity and completeness of information supplied. Costs are on average between £375 and £500 per annum. First meeting is free, with ongoing support by phone and email and regular email newsletter. Entirely UK-based staff accustomed to working with media industry clients. Advisory work during the year is billed on completion; rates vary depending on requirements. Standard spreadsheet template provided, and online accounts support available. Around 10-15% of clientele are actors or other entertainment industry professionals. Home or workplace visits can be arranged.

Bambridge Accountants LLP

1 Mercer Street, London WC2H 9QJ
tel 020-3757 9290
email info@bambridgeaccountants.co.uk
website www.bambridgeaccountants.co.uk
Accountants Alistair Bambridge, Jessica McKechnie, Callie Marles

Established in 2009. Usual fee is £295, but actors quoting *Actors and Performers Yearbook* receive a 25% discount. If bookkeeping is required there is an additional fee of £60 per hour. Offers a free initial consultation and free phone and email support throughout the year. Supplies a bookkeeping template in Excel, free of charge, which requires MS Office to operate. The template is suitable for Windows 95, Windows 98 & ME, Windows XP, Vista, Mac OS 9, Mac OS X, and Linux. 90% of clientele work in the entertainment and creative industries. The office is not wheelchair accessible, but will travel to client or another convenient location.

Breckman & Company

London office: 49 South Molton Street, London W1K 5LH
tel 020-7499 2292
email info@breckmanandcompany.co.uk
Brighton office: 95 Ditchling Road, Brighton BN1 4ST
tel (01273) 929350
website www.breckmanandcompany.co.uk
Accountants Kevin Beale, Graham Berry, Robert Breckman, Richard Nelson

Established for more than 50 years. Costs are dictated by complexity and time spent. Initial meeting is free during which the fee structure will be discussed. Client support includes face-to-face meetings, phone and email.

P O'N Carden

56-58 High Street, Ewell, Surrey KT17 1RW
tel 020-8394 2957 *fax*
email info@poncarden.com
Accountants Philippe Carden, Cathy Smith, Mondane Carden

Founded in 1977. Charges £400+VAT ('in the early years') for a complete set of accounts and tax return for sole traders. 'Time and complexity increase this. Tailor-made packages for complex cases and limited companies." Provides face-to-face meetings in central London. 'My actor clients make clear how much support they feel they need, and the programme of work is tailored accordingly.' Provides Excel spreadsheets appropriate to the client's needs. 50% of clients are actors and performers; 35% are other entertainment industry professionals. The offices are not wheelchair accessible, but meetings can be held in wheelchair-accessible locations. Advises actors *not* to "just give your accountant bags of receipts. Provide information about why you are claiming particular expenses. Do be obssessive about keeping payslips and remittance advices".

Mark Carr & Co.

Chartered Certified Accountants, 90 Long Acre, Covent Garden, London WC2E 9RZ
tel 020-7717 8474
email mark@markcarr.co.uk
63 Lansdowne Place, Hove, East Sussex BN3 1FL
tel (01273) 778802
website www.markcarr.co.uk

Providing Tax and Accounting services (including online accounting). Our fees are always competitive and can be paid by a fixed monthly amount. First meeting is free of charge. Represents the Actors Centre with regular Tax Surgery. Very popular free downloadable Excel spreadsheets available from the website to clients and non-clients alike. The London office has wheelchair access. "We have over 450 clients, who range from those starting out to those with celebrity status."

ClearSky Accounting

Optionis House, 840 Ibis Court, Centre Park, Warrington WA1 1RL
tel 0800-0149 596
email accountinginfo@clearskybusiness.co.uk
website www.clearskybusiness.co.uk/entertainment
Accountant Alex Fielding

Established in 1995. ClearSky is very experienced in dealing with entertainment accountancy and provides advice and recommendations on all tax issues, ranging from completing a standard self-assessment return to dealing directly with agents regarding VAT and payments. Fees start from £35 per month (+VAT) and there are a number of different packages available – details can be found on the website. The company offers support via telephone and email and is happy to provide Excel templates for book keeping, if required. The company's office is wheelchair accessible. "Our team of qualified experts have specialist knowledge of all Equity, PACT & BECTU rules and regulations – giving peace of mind that our work is fully compliant."

Count and See Ltd

219 Macmillan Way, London SW17 6AW
tel 020-8767 7882
email info@countandsee.com
website www.countandsee.com

Charges an annual fee of £250 (+ VAT) upwards, depending on the amount of work involved. Provides actor clients with face-to-face, phone and email support. The trading office is wheelchair accessible. "Before setting up my own practice, I worked for a number of firms specialising in the entertainment industry, so I have experience in advising such clients."

Crowe Clark Whitehill

St Bride's House, 10 Salisbury Square, London EC4Y 8EH
tel 020-7842 7100
website www.crowehorwath.net
Accountants David Ford, Tim Norkett

Established in 1982. Provides flexible solutions to clients' tax problems; initial meeting is offered free of charge. Supports clients via meetings, phone and email. Will supply software and/or spreadsheet templates that are tailor made to individual requirements. Current client list includes 20 actors and 20 other entertainment industry professionals. Offices are wheelchair accessible. Fees vary according to the complexity of the service(s) required: £400 (+ VAT) is the minimum. "The better the quality of the client's recordkeeping, the lower the fees."

Dub & Co.

7 Torriano Mews, Torriano Avenue, London NW5 2RZ
tel 020-7284 8686 *fax* 020-7284 8687
email office@dub.co.uk
website www.dub.co.uk
Accountants George Dub, Joyce Davies

Chartered, certified accountants established in 1979. Charges from £400 (+ VAT) for preparation of accounts for a tax return. Face-to-face meetings, phone and email support included in this fee. Does not provide software or spreadsheet templates to clients. Handles the tax and accountancy affairs of around 50 actors and 100 other entertainment industry professionals. The company's offices are wheelchair accessible.

Dunbar & Co.

70 South Lambeth Road, London SW8 1RL
tel 020-7820 0082 *fax* 020-7820 0806
email mason@equitax.co.uk
Accountants Nick Mason (Senior Partner), Bob Long

Founded in 1896. Fees are on a time-cost basis, depending on the complexity of the client's tax affairs, but a typical fee range for an actor would be £330-£420 per annum. Support is provided via various means, including face-to-face meetings, phone and email. Provides spreadsheet templates for clients, which require Microsoft Excel. 50% of clients are actors, with a further 15% other entertainment-industry professionals. Offices are wheelchair accessible.

"We offer a full accountancy service, including bookkeeping, VAT, tax returns, tax advice, assistance with Revenue investigations, limited company accounts, personal and corporate tax planning. Our sister company, Sandford Dunbar, is authorised by the FSA as an independent financial adviser specialising in personal financial and pension planning."

Fisher Packman & Associates in association with Simia Wall

Devonshire House, 582 Honeypot Lane, Stanmore, Middlesex HA7 1JS and Sir Robert Peel House, 178 Bishopsgate, London EC2M 4NJ (Simia Wall)
tel 020-8732 5500 *fax* 020-8732 5501
email nik@fisherpackman.com
website www.fisherpackman.com
Accountant Nik Fisher FFA FCCA

Established in 2005. Charges between £250 and £750 on average, depending on the amount of work involved. Offers actors face-to-face and email/phone support: "as much as they require; our policy is to teach actors how best to keep their books and records, to save on accountancy fees." Provides spreadsheet templates in Excel and for VAT analysis, suitable for a range of software platforms. Around 15% of clients are actors, and 25% other professionals in the entertainment industry.

Jonathan Ford & Co.

The Coach House, 31 View Road, Rainhill, Merseyside L35 0LF
tel 0151-426 4512
email info@jonathanford.co.uk
website www.jonathanford.co.uk
Accountant Jonathan Ford

Charges from £275 to £450, depending on the level of bookkeeping the client has done themselves. All fees are agreed in advance. Client service is comprehensive and includes face-to-face meetings, telephone and email support, all included within the fee. "Using the Internet we can meet the needs of clients all over the country." Supplies Excel spreadsheet templates, so MS Office is required; the software is suitable for all operating systems. Has around 10 actor clients and 40 other entertainment industry professionals. Offices are not wheelchair accessible. Advises actors to "see our 10 tax commandments!"

Goldwins

75 Maygrove Road, London NW6 2EG
tel 020-7372 6494 *fax* 020-7624 0053
email aepton@goldwins.co.uk
website www.goldwins.co.uk
Accountant Anthony Epton

Established in 1987. Specialises in the entertainment industry, handling the tax and bookkeeping affairs of around 200 actors. Charges around £400 for preparation of an actor's tax return, although this can vary from £250 up to £1,000 depending on the complexity of the job. Face-to-face meetings, phone and email support included in this price. Does not provide software or spreadsheet templates. The company's offices are wheelchair accessible.

Goodman Jones LLP

29/30 Fitzroy Square, London W1P 6LQ
tel 020-7388 2444 *fax* 020-7388 6736
email jrf@goodmanjones.com
website www.goodmanjones.com
Partner Julian Flitter

Founded in 1934. "Each person is different and we tailor our support to the clients needs, so costs can range from £250 to £500 for more complex returns involving international aspects and multiple categories of income." This amount would include any support required in the form of face-to-face meetings, phone calls, letters and emails. "The range of services we offer includes tax compliance services from personal tax returns and VAT returns, advice on whether or not to incorporate as a limited company, when to register for VAT, how to deal with working abroad, bookkeeping services, preparation of financial accounts (limited company, sole trader, LLP or partnership) as well as full personal tax planning and company secretarial and payroll services." Can supply software templates to clients as required, but recommends "keeping it simple". Offices are wheelchair accessible.

H & S Accountants Ltd

90 Mill Lane, West Hampstead, London NW6 1NL
tel 020-3174 1905 *fax* 020-7788 2984
email hstaxplan@gmail.com
website www.hstaxplan.com
Accountants David Summers, Chet Haria

Established in 1982. Charges start from £300 (+ VAT) for preparation of annual self-employed accounts and the self-assessment tax return. A quote is given at the initial meeting, which is free of charge. The services offered also include preparation of limited company accounts and corporate tax returns, VAT registration, payroll, tax-planning advice, etc. Client support includes face-to-face meetings, phone, email, and dealing with day-to-day queries as they may arise (all included in the price). Approximately 10% of clients are actors or members of the entertainment industry. "We tailor advice to each individual's requirements."

Hamilton Stewart & Co.

1A Little Roke Avenue, Kenley, Surrey CR8 5NN
tel 020-8763 1711 *fax* 020-8645 9550
email accounts@hamiltonstewart.co.uk
Accountant Tony Hamilton

Established in 1972. Charges £400 (+ VAT) to prepare an actor's accounts for the annual Inland Revenue tax return. If the gross turnover is below £15,000 a tax return only is prepared, for £200 (+ VAT). Provides first contact face to face, but continued contact may be by email or post – whatever is reasonably required for a client's circumstances. Additional services, such as payroll or VAT services, are negotiated by mutual agreement. Spreadsheet templates can be prepared for Microsoft Excel; this software is suitable for Windows 7 and 8 and can be ported to Mac. There is also a smartphone app available through Apple and Android app stores. Has approximately 107 actor clients. Offices are wheelchair-accessible.

Harris Coombs & Co.

5 Jaggard Way, London SW12 8SG
tel 020-8675 6880 *fax* 020-8675 7017
email mailbox@harriscoombs.co.uk
website www.harriscoombs.co.uk

Partners Graham Harris FCCA, Richard Coombs FCA

Charges to prepare actors' accounts for annual HM Revenue & Customs tax returns range from £500-

£1,000. Charges vary depending on figures and VAT. Client support includes: face-to-face meetings, phone, email (all included in the price). Personal service in all financial matters: tax, NI, VAT etc. Of client base 15% are actors and 20% are other entertainment industry professionals.

Harvey Mead & Co. Ltd

The Old Winery, Lamberhurst Vineyard, Lamberhurst, Kent TN3 8ER
tel (01892) 891572 *fax* (01892) 891892
email lynette@harveymead.co.uk
website www.harveysllp.com
Accountants Damian McGee, Lynnette Lawrence

Established in 2008. Charges £600 (+ VAT) per annum. Client support includes face-to-face meetings, telephone and email, as well as fee protection insurance and freepost record envelopes. Accounts support is charged at £40 per hour; tax compliance at £60 per hour; and partner at £90 to £150 per hour. Supplies clients with MS Excel spreadsheet templates suitable for Windows XP and Vista. 50% of the client base comprises actors, and 30% other entertainment industry professionals. Offices are wheelchair accessible.

Hayles & Partners Ltd

39 Castle Street, Leicester LE1 5WN
tel 0116-233 8500 *fax* 0116-233 7288
website www.hayles.co.uk
Accountants Geoff Banks, Amanda Jelley

Charges from £150 for preparation of a basic tax return. Provides face-to-face meetings, phone and email support. Initial consultation or advice is offered free of charge. Does not supply software or spreadsheet templates to clients. Advises actors to "open a separate business bank account and identify all receipts and payments, retaining all supporting documentation".

Hogbens Dunphy

First Floor, 104-108 Oxford Street, London W1D 1LP
tel 020-7016 2450 *fax* 020-7637 8219
email anything@hogbensdunphy.co.uk
website www.hogbensdunphy.co.uk
Accountant Richard Wadhams

Established in 1921. Offers complete support to actors and other theatre professionals in dealing with their accounts and for their tax return. Prices are dependent on each individual client's needs. Record book software and/or Excel spreadsheets are provided to the client as required, and this is suitable for all current computer operating systems. Offices are wheelchair accessible.

HW Lee Associates LLP – Accountants to the Creative Sector

New Derwent House, 69-73 Theobalds Road, Holborn, London WC1X 8TA
tel 020-7025 4600 *fax* 020-7025 4666
email rhusband@hw-lee.com
email srawal@hw-lee.com
email nstammers@hw-lee.com
website www.hw-lee.com
Accountants Robert Husband, Sudhir Rawal, Neil Stammers

Established in 1978. Charges in the region of £400 to prepare a set of accounts, depending on the complexity and condition of the information supplied. Package and ongoing support tailored to suit each client's requirements, and clients have access to their client partner by mobile at any time. Provides templates for clients to record their accounts information and expenditure, and also gives advice about setting up IT systems. Is able to work with any system used by the client. A creative-focused firm with about 50% of its client base from the creative sectors and 10% directly linked to the entertainment industry. Offices are wheelchair accessible. "Our role is to anticipate the advice you need and help you implement it. Thereafter, managing and maintaining your relationship with the Inland Revenue will be our focus so that you can concentrate on enjoying your roles and performances."

Nyman Libson Paul

Regina House, 124 Finchley Road, London NW3 5JS
tel 020-7433 2400 *fax* 020-7433 2401
email entertainment@nlpca.co.uk
website www.nlpca.co.uk

75 years in the entertainment industry.

Reddington & Co.

Four Sisters Farm Cottage, Stratford St Mary, Colchester CO7 6PE
tel (01473) 310238 and *mobile* (07563) 753318
email info@reddingtonandco.co.uk
website www.reddingtonandco.co.uk
Accountant Kate Reddington

Established in 1988. Average charge is £300 depending on individual circumstances. First consultation is free, fee thereafter includes accounts, tax return, NIC matters and general advice. Supports clients via phone call, email and Skype, though has no formal office hours. Can provide Excel spreadsheet templates as required, all of which are Windows compatible. 70% of clients are actors and entertainment industry professionals.

Shaw Walker Lees

26 Great Queen Street, London WC2B 5BB
tel 020-7242 1134
email a.mccarthy@shawwalkerlees.co.uk
website www.shawwalkerlees.co.uk
Accountants Mrs A. McCarthy, Mr P. Skinner, Mr T. K. Chong

Established in 1925, charges from £450 to prepare actors' accounts for the tax return, depending on the complexity of the accounts. Provides a face-to-face initial meeting; support thereafter is as convenient to the client and this is included in the fee. Provides a complete range of accounting services – VAT, tax, PAYE, business support, book keeping *et al.* Software and/or spreadsheets are provided to the client as required. Offices are not easily wheelchair accessible. Advice to actors: "Seek a *qualified* accountant."

Theataccounts LLP

The Oakley, Kidderminster Road, Droitwich, Worcestershire WR9 9AY
tel (01905) 823177 *fax* (01905) 799856
email info@theataccounts.co.uk
website www.theataccounts.co.uk
Accountant Alex Dyer

Entertainment Industry Accountants established in 1967. Charges are based on a sliding scale according to each client's requirements. Very basic package can start at £150. Offers support to clients through face-to-face meetings, phone, email, Skype, etc. No particular software is provided unless requested; tailored spreadsheets are emailed and are suitable for a wide range of software. Almost all clients are actors and other entertainment industry professionals. Offices are wheelchair accessible.

Wise & Co. Chartered Accountants & Business Advisers

Rm 245 Pinewood Studios, Pinewood Road, Iver, Bucks
tel (01753) 656770 and (01252) 711244
fax (01252) 737221
email info@wiseandco.co.uk
website www.wiseandco.co.uk
Accountants Colin Essex, Mandy Cornelius, Tom Mason

Established in 1972. Provides a full accounting service, business advice plus tax returns and staff payroll – "a personal, discreet and friendly service tailored to the needs of each individual". Prices vary, please phone to arrange a free initial consultation. Office at Pinewood Studios as well as in Farnham, Surrey. Works with Windows and MS Office, so Excel is widely used; spreadsheet templates can be provided if required. Offices at Farnham are wheelchair accessible. Coffee shop and restaurant at Pinewood.

Wyatts Accounts

247 Church Street, London N16 9HP
tel 020-7241 6779
email office@wyatts.co.uk

Friendly and clear service. Specialists with actors, artists and performers. Reasonable and transparent scaled fees and charges. Client base is 100% arts and entertainment industry professionals. Offices are wheelchair accessible.

Tax and National Insurance for actors

Philippe Carden

Actors are treated as self-employed for income tax purposes, but can benefit from certain advantages not generally available. Many actors choose to instruct an accountant to benefit from those advantages, and to avoid the pitfalls created by the complications.

The income tax advantages include being able to claim a deduction for expenses against income in arriving at taxable net profit (or allowable loss), provided that those expenses are incurred 'wholly and exclusively for the purposes of the trade'. *The Equity Tax and National Insurance Guide*, available free of charge to its members, provides a very helpful list of usually allowable expenses, with suitable notes to restrain the enthusiasm of actors to stretch definitions to their limits. Self-imposed restraint in claiming for expenses is sensible in minimising the risk of being selected for a HM Revenue and Customs (HMRC) enquiry. Some accountants produce their own list of generally allowable expenses.

It is helpful to assess the types of expense according to the risk of being challenged by the Revenue. Here are some examples:

Low risk or No risk
- Commission paid to agent (including VAT)
- Annual subscription to Equity
- Travel and subsistence on tour
- Photographs and publicity (repros, Spotlight entry)
- Classes to maintain skills, e.g. voice, movement
- Business stationery and postage
- Fee paid to accountant

Medium risk
- Professional library – scripts, books, CDs
- Publications – *The Stage, Time Out*
- Travel and subsistence when not on tour
- Visits to theatre and cinema

High risk
- Wardrobe – renewal, dry cleaning and repair
- Hairdressing and make-up
- Gratuities to dressers and stage door-keepers
- Home as office
- Osteopathy and other treatments
- Cosmetic dentistry

As the risk rises, so too must the care taken in deciding which to claim and which to discard. Engaging an accountant to use his or her experience, skill and judgement in carrying out a review of expenditure claims is a source of considerable reassurance to many actors. It is worth noting that entertaining, as in paying a meal for another person (even if a casting director), is never allowed.

An accountant's review may also be key in calculating the business proportions of motor car expenses, landline and mobile telephone charges (including internet access), television and film hire and television licence. An accountant's help in computing capital allowances for expenditure on capital items (computer, motor car, musical instruments) is appreciated by all but the most self-confident.

The emphasis so far has been on the income tax advantages of being self-employed. Whilst many actors are happy to register themselves as self-employed, others enlist the help of an accountant, even at that stage, to help with form-filling and provide a buffer-zone between themselves and the HMRC. Once registration is done, a Unique Taxpayer Reference (UTR) will be issued, often still referred to as a Schedule D number except by the HMRC. At the same time as registering as self-employed, actors should register to pay Class 2 national insurance contributions (NICs) calculated at the weekly flat-rate, currently £2.75. This can be paid quarterly, half-yearly or stress-free by monthly direct debit.

If an actor expects only a very modest net profit from his or her self-employment, say £6,000 net profit or so, the solution is to apply for small earnings exception (SEE) from Class 2 NICs by completing and submitting form CF10. Then you would still be registered correctly for Class 2 NICs but you wouldn't actually be paying them. It is always worth remembering, however, that paying Class 2 NICs is a cheap way of securing entitlement to certain basic state benefits such as maternity allowance and state pension.

For the sake of completeness, actors must pay Class 4 too. That class of NIC is the earnings-related charge borne by self-employed people in addition to the flat-rate Class 2. It confers no benefits to the payer and is collected by the HMRC as part of the self-assessment system.

The complexities of the NI regime, and especially the interaction of its different classes, encourage co-operation between actor and accountant almost as much as does the application of the criteria for acceptability of expenses for income tax purposes.

Core services provided by an accountant include the following:

- Annual income and expenditure account
- Capital allowances computations
- Advice on NI and the necessary form-filling
- Completion of the annual Tax Return
- Preparing a tax calculation and checking the Revenue's version
- Applying to reduce income tax payments on account, if appropriate

Additional services would include completing quarterly returns for actors successful enough to be registered for VAT, and advice on the tax and NIC implications of performing abroad. Student loan repayments and tax credit deadlines can also be discussed and planned for.

Most accountants charge according to time spent and the seniority and expertise of the persons doing the work. Here is an example of how this might work in practice for a young actor: he would need five hours of a bookkeeper, an hour for a manager's review and tax return and finally half-an-hour of the principal's/partner's time for overall review and quality control (£50). With perhaps a few telephone calls and shortish meeting, the annual fee would typically be £400 plus VAT, i.e. £480. Accordingly, careful sorting of expenses by expense type can save both time and money.

In my experience, as the cost of the initial meeting is rarely charged for, I make a loss in year one of a new client. I break even in year two, and only make a profit in year three and subsequent years. It is not a surprise, therefore, that I see my relationship with a client as a long-term one – one which has time and effort invested in it by both actor and accountant.

To an actor in the early years of his career, the accountant's annual fee of about £480 represents a significant expense. The decision to instruct an accountant is a personal one. Some actors are much more comfortable and confident than others in dealing with money matters, taxation and NIC. Others shy away from such a course of action and choose to have an ally in the form of an accountant.

In general terms, for an actor with gross earnings of less than £25,000 but who still makes a profit, having an accountant is optional. For one with smaller earnings and who makes a loss, having an accountant could be worthwhile to relieve that loss and seek a refund of income tax. For those with gross earnings in excess of £25,000, the choice is compelling.

Having made the decision to use an accountant, choose the firm carefully. The most desired method is word of mouth. A personal recommendation from another actor, from your drama school or indeed from the company manager works well. It is important that the accountant selected knows about the taxation and NIC of actors rather than being a general practitioner. It is also important that the accountant be a member of one of the professional bodies of accountants as an indication of quality – and just in case a dispute arises which cannot be resolved amicably. Most of the institutes have a system of arbitration for fee disputes, for example, which can be used as a last resort.

Another factor in the choice of accountant is the size of the firm. The range is huge: from a sole practitioner to a multinational firm employing thousands. The former will be suitable for an actor of modest means, while the latter might be a good match for a performer with very considerable earnings and royalties from several countries around the world. In between those extremes are smaller firms with one to five partners which specialise in the tax affairs of those who work in theatre, television and film, and larger firms which have an entertainment and media department with a similar specialism. The smaller firms are likely to provide a more personal service and lower fees. The larger are likely to have access to a greater breadth of related expertise (such as film finance, production accounting) but fees will be correspondingly higher.

Each accountant will have his or her favoured way for actors to keep records. The most important point is that an actor must co-operate with his or her accountant to save time and maximise the return on effort. Here are some guidelines and handy hints:

- Keep all agent's remittance advices, payslips and invoices.
- Only claim expenses incurred 'wholly and exclusively for the purposes of the trade'.
- Use the Equity list of usually allowable expenses for guidance.
- Keep receipts for all expenses and write explanatory notes on them (for example, 'for audition with X')
- File away carefully details of any other income such as interest or dividends received, P60/P45s from employments (for example, bar work), rental income as well as Gift Aid payments made and any other item which may be needed to complete your tax return.
- Deliver your accounts papers to your accountant *as soon as you can* after the end of the tax year (5th April) – never leave it until close to the 31st January deadline! The sooner your return is submitted, the earlier the warning of any tax liability payable 31st January and of any other payments on account due for the following year.

Philippe Carden is a chartered accountant specialising in the taxation of actors and other individuals working in theatre, film, television and dance, onstage and backstage, artistic and technical. He co-wrote *Investing in West End Theatrical Productions* (Robert Hale, 1992) and has written articles for the *Guardian*, *The Stage* and other publications.

Between engagements

or 'How to survive until the next job'
Andrew Piper

All the articles in this publication are one person's perspective, and as such need to be tested against your own judgement and experience. None more so than this article, because, like you, I'm an actor. Unless you are extremely lucky (or have only just graduated from drama school), you will have experienced periods of unemployment, and will have come up with your own strategies for coping with this. What follows is a collection of thoughts on what seems *to me* to be good advice for any actor finding themself temporarily out of work. I don't always follow this advice, but it does seem to help when I do. Not everything here will be right for you, but I hope that some of it will make it easier for you get to your next acting job with body and soul intact.

I've grouped the suggestions in this article under four headings: stay solvent, stay employable, stay visible, and stay sane. Do all these things, and acting work should never be too far away.

Stay solvent

It might surprise you that I start with this, but money problems can make all the other suggestions in this article so much more difficult to do. Your first priority as an actor, therefore, is to make sure that you can keep a roof over your head, food in your fridge, and your creditors (if any) off your back. Without these things it becomes next to impossible to present a confident face to the world, to maintain the self-esteem and self-belief that one needs to survive as an actor, and to plan any strategies for finding acting work. So with this in mind – and recognising that this is the least interesting bit – here are my tips for staying solvent:

• Save money when you are working. That's not easy if you're on the sort of wages that are common in theatre, but the more money you can save now, the more you'll have in reserve for the lean times ahead. Even if you have another job to go onto after this one, the chances are that there will be a few weeks between finishing one and starting the next, and that's time that potentially no one will be paying you for. Remember too that your wages will rarely have tax deducted from them, which means you will need something in reserve for when the tax bill is due. If you're doing a long theatre job, then consider setting up a standing order to a savings account – even if you only manage to save a few pounds a week, you may be glad of it further down the line.

• Live as cheaply as you can. The lower your overheads, the more you can save and the longer you can ride out a period of reduced income.

• Make your extravagances count. If you've been frugal during the week, then you can treat yourself at the weekend. Something as simple as making your own sandwiches may save you enough to pay for a meal out in as little as a few days. Skipping two or three nights of drinking and clubbing could even save you enough for a weekend in Paris or Prague.

• Probably the largest single expense you'll have is your rent or mortgage. This is generally unavoidable – unless of course you're still living with your parents – but if you're someone who does a lot of touring then it can be frustrating to be paying some exorbitant London rent for a room that you're hardly using. (Mortgages are different, of course, because at least you'll own something at the end of it.) However, for most people, having a place you can call home and look forward to returning to is immensely important. Whether or not you feel there are savings that can be made – by subletting while away, say, or moving to a cheaper area – don't leave it out of the equation when looking at keeping your costs down.

• Get a second phone. That might seem perverse, but if you don't have access to a landline (for example, if you're away from home) and you have an 'anytime minutes' contract with one of the operators, get yourself an old mobile phone (eBay is quite good for this) and put a pay-as-you-go SIM card in it for making all your off-peak calls. That way, all your long off-peak chats to your mum/partner/best mate won't eat up your valuable 'anytime' minutes. Shop around, and see what will work out best for you.

• Have a look at **www.moneysavingexpert.com**. Run by the journalist Martin Lewis, this website has all sorts of tips and tricks for making your money go further.

• Get a 'day job'. Even Kenneth Tynan's actor mistress once observed that "the worse thing about not working is having to work". And ain't that the truth! Sooner or later most of us – especially those who work mostly in theatre – have to knuckle down to something unrelated to acting in order to pay the bills. What form this takes will depend on your particular skills – it doesn't hurt to get some IT and typing skills under your belt when you get the chance – but consider office temping, waiting and bar work, call centres (one company, RSVP – **www.rsvp.co.uk** – is even run by actors), and shop work, for starters. If you have a teaching qualification, then you could make some slightly better money by doing 'supply teaching', covering for full-time teachers in case of illness. Many of the photographers listed in this book are (or were) also working actors – although this shouldn't be regarded as a way to a quick buck: those guys have worked long and hard at perfecting their skills. One of the most popular ways of earning cash between jobs is promotions work. Have a look at these sites for more information: **www.stuckforstaff.com**, **www.ays.co.uk** and **www.promojobspro.com** (this last one is run by the same people as CastingCall Pro). I've even turned my hand (if that's the right expression) to artists' life-modelling, although I've never managed to earn more than beer money for it. One friend of mine took a course in massage in order to have another string to his bow – although I'm generally cautious about diverting money, time and energy into training that won't actually improve your employment prospects as an actor. One job I wouldn't recommend is 'extras' work, unless what you aspire to be is a background artiste. Never did a job so eloquently encapsulate the meaning of the phrase, 'so near, and yet so far'. (*Note* This point doesn't really belong in the 'stay solvent' section, but while we're on the subject of day jobs: never take a job that you couldn't in good conscience drop at short notice to go to an audition or accept acting work, unless you want to be stuck doing that job for the rest of your life. Alas, almost any job that one could describe as 'interesting' or 'stimulating' also requires a degree of commitment. For this reason, most 'day jobs' that are suitable for actors are tedium incarnate. I wish it were otherwise. I really, *really* wish it were otherwise.)

• Don't sit around waiting for the money to run out. If you have managed to bring in a good chunk of money, paid off your debts, set aside enough for your tax bill, had a holiday, and still have enough left not to need to work for a while ... get a part-time job. Your savings will last you longer, and instead of turning into a couch potato (which can happen frighteningly quickly) you will retain a sense of yourself as a working, earning person. By all means do the other things you never had time to do before – take classes, see films, visit galleries, meet friends – but do these on your days off.

• Know what State Benefits you're entitled to, and claim them (and if you're not entitled, then don't). I loathe and detest signing on – Jobcentres are rarely beacons of hope and optimism – and will do almost any kind of work rather than do so, but if you do find yourself without work then it is worth taking the time to fill in the forms. Talk to Equity if the Jobcentre is sniffy about you signing on as an actor.

• Act quickly if you do get into financial trouble. If you find yourself borrowing money for your day-to-day living expenses (including using credit cards) or to make payments on existing debts, then you have a problem, and one that must be dealt with as soon as possible. This is too big an issue for me to tackle here, but you can get advice on dealing with unmanageable debts from your local Citizens' Advice Bureau, **www.citizensadvice.org.uk** (in Scotland this is **www.cas.org.uk**); from National Debtline, **www.nationaldebtline.co.uk** or *tel* 0808-808 4000; and from Consumer Credit Counselling Service, **www.cccs.co.uk** or *tel* 0800-138 1111. Whatever you do, don't be tempted to take out another credit card (even a zero interest one) or another loan unless this will allow you to cancel your existing credit cards, because you'll spiral even further into debt. Never *ever* touch those 'debt consolidation', 'one-easy-payment' companies that advertise on daytime TV – they just want to make money out of you and will make matters worse. It doesn't have to be scary – you have more power than you might think. The banks want their money back, of course, but would much prefer to accept a repayment plan which fits your budget, than go through the expense of legal proceedings when they know you can't pay.

Stay employable

This is perhaps the easiest section for me to write, because, well, we all know it all already. But do we do it? No, neither do I. Time and money are big factors, of course, but so are simple inertia and laziness. "Chance," said Louis Pasteur, "favours the prepared mind," so here's my list of best practices, given in the knowledge that I rarely get around to more than a handful of them when I'm between jobs.

• Brush up your skills – voice, dance, singing, stage combat, Shakespeare, Alexander Technique, etc. – and learn new ones. There are various places in London and around the country that offer professional-grade courses in these, such as the London and Manchester Actors Centres, The City Lit, and the drama schools and universities listed in the Short Courses section of this book. Get a driving licence if you don't already have one.

• Keep fit, whatever your preferred means is: sport, gym, dance, swimming, walking, martial arts – even regular bouts of acrobatic sex would do it, I suppose, as long as afterwards you didn't light up or order pizza. Aerobic fitness is most important as this provides both the stamina to get through an evening's performance (I'm talking theatre now, not sex) and the twinkle in the eye that says 'energy and vitality' to an auditioning director. (A twinkle that says 'regular, acrobatic sex' is probably quite effective too, in certain circumstances.)

• Brush up on your audition speeches and songs. How would you feel if, at short notice, you got an audition for a great job, and you fluffed it because your speeches or songs were rusty or tired? It's happened to me; don't let it happen to you.

• Read plays. Not because you *should* (because if that's your reason then you won't) but because they're *fun*. A lot of us came into this business because we loved plays – it's odd that once we got here we read so few of them. (Keep an eye open for good audition speeches while you're reading.)

• Keep in touch with what's going on in the business. Read *The Stage*, talk to your agent and your actor friends, keep your finger on the pulse. Know which theatres have new artistic directors, which casting directors are working on which projects, and so on. Remind yourself that you're an actor – not always easy after the umpteenth week of photocopying and filing in some awful temp job.

• Watch TV. And no, I don't mean *Trisha* or *Cash in the Attic* – watch drama on TV, and go to the theatre and cinema. Remind yourself of how it's done, and make a note of the performers, directors, casting directors and production companies whose work you most admire.

• Visit your dentist. That smile of yours is important, so look after it. You don't have to go getting expensive cosmetic work done (unless your gnashers are particularly hideous, or unless you're up for a lot of romantic leads in film and television), but get a check-up with your regular dentist and make sure any problems are spotted early. I had an abscess while on tour once, and was in agony for several days. This pain was as nothing, though, compared to the shock of the bill I had for a (private) emergency dentist to perform root canal surgery. Don't let it happen to you: get them sorted before you go away.

• Lastly, but perhaps most importantly: keep yourself **available.** Remember what your real job is. As I mentioned in the previous section, it's a sad fact that almost any job that's interesting will require a degree of commitment, but if you are so committed to your 'day job' that you can't drop everything for an audition or acting work then you are putting yourself and your acting career at a real disadvantage. Talk to your agent (if you have one) when you're planning a holiday – he or she must know your every movement, even if it's only a long weekend, because both you and your agent will look stupid if an audition is arranged for a time when you're actually going to be sunning yourself on some Mediterranean beach, or giving the Best Man's speech at your brother's wedding. Talk to your agent, too, if you're considering applying for Fringe work. In some circumstances this can be a good showcase for your talents, but this must be offset against the fact that it will put you out of the running for any paid work – talk it through with your agent and discuss what you hope to get out of it. Keep your mobile phone switched on whenever possible, and return calls from your agent immediately.

Stay visible

All the preparation in the world won't count for much if nobody knows you're there. There are thousands of us out there, all chasing too few jobs, and it can be hard enough to get noticed even when you're doing everything right. That means that being a wallflower just isn't an option, however much you might hate the idea of marketing yourself. So here are a few (relatively painless) suggestions for keeping your name and face in employers' minds.

• Keep your *Spotlight* CV up to date. An entry in *Spotlight* is essential for film, television and increasingly also theatre jobs. Unless your CV is up to date then (a) the casting director's picture of you is incomplete and (b) it will look like you haven't worked for the last x years.

• Keep your photo up to date. Angus Deuchar's excellent article on page 410 will tell you why, and what to do if it's not. It's significant that all the casting directors who have written for this book have stressed how important it is that your photograph actually looks like you.

• Keep in touch with past employers. Unless you've disgraced yourself while working for them, these people represent your best chance for further work. Send a friendly email or postcard to let them know what you've been doing, with perhaps a mention that you'd love to work with them again and would appreciate a call next time they're casting.

• The best time to write to other potential employers and casting directors is when you're working and can invite them to see you. Of course there's a pretty slim chance that any London-based employers will travel up to Pitlochry to see your Stanley Kowalski or Blanche Dubois, but that's not the point: they will see that you are working – not 'just finished' working (the meaning of which can be curiously flexible) – but actually working, right now.

• Keep covering letters brief, but as individual as possible. Most companies get stacks of CVs from actors with nothing but the baldest of covering notes, so a sentence along the lines of "I'm hoping to see your *Macbeth* when it comes to Leeds" or "My friend John Smith is having a great time working for you at the moment" may make yours stand out from the rest.

• Think about your marketing materials: photo, CV, covering letter. Are they well presented? They represent you: do they do a good job? Are the CV and letter on good-quality paper or the nasty, cheap stuff you get in photocopiers? Get someone who knows what they're talking about to give constructive criticism about them. There are differing opinions about this, but I think it's always worth printing your photo onto the CV itself. If it's well printed then many theatre companies are quite happy with this instead of a full 10x8. If you're sending out a lot of letters and CVs, then it might be worth asking your local printer to quote for some headed notepaper with your photo at the top. Don't get him to print the whole CV – it will go out of date long before you get round to mailing them all. (I should say that my agent completely disagrees with this idea – he reckons you should always send 10x8s, and leave printing your photo on your CV for when you've run out of photos. As I said, opinion is divided.)

• Additional marketing tools. Websites can be quite a good way of getting someone to spend time finding out about you, and of putting across a particular image. The cost of commissioning one from scratch can vary wildly, but someone with only a modicum of computer know-how should be able to knock together something quite presentable using a site like **www.moonfruit.com** or **www.easily.co.uk** (this latter also allows you to register quite cheaply your own domain name – e.g. andrew-piper.com). Don't fret if you haven't got one – your *Spotlight* web page already carries all the important information. Personal websites are currently a 'nice-to-have' not a 'need-to-have'.

• Postcards and business cards. Not a substitute for the CV and photo, but quite a useful additional tool – something to give or send someone who has met you, as a reminder of who you are. Postcards can also make quite good performance notices – something a casting director can read easily while eating breakfast. Have a look at **www.vistaprint.co.uk** (and there are many others) for business cards, including ones with your photo on. There are a number of companies which can produce postcards quite cheaply: **www.goodprint.co.uk** is one, but there are others if you hunt around.

• Apply for jobs. Sounds obvious, but plenty of actors wait for their agent to submit them for everything. Even if the agent is doing their job, in practice this will mean that your CV arrives with a pile of others, with little or nothing to indicate why you are (a) particularly good for this job or (b) interested in working for this company. Find out what's casting – the listings in this book will tell you how best to do that for each company, and your agent may also be happy to tell you – and make your own applications. Tell your agent who you're writing to, and make sure that the CV your agent sends out on your behalf is accurate and up to date.

• On the subject of agents, stay visible to yours. Quite a number of agents have far too large a client list (30 to 35 per agent is about right, I reckon) so it's easy for them to forget about those they haven't heard from in a while. Some form of contact – phone or email, say – every week or two isn't unreasonable when you're not working. Make it a constructive call – not just "have you got me any auditions?" – and talk about what you can be doing to generate work: what's casting, who to write to, ideas for people to approach for general auditions (especially if you're travelling), and so on. Remember that they work for you, so make the most of their skills.

• Write to directors, producers and casting directors whose work you have seen, and tell them how much you enjoyed or admired it.

• Network. Go to see friends in plays, especially first nights, and get yourself invited to the party or pub afterwards. No need to be pushy – just be sociable. When you meet the director don't be tempted to 'do an audition' – casting is almost certainly the last thing on his or her mind right now, and you'll just alienate them. Conversely, don't *not* talk to them just because they're the director – that can be just as irritating. Remember that they're human beings. You won't be able to forget that they're the director, but try to see them as just someone you're meeting at a party. Then follow it up with a CV or showreel in the post. (Have one to hand in case they ask for one.)

• Showcase your talents. The Actors Centre run showcase evenings to which casting professionals are invited, and there are various others around – although be careful, before you stump up too much cash, that they are reputable. One recent addition to the collection is Actors Platform (**www.actorsplatform.com**). Also worth considering is Fringe theatre. It is a huge commitment in terms of time and money (in lost earnings alone) to embark on a Fringe production, so make sure you'll get something out of it. If you want to work on *Holby City*, ask yourself if a Fringe production of *Godspell* is really the best showcase for you. Also, if you want casting directors to travel to see you, is it going to be worth your while doing something dark and disturbing in some tiny, God-forsaken flea-pit in the middle of nowhere? More problematic is the question, 'Is it likely to be any good?' – and for that you'll have to do your homework. Find out what the director (and writer if it's a new play) has done before, because you may not want to give up several weeks' earnings to work with a first-time director straight out of college. Everyone has to start somewhere, but you've a right to be able to make an informed judgement if you're working for next to nothing. Google, Whatsonstage.com and Theatre Record may be helpful here. (See the introduction to the Fringe theatre section for more pitfalls to watch out for.)

• Do a short film. These can be useful camera experience, and occasionally provide material for a showreel. Some of these are paid (often badly); a great many are not. These days every kid with a media studies degree wants to be the next Guy Ritchie, so again if you're working for nothing, make sure you have confidence in your director and producer before committing yourself. You're not a charity, and you're not an amateur who just does it for fun.

Stay sane

Being an actor should carry a mental health warning – working away from home, unemployment, rejection, failure, insecurity, poverty: all of these can take their toll on your psychological health and on your relationships. And the worse thing about that is that it makes it even harder to find and get acting jobs – few things kill your chances in an audition quicker than the smell of desperation. After all, if *you* don't have confidence in yourself, why should they? So look after yourself, and take responsibility for your own wellbeing. Here are my suggestions for psychological pick-me-ups ...

• Be sociable, even if you don't feel like it. It can be a lonely business when you're out of work – and often even when you're working – so make the most of the time to see as much of friends and family as possible. This is particularly important with partners, especially if the kind of work you tend to get means being away from home. Throw parties or invite your friends to dinner when you're feeling up, and call your actor friends for an understanding shoulder to cry on when you're not.

• Make time for things you enjoy, that make you feel good about yourself. Perhaps this may mean setting yourself challenges – do the garden, DIY around the home, learn French, run a marathon – or may just mean setting aside 'me' time. Yoga and meditation are particularly good for this, and some people draw great strength from religious observance.

• If (like me) you are a naturally anxious person, and meditation or yoga don't appeal, then consider getting some relaxation music and spend some time every day listening to it. If anxiety and self-image are your problem, don't go buying some motivational 'You too can be rich and famous' hypnosis tape, or you could make things worse: deal with the problem in hand. Have a look at **www.relax-uk.com** for some examples.

• Get out in the fresh air. Remember when you were younger, when adults urged you to switch off the telly and get outdoors? Well, they were right – exercise and sunlight are vitally important for both your physical and mental health, particularly in the winter months when daylight is in short supply. Even when we're working, often much of our time is spent in windowless boxes, so make the most of a nice day and go for a walk.

• Take a holiday. That's really not easy to do, especially at the start of one's career. A week away from the 'day job' is a week not earning money, which can be expensive if you've already used up your holiday pay subsidising those days or weeks of involuntary unemployment that often occur just before or just after an acting job. But everyone needs to recharge their batteries from time to time, even if it's just a long weekend visiting old friends.

• Detox. Most actors drink – I think it was Gene Hackman who once observed that all actors eventually become either directors or drunks – but if your last job involved a lot of boozing (or if you're currently waking up with one or more hangovers a week), then try a few weeks off the sauce. Drink two litres of water a day, get plenty of early nights, and try to make fruit and fresh veg a good fifty per cent of everything you eat. Some people also find it beneficial to give up bread or go veggie or vegan for a while. Go back to beer-and-burgers after that if you want, but notice the difference in your mood and concentration when you do.

• Keep a positive attitude. Remember, you're in this for the long term, so although six months or more can feel like a long time, compared with the 30- or 40-year career you have ahead of you, it's really not so long. Almost all actors are out of work for periods in their career – even very good ones – so don't panic.

• Don't give yourself a hard time about past failures: learn the lesson and move on. Make here and now your starting point, and plan for the future based on what *is* rather than what *might have been.*

• Silence your inner critic. Brendan Behan wrote that "Critics are like eunuchs in a harem: they know how it's done, they've seen it done every day, but they're unable to do it themselves." We all have a critic within us, but the less room we give it, the less we'll feel like eunuchs ourselves. Be generous to your fellow professionals, understanding of what they go through, and don't be threatened by their success. A friend of a friend of mine is doing very well for himself – very good-looking, great agent, lovely telly and film roles coming his way – and I so wanted to dislike him. But meeting him again at a party recently he was warm, relaxed, interested in what I was doing, remembered things I'd told him last time we met – in short, utterly charming. And I realised that that's actually what made him the star. Not just the looks or the talent – both of which he does have in spades – but also the generosity of spirit, the belief that 'I'm ok, you're ok'. It might be the acidic queen with the barbed tongue who gets the laughs at the party, but it's people like that actor who will in the end do well. So resist pressure to join in bashing reputations or impugning characters, and learn compassion for yourself and for others.

• Don't just wait for your agent to call. Be proactive. Take charge of your career. Keep doing the things listed above that will improve your chances of finding work.

• Finally – and you may be surprised that I give this advice in an actors' yearbook – if it really is getting too much for you, then it may be time to call it quits. Acting can be a very cruel business, and not everyone is built to withstand the emotional battering that visits most actors from time to time. If there is anything at all that you could be happy doing instead of acting, then do it: there is no shame at all in looking after your sanity. A very talented friend of mine who left the business after years of frustration described her new situation to me thus: "I'm doing a job that I hate and I'm happier than I've been in years." Many people who leave acting find related work – teaching, for example, or work in some aspect of production – but I know some who have found that proximity to what they've left behind to be too painful, and have opted for entirely unrelated occupations. In the end, it comes down to what makes you happy, where you feel at home, and what ultimately brings you peace. Enjoying acting is not the same as enjoying being an actor.

There's a 'prayer' that runs, 'Grant me the serenity to accept the things I cannot change, courage to change the things I can, and wisdom to know the difference.' This seems to me to be a good motto for any actor. A great many decisions affecting our lives as actors are out of our hands, but a great many more we *do* have control over. The trick to staying sane in this business seems to be knowing (and accepting) which are which.

Andrew Piper trained at the Bristol Old Vic Theatre School. More information can be found at **www.andrew-piper.com**. He edited the 2007 and 2008 editions of *Actors' Yearbook*.

Physical and mental fitness for actors

Alex Caan

The instrument or tool of the actor is the body. Like a musical instrument, if it is left idle it will become out of tune and lose its ability to function effectively.

Actors need to constantly develop their instrument to get the best out of it. Unlike a musical instrument, we carry our tool with us every day. With good habits and practice we can alleviate many of the problems that need to be fixed before they start. The work required to have a positive ongoing effect is not as great or as demanding as one would expect. Before we look at what we can do to make our bodies outstanding, let's look at what our bodies really are.

In a person of average weight and build, 70 per cent of the mass of the body is muscle and bone. Therefore we can have a large effect on our bodies, by focusing on our muscles and bones. Before we can affect change in our muscles and bones we need to understand how they work and what relationships they have with each other.

The structure of the body is extremely complicated but can be viewed in quite a simplistic manner. Originally we would have walked on all fours, which is why our upper limbs have very similar corresponding joints to our lower limbs. Each hand has five digits, with a dominant thumb; our corresponding lower body part is the opposite foot, with the big toe as the dominant digit. The wrist and ankle are similar multi-directional joints, whereas the elbow and knee are both hinged joints. The shoulder and hip are ball and socket joints.

The upper and lower limbs are also connected by corresponding groups of muscles. The quads, which are in the front of the thigh, are related to the upper body through the triceps, which are in the back of the upper arm. The hamstrings, at the back of the upper leg, are related to the biceps. The gluteus or buttocks are related to the pectorals or chest muscles. So rather than looking at muscular activity in isolation, we must see muscles as groups working together.

When the body moves forward, the opposite arm and leg swing. The combination of muscles working together propels our bodies. Muscles move limbs by shortening.

Muscles work together synergistically, and in a healthy, well-maintained body are balanced. If bad habits occur, this simplicity of movement can lead to long-term health problems by over-use of some muscles, and under-use of others. This constant over-use/under-use will lead to a tired or sore body part in a specific area, often one side of the neck or lower back.

As we move forward, the chain of movements pass through the centre of the body. This passing through the centre is a clue to the focus of long-term fitness and wellbeing for the actor.

The centre of the body is the place where all life stems from. It is here that a baby is connected to its mother through the placenta, that later becomes the belly button. In the centre of the body is the diaphragm, from which, through correct training, all breath should originate.

The movement of our bodies creates heat and energy. Contrary to what some directors believe, we are not beings that live in our head or brain space. We live in our bodies, and movement produces powerful emotional responses. This is encapsulated in the phrase 'Motion creates Emotion'. This is why actors talk about getting the walk of the character, because this allows them to get into the body of the character, which in turn allows them to get into the personality of the character. Some actors do this instinctively, but it is and can be a learned skill.

Actors communicate thoughts in the vast majority by speaking. There are, of course, actors who use mime and dance to communicate, but mainly thoughts are communicated verbally, using speech or song. Words are merely a manipulation of breath using the tongue, mouth and vocal cords. Without breath we have nothing to carry our thoughts over large theatrical space.

Coincidentally, breath or oxygen is the most important nourishment our bodies need. Without food one can live for 40 days or more; without water one can live for 7-10 days; but if you don't breathe for five minutes you will die.

Using this as our guide, the focus of the actors' fitness should be built around the development of a robust powerful tool that can create large amounts of powerful breath. Not just large volumes of breath, but outstanding control of the mechanism that delivers that breath.

The mechanism that delivers the breath is the lungs and diaphragm and their supporting muscles. These muscles need to be strong, but also need to be mobile and have excellent endurance.

Lastly, the value of water cannot be underestimated. A 5 per cent drop in hydration can lead to mild dehydration, which can lead to a large drop in bodily function, both mental and physical. Even a 2 per cent drop in hydration can have a very damaging and negative effect on our voice. In temperate climates we lose 2.5 litres of water throughout an average day. If we are performing, rehearsing or undertaking strenuous physical activity we will use much greater amounts of water than this. Therefore we must monitor our bodies and increase water intake when needed. Passing clear urine is a good indicator of hydration – if not first thing in the morning, then definitely throughout the day.

So where does one start in the nitty-gritty of training the actor's body? Actors come in all shapes and sizes. I am not advocating that all actors try to become slim and pert: who would play all the non-slim, non-pert roles? Equally, I am not advocating that all actors develop muscular physiques. We need to be limber in the joints and muscles, but there is no point in the serious actor developing big muscles at the expense of range of movement. I believe that you can be tall, short, slim, rotund, lanky or squat and at the same time be very fit. Olympic shot putters are very large but all can run great distances and move like ballet dancers.

Fitness for actors doesn't require a massive overloading of the body. To reach Olympic-standard fitness we would need to break the body down systematically over a period of time, in order to allow the body to regenerate stronger than before. This regeneration occurs during periods of rest. But this overloading is not really needed for general fitness for actors.

In all of our fitness development we need to place breath control and posture at the forefront. The ideas and concepts of the Alexander Technique are pivotal to this. Its values are based on excellent posture and good use of muscles, rather than overuse and bad postural habits. So when performing any movement, be aware of the alignment of the head, neck and back. Often actors strain their voices because they are tight in another part of their body, which pulls the head and neck out of alignment, resulting in a sore throat or strained voice. For those of you who are not familiar with the Alexander Technique, I would recommend that an awareness of posture and balance is vital to long-term fitness.

A simple starting point for general fitness for actors is walking. Walking is the most underused and undervalued exercise we can do. It involves a good pair of training shoes and a place to go! Between 20 and 60 minutes' continuous walking a day will increase lung capacity and make our heart a great deal stronger. I know many actors say that they walk at least that in a day – going shopping, walking to the bus or train, and so on. I am not discounting that, but I am advocating a steady brisk walk with arms swinging back and forth in time with the opposing leg. By doing this, the whole body is being exercised, and the core muscles through the centre of the body are activated. It is akin to the phase of human development that we know as crawling. The same benefits cannot be achieved through passive day-to-day walking.

Walking has a very effective return for the amount of effort expended, because there is little detrimental impact on the joints of the lower limbs. The swinging of opposing arms and legs also helps reinforce correct neurological pathways. This helps us to move our bodies more effectively and efficiently as a kinetic chain, rather than as disjointed isolated movements.

A walking regime three days a week is a good place to start. You will not only build your lungs and heart, but also the tissues around your joints in the legs, arms and back. These need time to adapt and grow to the new stresses being placed on them. Taking a day off in between will allow the tissues throughout your body to regenerate during the periods of rest.

If you are a fitness novice, then building up to an hour-long walk is an achievable goal. Start with a ten-minute walk that builds systematically over a period of between four and six weeks, rather than blazing into a brisk hour-long walk initially. Increasing your walks by three minutes each walk will let you achieve an hour-long walk from a ten-minute starting point in just six weeks. Three minutes may sound a lot, but since it requires adding just one and a half minutes to your outward journey, it is not an unrealistic amount.

Swimming is also an excellent way to work the heart and lungs without placing any stress on the joints, as it is a non-weight bearing form of exercise. However, it is important to swim using the front crawl and backstroke rather than predominantly using the breast stroke, so that we continue to move opposing upper and lower limbs to work our core muscles. A mixture of all swimming strokes would be best to work the greatest range of muscle groups and minimise the likelihood of housemaid's knee (a common breast stroke-related injury)! Learning to swim with your head partially submerged in the water is vital, in order to maintain correct alignment of the spine.

The same incremental approach to developing fitness through walking, as recommended above, should be applied when undertaking a swimming regime. Rather than using the increment of time, the number of lengths swum is a very simple starting point. Do bear in mind the length of each pool that you may swim in may vary! It is likely that the more often you swim, the quicker you will become. So increasing the number of lengths that you swim each session may require little or no extra time in the pool.

We have exercised the heart and lungs with walking and swimming. We need now to develop our range of movement and strength. Basic Yoga movements are also a simple and effective way to increase inner strength and develop range of movement and good posture. I am not looking at the more physical jumping around or sauna types of Yoga. I am advocating basic Yoga moves.

Yoga has many positive effects, which include large ranges of movement and mobility. By getting into certain Yoga positions, we are not only stretching the muscles, but also massaging the internal organs. Yoga also has the benefit of establishing excellent breath control. The breath floods into the centre of the body and has to be released with control and in a sustained manner. This has a very relaxing and meditative effect. This helps us switch off our overactive minds, the value of which cannot be underestimated.

Buying a book or DVD on Yoga or joining a Yoga class is an excellent place to start. If Yoga doesn't appeal to you, then Pilates is an excellent alternative. Both Yoga and Pilates are fantastic for developing breath control and posture control techniques.

Let us look at a sample week's exercise programme – for example, walking or swimming on Monday, Thursday and Saturday, with Yoga or Pilates on Tuesday and Friday. This gives you two days off, on Wednesday and Sunday, which follow either two or three days of activity. Rest is vital to regeneration. We only become fitter and stronger by allowing our bodies to recover and grow. These days off give the individual physical downtime, which can then be filled with mental stimulation of some kind, including meditation, vocal and singing practice, reading or other pursuits that aid the actor's development as a whole.

Further information

For more information about any of the suggested forms of exercise, see the websites listed below:

Alexander Technique **www.alexandertechnique.com**

Walking **www.thewalkingsite.com**

Swimming **www.britishswimming.org**

Yoga **www.bwy.org.uk** (British Wheel of Yoga)

Pilates **www.pilatesfoundation.com**

This is a brief overview of the most suitable and simple exercises to cover what is required for the stresses and strains of most acting jobs. All of these suggestions can be carried out from home or on tour. The time and effort required to train in this manner will not be detrimental to the actor's performance. By starting small, and increasing gradually, the actor will feel more invigorated and energised from undertaking an exercise programme.

The actor's body should be viewed as a communication tool. Bodies require stimulation to develop. Without stimulus, the body and mind will deteriorate. Permitting this to happen is an injustice to the craft of acting. We all only have one body, and we need to look after it and maintain it for our specific needs.

Alex Caan was an international athlete before training at RADA for three years. Since graduation, he has worked extensively in theatre, TV and radio. As a consultant Alex teaches business people powerful communication through effective use of the body. As a sports coach Alex has coached Premiership football and rugby players to international level. He has coached sportsmen and women to Olympic and World level in a range of different athletic disciplines. He is currently National Event Coach for High Jump in the UK, and prepared the group of talented high jumpers for the London 2012 Olympics.

Creating your own work: The four major hurdles and how to overcome them

Shaun Prendergast

There's an old joke which asks, 'Why don't actors look out of the window in the morning?' The answer? 'So they have something to do in the afternoon.'

Like all good jokes, there's truth in it. Although there's not enough work to go round, many actors prefer to complain about the situation, rather than make the effort to create work for themselves. But creating your own work is worth doing for a number of reasons.

Whether you write monologues or sketches and broadcast them on the net, or form your own company to produce Shakespeare, or teach communication skills to the corporate market, any effort you make will reap benefits. Extra income can support you till the next acting job comes along and, perhaps more importantly, any activity which nurtures your own creativity will increase your confidence and make it more likely that others will want to work with you. And, as we know, work breeds work.

Self-created work falls into two categories: a) work which will not make you any money, but will advance your career by giving you experience and broadening your list of contacts, and b) work which actually brings in an income. Either path requires the actor to step out of their comfort zone. This basic guide will take you through the problems associated with creating your own work, and help you overcome them.

The four main hurdles are as follows: let's deal with them individually.

Lack of time

If you're single, with no kids, you're in the best position of all. However hard you work to repay your debts or cobble together your Spotlight fee, you are essentially beholden to no-one. There will be time to work for yourself, although it may well have to be taken from other activities, such as mooching around doing nothing or bitching about being out of work. Come on folks, you know it's true. If you are in a relationship and find it hard to take time out to further your own needs, there are two simple strategies. Change your attitude. Or your relationship. If you have kids and a job and a relationship and all the other stuff which makes it genuinely difficult to find time for yourself, I have this hard nugget of advice. There is only one answer. Find the time somehow.

Whatever your commitments, follow these rules. Set aside *as much time as you can* every day. Once set aside, work for every minute of that time. Do not take time out for phone calls, checking Facebook or even cleaning. Get into a routine of working and stick to it. If, for example, you are writing something, remember there is no disgrace in writing fifteen pages of rubbish. There is a disgrace in not writing fifteen pages.

Lack of talent

Talent takes many forms. It may take a few goes to locate your true talent. You'll never know unless you try. If you try writing and it doesn't work for you, consider teaching. If not teaching, then produce. But whatever you choose, bear this principle in mind. You can learn.

There are others who have made this journey. Seek help. If you want to produce a show or write a script or direct a short, find others who have done the same thing and learn how they did it. Check out writers' groups, film makers' collectives. Contact people, hang out, ask questions, read books. Information is power. When you find your niche, you will surprise yourself. The willingness to learn is at least as important as inherent talent. Effort makes a difference.

Lack of opportunity

Here there is some good news. It is easier than ever to produce and create your own work. The most difficult and time-consuming route is to form your own company. The rewards can be extremely fruitful in terms of getting yourself noticed and producing work which makes you proud, but unless you are creating a market-driven product, (such as corporate training workshops or schools programmes) you won't make any money. An experienced and successful independent producer suggests following these simple principles:

a) Learn how to budget a production (there are books and Internet training forums galore on this), then raise the money and stick to the budget. Do not expect to make money. The best that most 'fringe' productions do is break even. Don't forget in your budget calculations that if you do sell tickets, you have to pay part of the ticket price in VAT back to the theatre. Forgetting this fact is the single most common mistake made by aspiring producers.

b) If you are paying your actors, make sure you can do so without bankrupting yourself. If you are not, make sure all other Equity conditions are in place and adhered to. Cast should work Equity hours, take proper breaks, etc. Fail to ensure this and you will soon see a breakdown in morale. Too often independent producers feel they are doing actors a favour. They are not. The actors are working for nothing. You are doing each other a favour. Treat casts and staff with respect, and they will repay you with (unwaged) loyalty and hard work.

c) At least a third of your budget needs to be spent on marketing.

If you do get a live production together, you can either present it at a Fringe venue for a limited run (expensive and ultimately bad value – you can easily end up playing to fewer people in the whole run than you could have crammed into your flat), or you can look to give the production a longer shelf life through festivals.

Edinburgh is hideously expensive and so slewed to comedy that many theatre pieces get no audience at all. Smaller festivals are a much better bet; if you can create a show with few props and little scenery, you can travel to festivals from Barnstaple to Prague (to name just two of the excellent smaller festivals) cheaply, gaining experience, building awareness and growing your audience. But an even more efficient way of getting your stuff out there is through new media. In many ways, this option for non-profit-making work is the most attractive.

It is now possible to record and edit (to pretty much broadcast quality) anything from a podcast monologue to a full-scale *Star Wars* pastiche on domestic equipment. By uploading your material to a hosting site or social networking sites, and spreading the word, you can quickly achieve a larger audience in a week than a Fringe production would in six. Best of all, casting directors and interested parties can view the material for evermore. This is the cheapest, fastest and most efficient method of creating your own work, and the opportunities increase exponentially every day.

And don't forget teaching. The interest in performing is greater than ever, and there are more stage schools than ever before. The most efficient ways of getting teaching work are by giving private tuition or group workshops. Experienced actors may well have amassed more expertise than they realise. The trick is to develop unique workshops which utilise any specific skills (e.g. Shakespeare in Performance or mask-work) and target a niche market – sixth form colleges or drama clubs for kids, for example. Then get together intelligent copy on what you have to offer and advertise, targeting every educational establishment or training H.O.D. you can identify. If you are seeking to get corporate work, you can offer yourself to companies who already have training contracts (role-play is very big) or you can launch yourself as an independent communication specialist. This can involve anything from speech training, confidence building or advanced communications techniques. Decide what expertise you have, design workshops, write copy that advertises them and send it out. You can also use your experience of various areas of the business to write articles like this one and sell them to magazines or trade journals.

Other markets that exist are taking work into schools. You need to find or create a text which is relevant to the needs of the curriculum, either by exploring a set text (preferably one out of copyright – no royalties to pay can make all the difference between profit and loss) or exploring issues which the curriculum demands be addressed: bullying, social pressures, etc. Then, again, you need to target schools with your product. Obviously, a two-handed, no-props show will be more feasible to tour than a full-scale version of *Aida*. But if you identify a gap in the market, there is money to be made.

Lack of money

Ah, money. For many actors, the perception is that finance (or the lack of it) is the biggest problem to overcome. This is not true.

Of course, if you are trying to mount a theatrical production you will have to raise funds. But bear in mind that all of the other options (particularly the new media/podcast/self-broadcast/self-publishing routes) will achieve a similar sized (or potentially much larger) audience than a Fringe production, for little or no cost at all. And if you develop a teaching or corporate training portfolio, you may even make a profit!

Finally, whatever you do, do something. Work breeds work, and any effort you put in that sharpens your skills and brings your profile to a larger audience will be worth it – and be much, much better for your career (and mental well-being) than standing around, looking out of the window, like an actor in an old joke.

Shaun Prendergast is an award-winning actor and writer. Recent acting work includes Mr Boo in *The Rise and Fall of Little Voice* in the West End (directed by Terry Johnson), Detective Superintendant Mike Evans in *Collision* for ITV (directed by Mark Evans), and Heinrich in the feature film *Fast Track No Limits* (directed by Axel Sand). His writing credits include *Eastenders*, *Roman Mysteries* and *The Lightning Kid* (all BBC), and *Rocket Man* (ITV Coastal).

Funding bodies

The competition for funding is so fierce that it is important to allow sufficient time for research, planning and proper presentation of your proposed project. It is well worth checking to see what information is available on the websites listed in this section. Many funding bodies are happy to advise on form-filling, what kind of projects stand a chance and what could constitute a realistic amount to ask for. It is also well worth going on one (or more) of the Independent Theatre Council's (ITC; see page 472) courses for assistance in the complex world of funding applications.

Bodies that offer individual funding should be approached with similar care and attention.

NATIONAL ARTS COUNCILS

Arts Council England

14 Great Peter Street, London SW1P 3NQ
tel 0845-300 6200 *fax* 0161-934 4426
textphone 020-7973 6564
email enquiries@artscouncil.org.uk
website www.artscouncil.org.uk

Arts Council England champions, develops and invests in artistic and cultural experiences that enrich people's lives. It supports a range of activities across the arts, museums and libraries - from theatre to digital art, reading to dance, music to literature, and crafts to collections. "Great art and culture inspires us, brings us together and teaches about ourselves and the world around us. In short it makes us better."

Between 2015 and 2018, Arts Council England plans to invest £1.1 billion of public money from government and an estimated £700 million from the National Lottery to help create these experiences for as many people as possible across the country. Grants for individuals and organisations through Grants for the Arts range from £1,000 up to a maximum of £100,000. Grants can cover activities lasting up to 3 years.

Application forms, guidance notes and information sheets can be downloaded from the website. A wide range of resources, publications, links and information about other funding sources is also accessible on the website.

Arts Council of Northern Ireland

MacNeice House, 77 Malone Road, Belfast BT9 6AQ
tel 028-9038 5200
email info@artscouncil-ni.org
website www.artscouncil-ni.org

The prime distributor of public support for the arts, the Arts Council of Northern Ireland is committed to increasing opportunities for artists to develop challenging and innovative work. In addition to funding schemes for organisations and community groups, the council has developed a special programme of schemes to extend support for the individual artist. This programme includes the General Arts Award, which provides funding for specific projects, specialised research and personal artistic development; and the Major Individual Award, which supports established artists in the development of ambitious work.

Arts Council of Wales

Bute Place, Cardiff CF10 5AL
tel 0845-8734 900 *fax* 029-2044 1400
email information@artscouncilofwales.org.uk
website www.artscouncilofwales.org.uk

Responsible for funding and developing the arts in Wales, using money from Welsh Government and the National Lottery. Provides arts organisations and individuals in Wales with the opportunity to apply for funding towards clearly defined arts-related projects. Scheme Guidelines for the funding programmes are available on the website.

Creative Scotland

249 West George Street, Glasgow G2 4QE
tel 0330-333 2000
Waverley Gate, 2-4 Waterloo Gate, Edinburgh EH1 3EG
tel 0330-333-2000
website www.creativescotland.com

In April 2010 the Scottish Arts Council merged with Scottish Screen to become Creative Scotland. Creative Scotland is the national leader for Scotland's arts, screen and creative industries. It helps "Scotland's creativity shine at home and abroad . . . We invest in talented people and exciting ideas. We develop the creative industries and champion everything that is good about Scottish creativity."

REGIONAL ARTS COUNCIL OFFICES

Arts Council England, East

Eastbrook, Shaftesbury Road, Cambridge CB2 8BF
tel 0845-300 6200 *fax* 0870-242 1271
textphone (01223) 306893

Area covered: Our East office covers Bedfordshire, Cambridgeshire, Essex, Hertfordshire, Norfolk and Suffolk.

Arts Council England, East Midlands

St Nicholas Court, 25-27 Castle Gate,
Nottingham NG1 7AR
tel 0845-300 6200 *fax* 0115-950 2467

Area covered: Derbyshire, Leicestershire, Lincolnshire (excluding North and North East Lincolnshire), Northamptonshire, Nottinghamshire, Rutland.

Arts Council England, London

14 Great Peter Street, London SW1P 3NQ
tel 0845-300 6200 *fax* 020-7973 6564

Area covered: Greater London.

Arts Council England, North East

Central Square, Forth Street,
Newcastle upon Tyne NE1 3PJ
tel 0845-300 6200 *fax* 0191-230 1020
textphone 0191-255 8585

Area covered: Durham, Northumberland, Tees Valley, Tyne and Wear.

Arts Council England, North West

The Hive, 49 Lever Street, Manchester M1 1FN
tel 0845-300 6200 *fax* 0161-934 4426
textphone 0161-834 9131

Area covered: Cheshire, Cumbria, Greater Manchester, Lancashire, Merseyside.

Arts Council England, South East

Sovereign House, Church Street, Brighton BN1 1RA
tel 0845-300 6200 *fax* 0870-242 1257
textphone (01273) 710659

Area covered: Berkshire, Buckinghamshire, East Sussex, Hampshire, Isle of Wight, Kent, Oxfordshire, Surrey, West Sussex.

Arts Council England, South West

Senate Court, Southernhay Gardens, Exeter EX1 1UG
tel 0845-300 6200 *fax* (01392) 498546
textphone (01392) 433503

Area covered: Cornwall, Devon, Dorset, Gloucestershire, the Isles of Scilly, Somerset, Wiltshire; unitary authorities of Bath and North East Somerset, Bournemouth, Bristol, North Somerset, Plymouth, Poole, South Gloucestershire, Swindon, Torbay.

Arts Council England, West Midlands

82 Granville Street, Birmingham B1 2LH
tel 0845-300 6200 *fax* 0121-643 7239
textphone 0121-643 2815

Area covered: Herefordshire, Shropshire, Staffordshire, Warwickshire, Worcestershire; metropolitan authorities of Birmingham, Coventry, Dudley, Sandwell, Solihull, Walsall, Wolverhampton.

Arts Council England, Yorkshire

21 Bond Street, Dewsbury,
West Yorkshire WF13 1AX
tel 0845-300 6200 *fax* (01924) 466522
textphone (01924) 438585

Area covered: Yorkshire and the Humber, which includes North and North East Lincolnshire.

NATIONAL FILM AGENCIES

Creative England

tel 0844-824 6042
email info@creativeengland.co.uk
website www.creativeengland.co.uk

Creative England is a national agency that invests in and supports creative ideas, talent and businesses in film, TV, games and digital media. We aim to grow the brightest, the best, and those with the most promise, so that individuals and businesses can achieve their full creative and commercial potential. We help identify future opportunities to grow the economy and generate jobs. With offices in Salford, Birmingham, Bristol, Leeds, Nottingham, Pinewood and Elstree, we are a national agency with strong local and regional links. For more information visit the website.

Northern Ireland Screen

3rd Floor, 21 Alfred House, Belfast BT2 8ED
tel 028-9023 2444
website www.northernirelandscreen.co.uk

Northern Ireland Screen is the national screen agency for Northern Ireland. Its aim is to accelerate the development of a dynamic and sustainable screen industry and culture in Northern Ireland.

Wales Screen Commission

1st Floor North, QED Treforest Ind. Est.,
Pontypridd CF37 5YR
tel 0300-061 5634
email enquiry@walesscreencommission.co.uk
website www.walesscreencommission.com

The Wales Screen Commission is the location service for Wales, offering comprehensive information and support on locations, facilities, crew and local services throughout Wales.

REGIONAL FILM AGENCIES

EM Media

Antenna Media Centre, Beck Street,
Nottingham NG1 1EQ
tel 0115-993 2333
email info@em-media.org.uk
website www.em-media.org.uk

EM Media is the Screen Agency for the East Midlands region of England, and invests in East Midlands based creative talent, supporting and developing projects and activities that meet its business aims.

Film London

Suite 6.10, The Tea Building,
56 Shoreditch High Street, London E1 6JJ
tel 020-7613 7676 *fax* 020-7613 7677
email info@filmlondon.org.uk
website www.filmlondon.org.uk

Film London is the capital's public agency for feature film, television, commercials and other interactive content, including games. "Our aim is simple: to ensure that London has a thriving film sector that enriches the capital's businesses and its people." The government has charged Film London with developing and managing a national strategy to generate inward investment through film production via a public-private partnership with key industry bodies, following its decision in July 2010 to abolish the UK Film Council.

Northern Film & Media

Baltic Centre for Contemporary Art,
South Shore Road, Gateshead NE8 3BA
tel 0191-440 4940
email info@northernmedia.org
website www.northernmedia.org

Northern Film & Media is the screen agency for the North East of England. "Our vision is to create a strong commercial creative economy in the North East, by investing in talent and ideas."

Screen South

The Wedge, 75-81 Tontine Street, Folkestone,
Kent CT20 1JR
tel (01303) 259777 *fax* (01303) 259786
email info@screensouth.org
website www.screensouth.org

Screen South is the film and media agency for the South East of England. "We aim to be a resource that helps people get their ideas off the ground, whether they want to make a short film, learn how to write successful scripts, set up a film festival or shoot a major movie here. We promote talent, preserve our film heritage and find ways of presenting exciting film to new audiences. Screen South is a Lottery distributor."

Screen Yorkshire

Studio 22, 46 The Calls, Leeds LS2 7EY
tel 0113-294 4410
email sally@screenyorkshire.co.uk
website www.screenyorkshire.co.uk

Screen Yorkshire's mission is to inspire, promote and support the development of a successful long-term film, broadcast, games and interactive media sector to grow the economic, social and cultural wealth of the region.

OTHER SOURCES OF FUNDING

Additional information about various entertainment charities and benevolent funds can be found on the website of The Actors' Charitable Trust **www.tactactors.org**. Unless explicitly mentioned, most of the organisations listed below and on the TACT website do not provide assistance with drama school fees or maintenance.

Actors' Benevolent Fund

6 Adam Street, London WC2N 6AD
tel 020-7836 6378 *fax* 020-7836 8978
email office@abf.org.uk
website www.actorsbenevolentfund.co.uk

Since 1882 the Actors' Benevolent Fund has provided financial assistance to actors unable to work due to poor health, an accident or old age. To be eligible for assistance, applicants need several years of professional acting experience.

Equity Charitable Trust

Plouviez House, 19-20 Hatton Place,
London EC1N 8RU
tel 020-7831 1926 *fax* 020-7242 7995
email info@equitycharitabletrust.org.uk
website www.equitycharitabletrust.org.uk

The Equity Charitable Trust provides educational bursaries to performers and industry professionals with a minimum of 10 years' professional adult experience who are looking to retrain, develop new skills and obtain valuable new qualifications. Depending on your circumstances, grants can cover some or even all of the course costs.

We also provide debt adive to industry members who are experiencing a financial or medical setback and who may qualify for a one-off financial grant. For information and to download an application form for either a Welfare or Education Grant visit the website **www.equitycharitabletrust.org.uk** or email **info@equitycharitabletrust.org.uk**

Evelyn Norris Trust

Plouviez House, 19-20 Hatton Place,
London EC1N 8RU
tel 020-7831 1926
website www.equitycharitabletrust.org.uk/evelynnorris.php
Secretary Keith Carter

The Evelyn Norris Trust is a charity that accepts applications for grants from members of the concert and theatrical professions. The Trust aims to help with the cost of convalesence or a recuperative holiday following illness, injury or surgery.

First Light

Studio 28, Fazeley Studios, Fazeley Street,
Birmingham B5 5SE
tel 0121-224 7511
website www.firstlightonline.co.uk

First Light is the UK's leading initiative enabling young people to realise their potential via creative digital film and media projects. It operates a number of youth funding schemes, including:

• The Young Film Fund – the BFI's Lottery-funded filmmaking initiative for 5-19 year olds.
• Mediabox – a Department for Children, Schools & Families fund to help young people establish a positive voice in the media. It offers disadvantaged 13-19 year olds the opportunity to develop and produce creative media projects using film, print, television, radio or online platforms. There are grants of up to £40,000 available now.
• Second Light – a talent development scheme which, through production-based training, will give 30 talented young people aged 18 to 23, from BME backgrounds, supported opportunities to move into the film industry.

The Foyle Foundation

Rugby Chambers, 2 Rugby Street,
London WC1N 3QU
tel 020-7430 9119
email info@foylefoundation.org.uk
website www.foylefoundation.org.uk

The Foundation operates a Main Grants Scheme supporting charities with a core remit of Arts or Learning and a Small Grants Scheme covering small charities in all fields. It has supported tours, festivals and education projects and helped to develop new work. It will also consider funding the building or updating of arts facilities. The majority of grants are in the range of £10,000 to £50,000. Capital projects seeking more than £50,000 are considered twice per year. Application forms and guidelines are available to download from the website.

The Jerwood Charitable Foundation

171 Union Street, London SE1 0LN
tel 020-7261 0279
email info@jerwood.org
website www.jerwoodfoundation.org

The Jerwood Charitable Foundation is dedicated to imaginative and responsible revenue funding of the arts, supporting professional artists to develop and grow at important stages in their careers. It works with artists across art forms, from dance and theatre to literature, music and the visual arts. For more information on the Jerwood Charitable Foundation, please visit the website.

National Endowment for Science, Technology and the Arts

1 Plough Place, London EC4A 1DE
tel 020-7438 2500 *fax* 020-7438 2501
email information@nesta.org.uk
website www.nesta.org.uk

Offers a variety of funding schemes to promote innovation within the fields of science, technology and the arts.

The Oxford Samuel Beckett Theatre Trust Award

PO Box 2637, Ascot, Berks SL5 8ZN
email info@osbttrust.com
website www.osbttrust.com
Director

The purpose of this annual award is, in particular, to help the development of emerging practitioners in the field of innovative theatre/performance and, in general, to encourage the new generation of creative artists. Artists from all disciplines are encouraged to apply.

The award is for a company or individual to create a show either for the Pit Theatre, Barbican, London, or a site-responsive, non-traditional show to take place in London. The winning show, either at the Pit or, if site-responsive, elsewhere, will be part of the Barbican Theatre season.

Performance Initiative Network

email contact@kerryirvine.co.uk
website http://kerryirvine.co.uk/consultancy/performance-initiative-network
Contact Kerry Irvine

Supporting the professional small theatre company and theatre artist to make and produce their work. Runs the GroundWork Festival, eVolve, and the PiLab series of projects.

The Ralph and Meriel Richardson Foundation

c/o 179 Great Portland Street, London W1W5LS
mobile (07733) 688120
email manager@sirralphrichardson.org.uk
website www.sirralphrichardson.org.uk

The Foundation was established by Lady Meriel (Mu) Richardson after the untimely death of the Richardsons' only son, Charles, to relieve the need, hardship or distress of British actors and actresses who have professionally practised or contributed to the Theatrical Arts (on stage, film, television or radio) and their spouses and children.

The Foundation has made grants for wheelchairs, for hospital treatment, residential care, surgeons fees, medication and a variety of short-term help to a large number of those seeking assistance. An applicant's request for a grant (with a CV and letters in support) is assessed on its merit in light of the objects of the Foundation. A majority of the Trustees is required for approval of every application. Applicants must have been active in the profession for a minimum of 15 years, save in exceptional circumstances.

The Royal Theatrical Fund

11 Garrick Street, London WC2E 9AR
tel 020-7836 3322 *fax* 020-7379 8273
email admin@trtf.com
website www.trtf.com

Founded in 1839, the Royal Theatrical Fund makes grants which will alleviate the suffering, assist the recovery, or reduce the need, hardship or distress of theatrical artists or their families/dependants. To be eligible to receive a grant, a person must have professionally practised or contributed to the theatrical arts (on stage, radio, film or television) for a minimum of 7 years.

Sophie's Silver Lining Fund

c/o Tony Scott Andrews, at Aplin Stockton Fairfax, 36 West Bar, Banbury, Oxon OX16 9RU
tel (01295) 251234
email office@sslf.org.uk
website www.sslf.org.uk

Provides assistance with the cost of their training to needy acting and singing students. "Please note that regretfully, we are no longer able to accept applications for funding from individual students. Awards are only made to students put forward by a small number of drama and music colleges selected by the trustees."

The Wellcome Trust

Arts Awards, 215 Euston Road, London NW1 2BE
email arts@wellcome.ac.uk
website www.wellcome.ac.uk/arts

The Wellcome Trust Arts Awards is the Trust's funding scheme that supports arts projects which engage with biomedical science.

"The Arts Awards provide funding for a range of projects that bring together any art form and any area of biomedical science. Projects must involve the creation of new artistic work and have biomedical scientific input into the process, either through a scientist taking on an advisory role or through direct collaboration. 2 levels of funding are available – small- to medium-sized projects (up to and including £30,000) and large projects (above £30,000) – primarily for artists or organisations with an existing track record with the Wellcome Trust or Wellcome Collection. Full details are available on our website, including details of pending deadlines for large and small grants, application guidelines, examples of previously funded projects, and the online application portal."

Publications, libraries, references and booksellers

This section lists the major sources for scripts and sheet music – and routes to finding that elusive script or score. While Internet search engines can be extremely useful in such a quest, it sometimes requires some lateral thinking to find what you want. It is possible to find out-of-print plays via libraries or book-finding services and by combing second-hand bookshops. Some publishers (even a few playwrights' agencies) will organise a photocopy – for a fee. Also, the British Library (in theory) has a copy of every play ever performed in this country, but there can be complications in actually getting hold of a copy. Start with your local library if you're determined to find a specific play; if they don't have it, they may well be able to get it from another library (via the inter-library loan system), but be prepared for it to take a long time. Another route is to try to find a theatre at which the play has been performed: they may be able to help.

AbeBooks.com

website www.abebooks.com

Excellent website which will search the catalogues of hundreds of second-hand booksellers in this country and around the world.

Actorsandperformers.com

Actors & Performers is a professional networking site for the acting community, containing must-have career information, and with authors, casting directors, actors and industry practitioners such as Richard Eyre appearing as guest bloggers and contributors, offering advice and insight into the profession.

Actors & Performers provides a community for actors to share events, ask questions, network, comment on blogs and events, and obtain career advice for free.

Register free for Actors & Performers at **www.actorsandperformers.com**.

Amazon.co.uk & Amazon.com

website www.amazon.co.uk or www.amazon.com

Remarkably useful not just for what is currently in print, but also for links to second-hand retailers who may have that out-of-print play or score you are seeking.

Barbican Library

Barbican Centre, London EC2Y 8DS
tel 020-7638 0569
website www.cityoflondon.gov.uk/barbicanlibrary

Situated on level 2 of the Barbican Centre, this is the largest lending library in the City of London. In addition to the general library, the strong arts and music sections reflect the Barbican Centre's emphasis on the arts. The library is fully accessible by wheelchair and has a number of other access facilities including hearing induction loops and a reading magnifier machine. *Opening hours*: Monday and Wednesday: 9.30am – 5.30pm; Tuesday and Thursday: 9.30am – 7.30pm; Friday: 9.30am – 2pm; Saturday: 9.30am – 4pm.

Bookbarn International

Units 1-2, Hallatrow Business Park, Hallatrow, Bath & Avon BS39 6EX
tel (01761) 452178
website www.bookbarninternational.co.uk

"The UK's largest used book warehouse," with many thousands of cheap second-hand scripts and a searchable catalogue online.

The British Library

St Pancras Building, 96 Euston Road, London NW1 2DB
tel 0330 333 1144 (switchboard), 020-7412 7676 (reader information, St Pancras), (01937) 546070 (reader information, enquiries, Boston Spa), 020-7412 7831 (humanities & sound archive), 020-7412 7702 (maps), 020-7412 7513 (manuscripts)
Legal Deposit Office: The British Library, Boston Spa, Wetherby, West Yorkshire LS23 7BQ
tel (01937) 546268 (books), (01937) 546267 (serials)
email legal-deposit-books@bl.uk
website www.bl.uk

The British Library is the national library of the United Kingdom and contains a substantial collection of plays and manuscripts from the UK and Ireland, as well as from other parts of the world. The sound

Resources

archive also includes just about everything from the sound of Amazonian tree frogs to classic recordings of Shakespeare's plays. Users need a Reader's Pass (details on how to acquire same are on the website) to access and read particular publications. The library will, for a fee, allow photocopying – subject to copyright legislation.

Contacts

See the entry for Spotlight under *Spotlight, casting directories and information services* on page 383.

Doollee.com

website www.doollee.com

An excellent free online guide to modern playwrights and theatre plays which have been written, or translated, into English since the production of *Look Back in Anger* in 1956.

Dress Circle

tel 020-7240 2227
email info@dresscircle.co.uk
website www.dresscircle.co.uk

Dress Circle formerly had a shop in London's Covent Garden; it now operates online only. It aims to supply the widest selection of musical theatre and cabaret-related products from around the world – CDs, DVDs, posters, cards, mugs, collectibles and more. "If we can't get it – no one can!"

Fourthwall (incorporating The Drama Student)

3rd Floor, 207 Regent Street, London W1B 3HH
tel 020-3371 0995
email editor@fourthwallmagazine.co.uk
website www.fourthwallmagazine.co.uk
Editorial Director Phil Matthews *Editor* Josh Boyd-Rochford

Fourthwall covers the whole journey, from auditioning for drama school through to graduation and beyond. Believes that to succeed in this industry, it is important that we constantly challenge ourselves, and often that means the training never leaves us. *Fourthwall* is at the forefront of that passion, delivering a magazine that is informative, amusing, intelligent, thought provoking, accessible and challenging. "Above all, we're a publication that is passionate about careers in the performing arts."

French's Theatre Bookshop (and Samuel French Ltd)

52 Fitzroy Street, London W1T 5JR
tel 020-7255 4300 *fax* 020-7387 2161
website www.samuelfrench-london.co.uk

Samuel French has been publishing, selling and leasing plays for performance since 1830. Today the company has more than 2,000 play scripts available to perform, covering all elements of performing theatre – from comedies to tragedies, sketches to full-scale musicals. In addition, the bookshop stocks a comprehensive range of play scripts and technical books on all aspects of theatre. The Samuel French *Guide to Selecting Plays* lists plays according to genre and cast size. French's Theatre Bookshop is wheelchair-friendly, staff are helpful and signage suitable for visually impaired. Enlarged print catalogue and lists are available on demand.

Internet Movie Database (IMDb)

website uk.imdb.com

A comprehensive database and news round-up of film and television around the world.

The Knowledge

Wilmington Business Intelligence,
6-14 Underwood Street London N1 7JQ
tel 020-7549 8666
email knowledge@wilmington.co.uk
website www.theknowledgeonline.com

Covering all aspects of production, The Knowledge Online contains contacts and services for the UK film, television, video and commercial production industry. The website features around 18,000 contacts, is free to use and does not require registration. Its new subscription service Production Intelligence features contact details of casting directors and line producers for forthcoming productions.

London Arrangements

30 Maryland Square, London E15 1HE
tel 020-8221 2381
email enquiries@londonarrangements.com
website www.londonarrangements.com
Director Stephen Robinson

London Arrangements specialise in the production of professional backing tracks ranging from stage and screen, swing and jazz, to classical and easy listening genres. Samples of all tracks can be listened to online, and the majority may be ordered in any key at no extra charge. We also produce bespoke backing tracks, piano rehearsal tracks and piano/vocal sheet music.

London Theatre

website www.londontheatre.co.uk

A website containing news, reviews, events, booking information and seating plans for London's theatre scene plus maps, hotels and general tourist information.

Mandy.com

website www.mandy.com

An online service providing a directory of 40,000 technicians, facilities and producers and a vacancy list for jobs in production, crew, art departments and post-production. Also posts casting calls for actors, classified ads and information about films for sale and distribution on its website.

Music Theatre International

website www.mtishows.com

A great resource for researching songs – some of which can be partially listened to and read about on this site.

Musicroom

email info@musicroom.com
website www.musicroom.com

The world's largest online retailer of sheet music, tutor methods, instructional DVDs & videos, music software and instruments & accessories.

National Theatre Bookshop

National Theatre, South Bank, London SE1 9PX
tel 020-7452 3456 *fax* 020-7452 3457
email bookshop@nationaltheatre.org.uk
website http://shop.nationaltheatre.org.uk/

Britain's leading specialist theatre bookshop. An inspiring selection of books, plays and design-led gifts. *Opening Hours*: Monday to Saturday: 9.30am – 10.45pm (this varies on certain public holidays); 12pm – 6pm on Sundays when there is a performance. Facebook – **nationaltheatrebookshop**; Twitter – **@ntbookshop**.

PlayDatabase.com

website www.playdatabase.com

US site that helps theatre-lovers find monologues and plays for production.

Project Gutenberg

website www.gutenberg.org

An online library of more than 18,000 books – and many classic plays – which have gone out of copyright in the US. Also a growing collection of music recordings and scores. Possibly the largest of its kind in the world.

Royal Court Theatre Bookshop

Sloane Square, London SW1W 8AS
tel 020-7565 5024
email bookshop@royalcourttheatre.com
website www.royalcourttheatre.com/your-visit/bookshop

Offers a diverse selection of contemporary plays and publications on the theory and practice of modern drama. The staff specialise in assisting with the selection of audition monologues and scenes. Royal Court playtexts from past and present productions cost £3 while stock available. The Bookshop is situated in the downstairs Royal Court Bar & Food area. *Opening Hours*: Monday to Friday: 4pm – 8pm; Saturday: 2pm – 8pm. It will also be open from 2pm whenever there is a midweek matinee.

Screen International

Greater London House, Hampstead Road, London NW1 7EJ
tel 020-7728 5000
email mike.goodridge@emap.com
website www.screendaily.com

International news and features on the film business. Subscriptions cost £175 per annum for:

- Screen International – 12 monthly issues delivered to your door
- ScreenDaily.com – instant access to the latest news, reviews and industry moves available online
- Global box office data available online – structured by territories, films and distributors
- Screen Base – the new online, interactive database providing vital production and financing information for the top five European territories

Script Websites

Although subject to rules on copyright, a number of websites make the scripts for films and television shows and suggestions for audition speeches available online. These sites tend to come and go, but here are some that are current at the time of going to press:

- **www.script-o-rama.com**
- **www.sfy.ru**
- **www.imsdb.com**
- **www.playscripts.com**
- **www.simplyscripts.com**
- **www.whysanity.net/monos**
- **www.singlelane.com**
- **www.filmsite.org/bestspeeches.html**

The Sheetmusic Warehouse

email pianoman@globalnet.co.uk
website www.sheetmusicwarehouse.co.uk

Specialists supplying old music, rare music, music from the shows, musicals and operetta, popular music, wartime music, jazz music, Deep South American music, music hall music, classical music, modern music . . . "You name it, we've probably got it. Music to play, music to sing to or music to frame and hang on your wall!"

Shooting People

PO Box 51350, London N1 6XS
email contact@shootingpeople.org
website www.shootingpeople.org

Shooting People allows thousands of people working in independent film to exchange information via a range of daily email bulletins. These include:

- Daily UK Filmmakers Bulletin – for directors, producers and crew to share information on the latest technologies, get advice, find crew, locations, production deals, events & screenings, training and more. Currently more than 22,000 members
- Daily UK Screenwriters Bulletin – writers all over the UK use this email network to discuss writing,

share ideas and hear about competitions, opportunities and training. Currently more than 13,000 members
• Daily UK Casting Bulletin – for actors to discuss their craft and receive casting calls from directors, producers and casting directors. Currently more than 14,000 members
• Weekly UK Script Pitch Bulletin – a weekly collection of script pitches offered to producers and directors by the writers on the Screenwriters Network. Currently more than 11,000 members

Both part- and full-membership are available. Part-membership allows subscribers to receive email bulletins only, and is free. Full-membership costs £20 per year and entitles users to a range of other services. Full-members can create an actor's personal profile with a photograph and be listed in the online directory, post to any bulletin and download guides on various confusing aspects of film-making such as actor contracts, health and safety and distribution. They are also entitled to create member cards and to browse other member cards to find potential local collaborators.

Shooting People also organises a number of parties, screenings, workshops and other events for which full members receive advanced notice.

Skoob Books

66 The Brunswick, Marchmont Street,
London WC1N 1AE
tel 020-7278 8760
website www.skoob.com

An excellent collection of second-hand plays, including many translated works and as-new titles at half RRP. Strong theatre, film, music and TV sections in a very large basement bookshop. All academic areas covered, and masses of paperback fiction. Lift access and knowledgeable, friendly staff. Thousands more books in its Oxford Warehouse, sent to the shop on request. Experienced in set-dressing, offering advice, samples and loan or purchase of books and ephemera.

The Stage

47 Bermondsey Street, London SE1 3XT
tel 020-7403 1818
and (01858) 438895 (Subscriptions)
email newsdesk@thestage.co.uk
website www.thestage.co.uk
Managing Director Hugh Comerford *Acting Editor* Alistair Smith

Online and weekly print publication for the entertainment industry. Established in 1880. Advice, news, reviews, features and recruitment for theatre, entertainment, opera, dance, TV, radio, backstage and technical, management, education and training. *The Stage* is also available on iPad, Android, Kindle and other tablet devices. *The Stage* Castings, the company's online casting service (**www.thestage.co.uk/castings**), offers access to hundreds of jobs for all kinds of performers.

Theatre Record – The continuing chronicle of the British Stage

131 Sherringham Avenue, London N17 9RU
020-8808 3656
email admin@trsubs.co.uk (subscriptions)
website www.theatrerecord.org

Established in 1981 as *London Theatre Record. Theatre Record* publishes the complete, unabridged reviews of all new shows in the UK covered by national press and leading magazines. As well as reviews, each show is represented by a full listing of cast, technical credits and, usually, production photographs. Issued fortnightly. Each annual volume is supplemented by a detailed Index which enables searching by production title or artist's name.

Theatrevoice

website www.theatrevoice.com

The leading site for audio content about British theatre, featuring journalists from across the UK press, and practitioners from across the theatre industry. It was set up in 2003 to see if theatre could be talked about in a new way – critics to be more expansive than what the usual space constraints of the print media allowed; to enable actors, writers, directors and designers to be heard talking in detail and at length about their work; and to help members of the public interact more directly with theatre-makers and commentators. The Theatre Museum, now V&A Theatre Collections, which provided technical assistance and a place for recording from the site's inception, assumed management responsibilities for the site in the summer of 2005, to ensure that Theatrevoice's growing archive of material would be preserved for posterity. In April 2008, V&A Theatre Collections and Rose Bruford College agreed to support the site in partnership. Theatrevoice acknowledges with gratitude all the input that has been and still is freely given.

Theatricalia

website theatricalia.com

Theatricalia is aiming to become "the repository of theatre productions on the Internet". In doing so, it will enable people to discover theatre that is going on around them, follow actors they have seen in previous productions and record memorable events of productions they have seen.

UK Theatre Network

PO Box 3009, Glasgow G60 5ET
tel 0870-760 6033 *fax* 0870-760 6033
email editor@uktheatre.net
website www.uktheatre.net

Established 2001. A weekly magazine in PDF, Kindle and eBook format is circulated to members by email.

In addition the company offers webmail, website hosting, reviews, contacts and listings of what's on. All services are provided free of charge. New members should contact **subscribe@uktheatre.net**.

Virtual Library of Theatre & Drama

website www.vl-theatre.com

Lists online versions of plays and resources in more than 50 countries.

Westminster Reference Library

35 St Martin's Street, London WC2H 7HP
tel 020-7641 5253
website http://www.westminster.gov.uk/services/libraries/special/perform/

West End public library specialising in arts and business, with 15,000 volumes, (5,000 of which can be borrowed), on the performing arts, including Spotlight and *The Stage*. There are regular talks, workshops, performances in support of Collections, with the library open to suggestion for future events. Opening Hours: Monday to Friday: 10.00am – 8.00pm; Saturday: 10.00am – 5.00pm.

Wikipedia

website en.wikipedia.org

A free, online encyclopedia with over 1 million articles. Originally created by an army of volunteers in 2001, it can be added to or edited by anyone at all – a very democratic publication. This democracy can sometimes mean that contentious or politically sensitive issues are not always presented in the most balanced way, although some measures are in place to prevent flagrant abuse of the system. Occasionally the editing process makes for some slightly disjointed articles. However, as a free source of information on just about any topic, it is unsurpassed. The theatre section can be accessed via: **en.wikipedia.org/wiki/Theatre**.

Organisations, associations and societies

This section contains details of all kinds of ways (not listed elsewhere) of getting involved, sourcing useful information, learning, finding interesting lectures, networking, and simply keeping in touch with what's going on. It is important for the 'jobbing' actor to keep up-to-date with developments within the industry, and getting involved in related activities can pay dividends in the future.

The Actors' Guild of Great Britain

website www.actorsguild.co.uk

The Actors' Guild is a community of professional actors who meet with leading acting tutors, casting directors, directors, artistic directors, producers and agents to develop their craft, maximise their career development and benefit from the professional networking opportunities that membership brings.

The Guild was formed as an antidote to the increasing number of enterprises that seemed to be taking advantage of actors. Providing a haven, a support network and the opportunity to work with the very people you meet in the audition room.

"Our unique set-up means we are able to swing the pendulum of power firmly back to the actor. Our programme is dictated purely by feedback from our membership; we never ask you to book casting director workshops in 'blocks', and believe quality does not have to cost the earth – workshops start at just £22 and never exceed £30 for a 3-hour workshop.

"We also offer an exclusive range of industry discounts for members; a bursary scheme which pays for all the essentials an actor could need for a year; a forum; and a support network that brings this often disparate, nomadic community together."

The Agents' Association (GB)

54 Keyes House, Dolphin Square,
London SW1V 3NA
tel 020-7834 0515
email association@agents-uk.com
website www.agents-uk.com

Established in 1927 to represent and enhance the interests of entertainment agents in the United Kingdom and to standardise practice. The membership covers all fields of the entertainment industry.

ASSITEJ (International Association of Theatre for Children and Young People)

Preradoviceva 44, 10000 Zagreb
tel +385 1 4667034 *fax* +385 1 4667225
email sec.gen@assitej-international.org
website www.assitej-international.org

ASSITEJ International (Association Internationale du Theatre pour l'Enfance et la Jeunesse) states: "Since the theatrical art is a universal expression of mankind, and possesses the influence and power to link large groups of the world's people in the service of peace, and considering the role theatre can play in the education of younger generations, an autonomous international organisation has been formed which bears the name of the International Association of Theatre for Children and Young People." Also see Theatre for Young Audiences (TYA), below.

ASSITEJ (International Association of Theatre for Children and Young People)

The Birmingham Repertory Theatre Ltd,
Broad Street, Birmingham B1 2EP
email secretary@tya-uk.org
website www.tya-uk.org
Contact Catherine Rollins

TYA-UK (UK Centre of ASSITEJ) is a network for makers and promoters of professional theatre for young audiences, linking the UK to theatres, organisations and individual artists around the world. Works for a fuller awareness of the value of theatre for young audiences.

British Academy of Film and Television Arts (BAFTA)

195 Piccadilly, London W1J 9LN
tel 020-7734 0022 *fax* 020-7292 5868
email reception@bafta.org
website www.bafta.org
Chief Executive Officer Amanda Berry OBE

Founded in 1947, BAFTA is the UK's pre-eminent independent charity supporting, developing and promoting the art forms of the moving image (film, TV and games) by identifying and rewarding excellence, inspiring practitioners and benefiting the public. BAFTA's awards are awarded annually by its members to their peers in recognition of their skills and expertise. In addition, BAFTA's year-round learning programme offers unique access to some of the world's most inspiring talent through workshops, masterclasses, lectures and mentoring schemes, connecting with audiences of all ages and backgrounds across the UK, Los Angeles and New York.

British Association for Performing Arts Medicine (BAPAM)

4th Floor, Totara Park House,
34-36 Gray's Inn Road, London WC1X 8HR
tel 020-7404 8444 (Helpline), 020-7404 5888 (Admin)
website www.bapam.org.uk

The British Association for Performing Arts Medicine is a unique medical charity helping performing arts professionals and students with work-related health problems, both physical and psychological.

BAPAM provides:

• Free confidential clinical advice from medical practitioners who have specialist understanding of industry professionals' needs
• Directory of Performing Arts Medicine Practitioners – a list of clinical specialists and practitioners in many branches of healthcare who have an interest in treating performing arts professionals
• Health-information resources enabling you to understand what you can do to keep in peak condition throughout a demanding career
• Healthy Performance talks and training for a wide range of audiences, including introductory sessions for student groups and educational institutions. Bespoke sessions for clients including performers, teachers, clinicians and employers.

British Council

Arts Group, 10 Spring Gardens, London SW1A 2BN
tel 020-7389 3194 *fax* 020-7389 3199
email arts@britishcouncil.org
Norwich Union House, 7 Fountain Street, Belfast BT1 5EG
tel 028-9024 8220 *fax* 028-9023 7592
email nireland.enquiries@britishcouncil.org
The Tun, 3rd Floor, 4 Jackson's Entry, Holyrood Road, Edinburgh EH8 8PJ
tel 0131-524 5714 *fax* 0131-524 5714
email scotland.enquiries@britishcouncil.org
1 Kingsway, 2nd Floor, Cardiff CF10 3AQ
tel 029-2092 4300 *fax* 029-2092 4301
email wales.enquiries@britishcouncil.org
website www.britishcouncil.org/arts

The British Council is the UK's public diplomacy and cultural organisation, and works in 100 countries, in arts, education, governance and science. The Arts Group supports around 2,000 arts events every year, encouraging international collaborations, performances and exchanges with some of the top UK artists. In addition they support arts-based workshops, seminars and online events.

The form of support which is offered varies according to the project. In most cases the Council acts as an advisory body, and brokers partnerships with overseas contacts such as artistic programmers and producers, venues, choreographers and festival directors. Although most work is geared towards young people aged 16-35, this isn't an exclusive emphasis, and classic or traditional work is supported, especially if it has a modern slant.

Resources available on the website include an annual directory of UK drama, dance, live art and street art companies that have work suitable for overseas touring; specialist information about drama/performing arts education in the UK; and *Britfilms* **www.britfilms.com** – a portal site for the UK film industry with information about international film festivals, UK film directors and films, making a film in the UK, training and careers advice.

Not open to the public except by appointment. Write, phone or email to establish contact, or get in touch with an artform specialist.

British Film Institute (BFI)

21 Stephen Street, London W1T 1LN
tel 0207-255 1444
email library@bfi.org.uk
BFI Southbank, Belvedere Road, South Bank, Waterloo, London SE1 8XT
tel 020-7928 3535
email nft@bfi.org.uk
website www.bfi.org.uk

Established in 1933, the BFI strives to increase the level of understanding, appreciation and access to film and television culture. In addition to the BFI Reuben Library, which provides access to the largest film archive in the world, the organisation runs BFI Southbank (formerly the National Film Theatre) and London Film Festival (see entry under Media festivals). It also publishes books, releases films in cinemas, on video and DVD, runs educational programmes, and has one of the largest collections of film stills and film posters in the world. The BFI also awards Lottery funding to film production, distribution, education, audience development and market intelligence and research.

British Music Hall Society

45 Mayflower Road, Park Street, St Albans, Herts AL2 2QN
tel (01727) 768878
website www.music-hall-society.com
Secretary Daphne Masterton

Founded in 1963, and with offices across England, the society aims to preserve the history of music hall and variety, to recall the artistes who created it and to support entertainers working today. Members receive copies of the society's quarterly magazine *The Call-Boy* containing news, views and information about the sector; they also have the opportunity to attend evening and weekend study group meetings. Arranges live theatre shows, and it is possible for members to take part in such performances on these occasions.

Casting Directors Guild of Great Britain and Ireland

website www.thecdg.co.uk

A professional organisation which represents casting directors working in film, television, theatre and commercials. The Casting Directors Guild aims to standardise professional working practice and to enable the exchange of information and ideas between members.

Election to the Guild is at the discretion of the Committee. Full members must have worked in one or more areas of the industry for at least 5 years, and are entitled to use the initials CDG after their name. Probationary members must have worked as an assistant to a casting director for 3 years.

Members are listed on the website with information about their areas of work and recent credits.

Casting Society of America

website www.castingsociety.com

The Casting Society of America is the premier organisation of theatrical Casting Directors in film, television, and theatre. Although it is not a union, its members are a united professional society that consistently set the level of professionalism in casting on which the entertainment industry has come to rely. Its more than 350 members are represented not only in the United States, but also in Canada, England, Australia and Italy.

Co-operative Personal Management Association (CPMA)

email cpmauk@yahoo.co.uk
website www.cpma.coop

Founded in 2002, the CPMA works to further and promote the interests of its members, who are acting agencies located across the UK. Backed by Equity, it seeks to raise the profile of co-ops with both employers and actors, and to represent the interests of co-ops with external bodies. Also works with members to identify and assist in solving the unique problems of a co-operative, to enourage good practice, to develop training skills and opportunities, and to act as an advocate for co-operative working.

The John Colclough Consultancy

tel 020-8873 1763
email john@johncolclough.com
website www.johncolclough.com

Practical independent guidance for actors and actresses. When Spotlight decided to end their advisory service in March 2005, John Colclough elected to carry on an 'advisory' service independently, using the knowledge he had gained at Spotlight and also from his shop-floor experience as an actor, director and producer. Sessions take place over the telephone. Please refer to the website for current charges. Payments may be made by Internet Banking or by cheque after the consultation had taken place. Telephone calls are free to landlines. Calls to mobiles will be charged for, unless the caller offers to return the call. For a consultation, telephone John on 020-8873 1763.

Conservatoire for Dance and Drama

Tavistock House, Tavistock Square,
London WC1H 9JJ
tel 020-7387 5101
email info@cdd.ac.uk
website www.cdd.ac.uk

The Conservatoire for Dance and Drama is eight specialist schools delivering world-leading vocational training within higher eduction. On stage and screen and behind the scenes, graduates are the actors, dancers, circus artists, choregoraphers, stage managers and theatre technicians shaping the indutry today.

All the Conservatoire Schools are small institutions with international reputations for high-quality training in dance, drama or circus arts. Publicly funded through the Higher Education Funding Council for England and students new to higher education can access Student Finance like other UK students. The Conseratoire Schools have strong traditions of providing student care and support services. Committed to admitting and supporting disabled students; warmly encourages students to inform the Schools so appropriate support can be put in place as soon as possible. Recruits on the basis of talent and potential, irrespepective of background.

The Conservatoire Schools are: Bristol Old Vic Theatre School, Central School of Ballet,London Academy of Music and Dramatic Art (LAMDA), London Contemporary Dance School, National Centre for Circus Arts, Northern School of Contemporary Dance, Rambert School of Ballet and Contemporary Dance, Royal Academy of Dramatic Art (RADA).

Culture.Info

website www.culture.info

The aim of Culture.Info is to be the first port-of-call for users seeking cultural information on a particular topic. Each Culture.Info sub-portal provides a carefully researched set of listings of links to information that is more focused and useful than can usually be obtained from the vast majority of existing listings or search engines.

Directors UK

3rd & 4th Floor, 8-10 Dryden Street,
London WC2E 9NA
tel 020-7240 0009
email info@Directors.UK.com
website www.directors.uk.com

Directors UK is the professional association for film, television and moving image directors in the UK. It also monitors, collects and distributes royalties on behalf of television and film directors. With over 5,000 members it represents the overwhelming majority of working film and television directors in the UK. Directors UK works to protect and enhance the creative, economic and contractual rights of directors in Britain and works closely with organisations in the UK, Europe and around the world to represent directors' rights and concerns. It also promotes excellence in the craft of direction both nationally and internationally. As a membership organisation, it offers a range of events, services and benefits to members including: screenings, masterclasses, workshops, legal services, advice, industry discounts and more.

Drama Association of Wales

Splott Library, Singleton Road, Cardiff CF24 2ET
tel 029-2045 2200
email chair@dramawales.org.uk
website www.dramawales.org.uk
Key contact Teri McCarthy (Chair)

Founded in 1934 and a registered charity since 1973, the Drama Association of Wales aims to increase opportunities for people in the community to be creatively involved in high-quality drama.

Its main activities include a mail-order library service for DAW Publications and training courses in all aspects of theatre, including a 5-day residential summer school.

Also runs a playwriting competition and workshops. Organises the Welsh National Drama Festival from March to June, culminating in the Wales Final Festival of One Act Plays.

UK membership costs £15 per year for individuals and £25 for groups, both professional and amateur. Overseas members are very welcome: contact Teri McCarthy for details.

Drama UK

Woburn House, 20 Tavistock Square,
London WC1H 9HB
email info@dramauk.co.uk
website www.dramauk.co.uk

Drama UK champions quality drama training in the UK through advocacy, assurance and advice, and provides a unique link between drama training providers in the UK and the theatre, media and broadcast industries.

The organisation gives a united, public voice to this sector; encourages the industry and training providers to continue to work together; offers help and advice to drama students of all ages through its website; and awards a quality kite mark to the very best drama training available.

Drama UK was formed in 2012 following the merger of the Conference of Drama Schools (CDS) and the National Council for Drama Training (NCDT).

Dramaturgs' Network

c/o Tinderbox Theatre Company, 72 High Street,
Belfast BT1 2BE
email info@dramaturgy.co.uk
website www.dramaturgy.co.uk

The Dramaturgs' Network is an organisation for UK theatre practitioners committed to developing dramaturgy and supporting practitioners' development in the field. Founded in 2001, it is a volunteer arts organisation created to share ideas, knowledge, resources and skills in current dramaturgical practices. The network aims to provide support for theatre makers functioning in the role of dramaturg and/or literary manager and educational professionals involved in dramaturgical practice.

Euclid

website www.euclid.info

Euclid provides a range of European and International information, research and consultancy services. It has been appointed by the UK Department for Media, Culture & Sport and the European Commission as the official UK Cultural Contact Point, in particular to promote the EU's funding programmes for culture.

Federation of Scottish Theatre

c/o Royal Lyceum Theatre, 30B Grindlay Street,
Edinburgh EH3 9AX
tel 0131-248 4842
email info@scottishtheatre.org
website www.scottishtheatre.org

The Federation of Scottish Theatre is the membership and development body for professional dance, opera and theatre in Scotland, bringing the sector together to speak with a collective voice, to share resources and expertise, and to promote collaborative working.

Highlands & Islands Theatre Network (HIN)

c/o HI-Arts, Suites 4 & 5, 4th Floor,
Ballantyne House, 84 Academy Street,
Inverness IV1 1LU
tel (01463) 717091
website www.hitn.co.uk

HITN has the following agreed aims:

• To promote the advancement of education and the arts in the Highlands and Islands of Scotland area for the benefit of the public
• To promote the professional theatre sector in the Highlands and Islands of Scotland area at regional, national and international levels
• To work with other organisations to encourage wider access to theatre across the Highlands and Islands of Scotland area

Independent Theatre Council (ITC)

c/o The Albany, Douglas Way, London SE8 4AG
tel 020-7403 1727 *fax* 020-7403 1745
email admin@itc-arts.org
website www.itc-arts.org

Founded in 1974, the Independent Theatre Council (ITC) is the management association and political voice of around 400 performing arts professionals and organisations. ITC provides its members with legal and management advice, training and professional development, networking, regular newsletters and a comprehensive web resource.

Working across a variety of art forms, including drama, dance, opera, music theatre, puppetry, mixed media, mime, physical theatre and circus, ITC members usually operate on the middle- and small-scale, and are dedicated to producing innovative work, often in unconventional performance spaces.

ITC has commissioned a wide range of publications which offer guidance on potentially difficult aspects of working in the performing arts, advice on good practice and further sources of information. For more than 20 years the Independent Theatre Council has been organising training for managers and staff across the performing arts.

For details of how to join and other benefits available to members, consult the website.

International Casting Directors Network (ICDN)

website www.shootingstars.eu/en/casting_directors_network.php

The idea for an informal international network was floated during a meeting of casting directors during European Film Promotion's ShootingStars event at the Berlinale. Until then, casting directors had only been organised in national associations, but ICDN offers them "the chance to exchange ideas on an international level about their different ways of working, to take advantage of synergies with international co-productions, and to attract greater attention to the work of casting a film".

International Federation of Actors (FIA)

Rue Joseph II 40, Box 4, B-1000 Brussels
tel +32 (0)2 234 56 53 / +32 (0)2 235 08 65 / +32 (0)2 235 08 74 *fax* +32 (0)2 235 08 70
email office@fia-actors.com
website www.fia-actors.com

The FIA currently represents 90 performers' unions and guilds in 66 countries around the world. Membership is limited to unions, guilds and professional associations – individual actors may not join. FIA works internationally to represent and co-ordinate the interests of performing artists and their professional organisations.

Services: Lobbying at European and international level on behalf of performers; defence of artists' freedom; trade union development; information exchange through confrerences and meetings; networking.

Objectives: To promote a better understanding of performers' concerns and challenges around the world; to ensure that all main decision-making processes take due consideration of the specific needs of performers; to contribute to improve the social and professional conditions of performers worldwide; to facilitate the sharing of knowledge and experience on all issues of common interest between member organisations.

Irish Theatre Institute

website www.irishtheatreonline.com

A comprehensive guide to professional theatre, dance and opera in Ireland, north and south.

National Campaign for the Arts

4th Floor, 17 Tavistock Street, London WC2E 7PA
tel 020-7240 4698
email nca@artscampaign.org.uk
website www.artscampaign.org.uk

The National Campaign for the Arts is the UK's only independent organisation campaigning for all the arts. Since 1985 they have worked to protect and promote the UK's world-class arts scene and acted as a powerful and effective advocate for the sector, able to influence the people who matter. With a growing UK-wide membership, the NCA is driven by the needs of the arts sector. "We believe that only speaking with a united voice can the arts truly be heard."

National Rural Touring Forum (NRTF)

tel (01904) 466527
email admin@nrtf.org.uk
website www.ruraltouring.org

The NRTF is the organisation that represents a number of mainly rural touring schemes and rural arts development agencies across England and Wales. "Our touring scheme members work with local communities to promote high-quality arts events and experiences in local venues."

North American Actors Association (NAAA)

mobile (07873) 371891
email admin@naaa.org.uk
website www.naaa.org.uk
Administrator Kelly Jeffreys

The North American Actors Association is an association promoting and supporting North American actors based in Britain, and is the largest non-Americas-based casting resource and database of genuine North Americans for the entertainment industry.

Membership is open to genuine North American professional actors who can work on both sides of the Atlantic without restriction, are full members in good standing of at least 1 entertainment union and have proof of professional contracts. Not an agency, but through the website provides agent and other contact details of members to those involved in casting.

Northern Ireland Theatre Association (NITA)

c/o The MAC, 10 Exchange Street West,
Belfast BT1 2NJ

email info@nitatheatre.org
website http://nitheatre.com
Coordinator Charlotte Smith

NITA is the representative body for professional theatre in Northern Ireland.

Pact (Producers' Alliance for Cinema and Television)

3rd Floor, Fitzrovia House,
153–157 Cleveland Street, London W1T 6QW
tel 020-7380 8230
email info@pact.co.uk
website www.pact.co.uk
Chief Executive John McVay

The UK trade association that represents and promotes the commercial interests of independent feature film, television, animation and interactive media companies. Headquartered in London, it has regional representation throughout the UK, in order to support its members. An effective lobbying organisation, it has regular and constructive dialogues with government, regulators, public agencies and opinion formers on all issues affecting its members, and contributes to key public policy debates on the media industry, both in the UK and in Europe. It negotiates terms of trade with all public service broadcasters in the UK and supports members in their business dealings with cable and satellite channels. It also lobbies for a properly structured and funded UK film industry and maintains close contact with other relevant film organisations and government departments.

Personal Managers' Association (PMA)

tel 0845-602 7191
email info@thepma.com
website www.thepma.com

The PMA is a membership organisation for agents who represent actors, writers and directors working mainly in film, television and theatre. It was set up over 60 years ago with the intention of encouraging good practice among agents by encouraging better communication between agents and better communication from agents to the industry.

The Radio Independents Group (RIG)

c/o Kim Mason (Administrator), 21 Pembroke Road, London N10 2HR
email chair@radioindies.org
website www.radioindies.org
Chair Phil Critchlow

A non-profit-making trade body funded through membership fees and other fundraising activities, representing the interests and needs of the UK's independent radio production industry. Formed in July 2004, RIG currently represents two-thirds of the industry, and membership continues to grow – to over 100 companies, from globe-spanning commercial giants through to one-person companies, partnerships and sole traders. As well as representing members' and the industry's needs in negotiations with the BBC, commercial radio and other groups, and the government, RIG offers support, resources, information, access and training. Its aim is to bring together the knowledge of the thousands of dedicated and skilled people in the independent radio production sector, making as much of it as possible available to all.

Royal Television Society (RTS)

3 Dorset Rise, London EC4Y 8EN
tel 020-7822 2810 *fax* 020-7822 2811
email info@rts.org.uk
website www.rts.org.uk

Provides the leading forum for discussion and debate on all aspects of the television industry, with opportunities for networking and professional development for people at all levels and across every sector. The RTS has 14 national and regional centres in the UK, which draw up an annual programme to suit the needs of their members.

Events organised by the RTS include dinners, lectures, conventions, conferences and awards ceremonies. In addition it produces a monthly magazine, *Television*, outlining key industry debates and developments.

Scene & Heard

Theatro Technis, 26 Crowndale Road,
London NW1 1TT
020-7388 9009
email info@sceneandheard.org
website www.sceneandheard.org

Scene & Heard is a unique mentoring programme that partners the inner-city children of Somers Town, London, with volunteer theatre professionals, to give them an experience of quality one-to-one adult attention and to enable them to write and sometimes perform their own plays.

The fundamental purpose of the project is to boost the self-esteem of the children involved by giving them a public platform for their voice and by providing a personal experience of success.

By introducing the children to a new way of working with language, Scene & Heard also strives to improve attitudes towards learning and literacy skills.

The Society of Teachers of the Alexander Technique (STAT)

Unit W48, Grove Business Centre,
560-568 High Road, London N17 9TA
tel 020-8885 6524 *fax* 020-8808 2135
email office@stat.org.uk
website www.stat.org.uk

The Alexander Technique has been taught for more than 100 years. In 1958, the Society of Teachers of the Alexander Technique (STAT) was founded in the UK by teachers who were trained by FM Alexander.

STAT's first aim is to ensure the highest standards of teacher training and professional practice.

Teaching members of STAT are registered (MSTAT) to teach the Technique after completing a 3-year, full-time training course approved by the Society or one of the Affiliated Societies overseas; they are also required to adhere to the Society's published *Code of Professional Conduct and Competence* and are covered by the professional indemnity insurance.

There are currently more than 2,500 teaching members of STAT and its affiliated societies worldwide. Graduates of STAT training courses are assessed by a system of external moderation; the Society also runs a postgraduate programme of Continuing Professional Development. STAT's further aims are to promote public awareness and understanding of the Alexander Technique, and to encourage research. The Society publishes a regular newsletter, *STATNews*, and *The Alexander Journal*.

Society of London Theatre (SOLT)

32 Rose Street, London WC2E 9ET
tel 020-7557 6700 *fax* 020-7557 6799
email enquiries@solttma.co.uk
website www.solt.co.uk

Founded in 1908 by Sir Charles Wyndham, the Society of London Theatre is the trade association which represents the producers, theatre owners and managers of the major commercial and grant-aided theatres in central London.

Today the Society combines its long-standing roles in such areas as industrial relations and legal advice for members, with a campaigning role for the industry, together with a wide range of audience-development programmes to promote theatre-going.

The Stephen Sondheim Society

265 Wollaton Vale, Wollaton, Nottingham NG8 2PX
email administrator@sondheim.org
website www.sondheim.org
Chairman Craig Glenday *Administrator* Lynne Chapman

The Stephen Sondheim Society is a registered charity promoting the works of the composer and lyricist Stephen Sondheim. Keeps track of all productions (professional and amateur) of Sondheim's musicals, publishes a newsletter, arranges theatre visits, runs an annual student competition and has an extensive archive housed at Kingston University.

At the time of writing, UK membership is £27 (single), £22 (concession) or £32 (joint), but please consult the website for the latest rates.

StartaTheatreCompany.com

email admin@startatheatrecompany.com
website www.startatheatrecompany.com

An online guide to starting and developing a performing arts company. An e-learning course with 6 comprehensive modules, covering all you need to know about building a successful and sustainable enterprise. Delivered through fortnightly video and audio lessons, the guide is presented by tutor Sinead Mac Manus. Sinead has many years of experience working with and training performing arts companies, and has brought this experience to the world of e-learning.

Studio Salford

King's Arms, 11 Bloom Street, Salford M3 6AN
website www.studiosalford.com

Studio Salford is an umbrella group representing and promoting several theatre companies, raising the profile of Salford as a viable artistic location, and promoting artists from all over Salford and Manchester. Their performance venue is the intimate and unique upstairs space at The King's Arms.

Theatre Chaplaincy UK

St Paul's Church, Bedford Street, London WC2E 9ED
tel 020-7240 0344
email actorschurchunion@gmail.com
website www.actorschurchunion.com
Administrator Libby Shaw *President* Bishop Jack Nicholls *Senior Chaplain* Rev'd Lindsay Meader

Provides pastoral support for all members of the entertainment world, regardless of beliefs. Runs a network of voluntary chaplains for theatres, clubs and studios, in the UK and overseas. Also runs a charitable trust for children of parents in entertainment.

Theatre in Wales

website www.theatre-wales.co.uk

"The only comprehensive Welsh theatre and performance website."

Theatres Trust

22 Charing Cross Road, London WC2H OQL
tel 020-7836 8591 *fax* 020-7836 3302
email info@theatrestrust.org.uk
website www.theatrestrust.org.uk

The National Advisory Public Body for Theatres, protecting theatres for everyone. Operates nationally in England, Wales, Scotland and Northern Ireland, providing an authoritative and knowledgeable source of expert advice and information on theatres. The Theatres Trust provides a range of advisory services, is a statutory consultee on planning applications and provides guidance on design, conservation, property and planning matters to theatre operators, local authorities and official bodies, and also runs an information service. Its archives include records of over 3,500 theatre buildings and some 30,000 images, as well as plans and other documents.

Total Theatre

University of Winchester, Faculty of Arts, Winchester SO22 4NR
tel (01962) 827107

website www.totaltheatre.org.uk

Total Theatre is a national agency with an international focus, developing contemporary theatre for both theatre makers and theatre audiences.

UK Theatre Association (TMA)

32 Rose Street, London WC2E 9ET
tel 020-7557 6700 *fax* 020-7557 6799
email enquiries@soltukt.co.uk
website www.uktheatre.org
Chief Executive Julian Bird

The UK Theatre Association is a membership organisation for theatre and the performing arts organisations. Its members includes theatres, arts centres and presenting venues, producers, opera, ballet and dance companies and now supports individuals who work professionally in the performing arts at all stages of their career. There are also membership schemes for sole traders, suppliers of goods and services to the industry and concert halls and members benefit from access to a range of professional services, high-quality training and events, and networking opportunities. As well as running the only awards scheme to recognise excellence in theatre throughout the UK, UK Theatre leads on audience development programmes and actively campaigns on behalf of theatres and their audiences.

UK Theatre shares a common staff with the Society of London Theatre (SOLT).

University of Bristol Theatre Collection

Vandyck Building, Cantocks Close, Bristol BS8 1UP
tel 0117-331 5086
email theatre-collection@bristol.ac.uk
website www.bris.ac.uk/theatrecollection

The University of Bristol Theatre Collection is one of the world's largest and most significant collections relating to the history of British theatre. It is an accredited museum and research facility that is open to the public. Its collection covers all spects of theatre from the seventeenth century up to the present day and includes original documents, photographs, artwork and artefacts.

V&A Department of Theatre & Performance Collections (formerly The Theatre Museum)

tel 020-7942 2697
email tmenquiries@vam.ac.uk
website www.vam.ac.uk/page/t/theatre-and-performance

The V&A's Department of Theatre & Performance Collections hold the UK's national collection of material about live performance in the UK since Shakespeare's day, covering drama, dance, musical theatre, circus, musical hall, rock and pop and other forms of live entertainment. In March 2009, the new Theatre & Performance galleries at the V&A opened to the public. The galleries replaced those at the Theatre Museum in Covent Garden, which closed in 2007. The new displays explore the process of performance, from the initial conception, through the design and development stages, to audiences' reactions.

Women in Film and Television (UK) (WFTV)

92/93 Great Russell Street, London WC1B 3PS
tel 020-7287 1400
email info@wftv.org.uk
website www.wftv.org.uk
Chief Executive Kate Kinninmont

A membership association open to women with a minimum of 1 year's professional experience in the television, film or digital-media industries. With more than 1,000 members including writers, actors, producers and directors, the WFTV promotes the interests and diversity of women working at all levels in these industries. Offers a network of national and international contacts with an online directory of members and provides a number of social forums, workshops, seminars and preview screenings.

WGGB - The Writers' Union

First Floor, 134 Tooley Street, London SE1 2TU
tel 020-7833 0777
email admin@writersguild.org.uk
website www.writersguild.org.uk

WGGB (Writers' Guild of Great Britain) is a trade union for professional and aspiring writers in TV, radio, film, theatre, books and games with 2,200 members; affiliated to the Trades Union Congress. The Guild negotiates collective minimum terms agreements with the main broadcasters and trade bodies for film and TV producers and subsidised theatre – these cover fees, advances, royalties, residuals, pension contributions, rights, credits and other matters. Guild members have access to free contract vetting, legal advice and representation in work-related disputes, and the Writers' Guild Welfare Fund gives emergency assistance to members in financial trouble. Also offered are professional, cultural and social activities to help provide writers with a sense of community, making writing a less isolated occupation. Members receive a weekly email bulletin containing news and work opportunities. The Writers' Guild Awards are presented every year.

An actor's guide to keeping sane

Tim Bentinck

This is not a flippant title. The psychological battle of being an actor/breadwinner is the war; doing the job is just the fighting.

If you're a good builder and you're not getting work, it's probably because you're being undercut by the East Europeans, but you still know you're a good builder.

If you're an actor, you have no such objective take on the matter. In order to be a professional actor, you *have* to believe you're bloody good, or you can't even get started, let alone continue. The problem is that your own estimation of your talent is inherently biased, because when a builder has finished a roof conversion that looks beautiful and doesn't leak, no one rings him to complain. When an actor has done a part on telly and no-one rings, is it because (a) they weren't watching? (b) they thought you were good but didn't bother to ring? (c) they thought you were crap? or (d) they didn't like you anyway and turned over the minute you appeared? Even when your best friends think you're crap, they almost never say.

Therefore, you have to rely on your own judgement, and as an actor it's extremely difficult to be objective, disinterested and honest about your own performance. On stage you get a good idea when your jokes fall flat and people talk about the set in the bar afterwards, but on screen and on radio, you really are not the best judge. Everyone, myself included, can believe they're being brilliant when they're not. When you start off as an actor you *have* to have at heart a naïve belief that your originality, eccentricity, new interpretation of a text, your life experience, your pain, your joy, your discovery of sex for the first time in history, your raw talent, or your chutzpah and charm will blow them all away.

This, dear actor, we all have. You can't *be* an actor without empathising with some part of the above.

The reality, *quel malheur*, is mostly down to luck – the right place, the right time, and almost nothing more. Oh, and probably being unconventionally good-looking or sexy. Being good at it is an added bonus.

I'm 52. About 25 years ago someone I knew fairly well said to me drunkenly at a party, "Oh I saw you in that thing on telly last night, you were *awful*! Jeremy did you see it? Wasn't Tim dreadful?! Ha ha ha." At the time I was really hurt. I was shocked and rocked to the core. I had to find a way to deal with it, so I just decided she was a cow and mad and had no taste and didn't get it, and got on with life. About a year ago, when I watched the episode in question again on DVD, I realised she was painfully closer to the truth than I'd realised. I'd never done telly before and had just done nine months as a pirate in the West End and I was way OTT — lots of *acting* going on. I hadn't learned the 'do nothing' rule. In my defence I was fairly dishy and the swordfights were good. Yes she was a rude cow for saying it, but the point I'm circumlocutorily trying to reach is this: at the time, everyone said I was brilliant. No – I was *alright*. Beware the flatterers. Make people tell you the truth and then do something about it. Never be afraid of criticism; it's usually well founded, and sometimes well meant.

So in order to remain sane in this business, it is important that you have a very strong belief – backed up by some rigorous interrogation of your most trusted friends, your family, your loved ones and your fans – that you have what it takes, if given the chance, to be an astonishingly brilliant actor. Because unless you're very lucky, you are going to be hurt, rejected, abused, disrespected, talked down to, patronised, dismissed, ignored, not appreciated, paid badly, not paid at all, taken for granted and generally ground down for the rest of your life ... so if you can't face that, forget it.

From then on, one of three things is going to happen. The first is that you become a megastar. End of story, read a different book. The second is that you become a professional actor, earning some kind of living. The third is that it's a total bloody disaster. Here are some suggestions for how to remain sane with option two.

About five years ago, I spent a good six months of that year worrying about what things were going to be like five years in the future. Here I am today and everything's pretty fine. So I had effectively *wasted* all that time of my life worrying about something that didn't happen. Absurd. You have got to seize the day, or the night if that's your thing – *carpe noctem,* even!

Depression is a killer – it killed someone close to me, and I've been down that road too. But you can talk yourself out of it. You can bully yourself. Buy a bike and ride it, swim, have more sex, go to the pub and meet new people, get drunk with them and solve the problems of the world, sign up for a rally driving course, use the credit card to pamper yourself and don't worry about tomorrow (if that doesn't work, take Prozac but don't do the drinking thing – it's unhealthy, expensive and doesn't work). Do that until you've stopped being depressed, then you can worry about the debt with a more sanguine view – sanguine and proactive (dreadful word but can't think of an alternative).

You have *got* to treat it as a business. You're the product and if someone else isn't selling you (PR or agent), then it's down to you. My very first agent came from the world of PR and said to me that he knew nothing about acting, but aimed to get my name on the desks of everyone who mattered, every day of the week. He made me a lot of money. You're up against the PR might of comedians, footballers, models, weather-girls, body-builders, basketball players, TV presenters, extras, personal fitness coaches to the stars, drunks, reality-show winners, reality-show runners-up, Pop Idols ... and many, many others.

Get a website, make a voicereel, make a video compilation, send them to Spotlight, send them to your agent, send a DVD to casting directors. Get yourself in the press, get yourself on radio, write plays, write songs, drive trucks, plant gardens, do classes, keep fit, look good, raise a family, change the nappies. Live a life, the experience of which you can bring to your acting. Be in trim and ready to grab the bits of luck that come your way with bold confidence.

Another thing: work on your memory, or carry a notebook. Remember the names of the casting directors; remember the directors you work for; be pleasant to the runner, because s/he'll be the producer/director in six years' time; remember what your agent looks like when you meet him/her at parties; remember the voice-overs you did and who directed them; also, get a copy of everything to add to your showreel. Remember to keep all your receipts and put money aside for tax; if you're VAT registered, you're being paid to be a tax collector, so do it yourself – keep the money and have a holiday.

If you're young – *do it now do it now*! Over 40? – you've learned the game, so play it; you're just a more mature version of you at 20. If you're over 50, this is the time to strike: be bold, we've learned it all, we've got it all to give. Young filmmakers take heed: we are what you will be in 30 years' time, so we represent what you aspire to. You're pretty bright now, but don't you reckon that after 30 years you'll have learned a whole shed-load more? Well that's *us*. Welcome to Saga and the days of low insurance, paid-off mortgages and, finally, the bus pass, which I admit is still hard, at my age, to contemplate. It's eight years away though. Hmmm.

All the bloody pain and insecurity and rejection is mitigated, though, by this: you could face a cavalry charge in the Crimea. You could star in a West End musical. You could fly an F3 Tornado simulator. You could fight duels and fire machine guns. You could sit on a rubber pad on the top of a mountain inside the Arctic circle in Norway for three days waiting for the fog to clear to shoot a commercial for beer and get frostbite. You could be protected at night from elephant and tiger by armed guards in the Masai Mara, filming an ad for ice cream – and get sunstroke. You could dice for the lead with Damon Hill in a Formula One Kart. You could re-voice Gerard Dèpardieu in a movie, be the voice of James Bond in a computer game and say "Mind The Gap" on the Piccadilly Line. You could be kissed by Kevin Kline or thrown overboard by Roger Moore. You could die in the arms of Sean Bean and snog loads of beautiful women. You could have Claudia Schiffer looking into your eyes saying, "Ich liebe dich, ich liebe dich...". You could dub the lucky guy who shags Sharon Stone in *Basic Instinct 2*. You could earn your living with an earring in your ear and a sword around your waist. You could star in sitcoms, television series and radio soaps. You could do live improvisation games on stage and be filmed on horseback, scuba diving, canyoning, parachuting and piloting a flying boat. You could time a kiss, on a beach on the Great Barrier Reef, so that the setting sun shines between your closing lips as the waves lap around your suntanned body.

Sorry, but look, we're all bloody show-offs after all, and if after 30 years I couldn't give a list like the above, I'd have given it up.

It's a great, great adventure. It's a business and you have to run it. If it isn't working, give it up. I know plenty of ex-actors who are hugely successful at their new jobs. When I was training at Bristol, I remember thinking that *everybody* should do this course – not just actors, but everyone. If you've acted professionally for a while, it's a brilliant intro to everything else. Look at politicians – crap actors. Local government – the same. Most businessmen talking to their staff – abysmal. Actors can turn their hands to anything, so if you give it up, it wasn't wasted; it was part of your life-training.

Downer. What I mean is this: I've seen the highs and I've dived down deep with the lows. I know the reality but I'm still fired by the dream. That's what keeps us going.

Churchill said it most accurately, with all the power of the struggle of the war behind him: "Keep Buggering On."

See you on the green.

More about **Tim Bentinck** can be found at **www.bentinck.net**.

Bibliography

Books for aspiring, student and young actors

Margo Annett, *Actor's Guide to Auditions and Interviews* (3rd edition, A & C Black, 2004). A useful guide outlining some of the techniques needed for success.

Simon Dunmore, *Alternative Shakespeare Auditions for Men* (A & C Black, 1997). A collection of 50 less-well-known speeches for men.

Simon Dunmore, *Alternative Shakespeare Auditions for Women* (A & C Black, 1997). A collection of 50 less-well-known speeches for women.

Simon Dunmore, *MORE Alternative Shakespeare Auditions for Men* (A & C Black, 2002). Another collection of 50 less-well-known speeches for men.

Simon Dunmore, *MORE Alternative Shakespeare Auditions for Women* (A & C Black, 1999). Another collection of 50 less-well-known speeches for women.

Alison Hodge (ed.), *Twentieth Century Actor Training* (Routledge, 2000). A valuable introduction to the lives, principles, and practices of fourteen of the most important figures in twentieth-century actor training.

Ellis Jones, *Teach Yourself Acting* (Hodder & Stoughton Ltd, 1998). A good overview of acting and the profession.

Jennifer Reischel, *So You Want to Tread the Boards: The Everything-you-need-to-know, Insider's Guide to a Career in the Performing Arts* (JR Books Ltd, 2007).

Anna Scher, *Desperate to Act* (Lions, 1988). Brilliant, basic advice for those so 'desperate', from a lady who should know.

William Shakespeare, *Hamlet, Prince of Denmark*. Especially Hamlet's advice to the players (Act 3, scene 2), which is some of the best advice on acting ever given.

Malcolm Taylor, *The Actor and the Camera* (A & C Black, 1994). Another good 'primer' for the beginner.

Other career advice books for actors

James Calleri and Robert Cohen, *Acting Professionally* (7th edition, Palgrave Macmillan, 2009). The first edition was published in 1972, and is now regarded as godfather of this genre in the USA.

Ed Hooks, *The Audition Book* (3rd edition, Back Stage Books, 2000). Excellent reading if you're thinking of trying your hand in the USA. It's also worth looking at Ed's website for his excellent 'Craft Notes' (**www.edhooks.com**).

Peter Messaline and Miriam Newhouse, *The Actor's Survival Kit* (3rd edition, Simon & Pierre, 1999). Well worth reading if you're thinking of trying your hand in Canada.

Books for any actor

Mike Alfreds, *Different Every Night* (Nick Hern Books, 2007). A top ranking director sets out his rehearsal techniques in this vital masterclass.

Brian Bates, *The Way of the Actor* (Century Hutchinson, 1986). Very interesting insights into the inner workings of the actor's psyche.

Nancy Bishop, *Secrets from the Casting Couch* (Methuen Drama, 2009). A practical workbook written from the point of view of a very experienced casting director.

Anne Bogart and Tina Landau, *The Viewpoints Book* (Nick Hern Books, 2014). The Viewpoints are an improvisation technique: a set of names given to certain principles of movement through time and space – they constitute a language for talking about what happens on stage.

Peter Brook, *The Empty Space* (Penguin, 1990). Written in the 1960s, but still essential reading.

Adrian Cairns, *The Making of the Professional Actor* (Peter Owen Publishers, 1996). A fascinating study of the history, and possible future, of the art of acting.

Simon Callow, *Being an Actor* (Penguin, 1995). Autobiographical books by famous actors are generally useless in terms of practical career advice. However, this one – part autobiography and part advice – has a great deal of down-to-earth common sense. His famous 'manifesto' on directors' theatre is spot on.

Dee Cannon, *In-Depth Acting* (Oberon Books, 2012). An essential guide to mastering the Stanislavski technique, filtering its complexities and offering a dynamic, hands-on approach.

Mel Churcher, *Acting for Film: Truth 24 Times a Second* (Virgin Books, 2003). Invaluable insights into the specific techniques involved.

Mel Churcher, *A Screen Acting Workshop* (Nick Hern Books, 2011). An excellent and comprehensive training course in screen acting which includes a DVD showing the work in action.

Declan Donnellan, *The Actor and the Target* (Nick Hern Books, 2005) A fresh approach to the actor's art from the artistic director of Cheek by Jowl.

Simon Dunmore, *An Actor's Guide to Getting Work* (5th edition, Methuen Drama, 2012). A practical, comprehensive guide covering all aspects of marketing yourself as an actor.

David Edgar, *How Plays Work* (Nick Hern Books, 2009). The distinguished playwright examines the mechanisms and techniques, which dramatists throughout the ages have employed to structure their plays and to express their meaning.

Gabriella Giannachi and Mary Luckhurst, *On Directing* (Faber & Faber, 1999). Twenty-one directors with very different styles, all working in the UK are interviewed to ascertain how they begin work on a play or performance, what methods they use in rehearsal and answer the question: 'is the modern director an enabler, collaborator or dictator?'

John Gillett, *Acting Stanislavski* (Methuen Drama, 2014). An excellent demystification of Stanislavski.

Bernard Graham Shaw, *Voice-Overs, A Practical Guide* (A & C Black, 2000). A useful guide which explains and teaches the skills of voicing radio and television commercials.

Uta Hagen, *A Challenge for the Actor* (Macmillan, 1991). One of the best books on acting ever written.

Keith Johnstone, *Impro: Improvisation and the Theatre* (Faber & Faber, 1979); and *Impro for Storytellers* (Faber & Faber, 1999). Keith Johnstone suggests a hundred practical techniques for encouraging spontaneity and originality by catching the subconscious unawares.

David Mamet, *True and False* (Faber & Faber, 1998). This book cuts through much of the mythology that surrounds acting.

Lorna Marshall, *The Body Speaks: Performance and Expression* (Methuen Drama, 2001). Lorna Marshall enables actors and performers to recognise and lose unwanted physical habits and discover new possibilities for the body.

Kelly McEvenue, *The Alexander Technique for Actors* (Methuen Drama, 2001). The Alexander Technique is a method of physical relaxation that reduces tension and strain throughout the body. F.M. Alexander (1869-1955) was an actor who developed this technique to conquer his habit of straining his voice. This book's exercises are linked to accurate anatomical drawings, showing where stress is most pronounced in the body.

Ros Merkin (compiler), *The Liverpool Everyman Theatre: Liverpool's Third Cathedral* (Liverpool and Merseyside Theatres Trust Limited, 2004). This book offers brief encounters with some of the people, the plays, the on-and-off stage dramas of the Everyman's first 40 highly eventful years.

Ros Merkin (ed.), *Liverpool Playhouse: A Theatre and its City* (Liverpool University Press, 2011). From its opening in 1911, Liverpool Playhouse has reflected the history of Liverpool – and at times the city itself has appeared on stage as a key character.

Patrick O'Kane (ed.), *Actors' Voices: The People Behind the Performances* (Oberon Books, 2012). Twelve experienced actors share their process, comment on their experiences and consider their role as theatre artists in the broader spectrum of Art and Culture.

Theresa Robbins Dudeck, *Keith Johnstone: A Critical Biography* (Methuen Drama, 2013). A fascinating account of Keith Johnstone's early years at the Royal Court Theatre and teaching at RADA, and a good assessment of his approach and contributions to theatre and improvisation.

Patsy Rodenburg, *An Actor Speaks* (Methuen Drama, 1997). An entirely practical guide with excellent advice and exercises to help develop the performer's voice.

Neil Rutherford, *Musical Theatre Auditions and Casting* (Methuen Drama, 2012). A performer's guide viewed from both sides of the audition table.

Michael Sanderson, *From Irving to Olivier – A Social History of the Acting Profession* (Athlone Press, 1984). A very expensive, but nevertheless fascinating, study of the actor's world over the last century.

Edda Sharpe and Jan Haydn Rowles, *How to Do Any Accent: The Essential Handbook for Every Actor* (Oberon Books, 2007).

Michael Shurtleff, *Audition* (Walker & Company, 1984). An American book which should be read. It contains brilliant insights and thoughts to help any actor.

Spotlight, *Contacts* (Spotlight, annually in October). Contact details for everything you can think of (and more) that relates to actors and performers.

Jane Streeton and Phillip Raymond, *Singing on Stage: An Actor's Guide* (Methuen Drama, 2014). Singing should be an essential part of every actor's toolkit. This book encourages each actor to explore their own authentic voice as opposed to offering a 'one-size-fits-all' or 'quick fix' approach.

Steve Waters, *The Secret Life of Plays* (Nick Hern Books, 2010). Covers the key elements of dramatic writing – scenes, acts, space, time, characters, language and images – to show how a play is more than the sum of its parts.

Webography

What follows is a selected collection of the most important websites for aspirants and professionals, and some others which the editors have found extremely useful, but don't quite fit elsewhere in this book.

Important websites for aspirants and professionals

www.actorscentre.co.uk – Actors Centre London
www.agents-uk.com – Agents' Association of Great Britain
www.bbc.co.uk – BBC homepage
www.bbc.co.uk/soundstart – advice on how to get work in radio drama
www.thecdg.co.uk – Casting Directors Guild
www.cpma.coop – The Co-operative Personal Management Association
www.cukas.ac.uk – Conservatoires UK Admissions Service (CUKAS) provides the facilities to research and apply for practice-based music, dance and drama courses at some UK conservatoires
www.dramauk.co.uk – Drama UK is the new body championing quality drama training in the UK
www.edfringe.com – Edinburgh Festival Fringe
www.eif.co.uk – Edinburgh International Festival
www.equity.org.uk – Equity
www.imdb.com – Internet Movie Database; catalogues all sorts of information on more than 250,000 films and the 900,000 people who helped to make them
www.itc-arts.org – Independent Theatre Council homepage with links to member companies' websites
www.thepma.com – Personal Managers' Association
www.spotlight.com – Spotlight publishes the most important actors' directories
www.thestage.co.uk – *The Stage*, contains news, information and job advertisements which are updated each Thursday
www.ucas.ac.uk – UCAS, the central organisation that processes applications for full-time undergraduate courses at UK universities and colleges

Other useful websites

http://accent.gmu.edu – the speech accent archive uniformly presents a large set of speech samples from a variety of language backgrounds
www.artsline.org.uk – Arts-Line, provides disability access information on arts venues
www.britfilms.com – an extensive source of information on the UK film industry
www.britishtheatreguide.info – lots of articles, reviews and links about British theatre
www.companieshouse.gov.uk – Companies House: useful for checking background details (like date of foundation) of individual companies
www.dialectsarchive.com – the International Dialects of English Archive (IDEA) is a useful collection of English-language dialects and English spoken in the accents of other languages
www.edhooks.com – contains some interesting articles on acting
www.excellentvoice.co.uk – information and advice for voice-over artists with examples of good voicereels online

www.its-behind-you.com – seemingly a comprehensive list of pantomimes and their producers

www.officiallondontheatre.co.uk – Society of London Theatre website with news, reviews and booking information

www.royalist.info – a database that provides biographical details of thousands of individuals who have either belonged to, or been connected with, the royal family of England and Scotland during more than 1,000 years of history

www.shakespeare-online.com – electronic copies of the plays and poems, along with other related material of interest. These copies of the texts should be checked against published editions before use in audition or performance, in order to gain the benefit of modern scholarship

www.shakespeareswords.com – an excellent resource for understanding Shakespeare

http://sounds.bl.uk/Accents-and-dialects – the British Library's archive of accents and dialects

www.theatredigs.com – a site aimed solely at touring professionals within the UK entertainment industry

www.theatrenet.com – news, events and special offers and links to agents, producers, theatre companies, venues and more

www.uksponsorship.com – an online database of UK sponsorship opportunities

www.uktw.co.uk – UK Theatre Web, with information, events and tickets for theatre in the UK

www.usefee.tv – a site which lets performers, their representatives and employers quickly calculate the appropriate use fee for featured players in TV commercials based on the established, industry-endorsed method approved by the Personal Managers' Association, the Association of Model Agents and Equity

www.visit4ads.com – a site where you can see recent television and cinema commercials and get details of the companies who created them

www.vocalist.org.uk – a site for singers, vocalists, singing teachers and students of voice of all ages, standards and styles. The site contains useful information on aspects of singing, performance, plus free online singing lessons and articles for vocalists related to singing and getting into the music industry

www.voiceovers.co.uk – a forum for voice-over artists to advertise themselves

www.wefund.co.uk – a fundraising platform for creative projects where people offer perks in exchange for pledges

www.whatsonstage.com – a UK theatre listing service with search facilities, a ticket-ordering service, reviews, news and debate

Index

Index